International Handbook
of Human Rights

International
Handbook
of Human Rights

EDITED BY

Jack Donnelly

AND

Rhoda E. Howard

Greenwood Press
NEW YORK
WESTPORT, CONNECTICUT
LONDON

Library of Congress Cataloging-in-Publication Data

International handbook of human rights.

  Bibliography: p.
  Includes index.
  1. Civil rights. 2. Human rights. I. Donnelly,
Jack. II. Howard, Rhoda E., 1948-
JC571.I587   1987   341.4′81   87-7529
ISBN 0-313-24788-9 (lib. bdg. : alk. paper)

British Library Cataloguing in Publication Data is available.

Library of Congress Catalog Card Number: 87-7529
ISBN: 0-313-24788-9

First published in 1987

Greenwood Press, Inc.
88 Post Road West, Westport, Connecticut 06881

Printed in the United States of America

The paper used in this book complies with the
Permanent Paper Standard issued by the National
Information Standards Organization (Z39.48-1984).

10 9 8 7 6 5 4 3 2 1

CONTENTS

PREFACE

During the last decade, a major scholarly literature on human rights has developed. The bulk of this literature deals with international law and politics. By contrast, this book contains nineteen case studies of *national* human rights practices, reflecting the fact that most human rights violations are perpetrated by states against their own citizens, and that improvements in practice must come principally at the national level. Our emphasis is on the politics of human rights, the sociopolitical bases of national practices, and the universality of human rights and human rights violations.

Unlike many previous efforts, most of the authors in this volume are not human rights specialists; most are social scientists with expert knowledge of their countries. This reflects the fact that human rights practices are embedded in social structure and politics. If we are to understand the bases for the respect and violation of human rights, we must understand power, wealth, and the relations of rulers to ruled. The study of human rights may be a newly emerging academic specialty, but it must be grounded in rigorous historical and social scientific analysis.

The majority of our contributors are political scientists and sociologists. Our authors include, however, two lawyers, a historian, a journalist, and three human rights activists. Most of our authors are North Americans. Several natives of countries we wished to include in the volume were recruited; most were lawyers and human rights activists. Unfortunately, many were unable to complete their chapters. For example, one East European lawyer withdrew for personal reasons and was unable to find a replacement, as to write a chapter for this volume could have invited political reprisals. One Asian lawyer, a defense attorney in a major political trial, withdrew when he found himself charged with criminal contempt by his government (see appendix 4).

But despite our authors' diversity of experience and perspectives, all accept the Universal Declaration of Human Rights as an authoritative international standard. In addition, all attempt a comprehensive assessment of the state of both civil and political, and economic, social, and cultural rights, although focusing more on those rights that are most problematic in their respective countries. This commitment provides the unifying structure of the volume.

In selecting the countries to be studied we tried to achieve a regional balance. Any underrepresentation is a consequence of the withdrawal of contributors, and of the special problems of finding authors in particular areas of the world (e.g., the Middle East) willing to discuss human rights matters.

Our first priority in selecting the nineteen countries under review was to cover all major world powers—the United States, the Soviet Union, and China.

Our second priority was to include many of the countries that have been the objects of international human rights concern in the last fifteen years. Chile, El Salvador, Lebanon, Nicaragua, Israel, the Philippines, Poland, South Africa, and Uganda represent countries in every region of the world and illustrate varying kinds of problems resulting from vastly different political, economic, social and cultural situations.

Of equal concern was the need to select countries that typify various types of political systems of special interest in the study of human rights. Canada, the United Kingdom and Japan represent the developed capitalist democracies; Canada also reflects concern with the ''group'' rights of indigenous peoples in settler societies. India is the largest underdeveloped democracy. Cuba and Jamaica are two neighboring Third World states that have chosen different political paths to development and human rights. Senegal is an African country that, with its comparatively good human rights record, belies the misleading stereotype of Black Africa as a human rights disaster area.

The volume is organized alphabetically. We considered other types of organization. Regime type was not chosen because of changes of regime in some countries (e.g., Uganda and the Philippines). There were also problems of classifying anomalous countries, especially South Africa. There might also be substantive disputes over some classifications: for example, we would argue that post-Somoza Nicaragua is social democratic rather than Soviet-style socialist. Regional organization seemed to be unhelpful and uninformative.

Before the individual case studies, we have included an introduction in which we provide background information on theoretical issues and international context and state our own position on the social structural causes of the respect for and violation of human rights. Our starting point is that human rights are universal, that they are the rights of individuals, and that they ground personal claims against the state. While all of our authors accept this starting point, they have not always agreed with all of our particular arguments. This theoretical diversity, we feel, enriches the volume.

International Handbook
of Human Rights

1

INTRODUCTION

Rhoda E. Howard and Jack Donnelly

WHAT ARE HUMAN RIGHTS?

The International Human Rights Covenants[1] note that human rights "derive from the inherent dignity of the human person." But while the struggle to assure a life of dignity is probably as old as human society itself, reliance on human rights as a mechanism to realize that dignity is a relatively recent development.

Human rights are, by definition, the rights one has simply because one is a human being. This simple and relatively uncontroversial definition, though, is more complicated than it may appear on the surface. It identifies human rights as *rights*, in the strict and strong sense of that term, and it establishes that they are held simply by virtue of being human.

The term "right" in English has a variety of meanings, but two are of special moral importance. On the one hand, "right" may refer to something that is (morally) correct or demanded, the fact of something being right. In this sense, "right" refers to conformity with moral standards; righteousness; moral rectitude. On the other hand, "right" may refer to the entitlement of a person, the special title one has to a good or opportunity. Such titles ground special and particularly strong claims against those who would deny the right; as Ronald Dworkin[2] puts it, rights in ordinary circumstances "trump" other moral and political considerations. It is in this sense that one *has* a right. And it is in this sense that one has human rights.

The sense of moral righteousness, conformity to moral standards, must be as old as the notion of moral standards themselves. In the Western tradition of moral and political discourse there have been a variety of theories resting on this sense of right, but perhaps the most popular has been the theory of natural law. Natural law theories hold that there is an objective moral law (given by God and/or grasped by human reason). This natural law binds all men and women and provides a standard for evaluating human practices, including political practices. A regime that transgresses the natural law is guilty of serious crimes and, in severe instances, loses its moral and political legitimacy.

Perhaps the most highly developed theory of natural law was that of St. Thomas Aquinas (1225–1274), who sought to combine Christian doctrine with the philosophical ideas of classical antiquity, especially those of Aristotle. For Aquinas, all law is the expression of divine reason, which is made available to mankind in two principal forms: "divine law," or the revelation of the Bible, and "natural law," the imprint of divine reason, directly available to all through the exercise of reason. What Aquinas calls "human law," the ordinary sorts of law made by legislators, is legitimate to the extent that it conforms to the natural law, of which it ought to be merely a practical political expression.[3]

Such theories in the Western world go back explicitly at least as far as Cicero (106–43 B.C.), and they may be seen as implicit in the writings of Plato and Aristotle. They also extend well into the modern era; even John Locke, one of the most important early modern natural rights theorists, has an explicit theory of natural law.[4] Today, natural law ideas still receive the support of a number of respected philosophers and have considerable popular appeal, particularly, but not entirely, in certain religious circles.

Furthermore, such ideas have been the norm in most premodern or preindustrial societies throughout the world. For example, the Chinese emperor was held to rule through a mandate from heaven, and thus was held to be accountable to heaven for his actions. Similarly, Islam provides a very detailed set of substantive norms, expressed in the Koran and in Sharia law, to which rulers are required to conform. In very few societies have rulers been conceived of as truly absolute and unconstrained; even the Ancien Régime monarchs of France who claimed to rule by divine right acknowledged an obligation to conform their rule to the dictates of divine justice. Whatever the deviations in practice, almost all rulers in preindustrial societies ruled under what in the West was usually referred to as natural law. Most traditional societies, Western and non-Western alike, have conceived of justice primarily in terms of conformity with substantive principles of right (although usually known through tradition, not apprehended directly by reason).

The political leverage that natural law provides citizens against the state— that is, the ability to indict a violator of natural law as one who transgresses objective principles of justice, not merely the preferences or interests of a particular person or group—should not be denigrated. For example, a tyrannical ruler in medieval Europe or imperial China would stand condemned in the eyes of God and the objective principles of law and justice; a ruler could be held accountable to objective standards. But the difference between natural *law* and natural or human *rights* indictments is quite important, both theoretically and practically.

A state that violates the natural law is guilty of moral crimes, but it has not necessarily violated the rights of its citizens. Natural law does not necessarily give rise to natural rights, rights one has "by nature," simply as a human being.

In fact, while some recent natural law theorists (most prominently, Jacques Maritain[5]) link natural law with natural or human rights, historically such a linkage is quite rare; it certainly is not made by figures such as Cicero, Aquinas, and Richard Hooker. Typically, regimes that stand condemned by the natural law do not face citizens whose natural *rights* have been violated, and thus the kinds of actions that are justified to remedy the injustice are quite different.

In particular, without natural (or legal) rights against the government, citizens are not *entitled* to seek redress; natural law by itself gives no one any right to enforce its injunctions. For that they must have natural or human (or legal) *rights* in the strong sense of entitlements that ground claims that have a special force. If the state violates their rights, citizens may claim not only that injustice is perpetrated against them but that their rights have been violated. This gives considerable additional force to these claims. In addition, and no less important, it puts the process of redress under their control, as rights-holders who are entitled to press claims of rights. When those rights are natural or human rights, rights one has simply because one is a human being, the moral offense is of the greatest magnitude.

This understanding of states being constrained by the *rights* of citizens, which are morally prior to and above the state, is historically of relatively recent date, distinctively "modern." Thomas Hobbes, in *Leviathan* (1655), speaks of the "right of nature," a precursor of our conception of natural rights, but he explicitly denies that such rights limit the sovereign's power.[6] By the time of Locke's *Second Treatise of Government* (1688),[7] a clear and explicit theory of natural rights exists side by side with a fairly traditional theory of natural law. By the time of the American and French revolutions, ideas of natural rights—or, in the language of the era, the rights of man—are not only politically central but have replaced natural law both in popular revolutionary discourse and in the writings of figures such as Thomas Jefferson and Thomas Paine.[8]

As is clear from the authors already cited, the human rights tradition is, in its inception at least, closely tied to contractarian political thought. In the social contract tradition, individuals are seen as possessors of natural rights entirely independent of the state; their basic rights derive "from (human) nature," not from the state, law, politics, God, or tradition. In fact, the state (and society) are seen as products of a contract among individuals to protect natural rights and provide the social and political conditions that will allow individuals to realize them. As such, the state is legitimate only if it respects, enforces, and permits the fuller realization of natural rights. And if it fails to discharge its part of the contract—if it grossly and systematically violates human rights—citizens, either individually or collectively, are entitled to revolt. For example, Locke recognizes and defends a right to revolution held by society against governments that systematically violate natural rights; Jefferson in the American Declaration of Independence justifies the revolution by the British denial of natural rights; and the French Declaration of the Rights of Man and the Citizen explicitly includes a right to revolution.

Natural law and other (nonhuman rights) theories of justice certainly are capable of denying the legitimacy of corrupt or vicious governments. The grounds of the denial, however, and the position of citizens in the face of such a government, are quite different in the absence of natural rights.

For example, Aquinas holds that tyrants are illegitimate because they have grossly and systematically violated the natural law. But citizens, lacking natural *rights* that this law be respected, are not entitled to revolt or even press rights-claims against the tyrant.[9] When, however, it is considered legitimate for citizens to react not only against the injustice of violations of the natural law but also in defense of their natural rights, the state is guilty of additional and particularly severe affronts to human dignity. Not only are its practices unjust, but they also violate human rights. And citizens are entitled to act to restore their rights. A natural or human rights conception of politics places individual citizens and their rights at the heart of politics, which is viewed as ultimately a device for the vindication of natural rights.

As we have already indicated, there is nothing necessary about such a conception of persons or politics. Elsewhere we have argued in some detail that most societies at most times (including Western society in previous eras) have had quite different views.[10] But this is what is entailed by a human rights conception. And the nearly universal acceptance of the idea (if not the practice) of human rights by virtually all states in all areas of the contemporary world gives this conception a validity that cannot be ignored. This book is a series of country studies that seeks to assess both how a fairly representative collection of the world's countries stacks up against the standard of human rights and, most important, why.

WHAT RIGHTS DO WE HAVE?

The definition of human or natural rights as the rights of each person simply as a human being specifies their character; they are rights. The definition also specifies their source: (human) nature. We have already talked briefly about human rights as rights. A few words are necessary about the claim that human *nature* gives rise to human rights, as well as the particular list that results.

What is it in human nature that gives rise to human rights? There are two basic answers to this question. On the one hand, many people argue that human rights arise from human needs, from the naturally given requisites for physical and mental health and well-being. On the other hand, many argue that human rights reflect the minimum requirements for human dignity or *moral* personality.[11] These latter arguments derive from essentially philosophical theories of human "nature," dignity, or moral personality.

Needs theories of human rights run into the problem of empirical confirmation; the simple fact is that there is sound scientific evidence only for a very narrow list of human needs. But if we use "needs" in a broader, in part nonscientific, sense, then the two theories overlap. We can thus say that people have human rights to those things "needed" for a life of dignity, for the full development of their moral personality. The "nature" that gives rise to human rights is thus *moral* nature.

This moral nature is, in part, a social creation. Human nature, in the relevant sense, is an amalgam consisting both of psycho-biological facts (constraints and possibilities) and of the social structures and experiences that are no less a part of the essential nature of men and women. Human beings are not isolated individuals, but rather individuals who are essentially social creatures, in part even social creations. Therefore, a theory of human rights must recognize both the essential universality of human nature and the no less essential particularity arising from cultural and socioeconomic traditions and institutions.

Human rights are, by their nature, universal; it is not coincidental that we have a *Universal* Declaration of Human Rights, for human rights are the rights of all men and women. Therefore, in its basic outlines a list of human rights must apply at least more or less "across the board." But the nature of human beings is also shaped by the particular societies in which they live. Thus the universality of human rights must be qualified in at least two important ways.

First, the forms in which universal human rights are institutionalized are subject to some legitimate cultural and political variation. For example, what counts as popular participation in government may vary, within a certain range, from society to society. Both multiparty and single-party regimes may reflect legitimate notions of political participation. Although the ruling party cannot be removed from power, in some one-party states individual representatives can be changed and electoral pressure may result in significant policy changes.

Second, and no less important, the universality (in principle) of human rights is qualified by the obvious fact that any particular list, no matter how broad its cross-cultural and international acceptance, reflects the necessarily contingent understandings of a particular era. For example, in the seventeenth and eighteenth centuries, the rights of man were indeed the rights of men, not women, and social and economic rights (other than the right to private property) were unheard of. Thus we must expect a gradual evolution of even a consensual list of human rights, as collective understandings of the essential elements of human dignity, the conditions of moral personality, evolve in response to changing ideas and material circumstances.

In other words, human rights are by their essential nature universal in form. They are, by definition, the rights held by each (and every) person simply as a human being. But any universal list of human rights is subject to a variety of justifiable implementations.

In our time, the Universal Declaration of Human Rights (1948) is a minimum list that is nearly universally accepted, although additional rights have been added (e.g., self-determination) and further new rights (e.g., the right to nondiscrimination on the grounds of sexual orientation or the right to peace) may be added in the future. We are in no position to offer a philosophical defense of the list of rights in the Universal Declaration. To do so would require an account of the source of human rights—human nature—that would certainly exceed the space available to us. Nonetheless, the Universal Declaration is nearly universally accepted by states. For practical political purposes we can treat it as authoritative. All the contributors to this volume have agreed to do precisely that. Therefore, a brief review of the list of rights contained in the Universal Declaration (reprinted as appendix 1) is appropriate here.

It is conventional to divide human rights into two major classes, civil and political rights, and economic, social, and cultural rights. Such a division is rather crude and unenlightening. It also has too often been the basis for partisan arguments, by left and right alike, for granting priority to one category or the other, arguments that often simply attempt to cloak the abuse of rights. Nevertheless, it is a common and convenient categorization.

The civil and political rights enumerated in the Universal Declaration include rights to life; nationality; recognition before the law; protection against cruel, degrading, or inhuman treatment or punishment; and protection against racial, ethnic, sexual, or religious discrimination. They also include such legal rights as access to remedies for violations of basic rights; the presumption of innocence; the guarantee of fair and impartial public trials; prohibition of ex post facto laws; and protections against arbitrary arrest, detention or exile, and arbitrary interference with one's family, home, or reputation. Civil liberties enumerated include rights to freedom of thought, conscience and religion, opinion and expression, movement and residence, and peaceful assembly and association. Finally, political rights include the rights to take part in government and to periodic and genuine elections with universal and equal suffrage. Economic, social, and cultural rights recognized in the Declaration include the rights to food and a standard of living adequate for the health and well-being of oneself and one's family; the rights to work, rest and leisure, and social security; and rights to education and to participation in the cultural life of the community.

There are occasional claims still made, especially by political conservatives in the West, that only civil and political rights are really rights.[12] Likewise, one still runs across no less one-sided arguments, made principally by Soviet bloc and Third World politicians and scholars, that economic and social rights have priority over civil and political rights.[13] But virtually all states are explicitly committed to the view that all the rights recognized in the Universal Declaration are interdependent and indivisible. And all the contributors to this volume have accepted such an understanding. While the particular coverage varies, as no author has the space to cover the full range of rights in his or her country, each chapter attempts a comprehensive assessment of the status of the full range of internationally recognized human rights in the country in question.

INTERNATIONAL HUMAN RIGHTS INSTITUTIONS

While this volume is made up of a series of country studies, the international context of national practices nonetheless deserves some attention.[14] There are, as we have already noted, international human rights standards that are widely accepted—in principle at least—by states. Thus the discussion and evaluation of national practices take place within an overarching set of international standards to which virtually all states have explicitly committed themselves. Whatever the force of claims of national sovereignty, with its attendant legal immunity from international action, the evaluation of national human rights practices from the perspective of the international standards of the Universal Declaration thus is certainly appropriate, even if one is uncomfortable with the moral claim sketched above that such universalistic scrutiny is demanded by the very idea of human rights.

In the literature on international relations it has recently become fashionable to talk of "international regimes," that is, norms and decision-making procedures accepted by states in a given issue area. National human rights practices do take place within the broader context of an international human rights regime centered on the United Nations.

We have already sketched the principal norms of this regime—the list of rights in the Universal Declaration. These norms/rights are further elaborated in two major treaties, the International Covenant on Economic, Social and Cultural Rights and the International Covenant on Civil and Political Rights, which were opened for signature and ratification in 1966 and came into force in 1976. Almost all of the countries studied in this volume have ratified (become a party to) both the Covenant on Civil and Political Rights and the Covenant on Economic, Social and Cultural Rights. (See appendix 2.) Even those countries that are not parties to the Covenants often accept the principles of the Universal Declaration. In addition, there are a variety of single-issue treaties that have been formulated under UN auspices on topics such as racial discrimination, the rights of women, and torture. These later Covenants and Conventions go into much greater detail than the Universal Declaration and include a few important changes. For example, the Covenants prominently include a right to national self-determination, which is absent in the Universal Declaration, but do not include a right to private property. Nevertheless, for the most part they can be seen simply as elaborations on the Universal Declaration, which remains the central normative document in the international human rights regime.

What is the legal and political force of these norms? The Universal Declaration of Human Rights was proclaimed in 1948 by the United Nations General Assembly. As such, it has no force of law. Resolutions of the General Assembly, even solemn declarations, are merely recommendations to states; the General Assembly has no international legislative powers. Over the years, however, the Universal Declaration has come to be something more than a mere recommendation.

There are two principal sources of international law, namely, treaty and custom. Although today we tend to think first of treaty, historically custom is at least as important. A rule or principle attains the force of customary international law when it can meet two tests. First, the principle or rule must reflect the general practice of the overwhelming majority of states. Second, what lawyers call *opinio juris*, the sense of obligation, must be taken into account. Is the customary practice seen by states as an obligation, rather than a mere convenience or courtesy? Today it is a common view of international lawyers that the Universal Declaration has attained something of the status of customary international law, so that the rights it contains are in some important sense binding on states.

Furthermore, the International Human Rights Covenants are treaties and as such do have the force of international law, but only for the parties to the treaties, that is, those states that have (voluntarily) ratified or acceded to the treaties. The same is true of the single-issue treaties that round out the regime's norms. It is perhaps possible that the norms of the Covenants are coming to acquire the force of customary international law even for states that are not parties. But in either case, the fundamental weakness of international law is underscored: virtually all international legal obligations are voluntarily accepted.

This is obviously the case for treaties; states are free to become parties or not entirely as they choose. It is no less true, though, of custom, where the tests of state practice and *opinio juris* likewise assure that international legal obligation is only voluntarily acquired. In fact, a state that explicitly rejects a practice during the process of custom formation is exempt even from customary inter-national legal obligations. For example, Saudi Arabia's objection to the provi-sions on the equal rights of women during the drafting of the Universal Declaration might be held to exempt it from such a norm, even if the norm is accepted internationally as customarily binding. Such considerations are partic-ularly important when we ask what force there is to international law and what mechanisms exist to implement and enforce the rights specified in the Universal Declaration and the Covenants.

Acceptance of an obligation by states does not carry with it acceptance of any method of international enforcement. Quite the contrary. Unless there is an explicit enforcement mechanism attached to the obligation, its enforcement rests simply on the good faith of the parties. The Universal Declaration con-tains no enforcement mechanisms of any sort. Even if we accept it as hav-ing the force of international law, its implementation is left entirely in the hands of individual states. The Covenants do have some implementation machinery, but the machinery's practical weakness is perhaps its most striking feature.

Under the provisions of the International Covenant on Civil and Political Rights, a Human Rights Committee of independent experts was created in the United Nations to supervise the Covenant's implementation.[15] The Committee's principal function, however, is simply to review periodic reports submitted by the different states who are party to the Covenant concerning their practices with respect to the enumerated rights. While the reports of states are examined in public, the most the Committee can do is raise questions and request further information. It is powerless to compel more than pro forma compliance with the requirement of periodic reporting, and even that sometimes cannot be achieved.

Furthermore, even this minimal international scrutiny applies only to the parties to the Covenant, which numbered only eighty—about half the countries of the world—in 1985.

An Optional Protocol to the Civil/Political Covenant permits the Human Rights Committee to receive and examine complaints from individuals. The Committee receives about two dozen complaints a year, about half of which are admissible and receive substantive scrutiny. But even here the most that the Committee can do is state its views on whether a violation has occurred. In other words, even in this, probably the strongest procedure in the international human rights regime, there is only international monitoring of state practice. Enforcement remains entirely national. And by 1985 only thirty-five countries had accepted the provisions of the Optional Protocol. Not surprisingly, almost none of those covered are major human rights violators. Thus relatively strong procedures apply primarily where they are least needed—which is not at all surprising given that participation in these procedures is entirely voluntary.

The procedures under the International Covenant on Economic, Social and Cultural Rights are even weaker. Periodic reports are reviewed not by an independent committee of experts but by a working group of the UN Economic and Social Council (ECOSOC), a body of political delegates representing the views of their governments. (A new committee of experts was established in 1986, but it has yet to meet.) In addition, there is no individual complaint procedure.

The single-issue treaties on racial discrimination, torture and women's rights also contain periodic reporting procedures, as well as various complaint procedures, but the coverage of the first two is narrow and their provisions not significantly stronger than those of the Civil and Political Covenant. The International Labour Organization, which provided the model for the reporting procedures adopted in the field of human rights, also has similar powers for the workers' rights issues within its purview, but once more the furthest the system goes is voluntarily accepted monitoring of voluntarily accepted obligations. There is no real international enforcement of any sort.[16]

The one other major locus of activity in the international human rights regime is the UN Commission on Human Rights. In addition to being the body that played the principal role in the formulation of the Universal Declaration, the Covenants, and most of the major single-issue human rights treaties, it has some weak implementation powers. Its public discussion of human rights situations in various countries can help to mobilize international public opinion, which is not always utterly useless in helping to reform national practice. For example, in the 1970s the Commission played a major role in publicizing the human rights conditions in Chile, Israel, and South Africa. Furthermore, it is empowered by ECOSOC resolution 1503 (1970) to investigate communications (complaints) from individuals and groups that ''appear to reveal a consistent pattern of gross and reliably attested violations of human rights.''

The 1503 procedure, however, is at least as thoroughly hemmed in by constraints as are the other enforcement mechanisms that we have considered.[17] Although individuals may communicate grievances, the 1503 procedure deals only with "*situations*" of gross and systematic violations, not the particular cases of individuals. Individuals cannot even obtain an international judgment in their particular case, let alone international enforcement of the human rights obligations of their government. Furthermore, the entire procedure remains confidential until a case is concluded, although the Commission does publicly announce a "blacklist" of countries being studied. In only four cases (Equatorial Guinea, Haiti, Malawi, and Uruguay) has the Commission gone public with a 1503 case. Its most forceful conclusion was a 1980 resolution provoked by the plight of Jehovah's Witnesses in Malawi, which merely expressed the hope that all human rights were being respected in Malawi.

In addition to this global human rights regime, there are regional regimes.[18] The 1981 African Charter of Human and Peoples' Rights, drawn up by the Organization of African Unity, provides for a Human Rights Commission, but it is not yet functioning. In Europe and the Americas there are highly developed systems involving both commissions with very strong investigatory powers and regional human rights courts with the authority to make legally binding decisions on complaints by individuals (although only eight states have accepted the jurisdiction of the Inter-American Court of Human Rights).

Even in Europe and the Americas, however, implementation and enforcement remain primarily national. In nearly thirty years the European Commission of Human Rights has considered only about 350 cases, while the European Court of Human Rights has handled only one-fifth that number. Such regional powers certainly should not be ignored or denigrated. They provide authoritative interpretations in cases of genuine disagreements and a powerful check on backsliding and occasional deviations by states. But the real force of even the European regime lies in the voluntary acceptance of human rights by the states in question, which has infinitely more to do with domestic politics than with international procedures.

In sum, at the international level there are comprehensive, authoritative human rights norms that are widely accepted as binding on all states. Implementation and enforcement of these norms, however, both in theory and in practice, are left to states. The international context of national human rights practices certainly cannot be ignored. Furthermore, international norms may have an important socializing effect on national leaders and be useful to national advocates of improved domestic human rights practices. But the real work of implementing and enforcing human rights takes place at the national level. Therefore, the case studies that make up this volume focus on individual nation-states, the central arena in which the struggle for human rights today takes place. Before the level of the nation-state is discussed, however, one final element of the international context needs to be considered, namely, human rights as an issue in national foreign policies.

HUMAN RIGHTS AND FOREIGN POLICY

Beyond the human rights related activities of states in international institutions such as those discussed in the preceding section, many states have chosen to make human rights a concern in their bilateral foreign relations.[19] In fact, much of the surge of interest in human rights in the last decade can be traced to the catalyzing effect of President Jimmy Carter's (1977–1981) efforts to make international human rights an objective of U.S. foreign policy.

In a discussion of human rights as an issue in national foreign policy, at least three problems need to be considered. First, a nation must select a particular set of rights to pursue. Second, the legal and moral issues raised by intervention on behalf of human rights abroad need to be explored. Third, human rights concerns must be integrated into the nation's broader foreign policy, since human rights are at best only one of several foreign policy objectives.

The international normative consensus on human rights noted above largely solves the problem of the choice of a set of rights to pursue, for unless a state chooses a list very similar to that of the Universal Declaration, its efforts are almost certain to be dismissed as fatally flawed by partisan or ideological bias. Thus, for example, claims by officials of the Reagan administration that economic and social rights are not really true human rights are almost universally denounced. By the same token, the Carter administration's serious attention to economic and social rights, even if it was ultimately subordinate to a concern for civil and political rights, greatly contributed to the international perception of its policy as genuinely concerned with human rights, not just a new rhetoric for the Cold War or neo-colonialism. Such an international perception is almost a necessary condition—although by no means a sufficient condition—for an effective international human rights policy.

A state is, of course, free to pursue any objectives it wishes in its foreign policy. If it wishes its human rights policy to be taken seriously, however, the policy must at least be enunciated in terms consistent with the international consensus that has been forged around the Universal Declaration. In practice, some rights must be given particular prominence in a nation's foreign policy, given the limited material resources and international political capital of even the most powerful state, but the basic contours of policy must be set by the Universal Declaration.

After the rights to be pursued have been selected, the second problem, that of intervention on behalf of human rights, arises. When state A pursues human rights in its relations with state B, A usually will be seeking to alter the way that B treats its own citizens. This is, by definition, a matter essentially within the domestic jurisdiction of B and thus outside the legitimate jurisdiction of A. A's action, therefore, is vulnerable to the charge of intervention, a charge that carries considerable legal, moral, and political force in a world, such as ours, that is structured at the international level around sovereign nation-states.

The legal problems raised by foreign policy action on behalf of human rights abroad are probably the most troubling. Sovereignty entails the principle of nonintervention; to say that A has sovereign jurisdiction over x is essentially equivalent to saying that no one else may intervene in A with respect to x. Because sovereignty is the foundation of international law, any foreign policy action that amounts to intervention is prohibited by international law. On the face of it at least, this prohibition applies to action on behalf of human rights as much as any other activity.

It might be suggested that we can circumvent the legal proscription of intervention in the case of human rights by reference to particular treaties or even the general international normative consensus discussed above. International norms per se, however, do not authorize even international organizations, let alone individual states acting independently, to enforce those norms. Even if all states are legally bound to implement the rights enumerated in the Universal Declaration, it simply does not follow, in logic or in law, that any particular state or group of states is entitled to enforce that obligation. States are perfectly free to accept international legal obligations that have no enforcement mechanisms attached.

This does not imply, though, that for a state to comply with international law it must stand by idly in the face of human rights violations abroad. International law prohibits intervention. It does, however, leave considerable room for *action*—perhaps even interference—on behalf of human rights.

Intervention is most often defined as coercive interference (especially by the threat or use of force) in the internal affairs of another country. But there are many kinds of noncoercive "interference," which is the stuff of foreign policy. For example, barring explicit treaty commitments to the contrary, no state is under an international legal obligation to deal with any other state. Should state A choose to deny B the benefits of its friendly relations, A is perfectly free, as a matter of international law, to reduce or eliminate its relations with B. And should A decide to do so on the basis of B's human rights performance, A is legally within its rights.

Scrupulously avoiding intervention (coercive interference) thus still leaves considerable room for international action aimed at improving the human rights performance of a foreign country. Quiet diplomacy, public protests or condemnations, downgrading or breaking diplomatic relations, reducing or halting foreign aid, and selective or comprehensive restrictions of trade and other forms of interaction are all actions that fall far short of intervention. Thus in most circumstances they will be legally permissible actions on behalf of human rights abroad.

An international legal perspective on humanitarian intervention, however, does not exhaust the subject. Recently, several authors have argued, strongly and we believe convincingly, that moral considerations in at least some circumstances justify humanitarian intervention on behalf of human rights.[20] Michael Walzer, whose book *Just and Unjust Wars* has provoked much of the recent moral discussion of humanitarian intervention, can be taken as illustrative of such arguments.

Walzer presents a strong defense of the morality of the general international principle of nonintervention, arguing that it gives force to the basic right of peoples to self-determination, which in turn rests on the rights of individuals, acting in concert as a community, to choose their own government. Walzer has been criticized for interpreting this principle in a way that is excessively favorable to states by arguing that the presumption of legitimacy (and thus against intervention) should hold in all but the most extreme circumstances. Nonetheless, even Walzer allows that intervention must be permitted "when the violation of human rights is so terrible that it makes talk of community or self-determination . . . seem cynical and irrelevant,"[21] when gross, persistent, and systematic violations of human rights shock the moral conscience of mankind.

The idea underlying such arguments is that human rights are of such paramount moral importance that gross and systematic violations present a moral justification for remedial international action. If the international community as a whole cannot or will not act—and above we have shown that an effective collective international response will usually be impossible—then one or more states may be morally justified in acting ad hoc on behalf of the international community.

International law and morality thus lead to different and conflicting conclusions in at least some cases. One of the functions of international politics is to help to resolve such a conflict; political considerations will play a substantial role in determining how a state will respond in its foreign policy to the competing moral and legal demands placed on it. But the political dimensions of such decisions point to the practical dangers posed by moral arguments in favor of humanitarian intervention.

If we search the historical record it is very hard to find a clear example of humanitarian intervention in practice. In the last twenty-five years, the two leading candidates are the 1971 Indian intervention in East Pakistan (which soon became Bangladesh) in response to the massacre of Bengalis by the government, and the 1979 Tanzanian intervention in Uganda to topple Amin. But even here it must be noted that India intervened so as to partition its archenemy, Pakistan, and Tanzania intervened only after almost a decade of extremely poor Ugandan-Tanzanian relations, and close on the heels of a failed Ugandan invasion of Tanzanian territory. By contrast, the use of the language of humanitarian intervention to cloak partisan political adventurism—for example, in the U.S. interventions in the Dominican Republic in 1965, Grenada in 1983, and Nicaragua in the mid–1980s—is distressingly common.

Reasonable people may disagree on whether the danger of abuse outweighs the benefits of openly acknowledging and advocating a right to coercive humanitarian intervention. At the very least it should be noted that such a right is at best a very dangerous double-edged sword. Our preference would be to keep that particular sword sheathed and focus the pursuit of human rights in national foreign policy instead on actions short of military intervention. Such nonmilitary actions are legally and morally relatively unproblematic, and far less subject to catastrophic political abuse.

Having selected the rights to be pursued and satisfied itself that the means to be employed in that pursuit are, all things considered, acceptable, a state still faces the fact that human rights are only one part of its foreign policy, and a part that is not always consistent with other parts of the national interest. The relationship between human rights and the rest of the national interest, however, is neither as clear nor as simple as critics often make it out to be. In fact, a concern for human rights may enhance the national security, as a few examples from recent U.S. foreign policy clearly indicate.

In the late seventies, the United States "lost" Nicaragua and Iran in large measure as a result of its support of repressive rulers who managed to alienate virtually their entire populations and provoke genuine popular revolutions. A few years earlier, Angola was "lost" because of the colonial policy and human rights abuses of the U.S.-backed Portuguese regime. More recently, the cost of supporting dictators has been underscored by the fall of Marcos in the Philippines: any problems faced by the United States in this strategically important country are not only almost entirely of its own making but also largely the result of a misguided subordination of human rights concerns.

Human rights may be moral concerns, but often they are not *merely* moral concerns. Morality and realism are not necessarily incompatible, and to treat them as if they always were can harm not only a state's human rights policy but its broader foreign policy as well.

Sometimes a country can afford to act on its human rights concerns; other times it cannot. Politics involves compromise, as a result of multiple and not always compatible goals that are pursued and the resistance of a world that more often than not is unsupportive of the particular objectives being sought. Human rights, like other goals of foreign policy, must at times be compromised. In some instances there is little that a country can afford to do even in the face of major human rights violations. For example, because of other interests in the relationship between the United States and the USSR, such as arms control and the avoidance of war, not much can be done about Soviet human rights violations—either in a period of détente or one of cold war.

If such variations in the treatment of human rights violators are to be part of a consistent policy, human rights concerns need to be explicitly and coherently integrated into the broader framework of foreign policy. A human rights policy must be an integral part of, not just something tacked on to, a country's overall foreign policy.

Difficult decisions have to be made about the relative weights to be given to human rights, as well as other foreign policy goals, and at least rough rules for making trade-offs need to be formulated. Furthermore, such decisions need to be made early in the process of working out a policy, and as a matter of principle. Ad hoc responses to immediate problems and crises, which have been the rule in the human rights policies of countries such as Canada and the United States, are almost sure to lead to inconsistencies and incoherence, both in appearance and in fact. Without such efforts to integrate human rights into the structure of national foreign policy, any trade-offs that are made will remain, literally, unprincipled.

Standards will be undeniably difficult to formulate, and their application will raise no less severe problems. Hard cases and exceptions are unavoidable. So are gray areas and fuzzy boundaries. Unless such efforts are seriously undertaken, however, the resulting policy is likely to appear baseless or inconsistent, and probably will be so in fact as well.

There are many opportunities for foreign policy action on behalf of human rights in foreign countries, but effective action requires the same sort of care and attention required for success in any area of foreign policy. Furthermore, outside actors, even with the best of intentions, resources, and skills, are not the crucial factor in the human rights practices of most countries. Therefore, we must now move to the level of the state, where the remainder of this volume is focused, and where, as we argued above, the principal struggles for human rights today take place.

THE INDIVIDUAL AND THE STATE

At the national level, the struggle for human rights is essentially a struggle between individual citizens and the state. All states, we contend, are obliged to grant their citizens human rights, though in practice few grant the entire range, and deliberate violations are rampant.

The Individual

Above we argued that human rights are universal. We reject the view that concepts of human rights pertain only to certain Western cultures. In premodern traditional societies, which were not incorporated into modern nation-states, the social conditions for human rights did not yet exist. As we argue below, people were not yet individualized, and they did not face the threats to their dignity posed by the modern state. Now, there is no society that has not been incorporated into such a state.

Amazonian Indians, for example, lived until very recently in their own small, isolated, and homogeneous communities, ignored by the larger Brazilian state. But in the 1960s, when the state began to "open up" the Amazon for its mineral and other natural wealth, officially sanctioned (or at least tolerated) mass murders of the Amazonian natives began.[22] However pristine and pure a traditional culture might seem, in the late twentieth century it is extremely vulnerable to the depradations of larger political entities. The individual within his own culture might base his everyday life on a system of reciprocal privileges and responsibilities with his kinsmen or fellow villagers; but his day-to-day life can be quickly ended once the state in legal charge of his society takes an interest in it.

All societies in the modern world, then, are incorporated into states. But are all people individuals? Our concept of human rights is grounded in the notion of individual rights—of rights of the single human person in his relations with the wider community. We argue that the processes sometimes called "modernization" or "Westernization" are now universal. As a result, almost everywhere in the world there are people who think of themselves and define themselves as individuals, and who objectively are individuals, although the process of individuation has proceeded further in some countries (e.g., the United States) than in others (e.g., Japan and China).

The individual is a social creation. We do not deny that in times and cultures past there have been societies in which to use the term "individual" would have been inappropriate. Nor do we argue that modern societies are somehow morally "better" than premodern societies. Rather, we merely maintain that, like it or not, all countries are now significantly modernized.

The term "modernization" is useful to describe certain social psychological processes of individuation which strongly imply the need for individual human rights. By *social* psychological we mean processes of change which affect the psychologies of entire groups of people; their modes of personal behavior, their belief systems, and their individual "needs." Human nature is malleable. Culture, similarly, is not static; rather the sum total of all the individual changes in psyche results in new cultural organization as well.

In traditional societies, to use a word that loosely encompasses all premodern societies, social roles are relatively undifferentiated. The villager who fulfills his role as husband is also fulfilling his role as farmer and as respected man in the community. But in modern society, now more typical of even the poorest of the world's nation-states, role segmentation is increasingly the norm. What one does in one aspect of one's life does not necessarily reinforce what one does in another. The roles of husband, economic man, and political man are differentiated; the good father who takes his child to the clinic when it is ill is the poor employee, who does not show up for work on time. A person's ascribed status, that is the status he was born with, no longer completely defines his role. The son of an Untouchable can enter the cabinet; a woman can run a corporation. One's biological sex and age are no longer such strong definers of the role one plays in life as they once were; one's achievement, in education, in occupation, in competition for political rewards, now has considerable bearing on one's life.

In the contemporary world the individual's life, with its multiplicity of non-complementary roles, is increasingly complex. The division of labor is infinite; modern individuals can create new occupations and roles for themselves. In the course of a lifetime, an individual can change occupations several times, move from the status of employee to self-employed, leave or return to a peasant existence.

The society the individual lives in is as complex as its division of labor: ethnically heterogeneous, stratified by class, and erosive of traditional status, age, and sex rankings. In this situation, the individual begins to rely less on his primary group and far more on secondary groups, characterized not by affective or kin ties but by commonality of purpose. New kinds of communities, formed by choice rather than by accident of birth, arise in modern cities. Even in the most supposedly alienating urban environments, people form social networks, often based on modern characteristics such as education or profession.

Even a country such as China exhibits these trends towards individuation. The "four modernizations" (of agriculture, industry, science and technology, and defense), which are the development slogan of the current regime, will not be possible without drastic changes in education, social mobility, and the division of labor. But education facilitates literacy, thought, individualism, and criticism. Far from being a monolithic society, China is a society whose government relies on a vast coercive apparatus to suppress individual dissent. The more "modern" artifacts (e.g., Coca-Cola) and ideas (e.g., the Democracy Wall of 1978–1979) are introduced into China, the faster individual Chinese adapt to them and incorporate them into their structure of "needs"—for material goods, for influence over government.

Urbanization is one of the most important characteristics of modernization, detaching many people from their primary kin/clan and village communities— in Central and South America, in Africa and Asia, even fairly recently in Eastern Europe—and removing them to heterogeneous, multiethnic, and culturally novel environments. Both the "push" of the rural areas and the "pull" of urban areas cause such migration. In many parts of the world, life in the rural areas is becoming increasingly unpleasant. For example, in El Salvador peasants have suffered for many years from land-grabbing landlords and multinational corporations. Urban areas, even when employment opportunities are few, generally offer far more facilities for education, medical care, social services, and an interesting cultural life than do rural areas. In Cuba, despite the regime's stated objectives of equality, social services still favor urban over rural areas.[23] Moreover, in the cities there is more personal freedom, the chance to attend the cinema, listen to new music, meet new people, and above all escape the often oppressive authority of family or village community. Individuals choose to go to the city—and once there they become more individualized.

National, modern societies are also facilitated by the spread of education and information. Literacy allows people—sometimes even forces them—to encounter new ideas. Even if government propaganda is the main function of schooling, the acquisition of literacy cannot help but increase both the modern aspects of an individual's psychology and his potential to think critically about the society in which he lives. India's relatively healthy system of competitive democracy, for example, undoubtedly emerged partly because of its large number of highly educated citizens. Schools are indeed a mechanism to socialize children into state-approved model citizens, but students are capable of turning received ideas to their own purposes, as Christian converts in colonial societies did in applying Christ's egalitarian doctrines to themselves. The literate person is individualized in the sense that he has not only the capacity to acquire a great deal of information but also the access to more varied and more complex modes of thought and expression, and can express his views to an audience wider than that which can be reached by the spoken word alone.

Urbanization and literacy are supplemented by the enormous spread of the mass media in all parts of the world. Radios and televisions, especially, can bring new ideas to people who are not yet able to read. Until the mid–1970s South Africa, aware of this, did not permit any television at all, even for white viewers. Cinemas are also important socializing mechanisms. The Third World urban dweller who sees imported Western films has a much closer encounter with the world of materialism and individualism than his rural counterpart. It is not surprising that during the so-called "Cultural" Revolution in China, almost all cultural creations were banned. Not only did the state consider it dangerous to allow its citizenry exposure to Western culture, but even the possibility of new Chinese culture—novels, operas, or films—threatened the ruling faction. A favorite tactic of some governments is to restrict the supply of newsprint, as in Guyana in the early 1980s and in India under Indira Gandhi. Then without actual censorship, the impression can be conveyed that since no opposition newspapers exist, there is an ideological consensus in the society.

The spread of mass media and education makes it extremely difficult for repressive governments to cut off their citizens from the rest of the world. The "revolution of rising expectations," which worried social scientists in the 1960s, was a revolution of material expectations. Almost everyone would like to live like a wealthy Westerner, if given the opportunity. That is why, while the Soviet Union restricts the right to emigrate, most Western countries restrict the right to immigrate.

There has been a revolution of moral expectations as well. The world over, individuals have higher expectations of their rights. They expect to be not only wealthier, but freer. It is not outside agitators who have caused revolutions in such poor countries as Nicaragua, or unrest in wealthier repressive countries such as Poland. It is the creation of one international community of modern men and women who are increasingly capable, however poor or oppressed they are, of recognizing the roots of their oppression—the state. The free communication of ideas is as threatening to ruling groups as the free commerce of guns.

The modern individual exists. And it is the modern individual who needs human rights.

Culture and Human Rights

This view of the creation of the individual, with individual needs for human rights, is criticized by many advocates of the "cultural relativist" school of human rights. They present the argument that human rights are a "Western construct with limited [universal] applicability."[24] But cultural relativism, as applied to human rights, fails to grasp the nature of culture. A number of erroneous assumptions underlie this viewpoint.

Criticism of the universality of human rights often stems from erroneous perceptions of the persistence of traditional societies, societies in which principles of social justice are based not on rights but on status and on the intermixture of privilege and responsibility. Often anthropologically anachronistic pictures are presented of premodern societies, taking no account whatsoever of the social changes we have described above. It is assumed that culture is a static entity. But culture—like the individual—is adaptive. One can accept the principle that customs, values, and norms do indeed glue society together, and that they will endure, without assuming cultural stasis. Even though elements of culture have a strong hold on people's individual psyches, cultures can and do change. Individuals are actors who can influence their own fate, even if their range of choice is circumscribed by the prevalent social structure, culture, or ideology.

Cultural relativist arguments also often assume that culture is a unitary and unique whole; that is, that one is born into, and will always be, a part of a distinctive, comprehensive, and integrated set of cultural values and institutions that cannot be changed incrementally or only in part. Since in each culture the social norms and roles vary, so, it is argued, human rights must vary. The norms of each society are held to be both valuable in and of their own right, and so firmly rooted as to be impervious to challenge. Therefore, such arguments run, the universal standards embodied in the main UN instruments are applicable only to certain Western societies; to impose them on other societies from which they did not originally arise would do serious and irreparable damage to those cultures. In fact, though, people are quite adept cultural accommodationists; they are able to choose which aspects of a "new" culture they wish to adopt and which aspects of the "old" they wish to retain. For example, the marabouts (priests), who lead Senegal's traditional Muslim brotherhoods, have become leading political figures and have acquired considerable wealth and power through the peanut trade.

Still another assumption of the cultural relativism school is that culture is unaffected by social structure. But structure does affect culture. To a significant extent cultures and values reflect the basic economic and political organization of a society. For example, a society such as Tokugawa Japan, that moves from a feudal structure to an organized bureaucratic state is bound to experience changes in values. Or the amalgamation of many different ethnic groups into one nation-state inevitably changes the way that individuals view themselves: for example, state-sponsored retention of ethnic customs, as under Canada's multicultural policy of preserving ethnic communities, cannot mask the fact that most of those communities are merging into the larger Canadian society.

A final assumption of the cultural relativist view of human rights is that cultural practices are neutral in their impact on different individuals and groups. Yet very few social practices, whether cultural or otherwise, distribute the same benefits to each member of a group. In considering any cultural practice it is useful to ask, who benefits from its retention? Those who speak for the group are usually those most capable of articulating the group's values to the outside world. But such spokesmen are likely to stress, in their articulation of "group" values, those particular values that are most to their own advantage. Both those who choose to adopt "new" ideals, such as political democracy or atheism, and those who choose to retain "old" ideals, such as a God-fearing political consensus, may be doing so in their own interests. Culture is both influenced by, and an instrument of, conflict among individuals or social groups. Just as those who attempt to modify or change customs may have personal interests in so doing, so also do those who attempt to preserve them. Quite often, relativist arguments are adopted principally to protect the interests of those in power.

Thus the notion that human rights cannot be applied across cultures violates both the principle of human rights and its practice. Human rights mean precisely that: rights held by virtue of being human. Human rights do not mean human dignity, nor do they represent the sum total of personal resources (material, moral, or spiritual) that an individual might hold. Cultural variances that do not violate basic human rights undoubtedly enrich the world. But to permit the interests of the powerful to masquerade behind spurious defenses of cultural relativity is merely to lessen the chance that the victims of their policies will be able to complain. In the modern world, concepts such as cultural relativity, which deny to individuals the moral right to make comparisons and to insist on universal standards of right and wrong, are happily adopted by those who control the state.

The State

Human rights ground claims of the individual on or against the state. Other social actors can of course violate an individual's rights. One can be mugged while jogging in the park, thus suffering an attack on one's liberty, or one can be denied maternity benefits by one's employer, thus enduring an attack on one's right to fair working conditions. But it is, or should be, the business of the state to ensure that these violations do not occur, by providing more street lamps and a better police force, or by enforcing the right of mothers and children to special protection, as provided in Article 25 of the Universal Declaration.

The legitimate functions of the state in modern society, however, produce many of its abuses of citizens' rights. The state, for example, is obliged to protect its own people and territory from foreign attack, as in Cuba or Nicaragua, but in the process of so doing, it frequently violates a variety of human rights. In Israel, which bases its claim to sovereignty partly upon an ideological definition of its existence as a homeland for the Jewish people, Arab citizens have fewer rights than Jewish.[25]

Another major function of the state is national integration; that is, the creation of a sense of common citizenship, of spiritual belonging, among people of often diverse and even conflictual origins. For example, in Canada persistent violations of basic civil liberties by the internal security force, the Royal Canadian Mounted Police, during the 1960s and 1970s (and possibly beyond) were in part a response to the independence movement in the French-speaking province of Quebec.[26] Uganda has suffered much more severely from lack of national integration. One of the underlying causes of the political chaos from 1971 to 1985 was the northern and other out-groups' fear that if the dominant ethnic group, the Buganda, obtained more power, the state would cease to represent any other ethnic groups. The state in Uganda was not capable of mediating among different ethnic or national groups and proved unable to create a sense of common belongingness in the new country.[27]

States often attempt to buttress their internal control by ideological unification. In Poland, the attempt by the Communist party to unify the country around its ideology was weakened by the compromise it made in 1956, when the party was obliged to permit the Catholic Church to continue its influence, especially through the presence of Catholicism in the schools.[28] The existence of such a strong, competing ideological organization as the Catholic Church facilitated the development of Solidarity. In contrast, the Soviet Union, which has never had to make such a compromise with an internally competitive ideological organization, has a much firmer grasp on its own citizens.

The state's function of providing internal order also can militate against human rights. Order is supposed to be one good which even the most repressive government can provide for its (law-abiding) citizens. Thus a common comment made by those who lived under, but were not persecuted by, Nazi rule, is that at least it was safe to walk in the streets. To those who value order, the United States often appears like a rights-protecting society run amok; while criminals are protected from the police, the people do not appear to be protected from criminals. Yet civil libertarians frequently interpret high crime rates as the social price for the scrupulous defense of the rule of law and the protection of citizens from possible violations of their rights by the police.

But the major reason why the state does not normally fulfill the entire range of its human rights responsibilities is that it is not a neutral entity. Rather in all societies, under all ideological regimes, the state is controlled by groups or classes that attempt to manipulate its organs in their own interests. Thus another reason for the necessary universality of human rights is the universal control or manipulation of the state by powerful groups in the society, in whose objective interest it is to deny rights to other groups.

Those who have power rarely willingly relinquish it. Rather, they strive to acquire more for themselves, their clients, friends, or kin. Even in socialist countries in which political power is (in principle) completely separate from economic power, there are many other resources for the accumulation of power— especially control of party and bureaucratic office and control of the military. In underdeveloped countries, even a university education is a resource which can be parlayed into a considerable amount of power.

Thus in the natural course of events, those who control the state will violate human rights in the pursuit of more power, wealth, and security for themselves. Any system of social stratification assumes that the wealthier and more powerful will have better access to basic economic (material) resources than the poor and the powerless. Thus we find that even in the United States of America there are strata of the population who do not have enough to eat and who do not have access to adequate medical care.[29] The existence of sufficient material resources for all by no means presumes that everyone is guaranteed basic subsistence rights.

Nor do those who control the state confine their rights violations to economic rights. "Cultural" or communal rights—to preservation of religion, language, or customs—are also frequently violated, especially in Third World countries in which the communal organization of politics assumes that competition for scarce goods can be ameliorated by simply ignoring—or perhaps excluding—the less powerful ethnic groups. Genocide is the most extreme form of such exclusion. But the creation of "stranger" or scapegoat groups, the creation of rightless categories of noncitizens, or the social exclusion of entire groups of people such as the *burakumin* of Japan[30] because of their ancestry or social origins, can also help limit competition for scarce material goods.

The natural concomitant of such categorizations is the exclusion of all except those who control the state and their allies from effective participation in politics. Even when the material goods for the satisfaction of basic subsistence needs are not scarce, those who control the state frequently fear any redistribution which might lessen their own privileges, access to material resources, or coercive power. Political rights of access to the state and participation in decision making are normally not permitted, even in countries—such as Cuba[31]—in which the state has an ideological commitment to providing basic economic rights. The ruling class prefers to organize the state as a benevolent dispenser of goods, rather than as an institution on which anyone and everyone in the populace can make legitimate claims.

When political rights are excluded, rights of freedom of expression and association are also likely to be violated. A free press or a free trade union is a threat to those who control power. In order to prevent such political organization, it is also necessary for the state to violate civil rights. Thus the rights to due process and to protection from arbitrary arrest, torture, and unlawful execution are the natural victims of political repression. State terrorism—the massive violations of the civil rights of the citizenry—is normally a last resort by a ruling class intent on preserving its power against pressure from below, although sometimes, as in Chile since 1973, it is the first weapon of a very brutal regime.[32]

The key question for social analysts of human rights, therefore, is not, why are rights violated, but rather, why are rights preserved? Power is very rarely used to support human rights, unless there are countervailing forces to which those controlling the state must defer. That is why societies with dispersed bases of power are the best protectors of human rights. An economic system which is substantially separate from the political system, competing political parties which have the right to assume office, a relatively independent judiciary, a free critical press, and a plethora of interest groups disperse power. Such dispersal provides a variety of means for citizens to protect themselves against the state's tendency to ignore at best, and violate at worst, human rights.

No state system, no political regime, no political philosophy is an absolute guarantor of human rights. Human rights are everywhere fragile and subject to constant assault by the state. Everywhere individuals are the victims of the very states that are supposed to protect them. The ideal of universal human rights provides philosophical legitimacy to the notion that an individual can, indeed ought to, protect himself against the state's tendency to deprive him of his material subsistence, physical security, and intellectual independence. Far too often, attempts to deny the philosophical legitimacy of universal human rights serve as handy tools for ruling classes whose real intent is to deny human rights in practice.

THIRD WORLD CRITICISMS

In recent years a number of commentators from the Third World have criticized the concept of universal human rights. Frequently, the intention of the criticisms appears to be to exempt some Third World governments from the standard of judgment generated by the concept of universal human rights. Much of the criticism in fact serves to cover abuses of human rights by state corporatist, developmental dictatorship, or allegedly "socialist" regimes.[33]

A common criticism of the concept of universal human rights is that since it is Western in origin, it must be limited in its applicability to the Western world. Both logically and empirically, this criticism is invalid. Knowledge is not limited in its applicability to its place or people of origin—one does not assume, for example, that medicines discovered in the developed Western world will cure only people of European origin. Nor is it reasonable to state that knowledge or thought of a certain kind—about social arrangements instead of about human biology or natural science—is limited to its place of origin. Those same Third World critics who reject universal concepts of human rights often happily accept Marxist socialism, which also originated in the Western world, in the mind of a German Jew.

The fact that human rights is originally a liberal notion, rooted in the rise of a class of bourgeois citizens in Europe who demanded individual rights against the power of kings and nobility, does not make human rights inapplicable to the rest of the world. As we argue above, all over the world there are now formal states, whose citizens are increasingly individualized. All over the world, therefore, there are people who need protections against the depradations of class-ruled governments.

Moreover, whatever the liberal origins of human rights, the list now accepted as universal includes a wide range of economic and social rights that were first advocated by socialist and social-democratic critics of liberalism. Although eighteenth-century liberals stressed the right to private property, the 1966 International Human Rights Covenants do not mention it, substituting instead the right to sovereignty over national resources. Indeed, much liberal thinking also now restricts property rights; for example, Henry Shue argues that property rights must always be subsidiary to subsistence rights.[34] To attribute the idea of universal human rights to an outdated liberalism, unaffected by later notions of welfare democracy and uninfluenced by socialist concerns with economic rights, is simply incorrect.

The absence of a right to private property in the Covenants indicates a sensitivity to the legitimate preoccupations of socialist and postcolonial Third World governments. Conservative critics of recent trends in international human rights in fact deplore the right to national sovereignty over resources, as some of them also deplore any attention to the economic rights of the individual.[35] We certainly do not share this view of rights; we believe that the economic rights of the individual are as important as civil and political rights. But it is the individual we are concerned with. We would like to see a world in which every *individual* has enough to eat, not merely a world in which every *state* has the right to economic sovereignty.

We are skeptical, therefore, of the radical Third Worldist assertion that "group" rights ought to be more important than individual rights. Too often, the "group" in question proves to be the state. Why allocate rights to a social institution that is already the chief violator of individuals' rights? Similarly, we fear the expression "peoples' rights." The communal rights of individuals to practice their own religion, speak their own language, and indulge in their own ancestral customs are protected in the Covenant on Civil and Political Rights. Individuals are free to come together in groups to engage in those cultural practices which are meaningful to them. On the other hand, often a "group" right can simply mean that the individual is subordinate to the group—for example, that the individual Christian fundamentalist in the Soviet Union risks arrest because of the desire of the larger "group" to enforce official atheism.

The one compelling use that we can envisage for the term "group rights" is in protection of native peoples, usually hunter-gatherers, pastoralists, or subsistence agriculturalists, whose property rights as collectivities are being violated by the larger state societies that encroach upon them. Such groups are fighting a battle against the forces of modernization and the state's accumulative tendencies. For example, native peoples in Canada began in the 1970s to object to state development projects, such as the James Bay Hydroelectric project in Quebec, which deprived them of their traditional lands. At the moment, there is no international human rights protection for such groups or their "way of life."

One way to protect such group rights would be to incorporate the group as a legal entity in order to preserve their land claims. However, even if the law protects such group rights, individual members of the group may prefer to move into the larger society in response to the processes of modernization discussed above. Both options must be protected.

If the purpose of group rights is to protect large, established groups of people who share the same territory, customs, language, religion, and ancestry, then such protection could only occur at the expense of states' rights. These groups, under international human rights law, do not have the right to withdraw from the states that enfold them. Moreover, it is clearly not the intention of Third World defenders of group rights to allow such a right to secession. A first principle of the Organization of African Unity, for example, is to preserve the sovereignty of all its member states not only against outside attack but also against internal attempts at secession.[36] Group rights appear to mean, in practice, states' rights. But the rights of states are the rights of the individuals and classes who control the state.

Many Third World and socialist regimes also argue that rights ought to be tied to duties. A citizen's rights, it is argued, ought to be contingent upon his duties toward the society at large—privilege is contingent on responsibility. Such a view of rights made sense in nonstate societies in which each "person" fulfilled his roles along with others, all of the roles together creating a close-knit, tradition-bound group. But in modern state societies, to tie rights to duties is to risk the former's complete disappearance. All duties will be aimed toward the preservation of the state and of the interests of those who control it.

It is true that no human rights are absolute; even in societies that adhere in principle to the liberal ethos, individuals are frequently deprived of rights, especially in wartime or if they are convicted of criminal acts. However, such deprivations can legitimately be made only after the most scrupulous protection of civil and political rights under the rule of law. The difficulty with tying rights to duties without the intermediate step of scrutiny by a genuinely independent judiciary is the likelihood of wholesale cancellation of rights by the ruling class. But if one has rights merely because one is human, and for no other reason, then it is much more difficult, in principle, for the state to cancel them. It cannot legitimate the denial of rights by saying that only certain types of human beings, exhibiting certain kinds of behavior, are entitled to them.

One final criticism of the view of universal human rights embedded in the International Covenants is that an undue stress is laid on civil and political rights, whereas the overriding rights priority in the Third World is economic rights. In this view, the state as the agent of economic development—and hence, presumably, of eventual distribution of economic goods or "rights" to the masses— should not be bothered with problems of guaranteeing political participation in decision making, or of protecting people's basic civil rights. These rights, it is argued, come "after" development is completed. The empirical basis for this argument is weak, as for example Rhoda Rabkin indicates in her chapter on Cuba. A number of other studies indicate that both in what is now the developed Western world[37] and in the Third World[38] civil and political rights are essential to obtaining economic rights from the state. Economic development per se will not guarantee future human rights, whether of an economic or any other kind. Often, development means economic growth, but without equitable distributive measures. Moreover, development strategies often fail because of insufficient attention to citizens' needs and views. Finally, development plans are often a cover for the continued violations of citizens' rights by the ruling class.

Thus we return to where we started: the rights of all men and women against all governments to treatment as free, equal, materially and physically secure persons. This is what human dignity means and requires in our era. And the individual human rights of the Universal Declaration and the Covenants are the means by which individuals today carry out the struggle to achieve their dignity. The chapters that follow are a series of individual country studies that attempt to assess the state of that struggle.

NOTES

1. The International Bill of Human Rights includes the Universal Declaration of Human Rights (1948; reprinted below as appendix 1), the International Covenant on Economic, Social and Cultural Rights (1966), the International Covenant on Civil and Political Rights (1966), and the Optional Protocol to the latter Covenant.

2. Ronald Dworkin, *Taking Rights Seriously* (Cambridge: Harvard University Press, 1977), pp. xi, 90.

3. Thomas Aquinas, *The Political Ideas of St. Thomas Aquinas*, ed. Dino Bigongiari (New York: Hafner Press, 1953).

4. John Locke, *Essays on the Law of Nature* (Oxford: Clarendon Press, 1954); *Two Treatises of Government* (Cambridge: Cambridge University Press, 1967), *Second Treatise*, para. 6, 12, 16, 57, 59, 60, 118, 124, 135, 172.

5. Jacques Maritain, *The Rights of Man and Natural Law* (New York: Charles Scribner's Sons, 1947); *Man and the State* (Chicago: University of Chicago Press, 1951).

6. Thomas Hobbes, *Leviathan* (Baltimore: Penguin Books, 1971).

7. Locke, *Second Treatise*.

8. Thomas Jefferson, *The Life and Selected Writings of Thomas Jefferson*, ed. Adrienne Koch and William Peden (New York: Modern Library, 1944); Thomas Paine, *Rights of Man* (New York: Penguin Books, 1984).

9. See Jack Donnelly, "Natural Law and Right in Aquinas' Political Thought," *Western Political Quarterly* 33 (December 1980); 520–35.

10. Rhoda E. Howard and Jack Donnelly, "Human Dignity, Human Rights and Political Regimes," *American Political Science Review* 80 (September 1986); 51–63; Jack Donnelly, "Human Rights and Human Dignity: An Analytic Critique of Non-Western Human Rights Conceptions," *American Political Science Review* 76 (June 1982); 303–16; Rhoda E. Howard, *Human Rights in Commonwealth Africa* (Totowa, N.J.: Rowman and Littlefield, 1986), chap. 2.

11. See Jack Donnelly, *The Concept of Human Rights* (London: Croom Helm; New York: St. Martin's, 1985), chap. 3 and the sources cited therein.

12. See, for example, Marc F. Plattner, ed., *Human Rights in Our Time: Essays in Memory of Victor Baras* (Boulder, Col.: Westview Press, 1984); Maurice Cranston, "Are There Any Human Rights?" *Daedalus* 112 (Fall 1983); 1–17; Jeane J. Kirkpatrick, "Establishing a Viable Human Rights Policy," in *Human Rights and U.S. Human Rights Policy*, Howard J. Wiarda, ed. (Washington, D.C.: American Enterprise Institute, 1982).

13. See, for example, H. Klenner, "Freedom and Human Rights," *GDR Committee for Human Rights Bulletin* 10, no. 1 (1984); 13–21; A. G. Egorov, "Socialism and the

Individual: Rights and Freedoms," *Soviet Studies in Philosophy* 18 (Fall 1979); 3–51; and UN document number A/C.3/32/SR.51.

14. This section is a very much abbreviated version of Jack Donnelly, "International Human Rights: A Regime Analysis," *International Organization* 40 (Summer 1986); 599–642.

15. See Farrokh Jhabvala, "The Practice of the Covenant's Human Rights Committee, 1976–82: Review of State Party Reports," *Human Rights Quarterly* 6 (February 1984); 81–106; Dana D. Fischer, "Reporting under the Covenant on Civil and Political Rights: The First Five Years of the Human Rights Committee," *American Journal of International Law* 76 (January 1982); 142–53; and Donnelly "International Human Rights," pp. 609–11.

16. See Donnelly, "International Human Rights," pp. 628–33 and the works cited there.

17. Howard Tolley, "The Concealed Crack in the Citadel: The United Nations Commission on Human Rights' Response to Confidential Communications," *Human Rights Quarterly* 6 (November 1984); 420–62.

18. See Donnelly, "International Human Rights," pp. 620–28 and the works cited there.

19. This section draws heavily on Jack Donnelly, "Human Rights and Foreign Policy," *World Politics* 34 (July 1982); 574–95, and "Human Rights, Humanitarian Intervention and American Foreign Policy: Law, Morality and Politics," *Journal of International Affairs* 37 (Winter 1984); 311–28.

20. See, for example, Jerome Slater and Terry Nardin, "Nonintervention and Human Rights," *Journal of Politics* 48 (February 1986); 86–96; Charles R. Beitz, "Nonintervention and Communal Integrity," *Philosophy and Public Affairs* 9 (Summer 1980); 385–91; and Robert Matthews and Cranford Pratt, "Human Rights and Foreign Policy: Principles and Canadian Practice," *Human Rights Quarterly* 7 (May 1985); 159–88.

21. Michael Walzer, *Just and Unjust Wars* (New York: Basic Books, 1977), p. 90. For criticisms of Walzer see Slater and Nardin, "Nonintervention;" Beitz, "Nonintervention"; and David Luban, "The Romance of the Nation State," *Philosophy and Public Affairs* 9 (Summer 1980); 392–97.

22. Shelton H. Davis, *Victims of the Miracle: Development and the Indians of Brazil* (New York: Cambridge University Press, 1977), p. 79.

23. See "Cuba," chapter 5, by Rhoda Rabkin.

24. Adamantia Pollis and Peter Schwab, "Human Rights: A Western Concept with Limited Applicability," in *Human Rights: Cultural and Ideological Perspectives* Pollis and Schwab, ed. (New York: Praeger, 1979), pp. 1–18.

25. See "Israel," chapter 8, by Raphael Israeli and Rachel Ehrenfeld.

26. See "Canada," chapter 2, by Robert Allan McChesney.

27. See "Uganda," chapter 18, by Edward Kannyo.

28. See "Poland," chapter 14 by Stefania Szlek Miller.

29. See "United States," chapter 20 by Robert Justin Goldstein.

30. See "Japan," chapter 10 by Lawrence W. Beer.

31. See chapter 5.

32. See "Chile," chapter 3, by Jinny Arancibia, Marcelo Charlin, and Peter Landstreet.

33. For our usage of these categories, see Howard and Donnelly, "Human Dignity."

34. Henry Shue, *Basic Rights: Subsistence, Affluence, and U.S. Foreign Policy* (Princeton: Princeton University Press, 1980), p. 127.

35. See Carnes Lord, "Human Rights Policy in a Nonliberal World," in *Human Rights in Our Time*, ed. Plattner, p. 132.

36. Howard, *Human Rights in Commonwealth Africa*, p. 5.

37. Robert Justin Goldstein, *Political Repression in Nineteenth Century Europe* (Totowa, N.J.: Barnes and Noble, 1983).

38. Jack Donnelly, "Human Rights and Development: Complementary or Competing Concerns?" *World Politics* 36 (January 1984); 255–83; Sylvia Ann Hewlett, "Human Rights and Economic Realities: Tradeoffs in Historical Perspective," *Political Science Quarterly* 94 (Fall 1979); Robert M. Marsh, "Does Democracy Hinder Economic Development in the Latecomer Developing Nations?" in *Comparative Social Research*, ed. Richard F. Tomasson (Greenwich, Conn.; JAI Press, 1979); and Han S. Park. "Human Rights and Modernization: A Dialectical Relationship?" *Universal Human Rights* 2 (January-March 1980).

SUGGESTED READINGS

Brown, Peter G. and Douglas Maclean, eds. *Human Rights and U.S. Foreign Policy*. Lexington: Lexington Books, 1979.

Donnelly, Jack. *The Concept of Human Rights*. New York: St. Martin's, 1985.

Falk, Richard. *Human Rights and State Sovereignty*. New York: Holmes and Meier, 1981.

Forsythe, David P. *Human Rights and World Politics*. Lincoln: University of Nebraska Press, 1983.

Howard, Rhoda E. *Human Rights in Commonwealth Africa*. Totowa, N.J.: Rowman and Littlefield, 1986.

Howard, Rhoda E. and Jack Donnelly. "Human Dignity, Human Rights and Political Regimes." *American Political Science Review* 80 (September 1986): 51–63.

Moore, Barrington, Jr. *Injustice: The Social Bases of Obedience and Revolt*. White Plains, N.Y.: M. E. Sharpe, 1978.

Pollis, Adamantia and Peter Schwab, eds. *Human Rights: Cultural and Ideological Perspectives*. New York: Praeger, 1980.

Shue, Henry. *Basic Rights: Subsistence, Affluence and U.S. Foreign Policy*. Princeton: Princeton University Press, 1980.

Thompson, Kenneth W., ed. *The Moral Imperatives of Human Rights: A World Survey*. Washington, D.C.: University Press of America, 1980.

Vasak, Karel and Philip Alston, eds. *The International Dimensions of Human Rights*. Westport, Conn.: Greenwood Press, 1982.

2

CANADA

Robert Allan McChesney

Canada is a stable parliamentary democracy in which human rights are guaranteed by custom, legislation, the Constitution, and increasingly by the courts. Despite abhorrent examples of legalized racism in its past, Canada has become a relatively tolerant multicultural society. Governments have enhanced the quality of life with an array of social programs such as public health insurance, universal primary and secondary education, and publicly supported pensions for older people. The legal system protects the rights of individuals, and in some instances, of collectivities as well.

The study that follows will not focus on such fundamental rights as freedom of expression and the right to a fair trial, which for the most part, Canadians and even non-Canadians in Canada can take for granted. Greater attention will be devoted to spheres of concern which are not so highly developed: economic and social rights; aboriginal and other collective rights; equality rights for women and for other economically or socially disadvantaged groups; and emerging issues in anti-discrimination law and practice.

Many readers will be aware that Canada is among the more fortunate nations with regard to income per capita and such social indicators as literacy, life span, and child mortality. Because of its predominantly aboriginal, British, and French heritage, Canada's multiracial and multicultural character is less well-known. The percentage of people who have native ancestry is not known, but widely divergent estimates range from 2 percent to 6 percent of the population. The 1981 census, which was not a precise measuring instrument, reported that roughly 40 percent of Canadians were of British origin, 27 percent of French origin, and the remainder from around the globe; the percentage of those with an ancestry traceable neither to Britain nor to France may prove closer to 50 percent in the 1986 census. English only is spoken by about 67 percent of the population, with about 32 percent speaking either French only (16.6 percent) or being bilingual (15.3 percent). Christianity is the predominant faith, with declared Roman Catholics and Protestants making up approximately 89 percent of the populace and Eastern Orthodox declarants numbering about 1.5 percent. Jewish adherents account for a bit more than 1 percent of the populace, which is also the approximate combined percentage of followers of other non-Christian religions (Muslims, Hindus, and Sikhs being the largest groups).

There are unequal opportunities and benefits in Canadian society for the various cultural groups within it. Adverse inequality is also faced by women as a group, by native peoples, by persons with a disability, and by other minorities. After outlining the general human rights picture in Canada, this chapter will focus on those classes of peoples whose rights have been realized least.

HISTORICAL BACKGROUND, 1867–1982

The British North America Act of 1867, the main constitutional document prior to 1982, contained no bill of rights.[1] In fact, the British North America Act made no reference to central characteristics of the largely unwritten Constitution by which Canada was governed, such as the existence of political parties and electoral democracy. All of these elements, as well as protection for civil liberties, flowed from a clause in the preamble to the 1867 act which refers to the Constitution as being "similar in principle to that of the United Kingdom."

This same provision later proved to be a foundation for some of Canada's most important civil liberties cases. There was no bill of rights having primacy over legislators, and Canadian courts generally found themselves powerless to interfere with harmful discrimination or restriction of civil liberties if these resulted from an unambiguous statute drafted by a legislature acting within its powers. Gradually, however, the question of discrimination came to be handled in courts and legislatures, and discrimination codes have come to play a significant role in Canadian law.

Despite some admirable civil libertarian decisions, until recently the human rights record of the judiciary in Canada with respect to safeguards against discriminatory practices left something to be desired. The case law included several judgments holding that discrimination on racial grounds was not a basis for invalidating legislation.[2] The leading example of this stream of judicial reasoning was the 1939 case of *Christie v. York Corporation*.[3] A season subscriber to ice hockey games at the Montreal Forum was denied service at a Forum tavern because of his color. The Supreme Court of Canada held that the management could refuse service on the basis of "freedom of commerce." Decisions following or paralleling this were taken elsewhere in Canada,[4] one as recently as 1961.[5]

In 1945 one judge in the province of Ontario, cognizant of the ideals espoused by the fledgling United Nations (UN) organization, held that a covenant not to resell land to "Jews, or to persons of objectionable nationality" was contrary to "public policy."[6] Despite this precedent, three levels of judiciary did not find a somewhat similar stipulation (also in Ontario) void in a subsequent case.[7] The

Supreme Court of Canada seemed to disregard the fact that before the case reached that judicial tier, Ontario had passed legislation invalidating such clauses.

During the 1950s and beyond, legislatures gradually enacted anti-discrimination legislation, filling the vacuum left by the inactivity or conservatism of the courts. About the time that legislators had begun outdistancing the judges in the combat against discrimination, some significant victories were being won in the courts on behalf of civil rights and fundamental freedoms. These cases tended to rely either on common law notions of the Rule of Law or on restriction of provincial powers under Canada's federal government system, rather than on explicit human rights principles.[8] One leading case arose from the harassment faced by adherents to the Jehovah's Witness religious sect in Quebec, a mainly Roman Catholic province. In 1959 Canada's Supreme Court found the head of the Quebec government, Premier Maurice Duplessis, personally liable for actions taken against Roncarelli, a man who had provided bail for fellow Jehovah's Witnesses when they were arrested. Duplessis acted outside his powers in arranging the cancellation of the liquor license for Roncarelli's restaurant, thus ruining the latter's business.[9]

In 1950 the Supreme Court of Canada interpreted an unclear definition of "Sedition" in the Criminal Code as not being applicable to the printing of scurrilous attacks against the Roman Catholic Church.[10] Although Canadian courts of that era would not intervene when civil liberties were restricted by unambiguous legislation promulgated by a legislature acting within its powers,[11] the judiciary would act when the restriction arose from improper exercise of authority, as in "the Padlock case" in 1957. The Supreme Court found that legislation authorizing the padlocking of any house used for the dissemination of Communist literature could not be passed by a province. The power to enact criminal law under the British North America Act rested solely with the federal (national) government.[12]

Commencing in the 1940s, a series of legislative enactments dealt directly with harmful discrimination. Although preceding statutes had contained some anti-discrimination provisions,[13] the first Racial Discrimination Act in Canada was passed by Ontario in 1944.[14] In 1947 Saskatchewan enacted the first detailed and comprehensive statute, the Saskatchewan Bill of Rights Act.[15]

These early statutes were quasi-criminal in nature, relying on the laying of charges and prosecution of offenders. Both victims and judges shied away from applying their provisions. During the 1950s Canadian jurisdictions gradually brought in Fair Accommodation and Fair Employment Practices acts which relied more on conciliation methods. In 1962 Ontario began the trend, since adopted by all provinces and the federal government, of consolidating all human rights legislation into a code, bill, or charter. By 1977 every province as well as Canada had set up a commission or similar structure to administer anti-discrimination legislation in its areas of responsibility.[16]

Anti-discrimination legislation has continued to progress,[17] gradually incorporating such notions as affirmative action, reasonable accommodation, and "systemic" approaches to discrimination (dealing with "unintentional," or "indirect," discrimination). Legislative protection in all parts of Canada covers employment, housing, education, advertisements, and access to government services.

Grounds of discrimination which are prohibited in almost all parts of Canada are race; color; origin; sex; creed, religion, or belief; family or marital status; a criminal record for which a pardon has been granted; and, more recently, physical or mental disability. Although "age" is a universally prohibited ground, many human rights statutes set age limits (for example, eighteen and sixty-five) below or above which discrimination is expressly permitted. A defense of "reasonable occupational requirement" is generally available.[18] Discriminating messages and hate literature are forbidden everywhere in Canada. Sexual orientation currently is a prohibited ground of discrimination only in Quebec. In some provinces, political or other opinions cannot lawfully be a reason to discriminate in non-political matters.

In recent years, the leading edge of development in the anti-discrimination field has been in "systemic" approaches to discrimination, particularly through "affirmative action." Whether by design or unintentionally there have always been practices in Canada, notably in matters of employment, which acted as barriers to the advancement of women and minority groups. Such pervasive, harmful practices are known in Canada as "systemic" effects, or "constructive" discrimination.

The object of "affirmative action" is to bring members of disadvantaged groups to the same starting line as those groups which have advantages related to systemic discrimination. In Canada, these attempts to provide "equal opportunity" are sometimes referred to as efforts toward "employment equity."[19] Virtually all jurisdictions authorize affirmative action, usually called "special programs," to eliminate or reduce disadvantages suffered by a group of individuals because of past discrimination.[20] Goals and timetables may be set and when the purposes are achieved, the program should be ended. Among the measures taken could be reassessment of criteria for hiring or for promotion and special recruitment methods or training. Section 15(2) of the *Constitution* declares that affirmative action is not "discrimination." While affirmative action plans usually are voluntary, some governments have legislated special programs for their own employees, and the ground has been broken for the ordering of affirmative action by a tribunal empowered to do so by statute. Most currently operating employment equity arrangements have been negotiated by governments acting jointly with employees and large employers.[21]

Advocates for the interests of women, native peoples, persons with a disability, and "visible minorities" (persons of non-European ancestry) argue that despite two decades of anti-discrimination laws, voluntary positive change has been quite unsatisfactory, and they call for mandatory affirmative action. In employment particularly there is a growing conviction that there is a need for "systemic" approaches to remedying employer-wide or industry-wide problems of inequality of opportunity and benefit.[22]

Governments have begun setting their own houses in order with respect to their own staffing. Moreover, the Supreme Court of Canada has ruled that discrimination need not be intentional in order to violate the law,[23] so that harmful *effects* of a practice are what matter most. Another high court has approved the principle that in an appropriate situation a complaint can be remedied by ordering that hiring goals be instituted (in this case for women) for an entire area of a company's operations.[24]

Another "systemic" approach to greater equity for all groups in society would be to require reasonable allowances or adjustments to be made for those differences among people which act as unnecessary barriers. This author believes that anti-discrimination statutes in Canada should mandatorily require that *reasonable* efforts to "accommodate" or adjust for cultural, ethnic, religious, health, gender, or other differences be undertaken by employers and others. When applied to the barriers faced by persons with a disability, "reasonable accommodation" describes adjustments made by an employer, educational institution, transportation facility, or those responsible for a public building to allow for greater equality of access or opportunity. The term is also applied to allowances made to permit adherence to beliefs of minority religions. Most Canadian human rights legislation, however, does not yet require reasonable accommodation, though the author of this chapter would recommend that it be obligatory.

Only a few of the currently challenging issues in Canadian anti-discrimination law and practice have been discussed here.[25] The problems covered by human rights codes potentially touch the majority of ordinary Canadians, but in constitutional terms, they are overshadowed by the Canadian Charter of Rights and Freedoms and by the embarrassing human rights concerns which are linked to its domain of guarantees.

Prior to the 1982 Canadian Charter of Rights and Freedoms, (Part 1 of the Constitution Act, 1982) the principal written instrument was the Canadian Bill of Rights, which applies only to federal laws, and is still in force.[26] Section 1 of the Bill of Rights recognizes and declares the civil liberties of speech, religion, assembly, association, and the press. It also contains clauses dealing with "due process" and "equality before the law." A major defect of the Bill of Rights is that it is not a constitutional document with supremacy over legislative or administrative action. It provides merely that laws of Canada shall "be so construed and apply" as not to be inconsistent with the rights and freedoms set forth in the Bill of Rights. Almost without exception, the Supreme Court has been able to find that the laws being challenged were not in conflict with the Canadian Bill of Rights.

The notable exception to the trend of judicial passivity was *Regina v. Drybones*[27] (1970). A native Indian man was arrested because he had become drunk at a hotel in a town. It was an offense for an Indian to be intoxicated off land reserved for Indians.[28] Section 1(b) of the Bill of Rights provides that an individual has the right to "equality before the law and the protection of the law." The Supreme Court applied Section 1(b) to the Indian Act and found the relevant provision to be inoperative.[29]

This judgment was heralded as the dawn of a new epoch in human rights, but decisions which dealt with equality issues over the next decade found some way to sidestep *Drybones* or to cut away at the progress it had made. The failure of the judiciary to employ the Bill of Rights to advance the position of disadvantaged individuals and groups provided some of the impetus for ensuring that the 1982 Constitution contained a broad equality rights clause. Among the unpopular judgments were *Lavell*,[30] in which a law was upheld which provided that a woman would lose her Indian status and benefits if she married a non-Indian (while an Indian man suffered no such loss by marrying a non-Indian woman); and *Bliss*,[31] in which adverse treatment of pregnant women was allowed under Canada's unemployment insurance scheme, because the Court felt that the distinction involved differences between pregnant women and all other people, rather than discrimination against women as a group.

One major catalyst to the creation of a constitution containing an "entrenched" or supreme charter of human rights was the desire of former Prime Minister Pierre Trudeau to ensure constitutional guarantees for the French language.[32] Commencing in the 1960s there had been a gradual effort, particularly in the federal government, to employ more Francophones and to increase the use and importance of the French language. The implementation of a program to ensure a bilingual civil service was the first example of a systemic approach to discrimination in Canada. It may be that this accommodation to minority interests prevented the breakup of Canada, for there were many in Quebec, the mainly Francophone province, for whom change was not swift enough.

In 1975 the Parti Quebecois, committed to achieving the eventual independence of Quebec, was elected as the provincial government. It did not achieve its goal, but it did increase the use and durability of the French language and in 1980 carried out a referendum on the question of independence. The Parti Quebecois lost the referendum, but the issue of Quebec's role within Canada remains unresolved. Quebec's leaders did not agree to the 1982 Constitution, and in 1986 were still negotiating the possibility of a veto to protect Quebec's interests in any future constitutional amending process.

Efforts to increase the power of Quebec or to sever ties with Canada were not always attempted through democratic means. More violent methods used by a tiny minority culminated in a dark chapter in Canada's human rights history, the October Crisis of 1970. Under the War Measures Act, enacted in 1914, the federal cabinet may assume extraordinary powers in time of "war, invasion or insurrection, real or apprehended." During the 1960s, Le Front de Liberation du Quebec (FLQ) acted in the inflamed political climate by directing violence at public property (such as postal boxes). In 1970 the FLQ kidnapped a British consular official and a Quebec cabinet minister, eventually killing the latter. The

War Measures Act permitted extraordinary detention powers, which the police used arbitrarily and excessively. Of almost 500 people arrested, only 18 were convicted of anything.[33]

THE CANADIAN CHARTER OF RIGHTS AND FREEDOMS (1982)

The inclusion of the Canadian Charter of Rights and Freedoms as Part 1 of Canada's constitution does not do away with the Canadian Bill of Rights of 1960. Unlike the Bill, however, the Charter does prevail over other laws. Furthermore, it applies to the provinces and territories as well as to the national government and its agencies. Nevertheless, the Bill remains in force, although some of its protections are *not* found in the Charter, notably the right of the individual to "enjoyment of property." If there were a conflict between the Bill and the Charter, the latter would prevail.[34]

The 1982 Constitution represents a series of political compromises. It incorporates and codifies many human rights considered as fundamental to Canadian society, while adding some protections not previously recognized. The Constitution Act, 1982 seeks to preserve historical bargains protecting French and English language, culture and educational rights. Among the rights retained or even enhanced were protections in the British North America Act for Protestants and Catholics in the organization of their own school system,[35] and for Anglophones and Francophones in the courts and legislatures of Quebec and Canada.[36] Nevertheless, those who framed the federal-provincial deal which resulted in the new Constitution were not able to obtain the participation of Quebec, because they were unwilling to give Quebec a veto power on certain issues to protect its identity within Canada.[37]

Most, but not all, of the Constitution's rights safeguards are found in Part 1, the Canadian Charter of Rights and Freedoms (the Charter). Anyone whose Charter rights or freedoms have been infringed or denied may apply to the proper court or tribunal to obtain an appropriate remedy, which usually means a declaration that a particular law is unconstitutional.[38] The Constitution is the supreme law and any law inconsistent with it is of no force or effect.[39] The Charter applies to the Parliament and government of Canada and to the legislature and government of each province. Some scholars hold to a minority view that the Charter applies to nongovernmental activities as well. The Constitution has been held to apply even to the deliberations of the federal Cabinet. In the *Operation Dismantle* case, peace activists sought to stop the testing of the (U.S.) Cruise missile in Canada. Although the applicants lost, some of the judges stated that Cabinet decisions are not immune to review under the Charter.[40]

One provision that is anathema to some human rights advocates is section 33, the "notwithstanding" clause, which allows any government to opt out of a part of the Charter, as long as it declares that it is doing so, giving potential voters a chance to judge its actions. Such a declaration loses its force after five years unless openly renewed or withdrawn by the government sooner. The necessity for section 33 was argued by government leaders wishing to maintain the overall paramountcy of legislatures over the judiciary. It was supported by some leading human rights proponents as being a necessary safety valve, and no doubt was a prerequisite to reaching a constitutional accord involving the federal government and nine of the provinces. Quebec chose initially to remain aloof from the Canadian Charter, and proclaimed a general opting out from the Charter's protections. In 1986 Quebec no longer seeks wholesale Charter exemption.

In February 1986, the Saskatchewan government used section 33 in a way that caused renewed cries for its removal from the Constitution. Having earlier lost an important constitutional case dealing with the rights of public sector workers, the government reinforced new restrictive legislation by declaring that it would operate notwithstanding the Charter of Rights.

Another catchall limitation on Charter rights is section 1, which guarantees the rights and freedoms set out in the Charter subject to ''such reasonable limits prescribed by law as can be demonstrably justified in a free and democratic society.'' Nonetheless, when challenged, the burden is on the party defending the offensive law to show that it can be justified as required by section 1.

Leading decisions have stated that in interpreting the Charter, it is appropriate to consider its background as well as relevant political, economic, social, and cultural developments in Canada. There must be a balancing of interests between the public purpose of restrictive legislation and the Charter right which is thereby limited.[41]

For the most part, the Charter of Rights records existing common law rights and freedoms and entrenches them in the Constitution. Section 2 sets out the ''fundamental freedoms'' of conscience and religion, of thought and expression, of assembly and of association. Sections 3 to 5 provide for ''democratic rights'': regular sittings of Parliament and each legislature, and universal suffrage and political participation rights.

Extensive legal rights are found in sections 7–14, which guard against deprivation of life, liberty, and security of the person; unreasonable search or seizure; and arbitrary detention or imprisonment. Also guaranteed are the right to be informed of the reasons for arrest, to instruct counsel and to have the option of habeas corpus proceedings, as well as all aspects of a fair trial. Witnesses are protected from self-incrimination and against cruel and unusual treatment or punishment.

Sections 16–22 preserve the special place given to the French and English languages in the public life and government services of the federal government and of the province of New Brunswick. In defined circumstances, section 23 guarantees the right of pupils to receive educational instruction in whichever of the official languages is preferred by the parents, regardless of whether the particular language group is the primary tongue of a minor part of a province or regional population.

SPECIAL CANADIAN PROBLEMS AND CONSTITUTIONAL
INNOVATIONS: EQUALITY RIGHTS AND COLLECTIVE RIGHTS

We have already noted the preservation of historical rights guarantees for established language and religious groups under Canada's 1982 Constitution. Certain aspects of the Constitution promote the interests of other collectivities which previously had not been constitutionally protected, namely, aboriginal peoples, women, ethnic cultures other than French or British, and persons receiving unequal benefit from Canadian society in general.

"The issue of aboriginal rights is the oldest question of human rights in Canada. . . . Aboriginal rights are simply the rights to which peoples are entitled because they are the original peoples of Canada."[42] In the 450 years since Europeans began occupying Canada, its first inhabitants have moved gradually from self-sufficiency and complete sovereignty to varying degrees of dependence upon governments of the dominant society. This dependence has not benefited the indigenous groups, who enjoy significantly worse education, health, incomes, and real power than most other Canadians. The aboriginal peoples (Indian, Inuit [sometimes called "Eskimo"] and Metis)[43] had their own "laws, systems for resolving disputes, cultures, religions, and languages" when the colonizers arrived, but these elements of civilization "are viewed by some as continuing only at the pleasure of the immigrant majority."[44]

Over the past fifteen years, native peoples have increasingly advanced claims to the lands they customarily occupied, and have demanded the right to continuation and control of traditional livelihoods of hunting, trapping, fishing, and gathering in these areas; the right to control and benefit from mineral and hydrocarbon extraction in aboriginal lands and waters; greater influence over education, adoption, and social services; and even self-government. There are varying notions of what self-government would entail, but important elements are the right to decide who is a member of the relevant native group and to determine the criteria for voting rights, such as length of residency.

One impetus for an intensified assertion of aboriginal rights was an early seventies land rights case which the Nishga Indians of the province of British Columbia barely lost at the Supreme Court of Canada. There was strong adverse reaction by native peoples (and eventually, the media) to the outcome of this case. This added fuel to the controversy created by an announcement of the federal government in 1969 that it intended to pursue a policy of assimilating native people into the mainstream of society.[45] Although a divided court ruled against the Nishga, three of the seven judges concluded that the general concept of "aboriginal rights" was valid in Canadian law.

At the time of the Nishga case, the government of British Columbia refused to recognize aboriginal rights, and a decade later, on the eve of the constitutional accord, many provincial leaders still refused to acknowledge that aboriginal claims were in fact rights. At the eleventh hour, provisions protecting aboriginal rights were removed from draft versions of the Constitution Act. In response to the outcry engendered, constitutional rights for native peoples were reinstated.[46] A key word was added to the original phraseology employed, so that only "existing" rights are now protected, leaving many native leaders concerned that this will be interpreted too restrictively.

Section 35 of the Constitution affirms "existing aboriginal and treaty rights" of the aboriginal peoples, and section 25 provides that rights pertaining to aboriginal peoples shall not be adversely affected by Charter rights and freedoms in general. Attempts to achieve a more precise meaning of "aboriginal rights" are the subject of a continuing series of national conferences involving native and government leaders.[47]

Another group whose interests were temporarily cast aside by political bargaining surrounding the Charter were women. The uproar caused when specific equality rights for women were left out of near-final drafts of the Charter produced a groundswell of organizing and lobbying. Section 28, the equal rights amendment, unequivocally states that Charter rights and freedoms "are guaranteed equally to male and female persons." This protection was set into place in addition to general equality rights assured by section 15, for fear that courts would not otherwise treat women's rights to equality seriously. Unlike some other portions of the Charter, Section 28 is not subject to limitation by governments wishing to make use of the "opting out" clause (section 33).

It was noted earlier that Canada increasingly is becoming a mosaic of different peoples and cultures. The federal cabinet and some provinces each have a minister in charge of "multiculturalism." To respond to this reality, section 27 states that the Charter must be interpreted "in a manner consistent with the preservation and enhancement of the multicultural heritage" of Canadians. Section 27 has been relied upon to strike down a Sunday business closing law based on recognition of the traditional Christian Sabbath,[48] but where the closing law focused instead on the need to provide a day of leisure for workers, the statute was upheld.[49] Nevertheless, section 27 was applied in that case to exempt businesses run by Jews who observed the Sabbath on Saturdays while their competitors remained open.

Perhaps the most far-reaching feature of the 1982 Constitution is the inclusion of four general equality rights in section 15. Well-publicized court decisions under the 1960 Bill of Rights, denying claims for equal treatment by women, together with public support for aboriginal and minority rights, led to intense lobbying for an enlarged "equality" provision in the Charter.

While the Constitution was being developed, a national survey sought opinions as to whether certain groups should be protected in a charter of human rights. Of those polled, 92 percent felt that the rights of the physically and mentally disabled should be specified, while 89 percent approved protection for senior citizens. There was agreement that particular provisions should cover rights of women (77 percent) as well as certain minorities: racial (69 percent); ethnic (64 percent); language (61 percent); and religious (58 percent). Support was given for such protection for those with a history of alcoholism or drug abuse (54 percent) and those with past criminal records (53 percent).[50]

Section 15, as enacted, reflects most of these concerns. It declares the right to equality in four formulations—equality *before* and *under* the law, and the right to equal protection and benefit of the law—and it permits challenges to unequal legislation and practice. It does not require positive government activity to overcome unjust distribution of the benefits of Canadian society, but a court order could have a similar indirect effect. Section 15(2) "does not preclude" any program designed to improve conditions for disadvantaged people, and thus reinforces the view that affirmative action is *not* discrimination against persons who are already in an advantaged position.

Aware that many existing laws and practices had the effect of creating or maintaining inequality, the parties to the constitutional agreement gave governments a moratorium during which to correct inequities. Section 15 came into force April 17, 1985, three years after the Constitution became law. On the eve of section 15's commencement, many organizations representing socially or economically disadvantaged Canadians (such as disabled people, women, and coalitions of ethnic groups) were poised to launch court actions. It is clear that these organizations think that the various governments did not do an adequate job in the interim of correcting imbalances found in or fostered by the law. The impression of grave imbalances within society has been amplified by three separate federal commissions which traversed the country during the 1980s to survey the extent of inequity for particular groups.[51] These commissions recommended large-scale changes in the way in which minorities, aboriginal peoples, and women were treated, particularly in employment. The federal government has begun to implement some of the recommendations, but not as swiftly as many human rights proponents would ask.

SOCIAL AND ECONOMIC RIGHTS AND THE CANADIAN CHARTER OF RIGHTS AND FREEDOMS

One can only speculate on the extent, if any, to which section 15 of the Charter could be used to ameliorate inequalities of wealth and opportunity as opposed to procedural unfairness. Although Canada is a party to the International Covenant on Economic, Social and Cultural Rights (ICESCR) and to conventions of the International Labour Organization (ILO) relevant to social and economic rights, these are barely touched on in the Charter.[52] One reason for this is the notion held by many lawyers and public officials that the only "real" rights are those which can be enforced in court, namely, "legal" or "political" rights. Some politicians labor under the misconception that social rights were an invention of communist states. In fact, the ILO had fostered international cooperation in economic and social rights since 1919, and the 1948 Universal Declaration proclaims inter alia that all people have the right to form and join trade unions; to education; and to adequate standards of living, health, and social services.

Since these rights have found their way into ICESCR, progressive implementation of them is a legal obligation of Canada,[53] a rather troublesome one in times of recession. Canada is among the foremost achievers of social goals on the globe,[54] but as one of the dozen richest nations,[55] its shortfalls in bringing about greater equality of opportunity and benefits among regions and groups may put it in breach of international obligations.

As required by ICESCR, Canada has presented reports to the United Nations on its progress in social and economic fields. One report concerns protections for the family and children, adequate standards of living, and the right to the highest attainable standard of physical and mental health. The report details social and economic support programs ranging from universal medicare and retirement pensions to occupational safety, but states that there are large disparities within the population and between regions.[56] The richest 20 percent of the Canadian population receive ten to eleven times as much personal income as the bottom 20 percent.[57] On average, women are paid about 40 percent less than men.[58] Unemployment for native Indians ranges from 35 to 75 percent, and in some communities approaches 100 percent.[59] In Halifax, Nova Scotia, a city of about one quarter million people, it is estimated that 40 percent of the young male black population is unemployed.[60] Canada is far behind other industrialized nations in encouraging the employment of employable disabled people.[61]

The previous paragraph highlights only a few of the inequities which have caused some scholars to propose that the Canadian Charter be amended to proclaim explicit safeguards for economic and social rights. It is possible that a court could be persuaded that the economic and social interests of disadvantaged groups are protected by some existing Charter sections. Experience to date however, suggests that the Charter as it stands is also likely to be used to benefit people who already enjoy favorable social and economic status.

Charter section 6 proclaims "mobility rights." Every citizen or permanent resident has the right to move to any part of Canada to live or to seek work. This is subject to reasonable limitations, including the priority of regional programs designed to improve job prospects where unemployment is higher than the national average. This section has been interpreted as not guaranteeing a right to obtain work, but it has been used to hinder attempts in one province to encourage doctors to settle in underserviced areas.[62]

Section 7 states that everyone has the right to "life, liberty and security of the person" and the right "not to be deprived thereof except in accordance with the principles of fundamental justice." It can be contended that section 7 requires that there be an adequate standard of living for everyone including recipients of social assistance. In Canada, as elsewhere, meaningful participation in political and cultural life requires some stability in one's circumstances and a basic assured level of sustenance and dignity. On the other hand, attempts have been made already (with minimal success) to seek an interpretation which includes guarantees of commercial private property rights which might possibly conflict with wider public interests.[63]

Section 2(d) protects "freedom of association." Nowhere in the Charter is there a distinct right of workers to form a union, to bargain collectively with employers, or to conduct a legal strike if necessary. It would be logical to assume that "freedom of association" includes these rights, and that assumption was held by trade union leaders and the relevant government ministers at the time the Charter was being drafted.

A number of enactments which inhibit the collective bargaining and strike rights of public sector workers have been challenged under section 2(d). The Supreme Court of Canada has yet to resolve differences of judicial opinion from lower courts. In those cases wherein judiciary have ruled that section 2(d) protects collective bargaining and the right to strike, judges have stated that without the strike weapon, collective bargaining is meaningless. Other judges have said that "freedom of association" guarantees only a right to join a union or other organization. Courts that have ruled in favor of workers note that a person joins an organization to carry out common actions for mutual interests. As one judge said, "*to be* in association means *to act* in association, for it is impossible for a human being to exist in a state of no movement."[64]

It can be argued that the freedom of workers to unite to seek improved social conditions for themselves and others, without undue government restriction, is a fundamental element of a modern democratic society. Any restrictions necessary in Canada would be permissible under section 1 of the Charter, e.g., legislation hindering strikes by truly essential employees in essential police or health services.

Not only is there uncertainty as to whether "freedom of association" protects collective bargaining rights, but there is a possibility that this term may include a freedom "not to associate" with the union that has the contract with one's employer, which would weaken existing union security. On a related point, different courts have diverged on the question of whether a union may spend money to support political causes that are opposed by an employee whose dues the union collects. Unionized workers may find that practices which were traditionally thought to be rights may be struck down as being unconstitutional. Increased worker militancy would likely result, as well as stronger demands for specific safety precautions in the Constitution for rights to collectively organize, bargain, and strike.

Uneven distribution of social and economic benefits affects people on a daily basis in a more direct way than infringement of many of the civil and political rights found in the Constitution, yet social and economic rights are not directly addressed in the Charter of Rights. The promotion and achievement of social and economic goals may simply be too dependent on the availability of finances and regional political pressures. A parliamentary committee which considered the inclusion of economic and social rights in an eventual constitution thought that the conversion of economic and social rights into legal values enforceable in the courts was an insurmountable problem; nevertheless, it did recommend that the preamble mention as one objective for Canada the promotion of "economic, social and cultural equality for all Canadians as individuals."[65]

By ratifying the ICESCR, Canada took on a legal obligation to abide by it. Before Canada accepted this obligation, all provinces agreed with the federal government to commit themselves to the implementation of economic and social rights as set out in ICESCR. Canada is a party to both the ICESCR and the International Covenant on Civil and Political Rights, and there is no legal priority between the covenants.[66] These two sets of rights are interdependent and should be more equally balanced in the Constitution. One cannot seek a fairer share of what a society might offer—spiritually and materially—without a minimum adequate standard of living as well as certain political freedoms.

A strong place for general social and economic rights in the Constitution would be imperative as a counterbalance, if those who lobby for constitutional property rights should succeed. An effort to add a "right to property" to the Charter in 1983 received strong backing from many politicians and influential interest groups, but was not warmly received by some legislators, who feared among other things that it would hamper highway, hospital, and school programs that depend on compensated expropriation of property. An unrestricted right of the ordinary person to own a home, farm, or business is protected in Canada by legislation and centuries of judge-made law. Inserting "right to property" into the Constitution might be both unnecessary and imprudent. (Such a right is *not* included in the ICESCR.) Some private interests could use the Charter to hinder inconvenient implementation of socially desirable objectives, such as pollution control or the location of a group home for mentally disabled adults in a particular community. A "property" clause might also be used by nonnatives to challenge settlements made by governments pursuant to aboriginal land claims.

If the Charter were amended to include social and economic rights, it would be impractical to inaugurate a stringent enforcement regime. Nevertheless, the Charter has important influence on society just by its existence. Most citizens, including members and agents of government, tend to act according to the law. "Given a publicly declared sense of values such as a Charter of Rights, few individuals are prepared to ignore a condemnation of their conduct when that conduct is deemed contrary to a proclaimed set of constitutional principles."[67]

CONCLUSION

Some institutions which enhance the climate of human rights in Canada have not been examined here. Most provincial governments have an ombudsman who handles complaints against government delay or insensitivity which is traceable not to discrimination, but to neglect, favoritism, or red tape.[68] The ability to defend oneself in a criminal case or to challenge human rights abuses (i.e., to exercise one's legal rights) is facilitated by Legal Aid plans in every jurisdiction which assure publicly funded legal representation for those who cannot afford a lawyer. In contrast to many countries, Canada allows open discussions of human rights issues, and governments widely distribute copies of international and Canadian human rights documents free of charge.

There is a danger that the progression of developments fostering human rights could make Canadians complacent about their human rights performance. These innovations are relatively recent and mask an undercurrent of the racism and intergroup conflict which exists in any society. It is worthwhile to recall that in Canada's early history slavery was permitted, that most of the land was wrested from its original inhabitants by Europeans, that until well into this century there was pervasive statutory discrimination against people of Asian origin, that Jews were not readily welcomed as refugees in the 1930s and 1940s, that for some purposes women were not considered full "persons" until the 1920s, that many indigenous people did not obtain a right to vote until 1960, and that even today some Canadians do not consider most disabled individuals to be capable of meaningful contribution to the community. It is fair to say that there was over-whelming support for the wholesale expulsion of Japanese Canadians from Canada's west coast during World War II,[69] along with confiscation of their property, despite the absence of concrete evidence of disloyalty and the fact that Canadians of German (white) origin suffered no such deprivation. With the benefit of hindsight and more progressive attitudes, the government of Canada may provide symbolic redress for the harm done to Canadians of Japanese ancestry. All of the official goodwill in the world, however, cannot change the attitudes of ordinary people, and there is much evidence of pervasive racism in the Canada of the 1980s.[70]

Optimistically, we can observe that people do draw moral lessons from what the law says is correct behavior and fair practice. There has been a laudable evolution in both legislation and tolerance in postwar Canada. One can hope that the protection of individual and collective rights through the Charter of Rights will prepare Canadians to accommodate each other in an increasingly multicultural land.

NOTES

1. There were safeguards in place for the principal linguistic groups, English and French (sec. 133), and for the main religious groups, Roman Catholic and Protestant (sec. 93).

2. *Union Colliery v. Bryden* [1899] A.C. 580; *Cunningham v. Tomey Homma* [1903] A.C. 151; *Quong-Wing v. The King* (1914) 49 S.C.R. 440. For a full exploration see W. S. Tarnopolsky and W. F. Pentney, *Discrimination and the Law* (Don Mills, Ont: Richard De Boo, 1985) chap. 1.

3. [1940] 1 S.C.R. 139.

4. *Rogers v. Clarence Hotel* [1940] 3 D.L.R. 583 (British Columbia).

5. *King v. Barclay and Barclay's Motel* (1961) 35 W.W.R. (New Series) 240 (Alberta).

6. Keiller MacKay, J. also found the covenant void for uncertainty and as a restraint upon alienation. *Re Drummond Wren* [1945] O.R. 778, 4 D.L.R. 674.

7. *Noble and Wolf v. Alley* [1948] 4 D.L.R. 123. The complainants eventually won, but on other grounds; (1951) 1 D.L.R. 321.

8. Leading cases were *Re Alberta Statutes* [1938] S.C.R. 100; *Boucher v. The King* [1951] S.C.R. 265; *Switzman v. Elbling* [1957] S.C.R. 285. For commentary, see W. S. Tarnopolsky, "The Historical and Constitutional Context of the Proposed Charter of Rights and Freedoms," *Law and Contemporary Problems* 44 (1981): 169–193 at 170–173.

9. *Roncarelli v. Duplessis* (1959) 16 D.L.R. (2d) 689.

10. In *Boucher v. The King*, [1951] 2 D.L.R. 369, the accused was also a Jehovah's Witness. The Supreme Court found that "sedition" contemplates actually inciting violence, and an acquittal resulted.

11. See, for example, *Co-operative Comm. on Japanese-Canadians v. Attorney General of Canada*, [1947] A.C. 87, wherein the Judicial Committee of the Privy Council (then Canada's highest court) upheld Orders-in-Council authorizing the deportation of Japanese-Canadians after World War II. On this see T. R. Berger, *Fragile Freedoms: Human Rights and Dissent in Canada*, rev. ed. (Vancouver: Clarke, Irwin, 1982).

12. *Switzman v. Elbling* (1957), 7 D.L.R. (3d) 337: [1957] S.C.R. 285.

13. Tarnopolsky and Pentney, *Discrimination and the Law*, cite examples in chap. 2, including a 1931 *Unemployment Relief Act* (B. C. [British Columbia]) wherein a clause dealt with discrimination because of "political affiliation."

14. S.O. 1944, c. 51. J. Keene, *Human Rights in Ontario* (Toronto: Carswell, 1983), refers to a Religious Freedom Act of 1897 (R.S.O. 1897, c. 306).

15. S.S. 1947, c. 35.

16. See Tarnopolsky and Pentney, *Discrimination and the Law*, chap. 2.

17. Ibid.

18. Ontario law now provides that employers cannot rely on the "reasonable and bona fide occupational requirement" (BFOR) defense without first attempting "reasonable accommodation" for certain minority groups.

19. This term was popularized by Judge Rosalie S. Abella in *Report of the Commission on Equality in Employment* (Ottawa: Ministry of Supply and Services Canada, 1984).

20. A typical example is sec. 15(1) of the Canadian Human Rights Act, R.S.C. 1976–1977, c. 33.

21. Special Committee on Participation of Visible Minorities in Canadian Society, *Equality Now!* (Ottawa: Queen's Printer for Canada, 1984).

22. W. W. Black, *Employment Equality: A Systemic Approach* (Ottawa: Human Rights Research and Education Centre, 1985).

23. *Bhinder and Canadian National Railway* (1986) 7 *Canadian Human Rights Reporter*, D/3093; *O'Malley (Vincent) v. Simpsons-Sears* (1986) 7 CHRR D/3102).

24. *Canadian National Railway v. Action Travail des Femmes*, Federal Court of Appeal, July 16, 1985.

25. Comprehensive sources are: Black, *Employment Equality*; Tarnopolsky and Pentney, *Discrimination*; Keene, *Human Rights in Ontario*.

26. See W. S. Tarnopolsky, *The Canadian Bill of Rights*, 2nd ed. (Ottawa: Carleton Library, 1975) for analysis.

27. [1970] S.C.R. 282.

28. *Indian Act*, R.S.C., 1970, c. I–6 s. 94 (now s. 95).

29. [1970] S.C.R. at 297.

30. *Attorney-General for Canada v. Lavell* [1974] S.C.R., 1349.

31. *Bliss v. Attorney-General for Canada* (1977) 77 D.L.R. (3d) 609; affirmed [1979], S.C.R. 183.

32. P. E. Trudeau, *Federalism and the French Canadians* (1968), 52–60 cited in W. S. Tarnopolsky, *Law and Contemporary Problems*, 169.

33. Berger, *Fragile Freedoms*, 209.

34. The Bill of Rights was somewhat rejuvenated by the Supreme Court of Canada in *Singh v. Minister of Employment and Immigration* [1985] 1 S.C.R. 177. In holding that Singh was entitled to the opportunity to state his case in a hearing, several judges relied on the Bill of Rights protection of "due process" in section 1(a).

35. British North America Act, 1867, sec. 93.

36. Ibid., sec. 133.

37. R. Romanow, "Making Canada's Constitution: Reflections of a Participant," in *The Canadian Charter of Rights: Law Practice Revolutionized*, ed. A. W. MacKay, C. F. Beckton, and B. H. Wildsmith (Halifax, Nova Scotia: Faculty of Law, Dalhousie University, 1982), 105–120.

38. Sec. 24. In the Canadian context, the normal response of the target government is to change the offending legislation.

39. Sec. 52.

40. *Operation Dismantle et al. v. The Queen* [1985] 1 S.C.R. 441.

41. Quebec's Act respecting the Constitution Act, 1982, which sought to oust the Charter entirely, was upheld as valid by the Quebec Superior Court in *Re Alliance des Professeurs* (April 27, 1983). The effect of this political maneuver was softened by the fact that, since 1975, Quebec's own Charter had included protections for a wide range of civil, political, economic, and social rights and freedoms.

42. Berger, *Fragile Freedoms*, 219.

43. The Metis are a distinct group formed from mixing between Indians and people of European origin several generations ago.

44. B. W. Morse, ed., *Aboriginal Rights and the Law: Indian, Metis and Inuit Rights in Canada* (Ottawa: Carleton University Press, 1985) xxi.

45. *Calder v. A. G. British Columbia*, [1973] S.C.R. 313. The Nishga sought a declaration "that the aboriginal title to ancient tribal territories [had] never been lawfully extinguished." Six judges divided 3–3 on the merits. The seventh held the action must fail on a procedural ground and, in the result, the Nishga lost.

46. Berger, *Fragile Freedoms*, 249–50.

47. One of the amendments arrived at pursuant to these constitutional conferences adds a subsection (4) to section 35 stipulating that aboriginal rights "are guaranteed equally to male and female persons."

48. *R v. Big M Drug Mart et al.* [1985] 1 S.C.R. 295.

49. *R v. Videoflicks et al.* (1984) 14 D.L.R. (4th) 10.

50. Canadian Human Rights Commission, *Selected Tables from a Survey of Public Opinion on Human Rights* (Ottawa, November 1981) and Canadian Human Rights Commission, *Canadians and Discrimination: An Analysis of the 1981 Opinion Poll* (Ottawa: September 1982).

51. *Abella Report*; J. P. Boyer, *Report of the Parliamentary Committee on Equality Rights* (Ottawa: Queen's Printer for Canada, 1985); Special Committee, *Equality Now!*

52. In contrast, the Quebec Charter of Human Rights and Freedoms (1975) contains

an entire Chapter on Economic and Social Rights. In the Northwest Territories, a "Charter of Founding Principles of Denendeh" proposed in 1976 by the Indian Brotherhood (now "Dene Nation") addresses environmental protection, group benefit from resource development, and the maintenance of "the traditional economy."

53. ICESCR Article 2.

54. See Appendix 3 in this book and the report cited at note 62 infra.

55. Ibid.

56. Department of the Secretary of State (Canada), *Report of Canada on the Implementation of the Provisions of Articles 10 to 12 of the International Covenant on Economic, Social and Cultural Rights*—December 1982 (Ottawa: Minister of Supply and Services, 1983).

57. Canadian Conference of Catholic Bishops, *Ethical Reflections of the Economic Crisis*, Ottawa, 1983.

58. A. McChesney, "Does the Charter of Rights Guarantee Equality for Everyone?" in *Take Care! Human Rights in the '80's*, ed. Human Rights Coalition (Canada) (Ottawa: Human Rights Research and Education Centre, 1983), 75–81 at 77.

59. Ibid., 76.

60. Mohammed Azhar Ali Khan, "The Economic Roots of Racism," in *Take Care!*, ed. Human Rights Coalition, 83–92 at 87.

61. D. Baker, "Equality Rights for Disabled People in Canada: An Overview," Proceedings of UNESCO Conference on Protection of Minorities, Quebec City, December 1985.

62. *Law Society of Upper Canada v. Skapinker* (1984) 9 D.L.R. (4th) 161; *Re Mia and Medical Services Commission of British Columbia* (1985) 17 D.L.R. (4th) 385.

63. Examples: *New Brunswick v. Fisherman's Wharf Ltd.* (1982) 135 D.L.R. (3d) 307. (property taxation); *Re Becker and Alberta* (1983) 148 D.L.R. (3d) 539 (expropriation).

64. Bayda, Chief Justice of Saskatchewan, in the *Dairy Workers* case, (1985) 19 D.L.R. (4th) 609. Since the foregoing text was written, the Supreme Court of Canada has issued a trio of decisions (on April 9, 1987) that conclude that the constitutional freedom of association does not include a right to strike. There were, however, strong dissenting judgments, and the value of collective bargaining within a democratic society was recognized.

65. Tarnopolsky, *Bill of Rights*, 220.

66. A. McChesney, "Promoting the General Welfare in a Free and Democratic Society: Balancing Human Rights and Development," *Netherlands International Law Review* 27 (1980): 283–334 at 292–296.

67. Justice of Appeal Walter S. Tarnopolsky, quoted in A. McChesney, "Economic and Social Rights in Canada: The International Bill of Rights and Canadian Human Rights Law," in *Take Care!*, 61–73 at 71.

68. The federal government does not have an "ombudsoffice," but there are four officials who perform ombudsfunctions with regard to official languages, penitentiaries (prisons), personal privacy, and access to government information.

69. Berger, *Fragile Freedoms*, 93–126. See also the novel by Joy Kogawa: *Obasan* (Markham, Ontario: Penguin, 1983).

70. Special Committee, *Equality Now!*

SUGGESTED READINGS

Abella, R. S. Commissioner. *Report of the Commission on Equality in Employment.* Ottawa: Ministry of Supply and Services Canada, 1984.

Berger, T. R. *Fragile Freedoms: Human Rights and Dissent in Canada.* rev. ed. Vancouver: Clarke, Irwin, 1982.

Black, W. W. *Employment Equality: A Systemic Approach.* Ottawa: Human Rights Research and Education Centre, 1985.

Boyer, J. P. Chairman. *Report of the Parliamentary Committee on Equality Rights.* Ottawa: Queen's Printer for Canada, 1985.

Caccia, I. *Charter Bibliography.* Ottawa: Human Rights Research and Education Centre; Saskatoon: Canadian Human Rights Reporter, 1985.

Gibson, D. *The Law of the Charter: General Principles.* Toronto: Carswell, 1986.

Keene, J. *Human Rights in Ontario.* Toronto: Carswell, 1983.

Morse, B. W., ed. *Aboriginal Peoples and the Law: Indian, Metis and Inuit Rights in Canada.* Ottawa: Carleton University Press, 1985.

Smith, L., G. Cote-Harper, R. Elliot, and M. Seydegart. *Righting the Balance: Canada's New Equality Rights.* Saskatoon and Vancouver: *Canadian Human Rights Reporter*, 1986.

Special Committee on Participation of Visible Minorities in Canadian Society. *Equality Now!* Ottawa: Queen's Printer for Canada, 1984.

Tarnopolsky, W. S. *The Canadian Bill of Rights.* 2d ed. Ottawa: Carleton Library, 1975.

Tarnopolsky, W. S. "The Equality Rights of the Canadian Charter of Rights and Freedoms." *Canadian Bar Review* 61 (1983): 242.

Tarnopolsky, W. S. and G. A. Beaudoin, eds. *The Canadian Charter of Rights and Freedoms—Commentary.* Toronto: Carswell, 1982.

Tarnopolsky, W. S. and W. F. Pentney. *Discrimination and the Law.* Don Mills, Ontario: Richard De Boo, 1985.

3

CHILE

Jinny Arancibia, Marcelo Charlin, and Peter Landstreet

HISTORICAL BACKGROUND

Until the 1973 military coup, the Chilean political system had been an unusual one in its Latin American context. In the first place, "coups d'état and military rule, common in other Latin American countries, had been almost completely absent in Chile since the 1830's."[1] In the second place, Chile was the closest of any Latin American country to having a "Southern European" party system similar to those of France, Spain, Italy, and Greece, in which parties representing a wide swath of the ideological spectrum existed and enjoyed substantial electoral support. By the 1941 congressional elections, an almost even division of the electorate into thirds, supporting the right, center, and left, was visible. With variations, this pattern repeated itself in electoral results through to the last elections in which parties participated (1973), and it still persists today, however opaquely. On the other hand, owing to fluctuations within this pattern, as well as parties' shifting electoral and coalition strategies, the Chilean government moved rapidly from right to left in the last three presidential elections. Thus the country had a conservative government, led by Jorge Alessandri, in 1958–1964; a reformist Christian Democratic one, led by Eduardo Frei, in 1964–1970; and a socialist one, led by Salvador Allende, from 1970 until the 1973 coup. From 1964 onward, the pace of change in the country became almost dizzying as reforms quickly followed one another, though usually meeting entrenched opposition at the same time.

The government in power during 1970–1973 was the Unidad Popular (UP, or Popular Unity), the world's first elected Marxist government. The left's success in the 1970 presidential election was due less to a secular trend over time toward the left among the electorate (though a case for that can be argued) than to a decision taken by the center and right parties to run separate candidates, which allowed the UP candidate, Allende, to win by a small plurality. The UP government was a coalition of two major, mass-based leftist parties (the Communist and Socialist parties), plus one smaller center-left "swing party" (the Radical party), plus several yet smaller leftist parties (mainly split-offs to the left from the Christian Democratic party).

Many reforms had already begun under the Christian Democratic administration from 1964 to 1970, but with the UP their pace heightened and they penetrated more deeply into the society.[2] Among the main UP reforms were the following: an intensification of agrarian reform, mainly benefiting peasants on large estates that were expropriated; the nationalization of key private industries and banks; the nationalization of the U.S.-owned sector of the country's copper industry (copper being Chile's most important export); expanded state services, especially in education, housing, and health; and a range of policy measures promoting income redistribution toward labor, both as a matter of social justice and as a means of increasing workers' purchasing power so as to support national economic growth.

As the society went through the traumas of these reforms, it became increasingly polarized. By 1973, side by side with the division of the population into thirds by party, there had also emerged a profound division among Chileans roughly into two halves, in terms of whether the government should be supported or terminated.

But the fate of the UP government was not decided in Chile alone. Both the U.S. government and U.S.-owned private corporations were involved in repeated attempts to keep the left from coming to power in the first place, and then to "destabilize" the socialist government. In the 1964 presidential election, an organization named the Business Group for Latin America—whose executive committee included leaders of major U.S. corporations with holdings in Chile—made covert donations to the campaign of Christian Democratic candidate Frei. In the 1970 presidential election, major funding was donated to the campaign of the conservative candidate Alessandri by the International Telephone and Telegraph Corporation (ITT), which owned and ran Chile's telephone system. It was the fear of nationalization of their Chilean holdings that led to these secret corporate donations. With regard to U.S. government policy, Central Intelligence Agency (CIA) penetration of Chilean society was already extensive in the early 1960s. The CIA funneled massive amounts of money to favored candidates, political parties, and mass media straight through to the time of the military coup. After Allende won the 1970 election, the U.S. government attempted to prevent him from taking office through a variety of means: a propaganda campaign, attempts to buy anti-Allende votes among members of the Chilean congress, and even an order by President Richard Nixon to have Allende assassinated. The CIA was unable to implement this latter order, but it did back a plan to kidnap the commander in chief of the Chilean army, General René Schneider, in October 1970. The objective was to blame the kidnapping on the left and thus persuade the Chilean congress to block Allende's accession to the presidency; the plan failed when Schneider was killed instead, and the slaying was revealed as the work of military officers associated with the far right. After Allende took power, the U.S. government, through the CIA, remained dedicated to the longer-term goal of promoting a coup by the military. Part of this policy involved a virtual declaration of economic warfare against the UP government: the persuasion of U.S. firms not to make new investments in Chile, the use of U.S. influence in international financial organizations (the World Bank, the Export-Import Bank, the Inter-American Development Bank) to block new financing to Chile, and the almost total cutoff of U.S. economic aid to Chile, while aid to its armed forces was increased yearly from 1970 to 1973. As another component of this policy the CIA actively engaged in propaganda and disinformation campaigns against the government through Chilean mass media, and financed opposition parties, organizations, strikes, boycotts, and demonstrations.[3] In short, though there is no solid evidence indicating direct American participation in the coup itself, the Nixon administration and its principal foreign policy activist, Henry Kissinger, committed itself to a course of action designed to bring about military rule in Chile. After the coup, the CIA even paid the expenses of spokespersons for the junta who traveled abroad to explain why the coup had been necessary.[4]

The destruction of the UP government and the operation of military rule have given Chile and its human rights situation an international profile and relevance far beyond that country's limited regional significance. This is for two main reasons. First, the coup "marked not only the demise of the Popular Unity government but also the violent breakdown of one of the world's oldest democracies."[5] Second, the UP experience magnetized many partisans of the left internationally who found it difficult to identify with existing state socialist regimes, precisely because of human rights issues. For them, the coup shattered their dreams, though it left them psychically energized to engage in extensive postcoup solidarity and human rights–support work around the issue of the military regime, which further brought the Chilean situation into international consciousness.[6] Broadly speaking, these are the reasons why Chile looms larger in international public consciousness than similar recent experiences with military rule in Brazil, Argentina, and Uruguay, even though the latter two countries experienced even deeper repressive processes than has Chile.

More than thirteen years have elapsed since the coup, and the country has been subjected to deep structural changes. The best and most extensive research on these changes has been done in Chile itself, as one component of that country's process of structural transformation has been the proliferation of "dissident" social science research centers outside of the formal university system, which have produced most of the systematic research on the effects of military rule on Chilean society.[7] Partly due to these research centers' activities, Chile represents an unusual case in terms of the amount and quality of the information on state repression, social adaptation, and opposition generated *while an authoritarian regime is still in power*. The Chilean experience also has been characterized by an unusually wide array of oppositional activities and organizations. The dissident academic centers are one example; others are the associations of relatives of victims of repression, and various church organizations, particularly the Catholic Church's widely known human rights organization, the Vicariate of Solidarity. Collectively, these and other organizations have amassed an impressive amount of documentation on human rights violations in Chile, most of which unfortunately remains untranslated.[8]

This chapter's primary emphasis is on the violation of civil and political rights in Chile. To that end, the next five sections identify five phases of state repression, as well as civil responses to it. It is important to bear in mind that when the military overthrew the UP government they aimed also at overturning the very system that had led—democratically—to that government. The repressive activities that ensued were thus guided by two imperatives: (1) to destroy, dismantle, or reorganize virtually everything that was considered to be an expression of support of the previous order (political parties, labor unions, grass-roots organizations, universities, etc.); and (2) to create the necessary additional conditions for prolonged military rule, together with its new economic policies.   ·

Periodization (the five phases) of the sort we use to guide the discussion of state repression has also been established from the standpoint of the economic policies that the military government has imposed on the country.[9] In full form (from 1975 onward), these are commonly described as the neo-conservative (or sometimes neo-liberal) "economic model." Within economics, this model is most closely associated with Milton Friedman and what is referred to as "Chicago School economics." The Chilean economists who promoted it in that country are commonly given the colloquial name of "los Chicago Boys," since many of them studied at the University of Chicago. Chile is generally considered to have adopted the "purest" version of neo-conservative economics of any country in the world, and thus many have regarded it as a form of test case.

The goals of the economic model . . . have been to establish a free market economy with a subsidiary role for the state, to promote stable economic growth, to increase the level of foreign and domestic investment, and to lower inflation to international levels. The main components of government policy to achieve these goals have been: removing government restrictions to allow the free fluctuation of prices; restrictive fiscal and monetary policies implying a reduction in government spending, especially for public investments and social spending; a general withdrawal of the state from intervention in the economy and the transferring of state enterprises to the national and international private sector; an "opening up" of the economy to the exterior by drastically reducing barriers to trade, investment and financial transactions; the provision of special conditions for the development of the financial and banking sector; and the suppression of trade unions and the restriction of the collective bargaining process in order to create a "free" labour market.[10]

This set of economic policies, serving certain big business interests, derived from no popular will; they were imposed from above with no consultative input outside of some elite circles. It is critical to understand that the imposition of these economic policies *required* political repression because they ran against the interests of much of the population, but they also *produced* repression of other sorts. That is, civil and political rights have been violated in order to implement certain economic policies, which in turn have meant the violation of a wide range of social, economic, and cultural rights (a topic we take up following the discussion of the five phases of state repression). Though analytically distinct, these two types of state repression are two sides of the same coin. By the same logic, it is apparent that the following analysis of state repression carries an important subtext dealing with economic, social, and cultural rights; human rights are too intertwined to be divided into two tidy packages.

ERUPTION OF REPRESSION, 1973–1974

When the military came out of their barracks and the coup arrived on the morning of September 11, 1973, it was as though the social system were discharging its accumulated, pent-up tensions in the form of anger and violence. To the UP supporters, it seemed the attack of maddened, unrestrained persons. No authorities seemed accountable for anything or to anyone. The previous government had fallen and President Allende was dead;[11] the new one which the officers were claiming to have formed still seemed unreal, and thus the state became to much of the civilian population a headless entity, about which little was known and from which in any case it was better to hide or try to go unnoticed. In these first days the state, in effect, was transformed into a military garrison in a state of war. Civilians lost their civil referents in a reign of terror mounted by the armed forces and police, who were under the influence of techniques derived from psychological warfare. These included the fabricated "Plan Z,"[12] under which military officers were led to believe that they and their families were about to be liquidated by the Socialist party. Thus many officers felt they were acting preemptively: strike first or be struck.

The initial ferocity of the repression was also fed by the retaliatory urges of the wealthy—and those who identified with them—who had been frustrated by the redistributive measures carried out by the UP government during 1970–1973.

This situation had distinct territorial features.[13] In the countryside repression took the form of almost indiscriminate murder, carried out not only by the police and the army, but also by the former owners of large landed estates who were in the process of recovering their property, much of which had been expropriated under the agrarian reform. Traditionally, peasants had been linked to the estate owners in personal relationships,[14] which the agrarian reform had been undermining. The rage which had been brewing among landowners was released by the new conditions brought about by the coup, and there was much private vengeance taken against their recently insubordinate inferiors.

In the cities, on the other hand, though repression also had a partially indiscriminate character, it is possible to trace some lines of orientation even from the first days. The primary victims of repression were the leaders of political parties and unions that had been associated with the UP movement, plus persons associated with the MIR (the Revolutionary Left Movement), an organization that stood outside and to the "left" (tactically) of the UP coalition. In second priority appear to have been those who, without being leaders, were directly or indirectly linked with the political parties of the left, especially the Socialist and Communist parties. Numerically, of course, this second category contributed the larger number of victims. In the main cities executions even took place in factories and shantytowns. And as in the countryside, vengeance could take private forms, such as by factory owners or managers.[15] Overall, estimates of the total number of political killings in the first few months range from 5,000 to 30,000.[16] The total of political detentions (excluding those of less than twenty-four hours) in the first six months has been estimated as between 60,000 and 70,000.[17]

After this first brief period, repression began to develop in more systematic ways. Within a week after the coup, the four-man Junta (Army General Augusto Pinochet, Air Force General Gustavo Leigh, Navy Admiral Toribio Merino, and Carabineros, or uniformed police, General César Mendoza) took steps toward self-legitimation by declaring first a state of siege, then a state of siege understood as a state of war, and finally a state of emergency (Decrees No. 3, 4 and 5 respectively, of the new government).

This was but a first expression of increasingly centralized military authority under conditions which now "legally" allowed for the establishment of military courts, detentions without charges, and the transfer of detained persons among different places of detention.[18] These three conditions also created the legal basis, so to speak, for detained persons to "disappear."

The aims of the decrees were (1) to create a fictitious "war" in which political opponents were assigned the role of the "enemy," and (2) to give a legal backing to heavy repressive sanctions, in that wartime convictions carry more severe sentences than the same crimes committed in peacetime. In this new perspective, Chile's allegedly seditious "internal enemy" was simply undergoing the experience of any army in the process of being defeated.

Even under these arbitrarily created conditions, however, the military war codes themselves were violated: political prisoners (the enemy) were not allowed a genuine opportunity to demonstrate their innocence, and military prosecutors functioned simultaneously as military judges. The abuses were such that in 1974 the Ministry of Defense created a committee charged with reviewing the military judges' sentences. Many cases were not even reviewed, as the prisoners had already been executed.

The real objectives of the military courts were to incapacitate and punish the political parties of the left and their leaders, not to uncover "crimes." All trials were brief and summary; in many cases whole groups of prisoners were sentenced in less than twenty-four hours. No evidence was given in proportion to the seriousness of the charges (e.g., treason), which in any case were of "crimes" allegedly committed before the military coup, and thus before the declaration of the state of siege. The legal principle of nonretroactivity of the law alone made these trials invalid. In addition, prisoners were held incommunicado and frequently under torture from the moment of their detention. In many cases the penalty was the death sentence, and there were also many cases in which prison terms were subsequently and summarily changed into death sentences by high-ranking officers.

These actions were sometimes accompanied by duly orchestrated accounts in the media, aimed at reinforcing the impression of a warlike situation created by the massive presence of heavily armed soldiers throughout the country. Arrests were labeled as "capture of the enemy," and military actions were glorified in dramatic and martial tones which distorted facts and their contexts. New, more convenient facts were also invented. There were even cases in which sets were prepared to film supposed armed confrontations, which were subsequently shown on national television. The sets were equipped with corpses of tortured prisoners, which were identified by their relatives.[19]

All this was happening at the same time that the Junta was making repeated public declarations that it wished to reestablish institutional order, peace, and unity among Chileans; that it would respect the rights of workers; that it was calling for patriotic cooperation and solidarity; that it would overcome divisions and not repress ideological tendencies of any kind; and that it would not permit personal retaliations.

These contradictions, in fact, reflected the tensions that existed within the bloc that had taken power through the coup, during what one Chilean researcher has appropriately called the initial "phase of ideological indefinition":

This phase was characterized by a surreptitious but decisive struggle between those authoritarian tendencies seeking to "refound" Chilean society, and the restoring tendencies linked to the political center and the moderate military officers. During this phase of indecision, discourse tended—perhaps through simple inertia—to refer to the immediate past, that of the struggle against the UP. . . . In fact, the first declarations were in a restoring language, emphasizing the transitory character of military rule.[20]

There was a great breach between the actual physical repression, of the sort we have described, and the improvised "legal" support given to it through decree-laws and the official statements justifying them. Shortly after the coup the first decrees declaring the national labor federation (Central Unica de Trabajadores, CUT) and the political parties of the left illegal were issued (the other parties were placed "in recess"); meanwhile, many of their leaders and members were being taken prisoner, tortured, executed, or forced into exile. These two fronts in the struggle—the physically repressive and the legal—and the chasm between them, were bridged by the mass media. In a "state of siege," understood as a "state of war," which had been "legally" declared, those murdered could be called "executed" or war "casualties." The government could state its principles, proclaim laws, kill, and issue a report on its killings, but the contin-

ually sympathetic and supportive description and interpretation of these phenomena by the media were necessary to impart to them a sense of connectedness
and wholeness, and to imbue them with legitimacy.

Thus the agents of repression were free to proceed, protected by this state of
affairs in which the ordinary courts and their legal procedures had no competence,
even where the will might have existed. Ordinary state institutions could no
longer protect the civilian population.

The repressive methods of this first phase set their mark on the entire period.
Almost all of the different modes of repression have been maintained subsequently, with variations in frequency of application; overall repression was simply at its greatest during the first part of this phase.

Initially, the leftist political parties and the labor movement were able to offer
only limited and short-lived resistance to the coup and then to the military
government; they were temporarily crushed by the weight of the repressive
apparatus. But as early as October 1973, Chilean churches began to take on the
protection of the victims of human rights violations, with the creation of the
Committee for Peace (Comité de Cooperación para la Paz en Chile), sponsored
by representatives of the Catholic Church and various Protestant churches, as
well as of the Jewish community. This centrality of religious forces in the
opposition to human rights abuses has been characteristic of the entire period of
military dictatorship.[21]

INSTITUTIONALIZATION OF REPRESSION, 1974–1977

After the initial onslaught against the left and the institutions which had allowed
it influence and finally power in Chilean society, systematic attempts to organize
repression in relationship to military and police hierarchies began to take place.
This meant a clarification of tasks and spheres of responsibility within and among
the three branches of the armed forces (army, navy, and air force) and the two
national police systems (Carabineros, uniformed, and Investigaciones, plain
clothed). Repressive functions thus began to be more professionally defined. In
addition, civilian participation and cooperation with the new government and its
agencies also began to wane, so political information by means of personal
denunciations became more difficult to obtain. These two problems found a
common solution in the creation of a specialized organization which would have
primary responsibility for both information gathering and professional repression:
the DINA (Dirección de Inteligencia Nacional, or National Intelligence Agency).
Created June 14, 1974, the decree-law that brought it into being "subordinated
all other intelligence services in the country to DINA and gave DINA agents
unlimited power to raid and search houses and take prisoners without charges."[22]
DINA represented, and in fact assisted, the consolidation of Pinochet's personal
power within the government. In theory, DINA took orders from, and reported
to, the four-member military Junta. In reality its director, General Manuel Contreras, was responsible only to Pinochet,[23] who by this time had already become

the executive head of state. The other three members of the Junta were deliberately kept in the dark about many of the details of DINA's activites. DINA put an end to spontaneous civilian participation in repression, and also allowed the armed forces to distance themselves somewhat from direct and flagrant involvement. More than an intelligence agency, DINA became the secret police of an all-powerful personalistic dictatorship.

This centralization of secret power and intelligence allowed the government to sharpen its aim. Repression became more selective, though it was still targeted mainly at the three political parties of the left that were seen as special threats to the government: the Communist and Socialist parties and the MIR.

DINA's modus operandi incorporated two methods, one stemming from the other. The first was secret action. Though the previous method of reporting and publicizing deaths as the results of confrontations was retained as a cover for some of the killings, DINA began operating whenever possible without witnesses and without press coverage. The victims were usually seized when they were alone, and kept in unknown detention places.

In this way the practice of disappearances began to operate in a more planned and expert way, the second new method. Previously, the government had not bothered much to disguise the fact that it had seized, and was holding, persons who subsequently disappeared. Now victims tended to be taken covertly and held without acknowledgment, making it unnecessary to explain their later whereabouts. The development of this method seems to have been a response to the need to clean up the government's image both internally and internationally. With regard to the latter, Chile had rapidly gained the image of a pariah country, and this conflicted with the requirements of the new economic model, which presupposed and counted on substantial foreign financial support. This support was initially slow in coming, due in part to the country's reputation abroad for turmoil and brutality.

New economic turbulence created new internal discontent toward the government, even among some who had originally supported the coup. The neo-conservative economic policy package was thrust upon the country in accelerated form in 1975, under the name of a "Shock Treatment" (*Plan Shock*—even its name was in English) needed by the economy. In that year, total government spending fell by 27 percent, and public investment by half. Tax revenues and rates charged by public enterprises were increased, real wages were reduced, interest rates charged by banks were freed, and tariffs were lowered. The ensuing recession included sharp falls in employment levels and industrial production, and a negative 12.9 percent economic growth rate for 1975. By early 1976 real wages and salaries were at 62 percent of their 1970 level.[24]

During this second phase, repression began to be exercised against a wider political spectrum, including the Christian Democratic party (though the techniques used against persons not associated with the left were generally "soft" ones—loss of employment, for example). The Christian Democratic party and the other nonleft parties, which previously had been placed "in recess," were ordered dissolved in March 1977. This phase also saw the Catholic Church draw more repressive attention as its spokespersons became increasingly critical of the regime's human rights abuses. This attention centered on (but was not limited to) its human rights organization, the Vicariate of Solidarity, created in January of 1976 after the Junta had pressured strongly to close down the Committee for Peace toward the end of 1975. The Vicariate in fact was a continuation of the Committee's work, and even personnel. Its creator, Cardinal Raúl Silva Henríquez, Archbishop of Santiago, placed it within the legal sphere of the Church, thus protecting it.[25] The Vicariate developed as the main public opposition force to the regime's human rights abuses, and in so doing, radically upset prevailing images of the nature of the Chilean Church. The parties of the left, having come close to being destroyed in the first phase, began the underground work of reconstructing themselves.

REPRESSIVE STABILIZATION, 1977–1981

In August 1977 DINA was legally dissolved and replaced by a new organization, the CNI (Central Nacional de Informaciones, or National Intelligence Agency). The immediate cause of this metamorphosis was the international scandal and political pressure against the Junta in the wake of DINA's assassination in Washington, D.C., of Orlando Letelier (a former UP ambassador to the United States and member of the Socialist party) and his American aide, Ronni Moffit.[26] Though the largest, this was but the latest in a series of international scandals involving the agency, and it coincided with (and helped foster) mounting resentment within the armed forces against DINA's increasing power at all levels of Chilean society. In fact, DINA had even been used to penetrate the armed forces themselves. More specifically, anger was focused against its director, Contreras, who used the agency he had built to amass enormous personal power, second only to that of Pinochet.

As a proper response to a human rights image crisis, it was said that the new agency, the CNI, would perform only intelligence functions. In fact, it continued many of DINA's lines of repression, including torture and executions. However, incommunicado periods for prisoners did shorten, and disappearances began to cease. Banishment (internal exile to remote regions within Chile) and compulsory foreign exile diminished as well. Methods which had been attracting the most national and international attention came under varying degrees of control. Now emphasis was placed on direct or indirect personal threats: following people, night searches of homes, threats involving family members, surveillance from cars parked in front of homes or places of work, anonymous phone calls during sleeping hours, and similar methods. These tactics had the advantage of being low-profile ways of warning people about possible consequences of their activities, with the aim of immobilizing them through fear. In general, efforts were made to maximize social control while minimizing the side effect of image-spoiling by giving primacy to psychological methods over physical ones.

On the other hand, the apparent relaxation of repression created enough sense of space for new opposition organizations to begin to develop. Some were directly supported by the Vicariate of Solidarity, such as the three Associations of Relatives of the Detained and Disappeared, of Political Prisoners, and of the Exiled. Others emerged independently of the Vicariate: the Association of Relatives of the Politically Executed, the Chilean Human Rights Commission, the Committee for Defense of the Rights of the People (CODEPU), Peace and Justice Service (SERPAJ), the National Committee for the Rights of Youth (CODEJU), and the National Labor Coordinating Committee (CNS). These organizations protected themselves as best they could with international political and religious connections, and their germination was in some degree insulated by the new human rights orientation of the Carter administration (1977–1981) in the United States, in contrast with the previous Ford and Nixon administrations.[27]

During most of this phase there was an impression of strong economic recovery, peaking in 1977–1980 with per capita economic growth rates of 6 to 8 percent (and labeled by some the Chilean Economic Miracle, by analogy with the previous apparent Brazilian one). This was largely accomplished by securing extensive lines of foreign credit (helped by the new, cleaner image of the regime), but rather than being productively invested in the country's economic infrastructure, it was mostly squandered on imported consumer goods for the middle and upper classes and on financial speculation. As one economist points out, the most dynamic activities in the economy were commerce, financial activities, and personal services.[28] The major winners were a small number of economic conglomerates which managed to concentrate great wealth in their direction. In 1978 five such conglomerates controlled 53 percent of the total assets of the country's 250 largest private enterprises, and no more than eighty individuals controlled 216 of these enterprises, while no more than fifty individuals controlled Chile's private banks.[29] Nevertheless, the 1976–1980 period saw increases in overall economic growth, industrial production, employment, real wages and salaries, exports, and foreign investment, while inflation decreased.[30]

The collapse would come during the next phase, but during this one, things seemed decidedly better, and not only economically. The transition from DINA to the CNI had meant more reliance on ''legal'' repression (that is, through the use of the ordinary court system, and with charges against the accused), and the growth of some more or less openly functioning opposition organizations. The combination of apparent economic growth and some measure of political stabilization was giving the government an almost credible impression of success.

But perhaps for these very reasons, around 1979 the ordinary courts began rejecting the CNI's charges against prisoners and ordering their release. Thus ''legal'' repression was not producing the expected results, and this, together with the upsurge of opposition organizations, induced the CNI to revert to older DINA-style methods beginning in 1980. On February 7, 1980, the Junta issued Decree No. 3168, allowing it to summarily banish persons into internal exile without sentencing, merely by order of the Ministry of the Interior. Several months later, in July, Decree No. 3451 raised from five to twenty the number of days during which detained persons could be held incommunicado before being brought before a court or released. This meant the CNI could hold persons in its secret detention places long enough both to torture them and have them recover from the visible effects before they reappeared publicly, something difficult under the previous five-day rule.

During this same year, 1980, repression mounted against the Catholic Church, which was assuming great visibility on the human rights front. Methods included threats to priests and other church members; the placing of bombs on church premises; arrests of priests and lay religious workers in poor neighborhoods; and a media campaign to discredit the Church hierarchy, especially Cardinal Silva Henríquez, who more than any other single public figure in Chile at this time symbolized in his person opposition to the military regime's human rights violations.

CONSTITUTIONAL REPRESSION, 1981–1983

This phase opened with the coming into force of a new Constitution, completed in 1980 but taking effect in March 1981, which now enshrined constitutionally much of what before had been ordered by decree.[31] The Vicar of Solidarity, Juan de Castro, issued an open letter[32] to Church officials expressing his concerns about the human rights implications in the Constitution, among which were the following:

—It renders the president immune from political judgment.
—It sets up a Constitutional Board, a majority of the members of which are appointed by the president, which can decide on the legality of political parties.
—It gives the Junta the power to decree "interpretations" of the Constitution.
—It gives the president the power to decree, by himself, a state of emergency, which in turn gives him exceptional powers.

But his gravest concern had to do with "Transitory Article 24," which would be in force for an eight-year period between 1981 and 1989. This article, which has since become infamous in Chile, gives the president the following powers (upon his own decree, and for periods of six months, renewable), in the event of "acts of violence aimed at affecting public order, or danger of disturbance to internal peace":

—To arrest and hold persons, incommunicado and without charges, for periods up to twenty days, in places of detention other than jails.
—To restrict freedom of assembly.
—To expel or prohibit the (re)entry to Chile of persons espousing certain doctrines (totalitarian, against the family, or supporting violence or the concept of class struggle), as well as persons "carrying out acts against the interests of Chile or representing a danger to internal peace."

—To banish persons into internal exile for periods up to three months.[33]

Beyond this, the Constitution maintains General Pinochet in power as president until 1989, and then allows the Junta to designate the next president, presumably Pinochet again, subject to "ratification" by a plebiscite (toward which the opposition is deeply skeptical). Thus the legal possibility is opened of Pinochet remaining in power for yet another eight years, for a grand total of twenty-four years from 1973 to 1997.

On the economic front there was disaster as the results of previous growth being built on the quicksand of foreign loans put to unproductive uses now were felt. Already by 1980 Chile had achieved the second highest per capita foreign debt in the entire Third World. Economic growth was weak in 1981, but in 1982 the economy registered a negative per capita growth of gross domestic product (GDP) of − 15.8 percent, followed by a smaller drop in 1983. Unemployment rose from 17 percent of the national labor force in September 1981 to 35 percent by March 1983. Between 1981 and 1983 gross investment fell by 47 percent, imports by 54 percent, private consumption by 19 percent, and the legal minimum wage lost 21 percent of its purchasing power. Bankruptcies of companies occurred in record numbers; the 810 in 1982 were about double the level of the two previous years, which in turn was about double the average level during the Christian Democratic and UP administrations.[34] Now the middle and upper classes were feeling the adverse effects of national economic policy.

The economic deluge caused further erosion of the government's political support base, and 1982 marked the beginning of an upsurge of large-scale opposition publicly expressed. The country's first major protest demonstrations since the coup occurred in this year, in the context of two massive funeral processions: the first in January, after the death of former Christian Democratic President Eduardo Frei, and the second in February after the assassination (throat cut and shot in the head, clearly to serve as a warning) of labor leader Tucapel Jiménez. Few arrests were made in these two demonstrations, but a subsequent one in March celebrating International Women's Day produced 198 arrests. Sporadic demonstrations occurred throughout the year, culminating with a particularly large one in December.

Oppositional activities also began mushrooming in working-class residential neighborhoods: open meetings were held, often on church premises and sometimes with the participation of clerics themselves, with speeches by those who dared (typically labor leaders and human rights activists, and even neighborhood party militants), the singing of protest songs, and the like. The opposition political parties themselves began to make a slow and somewhat cautious public reappearance—in spite of their illegality—in the form of public declarations, interviews with spokespersons and leaders, and eventually even press conferences. This process was easiest for the Christian Democrats, who had never really had to go underground. It was harder for the parties of the left, particularly for the Communist party, and impossible at this stage for the MIR.

The central changes in the nature of state repression during this phase were a direct result of the new forms that public opposition was taking. The Vicariate of Solidarity recorded more than a tripling of "mass arrests" (i.e., arrests associated with demonstrations) from 1981 to 1982. In addition, the Chilean Human Rights Commission (the country's other large human rights organization, formed in November 1978 by an agreement among representatives of the Christian Democratic party and certain parties of the left) was compelled to formulate a new recording category of "raid arrests," those resulting from raids on poor neighborhoods:

These operations are actually collective intimidations, included [in police statistics] under the item of arrests to maintain public order. During 1982 four such raids on poor neighborhoods [in Santiago] were reported, all with similar characteristics, by joint police and unidentified special civilian forces. [In two cases] both uniformed and plainclothed police, CNI agents and Air Force troops participated. They are carried out in the early morning hours [while the residents are still asleep]. They surround the sector and burst into the neighborhood, getting the residents out of bed or out of their homes. They break into the homes, looking for "weapons" or clandestine printing machinery. . . . Violence is another common characteristic of these raids. In the case of Nuevo Amanecer neighborhood, some 1,550 persons were arrested. Only the small children were left, without their mothers, as the mothers had been arrested too.[35]

The Chilean Human Rights Commission reported 8,991 known raid arrests in 1982.

REPRESSION AND MAJOR CIVIL RESISTANCE, 1983-PRESENT

What is perhaps most striking about the most recent phase is the simple fact that the military regime is still in power, even amidst the regional movement toward redemocratization (Brazil, Argentina, Uruguay, etc.) and the almost volcanic eruption of anti-government protest in Chile.

In 1983, a decade after the coup, both opposition and repression peaked. Beginning in 1982, the regime was showing signs of losing control of the situation, at first economically and then politically. The intensification and spread of opposition are understandable in terms of the disastrous effects of the government's economic policy registering in the context of the relatively relaxed repression of the previous two phases. In fact, 1983 became known in Chile as "the year when people lost their fear." One might also say that there was an energetic conversion of fear into anger, which now fueled massive and repeated mobilizations against the government. Since the category of "victims" was now less confined to the political left and the poor, the ranks of the opposition began to be joined by those to whom fear—whether politically or economically induced—had previously been a stranger. Now for the first time state repression took place in direct response to widespread challenges to the government's authority and legitimacy.

The clearest expression of the new opposition trend was a set of key political events that took place between May and November 1983: a series of social mobilizations known as "Days of National Protest." These were actions called by different organizations, both labor and political, that would last as little as a day or as long as four or five, which included a range of activities and nonactivities: the sealing-off and defense of working-class neighborhoods by their own residents, street demonstrations, deliberate traffic congestion and horn-honking, pot-banging,[36] work and school absenteeism, and the like. Public protest meetings were called, the largest, on November 18 in O'Higgins Park in downtown Santiago, reaching a turnout estimated at close to a million persons. During these months, the situation was reaching a critical point for the government, which many mistakenly believed was facing an imminent breakdown of its control of political life.

There also began a proliferation of attempts to create organizational alliances among the different political parties and other groupings that now composed a very disparate opposition movement ranging from armed sectors of the left to democratic sectors of the right. The aim was, and still is, to build an opposition front sufficiently broad and strong to force the military regime to abdicate (or at least to transform itself substantially), as well as one uniting enough of the society to be able to present itself as a viable alternative to continued military rule. This task has been unsuccessful up to the present time, for two main reasons.

First, the problem from the point of view of the opposition may be stated by inverting an old cliché: *les extrêmes ne se touchent pas*. Not only that, but important sectors even of the centrist Christian Democratic party have been unwilling to engage in alliances with the Marxist-Leninist left, which in turn has a long history of ideological condescension and hostility toward the center. Alliances embracing up to half or even two-thirds of the political spectrum have been constructed, but its totality has escaped cementing together. The issues at stake are not only ideological, however; they also include the (so far) very hypothetical questions of who would actually participate in a transition government and whether certain parties of the left would remain proscribed.

The second reason is that the government has proved itself very adept at divide-and-rule tactics. Examples include its attempts to divide the labor movement by inviting some of its leaders to confer while arresting others; sporadic dialogues between some individual government officials (normally cabinet members but never Pinochet himself) and selected opposition leaders, but always with the purposeful exclusion of certain political sectors, particularly the Communist party; and the calling on government supporters to organize "self-defense squadrons" to act in the more affluent neighborhoods of Santiago, thus intimidating members of the middle class from joining in protests.

Just as the level of opposition to the government during the current phase from May 1983 onward is the highest it has been since the coup, the level of state repression is the highest it has been since the end of the second phase in 1977; the repression has been a direct response to the opposition. The Vicariate of Solidarity's Legal Department attended 46,311 cases in 1983 (an average of 180 daily), which was an increase of 105 percent over the cases in 1982.[37] The Chilean Human Rights Commission's statistics show increases in every single repressive indicator from 1982 to 1983: individual arrests more than doubled, mass arrests increased tenfold, raid arrests doubled, political deaths increased fourfold, reported cases of torture more than tripled, cases of exile more than doubled, cases of banishment almost doubled, and reported cases of intimidation more than tripled.[38]

This stepped-up level of repression took its toll on the protest movement, which by the end of 1983 had found itself incapable of dislodging the government, and which by now was suffering from a serious loss of energy and morale. Thus the Chilean Human Rights Commission's recorded cases of mass arrests (associated with demonstrations) for 1984 were half the 1983 level. A case for generally lower repression would be hard to make, however, because although the recorded incidence of political deaths, torture, and intimidation did decrease in 1984, the incidence of individual and raid detentions, exilings, and banishings increased.[39]

A state of siege was also imposed in late 1984, following violent demonstrations and subsequent killings of six policemen in terrorist attacks. This state of siege, referred to by Pinochet as his "second September 11th" (the day of the coup), gave the president his strongest powers since the prolonged state of siege following the coup was lifted in 1978. Coming on top of two other "states of exception" that were already in place—a state of danger of disturbance to internal peace, and a state of emergency—it ran from November 6, 1984, to June 16, 1985.[40] Pinochet explained that it was necessary because "the country cannot continue allowing an institutionalized sequence of subversive practices to block the way to the achievement of full democracy."[41] In practice, the most important additional legal powers that the state of siege allowed Pinochet were (1) to seize and hold persons incommunicado, in secret detention places (mainly those of the CNI), for as long as the state of siege was in effect, and (2) to close down the (opposition) news media. Additionally, it empowered him to censor *all* media, ban meetings and associations, suspend the right of freedom of opinion, restrict travel, open mail, and tap telephones, with no right of appeal to the courts. In fact, the state of siege ushered in an immediate crackdown on the opposition: a curfew was imposed; most of the important opposition publications were banned, and all media were placed under censorship; and raids were carried out both on the offices of opposition organizations and in poor neighborhoods, where hundreds and even thousands were arrested in each raid.

Subsequently there has occurred a series of very high-profile repressive actions. In November 1984 the head of the Vicariate of Solidarity, Ignacio Gutiérrez, a Jesuit priest, was barred from reentering the country after making remarks critical of Chile's human rights situation during a trip to Europe; the Church had to replace him with a new Vicar. In March 1985 three communists—including the widely respected human rights researcher José Manuel Parada—were abducted in Santiago and found later beside a road with their throats cut; this was later revealed as the work of a police (Carabineros) intelligence agency. In May 1986 two professionals on the staff of the Vicariate of Solidarity were arrested, causing the other staff members to mount twenty-four-hour guard duty on the premises of its church building, in fear of a possible police raid. In July 1986 security forces raided the home of three alleged guerrillas, who died along with two sisters and a nephew; the police reported that they had fired only one shot, and that the six had committed suicide. Also in July a nineteen-year-old Chilean-born photographer from Washington, D.C., died of burn wounds sustained during an anti-government demonstration in a shantytown. Witnesses said he and an eighteen-year-old female friend were chased by soldiers, then both were doused with a flammable liquid and set on fire; Pinochet suggested that the man accidentally might have set fire to himself. Riot police later attacked the man's funeral procession with tear gas and water cannon (the badly wounded woman survived). A week after these two torchings, men in civilian clothing carried out a third one.

Actions such as the ones above carry significance that extends far beyond the fates of the direct victims, since they carry cautionary messages to different sectors of the opposition. As actions, they deal not only with a given "problem" (person/s or situation); they also operate as a form of behavior control by instilling fear among those whose knowledge that "such things happen" is reinforced.

THE VIOLATION OF ECONOMIC, SOCIAL, AND CULTURAL RIGHTS

This section presents, in capsule form, some basic additional information on how certain fundamental economic, social, and cultural rights have been contravened in Chile since the establishment of military rule. Given the summary nature of this chapter, the range of rights covered is truncated, and the aim of the comments is essentially illustrative. Care has been taken not to evaluate Chile by First World standards; the relevant comparisons are with the country's own past performance.

a. *Firing of employees for political reasons.* This has been continuous, but there have been certain notable waves. The first was right after the coup; it has been estimated that within one and a half years (until March 1975) some 300,000 public and private employees were dismissed for political reasons.[42] In 1984 the number of participants in Metropolitan Santiago in the government's work program known as the PEM (Programa de Empleo Mínimo) was cut from 67,000 in January to 8,194 in February. This was the government's response to demands for higher pay by the participants, who were receiving well under the legal minimum wage. It has been characterized as "the largest mass firing in national history, and perhaps in world history."[43]

b. *Maintenance of massive unemployment.* During the UP years, unemployment averaged some 4 percent. Subsequently it rose as high as 35 percent in mid–1983, declining to 25 percent by early 1985. Government economic policy has heavily favored capital over labor; as labor specialists have pointed out, in this "free market" policy, the labor market is in fact a *captive market.*[44]

c. *Regressive income redistribution.* The major study on this topic concludes that between 1969 and 1978, income was redistributed toward the top 20 percent of the population and away from the bottom 60 percent of the population.[45]

d. *Loss of purchasing power among the poor.* Government statistics, using the official consumer price index (CPI) to adjust for inflation, show that between December 1981 and June 1985, wages and salaries lost 21 percent of their purchasing power. But to measure the impact among the poor, a research center specializing in labor issues has constructed a "CPI of the Poor" based on the products and services most consumed by them specifically, the cost of which has increased disproportionately. Using this measure, their results show that the purchasing power of the legal minimum wage dropped by *52 percent* between September 1981 and September 1985.[46]

e. *Pauperization of the peasantry.* The military government carried out what has been called an agrarian "counterreform." Of the land expropriated from large estates during the previous two administrations, most was returned to its former owners or sold at discount prices to corporations; less than half remained with the peasantry. The government also eliminated almost all of the resources and services (credits, machinery, technical assistance, etc.) that the state formerly had provided to peasants, who now had to purchase these—when possible—in the market. Price controls were eliminated, and tariffs were reduced to such low levels that Chile was flooded with inexpensive foreign food products, and the peasantry became largely confined to growing low-priced agricultural staples. The main consequences have been pauperization and out-migration from the countryside.[47]

f. *Nutritional deterioration.* Between 1971 and 1983 the average caloric intake of the Chilean population fell by an estimated 20 percent, while the average protein intake fell by some 28 percent.[48] The Chilean Medical Association has estimated that in the mid–1980s, 46 percent of children under six years of age are malnourished.[49]

g. *Authoritarian control of higher education.* (Within the field of education we restrict ourselves to universities for the sake of brevity.) At the time of the coup, the universities were occupied militarily, and officers were placed in charge of them; as of 1984 only one university had a civilian president. By conservative estimates, about one-third of faculty members were purged and some 15 to 18 percent of students were expelled within the first several months alone.[50] Entire academic units (departments, faculties, research centers) were eliminated or reorganized, for political reasons. Strong ideological control over curricula was implemented, which began weakening only in the 1980s. Budgets were cut and market principles were applied, compelling the universities to move toward greater self-financing by increasing fees, thus making access to them more difficult for students from low-income families.[51]

h. *Housing shortage*. The withdrawal of the state has been particularly notable
here. Even the military government, in its first full year of rule (1974), spent
an average of 1,815 pesos per capita on housing. By 1982 the per capita state
expenditure had declined by three-quarters, to 419 pesos per capita. Total housing
construction (private and public) averaged 4.0 homes per 1,000 population annually during the Christian Democratic and UP administrations (1964–1973),
while from 1974 to 1982 it averaged 2.7, a decrease of one-third. Another
indicator of the same phenomenon is that by 1982, unemployment among Chilean
architects was running around 70 percent. The country's total housing shortage
rose from an estimated 664,000 homes in 1976 to 807,000 in 1984, and a major
earthquake in 1985 further aggravated the problem.[52]

i. *Native peoples' cultural survival at risk*. The principal native people of
Chile are the Mapuche, who live in the south-central region of the country. Their
numbers are very difficult to determine, for the military government concedes
them no special identity, and the 1982 census included no question on ethnicity;
recent estimates run the gamut from 400,000 to 1,000,000, i.e., from about 4
to 10 percent of the Chilean population. Their propensity toward militancy during
the UP period meant that their leadership was struck particularly hard after the
coup. In addition, like other peasants who had benefited from the agrarian reform,
after 1973 much of their newly acquired land was taken away from them. Their
material conditions of life are such that even the government recognizes that
they are living in a state of "extreme poverty." Most rural Mapuche live on
reservations, and their culture involves communally owned land. Legislation
dating from 1961 prohibited non-Indians from buying reservation land, and
forbade its division into privately owned units unless so requested by at least
one-third of the inhabitants of the reservation. Legislation decreed by the Junta
in 1979 reflects the government's dedication to economic privatization: it allows
reservations to be divided into private units upon the request of one single
occupant. This has opened the way for non-Mapuches to buy the newly privatized
land, and given the Mapuche's grinding poverty and the general difficulties that
small peasants have competing in the market with large agricultural enterprises,
there are strong pressures for Mapuche small owners to sell. These pressures
are reinforced by legislation which provides economic incentives (through taxes
and access to credit and other services) for land division, and penalties for
retention of land on a communally owned basis. Among supporters of the Mapuche there is general agreement that maintenance of the existing legislation will
doom the Mapuche to cultural disappearance.[53]

CONCLUSION

The main problem in understanding Chile's profile with regard to civil and
political rights is that internationally there is confusion about two different images
of the country. On the one hand there is the image of an omnipotent "regime
of terror" with no substantial opposition to it; and on the other hand, an image

of an "authoritarian regime" which both permits and is regularly confronted by a certain range of opposition. Both images are approximations of the truth, but they correspond to two different time periods: 1973 to 1977 was a period of relatively unchecked state terrorism, whereas from 1977 to the present repression has been generally more selective, the military regime has been more attentive to its image, and organized opposition has both built over time to massive proportions and virtually institutionalized itself. Thus in the 1980s we have, for example, a situation in which political parties are illegal but exist in active form. What complicates this attempt to clarify conflicting perceptions of the country, however, is the fact that throughout the second period, the regime periodically has unleashed waves of repression that are reminiscent of the first period, though at generally lower levels of brutality.

What accounts for the continuing violation of civil and political rights in Chile? One must recall that the original point of the coup d'état was to remove the left from power, bring it under permanent control, and thus safeguard an endangered capitalist economic system. State terrorism, and state repression in general, have been rational policies designed and implemented by the military government in pursuit of these objectives. These objectives *required* the suspension of democracy. The Junta sees the nonleft parties as a threat, because by and large they functioned within a political system whose norms involved the legitimacy of the left as a set of political actors. Thus the democratic system as such had to be eliminated and its principal actors (parties) made illegal, lest they eventually re-create the very system which allowed the left to come to power in the first place. Freedom of information, of speech, of peaceful assembly, the right to a fair trial, and the like carry the same type of risk.

The violation of the citizens' economic, social, and cultural rights has mainly been the result of the Junta's economic model and its derivative social policies. The state has largely abandoned claims to be a protector of the interests of the disadvantaged, and has left those who stand in a weak relationship to the market undefended. The results have included a great concentration of private economic power and the correlative aggravation of problems such as unemployment and deteriorating incomes among much of the population.

Thus the Chilean state is characterized by a massive *withdrawal* from the economy and a massive *intervention* in other areas of the society. The former would have been impossible without the latter, because the majority of Chileans would not voluntarily have accepted the Junta's economic model. Chile's "free market" economy is based on political unfreedom.

It would be foolhardy to predict the future of the military regime, but it is worthwhile underscoring an issue that is central to questions of its longevity. For the coup to happen originally, a series of interests had to coalesce: domestic civilian interests, military interests, and foreign interests. But the state was captured by *one* set of institutions, and only one: the armed forces. That they need allies to govern effectively, and that they serve class interests external to themselves, is clear. But those allies and the holders of those interests do not control the state; the control is exercised by a highly centralized, hierarchically organized and disciplined set of specialists in the use of violence. The high command of the armed forces assures its rule through well over one hundred thousand armed personnel—soldiers and police—most of whom, if ordered to, presumably will kill. Many scenarios for an end to the current regime are predicated on divisions opening up within the military, and rumors of such divisions constitute part of the lifeblood of the opposition. In fact, there are strong grounds for believing that divisions of this sort exist. But such discontent as may exist around and under Pinochet in the armed forces has so far been kept in check by at least four factors: the verticality of command within the military, the continual use of the secret police for surveillance work against dissidents and would-be plotters within the armed forces, the uncertainty about what an acceptable alternative to the present government might be, and the armed forces' fear of eventual prosecution under a civilian regime for human rights violations—the Nuremberg scenario.

NOTES

The research for this chapter is jointly sponsored by the Centre for Research on Latin America and the Caribbean and the LaMarsh Research Programme on Violence and Conflict Resolution, both of York University, Toronto. Financial support is gratefully acknowledged, as follows: Arancibia, from the LaMarsh Programme; Charlin, from the Social Sciences and Humanities Research Council of Canada (SSHRC); and Landstreet, from SSHRC and York University. Personal acknowledgments are too numerous to list; those who have helped us know of our gratitude. We do, however, wish to thank, and to record our great respect for, the Vicariate of Solidarity and the Chilean Human Rights Commission.

1. Arturo Valenzuela, *The Breakdown of Democratic Regimes: Chile* (Baltimore: Johns Hopkins University Press, 1978), xi.

2. On Christian Democratic and UP reforms, see Barbara Stallings, *Class Conflict and Economic Development in Chile, 1958–1973* (Stanford: Stanford University Press, 1978), and Stefan de Vylder, *Chile 1970–73: The Political Economy of the Rise and Fall of the Unidad Popular* (Cambridge: Cambridge University Press, 1977).

3. This section on U.S. intervention in Chile draws primarily on Seymour Hersh, *The Price of Power: Kissinger in the Nixon White House* (New York: Summit Books, 1983). See also James Petras and Morris Morley, *The United States and Chile: Imperialism and the Overthrow of the Allende Government* (New York: Monthly Review Press, 1975); Donald Freed and Fred Landis, *Death in Washington: The Murder of Orlando Letelier* (Westport, Conn.: Lawrence Hill, 1980), chaps. 5–12; and the references these three works contain to published U.S. government information sources from congressional hearings on CIA activities in Chile.

4. Information from a U.S. Senate Committee on Intelligence report, cited in Valenzuela, *Breakdown*, 133.

5. Valenzuela, *Breakdown*, xi.

6. For an examination of how this happened in the United States, see Paul Hoeffel

and Peter Kornbluh, "The War at Home: Chile's Legacy in the United States," *NACLA Report on the Americas* 17 (September-October 1983): 27–41.

7. See Harry Díaz, Peter Landstreet, and María Teresa Lladser, *Centros Privados de Investigación en Ciencias Sociales en Chile* (Santiago: Academia de Humanismo Cristiano, Centre for Research on Latin America and the Caribbean, and Canadian Association for Latin American and Caribbean Studies, 1984).

8. There are two primary sources of information on human rights violations in Chile, on which most other sources, in Chile and abroad, rely. They are the various publications of the Vicariate of Solidarity (since 1976) and of the Chilean Human Rights Commission (since 1978). Beyond these, the following Spanish-language sources originating in Chile may be consulted: *Un Año y Medio de Labor* (Santiago: Comité de Cooperación para la Paz en Chile, 1975); Bernarda Elgueta et al. (pseudonyms), "Cinco Años de Gobierno Militar en Chile: 1973–1978" (Santiago, mimeo, 1978); Hugo Frühling, "Limitando la Acción Coercitiva del Estado: La Estrategia Legal de Defensa de los Derechos Humanos en Chile" (Santiago: Facultad Latinoamericana de Ciencias Sociales, Serie Contribuciones no. 12, November 1982); and the publications of the Programa de Derechos Humanos of the Academia de Humanismo Cristiano, Santiago, especially its *Revista Chilena de Derechos Humanos*. In English, see the periodic reports by Amnesty International, Washington Office on Latin America, Americas Watch, and the Ad Hoc Working Group on Chile, and the Special Rapporteur on Chile from the United Nations; C. G. Brown, *Chile since the Coup: Ten Years of Repression* (New York: Americas Watch, 1983); Hugo Frühling, "Stages of Repression and Legal Strategy for the Defense of Human Rights in Chile: 1973–1980," *Human Rights Quarterly* 5, no. 4 (1983): 510–33; and Jinny Arancibia, Marcelo Charlin, and Peter Landstreet, *State Repression and Civil Opposition in Chile: 1973–1984* (Toronto: LaMarsh Research Programme on Violence and Conflict Resolution, York University, 1985).

9. For phases of state economic policy see Pilar Vergara, *Auge y Caída del Neoliberalismo en Chile* (Santiago: Facultad Latinoamericana de Ciencias Sociales, 1986). Another effort at establishing phases of state repression is found in Frühling, "Limitando" and "Stages"; his and ours coincide in some of their dating but were arrived at independently of each other.

10. Robert Carty, "Miracle or Mirage? A Review of Chile's Economic Model, 1973–1980," *LAWG Letter* (Toronto) 7, no. 5–6 (1982); 2. This article provides an excellent summary discussion of its topic. For more information see Alejandro Foxley, *Latin American Experiments in Neo-conservative Economics* (Berkeley: University of California Press, 1983), and Vergara, *Auge y Caída*. See also the many relevant articles published from 1979 onward in the journal *Colección Estudios CIEPLAN*, as well as the publications of the Programa de Economía del Trabajo (PET), especially their serial *Coyuntura Económica*, published since 1980.

11. After the coup there was a debate over whether Allende had committed suicide or been shot by the military. Recent information seems to put an end to this debate; see the account of his being killed in Taylor Branch and Eugene Propper, *Labyrinth* (New York: Penguin Books, 1983), 63–66.

12. Freed and Landis, *Death*, chap. 12.

13. Arancibia, Charlin, and Landstreet, *State Repression*, 35–40.

14. José Bengoa, "Trayectoria del Campesinado Chileno" (Santiago: Grupo de Investigaciones Agrarias, Documento de Trabajo, 1982).

15. See accounts in the various reports issued by the Fundación de Ayuda Social de

las Iglesias Cristianas (FASIC, Christian Churches Social Aid Foundation), such as "Relatos de Ocho Familiares de Ejecutados Políticos" (Santiago, mimeo, 1981).

16. The lower estimate is from the U.S. embassy in Santiago, as cited in John Dinges and Saul Landau, *Assassination on Embassy Row* (New York: Pantheon Books, 1980), 71. The higher estimate is from the Inter-Church Committee on Human Rights in Latin America *Newsletter* entitled "Chile: Ten Years after the Coup" (Toronto: summer 1983), 16.1.

17. Elgueta et al., *Cinco Años*, 527.

18. Frühling, "Limitando," 15.

19. *Enfrentamientos y Falsedades* (Santiago: Fundación de Ayuda Social de las Iglesias Cristianas, 1981).

20. Vergara, *Auge y Caída*, 18–19. Her "phase of ideological indefinition" is from September 1973 to April 1975.

21. Brian Smith, *The Church and Politics in Chile: Challenges to Modern Catholicism* (Princeton: Princeton University Press, 1982).

22. Dinges and Landau, *Assassination*, 21. Another good and accessible source of information on DINA is Branch and Propper, *Labyrinth*.

23. Dinges and Landau, *Assassination*, 133.

24. Foxley, *Latin American Experiments*, 43–57.

25. For the government to have attacked a unit of the Church directly and openly—even one such as the Vicariate of Solidarity—it would have had to be prepared to risk major internal and international consequences, including possible ecclesiastical sanctions such as excommunication of one or more members of the Junta. Attacks on Church personnel and institutions involved in human rights work and support activities for the poor have occurred frequently, but they have tended to be clandestine. Enrique Palet, current Executive Secretary of the Vicariate of Solidarity, has referred to the Church suffering "degrees of harassment carried out by 'civilians,' whose identities are not always possible to establish because of their skill in keeping their identity a secret. Nevertheless, when identities have been determined, the 'civilians' have always turned out to be people linked to the armed forces." Enrique Palet, "Repression of the Church in Chile," in *Chile: Human Rights and U.S. Policy* (Washington, D.C.: Washington Office on Latin America, 1985), 16.

26. On the Letelier-Moffit assassination and its aftermath, see Dinges and Landau, *Assassination*; and Branch and Propper, *Labyrinth*.

27. On U.S. policy toward Chile, see *Chile: Human Rights*.

28. Foxley, *Latin American Experiments*, 80.

29. Fernando Dahse, *Mapa de la Extrema Riqueza* (Santiago: Editorial Aconcagua, 1979), 146, 150.

30. Berta Teitelboim, "Indicadores Económicos y Sociales: Series Anuales, 1960–1982" (Santiago: Programa de Economía del Trabajo, 1983).

31. The new Constitution and interpretations of it can be found in *Constitución de 1980: Comentarios de Juristas Internacionales* (Santiago: Centro de Estudios Sociales—CESOC, 1984). For additional interpretation from the standpoint of human rights, see *Informe Anual 1982* (Santiago: Comisión Chilena de Derechos Humanos, 1983).

32. "Carta del Vicario de la Solidaridad a los Agentes Pastorales de la Iglesia de Santiago" (Santiago: Vicaría de la Solidaridad, Arzobispado de Santiago, October 1981).

33. The full wording of "Transitory Article 24" is found in *Constitución de 1980*, 166.

34. Chile's foreign debt ranking from Carty, "Miracle," 34; bankruptcy and 1981–1982 GDP figures from Teitelboim, "Indicadores," 2, 17; all other indicators from Jorge Leiva, "Las Dos Fases de la Crisis Económica en 1984," *Coyuntura Económica*, no. 11 (January 1985): 5, 30. Unemployment figures include persons involved in the government's two work programs, the Programa de Empleo Mínimo (PEM) and the Programa de Ocupación para Jefes de Hogar (POJH), both of which pay well below the legal minimum wage (the equivalent of U.S. $18 and $31 respectively per month, in 1985). This inclusion of PEM and POJH members in total unemployment figures is conventional among Chilean economists working in that country's private ("dissident") research centers.

35. *Informe Anual 1982* (Santiago: Comisión Chilena de Derechos Humanos, 1983), 74.

36. Pot-banging refers to a technique of expressing discontent and dissent that had been used by middle-class housewives during the UP government. In recent years it has been widely used against the military government. It involves collectively banging pots and pans in front of houses or out of windows at a fixed time across the city.

37. *Vicaría de la Solidaridad: Octavo Año de Labor, 1983* (Santiago: Vicaría de la Solidaridad, Arzobispado de Santiago, 1984), 82.

38. *Informe Anual 1983* (Santiago: Comisión Chilena de Derechos Humanos, 1984), 41.

39. *Informe Mensual* (Santiago: Comisión Chilena de Derechos Humanos, December 1984).

40. A full legal description of the nature of the three states of exception (of siege, of emergency, and of danger of disturbance to internal peace) is found in *Vicaría de la Solidaridad: Décimo Año de Labor, 1985* (Santiago: Vicaría de la Solidaridad, 1986), 121–23.

41. "Pinochet puts Chile under State of Siege," *The Sun* (Vancouver), November 7, 1984.

42. "Un Año y Medio de Gobierno Militar" (Santiago, mimeo, March 1975), 13.

43. Jaime Ruiz-Tagle, "Informe sobre la Situación de los Derechos Económicos y Sociales en Chile," Documento de Trabajo no. 40 (Santiago: Programa de Economía del Trabajo, November 1985), 3. Also Leiva, "Las Dos Fases," 30–32.

44. Humberto Vega and Jaime Ruiz-Tagle, "The Economic Model: Authoritarian Capitalism," in *By Reason of Force: Social Science Perspectives on Contemporary Chile*, ed. Peter Landstreet and Jorge Nef (in preparation). Unemployment figures from Jorge Leiva, "La Deuda Externa y la Coyuntura Económica Actual," *Coyuntura Económica*, no. 12 (August 1985); 45. For reasons explained previously, the 1983 and 1985 figures include members of the PEM and POJH.

45. René Cortázar, "Income Distribution, Employment and Real Earnings," in *By Reason of Force*, ed. Landstreet and Nef. This study took Santiago households' proportional participation in total household consumption as a proxy for income, since direct data on income was lacking.

46. Ruiz-Tagle, "Informe sobre la Situación," 15–16.

47. Summarized from Harry Díaz's contribution to Peter Landstreet et al., "Human Rights Advocacy in a Repressive Context: Chile, 1973–1985," in *Advocacy and Practice*, ed. Peter Harries-Jones forthcoming.

48. Jorge Echenique, "La Situación Nutricional de los Chilenos," *Agricultura y Sociedad* 2 (Santiago: Grupo de Investigaciones Agrarias, 1985), 8.

49. Reported in *Vicaría de la Solidaridad: Décimo Año de Labor*, 78.
50. Elgueta et al., *Cinco Años*, 416.
51. For more detail on education, see *Education and Repression: Chile* (London: World University Service, 1982), and *Las Transformaciones Educacionales bajo el Régimen Militar*, 2 vols. (Santiago: Programa Interdisciplinario de Investigaciones en Educación, 1984).
52. State expenditure figures reported in, and construction figures calculated by the authors from, statistics in Teitelboim, "Indicadores," 44, 48. Construction figures are based on a sample of eighty communities. Housing shortage figures from *Vicaría de la Solidaridad: Décimo Años de Labor*, 76.
53. Jacques Doyer, "Inter-Ethnic Relationships in the South of Chile: Mapuche Resistance to Domination from Pre-Spanish Times to the Military Regime" (M.A. thesis, York University, Toronto, 1985); Brown, *Chile since the Coup*, chap. 4; *Mapuches: People of the Land* (Toronto: Inter-Church Committee on Human Rights in Latin America, 1980). In Spanish, see the publications of the Centro Asesor y Planificador de Investigación y Desarrollo (CAPIDE), in Temuco, which specializes in Mapuche research.

SUGGESTED READINGS

Arancibia, Jinny, Marcelo Charlin, and Peter Landstreet. *State Repression and Civil Opposition in Chile*. Toronto: LaMarsh Research Programme on Violence and Conflict Resolution, York University, 1985.
Branch, Taylor and Eugene Propper. *Labyrinth*. New York: Viking Press, 1982.
Brown, C. G. *Chile since the Coup: Ten Years of Repression*. New York: Americas Watch, 1983.
Chavkin, Samuel. *Storm over Chile: The Junta under Siege*. Westport, Conn.: Lawrence Hill, 1985.
Dinges, John and Saul Landau. *Assassination on Embassy Row*. New York: Pantheon Books, 1980.
Foxley, Alejandro. *Latin American Experiments in Neo-conservative Economics*. Berkeley: University of California Press, 1983.
O'Brien, Phil and Jackie Roddick. *Chile: The Pinochet Decade*. London: Latin America Bureau, 1983.
Petras, James and Morris Morley. *The United States and Chile: Imperialism and the Overthrow of the Allende Government*. New York: Monthly Review Press, 1975.
Smith, Brian. *The Church and Politics in Chile: Challenges to Modern Catholicism*. Princeton: Princeton University Press, 1982.
Valenzuela, Arturo. *The Breakdown of Democratic Regimes: Chile*. Baltimore: Johns Hopkins University Press, 1978.
Valenzuela, J. Samuel and Arturo Valenzuela, eds. *Military Rule in Chile: Dictatorship and Oppositions*. Baltimore: Johns Hopkins University Press, 1986.

4

CHINA

James D. Seymour

The People's Republic of China (PRC) was founded one year after the adoption of the Universal Declaration of Human Rights by the United Nations.[1] Thus, that government played no role in its promulgation. Nonetheless, the document's terms have not been rejected by the PRC, and indeed the country's constitutions have generally been consistent with its terms. Constitutional provisions, however, have done little to overcome political realities and cultural inertia.

HISTORICAL BACKGROUND

In viewing traditional Chinese political culture, one does well to distinguish between elite and mass culture, even though there was much overlap between the two. The elite believed in and promoted Confucianism, which called for social harmony based on a hierarchical ordering of individuals and groups. Although the Confucian social system provided for some social mobility, in practice there was barely enough to provide the elite with essential new blood. For those who fared poorly under this system, more egalitarian philosophies (associated with Buddhism, Taoism, and various folk religions) tended to have more appeal. But these faiths were not particularly political, and even Confucianism, as a political culture, failed to provide a system of conflict resolution. The emphasis, rather, was on conflict avoidance.[2]

When Chinese intellectuals began exploring Western political ideas, they naturally perused the writings of the greats such as Rousseau and Hegel, but they often had difficulty coming to grips with the essences of such works. For example, Liang Qichao (1873–1929), considered China's first great liberal, nonetheless ended up much more at home with organic theories of the state than with permissive liberalism. His firsthand observations of political incompetence and corruption in American cities soured him on the idea of introducing republicanism into China.

Many Chinese have traveled the same intellectual route as Liang: infatuation with Western democracy, followed by disillusionment. China's problems have often seemed too intractable to be resolved by the ignorant masses through alien institutions. Even many of those who participated in the democratic movements of 1919 and 1978–1979, and who fought for free elections in the early 1980s, feared that if political decision making were left to the peasants, they would end up choosing another dictator. Better to leave politics to a reliable corps of intellectuals.

One of modern China's phobias has concerned imperialism, which has handed those who would deny human rights a tailor-made excuse to do so. Sun Yat-sen (1866–1925), credited with being the father of the republic and now honored by both the Chinese Communists and the Nationalists on Taiwan, is an example of a political thinker who put nationalism ahead of democracy. He preferred the Soviet "dictatorship of the people" to Western democracy.

With the advent of nationalism, Chinese attitudes toward the country's place in the world have changed. Traditionally, the Chinese had been condescending toward foreigners. It was assumed, even when the country was overrun by outsiders, that they would either be expelled in due course or (more often) absorbed. Thus, the Manchu rulers were tolerated from 1644 to 1911 because they adopted Confucianism and ruled through the traditional Chinese scholar-gentry class. But with the arrival of Western and Japanese armies in the nineteenth century, it was clear that China was up against a new sort of foreign threat. Chinese reacted by placing anti-imperialism paramount in their hierarchy of values. Thus, few Chinese have questioned Liang Qichao's conclusion that even if a governmental system deprives the people of much or all of their freedom, it is a good system so long as it meets national security requirements.

There is one important exception to the generalization that democracy and nationalism have been antithetical in China. In 1919 when Japan seemed to be benefiting from the territorial spoils of World War I at China's expense, students and other intellectuals mobilized to insist that the government not yield on the question of China's territorial integrity. The incensed youths were often icon-oclastic and saw no contradiction between denigrating traditional Chinese values and upholding nationalism. Most of the participants in this "May Fourth" move-ment considered themselves liberal democrats, though democracy was poorly understood.

During the 1920s three groups sought to establish themselves in Chinese political life. Least powerful (because they eschewed armed force) were the liberals. Thus, the great decisions about China's future were fought out by the right-wing Kuomintang (Nationalist party), which would reign temporarily, and the Marxists, who would emerge triumphant in 1949.

Notwithstanding various liberal-sounding constitutions and visionary eco-nomic programs, the human rights record of the PRC has been disappointing. Communist rule has seen periods of extreme repression (1950–1953, 1957–1961, and 1968–1976), with most of the years between characterized by tight controls and little opportunity for the exercise of individual political rights. There have been only two moments of relatively free expression—1956–1957 and 1978–1979. Even at such times, the public was aware that the prisons still contained large numbers of people whose crimes were purely political. It is claimed that the deprivation of civil liberties is necessitated by the need to achieve social and economic reforms. But as we shall see, China has remained a poor nation with striking inequalities.

Beginning around 1966, in an effort to deal with the problems of bureaucratism and elitism (similar to the "new class" of European communism), Mao launched his Great Proletarian Cultural Revolution.[3] At first, this looked like an affirmation of human rights. The goal was realizing the economic rights of the underprivileged; the intended means was unleashing the masses in an orgy of poster writing. Mao insisted that the people had the right to "speak out freely, air views fully, hold great debates, and write posters," and these Four Great Rights were temporarily enshrined in the Constitution.

But the Cultural Revolution turned chaotic, and the result—a decade of disaster—seemed to confirm the view that political freedom was not good for the country. According to official statistics (which are conservative), 34,274 men and women were killed, and 700,000 were subjected to other forms of persecution. The perpetrators were "red guards" and other upstarts, unleashed by Mao to attack the establishment under him. There is no way of counting the actual number who suffered from the radicals' actions; targeted were not only allegedly corrupt officials but all those who seemed to represent traditional cultural values. Inevitably, there was a Thermidorian reaction. The repudiation of the Cultural Revolution would be led by onetime party secretary-general Deng Xiaoping. Deng had been condemned as a "capitalist roader," but in something akin to a coup d'état he reemerged as China's strongman after Mao's death.

In 1978 Deng began to institute major reforms involving both political and economic thawing. Since then, there has been greater respect for the dignity and autonomy of the individual than during the Mao years. The press has been slightly less monolithic, and the imprisonment of independent thinkers has been sporadic, rather than universal. Still, the real relaxation that began in 1978, when "democracy walls" could be plastered with dissidents' essays,[4] lasted scarcely a half year. The democratic movement which the episode spawned quickly backfired when some of the dissidents, the most outspoken being Wei Jingsheng, turned their fire on Deng himself. Wei was arrested immediately, and eventually sentenced to fifteen years. By 1981 most of the other leading participants in the movement had been imprisoned.[5]

The *economic* liberalization has been more enduring, but its relevance to human rights is not easy to characterize. There has been little recognition of workers' rights. Property rights are shown greater respect, and agriculture has become privatized in practice (but not in theory). There is less concern with preventing inequalities than there was during Mao's time. The hope now is that if the size of the pie is increased, there will be more for everyone. There is a recognition that "some will have to get rich before others," but little has been done to provide a minimal standard of living for those unable to make it in the new rough-and-tumble economic order influenced by free-market mechanisms.

THE INTELLECTUALS

By law and custom, Chinese society is rigidly stratified, though the class labels often conceal as much as they describe. Propertyless "landlords" have been discriminated against, and "counterrevolutionaries" are imprisoned—though all this is supposed to have ended in 1984. "Workers," "peasants," and "cadres" are generally favored groups. "Intellectuals" have had uneven treatment. The educated have always occupied a special place in Chinese society. Traditionally, they have monopolized political power. To a greater extent than in the West, the term "intellectual" has indicated noninvolvement in physical activity. Maoism was in part a reaction against such privilege. Especially during Mao's later years, intellectuals were demeaned and often persecuted.

The struggle for civil liberties in China has been conducted by certain groups within this amorphous, embattled community of intellectuals. To outsiders, the most spectacular drive was that of the Democracy Wall–era dissidents. Many of these people were young "radicals" in the sense that they unabashedly sought fundamental change. They did not care about whom they offended as they promoted their cause, which is why they were repressed.

By the mid–1980s, a different element was carrying the banner, and the issue had been drastically redefined. The spokesmen were moderate liberals, not radicals. Most were party members—what we might call "official" or "establishment" intellectuals. But they viewed themselves as people of integrity. They rejected the notion that the party was invariably correct, with mistakes made only by errant individuals. The Cultural Revolution, they realized, was not the doing of a handful of villains. Even though people at all levels of the party were victims of the movement, they also bear responsibility for the fact that it happened. People of this view want the system to be opened somewhat, but not destroyed. Their watchword became "humanism"—as opposed to class struggle.

In past years, much of the violation of human rights in China occurred in the name of "class struggle." Thus, for human rights advocates, the most worrisome aspect of any campaign mounted by conservatives against humanism is the implication for class struggle. According to one party spokesman, bourgeois humanism "is a theoretical tool for advocating the theory that class struggle is dying out." It would be a historic mistake "to regard . . . bourgeois humanism as supra-class, supra-era ideological trends or absorb them into Marxism."[6] This is a convoluted way of saying that the rights of the individual must be eclipsed by the authority of the party of the working class.

In its efforts to squelch the idea of abstract humanism, in 1984 the Party rolled out its big theoretical guns. On January 27, *People's Daily* carried a lengthy piece by official theoretician Hu Qiaomu, in which he indicated a concern that humanism, even "socialist" humanism, would lead inevitably to individualism. Sloganeering about humanism, Hu argued, "will only encourage all kinds of unrealistic demands for individual well-being and freedom, and create a false impression that once the socialist system is established, all personal demands will be satisfied—for otherwise, the socialist system would be proven 'inhumane.' . . . Some of those who preach humanism have set the value of individuals against the development of the cause of socialist construction." But in 1985 other official intellectuals openly argued that there is a place for "individualism under socialism" in both politics and economics[7]—an idea that was immediately attacked by conservatives (leftists).[8]

Though the authorities, with their control over the media, appear to have the upper hand in these matters, the fact that they feel compelled to respond to the "humanist" and "socialist individualist" schools indicates that the latter must have a substantial following in China—among everyone from official intellectuals to outcasts. If this is so, then a demand for human rights lies close beneath the surface.[9] However, there is no consensus as to just which rights should be emphasized. We turn, then, to the specifics.

CIVIL LIBERTIES

Traditional Chinese culture placed a premium on harmony. The harmonious was ipso facto the truth; dissension signaled falsehood.[10] Although many Chinese no longer think in such terms, some continue to be burdened by this legacy.

Flow of Ideas and Information. Book publishing became common in China during the Song Dynasty (960–1127). The ruling elites quickly realized the political implications and sought to control the publishing industry. From that time through the Republican period (1911–1949), such efforts to control the flow of ideas and news were constant but never completely successful.

To what extent is a Chinese citizen's right to information about society and politics honored now? Insofar as the Chinese Communists advocate or tolerate freedom of expression, the rationale is usually stated in terms of Mao Zedong's "hundred flowers" principle—pursuant to which political criticism was briefly allowed in 1957. More recently, during the anti-spiritual-pollution campaign (1983–1984), this principle was given a restrictive reading. The hundred flowers line, people were told, was subordinate to the requirement that people be politically correct. But the signals thereafter were very mixed, and there were assurances that sincere criticisms would be welcome. The media even contained complaints that local party secretaries were "stifling democracy" and retaliating against whistle-blowers. "Our Party has repeatedly exhorted all comrades of the Party, especially the Party's leading cadres at all levels, not to abuse functions and powers to stifle criticism or to retaliate against others."[11]

National politics is shrouded in secrecy, which means that the Chinese people are not well informed about their government. Information which would be public in democratic countries is treated in China as the private property of the ruling group. Occasionally, an official document does find its way into the "wrong hands," causing the media to remind people of the need to safeguard secrets.

Even when news is not secret, what Chinese read and hear is carefully controlled. For ideas and information, Chinese rely largely on the official media. Until recent years, this meant primarily a few national newspapers. These were more authoritative than provincial and local publications. But the erstwhile efforts of certain officials notwithstanding, it is frequently admitted that there has been a serious credibility gap. In particular, the media have often been notorious for claiming unreal gains for the economy, though this has been less so in recent years. Still, the less politically embarrassing to the leadership, the more likely the information is to be published. When there is a power struggle or shakeout of high-level personnel, press accounts, if any, are Aesopian.

Despite the improvements, the national media have been so ideological and devoid of real news for so long that people generally would prefer alternatives if available. Occasionally there have been remarkable examples of muckraking, though these tend to involve local issues reported by journalists from national publications.[12] (It is unlikely that locals would condemn corruption in their midst, and those who have tried have often been rebuked.) There has also been a growth of provincial and rural newspapers which concentrate on subjects of interest, especially agricultural news. There are two categories of such newspapers. First, there are about 400 provincial and local papers. Second, there are another 600 newspapers published by units, departments, and enterprises. The total circulation is 110 million. The medium of wall posters as a mode of free expression is no longer legal, and violators are subject to at least brief detention. For example, in August 1984 a Hunan couple was sentenced to a month's imprisonment for writing a poster critical of the judiciary. Foreign political publications are virtually unavailable, and there are limits on outsiders' ability to gather news in China. Zealous writers from abroad have sometimes been expelled, and occasionally have been imprisoned.[13]

The Role of Law. In the 1950s China began building a Soviet-style judicial system, though little progress was made codifying laws. The legal apparatus fell apart during the Cultural Revolution, but much progress has been made in restoring the system, albeit a still somewhat politicized one. A defendant's politics can still be a factor in the outcome of his case, and the issue of whether or not the courts should be independent or be used to achieve political goals remains a controversial one. Often, the courts' role is purely nominal, especially in civil matters. Party functionaries sometimes have blank paper with the court's seal already affixed. Thus, a party secretary can issue a "judicial" decision without the court being involved in any meaningful way.

The number of "counterrevolutionary" cases has dropped to well under one percent. The authorities have also continued to correct many past injustices. By the end of 1981, 1.2 million "criminal" cases of the Mao era had been reviewed, and 326,000 people were granted retrials. However, in the mid–1980s efforts to correct unjust verdicts seemed to flag, and many intellectuals who were banished to the countryside remain there living a hopeless existence. Supreme Court president Jiang Hua told the National People's Congress in 1983: "Some major, important, difficult, and complicated cases still have to be reviewed. Among the cases that have been reviewed, some have not been redressed that should be, some have not been thoroughly redressed, . . . and there are those that require efforts to bring the case to completion."[14]

Thus, some of China's leaders appear to have been making a serious (if uphill) effort to improve the legal system, which was never viable and was in total shambles by the end of the Cultural Revolution. They appear to be having some success. But many functionaries are simply not interested in (or do not understand the meaning of) operating within a legal framework. Furthermore, they are in an awkward position in deciding whether to adhere to the law or obey their superiors in the party.

There has been discussion of the extent to which foreign legal standards should be allowed to influence China's legal process. A commentary in the party journal would allow "reference to be made to foreign laws and legal theories," but insisted: "With regard to 'democracy' and 'humanism,' under no circumstances can we let bourgeois legal viewpoints and theories obstruct the implementation of law in our country."[15]

Criminal trials are not allowed to founder on legal technicalities. They are often conducted with lightning speed, sometimes with no advance indictment. In the early 1980s, executions were being carried out within as few as eight days from the commission of an offense. There was some improvement in 1984. Bail provisions were established, and the period between arrest and trial was lengthened.[16]

Political Participation. The political system built after 1949 was patterned after the Soviet model. Although all citizens were required to involve themselves in campaigns and elections, there was no choice but to support the status quo. This system broke down during the Cultural Revolution, with Mao Zedong encouraging people to attack party and government establishments, but providing no institutions to regularize such activities. With order restored, there was some degree of political participation after 1979. This was especially true in the period 1980–1981, during which time the local electoral process was relatively unmanaged.[17] (National and provincial leaders are not elected.) Since that time, the voters have occasionally been allowed some choice of candidates, but there has been little genuine spontaneity or freedom to run for office.

Political Imprisonment. Four groups of people appear to be affected by systematic political imprisonment: democratic activists, certain religious believers, unsubmissive ethnic minorities, and leftists.

China's democracy movement of the late 1970s was so effectively suppressed that there has been no attempt at a repetition. Although some participants have been released, many of them remain in labor camps and prisons.

Most of the reported noncriminal arrests during the mid–1980s were of religious figures, particularly Roman Catholics. But one Catholic leader, Bishop Gong Pinmei, was conditionally released in 1985, after thirty years imprisonment.

Among imprisoned ethnic minorities, the most information is available about the Tibetans. According to some reports, one in every ten Tibetans has been imprisoned at one time or another since 1959. Lhasa has five prison camps in all holding 7,000, or one-fifth of the city's Tibetan population. (The questions of religious freedom and ethnic minorities will be further discussed below.)

Deng Xiaoping has been relatively restrained in dealing with the leftists whom he overthrew, and only a tiny fraction of them were imprisoned. Many of the detainees were responsible for acts of violence, but some appear to have been arrested simply for having engaged in internationally protected political activity. For example, former Central Committee member Zhai Decheng was given a fifteen-year term simply for writing objectionable posters.[18]

Capital Punishment. In 1983 and 1984 there was a major crackdown on crime. As part of this effort, there were widespread reports, unconfirmed but not incredible, of quotas for executions. At any rate, many thousands, and possibly tens of thousands, of people were executed during this period, usually after perfunctory trials. Most of those subjected to capital punishment were accused of internationally recognized crimes, but often the offenses were economic crimes which would result in only a short prison term in the West. A few of the cases appear to have been largely political.[19]

Torture. Though prohibited by law, torture of prisoners occurred during the Mao years, especially during the Cultural Revolution. Since 1976, reports of actual torture have been relatively rare. It is not unheard of, however, for there have been a few documented instances of beatings of prisoners.

According to the criminal code, confessions must be voluntary and cannot be the sole evidentiary basis of conviction. However, the great weight that courts place on confessions gives rise to temptations to use heavy-handed methods of interrogation. This appears to have been especially true during the anti-crime drive of 1983–1984.

Prison conditions are often extremely harsh and sometimes result in mental deterioration. Obstreperous prisoners are placed in solitary confinement for long periods, even years. The administration of drugs for nonmedical purposes has been reported.

CULTURAL RIGHTS

Cultural freedom varies considerably over time. The year 1983 saw escalating controls on the cultural life of the country. These began with inconspicuous, often local measures, and eventually merged with a national campaign aimed at the "spiritual" life of the country. During 1984, these controls eased considerably.

In the past, culture has been the responsibility of the bureaucracy. Each province has a culture department, usually staffed by 5,000 or more. But, as in industry and agriculture, in recent years there has been a tendency for the arts to be commercialized. Although this makes more culture available to the public, the authorities see social costs. According to a writer in the party theoretical journal *Red Flag*, turning literature and art into commodities would lessen the artists' sense of social responsibility. "While we do not object to a higher remuneration of artists on account of their arduous creative work, the results for society must be considered as a prerequisite for giving remuneration for their work. . . . The social value of literature and art cannot be measured by economic results."[20]

How this has played out can be seen in the field of book publishing. Until a few years ago the distribution of books was almost entirely a government operation. However, as more books were published, the inefficient state and collective distribution facilities could not handle the load, especially outside the large cities. With others getting into the act, political controls have been more difficult to maintain, though the authorities still go to great lengths to do so.

Many artists and writers have objected to the party's heavy hand over creativity. They enjoy being able to expound on such "unacceptable theories" as social Darwinism, to name just one. Arguments have been raised that only with intellectual independence can "abilities be fully realized." Another slogan is a throwback to Taoism: "In running the government, do nothing that goes against nature." An article in *Red Flag* (March 16, 1984) insisted that this was all erroneous. "It is wrong to adopt this passive ideology which publicizes 'running the government by doing nothing that goes against nature' in our Party's leadership over literature and art. . . . [This] can only hasten the development of the sinister trends of laxity in leadership and being afraid to criticize or struggle against bourgeois liberalism." But even the officially approved writer Ba Jin expressed his belief that "ultimately, a writer alone is responsible for the development of his own works."[21]

Although many recent Western novels have been published in China, it appears that the literature of earlier years, primarily the 1920s to the 1950s, has had greater influence on Chinese intellectuals. The Chinese generally refer to this genre, ranging from Joyce and Eliot to Sartre and Beckett, as "the modernist school." Writers are attracted to modernism because, unlike socialist realism, it permits writers to express honest emotions without regard to their political "correctness." It is unsurprising that this would raise the ire of conservatives. On November 16, 1983, *Red Flag* carried an article which made it clear that no liberalization was in the offing. By the end of 1983, with the national campaign against spiritual pollution getting underway, it looked as though there would be a serious impact on cultural affairs. Some cultural activities and publications were curbed or even terminated, but the campaign fell short of people's worst fears. For the next two years, China's artists and writers would receive a series of very mixed signals.

Education. The school-age population (six to eighteen years old) already numbers three hundred million, and is still increasing. It is claimed that 95 percent attend six-year primary schools; only two-thirds enjoy the next three years of junior high school. China's record is good by Third World standards, and also considering the Chinese tradition of education being only for a small socioeconomic elite. (Women received no education until foreign missionaries enrolled them in Christian schools in the nineteenth century.) The goal now is to make the nine years of education universal by 1995. However, education is to be primarily a local responsibility, and it is implicitly admitted that poorer areas will be unable to meet this target. This is a departure from the Maoist principle of insisting that rural areas be brought up to the national standard. And Maoist egalitarianism is being relinquished in other ways as well, for advancement is to be primarily on the basis of academic achievement, and supposedly not social background or political correctness.

To improve the quality of education, an article in *People's Daily* (May 25, 1984) called for legislation concerning the qualifications, obligations, and social status of teachers. Although 31 percent of all college graduates are involved in education, only 13 percent of all people involved in education are college graduates. The low quality of education is also due in part to the reluctance of intellectuals to teach in the countryside. (Those few who do go often face large classes of students of many grades.) The government claims that it will meet this problem by favoring college applicants from the countryside over urbanites. Even where teachers are natives of the locality, however, they sometimes are hampered by political interference or discrimination against them as intellectuals.

A factor contributing to the lack of primary education is the new incentive-based agricultural system, which in effect encourages absenteeism from school. Children's labor is needed at home for farm work, and would-be teachers often would rather farm. Also, some brigades now lack funds to finance schools.

The result of these various problems has been that about one-third of the people are illiterate. In ethnic minority areas (see below) the situation is worse (and sometimes often compounded by erratic language and script changes). In Tibet, three-quarters of the people are illiterate.

Although provisions for higher education have been inadequate by any standard, the situation is improving. In 1984–1985 there were 1.3 million university students, and the number of newly enrolled students was growing at an annual rate of 13 percent. Equally important, the quality of education is improving, as political studies are deemphasized and as higher intellectuals are allowed to teach with less interference.

Admission to college has generally been by national examination. Nonetheless, before the Cultural Revolution there was much abuse. When colleges were first reopened after the Cultural Revolution the system seemed quite fair, with minimum passing scores announced, and individuals told their grade. But after 1980 the minimum passing scores ceased to be announced, and the right to request reconsideration of one's case was withdrawn. It appeared that higher education was to be increasingly for the privileged few. A certain percentage (8 percent at Peking University, higher elsewhere) are even admitted on the recommendation of high school teachers, regardless of the grade on the examination. More worrisome from the point of view of human rights has been the reintroduction of the dossier system, which facilitates holding political mistakes against a student or would-be student. How this all works out in practice sociologically is difficult to determine, inasmuch as the social composition of colleges is not revealed. However, there is considerable anecdotal evidence of favoritism, which must inevitably be detrimental to qualified applicants.

Once admitted, most students are required to pay some tuition. Though there are exceptions and scholarships are available, only the elite schools (aimed at training high-level scientists and engineers) are heavily supported by the central government. Other colleges, in which general educational skills are taught, are expected to rely on local or private funding.[22]

Religion. The Communists came to power promising freedom of religion. This guarantee has never been fully honored, and at times has been renounced. During the Cultural Revolution there was much religious persecution. Since Mao's death there have been improvements, but some religions are still proscribed. An example is Roman Catholicism (though Catholics not recognizing the Vatican may practice their religion). Islam and Buddhism, not seen as linked with foreign imperialism, have fared better. This new official leniency is partly to appease the devout populations of colonial areas such as Tibet (Xizang) and Eastern Turkestan (Xinjiang), the problems of which will be discussed later under Ethnicity.

In some parts of China, cadres forbid youths under eighteen to practice religion (particularly Christianity). Indeed, a purported internal party document of 1982 cites the constitution (apparently incorrectly) to the effect that it is "citizens who have reached the age of eighteen" who have freedom of religion, and adds that it is unacceptable to propagate a faith to those younger.[23] But the public stance is that those under eighteen may be proselytized.

With the publication of the Law on Regional Autonomy for National Minorities (1984), it was apparent that the moderate religion policy remained in place. Article II of that law states:

Autonomous organs in the areas of national autonomy should protect the freedom of the citizens of various nationalities for religious belief. State organs, social organizations, and individuals are not allowed to compel citizens to believe, or not to believe in, religion. They are not allowed to discriminate against citizens who believe in, or do not believe, in religion. The state protects normal religious activities. No person is allowed to make use of religion to carry out activities of disrupting social order, harming the health of citizens, or obstructing the educational system of the state. Religious organizations and religious affairs should not be controlled by any foreign force.

Thus, for the time being, those non-Communists who elect to do so are fairly free to practice a faith. (Party and Youth League members are expected to eschew religion.) According to the above-mentioned 1982 internal document: "Comrades of the whole Party must clearly understand that the problem of religion will exist for a long time under socialism." Religion is still seen as an "opiate," and its "abolition" is still seen as a long-term goal.

ECONOMIC RIGHTS

China's per capita income is about U.S. $300 per year, better than double that of Bangladesh, but less than half that of Nigeria. At the end of Mao Zedong's rule, per capita rural income, though extremely low, was quite evenly distributed. Now, incomes are rising, with almost everyone making more than before, but some doing much better than others. Continued progress depends on curbing population growth, which means limiting people's right to have children. This is a controversial matter, especially the attempt to impose a single-child rule uniformly. Abortion (occasionally coerced) is unpopular and causes adverse international reactions. Birth control is almost universally promoted, but numerous exceptions to the one-child rule are permitted.[24]

Health and Nutrition. Although China still has serious deficiencies in terms of health care, the situation has vastly improved since 1949. The average life expectancy is sixty-seven, though it is lower among many minority groups (under forty-five in the case of Tibetans). The mortality rate in Beijing (surely better than the national average) is reported to be five per thousand.[25] China's infant mortality rate is said to have dropped to below thirty-four per thousand in 1985, but again, the picture is much worse in poor and minority ethnic areas, where the rate is often over one hundred per thousand. In the cities, the record is not bad by world standards. In Beijing, the infant mortality rate is put at twelve per thousand in 1983,[26] which is equal to the national average in the United States.

There has been considerable, though uneven, progress against disease. Venereal disease and drug addiction, common before 1950, are now virtually unknown. Though still problems, typhoid, dysentery, measles, polio, diphtheria, whooping cough, and viral hepatitis are on the decline. Otherwise, progress has been less than spectacular. For example, in 1985 the number of leprosy cases was 100,000, down from a pre–1949 500,000. Snail fever cases declined to one million (down from eleven million). Some diseases continue to be very widespread, especially parasitic ones such as filariasis (still five million cases in 1985). Malignant malaria also continues to be a problem in some provinces. The head of the government's Epidemic Prevention Department has cited various problems in controlling infectious diseases, including poor management, inefficiency, lack of money, and outdated equipment.

Only state employees receive free health care, but for a nominal charge rudimentary health care is available for most peasants. In the rapidly expanding private industrial and commercial sectors no such benefits are automatic. For those who can afford them, private medical practitioners are often available. The possibility of establishing a health insurance plan has been discussed. Under one proposal, health care would be subsidized by the state and enterprises, but primarily financed through the collection of insurance premiums. Minor illnesses would not be covered, and "intermediate illnesses" would be only about two-thirds covered.[27]

An important reason that the health picture has gained is improved nutrition. In traditional China, malnutrition was commonplace, and famines occurred from time to time. The record since 1949 has been erratic. A serious famine in the early 1960s cost the lives of between fifteen and thirty million people. As late as 1981 there was serious hunger in certain provinces. For the next three years, the amount of food available increased markedly as a result of the dismantling of the communes and the partial adoption of a market system in agriculture. There continue to be inequalities among regions, and in 1985 overall yields declined markedly. Nonetheless, reserves remained adequate, and the state was able to provide deficit areas with grain. The state tries to insure that everyone receives sufficient food to sustain life, but the floor has generally been only 1,400 calories per day. A somewhat patchwork welfare plan exists (see below). There is a system of emergency grain distribution where shortages arise, but corruption often curbs its effectiveness. Thus, there is still some malnutrition, notably among children in poor areas. (In these regions, which are off-limits to foreigners, begging and scavenging are not unknown.)

Employment. The problem of unemployment in China was not recognized for what it is until recent years. This is still true in the case of peasants, who comprise 80 percent of the population and are deemed "employed" whatever their income. Among urbanites, the government once denied that any unemployment existed, and there were no statistics to prove otherwise. In the late 1970s, with the new spirit of "seeking truth from facts," it was acknowledged that urban unemployment did exist. Economists have put the figure for 1979 at between fifteen to twenty million; the larger figure would be more than 20 percent of the urban labor force. At that time, the ranks of the unemployed were swelled by youths who had been sent off to the countryside during the Cultural Revolution and were now returning to the cities. During the next few years progress was made at reducing unemployment, but by the mid–1980s the number of unemployed appeared to be growing again due to the entry into the job force of "baby-boomers" born in the mid–1960s. Even with the expected decline in population growth, it is estimated that to maintain full employment China would have to create five hundred million new jobs between 1986 and 2005.[28] With the state sector already bloated, there is little thought of having public enterprises solve the employment problem. Rather, the post-Mao leadership is pinning its hopes on the emerging private sector. Unemployed people are urged to arrange "self-employment" if possible.

The state does not recognize any right to employment, nor does it guarantee jobs (except for graduates of the elite universities). There is little protection for the unemployed, who are generally forced to live off relatives. There are plans to establish an unemployment insurance program.

Urban people can often hope to earn $400 per month, but the average earned by agricultural workers is $122. It is considerably lower in minority areas, where prices are sometimes higher than in China proper.

Mobility. China's billion people are officially comprised of three main social categories: peasants, workers, and "intellectuals." The largest group by far is the peasantry (about 850 million people). Although the system is beginning to change (or break down), for the vast majority of Chinese, peasant or worker status is still determined at birth on the basis of inheritance. It is possible for a young person to graduate to the intellectual category; this is exceptional, however, and most intellectuals grew up in intellectual families.

This curious social system is explained by history and economics. In the 1950s China's leaders felt obliged to create a formal division between urban workers and rural farm folk. This was to prevent a mass migration from the countryside to the cities, which might have resulted in widespread starvation. Thus, generally speaking, people classified as peasants have been forbidden to leave the land. Surprisingly, the designation "peasant" or "worker" is not determined by the type of work a person does. Indeed, it is common for most of a village's income to be derived from nonagricultural enterprises. If a peasant has skills and can arrange a job and accommodations, he or she may be allowed to live in a town, but even then the peasant does not thereby graduate to worker status. If one's mother was a peasant, one is probably a peasant for life. If the father should happen to be a worker, he cannot pass worker status on to a child. However, a male child generally "inherits" his village (to which he will almost certainly be attached permanently) from his father. Conversely, if a worker or intellectual is sent to engage in farm work, the original classification is usually retained.[29]

A peasant has had three possibilities for upward mobility: gaining an education and becoming an intellectual, or joining either the party or the army. By the early 1980s the latter ceased to be a promising alternative, as discharged soldiers were now required to return to their villages. At any rate, perhaps one in a hundred boys takes one of these steps. (Girls almost never do.) Intermarriage is rare and does not change one's status.

Otherwise, Chinese are not generally permitted to change their domicile. The police and special domicile inspection committees try to make sure that people live where they are supposed to.

Although it is not easy for citizens of the PRC to emigrate, restrictions have eased somewhat in recent years. The government claims, for example, that Tibetans have free exit and entry at Indian border stations.

Welfare and Social Security. In traditional China, the extended family was expected to care for the aged, and the lineage (same-surnamed villagers) took care of its poor. However, this arrangement could not cope with the more serious natural and man-made disasters.

Today, according to the constitution, each person is to be paid according to the labor he or she contributes. Regarding social insurance, the constitution promises to "expand" such services but stops short of making guarantees. In the cities, welfare needs are, by Third World standards, well met, but in rural areas services are uneven. In fact, the country has no comprehensive welfare system. Destitute people, especially children and the elderly, are still normally cared for by their relatives. Although rarely imposed, jail sentences of up to five years theoretically await those who fail to support an aged parent. (More commonly, one's pay will be docked.) In recent years the central government appears to have provided only $6 million annually for all rural aged, orphaned, and disabled. (This figure represents the average per annum and does not include pensions or assistance for veterans and military dependents.) More—at least $64 million—has been provided by collective enterprises, but a poor person is not automatically eligible for help from collectives.

In the case of old people who cannot provide for themselves and have no offspring to provide for them, the state sets a standard for their care, known as the "Five Guarantees" (food, housing, clothing, medical care, and burial). However, the financial responsibility for this falls almost entirely on the local community. In the past, this has usually meant that the production brigade (one or more villages) had to finance welfare. Thus, poor people in poor villages received little or no help, and often fell back on begging. As of 1984, there were only 153,000 people being cared for in homes for the aged,[30] 6 percent of those theoretically eligible (those childless, etc.). Apparently, most of the others were receiving some "five guarantee" benefits, but they lived with relatives. The government has called for 13,000 more homes for the aged to be opened by 1990. Because of the abandonment of collective agriculture and the accompanying loss of funds to the public sector, such a goal could not be attained without a massive (and unlikely) infusion of state funds.

The policy of each couple having only one child has important long-term implication for the problem of caring for the aged, for it implies that eventually many young or middle-aged couples will be obliged to provide for up to four old people in addition to a child. Pensions have been suggested to relieve the financial burden. Only a small number of Chinese are covered by pension programs—primarily those who work in large urban collective or state enterprises. New units can handle the situation without problem, but each employee of an old factory may have to support as many as 1.5 pensioners. Retirees receive from 60 to 90 percent of their former wages, depending upon political considerations and length of service. (Those who failed to support the Communists before 1949 have generally received no more than 70 percent, but otherwise there are no political considerations involved.) The whole system is admittedly flawed, and in 1986 there was talk of replacing it with a general system of social security to cover retired people and those left unemployed by failed enterprises.

There are already certain special forms of relief. The state seems to respond quickly when there is a natural disaster. There are also locally administered programs for people who cannot work for special reasons, such as injury, but there is pressure to limit the benefit period.

Poverty is often associated with mental and physical deficiency. The number of physically handicapped people in China is put at twenty million. The number of mentally deficient is not known, but in one prefecture (perhaps an extreme case) 10 percent of the population were found to be retarded.[31] There is doubtless a direct relationship between economic deprivation and mental retardation. However, except for military-related disabilities and a few additional showpiece efforts, in past years China's physically and mentally handicapped were paid scant attention. Such institutions for the disabled as exist once tended to serve only the urban minority, but now rural blind, deaf, and mute children are often sent to special urban schools. Disabled persons among the rural majority have had to rely on the goodwill of relatives and other neighbors. Now, handicapped people are promised better care. A welfare fund for the handicapped has been established (with funding coming from overseas Chinese). The aims of the organization are still not grandiose. "In running welfare services for the handicapped, we must do what we are capable of, and not indiscriminately copy and apply foreign practices; we have to rely on our own efforts and the strength of the masses and society rather than relying entirely on the state."[32] Thus, the central government does not intend to shoulder the main financial burden. Under the evolving system (still largely confined to the cities), these responsibilities are shared by "the state, the collective and the individual."[33]

Property. The right of possession is now given greater respect than at any time since 1949. A substantial body of case law has been built up around this subject, many of the disputes having arisen as a result of property previously confiscated.[34]

In agriculture, there has been a virtual counterrevolution in the landholding situation. Until recent years, all but a tiny percentage of the land (the private plots) was collectivized; there could be no thought of renting out farmland. Now, with the new responsibility system of de facto private ownership, people sometimes find it advantageous to subcontract their land to others to cultivate. In theory the land is not owned, and therefore not rented. Instead, one is authorized to sublet to another family his "contract" (by means of which the government originally gave him the right to farm the land). In practice there seems to be little distinction between this and a system of private property.

It is still officially insisted that China has a "socialist public ownership" land system. People are not supposed to be free to do with their land whatever they wish. Nonetheless, when it comes to determining land use, the government often appears to be losing control. In Hubei, farm acreage is declining at the rate of 83,000 hectares a year, much of the former farmland being used for other businesses or for housing. According to radio Wuhan,

This is a really shocking fact showing that the strengthening of land control is a task which cannot afford delay. There is a saying, "All things come from the earth, and the earth produces again." But our country has a large population and limited farmland. This has long been a conspicuous contradiction. . . . The efficient control and use of farmland has an important bearing on the realization of the magnificent goal of socialist modernization. How well we do this will determine the quality of the environment we leave to our descendants. Therefore, this task is a key matter of fundamental, overall importance. If we continue to shut our eyes to the arbitrary occupation and use of farmland, we will certainly be punished by history and be scolded by our descendants.[35]

Thus, it is argued that property rights must yield to larger social and ecological concerns.

Although small businesses are now supposed to be permitted in China, many cadres have been slow to get the message. In February 1983 the heads of two Henan "specialized households" who had engaged in food processing and fishing were detained because of their business activities. They were sharply criticized, fined, and their newly built workshops were torn down. After their release, they appealed to higher party authorities, who found in their favor. In January 1984 the secretary of the prefectural party committee visited their town and declared that an "extreme wrong" had been done and demanded that the local officials apologize, which they did.[36]

As the bureaucratic problems are ironed out, private enterprise can be expected to grow. According to official statistics, in 1984 there were already 9.3 million private businesses (mostly small), employing thirteen million people.

Four Chinese cities, including Changzhou (Jiangsu Province) and Siping (Jilin), have been experimenting with a new legal form of home holding. Housing is being sold (rather than rented as in the past). A two-room apartment (fifty square meters) apparently costs about U.S. $3,000 to build, but is subsidized and sold for $500 to $1,100 (depending on whether it is bought on the installment plan or with cash). One occasionally sees the sensitive words "own" and "ownership" used to describe the new setup, which, however, is still described as "socialist."

SOCIAL RIGHTS

Women and the Family. Although Chinese women are not demeaned to the extent that they were in traditional China (when they were not educated, and often had to suffer through life on deliberately deformed feet), their lives are nonetheless largely defined by their gender.[37] Notwithstanding repeated campaigns, such as that underway in early 1984, the struggle for women's equality has not progressed quickly. As one member of the National Federation of Women told a Hong Kong reporter, "the very fact that now, more than 30 years after Liberation, we feel compelled to launch such a movement shows beyond doubt that there's something seriously wrong."[38]

In traditional China, marriages were generally arranged by parents and intermediaries. The Communists have tried (with considerable but not total success) to abolish this system, and in general there is freedom to choose marriage partners. However, early marriages are virtually forbidden. Even after marriage, work assignments have sometimes made it impossible for spouses to live together.

The government discourages divorce, which is especially difficult to obtain when one party is opposed.

In education, girls and women are still disadvantaged. Seventy percent of China's illiterates are female. Girls often drop out of school after one or two years.[39] However, in at least some areas the local authorities are insisting that "the rights of school attendance and employment of girls should be protected on equal terms."[40] As for higher education, only 24 percent of China's college students are women.[41] (Japan and South Korea have slightly lower figures, but many other countries have higher—52 percent in the case of the United States.)

In past years, all-female work teams have been common, but many of these have been abolished. It is now claimed that because of the different physical characteristics and problems arising from menstruation, pregnancy, and nursing, work teams generally perform better if they include men. Old leftist slogans, such as "what men can do, women can do," have been quietly abandoned. While "equal pay for equal work" is the rule, women tend to have lower-paying types of work than men. Often, even when they outperform men, they are paid less. They also have difficulty advancing to better jobs. The official *Beijing Review* (Sept. 10, 1984) comments: "The habits formed over thousands of years and the current lack of conveniences leave most women workers tied up with family chores. This adversely affects their work and study. Today, a mere third of all scientists and technicians in Chinese industry are women. Of these, few hold senior posts."

Only 13 percent of Communist party members are women, and even this figure hides a somewhat gloomy reality of the role of women in Chinese politics. There are hardly any women in high positions, and a woman's political role is often husband-dependent. There have been complaints about women taking advantage of their husbands' positions and power to advance private interests, sometimes committing illegal acts in the process. Although women still rarely hold powerful political office in their own right, in 1985 for the first time a woman was appointed to head a provincial party committee.

Sexual Preference. Although homosexuality exists in China as elsewhere, and there are references to it down through the ages, Chinese culture today does not regard it favorably. There has been no gay rights movement, and the issue is never aired in the media. Indeed, any mention of the subject is extremely rare. One such news item (the only one I have seen) appeared in *Hunan Daily* and was broadcast by the provincial radio service on July 26, 1984. It reported (unsympathetically) on a homosexual man driven to suicide.[42]

Ethnicity. China has more than fifty-five ethnic minority groups, with a population of about seventy million. Although less than 7 percent of the country's total population, minority groups occupy more than half of the territory. During various historical epochs, many of these nationalities were very powerful, and some of them actually ruled all of China. But in recent centuries these groups have been on the decline. They tend to live in barren but sensitive border homelands and are sometimes targets of Soviet or Vietnamese propaganda. As a gesture of recognition of these people's cultural rights, their areas have been designated "autonomous" by the Communists, but this has never implied political autonomy. Conditions were worst during the Cultural Revolution, when most ethnic minorities endured persecution (approaching genocidal levels in the case of the Mongols).

In 1984 a new Law on Regional Autonomy for Minorities went into effect.[43] In the law's preamble it is implicitly admitted that ethnic minorities have been subjected to some discrimination. "In the struggle to uphold unity among nationalities, we should oppose big-nationality chauvinism, Han [ethnic Chinese] chauvinism in particular." Article 9 elaborates: "Any discrimination against and suppression of minority nationalities . . . should be prohibited." But it is also emphasized that minorities will not be allowed to go their own way. Specifically prohibited are local nationalism and any "undermining national unity or creating ethnic disunity." All nationalities are expected to abide by Marxism-Leninism-Mao Zedong thought and to protect national unity.

According to the preamble of the minorities law, autonomous regions are governed "under the unified leadership of the state." Thus, these peoples do not enjoy any political independence (though before they came to power the Communists promised that this would be allowed). In some "minority regions" the Hans (Chinese) are actually in the majority; to help maintain the fiction of minority control over minority affairs, even in such areas the regional congresses have a majority of non-Hans. For example, in the Ningxia Hui Autonomous Region, where only 32 percent of the population is Hui (Muslims of the Chinese race), the standing committee of the regional congress is 56 percent Hui. In fact, the law requires that the administrative heads of nationality areas be citizens of a nationality "exercising regional autonomy in the area concerned." However, this principle does not apply within the Han-dominated Communist party, where the real power resides. The party has been trying to train "reliable" cadres belonging to ethnic minorities. In Tibet, there are 36,000 cadres (59 percent of the total) belonging to the Tibetan and other minority races. Elsewhere, however, figures published are so selective that one suspects that progress has been slow. For example, in the Turkic region of Xinjiang, we are told that "in the 10 leading prefecture and city organizations" the percentage of minority cadres has increased from 33 to 44. The best progress appears to have been made in "minority" areas where Hans are actually in the minority. In Inner Mongolia, for example, the proportion of Mongol cadres is higher than the proportion of Mongols in the general population. Throughout the country, there are over a million minority cadres, who are described as occupying leadership posts at all levels. Although this represents an increase of 30 percent over 1978, few non-Hans yet occupy positions of real power.

Population growth is a sensitive racial issue in China. Historically, fertility rates have been much higher among Hans than other groups, which accounts for the present 14–to–1 population ratio. But minority nationalities, after a period of numeric stability or (in some groups) decline, have recently been growing at an annual rate of almost 3 percent, compared with 2 percent for the Hans. (This may be due in part to the fact that in order to take advantage of affirmative action programs, those of mixed parentage now often choose to be counted as minority.) Thus, in 1982 it was decided that birth control should normally be required of minorities as well as Hans, but the policy has been difficult to carry out. In practice, minorities are often allowed larger families than Hans. Koreans are allowed two children, and both the Miao and Li of Hainan are often allowed three. Birth control is also stressed for large nationalities, such as the Zhuang of Guangxi, and sometimes for small ones, such as the Dai of Yunnan. The policy regarding Tibetans is not altogether clear, but it is evident that they are allowed more children than Hans. On August 9, 1984, Lhasa radio emphatically denied a rumor that local Hans could have more than one child, but was vague about *Tibetan* couples' rights. Among Xinjiang's Uygurs and Kazakhs, the Chinese appear unable to limit population growth.

The minorities law asks ethnic groups to "concentrate their efforts to carry out socialist modernization," but promises "flexible measures" that harmonize with local conditions. To further their development, minorities receive some special help from the state. In particular, investment in these areas is being stepped up. Article 35 also calls for certain tax breaks. However, China is not a rich country, and there can be no massive subsidies. Thus, minorities are left largely to their own resources.

These peoples, to the extent that they are integrated into the national economy at all, tend to serve as suppliers of raw materials. Maoists once called for breaking down the distinctions and separateness of the economies of the various races. Apparently, the government is now content for traditional divisions of labor to continue. At the same time, it is hoped that these areas will become integrated into the national economy (rather than self-sufficient as Maoists would have had them).

"Autonomy" for minorities means primarily that traditional national cultures may persist. Local governments "should ensure that minority nationalities living in their areas enjoy the freedom of using and developing their own spoken and written languages, and the freedom of maintaining and changing their customs and habits." This reference to "changing" culture is only one of several hints that signification will not be discouraged. In this regard, educational policy is particularly noteworthy. "In schools which mainly recruit students of minority nationalities, textbooks in languages of minority nationalities concerned should be used where appropriate conditions exist. Languages for instruction should also be the languages of the minority nationalities concerned. Primary school students of higher grades and secondary school students should learn Chinese. Mandarin, which is commonly used throughout the country, should be pop-ularized among them." In practice, 80 percent of Mongol primary school students are taught in their native language.[44] The percentage is probably much lower among many other minorities, for whom use of Mandarin has often been nec-essary. In general, educational opportunities for minorities are far inferior to those for the Han. The best educated are the Mongols and Koreans. By comparison, in one Miao (Hmong) village, only 12 percent of the school-age children are in school.

Until recently, it has not been possible to send a telegram in the Tibetan language,[45] even though, being alphabetic, it is much more suitable to telegraphy than is Chinese.

China has made some progress in realizing human rights, but on balance one is struck by the low priority these issues have received. The reasons for the situation are partly economic (the unfavorable population-resource ratio) and partly cultural. But in the final analysis, the poverty of rights probably has the same explanation for China as elsewhere: Those who have power are unwilling to have their authority compromised. Their power base—the privileged class of cadres and official intellectuals—naturally tends to support the status quo. Thus, with both economic rights and civil liberties, the masses have what the leaders decide they should have. In this respect China is not unusual. Considering the ecological and historical problems, the current standing of economic rights may be the best that could be expected, but in terms of civil liberties the country falls far short of international standards.

NOTES

1. This chapter only discusses human rights in territories controlled by the Beijing government. For information on Taiwan, the reader is referred to the periodical *Taiwan Communiqué* (POB 45205, Seattle WA 98105 USA). See also James D. Seymour, "Taiwan's Thought Police," two-part series in *Index on Censorship* 14 (June 1985): 44–47; (Oct. 1985): 31–34.

2. See Andrew J. Nathan, *Chinese Democracy* (New York: Alfred A. Knopf, 1985), 58 passim.

3. For one participant's account of the Cultural Revolution, see Liang Heng and Judith Shapiro, *Son of the Revolution* (New York: Random House, 1983).

4. For documents with commentary, see James D. Seymour, *The Fifth Modernization: China's Human Rights Movement, 1978–1979* (Crugers, N.Y.: Earl Coleman Enterprises, 1980).

5. These developments are chronicled in the quarterly *SPEAHRhead: Bulletin of the Society for the Protection of East Asians' Human Rights* (P.O. Box 1212, New York, 10025).

6. Ru Xin, quoted in *People's Daily*, Jan. 9, 1984, trans. in U.S. Foreign Broadcast Information Service, *Daily Report* (hereafter: "FBIS"), Feb. 1, 1984.

7. Zhao Fushan, "Socialist Culture and Ethics in the Making," *Beijing Review*, Nov. 18, 1985, 15 (summary of an article from *People's Daily*).

8. See, for example, article in the army newspaper *Jiefangjun Bao*, Oct. 23, 1985, summarized in FBIS, Oct. 24, 1985, K–3.

9. For more information, see Liang Heng and Judith Shapiro, *Intellectual Freedom in China after Mao, with a Focus on 1983* (New York: Fund for Free Expression, 1984), followed in 1985 by a separate *Update*.

10. See David E. Mungelo, "The Reconciliation of Neo-Confucianism with Christianity in the Writings of Joseph de Prémare, S. J.," *Philosophy East and West*, Oct. 1976, especially 395.

11. Tianjin radio, Dec. 31, 1983, FBIS, Jan. 4, 1984.

12. The best known journalist of this sort is Liu Binyan. Among his published articles is a detailed analysis of corruption in the Manchurian town of Shuangyashan. *Baogao Wenxue* (June 1984, U.S. Joint Publications Research Service [hereafter, "JPRS"], CPS–84–064), 31–54. Of past abuses, Liu notes: "Had China's nobodies had a little more power, things would have been much easier to handle." Ibid., 50.

13. For more on China's press, see Rudolph Jörg-Meinhard, "China's Media: Fitting News to Print," *Problems of Communism* (July 1984).

14. New China News Agency, June 25, 1983; FBIS, June 27, 1983.

15. *Red Flag* (Sept. 16, 1983, JPRS 84675), 8.

16. For further analysis of Chinese law and its relevance to human rights, see R. Randle Edwards, Louis Henkin, and Andrew J. Nathan, *Human Rights in Contemporary China* (New York: Columbia University Press, 1986).

17. These developments are described in *SPEAHRhead*, no. 3/4; and nos. 12/13 20–22.

18. For information on political prisoners, see Amnesty International, *China—Violations of Human Rights: Prisoners of Conscience & the Death Penalty in the People's Republic of China* (London and New York: Amnesty International, 1984).

19. For details, see ibid.

20. *Red Flag*, July 1, 1983, JPRS 84307.

21. *Asiaweek*, June 8, 1984.

22. See Stanley Rosen, "Recentralization, Decentralization, and Rationalization: Deng Xiaoping's Bifurcated Educational Policy," *Modern China*, July 1985. For background, see Suzanne Pepper, *China's Universities: Post Mao Enrollment Policies and Their Impact on the Structure of Secondary Education* (Ann Arbor, Mich.: Center for Chinese Studies, 1984).

23. *Issues and Studies* (Taipei), Oct. 1983, 89. (Because this document was released by the Chinese Nationalists, its authenticity is open to question.)

24. Rules vary among localities. For one set of eight exceptions (in Hainan), see Haikou radio transcript, Oct. 17, 1985; FBIS, Oct. 22, 1985, P–1.

25. Beijing Broadcast (June 6, 1985, JPRS CPS–85–084), 105.

26. *China Daily*, August 8, 1985, 3.

27. See Huang Fanxing, "Medical and Health Work and Medical Insurance," *People's Daily*, Feb. 15, 1985, 5; FBIS, Feb. 26, 1985, K–13.

28. The estimate is that of Leo A. Orleans, *New York Times*, Aug. 1, 1985.

29. See Sulamith Heins Potter, "The Position of Peasants in Modern China's Social Order," *Modern China* (Oct. 1983).

30. Nov. 7, 1984; FBIS, Nov. 8, 1984, K–31.

31. Bai Jinian, "It Is Necessary to Support Poor Rural Areas While Helping Them to Get Rich," *Shaanxi Daily*, Oct. 17, 1985, 1; FBIS, Nov. 5, 1985, T–5.

32. New China News Agency, March 13, 1984; FBIS, March 13, 1984.

33. Wu Xiaoming, "Spring Has Arrived for Social Security in China," *Liaowang*, Feb. 4, 1985, JPRS, CPS–85–054, 47.

34. See *Collection of Cases on General Principles of the Civil Law* (Civil Law Teaching

and Research Office, Beijing Political and Legal Institute), trans. in *Chinese Law and Government*, Fall-Winter 1985–1986.
  35. August 7, 1984; FBIS, August 7, 1984.
  36. Henan Radio, Jan. 29, 1984; FBIS, Feb. 8, 1984.
  37. See Margery Wolf, *Revolution Postponed: Women in Contemporary China* (Stanford: Stanford University Press, 1985), and Judith Stacey, *Patriarchy and Socialist Revolution in China* (Berkeley: University of California Press, 1984).
  38. *Asiaweek*, Jan. 13, 1984.
  39. *Beijing Review*, Oct. 17, 1983, 19.
  40. Gansu Radio, Dec. 17, 1983; FBIS, Dec. 21, 1983.
  41. *Guangming Daily*, June 17, 1984, JPRS, CPS–84–050, 5.
  42. For details, see James D. Seymour, *China Rights Annals—1: Human Rights Developments in the People's Republic of China from Oct. 1983 through Sept. 1984* (Armonk, N.Y.: M. E. Sharpe, 1985), chap. 16. A good source on homosexuality and Chinese culture is Xiaoming Xiong (Samshasha), *Zhongguo Tongxing Ai Shilu* (Hong Kong, 1984).
  43. For a detailed discussion, see Seymour, *China Rights Annals—1*, 79–83. For text of the law, see *People's Daily*, June 4, 1984, JPRS CPS–84–045.
  44. *Beijing Review*, Oct. 17, 1983.
  45. *Beijing Review*, May 6, 1984.

SUGGESTED READINGS

Amnesty International. *China—Violations of Human Rights: Prisoners of Conscience & the Death Penalty in the People's Republic of China*. London: Amnesty International, 1984.
———. *Political Imprisonment in the People's Republic of China*. London: Amnesty International, 1978.
Edwards, R. Randle, Louis Henkin, and Andrew J. Nathan. *Human Rights in Contemporary China*. New York: Columbia University Press, 1986.
Gastil, Raymond, et al. *Freedom in the World: Political Rights and Civil Liberties, 1983–1984*. Westport, Conn.: Greenwood Press, 1984.
Liang Heng and Judith Shapiro. *After the Nightmare: A Survivor of the Cultural Revolution Reports on China Today*. New York: Alfred A. Knopf, 1986.
Liang Heng and Judith Shapiro. *Cold Winds, Warm Winds: Intellectual Life in Post-Mao China*. New York: Wesleyan University Press, 1985.
Nathan, Andrew. *Chinese Democracy*. New York: Alfred A. Knopf, 1985.
Rudolph, Jörg-Meinhard. "China's Media: Fitting News to Print." *Problems of Communism*, July 1984.
Seymour, James D. *China Rights Annals—1: Human Rights Developments in the People's Republic of China from October 1983 through September 1984*. Armonk, N.Y.: M. E. Sharpe, 1985.
———. *The Fifth Modernization: China's Human Rights Movement, 1978–1979*. Crugers, N.Y.: Earl Coleman Enterprises, 1980.
SPEAHRhead: Bulletin of the Society for the Protection of East Asians' Human Rights. P.O. Box 1212, Cathedral Station, New York, N.Y. 10025.
Stacey, Judith. *Patriarchy and Socialist Revolution in China*. Berkeley: University of California Press, 1984.
Xu Wenli. "My Self-Defence." *Index on Censorship* (London) (May 1986): 18–25.

5

CUBA

Rhoda Rabkin

The human rights situation in Cuba leaves much to be desired. Freedom of speech and association do not exist. All the mass media, both print and electronic, are under Communist party control. Cuban jails hold approximately one thousand political prisoners, including several hundred long-term inmates subject to appalling prison conditions and abuse.

This dismal human rights record is only partially offset by the Cuban revolution's accomplishments in the field of economic and social development. The revolution has certainly brought a more egalitarian distribution of income and has broadened access to health care and education. It can be questioned, however, whether these gains, which build on the achievements of the past, are so dramatic as Cuban propaganda claims. There is even more doubt as to whether these gains can justify the sacrifice of political rights and individual freedom that has been entailed by the Cuban revolutionary process.

HISTORICAL BACKGROUND

Before ceasing to be a colony, Cuba fought two destructive, bloody wars, marked by atrocities on both sides and immense human suffering. Independence from Spain was not achieved until 1898, and then only after U.S. military intervention.

In 1902, the new Cuban constitution incorporated, on Washington's insistence, a provision (the famous Platt amendment) allowing U.S. intervention in Cuba to guarantee the island's independence and to maintain its public order. The Americans hoped by this means to curb the Cuban tendency to resolve political conflict through violence. The limitation of Cuban sovereignty, however, appears to have encouraged the very political irresponsibility and cynicism that it was meant to allay. In the years that followed, whenever their political fortunes were threatened, Cuban leaders called for U.S. intervention as the means of redressing the power balance inside Cuba.[1] In the absence of respected, legitimate national political institutions, the tradition of violent protest became that much more deeply embedded.

The period between the abrogation of the Platt amendment in 1934 and the triumph of Castro's revolution in 1959 were years of economic and social progress, coupled, paradoxically, with political stagnation and failure.[2] The era was dominated by the military-politician Fulgencio Batista. At first Batista ruled from behind the scenes, but in 1940 he was elected president, legally and democratically, in his own right. Also in 1940, a new Cuban constitution, incorporating many advanced social provisions, such as the minimum wage and eight-hour day, was adopted. In 1944 Batista was succeeded in office by an elected civilian, who was in turn followed in 1948 by another civilian. These years of corrupt, but democratically elected, governments provided Cuba with the most significant experience of democratic, constitutional rule that it would have.

The blatant corruption of the political class during this republican era did not totally destroy the democratic ideal in the minds of the Cuban people, but it greatly weakened it for many. In 1952, when Batista seized power and began to rule dictatorially, many Cubans welcomed his intervention. Soon, however, it was seen that the old vices of corruption and gangsterism in Cuban politics continued, and that in the absence of democracy, would only worsen.

Opposition to Batista was at first concentrated among students, but soon spread to urban workers and middle-class elements. The resistance to Batista's dictatorship followed the time-honored practices of previous political opposition in Cuba: strikes, demonstrations, clandestine meetings, bombs, assassinations, etc.

In December 1956 the struggle took a new turn when Fidel Castro and a small group of followers began guerrilla operations against Batista from the mountains in Oriente province. With the help of poor peasants in the region, they attacked military outposts and harassed the troops sent to find them. Castro's guerrilla fighters in the mountains received assistance (recruits, supplies, intelligence, etc.) from a network of supporters (loosely organized as the "Movement of the 26th of July") in the cities.

Batista's soldiers had not been trained for guerrilla warfare, and they responded to Castro's challenge ineffectively, with intermittent and undiscriminating cruelty. And as a Cuban novelist scathingly observed: "Batista turned out to be only a part-time tyrant—the rest of the time he was too busy being a thief and a canasta player."[3] Without the guidance of any overall political or military strategy, the army and the police resorted extensively to the use of torture, as a method of both interrogation and reprisal. Repression inspired fear, but to an even greater extent, revulsion. At the end, no sector of Cuban society saw any advantage to Batista's continued rule. In the last months of 1958, the army was thoroughly demoralized, with many units either surrendering or refusing to fight. On December 31, 1958, the dictator and his closest associates secretly left Havana by airplane, never to return.[4] The most fundamental factor shaping the negative human rights situation in Cuba today is the ideology of revolutionary transformation held by the country's political elite. Cuba's twentieth-century political traditions cannot be directly blamed. Their failings, which were many, did not include the all-encompassing centralization of power practiced by the Cuban revolution. Before the Castro era, infringements of political rights were linked to instability and conflict. Today, the denial of freedom is part of an institutionalized political order that has shown remarkable staying power.

CONFLICT WITHIN THE REVOLUTION

In 1959 the vast majority of the Cuban public, especially those in the middle class, expected the revolution to restore democracy and to rid government of dishonesty and corruption. During the war Castro had pledged to restore the rights and freedoms enshrined in the Constitution of 1940. During his first months in power, he promised that the revolution would bring needed social reforms without sacrificing political freedoms or democracy: "Regardless of how revolutionary the laws we propose to enact may be, they will be enacted without violating one single right, without suppressing even one public liberty, without beating anyone, and without even insulting anyone."[5] His popular slogan was "Neither bread without liberty, nor liberty without bread."[6]

But it was not to be. The Castro government's radical economic policies, its confrontational stance toward the United States, and the promotion of communists into positions of responsibility alienated important sectors of Cuban public opinion. Castro responded to the growing political polarization by curtailing political freedoms. All who dared criticize or dissent from any of Castro's policies were branded enemies of the people, "counterrevolutionaries." In June 1959 Castro postponed elections indefinitely with the slogan "Revolution first, elections later!" In January 1960 the government seized two major newspapers, *Avance* and *El Mundo*. Later, all television and radio stations were expropriated. Labor unions and student organizations were compelled to accept leaders chosen by Castro.

Many Cubans expressed their disillusionment with the revolution by simply emigrating. Some of the emigrants, however, and others remaining in Cuba, took the road of violent opposition. By the end of 1960 the U.S. Central Intelligence Agency (CIA) was giving several thousand anti-Castro exiles military training in preparation for a landing in Cuba. In theory, the landing was supposed to be aided by an underground based inside Cuba, but although underground activities existed, the CIA did little to coordinate them.[7]

The revolutionary government, alarmed by news reports of the training camps, decided to eliminate the danger posed by underground sabotage activities. In the fall of 1960, Castro organized his supporters at the neighborhood level into Committees for the Defense of the Revolution (CDR), which kept close watch on the political activities and tendencies of every resident. In April 1961, just prior to the Bay of Pigs exile invasion, these committees helped to arrest perhaps 100,000 suspected counterrevolutionaries, who were herded into sports stadiums, public buildings, and schools for interrogation. About a half dozen suspected leaders were summarily executed.[8] Most of the detained were soon released, but thousands languished in prison for lengthy terms. The revolution's methods were effective. No urban underground movement ever since has been able to organize inside Cuba.

The exile invasion, which was poorly planned, came on April 17, 1961. It was quickly defeated, thanks to the action of Castro's air force, which had not been destroyed on the ground prior to the landing.

The crushing defeat at the Bay of Pigs did not, however, put a stop to counterrevolutionary violence. In 1960 and for several years thereafter, anti-Castro guerrilla bands operated in the mountainous regions of Las Villas and other provinces.[9] According to Cuban sources, the rebels numbered about 3,500 men at their height. The government resorted to harsh methods, including executions, imprisonment, and forced removal of the rural population from the Escambray mountain region.[10] By 1965 the anti-Castro guerrillas had been completely defeated. With the peasant rebellion crushed, Castro and his fellow revolutionaries never again faced a comparable domestic challenge to the implementation of their philosophy and programs.

CIVIL AND POLITICAL RIGHTS

Castro's strategy called for the creation of a mobilized society and a strong centralized state, all under the direction of a single revolutionary vanguard party. The vanguard has been organized since 1965 as the Communist party of Cuba (PCC). Decision making in Cuba is dominated by the general secretary of the party, Fidel Castro, and a small circle of his close associates. The formal institutions of government, known collectively as the Organs of Popular Power, consist of a 500-person National Assembly and local government units at the provincial and municipal level. In addition, interest-oriented associations, called mass organizations, are responsible for channeling the concerns of workers, peasants, women, etc., to the highest political leadership. There is no freedom to organize independently of the government-sponsored institutions.

In theory, the great variety of participatory mechanisms permits extensive popular influence on policy. In practice, however, the opportunities for genuine participation in Cuba are significantly constrained by the vanguard party's leadership role in all such institutions. Individuals reach senior leadership positions within government and the mass organizations through a process of elite cooptation. Important political issues are debated, if at all, by a small circle of top leaders in great secrecy. At no level of the political system does competition for office involve the airing of political issues or appeals for mass support.[11]

Political freedom, understood in the Western sense, does not exist in Cuba. The Cuban constitution mentions freedom of speech, freedom of the press, and the rights of assembly, demonstration, and association. All of these rights and freedoms, however, are explicitly limited by Article 61 of the constitution which provides: "None of the freedoms which are recognized for citizens can be exercised ... contrary to the existence and objectives of the socialist state, or contrary to the decision of the Cuban people to build communism." The restrictive constitutional framework is supplemented by various sections of the Penal Code. The most important is Article 108, according to which a person who "incites against the social order, international solidarity, or the Socialist state, by means of oral or written propaganda, or in any other form" risks a prison sentence of from one to eight years. These restrictions are by no means of merely theoretical significance, but are strictly enforced. Repression of "counterrevolutionary" writings, speech, demonstrations, meetings, etc., is complete and well institutionalized.

This does not mean that all criticism is forbidden. Complaining, both informally to one's neighbors on the street, and formally through government channels, is an accepted part of Cuban life. So long as grousing is focused on specific deficiencies, such as overcrowded buses, dirty beer bottles, and rude treatment at clinics, it is tolerated, and even promoted by the government. For those Cubans, however, who direct their criticism toward the system as a whole, or to particularly sensitive aspects of it, the penalties can be severe.

One well-documented case is that of Ricardo Bofill Pages, once a professor of philosophy at the University of Havana. Bofill was first arrested in 1967, apparently in connection with his involvement in an anti-Castro faction of the Cuban Communist Party. Released after five years, he worked as a floor-sweeper until 1980, when he was again arrested. After serving another two and a half years in prison Bofill was released, but not permitted to work or emigrate. In 1983 Bofill was back in prison, this time in reprisal for granting an interview to two French journalists concerning the situation of human rights in Cuba.[12]

Another example illustrative of the government's refusal to tolerate dissent is the case of Ariel Hidalgo, a forty-year-old leftist historian. Hidalgo was first arrested in 1980 when he confronted a rock-throwing group that was attacking a student who wanted to emigrate. Although freed, Hidalgo was again arrested in 1981 and sentenced under Article 108 of the Penal Code. Hidalgo, who dared to criticize the Castro government from an egalitarian standpoint, is now serving his sentence in the Combinado del Este prison near Havana.[13]

It is important to keep cases such as these in mind, because Castro and other government spokespersons often deny that there are any political prisoners in Cuba. For example, a recent exchange between Castro and a Western journalist went like this:

Lehrer: Is there anybody in jail simply because his political beliefs are—he dissents from you politically?

Castro: No one. Not because of political beliefs, nor because of religious beliefs that are in prison.[14]

Castro told another interviewer,

No one in our country has ever been punished because he was a dissident or held views that differed from those of the Revolution. The acts for which a citizen may be punished are defined with precision in our penal code.[15]

But Castro also has generally been quite forthright concerning the absence of freedom in Cuba to oppose the revolution:

We don't understand the concept of liberty in the same way as you and, as a matter of fact, the opportunities to carry out opposition against the Revolution are minimal. They do not exist legally.[16]

The key to interpreting Castro's answers would seem to be with the emphasis on "beliefs" and "ideas." No one is punished for purely inner convictions. But to voice dissident ideas, or to seek to persuade others of their truth, is to leave the realm of ideas and enter the world of criminally punishable action.

In the early 1960s, as a consequence of severe security measures, the Cuban government was burdened with a large number of supposedly counterrevolutionary prisoners. By 1965 there were still, by Castro's own estimate, 20,000 political prisoners in Cuba.[17] Ten years later, again by Castro's estimate, there were about 4,500 such prisoners.[18] These reductions were achieved through a government-sponsored rehabilitation program which offered early release to those engaging in labor and political study.

Even this greatly reduced number represents a high ratio of prisoners to population—more than 40 per 100,000. As one specialist on Latin America has observed, even as early as two years after the Pinochet coup, Chile had no more than 47 political prisoners per 100,000 population.[19] In 1979 Castro freed some 3,600 prisoners after a dialogue with Cuban-Americans. According to the Inter-American Commission on Human Rights, there are still some 1,000 political prisoners remaining in Cuban jails.[20]

There has never been on-site inspection of Cuban prisons by independent outside groups such as Amnesty International, the Red Cross, or the Inter-American Human Rights Commission. In this respect, Cuban prisoners are more disadvantaged than even those of Chile, Uruguay, or Haiti. Castro denies that he has anything to hide: "Throughout the twenty-five years of the Revolution in spite of the difficulties and dangers we've experienced, there has never been a person tortured."[21] Outside observers, however, believe that torture was employed in the early 1960s.[22] Even when outright torture is not employed, mistreatment of prisoners has taken the form of poor prison conditions and severe harassment. Prisoners in recent years have suffered from overcrowding, unsanitary conditions, and inadequate food. Certain prisoners, singled out for special abuse, are subjected to sleep deprivation, special punishment cells, lack of medical care, and denial of family visits and mail.[23]

Physical abuse over the years has, not surprisingly, resulted in the disfigurement and physical incapacitation of prisoners. Eloy Gutierrez Menoyo, a fearless guerrilla leader who fought first against Batista and then against Castro (in the Escambray), reportedly became deaf in one ear and blind in one eye as a result of prison beatings. Armando Valladares, a student oppositionist imprisoned in 1960, received no medical attention for a fractured ankle, contracted polyneuritis in 1974 after months on a starvation diet, and was subsequently deprived periodically of therapy for paralysis of his legs. Miriam Ortega, a former president of a Catholic youth organization, became a semi-invalid as a consequence of prison beatings.[24] Many less well-known inmates have suffered similar experiences.

Today the most abused inmates are those several hundred who for political reasons refuse to participate in the government-sponsored rehabilitation program. Nicknamed "plantados" from the Spanish for "to stand firm," these prisoners do not accept political reeducation and insist on their rights under an International Labor Organization (ILO) convention (number 29) ratified in 1930 by Cuba which forbids the use of forced labor as a means of education or punishment.[25]

One particularly cruel aspect of the situation of Cuban political prisoners is the arbitrary reimposition of sentences on prisoners who have completely served their terms. Amnesty International reported in 1982 that it knew of more than fifty political prisoners who had, since 1977, received additional sentences for having manifested a "rebellious attitude" while in prison. In some cases these further terms were handed down by special security courts; in other cases the court system appears to have been bypassed.[26]

Although a very occasional act of economic sabotage is still reported, the Cuban government has not faced armed internal resistance since the early 1960s. Thanks to the thorough and efficient labors of the internal security organs, there is no organized underground resistance in Cuba to be rooted out by "dirty war" methods as in Argentina. Nevertheless, arrests for political causes, mistreatment of prisoners, and arbitrary extension of prison terms continue to take place. These, together with the extensive curtailment of individual freedom, enforced through a highly organized system of surveillance, amply justify Cuba's reputation as a major violator of human rights.

The Castro government has not only intensified the use of ordinary techniques of repression, familiar from Cuba's past, but has also introduced forms of regimentation wholly new to Cuba. With the advent of Cuban socialism, every sphere of life formerly deemed private, including the economy, religion, emigration, and even sex, became politicized and subjected to rigid norms of conduct. This politicization is the consequence of a revolutionary ideology which views the old division between private and public as no longer legitimate.

The CDR block committees, which originally monitored the political activities and associations of citizens to prevent acts of violence and sabotage, soon became an all-purpose institution for repression. Surveillance became multifaceted, intrusive, and petty. Vigilance came to mean, for example, taking note of one's neighbor's cooking odors (too-frequent roasted meat might indicate black market dealings). The CDRs were also made responsible for listing inventories of would-be emigrants' furniture and valuables, to prevent their sale before departure (since these items would be confiscated by the state). Admission to university and even technical schools became contingent on a favorable evaluation from the local CDR.

One of the previously private spheres most affected by the revolution's expanded definition of the political is that of religion. On paper, the Cuban constitution "guarantees freedom of conscience and the right of everyone to profess any religious belief and to practice, within the framework of respect for law, the belief of his preference." However, with the triumph of the revolution, religion almost immediately became a battleground between the Castro government and more conservative elements of Cuban society.

In 1960 the Roman Catholic Church, Cuba's largest religious denomination, went on record denouncing the advance of communist influence in Cuba. This was not, however, a conflict that the Church was in a position to win. Even before 1959, the Catholic Church had very weak roots in Cuban society: few priests were native Cubans, attendance at mass was minimal, and many lower-class Cubans did not even bother with the sacrament of marriage.[27]

After the Bay of Pigs invasion, Castro closed the Catholic university and more than three hundred private religious schools, thereby making Cuban education state-run and secular. In September 1961 a religious procession developed into an anti-government political demonstration in which one layman was killed. After the incident, traditional religious processions were banned, and more than one hundred priests (about half of the remaining Catholic clergy in Cuba) were expelled from the country.[28]

Since then, religious activities have been restricted to church premises: government permission must be obtained even to hold a church-sponsored picnic.[29] Thanks to the efforts of the CDRs, schools, and sports organizations, Sundays are heavily programmed with activities for children which compete with Sunday school. Few Cuban children have significant exposure to Christian teachings or observances. Those young adults who do surmount these obstacles, and who consider themselves believers, encounter discrimination in school and employment.[30] Cuba has become effectively a de-Christianized country.[31]

In the sphere of sexual conduct, the revolution's impulse to purge Cuban society of "capitalist vices" has brought persecution of homosexuals. In late 1965 homosexuals, along with others considered socially deviant, were drafted into the army in special groups called Military Units to Aid Production. Treatment of the draftees was always harsh and sometimes brutal. Many writers and university faculty at this time were denounced as homosexuals (sometimes at public meetings convened for this purpose) and removed from their jobs. The hard-hit Union of Writers and Artists protested to Fidel Castro, who eventually agreed that the program was excessive. The units were phased out in 1967. Homosexuals continue, however, to experience officially sanctioned job discrimination in certain fields, and other forms of harassment.[32]

Another potent new mechanism of social control introduced by the Castro government has been restriction of the right to emigrate. No previous government of Cuba, no matter how tyrannical, saw fit to adopt this kind of measure. Revolutionary policy has been not consistently to forbid emigration but to control it, turning the flow of people on and off, in accordance with government goals. At times, emigration has been tolerated as a means of "cleansing" Cuban society of dissenters and "scum."[33] At other times, emigration has been prevented so as to leave the discontented with no alternative but external conformity to revolutionary norms. Always, however, emigration has been regarded as an act of disloyalty, and the would-be emigrant has been subjected to various official and semiofficial acts of retaliation.

ECONOMIC RIGHTS

The purpose underlying all the mechanisms of social control in Cuba is to harness popular energies to construct socialism, defined as an egalitarian social order in which all citizens enjoy economic security, a rising standard of living, and the opportunity to have their talents put to use by society. In place of "formal," "bourgeois" liberties are "concrete" socialist rights understood as entitlements to goods such as employment, paid vacations, education, health care, etc.[34]

All observers can agree that Cuba in the 1950s stood in need of major economic and social reforms. The prerevolutionary economy, although prosperous by Latin American standards, was marred by massive unemployment and by a considerable disparity in living standards between urban areas and the countryside. Urban workers enjoyed job security, vacations, and various wage and health benefits, but rural workers and the unemployed experienced considerable deprivation. Inequality also had a racial component, since black Cubans were more likely than whites to have low incomes.

There is no question that the Cuban revolution has benefited those who were most underprivileged before 1959. Although systematic data on Cuban income distribution do not exist, most scholars agree that it is more egalitarian than in Cuba's past or in other Latin American countries.[35] Rationing, price subsidies, and rent ceilings play an important role in maintaining minimum levels of consumption. The Castro government has expanded social security coverage and has made new services available, such as guaranteed milk rations for children, reduced-price meals at work centers, day-care facilities, etc. One of the revolution's greatest successes has been in the field of education. Whereas only about one-half the school-age population in 1953 was enrolled in school, primary education was nearly universal in Cuba by the mid–1970s. In 1958 the national rate of illiteracy was around 21 percent. In 1970, according to Cuban census data, the rate was 12.9 percent.[36]

Another important area of great progress has been in combating unemployment. During the 1960s expansionary policies put an end to open unemployment, which in 1958 had stood at about 12 percent.[37] This revolutionary success, however, came at a heavy price. Many of the new jobs were "make-work," and labor productivity declined. Since 1970 there has been renewed emphasis on efficiency, and excess labor has been "released." But although unemployment has returned as a problem, it is much less serious than in the past.[38]

Black Cubans have also benefited from the revolution, although complete equality is still some way off. In prerevolutionary Cuba, racial discrimination was practiced openly by exclusive white social clubs, and blacks were excluded from some of Cuba's best beaches. Blacks were also disproportionately concentrated in the ranks of those holding menial and low-paying jobs. In 1960 Fidel Castro pledged to end discrimination in employment. The revolutionary government also ordered the private beaches, hotels, and restaurants open to the public of all races. Segregated white social clubs were disbanded.

The official view of the Cuban revolution is that government should be color-blind.[39] Affirmative action, racial quotas, and preferential hiring are not employed. Instead, policies aimed at raising the living standards of all the poor are expected to place the life chances of blacks on a par with those of whites.

It is difficult to evaluate the impact of the revolution's policies because, although data on race is collected by Cuban census takers, published data is almost never broken down by racial categories. The information that we do have, however, suggests that although overt discrimination has been eliminated, black Cubans are still not fully represented at the highest levels of Cuba's socioeconomic stratification, and they are still overrepresented at the lowest. The top leadership of the Cuban revolution has been disproportionately white.[40] Black American vistors who have toured Cuba's schools have noted that few black students attend the most elite schools, such as the Lenin Vocational School.[41] Overrepresentation of whites among military officers was found by one scholar who compared photographs of officers and soldiers published in a Cuban military magazine.[42] There is also some evidence that blacks suffer disproportionately from diseases typical of poor people.[43] The Cuban experience thus suggests that when racial and class stratification overlap, the resulting pattern of racial inequality is very difficult to eradicate.

The status of women in revolutionary Cuba also illustrates the difficulty of transforming ingrained traditional attitudes and social practices. Since the revolution, more women hold paying jobs outside the home (only 13 percent of the labor force was female in 1958, compared to 30 percent in 1980).[44] By Latin American standards, however, this rate of participation is not exceptional. More women participate in politics at the leadership level than ever before, although as might be expected, women are still significantly underrepresented in top positions. Women were about 18 percent of the Central Committee in 1986.[45] Women have also somewhat improved their educational status relative to men, although not dramatically. In prerevolutionary Cuba, girls were more likely than boys to receive at least some grade school instruction. Once the revolution brought about almost universal enrollment at the primary level, the female "advantage" disappeared. At the university level, women have gone from 34 percent to 40 percent of those attending classes.[46]

Despite the revolution's genuine achievements in improving the incomes, educational opportunities, and health standards of the disadvantaged, it may still be doubted whether the mobilization model adopted has really been the best one for achieving socioeconomic development. Cuba's gains in equality have come at a considerable sacrifice in economic growth. According to one estimate using World Bank figures of per capita national product, Cuba between 1952 and 1981 dropped from third to fifteenth place in Latin America.[47] The negative impact of low economic efficiency and sluggish growth on Cuban social progress is not always fully appreciated.

Furthermore, it is often overlooked, amidst glowing reports concerning the revolution's progress against illiteracy and infant mortality, that in 1959 Cuba, by Latin American standards, already enjoyed high educational and health standards. In the 1950s, Cuba ranked with at least the top three or four countries in the region on almost every socioeconomic indicator, including per capita income and literacy. It was also the country in Latin America with the lowest rate of infant mortality.[48]

Since the revolution, Cuba has made impressive advances in education, but such progress is not unique to Cuba. Between 1960 and 1976, Chile, Costa Rica, and Panama increased primary school enrollment by similar or greater percentages than Cuba, and also made comparable progress in expanding high school enrollment.[49] And although the quantitative expansion of education in Cuba has been impressive, the quality of schooling has not always kept pace. School buildings are often in poor repair, and textbooks and other materials are in short supply. Students above the sixth-grade level work in agriculture, sometimes for half the day, presumably with an impact on their ability to learn. Educational morale seems to be low. For example, in 1980 more than one-third of secondary schools were found to have engaged in some form of academic fraud or cheating on the part of students and faculty.[50]

Standards of health have improved since the revolution, but the rate of progress is not unique. In the 1950s Cuba had the third longest life expectancy in Latin America. Today, with a life expectancy of 73.5 years, Cuba is in first place in the region. However, Cuba's advance in the Latin American ranking owes more to the faltering performance of Argentina and Uruguay than to spectacular progress in Cuba. More than half of the countries of Latin America have equaled or exceeded Cuba's accomplishment of extending life by 14.7 years. Both Costa Rica and Panama (each by adding 15.7 years to life expectancy) rival Cuba's accomplishment of moving up two places (to second and third, respectively).[51]

There remains a considerable disparity in health facilities in different regions of Cuba. In 1958 Havana province had one physician for every 420 persons, while Oriente had only one doctor for every 2,550.[52] Administrative boundaries changed in 1976, so exact comparisons are not possible. But in 1980, in a developed urban area (Matanzas), there was one doctor for 263 inhabitants, while in mostly rural Granma province the ratio was one physician for 1,750 people.[53]

Differences in general socioeconomic conditions also contribute to health disparities between rich and poor regions. In 1985 the infant mortality rate in the worst performing provinces (Isle of Youth and Las Tunas) was about 75 percent higher than in the best performing province (Matanzas). In the poorer provinces, higher infant mortality is associated with earlier maternal age and unsanitary water supplies.[54]

In respect to basic material necessities, such as food and shelter, per capita growth has been virtually stagnant. According to the United Nations Food and Agriculture Organization (FAO) daily per capita intake in 1980 was 2,795 calories. But this is not above the average 2,740–2,870 reported for the 1950s.[55] Moreover, according to one study, in 1956, even a poor agricultural worker consumed at least 2,500 calories.[56] Given a stagnant per capita food supply, nutritional improvement in the diets of the poor has come about through two major mechanisms: a rationing system that assures minimum intake of basic foods, and increased availability for sale of inexpensive, nontraditional (and also unpopular) foods (e.g., yogurt, eggs, and fish).[57] Cuban officials estimate that rationed foods, which constitute about 80 percent of the average Cuban diet, provide every Cuban with a daily average of 2,100 calories.[58] Many urban working-class Cubans complain that food supplies are inadequate and that they ate better before the revolution.[59]

Housing was in short supply before 1959, but the problem of overcrowding has worsened since the revolution. According to the Cuban government in 1960, 655,000 new housing units were needed to give adequate shelter to the population.[60] By 1970, because of population growth, inadequate new construction, and deterioration of the existing stock, the housing deficit had grown to one million units.[61] According to one estimate, the housing deficit by 1980 had reached 1.5 million units.[62]

In view of the Cuban government's well-known commitment to meeting basic economic needs, it is perhaps surprising that practical results have not been greater. Cuba's poor economic growth record can be attributed to various causes, among them the emigration of professionals and skilled workers, low world prices for sugar, and the U.S. trade embargo. But a large part of the blame must surely be placed on features inherent in the Cuban development model itself. These include an inefficient centrally planned economy, poor incentives leading to chronic low labor productivity, and continued excessive concentration on sugar exports.

Political centralization in Cuba also contributes to shortcomings in economic management. The most extreme instance of this was Castro's misguided decision in the 1960s to produce ten million tons of sugar by 1970. Not only was the goal not reached, but the effort seriously disrupted the entire economy. Castro and the Communist party exercise a dominant role in all economic decisions, from the largest to the smallest, with a detrimental impact on the initiative and sense of responsibility at lower levels.[63]

Growth rates in the 1980s have been financed by grant-aid and debt, not by advances in productivity which can be counted on to sustain prosperity in future years. Since 1959, Cuba has become one of the largest per capita recipients of external financing in the world. It is estimated that as of 1983, Cuba owed about $8 billion to the USSR (the exact figure is a secret).[64] Exceptional Soviet generosity toward a politically valuable and militarily useful ally suggests that "the Cuban model" is not one that can be easily replicated by other countries. The obligation to Western countries in 1983 was about $3.3 billion. Loans, however, constitute only about one-third of Soviet economic assistance to Cuba. Another two-thirds has been transferred in the form of subsidized trade, with the Soviet Union buying sugar and nickel at above-market prices and selling petroleum at below-market rates.[65]

Cuban economic officials readily acknowledge that the economy operates below acceptable limits of economic efficiency.[66] Castro is well aware that to avoid economic strangulation, Cuba must promote nonsugar exports, which in turn requires increased productivity and international competitiveness. But despite a rhetorical commitment to economic liberalization, Castro is averse to market-oriented reforms. The long-run efficiency gains associated with market mechanisms are desired, but the short-run social costs (inequality and acquisitiveness) are considered prohibitive. Consequently, the economic future of Cuba's socialist experiment is very uncertain.

CONCLUSION

It is sometimes argued that the negative Cuban record regarding political rights is offset by exemplary social progress.[67] The notion that a trade-off exists under certain circumstances between political liberties and socioeconomic progress is one which, despite meager empirical support, has long enjoyed a certain vogue. Even before Castro turned to communism, he seemed to subscribe to such a view, when he referred to "capitalism under which people starve to death, and communism, which solves economic problems but suppresses the liberties that are so dear to mankind."

The economic performance of the Cuban revolution suggests, however, that it is at the very least premature to assert that communism "solves" economic problems. Cuba demonstrates that ringing declarations of "concrete" rights do not automatically produce results. Despite the extensive mobilization of society in pursuit of economic and social goals, the achievements of the Cuban development model are more limited, and the economic costs of the system higher, than is often recognized. Many of Cuba's economic achievements have been equaled or surpassed by other Latin American countries—without the extensive suppression of political liberties entailed by the Cuban development model.[68] Therefore, it must be questioned whether Cuban social progress really required the economic and political sacrifices that have characterized the revolutionary process under Castro's leadership. Indeed, it is even possible that demagogic promises, overcentralized decision making, and social regimentation are all aspects of a syndrome that contributes to economic mismanagement, which in turn hinders social progress. For these reasons, an allegedly superior record of fulfilling economic rights cannot justify the absence of political freedom in Cuba today.

NOTES

1. As one scholar notes, "The low but persistent level of organized political violence in Cuba can be directly linked to the opposition's need to provoke United States intervention." Jorge I. Dominguez, *Cuba: Order and Revolution* (Cambridge: Harvard University Press, Belknap, 1978), 18.

2. For a concise description, see Juan M. del Aguila, *Cuba: Dilemmas of a Revolution* (Boulder, Col. Westview Press, 1984), 25–28.

3. G. Cabrera Infante, Foreword to *Family Portrait with Fidel*, by Carlos Franqui, trans. by Alfred MacAdam (New York: Vintage Books, 1985), vii.

4. For a fuller account of this revolutionary period, see Hugh Thomas, *Cuba: The Pursuit of Freedom* (New York: Harper and Row, 1971), and Ramon L. Bonachea and Marta San Martin, *The Cuban Insurrection 1952–1959* (New Brunswick, N.J.: Transaction Books, 1974).

5. Loree Wilkerson, *Fidel Castro's Political Programs* (Gainesville, University of Florida Press, 1965), 54.

6. Quoted in ibid., 55.

7. Peter Wyden, *Bay of Pigs* (New York: Simon and Schuster, 1979), 111–14 and 245–48. According to one source, the CIA, fearing the leftist leaning of many resisters, actually obstructed cooperation. "The Military Dimension of the Cuban Revolution," in *Cuban Communism*, ed. Irving L. Horowitz, 3d ed. (New Brunswick, N.J.: Transaction Books, 1977), 537.

8. Herbert L. Matthews, *Revolution in Cuba* (New York: Charles Scribner's Sons, 1975), 203.

9. Bonachea and San Martin, 394.

10. Lee Lockwood, *Castro's Cuba, Cuba's Fidel* (New York: Random House, 1969), 260.

11. For a fuller discussion, see Rhoda P. Rabkin, "Cuban Socialism: A Case Study of Marxist Theory in Practice" (Ph.D. diss., Harvard University, 1983), 112–256.

12. *Le Matin de Paris*, October 7, 1983, and *New York Times*, September 29, 1983. Bofill was adopted as a prisoner of conscience by Amnesty International; see *Amnesty International Report 1984* (London: Amnesty International Publications, 1984), 146. As of this writing, he is once again free and living in Havana.

13. Carlos Ripoll, "Harnessing the Intellectuals: Censoring Writers and Artists in Today's Cuba" (Washington, D.C.: Cuban-American National Foundation, 1985), 39–40.

14. "MacNeil/Lehrer Newshour," February 12, 1985, transcript 2447, 2.

15. "*Playboy* Interview—Fidel Castro," *Playboy*, August 1985, 67.

16. Frank Mankiewicz and Kirby Jones, *With Fidel* (New York: Ballantine Books, 1975), 84.

17. Lockwood, 230.

18. Organization of American States (OAS), Inter-American Commission on Human Rights, *Sixth Report on the Situation of Political Prisoners in Cuba* (Washington, D.C.: 1979), 15.

19. Dominguez, *Cuba: Order and Revolution*, 254.

20. OAS, *Sixth Report*, 38.

21. Fidel Castro, *Talks with Us and French Journalists, July-August 1983* (Havana: Editora Politica, 1983), 54.

22. *Amnesty International Report on Torture* (London: Gerald Duckworth, 1973), 191. Some officers guilty of brutality toward prisoners were court-martialed. *Granma*, April 14, 1966, 8.

23. Ibid., 17–25. See also the testimony of Basilio Guzman Marrero at the Amnesty International Forum, Maryland University, September 26, 1984; reprinted in *Of Human Rights, 1984–85* (Washington, D.C.: Georgetown University), 23–25.

24. Carlos Alberto Montaner, *Secret Report on the Cuban Revolution*, trans. Eduardo Zayas Bazan (New Brunswick, N.J.: Transaction Books, 1981), 222.

25. OAS, *Sixth Report*, 12–13.

26. *Amnesty International Report 1982* (London: Amnesty International Publications, 1982), 129.

27. Almost all Cubans, however, were baptized, and about half of Cuban children received first communion. Education in Church-run schools was common for middle-class youth. Dominguez, 471.

28. Mateo Jover Marimon, "The Church," in *Revolutionary Change in Cuba*, ed. Carmelo Mesa-Lago (Pittsburgh: University of Pittsburgh Press, 1971), 404.

29. *Freedom at Issue*. March-April 1983.

30. John M. Kirk, "From Counterrevolution to Modus Vivendi: The Church in Cuba," in *Cuba: Twenty-Five Years of Revolution*, ed. Sandor Halebsky and John M. Kirk (New York: Praeger, 1985), 107.

31. In recent years, Castro has been very public in expressing his respect for Christians who agree with Marxists on the urgent need for social change benefiting the poor in Latin America. In view of the contribution of "liberation theology" to revolutionary activism in Central America, this is not surprising. It remains to be seen, however, whether this positive attitude toward revolutionary Christianity will translate into greater freedom for more traditional Christians inside Cuba.

32. Luis Salas, *Social Control and Deviance in Cuba* (New York: Praeger, 1979), 150–77; and Montaner, 143–47.

33. It has been alleged, though denied by Castro, that Cuba emptied mental hospitals and placed patients on boats for the United States during the 1980 Mariel crisis. The truth seems to be that local CDR units rounded up noninstitutionalized persons with mental defects for this purpose. See Margarite Garcia, "Last Days in Cuba—Personal Accounts of the Circumstances of the Exit," *Migration Today* 11, no. 4/5 (1983): 21.

34. Cuba's "concrete" rights are narrower than the economic and social rights in the UN Universal Declaration of Human Rights. (Cuba has not signed the International Covenant on Economic, Social, and Cultural Rights, or the International Covenant on Civil and Political Rights.) The Declaration requires that parents have the "prior right to choose the kind of education that shall be given to their children" (Article 26), but

this is incompatible with the Cuban view that education is determined by the government and party. The Declaration also includes the right to form trade unions (Article 23), but this conflicts with the practice in Cuba of preventing independent unionism. In 1983 more than a dozen Cubans who had discussed founding an independent trade union were tried and sentenced (reportedly, five of them originally to death) for "industrial sabotage." Their lawyers were subsequently arrested, apparently for reporting the death sentences to outside human rights agencies. See *Amnesty International Report 1984*, 147.

35. Carmelo Mesa-Lago, *The Economy of Socialist Cuba* (Albuquerque: University of New Mexico Press, 1981), 144; Claes Brundenius, *Revolutionary Cuba: The Challenge of Growth with Equity* (Boulder, Col.: Westview Press, 1984), 122; and Susan Eckstein, "Income Distribution and Consumption in Revolutionary Cuba: An Addendum to Brundenius," *Cuban Studies/Estudios Cubanos* 10, no. 1 (January 1980): 91–98.

36. Mesa-Lago, 164–65.

37. Mesa-Lago, 189.

38. By the end of the 1970s, unemployment had crept back up to an estimated 5.4 percent. Claes Brundenius, "Some Notes on the Development of the Cuban Labor Force, 1970–1980." *Cuban Studies/Estudios Cubanos* 13, no. 2 (Summer 1983), 69.

39. This continues an earlier Cuban tradition. In prerevolutionary Cuba, both whites and blacks subscribed to a value system that branded references to race as gravely impolite and open discussion of racial issues as offensive. Geoffrey Fox, "Race and Class in Contemporary Cuba," in *Cuban Communism*, ed. Irving L. Horowitz, 4th ed. (New Brunswick, N.J.: Transaction Books, 1981), 309–330.

40. Castro reported in 1986 that blacks and mulattoes made up 26.4 percent of the membership of the Central Committee of the Cuban Communist party. *Latin American Weekly Report*, February 14, 1986, 9. This is twice the percentage that obtained in the 1970s; see Montaner, 88. Cuba's 1981 census classified 34 percent of the population as either black or mulatto.

41. Lourdes Casal, "Race Relations in Contemporary Cuba," (Unpublished manuscript, 1979).

42. Jorge I. Dominguez, "Racial and Ethnic Relations in the Cuban Armed Forces: A Non-Topic," *Armed Forces and Society* 1, no. 2 (February 1976): 273–90.

43. See Dominguez, *Cuba: Order and Revolution*, 226–27 and appendix C.

44. Mesa-Lago, *The Economy of Socialist Cuba*, 117; and *Granma Weekly Review*, March 15, 1980, 2.

45. *Latin American Weekly Report*, February 14, 1986, 9.

46. Rabkin, 234.

47. Hugh S. Thomas, Georges A. Fauriol, and Juan Carlos Weiss, *The Cuban Revolution: Twenty-five Years Later* (Boulder, Col.: Westview Press, 1984), 29.

48. Carmelo Mesa-Lago, "Economic Policies and Growth," in *Revolutionary Change in Cuba*, ed. Carmelo Mesa-Lago (Pittsburgh: University of Pittsburgh Press, 1971), 280.

49. *World Development Report 1979* (Washington, D.C.: World Bank), Table 23, 170–71.

50. Sergio Roca, "Cuba Faces the 1980s," *Current History* 82, no. 481 (February 1983): 76.

51. Economic Commission for Latin America and the Caribbean, *Statistical Yearbook, 1984*, (Santiago, Chile: ECLA, 1984), 88.

52. Ricardo Leyva, "Health and Revolution in Cuba," in *Cuba in Revolution*, ed.

Rolando E. Bonachea and Nelson P. Valdes (Garden City, N.Y.: Doubleday, 1972), 473.

53. Roca, 76.

54. *Granma Weekly Review*, January 12, 1985, 8.

55. ECLA, *Statistical Yearbook, 1984*, 117; Leyva, 463.

56. See Antonio M. Gordon, Jr. "The Nurtiture of Cubans: Historical Perspective and Nutritional Analysis," *Cuban Studies/Estudios Cubanos* 13, no. 2 (Summer 1983):8.

57. It is sometimes claimed, citing a World Bank study conducted in 1950, that malnutrition was rampant in prerevolutionary Cuba, see Leyva, 459. This, however, misconstrues the report. The experts consulted by the Bank estimated that 30 to 40 percent of the city population and more than 60 percent of rural Cubans suffered from vitamin deficiencies, ranging from mild to severe. The experts did not, however, allege that protein-calorie malnutrition was a widespread problem. Instead, they attributed the undernourishment to the Cuban preference for milled, polished rice that is stripped of vitamins and minerals during processing. International Bank for Reconstruction and Development, *Report on Cuba* (Washington, D.C.: IBRD Special Publication, 1950), 441–50. For a fuller discussion, see Antonio M. Gordon, Jr., "The Nurtiture of Cubans: Historical Perspective and Nutritional Analysis," *Cuban Studies/Estudios Cubanos* 13, no. 2 (Summer 1983): 1–34; Howard Handelman, "Comment on the Nurtiture of Cubans," ibid., 35–37; and Howard Handelman, "Cuban Food Policy and Popular Nutritional Levels," ibid. 11/12 (July 1981-January 1982): 130.

58. Handelman, "Cuban Food Policy," 137.

59. Oscar Lewis, Ruth M. Lewis, and Susan M. Rigdon, eds., "Four Men: Living the Revolution" in *Living the Revolution: An Oral History of Contemporary Cuba* (Urbana: University of Illinois Press, 1977), 243–51; Lorrin Phillipson and Rafael Llerena, *Freedom Flights* (New York: Random House, 1980), 12, 21, 122, and 130.

60. Sergio Diaz Briquets and Lisandro Perez, "Fertility Decline in Cuba: A Socio-Economic Interpretation," *Population and Development Review* 8, no. 3 (September 1982): 525.

61. Ibid.

62. Ibid.

63. Sergio Roca, "Management of State Enterprises in Cuba: Some Preliminary Findings," in *Latin American and Caribbean Contemporary Record*, vol. 3, *1983–1984*, vol. 3, ed. Jack W. Hopkins (New York: Holmes and Meier, 1985), 228–30.

64. Economist Intelligence Unit, 1983 *Annual Supplement*, (London: The Unit, 1983), 22.

65. Lawrence M. Theriot, "Cuba Faces the Economic Realities of the 1980s" (Study prepared for the Joint Economic Committee of Congress, 97th Congress, 2d session, March 22, 1982), 16. These figures do not include the value of Soviet military assistance, which is substantial.

66. *Granma Weekly Review*, January 13, 1985, supplement, 13.

67. Patricia Weiss Fagen, "Reporting about Cuba from the United States" (Paper presented at National Cuba Conference, New York, November 1979).

68. As Hugh Thomas has written, "Costa Rica, an open pluralistic, nonmilitarized democracy in Central America is a notable example of the fact that a society need not be politically repressive to be socio-economically progressive." Thomas, Fauriol, and Weiss, 46. The experience of Venezuela and the Dominican Republic, although not as notable as that of Costa Rica, also illustrates the same point. Even Panama, although it

cannot be considered democratic, has achieved impressive social and economic progress without the near total curtailment of political and personal freedoms found in Cuba.

SUGGESTED READINGS

Casal, Lourdes, ed. *El Caso Padilla: Literatura y revolution en Cuba*. Documentos Miami: Nuevo Atlatida, 1971.

Dominguez, Jorge I. *Cuba: Order and Revolution*. Cambridge, Mass.: Harvard University, Belknap Press, 1978.

Echevarria, Roberto Gonzalez. "Criticism and Literature in Revolutionary Cuba." In *Cuba: Twenty-Five Years of Revolution 1959–1984*. Ed. Sandor Halebsky and John M. Kirk. New York: Praeger Publishers, 1985: 154–73.

Inter-American Commission on Human Rights. *Sixth Report on the Situation of Political Prisoners in Cuba*. Washington, D.C.: OAS General Secretariat, 1979.

Jacqeney, Theodore. "The Yellow Uniforms of Cuba." *Worldview* (January-February 1977): 4–10.

Mesa-Lago, Carmelo. *The Economy of Socialist Cuba*. Albuquerque: University of New Mexico Press, 1981.

Montaner, Carlos Alberto. *Secret Report on the Cuban Revolution*. Trans. Eduardo Zayas-Bazan. New Brunswick, N.J.: Transaction Books, 1981.

Neier, Aryeh. "Castro's Victims." *New York Review of Books* 33, no. 12 (July 17, 1986): 28–31.

El presidio politico en Cuba comunista. Miami: Instituto Internacional de Cooperacion y Solidaridad Cubana, 1983.

Thomas, Hugh S., Georges A. Fauriol, and Juan Carlos Weiss. *The Cuban Revolution: Twenty-Five Years Later*. Boulder, Col.: Westview Press, 1984.

Valladares, Armando. *Against all Hope: The Prison Memoirs of Armando Valladares*. Trans. Andrew Hurley, New York: Alfred A. Knopf, 1986.

6

EL SALVADOR

Liisa Lukkari North

In the late seventies, El Salvador achieved the grisly distinction of ranking among the worst violators of political human rights in the world. The situation deteriorated further in the 1980s in the midst of civil war. Of the approximately fifty thousand "war casualties" recorded between early 1980 and mid–1985, at least thirty-eight thousand (or 76 percent) were noncombatant civilians assassinated and often tortured by death squads and government security forces, or massacred in army sweeps of villages and indiscriminate bombings of civilians in guerrilla-controlled and contested areas.[1] The massive scale of the violence was further reflected in the floods of refugees pouring from the rural areas to the cities and from El Salvador to neighboring Central American countries, Mexico and the United States. By mid–1985, according to U.S. Agency for International Development (AID) estimates, up to 20 percent of the total population of 4.8 million may have been "displaced" within the country. External refugees are estimated to number more than five hundred thousand.[2] The combined figures on internal and external refugees add up to at least 25 percent of the total population.

The devastation was worsened by increasing amounts of military aid from the United States. This aid and the foreign policy of the Reagan administration reinforced the power of the armed and security forces responsible for most of the violence against the civilian population. Thus both national and international factors and power relationships were involved in the escalation and perpetuation of human rights violations.

While El Salvador's abysmal human rights record began to receive worldwide attention only in the late 1970s, the systematic use of force to maintain political control dates back to the sixteenth-century Spanish conquest. If the discussion is limited to more recent history, the socioeconomic and political processes tied to the organization and growth of the country's coffee export economy (1880s–1930s) represent a turning point for explaining the origins of the current situation. The rapid expansion of coffee production was accomplished through the political and cultural repression of the indigenous peasant majority whose community lands were expropriated by a landlord-merchant oligarchy which controlled the state. Subsequently, the diversification of primary export production and the promotion of import substituting industrialization following World War II were accompanied by further concentration of land and income in the context of rapid population growth.

Since both the prewar and postwar economic development models adopted by the Salvadorean ruling classes forced stagnant or deteriorating living standards on the majority of the population, and also involved the withdrawal of "rights" previously enjoyed (access to land ownership most important among them), they could be implemented only through sustained political repression. Consequently, the army and state security forces acquired an increasingly critical role in the maintenance of an exclusionary system which denied the great majority of the population access to the political process and the benefits of economic growth. In 1980, according to a study carried out by the United Nations Economic Commission for Latin America (UN-ECLA), 50.6 percent of the Salvadorean population could not satisfy its basic nutritional needs.[3]

This, in brief, was the context in which state violence exploded in the late seventies against a broad range of opposition groups seeking redistributive social and economic reforms. Following a description of gross human rights violations since 1979, the chapter will turn to analysis of the historical sequence outlined above in order to probe causes. It will conclude with an evaluation of the apparent decline in violations since the inauguration of Christian Democratic President José Napoleón Duarte in June 1984.

HUMAN RIGHTS VIOLATIONS IN EL SALVADOR—THE DIMENSIONS OF THE PROBLEM

There are four functioning human rights and documentation offices in San Salvador which collect information on violations. International human rights organizations such as the Americas Watch Committee (the principal source used here) and Amnesty International rely, in great part, on these local organizations for preparing their reports. The U.S. government, especially after the election of Republican President Ronald Reagan, repeatedly contradicted and also attempted to discredit the reports of the independent human rights organizations. A brief description of the local organizations and their modus operandi is therefore necessary not only to establish the degree of reliability of the data but also to identify the U.S. role in the exacerbation of human rights violations.

Two of the functioning human rights offices, the *Oficina de Tutela Legal del Arzobispado* (the Archdiocese Office for Legal Protection) and the *Socorro Jurídico Cristiano* (Christian Legal Aid Office), emerged from the reorganization of archdiocesan services by Bishop Rivera y Damas in May 1982. (Prior to this date, a single Archdiocese Legal Aid Office had collected data on human rights violations since 1975.) The Salvadorean Human Rights Commission, which is independent, has functioned since 1978. The Documentation and Information

Centre of the (Catholic) Central American University also collects and analyzes information on human rights violations as well as political developments in general, and publishes its findings in the magazine *Proceso*.

In addition, the Salvadorean government established a human rights commission in December 1982 and named the then director of the National Police, Col. Carlos Lopez Nuila, a member. Since the National Police as well as other state security forces had been implicated in gross human rights violations, and since the government had a strong interest in denying the severity of the problem, the reliability of the government commission's reporting has been highly questionable since its foundation.

The church-related and independent human rights organizations have functioned under severe threat and repression. Their staff members have been harassed, abducted, reported missing and assassinated, and their offices raided and bombed.[4] Since these organizations work in conditions of generalized repression, maintain offices only in the capital city (San Salvador), and adhere to strict data collection standards, it is highly likely that their reports actually underestimate the numbers of violations. For example, *Tutela Legal*'s figures on noncombatant deaths due to right-wing death squad violence and military operations are based on information provided by eyewitnesses and relatives who have traveled to its office to testify. Even widely publicized cases which have not been verified in this manner are not included in *Tutela Legal*'s statistics.

The figures cited in the reports prepared by Americas Watch together with the American Civil Liberties Union and the Lawyers Committee for International Human Rights come from *Tutela Legal*. The Americas Watch Committee also draws on information gathered by a broad range of public and private agencies, and fact-finding missions organized by the Committee as well as other institutions. In January 1983 alone, in addition to Americas Watch, the New York Bar Association, the Lawyers Committee for International Human Rights, the American Academy of Science, the American Public Health Association, and Faculty for Human Rights in El Salvador were involved in sponsoring missions to El Salvador. In short, the information on human rights violations comes from a variety of highly reputable sources which maintain strict standards of data collection and verification.

To review the yearly statistics, the toll from right-wing death squad violence and army massacres, as reported by Americas Watch, reached approximately 1,000 in 1979 and 9,000 in 1980, 12,501 in 1981, 5,399 in 1982, 5,142 in 1983, 2,881 in 1984, and 1,913 in 1985.[5] The 1979–1982 statistics refer primarily to death squad victims who included the archbishop of the country, assassinated while saying mass in March 1980. In 1981 violence shifted from the urban to the rural areas, making data collection and verification more difficult. Then in 1983 death squad activity began to decline while the armed forces adopted razed-earth tactics involving indiscriminate bombing and shelling of civilians together with massacres of people escaping from zones of conflict. The men and women who disappeared following abduction or arrest numbered approximately 300 in

1979; 602 between October 15, 1979, and March 1981; 535 in 1983; 195 in 1984; and 63 during the first six months of 1985. The numbers are astounding, especially when the small size of the total population—4.8 million—is considered. Moreover, as noted earlier, these figures in all likelihood underestimate the scale of the violence.

The judicial system—corrupted, threatened, and penetrated by extreme right-wing forces—failed to provide protection and prosecute violators. The opposition press was decimated between January 1980 and June 1981: "17 news offices and radio stations were bombed or machine gunned, twelve journalists killed, eleven by official security forces, and three disappeared."[6] The independent newspapers consequently ceased publication. The armed forces invaded and closed down the National University in 1980—twenty-five students were killed in the operation, and much of the physical plant was destroyed. The rights to assembly and association, historically restricted in El Salvador, were effectively eliminated by threat and repression. Union and peasant leaders, clergy and community organizers, and opposition political figures were specifically targeted for elimination. In sum, state security forces together with death squads waged a veritable war against the institutions of civil society.

In 1983 *Tutela Legal*, under criticism of bias in its reporting, began to systematically gather information on the murder of noncombatant civilians by guerrilla forces; sixty-seven cases were verified for that year, twenty-nine during the second half of 1984, and fifty-three during the first six months of 1985. While these acts must also be condemned, they hardly compared with the scale of the human rights violations perpetrated by right-wing death squads, the armed forces (army and air force), and the state security forces (National Police, Treasury Police, and National Guard). Moreover, the linkages and cooperation between death squads, state military and police organizations, the extreme right political leadership and sectors of the business community, have been corroborated by a large number of sources.[7] It is thus established that human rights violations were condoned, authored, and executed by individuals and groups occupying the highest levels of military, political, and economic power in El Salvador.

The U.S. government committed itself to supporting the Salvadorean regime during 1980, the last year of Carter's presidency. The Reagan administration increased military aid (from $9.59 million in 1980 to $35.5 million in 1981, $81 in 1982, $81.3 in 1983, $196.55 in 1984 and $146.25 in 1985), claiming that a fledgling centrist democracy was under attack by subversive forces sponsored by the Soviet Union via Cuba and Nicaragua. Attributing the human rights violations to a "terrorist left" and to right-wing extremists outside government control, the U.S. government denied the culpability of powerful sectors of the Salvadorean civilian and military elite. The Reagan administration in effect provided encouragement to those responsible for the violations by repeatedly contradicting the evidence presented by independent human rights organizations. This was done to justify the sharply increased military assistance before Congress and the American public.

In late 1981, under public pressure, the U.S. Congress passed legislation that made military aid to El Salvador conditional upon improvement in the status of human rights. The president was required to certify this in a report to Congress every 180 days from January 1982 to July 1983. The pattern of violence during the two years that the legislation was in effect proved that human rights violations could be controlled by El Salvador's military and civilian authorities. The number of cases regularly declined in the weeks immediately preceding the submission of the president's report, thereby permitting President Reagan to "certify" improvement and Congress to approve the continuation of military aid.

After the certification law expired and the last presidential report had been presented in July 1983, death squad violence exploded once again, reaching a scale which threatened the U.S. administration's capacity to sustain its Salvadorean and Central American policies. Apparently, the most reactionary and violent sectors among the ruling groups took President Reagan's declaration that he would veto any new Congressional initiatives to condition military aid on improvements in the human rights situation for a license to eliminate even their most moderate opponents. Fall 1983 death squad victims included Salvadoreans working for U.S.-sponsored organizations and programs. Meanwhile, no progress had been made in bringing to trial the assassins of four American churchwomen killed in December 1980, and two U.S. agrarian reform advisers killed in January 1981. In both cases, members of the state security forces were implicated, and U.S. public opinion was highly agitated.

In this context, the Reagan administration finally decided to criticize the Salvadorean regime in public. U.S. Ambassador Thomas Pickering, addressing a business group, called the death squads "fascists serving the communist cause" who killed "university professors, doctors, labor leaders, peasants and government workers." He added, "none of us can continue in the self-deluding belief that nothing is really known about the shadowy world of these individuals—and therefore nothing can be done."[8] Visits to San Salvador by Vice President George Bush and Under Secretary of Defense for Policy, Fred Iklé, followed. The American Embassy also presented to the Salvadorean government a list of military officers involved in death squads. Thus the U.S. government effectively admitted its knowledge of the networks linking the death squads to the military and civilian political elites, networks whose existence it had denied during the previous years.

During the following months, death squad activity declined sharply. *Tutela Legal* verified 185 death squad killings during the first six months of 1984 in comparison to 810 from January to June of 1983; disappearances fell to 139 in comparison to the 326 of the previous year's first six months. These figures, of course, were still enormous. Nevertheless, the noticeable decline prompted Americas Watch and the Lawyers Committee for International Human Rights to conclude: "Pressure from the United States is vital—far more important than we previously realized—in shaping human rights practices in El Salvador."[9]

Following the June inauguration of Christian Democrat José Napoleón Duarte as president, death squad activity continued to decline during the second half of 1984 although the numbers remained gruesome by any non-Salvadorean standard—thirty-nine assassinations and fifty-six disappearances were recorded by *Tutela Legal*. Simultaneously, deaths from indiscriminate aerial bombing, shelling of civilians in guerrilla-controlled areas and in conflict zones, and army ground sweeps claimed at least the 2,657 victims reported to *Tutela Legal* during the year.[10] Evidence on the use of anti-personnel weapons by the Salvadorean armed forces also kept mounting.[11] As in Vietnam, so in El Salvador, the military effort turned to "emptying the pond" from which the guerrillas drew their sustenance in the countryside. The new aggressive strategy and the escalation of the war against the guerrilla forces were made possible by increased U.S. economic and military aid (advisers, training, and weapons). For example, the size of the military's combat helicopter fleet almost tripled during the year following Duarte's election. Much of the $432 million economic aid package provided in 1985 contributed directly to the war effort.

As for the prosecution of human rights violators, only the National Guardsmen who had raped and murdered the four American churchwomen were eventually brought to trial and convicted. A few officers were sent into gilded exile at postings abroad or were reassigned within the country. None of the well-known death squad leaders or their collaborators in the officer corps was tried.[12] Consequently, there was no evidence to argue that the death squad networks were being dismantled. This, in turn, meant that the groups within the power structure which were responsible for the massive and brutal political repression of 1979 onwards remained intact.

THE CONSTITUTION OF AN EXCLUSIONARY POLITICAL SYSTEM: 1880s–1930s

The contemporary characteristics of El Salvador's exclusionary political system emerged from the social changes involved in the organization of the country's coffee export economy. As world markets for primary exports expanded rapidly during the second half of the nineteenth century, the landed and commercial-financial elites turned to coffee production. However, they faced an obstacle—much of the most suitable land for coffee cultivation, in the central and western highlands, was still retained by Indian peasant communities engaged in food production and with collective tenure rights dating back to the Spanish colonial regime. In a series of decrees beginning in 1881, communal forms of land ownership were legally abolished as inimical to individual entrepreneurship and socioeconomic progress. During the following fifty years, the indigenous peasantry was dispossessed of its lands by landowning, merchant, and banking families who formed the coffee export oligarchy and concentrated political power into the hands of a small group of interrelated families.

The estimates of the proportion of the country's land which passed from the peasantry to the coffee oligarchy during this period range from 25 to 45 percent.[13]

The proportion of the population affected was certainly higher since it was concentrated in the regions most suitable for coffee production.

The conversion of community lands into large, privately owned estates and of peasant community members into landless laborers and *minifundistas* (owners of plots too small to provide subsistence for a family) was accomplished through the employment of physical violence as well as legal chicanery. A series of bloodily repressed peasant rebellions punctuated the process. Before the most well known of these uprisings, which led to the *matanza*, or massacre, of 15,000–30,000 peasants in 1932, revolts took place in the coffee-growing region in 1872, 1875, 1880, 1885, and 1898. New rural police forces were established to evict peasants, repress unrest, and control the increasingly landless rural population. These police forces were consolidated in 1912 in the National Guard. The Guard, together with *patrullas cantonales* (consisting of army reserve units), carried out regular police functions, often at the direct request of landlords who could also call on "agricultural judges." These were officially appointed to "keep lists of all day workers, arrange for the capture of those who left an estate before fulfilling their [work] obligations, and to visit private estates regularly to check the need for workers."[14] Landless laborers had to carry a record of their work obligations and could be arrested for vagrancy.

A distinction between public and private power could hardly be made. The judicial system and state security forces functioned to buttress and expand the labor-repressive economy and the system of large, privately owned estates. The coffee export oligarchy, together with allied and often related urban commercial families, monopolized political power. (From 1913 to 1927 the presidency rotated among members of a single family, the Meléndez Quiñónez.)[15] Enrique A. Baloyra describes the political system succinctly: "The government was under the control of planters, and the control and execution of public policy were by and for them."[16]

Finally, it must be noted that communal land ownership was rooted in a distinct culture which, still in the late nineteenth century, was based on indigenous traditions. These were progressively destroyed since the elites regarded them as backward, even barbaric, remnants, incompatible with "progress" and modernization. Although the Salvadorean population today is quite homogeneously ethnically mixed, or mestizo, strong racial prejudices against the rural population as being close to Indian, and therefore inferior, remain.

As for social and economic progress, the surplus generated in the coffee export sector was largely retained by the landed and merchant groups (interrelated family networks) which formed the oligarchy. Some of the surplus filtered into the local urban economy but most was spent on luxury consumption and nonessential imports or invested abroad.[17] The extreme concentration of land and income within the oligarchy also blocked the diversification of the economy and the development of a strong domestic market, since most of the population was denied sufficient wage income or productive property to generate increasing demand for locally produced agricultural and industrial commodities. In short, the "vicious cycle" of underdevelopment characteristic of low-wage export economies was structured into place. El Salvador's ruling elite effectively closed off the possibility of a more egalitarian and democratic path to capitalist development that could have been based on widespread access to income-earning property in the rural areas.

Finally, dependence on international market forces increased as the country's patterns of economic growth and decline came to be determined by the volume and prices of coffee exports. These reached approximately 75 percent of the value of all exports by the turn of the century and hit their peak of 96 percent in 1933. Moreover, the increasing concentration of the most fertile land in export production eventually led to declines in domestic food production together with sharp price increases and, beginning in the 1920s, to dependence on food imports.[18]

In sum, the contemporary dominance of police and military institutions within the Salvadorean state dates to the formative years of the coffee export economy. Widespread and ruthless coercion was employed to dispossess the peasantry and convert it into a servile labor force. Coercion continued to play a key role in controlling the labor force at the service of a narrow elite which considered itself the carrier of progress and viewed the rural population as hopelessly backward if not racially inferior. It hardly needs stating that the rights to life, humane treatment, personal liberty, due process and fair trial, assembly and association, were systematically denied to the great majority of the population.

The system's foundation on coercion was demonstrated once again in the social and economic crisis provoked by the Great Depression. As the volume of coffee exports plummeted from 58.5 to 39.5 million kilograms between 1930 and 1932, the average price per quintal dropped by half,[19] and local stocks grew, coffee growers decided in 1931 to cut their losses by not harvesting the crop at a moment when economic activity was already sharply depressed. Unemployment increased to over 40 percent of the adult male population in the rural areas and to over 15 percent in the cities while wages were also reduced.[20] Without access to land or work, the peasantry of the coffee-growing region rebelled in early 1932 to regain possession of its lands.

The recently formed and small Communist party of El Salvador was held responsible for the uprising. Its leader and his close collaborators, who had been arrested prior to the revolt, were executed following it; others were jailed or went into exile. But it was in the coffee-growing rural areas that state repression took on the dimensions of a racial war. From 15,000 to 30,000 peasants were massacred *after* order had been restored. "All those who were carrying machetes" or "of a strongly Indian cast of features" and wearing typical peasant costumes were considered "guilty."[21] In an article published by a local newspaper, a landowner wrote: "There was not an Indian who was not afflicted with devastating communism."[22] Another commentator remarked: "We'd like this race of the plague to be exterminated . . . they did it right in North America, having done with them by shooting them in the first place before they could impede the progress of the nation.''[23]

This *matanza* was a formative event in El Salvador's history. Confronted with widespread popular unrest, the ruling elite chose repression rather than social, political, and economic reforms. Land reform, especially, became a taboo issue. While a "dictatorship of notables"[24] which maintained at least a facade of democracy in the urban areas had ruled the country until 1931, military dictatorship (a co-government of the oligarchy with the heads of the military institutions created earlier in the century) was installed with the Depression.

MODERNIZATION WITHOUT REFORM: 1940s–1970s

Unlike the regressive Depression dictatorship of General Hernández Martínez (1931–1944), the post–World War II military regimes presented themselves as "modernizers" and "developmentalists" favoring "moderate reforms" which were to be made possible by economic growth. Civilian technocrats were incorporated into state agencies to formulate policies for economic and social transformation. Those policies, despite some variations in the political orientation of the different military governments, were consistently geared toward agricultural export diversification (to reduce the dependence on coffee) and import-substituting industrialization.

The economic growth and diversification policies were quite successful. Until the mid–1970s, the Salvadorean economy achieved respectable per capita growth rates (3.6 percent per annum between 1960 and 1965, 0.8 between 1965 and 1970, and 2.4 between 1970 and 1975, at market prices).[25] The country still remained in the group of poorest Third World countries with a per capita gross national product (GNP) of $340 in 1972, before the economy began to experience difficulties. Sugar and cotton became important export crops, and the share of manufactures in total exports increased from 5.6 percent in 1960 to 28.7 percent in 1970 with most of the latter sold to the Central American Common Market member countries. Urbanization accelerated—34 percent of the population lived in cities of 20,000 or more by 1971, in contrast to 21 percent in 1931 and 26 percent in 1950. A middle class emerged in the cities which, together with the upper classes, made up 13.6 percent of the population in 1970 while the working class engaged in manufacturing constituted 11.1 percent.[26]

The distribution of the benefits obtained from growth, however, was highly inegalitarian. Around 1980, 50.6 percent of the population subsisted in a state of "extreme poverty," defined by UN-ECLA as a situation in which income is not sufficient "to pay for the minimum shopping-basket of food considered necessary to meet their biological nutritional requirements."[27] Another 17.5 percent could not satisfy their "basic needs" (defined as including housing, clothing, and basic services). In the same year, the poorest 20 percent of the population with an average income of U.S. $46.5 (at 1970 prices), received 2.0

percent of national income, while the richest 20 percent with an average income of $1,535.5 received 66 percent.[28] The average income of the richest 20 percent was thirty-three times the average income of the poorest 20 percent.

Malnutrition reached shocking levels. Between 1971 and 1975, 48.5 percent of Salvadorean children under five were estimated to suffer from mild malnutrition (requiring more and/or better quality food), 22.9 percent from moderate malnutrition (needing medical attention), and 3.1 percent from severe malnutrition (requiring hospitalization for recovery). Moreover, trend data indicated deterioration with reference to 1965.[29]

While at least a significant minority of the urban population did improve its living standards, conditions in the rural areas became critical. In the prosperous years of the early 1970s, 58.3 percent of the agricultural labor force, which constituted 60 percent of the total, was either unemployed or underemployed.[30] Between 1961 and 1975 the proportion of rural families without land or with access to less than one hectare moved up from 53.4 to 75 percent.[31] As for the distribution of public expenditure, only 15 percent of the country's schoolteachers served in the rural areas where most of the 40 percent illiterate population lived; around 1970, 45.4 percent of the economically active population had received no formal education, and another 24.7 percent had completed only one to three years of schooling.[32] In 1977 only 36.8 percent of the rural population had access to piped water in contrast to 82.4 percent in urban centers.[33] Medical services were close to nonexistent in the countryside—67 percent of the country's doctors practiced in the capital city. "Extreme poverty" afflicted 44.5 percent of urban residents, while another 13.1 percent could not satisfy "basic needs"; as socially unacceptable as this was, conditions in the rural areas were considerably worse with 55.4 percent in a state of "extreme poverty" and another 21.0 incapable of satisfying "basic needs."[34]

It is not necessary to belabor these statistics. The failure of the economic growth and modernization policies implemented by El Salvador's ruling elites to satisfy the "basic needs" of approximately 70 percent of the population is only too evident. Although a socioeconomic system's capacity to ensure a "full belly" and minimally satisfactory living conditions does not justify violation of civil and political human rights,[35] adequate nutrition is certainly a precondition to their enjoyment.

The reasons for the dismal social consequences of economic growth in El Salvador deserve closer examination. In general terms, they lie in economic policies designed only to maximize growth, coupled with political repression to prevent the poor from organizing to obtain a share of the benefits of growth.

To begin with the rural areas, the post–World War II diversification of agricultural export production involved yet another phase of increasing land concentration—the displacement of tenant farmers and the expropriation of small producers who were primarily engaged in food crop cultivation.[36] The expansion of cotton production took place on large estates which were established in the "one remaining area of fertile coast land into which formerly the dispossessed and landless cultivators of the interior were able to move."[37] Sugar export production was similarly concentrated on large estates. Both crops occupied land previously dedicated to food crop cultivation and both adopted mechanized capital-intensive methods of production. In contrast to food agriculture, their year-round labor requirements were therefore low, but seasonal needs for harvesting were high. Consequently, large-scale commercial farmers developed a vested interest in the existence of a large unemployed and underemployed rural population to provide cheap labor during the short and critical picking season. Thus, both land for food production and stable work opportunities were increasingly denied to the rural population. Income from women's handicraft production—a traditional supplement to agricultural earnings in the rural areas—also declined in the face of competition from manufactured goods.[38]

The economic irrationality as well as the social inequity of El Salvador's agricultural system deserves a brief comment. While large estates were dedicated to the production of exports whose prices fluctuated sharply in world markets, half of the country's total goods purchased in 1972 consisted of wheat, milk, vegetables, and fruits[39] whose equivalents could have been produced more cheaply locally.

This rural socioeconomic system continued to be maintained through coercion. A separate legal code (the Ley Agraria) "stipulated that National Guard members keep order on private estates and that law enforcement officials be appointed by the landowners themselves."[40] Vagrancy continued to be a punishable offense and union organization was proscribed. Tenants could be summarily evicted and the local mayor and police were instructed by law to destroy the houses of "malefactors." In the late 1960s, yet another element was added to the system of repression in the countryside. A paramilitary civilian vigilante network, OR-DEN, was established under the leadership of a National Guard director to defend "democracy" and to identify and punish "communists"—defined in practice as anyone who protested against the system.[41] It is clear that a situation approximating serfdom existed in the rural areas and that no civil or political rights were respected.

To turn to the urban sector, the average annual growth rate of manufacturing industry climbed to over 5 percent in the 1950s, peaked at 10.7 percent during 1960–1965, averaged 5.7 percent during 1965–1975, with negative growth (−0.6 percent) during 1975–1980.[42] Much of the output, as indicated earlier, was sold in the Central American Common Market. The capital-intensive forms of production chosen by domestic and foreign investors (the latter, primarily U.S.-based transnational corporations)[43] did not permit parallel increases in industrial employment. According to UN-ECLA statistics, the proportion of workers in the total labor force engaged in manufacturing actually declined from 13.1 to 11.1 percent during the period of rapid growth between 1960 and 1970. Moreover, the industrial sector was heavily dependent on imported raw materials, intermediates, and capital goods, thus increasing the country's dependence on foreign markets without inducing ancillary local economic activity. The proportion of the labor force employed in basic services increased from a mere 0.2 percent in 1950 to only 0.4 percent twenty years later. A large unemployed and underemployed population, swelled by migrants escaping the misery and repression of the countryside, pushed down the wages of the lucky who obtained stable work.

In contrast to the daily repression in the countryside, a restricted but nevertheless real political opening took place in the cities during the "prosperous" 1960s. Industrial workers, teachers, public and private employees organized unions. The Christian Democratic party (founded in 1960) contested elections with a mildly reformist program and even won control of municipal governments in addition to representation in Congress. Some political activity also began to spill over into the countryside in the late sixties, importantly so through the aegis of a radicalized and activist Catholic clergy.[44] Following El Salvador's brief border war with Honduras in 1969, debate on the need for reform, including for the first time demands for land redistribution, picked up as some 130,000 of the estimated 300,000 Salvadoreans (mostly peasants) who had migrated to Honduras were forced to return.[45]

Reformist political activity reached a peak during the 1972 presidential elections. By all accounts, they were won by the opposition coalition of the Christian Democratic party headed by José Napoleón Duarte (the presidential candidate), and a smaller socialist party headed by Guillermo Ungo (the vice presidential candidate). The military government, however, declared its own choice, an army colonel, the victor. An attempted coup in favor of Duarte was followed by his arrest, torture, and exile. During the following years, the Christian Democratic party became a principal target of repression, and as the electoral route to reform was closed off, a revolutionary opposition emerged during the 1970s. In 1979, when the country was heading rapidly toward civil war, this opposition was composed of four relatively small guerrilla groups backed by loosely forged and shifting coalitions of popular organizations and unions. In this context, human rights violations—arbitrary arrests, torture, disappearances, assassinations—escalated dramatically in the cities as well as the rural areas. Radical clergy and lay religious activists involved in community self-help projects were among the principal targets.[46]

In summary, during the post–World War II modernization drive, the majorities in the urban as well as the rural sectors were structurally blocked from sharing in the benefits of economic growth. With the exception of the brief interlude of restricted democracy extending from the early sixties to the early seventies, systematic political repression prevented them from organizing or influencing state policy-making in any meaningful way. The economic policies implemented by the civilian-military ruling elite (family networks of landowners, financiers, merchants and industrialists, and the higher ranks of the officer corps) did not generate employment or opportunities for self-employment. Compensatory welfare policies were never seriously considered, much less implemented. The elites did not even tax themselves. Coffee producers, for example, were exempt from income taxes; while they did pay a modest export tax, it was not progressive and consequently penalized small producers.

Redistributive policies which would have increased popular purchasing power and led to domestic market development, employment generation, and improvements in social conditions were blocked by the power structure inherited from the previous historical period. People who could not satisfy their basic needs (some 70 percent of the population) could not be expected to become consumers of the factory production encouraged by government policy. Thus the industrial growth rate, predictably, was going to stagnate in a market reduced to, at most, 30 percent of the population. The growth of the regional Common Market was also limited by a similar pattern of extreme income concentration among its members.[47] It bears repeating that, as bad as the social conditions were in the urban areas, rural conditions were considerably worse. The average nonagricultural income was 2.9 times the average in agriculture in the late sixties. The lowest 20 percent of income earners were all semioccupied in agriculture and 87.9 percent of rural income units were below the median income in contrast to 12.1 percent in the cities.[48] Moreover, public investment in education and basic services was concentrated in the urban sector.

A redistributive effort implied both a profound transformation of the agricultural sector (land reform, incentives for food production, labor-intensive public works, etc.) and a redirection of public investment toward rural areas together with tax reform. Such policies ran against the interests of the large landholders and merchants involved in export crop production. They also ran against the interests of industrialists who manufactured what in the Salvadorean context were luxury and semiluxury goods for a restricted urban market and, certainly not least, the officers of the armed and security forces who had translated their control of a significant portion of the public budget into private undertakings. It was this coalition of interests which blocked social and economic reform by maintaining a closed and repressive political system. Thus the violation of civil and political rights formed an integral part of the maintenance of an economic system which denied minimally satisfactory living conditions to the majority of the population. The sources of the unspeakable savagery and indiscriminate character of the repression during the last few years call for social-psychological as well as political-economic analysis. This cannot be undertaken here but racism suggests itself as an element.

RECENT DEVELOPMENTS

As noted earlier, death squad activity declined considerably after the ascension of Christian Democratic leader José Napoleón Duarte to the presidency in June 1984. A sector of his party had split in 1980 to join the revolutionary opposition—the Frente Democrático Revolucionario (FDR) headed by Duarte's former running mate in the 1972 elections, Guillermo Ungo. Duarte, however, returned to El Salvador to collaborate with the military, arguing that his party and his presence within the government would act as a moderating force. In fact, the numbers of civilian victims peaked while Duarte was first member and then titular head of the military-civilian junta which governed the country from early 1980 to early 1982. A right-wing coalition won the elections held in 1982. The question therefore arises whether Duarte's election in 1984 and his party's subsequent victory in congressional elections held in 1985 represented an effective ascendancy of moderate civilian forces in the power structure of the country and the beginning of a long-term trend toward improvement in respect for social, economic, and political human rights.

Several sets of factors cautioned against optimism. First, with reference to the military situation, the civil war continued at a more destructive level with the adoption of razed-earth tactics and the introduction of sophisticated new weaponry, including helicopter gunships, in late 1984. Ironically, the improved image created by Duarte's election and the decline in urban violence made the U.S. Congress sympathetic to increasing military aid. Consequently, the military and security institutions which, together with the death squads, were responsible for torturing, assassinating, and massacring more than 38,000 civilians between 1979 and mid–1985, were strengthened. Duarte argued that he could transform the orientation of the armed forces and pointed to the reduction of indiscriminate violence in the cities. However, the New York Times reported in July 1985 that a military officer who had played an important role in the events since 1979 stated that the military accepted the Duarte government only because it had " 'demoralized' the guerrillas while making it easier to get outside military assistance."[49] Also, no officers involved in the gross human rights abuses of the previous years were brought to trial. In early 1986 researchers at the Central American University in San Salvador concluded that the military was becoming "increasingly autonomous" and was "likely to exercise even greater direct control over government policy."[50]

Second, the much publicized elections of 1982, 1984, and 1985 were held only among political groups on one side of a civil war. The representative political force of the poor and marginal, the FDR, was not allowed to participate. To be sure, President Duarte held a "dialogue" with the Farabundo Martí National Liberation Front (FMLN)—the guerrilla arm of the FDR—in the fall of 1984. However, the Salvadorean business elite and armed forces expressed their "opposition to the very idea of peace talks"[51] and the "dialogue" was not continued in 1985. Fortified by increasing military aid from the United States, the army was convinced that it could "grind down the guerrillas once and for all. To maintain morale, they want[ed] no truly serious discussions on the mechanics of peace, or the possibility of a cease fire."[52] Without FDR-FMLN participation in the national political and economic policy-making process, the prospects for long-term improvement in respect for political, social and economic rights of the majorities remained extremely dim.

Third, the U.S. government was committed to a military victory and to preserving the basic contours of the country's traditional socioeconomic and political power structures.

The continuation of the war meant more razed-earth tactics, more refugees, and the impossibility of beginning social and economic reconstruction. The fact that death squads were not dismantled and that officers linked to them continued in active service meant that a resurgence of violence against civilians could be expected. Finally, it must be noted that despite the decline in death squad activity during Duarte's first eighteen months in office, the frequency of gross violations remained at an unacceptable level.

NOTES

1. The data on assassinations, torture, massacres, and indiscriminate bombings is available in Americas Watch Committee and the American Civil Liberties Union, *Report on Human Rights in El Salvador* (New York: Vintage Books, January 1982), *Second Supplement to the Report on Human Rights in El Salvador* (Washington, D.C.: Center for National Security Studies, January 20, 1983), *Third Supplement to the Report on Human Rights in El Salvador* (Washington, D.C.: Center for National Security Studies, July 19, 1983), and *As Bad As Ever: A Report on Human Rights in El Salvador, Fourth Supplement* (Washington, D.C.: Center for National Security Studies, January 31, 1984); Americas Watch and Lawyers Committee for International Human Rights, *Free Fire: A Report on Human Rights in El Salvador, Fifth Supplement* (Washington, D.C.: Americas Watch Committee, August 1984), and *El Salvador's Other Victims: The War on the Displaced* (April 1984); Americas Watch, *Draining the Sea . . . Sixth Supplement to the Report on Human Rights in El Salvador* (Washington, D.C.: Americas Watch Committee, March, 1985), and *The Continuing Terror: Seventh Supplement to the Report on Human Rights in El Salvador* (September, 1985). See also various issues of *Update Latin America* and special reports published by the Washington Office on Latin America (WOLA).

2. In addition to the Americas Watch reports noted, see Latin American Working Group, *LAWG Letter—Central American Refugees: The Crisis and the Context* (Toronto) 8, no. 1 (December 1982); and *New York Times* (January 23, 1983).

3. ECLA Mexico City Office, "The Crisis in Central America: Its Origins, Scope and Consequences," *CEPAL Review* 22 (April 1984): 53–80.

4. See, for example, Washington Office on Latin America (WOLA), *Common Questions: El Salvador and Certification* (Washington, D.C.: WOLA, January 1983), p. 6, in addition to the Americas Watch reports; these regularly include a section on the suppression of human rights groups.

5. These and the following figures are drawn from the reports cited in note 1, and compiled by *Tutela Legal*. Figures from other nongovernment sources are higher. For example, in 1982, *Socorro Jurídico* reported 5,967 deaths rather than the 5,399 verified by *Tutela Legal* on the basis of eyewitness and/or relatives' reports.

6. Americas Watch and American Civil Liberties Union, *Report* (January 1982), xxxix.

7. See, for example, Raymond Bonner, *Weakness and Deceit: U.S. Policy and El Salvador* (New York: Times Books, 1984), especially chaps. 1, 4, and 9; the series of articles by Laurie Becklund and Graig Pyes in the *Los Angeles Times* and the *Albuquerque*

Journal, beginning December 18, 1983; WOLA, *An El Salvador Chronology: Death Squads as a Political Tool* (Washington, D.C.: WOLA, February 1984).

8. "Another Warning to the Death Squads," *Newsweek* (December 5, 1983); see also "Attacking the Death Squads," *Newsweek* (January 16, 1984).

9. Americas Watch and Lawyers Committee, *Free Fire*, 3.

10. In addition to the Americas Watch reports, see Inter-Church Committee on Human Rights in Latin America (ICCHRLA), *Newsletter* (Toronto, Fall 1984): 2–3.

11. Concerning the use of napalm, see the *New York Times* (September 30, 1984); concerning the military situation, in general see the *Strategic Survey*, published yearly by the International Institute for Strategic Studies, London.

12. Shirley Christian, "Has Salvador's Army Done an About Face?" *New York Times* (July 28, 1985).

13. David Browning, *El Salvador: Landscape and Society* (Oxford: Clarendon Press, 1971), and Rafael Menjívar Larin, *El Salvador: El Eslabón Mas Pequeño* (San José: EDUCA, 1980).

14. Browning, 217.

15. For a discussion of this "exclusionary civilian dictatorship," see Rafael Guidos Vejar, *El ascenso del militarismo en El Salvador* (San Salvador: UCA Editores, 1980).

16. Enrique A. Baloyra, "Reactionary Despotism in El Salvador," in *Trouble in Our Backyard*, ed. Martin Diskin (New York: Pantheon Books, 1983), 103–104.

17. Guidos Vejar.

18. William H. Durham, *Scarcity and Survival in Central America* (Stanford: Stanford University Press, 1979), 36; and Guidos Vejar, 84–85.

19. Guidos Vejar, 102.

20. Menjívar, 55.

21. Thomas P. Anderson, *Matanza: El Salvador's Communist Revolt of 1932* (Lincoln: University of Nebraska, 1971), 25.

22. Cited by Anderson, 17.

23. Cited by Anderson, 17.

24. Baloyra, "Reactionary Despotism," 103.

25. Economic Commission for Latin America (ECLA), *Statistical Yearbook for Latin America, 1983* (Santiago: UN-ECLA, June 1984), 121.

26. ECLA, *Statistical Yearbook for Latin America, 1979* (Santiago: UN-ECLA, December 1980), 18, 22.

27. ECLA, "The Crisis in Central America," 61.

28. Ibid., 60.

29. Inter-American Development Bank (IADB), *Economic and Social Progress in Latin America: Annual Report* (Washington, D.C.: IADB, 1973), 138.

30. Max Alberto Soto, "The Labor Markets in Central America," in *Employment and Labor Force in Latin America: A Review at National and Regional Levels*, ed. Juan J. Buttari (Washington, D.C.: Organization of American States, 1979), 49–50.

31. Carlos Samaniego, "Movimiento campesino o lucha del proletariado rural en El Salvador?" *Revista Mexicana de Sociología* 42, no. 2 (April-June 1980); 661.

32. ECLA, *Statistical Yearbook* (June 1984), 113.

33. Ibid., 117.

34. ECLA, "The Crisis in Central America," 62.

35. See Rhoda Howard, "The Full-Belly Thesis: Should Economic Rights Take Prior-

ity Over Civil and Political Rights? Evidence from Sub-Saharan Africa," *Human Rights Quarterly* 5, no. 4 (Fall 1983): 467–490.

36. See Durham, *Scarcity and Survival*, 30–62 passim and graph, 45.

37. Browning, *El Salvador*, 235.

38. Alastair White, *El Salvador* (New York: Praeger Publishers, 1973), 194.

39. IADB, *Economic and Social Progress*, 207.

40. Americas Watch and American Civil Liberties Union, *As Bad As Ever* (January 1984), 7. See also White, *El Salvador*, 208–209.

41. White, *El Salvador*, 207; Stephen Webre, *José Napoleón Duarte and the Christian Democratic Party in Salvadoran Politics, 1960–1972* (Baton Rouge: Louisiana State University Press, 1979), 162.

42. ECLA, *Statistical Yearbook* (June 1984), 141.

43. See Robert Armstrong and Janet Shenk, *El Salvador: The Face of Revolution* (Boston: South End Press, 1982).

44. Space does not permit an analysis of the transformations within the Catholic Church. The reader should consult Tommie Sue Montgomery, *Revolution in El Salvador: Origins and Evolution* (Boulder, Col.: Westview Press, 1982), 97–117; and Penny Lernoux, *Cry of the People* (New York: Penguin Books, 1982).

45. See Durham, *Scarcity and Survival*, for a discussion of the origins and consequences of the war, which was dubbed by journalists "The Soccer War" since it took place immediately after three hotly contested soccer games in the qualifying rounds for the 1969 World Cup.

46. For a detailed discussion of the political developments described here, see Montgomery, *Revolution*.

47. For a discussion of the socioeconomic consequences of growth first or redistribution first policies, see Jack Donnelly, "Human Rights and Development: Complementary or Competing Concerns?" *World Politics* 36, no. 2 (January 1984): 255–283.

48. Alan Gilbert, *Latin American Development: A Geographical Perspective* (Middlesex: Penguin Books Ltd., 1974), 129.

49. Christian, "Has Salvador's Army Done an About Face?"

50. "Duarte: Prisoner of War," *NACLA Report on the Americas* 20, no. 1 (January-March 1986); 20.

51. *Globe and Mail* (November 29, 1984). "Politics Mar Peace Hopes in El Salvador."

52. Ibid.

SUGGESTED READINGS

Americas Watch Committee and the American Civil Liberties Union. *Report on Human Rights in El Salvador*. New York: Vintage Books, 1982.

Baloyra, Enrique. *El Salvador in Transition*. Chapel Hill: University of North Carolina Press, 1982.

Bonner, Raymond. *Weakness and Deceit: U.S. Policy in El Salvador*. New York: Times Books, 1984.

Brown, Cynthia, ed. *With Friends Like These. The Americas Watch Report on Human Rights and U.S. Policy in Latin America*. New York: Pantheon Books, 1985.

Donnelly, Jack. "Human Rights and Development: Complementary or Competing Concerns?" *World Politics* 36 (January 1984); 255–83.

Farer, Tom J. "Human Rights and Human Wrongs: Is the Liberal Model Sufficient?" *Human Rights Quarterly* 7 (May 1985): 189–204.

Franco, Jean. "Death Camp Confessions and Resistance to Violence in Latin America." *Socialism and Democracy* (Spring-Summer 1986): 5–17.

Fuentes, Carlos. *Latin America at War with the Past.* Montreal: CBC Enterprises, 1985.

Montgomery, Tommie Sue. *Revolution in El Salvador: Origins and Evolution.* Boulder, Col.: Westview Press, 1982.

North, Liisa. *Bitter Grounds: Roots of Revolt in El Salvador.* 2d ed. Toronto: Between The Lines, 1985.

Shue, Henry. *Basic Rights: Subsistence, Affluence, and U.S. Foreign Policy.* Princeton: Princeton University Press, 1980.

7

INDIA

Barnett R. Rubin

Although today India is a sovereign nation-state, juridically equal to the other members of the United Nations, it is also the home of one of the world's handful of great civilizations. Besides the Republic of India, historic India includes the nations of Pakistan, Bangladesh, Nepal, Bhutan, and at least parts of Afghanistan. The Republic of India alone, with more people than Latin America and Africa combined, and with more languages in official use than all the members of NATO, contains regions larger than most nations. These regions possess distinct social systems and different human rights practices, despite their incorporation into a common administrative and legal framework.

This diversity has deep roots in Indian history and ecology. The heart of the subcontinent is the Indo-Gangetic plain of the north, watered by the immense snow-fed river systems of Punjab-Indus and Ganges-Brahmaputra. Surrounding the plateaus, hills, and forests south of these plains are the tropical coasts of Malabar and Madras. Across the North, from the Khyber pass in the West across the peaks of the Himalayas to the remote jungles of upper Burma, the world's highest mountains largely cut off the region from land communications. Only through the passes of the Northwest did the invaders continually stream from Central Asia, and they, as well as the two great empires that came by sea—the Arabs and the British—brought new races and religions, which continually mixed with the indigenous to form the spectrum of syncretisms that is Indian civilization.

CULTURAL AND HISTORICAL BACKGROUND

So continual has the process of syncretism and cultural transformation been, and so great has the spectrum been at any one time, that one cannot easily speak of "Indian culture" or "Indian values" in general. "Indian culture" owed its beginning to the synthesis that developed when the nomads speaking an Indo-Aryan language (Sanskrit), and worshipping a pantheon akin to that of the ancient

Hellenes, conquered a sedentary population, apparently of Dravidian language (linked to the modern languages of South India such as Tamil), that venerated the cow and the lingam (phallus). Out of this synthesis developed the social arrangements known as the caste system and the vast range of beliefs and practices grouped together, initially by outside observers, as "Hinduism." The canons of Hinduism as interpreted by the priestly stratum, the Brahmans, sanctify inequality as institutionalized in caste.[1]

According to the social teaching of the classic Brahmanical texts, especially the *Laws of Manu*, society is based on legitimate human inequality. Each person is first and foremost a member of one of the four *varnas*, or strata (literally, "colors"); the Brahmans (priests), Kshatriyas (warrior-rulers), Vaishyas (cultivators and traders), and Shudras (servants of the other three "twice-born" strata). Membership in such a stratum derives primarily from birth, and confers a particular set of duties—the *dharma*, or code for conduct, of a particular stratum. This doctrine is known in Sanskrit as the *varnashrama dharma*.

These strata form a moral hierarchy continuous with the natural world. Each living physical being is essentially a soul that is reborn continually. The level of being into which the soul is reincarnated depends on the objective moral law of *karma*, according to which the better one fulfills one's *dharma* in this life, the higher one will be born in the next life. The role of the just ruler is both to protect *varnashrama dharma* by insuring that each stratum carries out its role, and to carry out his own *dharma* by expanding his kingdom.

At the popular level, however, "Hinduism" and the "caste system" have borne at most a family resemblance to the teachings of the Brahmans. Furthermore, some of the spiritual teachings of Brahmanical philosophy, in particular the doctrine that each soul could potentially enter into unity with the absolute, contained the seeds of heterodoxical, egalitarian movements.

Finally, major variants of Indian civilization, including parts of "Hinduism," have been indelibly marked by Islam.[2] Some popular religious leaders, whether Muslim pirs or Hindu or Sikh gurus, have preached the equality of men and women and the unity of all faiths, and their followers have been from all origins. Mahatma Gandhi drew on this tradition.

Within Indian society, even among "Hindus," the *varnashrama dharma* is thus but one of several sources of legitimacy. The actual "caste" system varies by region and is far more complex than the fourfold schema of the laws of Manu. The actual unit of the caste system is the *jati*, an endogamous unit all of whose members speak the same language and have a traditional occupation, which they may or may not practice. A single village may have twenty or thirty *jatis*. Within each village or region, it is clear which *jatis* are ranked high and which low, but the middle area may be unclear. People believe that *jatis* either belong to one of the four *varnas* or do not; in the latter case they are "untouchables" or "outcastes." Membership in a *varna* is a political claim; *jatis* can try to change their status by claiming membership in a higher *varna* and adopting an appropriate *dharma*. *Jatis* also join coalitions of similar *jatis* for political purposes.[3]

Modified forms of the caste system also exist among the 11 percent of India's population who are Muslims and among other minorities. The tribal population, largely in the hills, mountains, and forests, is outside the caste system.

The institutionalized inequality of caste is obviously inimical to human rights, but respect for human rights in India need not require the abolition of caste *per se*. Caste, especially when articulated with class, is also a basis for political mobilization, even empowerment, of disadvantaged groups, who use the group identities inherent in the system as resources to challenge its hierarchy. The plurality of *dharma* can also legitimate rights to social and political pluralism. Probably the biggest obstacle to human rights is not caste itself but untouchability, which, while outlawed, is still widely practiced and relegates a whole section of the community to "unclean" status.[4]

The basic unit of membership in a *jati* is not so much the individual as the patriarchal, patrilineal family (although at least one group of *jatis*, the Nayyars of Kerala, are matrilineal). As in other pre-modern societies, women belong first to their fathers and then to their husbands. Women have a somewhat higher status in Hinduism than in some cultures, as their participation is required in some rituals (not only "women's" rituals) and some variants place great importance on *shakti*, or female power, as incarnated in goddesses such as Kali and Durga. Orthodox teachings of all religions firmly emphasize woman's subordinate role within the family and the importance to male honor of defending female chastity, but there are also cults and traditionally recognized "deviant" groups of women, such as temple dancers, as well as some mystic (Tantric) sexual practices, that provide elements on which indigenous feminism can draw.[5]

The ecological and cultural diversity of India has been reflected in the weakness of state formation, especially as compared with the other great Asian civilization, China. Accumulation of power has occurred at roughly three levels in India: village, regional kingdom, and empire. The life of the villages has been relatively independent of the higher levels of state formation. Villages were patriarchal, oligarchical republics run by the locally dominant castes, whose relations to states have been mainly collective and external. Direct taxes, for instance, as in most pre-capitalist states, were levied on the village as a whole through the village's authorities.

The complex dynamics of regional kingdom and continental empire have defined much of the large-scale political changes of Indian history.[6] Empires often emerged from the expansion of regional kingdoms, and they fell as they disintegrated into such kingdoms. Indian empires were ruled by pluralistic, multiethnic elites created from alliances of regional rulers. Imperial officers, on the other hand, tried to transform themselves into independent rulers. The Indian subcontinent thus underwent cycles of imperial rule and dissolution into regional kingships, punctuated by invasions from Central Asia. Today the Republic of

India continues the imperial tradition, and the revolts of culturally distinct regions resemble processes that threatened imperial unity in the past; Sikh leaders, for instance, challenged the centralizing rule of the "throne of Delhi" under the Mughal Aurangzeb, as some do today. Bangladesh and Nepal resemble regional kingdoms, while Pakistan, with its four distinct regions dominated by Punjab, falls somewhere in between, even as troops based in Central Asia, now part of the Soviet Union, press against and sometimes violate its borders.

Colonialism reached India in force during a period of imperial dissolution. Although they came to trade (or plunder, a distinction even less clear then than now), the British of the Honourable East India Company found themselves drawn into the battles among regional rulers as the Mughal empire dissolved in the eighteenth and early nineteenth centuries. Imposing central rule here, deputizing a Nawab, Nizam, or Maharaja there, their office in Calcutta gradually displaced the decaying throne of Delhi, whose suzerainty they nominally acknowledged.

When the displaced elites of Bengal and the United Provinces revolted in what the British called the Sepoy Mutiny of 1857 (and which modern Indians call the First War of Independence), the British first repressed the revolt with the aid of allies, especially the Sikhs, who relieved Delhi. Next, after officially deposing the last Mughal, a poetic drunkard who had been induced against what judgment he had to support the anti-foreign revolt, they erected a new sovereignty in the land, the Government of India, ruled by a Viceroy on behalf of that Imperial Crown wherein it became the most precious jewel. The national government of today's Republic is the direct institutional descendant of that Government of India, whose name it retains.

Thus in the train of the capitalist world market came the sovereign, bounded, census-taking nation-state to the sub-continent of India. In the struggle to make that state the expression of Indian national identity rather than foreign domination, "human rights" entered the political vocabulary of India. To understand how, one must appreciate four effects of British rule: effective state-building, the growth of an English-educated middle class oriented toward state employment, the stymied growth of Indian manufactures, and the development of parasitic landlordism and landlessness.

With their industrialized weaponry, railroads, and telegraph, the British imposed on India the most extensive domestic peace it had known. They established a bureaucratic apparatus of administration and surveillance, headed by the Indian Civil Service. They created the Indian Army and the Indian Police Service. In order to carry out its tasks the administration needed information on its subjects and therefore, from 1881, carried out the first censuses of the Indian population.[7]

To run the state the British needed assistants and intermediaries. They therefore began to propagate English education among a limited class of Indians. On the basis of this education, used for state service and the new liberal professions introduced by the state (law, medicine, journalism) there developed a bi-cultural class, more and more of whose members had travelled abroad. These middle-class Indians learned of the philosophies of right legitimating British legal practices even as they observed the wealth and power produced by the industrial revolution.[8]

Members of this class, together with some reformist Englishmen, founded the Indian National Congress in 1885, initially to campaign for greater Indian participation in British rule. The leaders of the nationalist and reformist movements that developed subsequently came almost without exception from this class. Motilal Nehru, Jawaharlal Nehru, and Mohandas Gandhi, leaders of the Congress, and Mohammad Ali Jinnah, leader of the Muslim League, all read law in England, while Dr. Bhimrao Ambedkar, leader of the "untouchables" and chief drafter of the Indian Constitution, studied at Columbia University.

The discourse these leaders shared with the state they opposed—or, more accurately, wished to control for their national ends—led them to articulate their nationalist claims in terms of rights unjustly denied on the basis of race. They could oppose the British on the basis of ideals the British claimed to represent. They were able to mobilize social support from wider groups, however, only because Gandhi, in particular, developed an indigenous cultural idiom for mass politics and because of the economic grievances these groups had against colonialism.[9]

The British imposed on India what some have called a policy of "one-way free trade." While British manufactures, especially textiles from the Manchester mills, flooded the Indian market, fine Indian fabrics and other products were kept out of world markets. As a result, the craft-based manufacturing industries were largely destroyed. Indian businessmen, mostly from the traditional trading castes of Western India, did establish some modern industries, but they suffered from restrictive trade and investment policies and lack of government patronage and protection. This weak but growing bourgeoisie supported the nationalist movement.

Finally, British policies of introducing full property in land and thus capitalist relations of production in agriculture and of requiring that land cess (tax) be paid in cash led to a growth in agrarian debt and landlessness, and the concomitant accumulation of land in the hands of those who had access to cash or state power. As peasants lost the traditional rights that had guaranteed more of them access to land and a chance at subsistence, they accumulated grievances that made them potential, and at times actual, allies of the nationalist movement.

The nationalist movement thus claimed full civil and political rights for the people of India, rights which would enable that "people" to control the administrative apparatus of the (formerly) colonial state. Such control would enable the new government to pursue policies leading to both economic growth and protection of the economic rights of the masses, both of which were ignored or trampled on by the colonizer. Much of the Muslim minority feared that political rights (democracy) would only empower the Hindu majority, and thus gave its support to the establishment of the new nation of Pakistan. In the rest of India, however, a new government came to power based on the Indian National Congress, led by legal-minded high-caste professionals, allied with rising industrialists (mostly from traditional business castes) and supported by the upper peasantry. This government appointed itself the task of framing a new constitution (in the English language), under which India became a republic in January 1951.[10]

LEGAL FRAMEWORK OF RIGHTS IN THE REPUBLIC OF INDIA

The Republic of India is a federal, parliamentary democracy. The national Government of India is officially headed by an indirectly elected President, but the President must follow instructions of the Council of Ministers. The Prime Minister heads the Council of Ministers, which is chosen or approved by the House of the People (Lok Sabha), the lower house of parliament. The upper house, known as the Council of States (Rajya Sabha) is mostly composed of representatives elected by state legislatures, with a dozen prominent people appointed by the President. It has few powers.

The Lok Sabha is elected from single member districts in which the candidate with the plurality of votes wins. Every adult has the right to vote, and the independent Election Commission has made extraordinary efforts to enable illiterates to participate by, for instance, requiring that each party have a visual symbol such as a cow or a hand. There are no legal restrictions other than age and citizenship on participation in elections by either candidates or voters.

Each state government has a parallel system, with a Governor, Chief Minister, and State Legislative Assembly. The Constitution defines a division of powers between the levels, with residual powers vesting in the national government. The President has the power to dissolve state governments and place them under "President's Rule" until new elections can be held, if he finds that the state government cannot govern (Article 356).

To the extent that this system of government functions as a meaningful democracy, it is because of the effective protection of many rights in law and practice. The Indian Constitution defines both civil and political rights (the Fundamental Rights) and socio-economic goals (the Directive Principles of State Policy).

In the Fundamental Rights, the Constitution provides for equality in law and public employment and for protection against discrimination of all kinds, noting that this provision may not be invoked against either protections for women and children or the advancement of "any socially and educationally backward classes of citizens or for the Scheduled Castes and the Scheduled Tribes."[11] It abolishes "Untouchability." It protects rights to freedom of speech and expression, to assemble peaceably, to form associations or unions, to travel and settle freely in India, and to practice any profession or business. The Constitution also provides, however, that nothing shall prevent the State from imposing "reasonable restrictions on the exercise of these rights" in the interests of the security of the State, national sovereignty, friendly relations with foreign states, public order, or public morality.

The Constitution provides for some legal protections against arbitrary arrest, but these are weaker than in Anglo-Saxon law. The concept of "due process of law" is somewhat diluted in Article 21: "No person shall be deprived of his life or personal liberty *except according to procedure established by law.*" (My emphasis.) While "no person accused of any offence shall be compelled to be a witness against himself" (Article 20(3)), there is no specific prohibition of torture or mistreatment. Those arrested must be informed of the charges against them, have the right to counsel, and must be produced before a magistrate within twenty-four hours, but these rights are suspended for those "arrested or detained under any law providing for preventive detention" (Article 22 (3) (b)). The Constitution gives wide latitude to the Parliament in drawing up laws for preventive detention.

The Fundamental Rights include a right against "exploitation," defined as "traffic in human beings," forced labor, or the employment of children in factories, mines, or dangerous occupations. The Constitution protects religious freedom, but reserves to the government the right to regulate economic, financial, or political activities connected with religion and to institute certain reforms. It protects the rights of minorities to retain their language, culture, and educational institutions.

The Constitution provides for remedies for violations of these rights through the Courts. The Supreme Court, in particular, has the power to respond to writ petitions claiming violations of the Fundamental Rights by issuing various writs and orders, including *habeas corpus, mandamus,* and others.

The Constitution also lays down Directive Principles of State Policies, which parallel many of the rights found in the International Covenant on Social, Economic, and Cultural Rights. These do not have the status of legal rights, however. Rather, "The [Directive Principles] shall not be enforceable by any court, but [they] are nevertheless fundamental in the governance of the country and it shall be the duty of the State to apply these principles in making laws" (Article 37). The Directive Principles thus confer duties on the state without granting rights to citizens.

The Directive Principles enjoin the State to promote justice, equality, and welfare. The Principles do refer to the "right to work, to education, and to public assistance in cases of unemployment, old age, sickness and disablement, and in other cases of undeserved want." The state is to work "within the limits of its economic capacity and development" for these rights (Article 41). Otherwise, the Directive Principles make no reference to rights, but call for policies to promote public health, the well-being of workers, and the uplift of disadvantaged groups.

As noted, many of the Fundamental Rights are hedged about with rather vague provisions allowing the government to violate them. The desire to endow the state with sufficient power to uphold public order, national security, and the unity of the country also led to the inclusion of provisions enabling the President to suspend most of the Fundamental Rights by proclaiming a State of Emergency in the whole or part of the territory of India in the event of war or internal disturbance.[12] Even under an Emergency, detainees enjoy freedom from forced self-incrimination and rights to be informed of charges against them, to consult counsel, and to be brought before a magistrate. The latter three rights may be suspended for those held under a law providing for preventive detention.

The relationship between the Fundamental Rights and the Directive Principles was one of the issues that preoccupied the Constitutional Assembly. The members of the Assembly expressed concern over limiting the state's power to enact social reforms. This conflict was the backdrop to the major legal controversies over rights since the establishment of the Republic.[13]

During the period of the "Congress System" (1951–1967), when the undivided Indian National Congress dominated politics both nationally and in nearly all states, the major political conflict over rights involved the compensation to be paid to *zamindars* (feudal landlords) by states that had enacted land ceilings. Landlords brought to court claims that the ceiling acts deprived them of due process and just compensation, until a constitutional amendment removed such questions from judicial jurisdiction. Subsequently a further amendment restored compensation at fair market value as a fundamental right. In addition, in the Golak Nath case the Supreme Court ruled that Parliament could not amend the Fundamental Rights, which were a part of the "basic structure" of the Constitution, except by calling a new Constituent Assembly.

Under Indira Gandhi's first term as Prime Minister (1967–1977) conflicts over the relation of the Fundamental Rights to the Directive Principles intensified. In a series of contests between Mrs. Gandhi's government and the courts, the courts overturned policies basic to the political position she was staking out for herself, such as nationalization of banks and ending the "privy purses," or private incomes the government had agreed to pay Indian princes.[14]

After winning more than two-thirds of the parliamentary seats in the 1971 elections, Prime Minister Gandhi could respond to court decisions overturning her policies by amending the constitution. She and her followers passed constitutional amendments that forbade the courts from ruling unconstitutional, on the grounds of violation of the Fundamental Rights, any legislation declaring as its aim the fulfillment of the Directive Principles. In a case challenging these amendments, the Supreme Court held that Parliament could amend any provision of the constitution, including the Fundamental Rights, but could not "abrogate" the constitution or alter its "basic structure or framework" by, for instance, abolishing federalism or elections. Prime Minister Gandhi responded to this partial defeat by appointing a new chief justice, who agreed with her legal doctrines, over the heads of three senior justices, contrary to established practice. All three superseded justices resigned.

From June 1975 to March 1977 Prime Minister Gandhi suspended the Fundamental Rights by declaring a State of Emergency, which she justified by claiming that powerful citizens were using these rights to prevent her from carrying out programs in the interest of the "majority." Under the Emergency Prime Minister Gandhi's government passed major constitutional amendments, removing the Prime Minister from the jurisdiction of the courts, strengthening the prohibition against overturning laws intended to fulfill the Directive Principles, and declaring that no court could find an amendment unconstitutional on any grounds whatsoever. The Supreme Court subsequently ruled that both provisions are unconstitutional. The conflict has clearly attained the limits of what formal legality can resolve. However, since the Emergency of June 1975 to March 1977 failed to realize any of the Directive Principles, despite suspension of nearly all the Fundamental Rights, this conflict has ceased to be an active issue.

HUMAN RIGHTS PRACTICES

Respect for and violations of human rights in India are as varied as the country itself. The Constitution makes ample provision for both. Actual practices reflect four major factors: the vital but ambiguous legal framework, which offers resources to both those who would violate and those who would defend human rights; the broad, and, over time, broadening acceptance of democratic legitimacy as the only formula able to produce national unity, backed by a growing middle class, some of whose members are willing to commit resources to defense of democracy and human rights; the intensity of social conflicts over the linked issues of ethnicity, religion, caste, and class, against a background of mass poverty and extreme differences in access to slowly growing resources; and the presence of a population of several hundred million destitute people lacking the basic political, economic, and social resources to claim rights.

These factors create distinct political arenas in which rights practices differ. National politics conducted within the mainly English-speaking elite generally respects both the rules of democratic procedure and civil and political liberties, especially freedom of expression. The major exception to this was during the period of the Emergency. Regional politics, often revolving around ethnic, religious, caste, and class issues, frequently becomes violent. Regionally based ethnic protests in some cases have turned into insurgencies, which the central government has repressed with suppression of civil and political liberties and counter-insurgency tactics that involve some torture and arbitrary killing. Local politics in some rural areas involves conflict over land, exacerbated by extreme caste disparities. Sometimes the landless laborers, often "untouchables" or tribals, are mobilized by political groups, some of them using violence, and either activists or those suspected of supporting them may suffer extremes of police violence without meaningful recourse to local judicial authorities. Members of relatively powerless social groups in both urban slums and the villages, and, in particular, the women members of such groups, may also be subjected to police violence as a result of various corrupt practices not necessarily connected to explicitly political struggles.[15]

Various forms of human rights violations occur in all these arenas, especially the peripheral ones, as described below. Nevertheless, the frequency of most such violations is probably less in India than in other countries with comparable levels of poverty and conflict.

Political Killings

The Indian national government or ruling party have not killed members of the political opposition, even during the Emergency. Nevertheless, the police and army have carried out summary executions of suspected armed insurgents, including suspected "Naxalites"[16] (members of various "Marxist-Leninist" groups to the left of the established Communist parties), Sikh separatists in Punjab, and tribal insurgents in the Northeast. The most common form of such summary execution in India is the death of a suspect "in an encounter with police [or army]," which has come to be known as an "encounter killing."

"Encounter killings" developed from police practices in dealing with "dacoits" (armed bandits in gangs). When the "Naxalites" split from the Communist Party of India (Marxist) in 1969 and began a strategy of "people's war," including the annihilation of "class enemies," police responded to their campaign of rural and urban terrorism with "encounter killings" of suspects. West Bengal, especially Calcutta, was the main center of this practice from 1969 to 1971. Since then encounter killing and allied practices have spread to other regions where extreme caste and class disparities have led to rural conflicts. Amnesty International, for instance, has continued to receive such allegations:

In Uttar Pradesh those killed were criminal suspects, especially from among the *Harijans*, "scheduled castes." "Encounter" killings of political activists were reported from Andhra Pradesh, Bihar and Punjab. In one such incident in Andhra Pradesh in April [1985], five alleged Naxalites were killed and a survivor stated that they had been surrounded by police in plain clothes, stripped naked, stood in a row with their hands behind their backs and shot.[17]

There are many claims of such killings during army operations in Punjab. During the army assault on the Golden Temple in Amritsar on June 4, 1984, in which over 1,000 civilians and 100 soldiers were killed, a journalist for the Associated Press reported that a doctor had told him that some prisoners had been shot in the back of the head with their hands tied. There have been other, less detailed accounts of other encounter killings in Punjab as well, but there have been no adequate independent investigations to establish the facts.[18] There is better documentation of summary executions in the tribal northeast, where several insurgencies have been in progress since the 1950s.

There are also frequent reports of deaths in police custody due to torture. The victims include both political detainees (mainly suspected terrorists or insurgents, such as Sikhs suspected of planting bombs in Delhi or tribal guerrillas in Manipur) and common criminal suspects.[19]

There has not been a complete accounting of the numbers of such deaths. Estimates of the number of "encounter killings" are in the hundreds or low thousands since the late 1960s. Without meaning to minimize the severity of these violations, one should bear in mind the size of the Indian population in assessing them.

Many more people have died in other forms of political and social violence in India, for which the degree of official responsibility varies and is disputed. Such violence generally takes the form of the "communal riot" in which members of different religious, ethnic, or caste groups attack each other. Sometimes the government attempts to stop the fighting. In other cases officials seem to refrain from acting, thereby implicitly supporting the more powerful group, while in some cases police and politicians belonging to the dominant community may actually participate in or even lead the killings.

Among the largest of such killings in recent years were the massacres of Sikhs in Delhi and other north Indian cities after two Sikh bodyguards assassinated Prime Minister Indira Gandhi on October 31, 1984. According to the Indian government, 2,987 people died in these disturbances, but others put the figure much higher. Indian human rights groups published a detailed report claiming that in Delhi, the police at best refrained from acting and at times directly participated in the killing, and that local leaders of the Congress (I), the ruling party, led the mobs in some areas or intervened to obtain the release from custody of people detained for participating in the violence. Only after considerable political pressure did the government agree to an inquiry. The inquiry, released in February 1987, found the police guilty of negligence but exonerated politicians. Human rights groups charged that the inquiry commission's conclusion was inconsistent with the evidence it collected.[20]

Government complicity is sometimes less clear. In Assam, where perhaps 4,000 people died in political violence over religious-ethnic issues, and in Gujarat, where hundreds have been killed over caste issues, political leaders may have exploited the conflicts, but do not seem to be as directly responsible.[21]

Another form of killing of members of relatively powerless groups in India is the so-called "dowry death," or "bride burning," in which a newly married young woman's in-laws kill her, usually trying to disguise the death as a kitchen accident, because her parents did not supply a large enough dowry. These generally occur in urban middle class families of north and northwest India, especially Delhi, apparently as a result of the lower status of women in that area, the growth of consumerism, and the devaluation of women's economic contribution as a result of urbanization. The police and even the victim's parents have been reluctant to prosecute in many cases, as a result of shared patriarchal values and the shame attached to being victimized in this way. In recent years, thanks to campaigns by women's organizations and some new legislation, prosecutions have increased. In 1985 the Minister of the Interior estimated that more than 1000 women had died under such circumstances in the previous three years.[22]

Torture

The Indian Constitution does not explicitly prohibit torture or mistreatment, although there are laws prohibiting torture by the police and army and case law prohibiting the use of forcibly extracted confessions. Torture and mistreatment of detainees, including both political and criminal suspects, are widely reported in India, although it is impossible to state precisely how prevalent the practices are. Torture does not always result from a government policy to torture suspects. Sometimes it is due to lack of adequate legal safeguards and the vulnerability of certain groups, generally the same groups who may be victims of summary execution. Some state governments, however, clearly condone torture.

There are frequent reports of extreme police brutality, sanctioned by the state governments, against "untouchables" and tribals in Bihar and Andhra Pradesh. In 1980 and 1981 police in Bhagalpur, Bihar, blinded 31 prisoners awaiting trial by piercing their eyes with needles and pouring acid on the eyes. (The victims were low-caste criminal suspects.) Only in 1985 were 15 officers finally suspended, and there have not been any criminal convictions. In a 1985 petition to the Supreme Court, 238 tribal people from an area of Andhra Pradesh where Naxalites are active claimed to have been tortured. After bomb explosions in Delhi that killed 86 people in May 1985, a number of young Sikhs were arrested. At least one died in custody, and others showed signs of injury when they were produced in court. There are also frequent reports of torture of suspected terrorists or guerrillas in Punjab or the northeast. Finally, police in some areas seem almost routinely to work over criminal suspects in order to obtain confessions or to administer summary punishment. Such summary punishment has a certain degree of popular support, because of the slowness of the court system.[23]

In recent years reports have begun to emerge of custodial rape, sometimes leading to murder, of women detainees. Again, the victims are often "untouchables" or tribals, whose sexual victimization is part of social life in some areas. Police sometimes collaborate with rape, assault, and humiliation of women from these backgrounds by refusing to prosecute or register cases against the high-caste perpetrators. Rape and threat of rape are used to control not only women, but also the men belonging to the family or social group of the victim.[24]

Arbitrary Arrest and Detention

India currently has several laws providing for preventive detention, including the National Security Act (NSA), the Terrorist Affected Areas (Special Courts) Ordinance, and the Terrorist and Disruptive Activities Act. Under these laws detainees may be held for as long as two years without trial. "Terrorists" are defined as anyone "causing disruption of services or means of communication essential to the community" for purposes of coercing the government. Such "terrorists" can receive summary trials in which the presumption of innocence is reversed and in which the judges are directly appointed by the government.

"Disruptive activities," punishable by three years to life imprisonment, are defined as "any action taken, whether by act or speech or through any other media, which questions, disrupts or is intended to disrupt, whether directly or indirectly, the sovereignty and territorial integrity of India." Advocating or inciting disruptive activities are also punishable.[25]

Several thousand people were arrested under the NSA in Punjab following the assault on the Golden Temple. Many, perhaps most, were released without trial after Punjab elections that brought to power in September 1985 a government of the Akali Dal, a non-violent Sikh political party whose most important leaders had also been detained. Three hundred and sixty-five such Sikh detainees remain in jail in Jodhpur, Rajasthan, more than two years after their arrest, despite the expiration of the maximum term of detention under the NSA.

The Government of Andhra Pradesh arrested several hundred accused "Naxalites" under the Terrorist and Disruptive Activities Act. One of those arrested, in November 1985, was Dr. Balagopal, General Secretary of the Andhra Pradesh Civil Liberties Committee, which had documented police atrocities in the state. In September 1985 the Government arrested three other civil liberties activists under the same Act for having written the report *Oppression in Punjab*, which the government ordered banned. The three were released on bail when a magistrate ruled the government had failed to bring evidence of publication of seditious materials.[26]

In some of the more peripheral arenas of conflict, police enjoy wide discretion in arresting members of powerless groups, despite the existence of formal legal protections. Threat of such arrest may be used to extract bribes or enforce social hierarchy. Prisoners arrested for doubtful reasons can sometimes be held for years without trial, sometimes for far longer than the maximum prescribed punishment for their supposed offenses. The State of Bihar, in particular, at one time held thousands of such long-term "undertrial" prisoners, and some apparently still remain.

Freedom of Expression

There is extensive freedom of speech and publication in India, although under the Emergency, Prime Minister Gandhi instituted stringent censorship. The regional press in vernacular languages may be subject to greater harassment than the national press in English. State governments may, for instance, withhold advertising. Broadcast media are owned and controlled by the government and reflect official positions.

The law against "sedition" has been used by police, at least in Andhra Pradesh and Tamil Nadu, to prevent public meetings protesting police killings and torture. The central government used both that same law and the newer legislation mentioned above to ban the report *Oppression in Punjab* in September 1985. The report is now widely circulating in pirate editions, and it does not appear that the judicial proceedings against the authors will amount to anything.

Brahma Chellaney, the Associated Press reporter who reported executions of prisoners in the Golden Temple assault, was similarly arrested. Eventually he was freed, and it does not appear that the government will pursue the case. In May 1985 police burned down the offices of two newspapers in Ahmedabad, Gujarat, and beat several journalists in retaliation for the newspapers' reporting of police violence in the context of the long-standing caste conflict in that state.[27]

Political Participation

Despite everything else reported here, India is a functioning democracy in which elections have led to meaningful changes of power in both the national and state governments.[28] Besides the dominant Congress Party (which has split several times), Communist parties, regional parties with strong separatist leanings, and Hindu communalist parties have all had the opportunity to form governments, either alone or in coalitions. The elections of 1967, which left Congress with a greatly reduced majority in the center and swept it out of power in most states, spelled the end of an era of unchallenged one-party dominance. The elections of 1971, in which Indira Gandhi asserted her domination of national politics, made poverty a national political issue for the first time. The 1977 elections deposed Indira Gandhi and ended the Emergency, but she was returned to power in the 1980 elections. The 1984 elections gave a clear mandate to Rajiv Gandhi after he was appointed to succeed his assassinated mother and changed him overnight from a drab figurehead to a charismatic leader.

Under the Emergency the activities of opposition parties (as well as of dissidents within Mrs. Gandhi's Congress) were curtailed, as political leaders were arrested, and national elections were postponed for an additional year beyond the normal five. During her second term (1980–1984) Prime Minister Gandhi made use of the provision for President's Rule to bring down opposition governments in several states, even when it was clear that they were, in fact, able to govern. Rajiv Gandhi, however, has clearly repudiated this portion of his mother's legacy. He introduced several measures to strengthen democratic legality, such as a law forbidding representatives from changing parties after election. (Bribery to induce such defections was an important way of undermining state governments.)[29]

In the conflict-torn states of Punjab and Assam, Rajiv Gandhi succeeded in arriving at settlements with local opposition groups that allowed elections to take place and state governments, headed by regional parties opposed to Congress, to take office.

An important form of democracy that has, however, dwindled, is democracy within the Congress Party itself. Since this party dominates so many institutions, the personalization and centralization of power within it that began with Indira Gandhi, who never held internal party elections, has affected much of the political system. Rajiv Gandhi has not thus far been able to make any substantial improvements, although he has indicated his intention to hold party elections.

Right to Food

India is a very poor country, with a per capita income of about $260 per year. India is now self-sufficient in food production, while in the 1960s it was dependent on massive imports of wheat, mainly from the United States. This self-sufficiency, however, reflects not only increased production but also the inability of many Indians to purchase what they need. Estimates of average daily caloric intake are around 90 percent of nutritional requirements, which means that there are probably hundreds of millions of malnourished people, including perhaps a third of the rural population. This is probably the main reason for India's life expectancy of 55 years and infant mortality rate of 110 per 1000 live births. Because of patterns of food distribution within families, a disproportionate number of these malnourished people are women and girls. Baby girls are the most likely to be deprived of food.[30]

On the other hand, India since independence has avoided massive famines, which had occurred periodically under the British and previously, most recently in Bengal in 1943, when an estimated 3 million people died. Some analysts attribute this success largely to democratic government and freedom of expression, which have made it politically impossible for the government to ignore pockets of extreme hunger that have begun to develop from time to time.[31]

In view of India's overall poverty, there is some debate as to whether it could realistically feed all its people now. Amartya Sen has cited the example of neighboring Sri Lanka, with a per capita income of only about $330 per year, and a similar political and social system, but where government programs have raised average caloric intake to 107 percent of requirements, a major reason why life expectancy is 69 years and the infant mortality rate is 37 per 1000 live births. Sen has estimated that a comparable effort in India would cost about 5 percent of GNP.[32]

There are major regional differences in nutrition in India. The differences reflect both different rates of food production and government food distribution policies. In some states the governments have distributed surplus food as wages on public works projects under the Food for Work program.

Right to Health

Nutrition, of course, is a major determinant of the overall health of a population, and we have already noted India's low life expectancy and high infant mortality rates, both of which have, however, improved considerably since independence. In recent years the government has concluded that its health expenditures, averaging around 4–5 percent of public expenditure (about $3 per year per capita), have concentrated too much on Western curative medicine. There are plans for constructing networks of local health centers, but many rural areas are not served. As with everything else in India, there are major regional differences.[33]

The government has promoted family planning since the 1950s. In areas with higher female literacy, in particular Kerala, it has been more successful. Some of the worst abuses of the Emergency arose from the imposition of quotas for vasectomies. There were many reports of coercion and abuse, especially of Muslims and "untouchables" in North India, and this was a major reason that Indira Gandhi lost her traditional high level of support among these groups in the 1977 elections.[34]

Women's health is significantly worse than men's health in India, which reflects food distribution in the family, work patterns, and differential access to health care. Male life expectancy is 56 years, compared to 54 years for females, contrary to the usual pattern. Furthermore, as Sen notes:

The so-called sex ratio—the percentage of females to males—has declined from around 97.2 percent in 1901 to 93.5 percent in the last census in 1981. . . . It appears that with the progress of modern medicine and health services in India, the opportunities have been much more effectively—and unequally—seized by men than by women. The traditional differences have been heightened by new opportunities, and as the absolute positions of both men and women have slowly improved in health and longevity, the *relative* position of women has fallen behind. This does not of course happen among the elite—not much, anyway.[35]

The Indian government has proven unable to meet the health needs of the victims of the 1984 disaster at the Union Carbide plant in Bhopal, Madhya Pradesh. Official sources claim that 1,754 people died from inhaling poison gas as a result of that industrial accident. Other sources, basing themselves on reports of bodies being dumped in the river and on estimates of the quantity of shroud cloth sold for the mostly Muslim victims, cite higher figures, such as 2,500. The total affected may be as high as 200,000 out of the 350,000 residents of Bhopal. Symptoms among the survivors include blindness, stillbirths, and birth defects.

The introduction of proper treatment was delayed by the reluctance of the company and the government to admit that the accident had created cyanide poisoning, although limited quantities of antidote were made available to local elites. Police broke into a private clinic run by medical activists who were trying to implement mass detoxication. They confiscated the clinic's records as well as supplies of the antidote. The Government of Madhya Pradesh planned to use most of the money collected for rehabilitation for "urban beautification" schemes and ended food distribution to affected families in January 1986 although 15,000 families still needed support. There has as yet been no compensation to the victims.[36]

Right to Work

In an economy such as India's, "unemployment" is not always a meaningful concept. More than 80 percent of the labor force is still employed in agriculture (although many such workers also have part-time non-agricultural jobs). In family-based subsistence agriculture, which still predominates in much of India, there is no institutional separation between employment and unemployment.

Some estimates, including partial (largely seasonal) unemployment in the total, showed that 8.8 percent of the total labor force of 276 million were unemployed in 1984. About 4.6 percent of the labor force were totally without access to income. There is no unemployment insurance in India.

In the rural areas, landlessness is the major factor contributing to unemployment. The pattern of increasing concentration of land ownership that began under the British has continued, despite some redistributional land reforms. Nationally about 30 percent of rural families are landless and thus depend on largely seasonal agricultural employment for their livelihood. Even in those states, such as Kerala and West Bengal, where land reform has proceeded further than elsewhere, the main result has been greater security for tenants, rather than distribution of land to those who are completely landless. In fact, there is not enough land to provide adequate holdings to all families. The result has been an increase in urbanization and urban unemployment, as employment in services and industry is not expanding quickly enough to absorb the surplus labor from the rural areas. From 1982 to 1988 the labor force is expected to grow by about 59 million, which is twice the total employment in the modern sector of the economy.[37]

The urbanization of employment (and unemployment) has tended to eliminate women from the labor force. Statistically this lowers their unemployment rate, but it appears that this may be an artifact of the definition of "labor force." Women play a vital role in subsistence agriculture but can get only low-paying and sometimes "dishonorable" urban employment. (Naturally this does not apply to educated professionals.) The result has been a devaluation of the economic role of urban women, which, as noted above, contributes to the phenomenon of "dowry death."

Some states operate Employment Guarantee Schemes, which also utilize surplus food as payment, and which have made particular efforts to employ women. In Maharashtra, for instance, 43 percent of those hired under the scheme were women.[38]

Rights of Labor

Bonded or forced labor remains a problem in India. Estimates of the number of bonded laborers, partly depending on the definition, range from 500,000 to 6 million. Bondage most commonly arises when laborers borrow money at usurious rates and, lacking collateral, agree to work for the creditor in lieu of repayment. Such debt bondage can last a lifetime and even be inherited. Bonded laborers are found in agriculture, quarries, carpet-weaving, and other small industries. Some of them are children. Most of them belong to scheduled castes and tribes. The Indian government specifically outlawed bonded labor in 1976 (it was already a violation of the fundamental rights in the Constitution) and has supported state programs to eliminate it. However, in September 1985 it confiscated the passport of Swami Agnivesh, leader of the Bonded Liberation Front, upon his return from testifying before the UN Subcommission on the Prevention of Discrimination and the Protection of Minorities in Geneva, on the ground that his testimony was "anti-national."

The Indian Supreme Court has given a broad interpretation to "forced labor" as prohibited in the fundamental rights; in its decision on the conditions of construction workers building facilities for the Asian Games in 1982, it ruled that working for less than the legal minimum wage was *prima facie* evidence of "forced labor." There is no national minimum wage in India, but the states have established different minimum wages for different kinds of employment, with the women's minimum wage generally being lower. In agricultural and other small-scale sectors of the economy, the minimum wage laws are generally not enforced.

There is no child labor in India's modern factory sector, as there was for instance in England during the early stages of industrialization, but about a third of children aged 5 to 15 are employed in one way or another. Many of these children work in subsistence agriculture with their families, but some are engaged, contrary to law, in dangerous or unhealthy occupations.[39] A November 1986 Supreme Court decision ordered the release of 319 child bonded laborers employed in carpet weaving in Mirzapur, Uttar Pradesh. Chief Justice P. N. Bhagwati described them as "non-beings, exiles of civilization, living a life worse than that of animals."

Indian workers have the right to form trade unions and, subject to certain restrictions, the right to strike. Trade unions generally represent workers only in the more highly paying modern sectors of the economy, namely industry and government services. Trade unions are usually associated with political parties, and there are four trade union confederations, belonging to all of the major international union associations. Strikes are frequent in India.

Legislation introduced since 1979, especially the Essential Services Maintenance Act of 1981, limits the right to strike by empowering the government to intervene by banning strikes and arresting and dismissing strikers. The government has used the provisions of the act against strikes or threatened strikes in, for instance, coal, textiles, and public broadcasting, but it has not used it to try to break the trade union movement as a whole.[40]

Right to Education

Education in India is as polarized between the elite and the masses as other aspects of society. While fully 8 percent of the appropriate age group is enrolled in institutions of higher learning (compared to about 1 percent in China), 56.5 percent of the population over 15 years old is illiterate, including 42.8 percent of the men and 71.1 percent of the women. Only a third of total educational expenditures go for elementary education.

Although the Directive Principles (Article 45) provided that the government should try to establish free and compulsory education for all children within 10 years of the adoption of the Constitution, education is still far from universal. Nearly all boys now enroll in school, as do about two thirds of the girls. A quarter of those who enroll do not finish the first year, and only half complete four years of education, generally considered the minimum required for basic literacy. Far fewer children attend school in the rural areas, where parents see less need for education and may need the children's labor.[41]

The government has various programs to promote the education of scheduled castes and tribes. These programs have greatly increased literacy and white collar employment in these groups, although they continue to lag behind.

Rights of Minorities and Disadvantaged Groups

The Indian government has attempted to accommodate demands by linguistic minorities by redrawing the boundaries of the states to coincide, as far as possible, with territories where a single language is spoken. The government has repeatedly defused regional agitations by redrawing state borders or splitting states into smaller units so that leaders of separatist organizations, even former guerrillas, can become chief ministers. Indira Gandhi at times resisted regional demands to the point that critics blamed the exacerbation of conflicts in Punjab and Assam on her insistence on strengthening the center. Her son's government may now be in the process of resolving those conflicts, although, especially in Punjab, a peaceful outcome is still far from certain.

The creation of linguistic states has created problems for some members of linguistic minorities within the states. In some states, affirmative action programs for public employment of speakers of the regional language (the so-called "sons of the soil" or *bhumiputra*) in effect discriminate against speakers of minority languages.[42]

The Muslims, amounting to 11 percent of the population, are the major religious minority in India. The areas where Muslims had a territorial base (except for Kashmir) exercised the right of self-determination by forming the new nation of Pakistan, including what is now Bangladesh, rather than by becoming states in a federal India. The government's policy of secularism and the strong ties between Muslims and the Congress, particularly the Nehru family, long helped to incorporate the remaining minority into the polity. In recent years, however, conflicts with Hindus in many areas, combined with an apparent revival of Hindu consciousness, seem to have increased the feelings of Muslim insecurity. In some cases police seem to join or at least ignore Hindu violence against Muslims.

Muslim insecurity recently came to a head over the Shahbano Begum case. An elderly Muslim woman, Shahbano Begum, sued her former husband, a wealthy businessman who had divorced her, for support. Her husband contended that under Islamic law he had discharged his obligation to her by returning her *mahr*, or brideprice. A Hindu judge ruled not only that the husband should pay alimony on the basis of Indian civil law, but that such payment was consistent with the *shari'a*, the Islamic code. Muslim scholars and community organizations throughout India opposed the ruling, while some Islamic modernists, feminists, and others defended it. (The Directive Principles call on the state to establish a uniform civil code for all Indian citizens.) Shahbano Begum herself withdrew the suit when she was informed that it contradicted Islamic principles. The government took pains to conciliate the Muslims on this case. One paradoxical result was the resignation of a Muslim modernist from the cabinet.

This case illustrates one of the many conflicts over women's rights in India. As noted above in several places, women are often victims of extreme abuse, ranging from discriminatory access to food and health care to custodial rape and dowry death. Elite women do participate extensively in public life in India, including government and the professions. In a way, the depressed position of other women in the society enables them to do so without confronting men on issues of power in the family: virtually all such women have access to cheap child care and home labor.

The "untouchables" and tribals are the most consistent victims of most forms of human rights violations. The government has extensive programs, sanctioned by the constitution, for assistance to these groups. It reserves places for them in all educational institutions, in public employment, and in parliament.[43] Although discrimination remains pervasive in the private sector, the government's efforts have created an educated stratum in groups that never had one before, and in some cases this new stratum has exercised leadership in the community. Upper castes have at times protested these measures violently, even resorting to forms of mass terror against the depressed communities. In Gujarat a protest against reserved seats in a medical college in Ahmedabad blew up into a statewide caste conflict that cost hundreds of lives and lasted for several years.

Policies of economic "development" often destroy the land of the estimated 40 million tribal people. Peasants, lumber contractors, and the government forest service encroach on their forests with the approval of the authorities.

HUMAN RIGHTS MOVEMENT

From the forests of the Himalayas to the tip of Cape Cormorin India is teeming with movements. Every offense listed above has an organized opposition. One of the legacies of Mahatma Gandhi was his concept of *swaraj*. *Swaraj* was Gandhi's word for the goal of the freedom movement. It literally means "self-rule," and sometimes is translated simply as "independence." For Gandhi, however, *swaraj* meant not only that Indians rather than British should control the state; he opposed what he called the continuation of British rule by Indians. True *swaraj* meant self-regulation of an autonomously organized society, as well as self-control by a morally autonomous individual. The Indian human rights movement grew out of this tradition of autonomous social organization and is linked to other social movements, many also of Gandhian inspiration, both through shared personnel and because the victims of human rights violations are often activists in those movements.

In keeping with the diversity of Indian society, there are numerous organizations in India concerned with human rights or civil liberties. Here we will mention only the two most prominent nationwide ones, the People's Union for Civil Liberties (PUCL) and the People's Union for Democratic Rights (PUDR).[44] PUCL was first founded by Jayprakash Narayan, the most prominent Gandhian leader of independent India, after he was released from prison in 1976, under the Emergency. Originally its goal was to oppose the overt suppression of civil and political liberties under the Emergency. After Narayan's death and with the accession to power of the Janata party, which promised to carry out most of the PUCL's original demands, the PUCL was in disarray for a while, but it, together with PUDR, acquired its present form in 1980, after Indira Gandhi's return to power.

Both PUCL and PUDR reacted against the idea, used by Indira Gandhi to justify the Emergency, that it might be necessary and justifiable to violate fundamental rights in order to realize some of the directive principles in the interest of the poor and powerless. They have concentrated on defending the fundamental rights of the poor and have endorsed models of social change and protection of social and economic as well as civil and political rights which concentrate on organizing and empowering the poor rather than on state initiatives conceived by supposedly enlightened elites.

The PUCL and PUDR have brought suits in the Supreme Court against the practice of encounter killings and sent study teams to troubled areas in Andhra Pradesh, Bihar, and elsewhere. Their work has also inspired a new kind of investigative journalism. Beyond this type of work, they have organized camps and workshops bringing together political activists and lawyers to instruct the activists in how to defend their rights.

PUDR has been particularly active in defending the most abused workers. Their litigation, in collaboration with sympathetic members of the Supreme Court, in particular Chief Justice P. N. Bhagwati, has led to the development of important legal doctrines. In the 1982 case of the Asiad workers, the Court accepted the right of PUDR to petition on behalf of the workers, even though they lacked the traditional *locus standi* of being the aggrieved party. The court ruled that in a country where many people lack the resources to make use of the legal system on their own behalf, any member of the public may move the court, even by writing a letter, and the court will accept such a letter as a writ petition. In the same case the court interpreted "forced labor" to include labor at below the legal minimum wage. In a case brought by PUCL to stop the Government of Maharashtra from removing pavement dwellers from the streets of Bombay without providing alternative shelter, the court ruled that the "right to life" includes not just the right not to be killed, but the right to a life with some degree of dignity, thus greatly enlarging the potential scope of social action litigation.

PUCL and PUDR together documented the participation of police and politicians in the killing of Sikhs in Delhi after Prime Minister Gandhi's assassination. Their joint pamphlet, *Who Are the Guilty?*, combined with a court case they filed, was probably the main reason the government was finally forced to form a commission of inquiry.

Many other organizations also deal with human rights questions. India's women's movement, in particular, has publicized issues of bride burning, wife beating, and custodial rape.

CONCLUSION

India's freedom of expression enables us to see its flaws all too clearly. The government of India is sensitive about this and is generally inhospitable to international inspection of its human rights performance; except under the Janata Party immediately after the Emergency, it has never admitted an Amnesty International research mission, and it has refused entry to Norwegian researchers working on the report *Human Rights in Developing Countries*.

India poses as big a test for the human rights movement as any country in the world. In such an enormous country, wracked by deprivation and conflict, culturally seemingly at the opposite pole from the philosophy of human rights, any success of human rights protection is a strong argument for the potential universality of the movement. Failure of human rights in India, however, could mean that the movement does not have the capacity to deal with some of the most important questions; after all, one-sixth of humanity is involved. Finally, however, the criteria of success and failure may be too absolute. Instead, we can say with the Urdu poet Ghalib:

> Hazaron khvahishen aisi ke har khvahish pe dam nikle;
> Bahut nikle mere arman, lekin phir bhi kam nikle.

> Thousands of desires, each of which could consume a lifetime;
> Many of my wishes were granted, but even those were too few.

هزاروں خواہشیں ایسے کہ ہر خواہش پہ دم نکلے
بہت نکلے میرے ارمان، لیکن پھر سے کم نکلے

NOTES

1. On ancient Indian civilization see A. L. Basham, *The Wonder That Was India: A Survey of the History and Culture of the Indian Sub-continent before the Coming of the Muslims*, Third Revised Edition (London: Sidgwick and Jackson, 1967).

2. For a study of Islam in India, which also discusses syncretism with Hinduism, see Aziz Ahmad, *Studies in Islamic Culture in the Indian Environment* (Oxford: Oxford University Press, 1964).

3. There is a vast anthropological literature on caste and related subjects. Some seminal works are Andre Beteille, *Caste, Class*, and *Power: Changing Patterns of Stratification in a Tanjore Village* (Berkeley: University of California Press, 1965); M. N. Srinivas, *Caste in Modern India* (London: Asia Publishing House, 1962); McKim Marriot and Ronald B. Inden, "Caste Systems," *Encyclopedia Britannica* (1973), 3: 983–991; and Louis Dumont, *Homo Hierarchicus* (Chicago: University of Chicago Press, 1970).

4. On the modern politics of caste see Lloyd I. Rudolph and Susanne Hoeber Rudolph, *The Modernity of Tradition: Political Development in India* (Chicago: University of Chicago Press, 1967) and Rajni Kothari, *Caste in Indian Politics* (New Delhi, Orient Longman, 1970). On untouchables see J. Michael Mahar, ed., *The Untouchables in Contemporary India* (Tucson: University of Arizona Press, 1972).

5. Gail Omvedt, *We Will Smash This Prison* (London: Zed Press, 1980), gives a personal account of contemporary Indian feminism.

6. Lloyd I. Rudolph and Susanne Hoeber Rudolph, *In Pursuit of Lakshmi: The Political Economy of the Indian State*, forthcoming, provides a survey of state formation in India.

7. An influential analysis of the colonial state is in Hamza Alavi, "The State in Post-Colonial Societies," *New Left Review* 74 (1972), pp. 59–81. Philip Woodruff, *The Men Who Ruled India* (London: Cape Press, 1954), describes the state from the viewpoint of the British who ran it.

8. On the origins of this class see Anil Seal, *The Emergence of Indian Nationalism* (Cambridge: Cambridge University Press, 1968); John R. McLane, *Indian Nationalism and the Early Congress* (Princeton: Princeton University Press, 1977); or Peter Hardy, *The Muslims of British India* (London: Cambridge University Press, 1972).

9. The section on India in Barrington Moore, *Social Origins of Dictatorship and Democracy: Lord and Peasant in the Making of the Modern World* (Boston: Beacon Press, 1966), describes the effect of colonialism on Indian society and how it therefore shaped the nationalist movement. Amiya Kumar Bagchi, *The Political Economy of Underdevelopment* (Cambridge: Cambridge University Press, 1982), places the socio-economic effects of colonialism in a Marxist theoretical framework. It is also still worthwhile to read Marx on India, in, for instance, *The Marx-Engels Reader*, 2d ed. Robert Tucker, ed. (New York: Norton, 1978), pp. 653–664.

10. Granville Austin, *The Indian Constitution: Cornerstone of a Nation* (Oxford: Clarendon Press, 1966), describes the framing.

11. "Scheduled Castes" and "Scheduled Tribes" are the legal terms for officially recognized "untouchable" and tribal groups. Gandhi called the "untouchables" "*harijans*," or "children of God," but the more militant of them have rejected the term as patronizing. Instead they call themselves "dalits," "the oppressed," which includes tribals, and sometimes any oppressed group in the world, such as American blacks. Here they are called "untouchables" in quotes, indicating that others still treat them as untouchable, despite legal abolition of the status.

12. In 1977, in reaction against the authoritarian powers assumed by Prime Minister Indira Gandhi under the emergency provision of the Constitution, the Janata Party government amended the provision so that only "armed rebellion" could justify an internal emergency.

13. On these controversies see Francine Frankel, *India's Political Economy 1947–1977: The Gradual Revolution* (Princeton: Princeton University Press, 1978), and Lloyd I. Rudolph and Susanne Hoeber Rudolph, "Judicial Review *versus* Parliamentary Sov-

ereignty: The Struggle over Stateness in India," *Journal of Commonwealth and Comparative Politics* 19 (November 1981), pp. 231–256.

14. Under the British, some Indian rulers (maharajas, nizams, and so on) continued to rule their realms, under British suzerainty. After independence, these rulers ceded their rule to India or Pakistan, but the Indian government compensated them by granting the "privy purses."

15. For a more detailed analysis of the social contexts of human rights violations in India, see Barnett R. Rubin, "The Civil Liberties Movement in India: New Approaches to the State and Social Change," *Asian Survey* (March 1987).

16. The Naxalites took their name from Naxalbari, a district in West Bengal where a group of Maoists started "armed struggle" among the peasantry in 1967.

17. Amnesty International, *Annual Report 1986*, pp. 223–224. On earlier practices see Amnesty International, *Political Killings by Governments* (London: Amnesty International, 1983), pp. 61–68.

18. Tor Skalnes and Jan Egeland, eds., *Human Rights in Developing Countries, 1986: A Yearbook on Countries Receiving Norwegian Aid* (Oslo: Norwegian University Press), p. 170; Citizens for Democracy, *Oppression in Punjab* (September 1985), U.S. Edition, Sikh Religious and Educational Trust, Columbus, Ohio. For background on the Punjab conflict see Paul Brass, *Language, Religion, and Politics in North India* (London: Cambridge University Press, 1974). An account through June 1984 is in M. J. Akbar, *India: The Siege Within* (Middlesex: Penguin, 1985).

19. Amnesty International, "India: Some Reports Concerning Deaths in Police Custody Allegedly as a Result of Torture or Shooting during 1985," ASA 20/03/86, January 1986; Amnesty International, *Annual Report 1986*, p. 223.

20. The report on the killings of Sikhs was People's Union for Democratic Rights and People's Union for Civil Liberties, *Who Are the Guilty? Report of a Joint Inquiry into the Causes and Impact of the Riots in Delhi from 31 October to 10 November* (Delhi, 1984).

21. On the Assam conflict see Myron Weiner, *Sons of the Soil: Migration and Ethnic Conflict in India* (Princeton: Princeton University Press, 1978), and Sanjib Baruah, "Immigration, Ethnic Conflict, and Political Turmoil—Assam, 1979–1985," *Asian Survey* 26 (November 1986), pp. 1184–1206.

22. Skalnes and Egeland, *Human Rights in Developing Countries*, p. 172.

23. On the Bhagalpur blindings see Arun Shourie, *Mrs. Gandhi's Second Reign* (New Delhi: Vikas, 1983). On Andhra and the Sikhs see Amnesty International, *Annual Report 1986*, p. 223. On torture as summary punishment see *Fourth Report of the National Police Commission* (New Delhi: Government of India, June 1980).

24. See the special issue on women of *PUCL Bulletin* (September 1982).

25. Amnesty International *Annual Report 1986*, pp. 220–222; Skalnes and Egeland, *Human Rights in Developing Countries*, pp. 173–175; People's Union for Civil Liberties, *Black Laws 1984* (Delhi, 1984).

26. Amnesty International *Annual Report 1986*, p. 221.

27. *PUCL Bulletin* (November 1982); *Ibid.* (January 1983); *Ibid.* (February 1983); Skalnes and Egeland, *Human Rights in Developing Countries*, pp. 175–176.

28. There is a vast literature on Indian politics, parties, and elections. A basic survey is Robert Hardgrave, *India: Government and Politics in a Developing Nation* (New York: Harcourt, Brace Jovanovich, 4th Edition, 1985). See also Rajni Kothari, *Politics in India* (New York, Little Brown and Co., 1970); Myron Weiner, *Party Building in a New*

Nation: The Indian National Congress (Chicago: University of Chicago Press, 1967); Henry C. Hart, ed., *Indira Gandhi's India* (Boulder, Colo.: Westview Press, 1976); Rudolph and Rudolph, *In Pursuit of Lakshmi.*

29. Skalnes and Egeland, *Human Rights in Developing Countries*, p. 176–180.

30. *Ibid.*, p. 167; Department of State, *Country Reports on Human Rights Practices 1986*, "India."

31. Amartya Sen, "How is India Doing?" *New York Review of Books* 21 (Christmas Number, 1982), p. 45.

32. *Ibid.*, p. 44. Data on Sri Lanka are from Skalnes and Egeland, *Human Rights in Developing Countries*, p. 227.

33. *Ibid.*, pp. 182–184.

34. Myron Weiner, *India at the Polls: The Parliamentary Elections of 1977* (Washington: American Enterprise Institute for Public Policy Research, 1978).

35. Sen, "How is India Doing?" p. 44.

36. Skalnes and Egeland, *Human Rights in Developing Countries*, pp. 184–186.

37. Employment data from *Ibid.*, pp. 186–188. On land reform in India see Ron Herring, *Land to the Tiller* (New Haven: Yale University Press, 1984).

38. Skalnes and Egeland, *Human Rights in Developing Countries*, p. 189. On these and other anti-poverty schemes see Atul Kohli, *The State and Poverty in India: The Politics of Reform* (New York: Cambridge University Press, 1987).

39. Skalnes and Egeland, *Human Rights in Developing Countries*, pp. 189–190; Department of State, *Country Reports 1986*, "India."

40. Skalnes and Egeland, *Human Rights in Developing Countries*, p. 190.

41. *Ibid.*, pp. 191–192; Sen, "How Is India Doing?" p. 46.

42. Myron Weiner, *Sons of the Soil.*

43. Marc Galanter, *Competing Inequalities: Law and the Backward Classes in India* (Berkeley: University of California Press, 1983).

44. For a fuller treatment of these organizations see Rubin, "The Civil Liberties Movement in India."

SUGGESTED READINGS

Bardhan, Pranab. *The Political Economy of Development in India*. Oxford: Blackwell, 1984.

Basham, A. L. *The Wonder That Was India: A Survey of the History and Culture of the Indian Sub-continent before the Coming of the Muslims*. Third Revised Edition. London: Sidgwick and Jackson, 1967.

Basu, Dilip K. and Richard Sisson, eds., *Social and Economic Development in India: A Reassessment*. New Delhi: Sage, 1986.

Freeman, James M. *Untouchable: An Indian Life History*. Stanford: Stanford University Press, 1979.

Herring, Ron. *Land to the Tiller*. New Haven: Yale University Press, 1984.

Nehru, Jawaharlal. *The Discovery of India*. Second Edition. New York: Oxford University Press, 1982.

Omvedt, Gail. *We Will Smash This Prison*. London: Zed Press, 1980.

Rudolph, Lloyd I. and Susanne Hoeber Rudolph. *In Pursuit of Lakshmi: The Political Economy of the Indian State*. Forthcoming.

Rushdie, Salmon. *Midnight's Children*. New York: Alfred A. Knopf, 1981.

Srinivas, M. N. *Social Change in Modern India*. Berkeley: University of California Press, 1966.

Wolpert, Stanley. *A New History of India*. Second Edition. New York: Oxford University Press, 1982.

8

ISRAEL

Raphael Israeli and Rachel Ehrenfeld

CULTURAL AND HISTORICAL BACKGROUND

Israel is a democratic country where the rule of law prevails, where legal institutions enjoy authority and prestige, and where concern for human rights is one of the overriding preoccupations and sensitivities of Israeli society. However, many built-in contradictions, cleavages, clashes, and constraints between various norms—legal, social, religious, ethnic, and political—tend to erode the fringes of the otherwise strong fabric of Israeli commitment to human rights.

This state of affairs is generated by the fact that modern Israel comprises not only a heterogeneous Jewish population, a factor which in itself creates social tensions and vocal recriminations regarding alleged breaches of human rights, but also a large minority of Arab citizens (17 percent) which is basically at odds with the Jewish majority. What is more, Israel has been administering since June 1967 large tracts of previously Arab-held territories (the West Bank, the Gaza District, and the Golan Heights) where the population is predominantly Arab.

In an intricate situation of this sort, how does one gauge the effectiveness of the protection of human rights or the infringements thereupon? By the degree of the subjective sense of grievance incurred by those who feel they are discriminated against, or by the strictness of the enforcement of the law of the land? By the escalation or attenuation of human suffering, or by the means of legal relief that the victim of oppression can resort to when seeking redress? For the commitment of the authorities to legal enforcement, to goodwill, to humane attitudes, and to a fair enactment of laws and regulations can be easily offset by subjective feelings of discrimination on the part of certain sections of the population.

For example, many religious Jews in Israel feel that their rights are being encroached upon by secular Israel which does not officially close down the country altogether on Sabbath and Jewish festivals. Other Israelis feel that their religious rights are abridged by the fact that a mosque had been built by Muslims on the site of the ancient Jewish Temple. Inquire of some women groups in the country and you will hear loud clamoring for equal rights and a stringent denunciation of the male chauvinism of the Israelis. Ask Arabs in Israel and they would enumerate a long list of abridgments of their civil rights, from the military government under which they used to live to their deprivation of the right to get veteran benefits since it is not their fault that they cannot serve in the Israeli Army. They would bitterly resent their de facto discrimination in job opportunities, in choosing their housing areas, in pursuing political careers, etc. If you ask Sephardic Jews, some of them would criticize the patronizing attitude of Ashkenazim towards them, deplore Ashkenazi domination of the political, economic, social, and intellectual systems in the country, and denounce the Ashkenazi predominance which has made them abandon their own cultural heritage. Secular Jews would voice a long litany of claims and grievances against the religious takeover of the country, the disproportionate influence of the religious parties in Israeli politics, and the ensuing infringement of human rights with regard to personal status (no civil marriages are allowed in Israel) or public services (no public transportation, shopping centers, and amusements are available on Sabbath).

The Arabs in the occupied territories would enumerate an even more formidable list of recriminations against the Jewish state which they perceive as undermining their Holy Places, demolishing their houses, deporting their leaders, censoring their newspapers, curtailing their free movement, etc.

Who is right and what is right in this maze of contradictions, perceptions, and claims? Maybe our only recourse is to try to sort out what the moral norms and the laws of Israel say about human rights, and how law is applied in practice in everyday life under the existing constraints.

The Jewish Tradition of Human Rights

A rabbinical saying enjoins Jews: "If you aspire to greatness, erect a peak for yourself; dig not a pit for others." Namely, exactly as one has the right to achieve for oneself, one is under the obligation not to hinder others. In Judaism, respect for the right of others is a binding and enforceable religious norm. Justice H. H. Cohn, the distinguished advocate of civil rights in Israel, has aptly remarked, "While in secular legal systems a man who does not commit any offense and does not infringe the rights of others may trust, at best, to be left unmolested by the law enforcement agencies, in Jewish law, even the man who just refrains from infringing the others' rights is assured of divine reward."[1]

True, harsh measures against idolaters, as against others, were prescribed by the Bible, but in general, Jewish law came to treat the adherents of the monotheistic faiths as gerim (strangers), namely, that they should be governed by the same laws and rules of conduct as the Jews. Similar injunctions are found in Jewish law regarding equality before the law and the administration of justice.

The Jewish codes of law not only enjoin individuals and the state to pursue justice, to give a fair hearing to all parties, to assume a person innocent unless proven guilty, and to intervene when the life of another human being is in danger, but also recognize the right of all men to education and to a fair reward for labor and rendered services. It is noteworthy that the great Jewish prophets lay more emphasis on social justice towards one's fellow man, widows, and orphans and on succoring the oppressed than on the worship of God and the fulfillment of all rituals.

It is this long and unbroken tradition of the Jews, coupled with their sad history of persecution, annihilation, and oppression that culminated in the Holocaust, which reinforces the human rights awareness of Israelis. There is an underlying assumption in Israeli society that the Jewish state should put an end to all forms of discrimination, oppression, injustice, and persecution of which the Jews have been the victims and still bear the sad historical memory. The lofty principles deriving from the prophets' visions of freedom, justice, and peace came to be incorporated in Israeli's Declaration of Independence which, in the absence of a formal Israeli constitution, constitutes the basic document of human rights promulgated by the nascent State of Israel (1948). It declares, inter alia,

The State of Israel . . . will be based on freedom, justice and peace as envisaged by the Prophets of Israel; it will ensure complete equality of socio-political rights to all its inhabitants irrespective of religion, sex or race; it will guarantee freedom of religion, conscience, language, education and culture; it will safeguard the Holy Places of all religions and it will be faithful to the principles of the Charter of the United Nations.

Legal Standards

The Declaration of Independence is not a law per se, but it does provide a guideline and a yardstick for the interpretation of all Israeli laws whether they were enacted by the State of Israel or prior to the foundation of the State. As such, the Declaration of Independence is assumed by the courts of Israel as a safeguard of the supreme principles of liberty, equality, and justice, and as a guarantee that the Israeli legislature (the Knesset) will not enact any law that runs counter to its spirit. This is all the more important since Israel does not have as yet either a formal written constitution or a Bill of Rights.

Initially, upon the establishment of Israel, a constitution was drafted, but due to the inability of the first Constitutional Assembly to resolve basic political differences between various constituting groups, it was decided, after long and exacting deliberations, that the constitution would be enacted piecemeal. Constitutional matters, including a bill of rights, were to be incorporated in a series of "Basic Laws," the sum total of which would ultimately amount to a constitution. Indeed, such Basic Laws have been enacted over the years, covering most aspects of what a constitution would incorporate, but the Basic Law on Civil Rights has been discussed in parliamentary committees for a number of years without conclusion. This bill, when adopted, would cover most aspects of civil rights, including the clause that they may not be curtailed by the legislature except in the context of ensuring the maintenance of a democratic government, preserving the security of the state, safeguarding moral values, preventing the profanation of religion, protecting the rights of others, or ensuring orderly judicial process.

The lack of a formal constitution or a Bill of Rights in Israel does not mean, however, that human rights are not duly safeguarded under the present legal system. For not only are there statutory laws governing many aspects of human rights, but the judicial system, and especially the institution of the Supreme Court, are in themselves alert and awesome watchdogs of the due application of those laws.

As regards statutory laws, they extend over a wide gamut of domains; several laws, such as the Labor Act, explicitly prohibit discrimination on the basis of race, color, sex, language, religion, political and other opinion, party affiliation, and country of origin. All institutions of education are bound by the same obligations vis-à-vis both applicants and teachers. Privacy and the right of election and representation are all covered by the Basic Laws that have already been adopted by the Knesset. Similarly, the existing laws provide for social rights such as medical care, education, equal participation in social activities, the right to housing, the right to access to any place or service intended for the use of the general public, and the right to the preservation of the identity and cultural heritage of the different communities. The rights of persons accused of crime, the freedom from arbitrary arrest and torture, and the right to life, liberty, and personal security are laid down in the codes of criminal law and criminal procedure. The rights of nationality and citizenship, to social security and work, to rest and leisure, to join trade unions and other organizations, are all part of the Israeli legal code. The right of property, even though it is qualified by the right of the state to expropriate for public purposes, is firmly safeguarded by law.

Laws of personal status, such as marriage and divorce, are administered by religious courts so as to accommodate the various religious communities of Israel: Jews, Muslims, Christians of different denominations, and Druze. This legal arrangement was inherited from the Ottoman Empire's millet system and continued through the British Mandate in Palestine (1918–1948). But since the foundation of Israel (1948) universal civil laws have governed such matters as equality of women in inheritance, dissolution of marriage against the wife's will, polygamy, matrimonial property relations, and the like, all pertaining to human rights. The net result is that while the protection of human rights is ensured inasmuch as the personal choice of Israeli citizens is respected in these matters, the civil law applies whenever the traditional customs and laws are deemed in contradiction to the Universal Declaration of Human Rights.

Besides enacted laws, however, there are recognized basic freedoms—such as the freedom of the press, freedom of movement and worship, freedom of religious belief and ethnic affiliation, freedom of expression and peaceful assembly—which are upheld by the courts in Israel despite the absence of a Bill of Rights or a formal constitution, sometimes of even specific statutory laws. The Supreme Court in Israel is, in this regard, perhaps the foremost institutional guarantor of civil rights. For it is empowered, when it sits as the High Court of Justice, to issue an *order nisi*, at the behest of any citizen, against any institution or official, to show cause why it took, or refrained from taking, any particular measure which might be deemed harmful to the interested party.

In fact, Israeli citizens of all creeds, ethnic origins, and walks of life, when it comes to matters pertaining to basic freedoms, often petition the High Court and find relief when they are justified by the bench, and the governmental agency concerned is ordered to redress the wrong.

In addition to its statutory laws, Jewish tradition, and moral norms, democratic Israel also relies on accepted international conventions of human rights. The Universal Declaration of Human Rights (1948) and the International Covenant on Civil and Political Rights (1966) have been cited and given effect by Israeli courts under the rationale that they have become "nowadays the common property of all enlightened nations whether or not they are members of the United Nations, and whether or not they have already ratified the 1966 Covenant."[2]

Israel has not yet ratified the International Covenant on Economic, Social and Cultural Rights, probably due to political reasons, both domestic and external. But most other human rights conventions were ratified, e.g., those on racial discrimination, discrimination in education and employment, prevention and punishment of genocide, war crimes and crimes against humanity, abolition of slavery and the slave trade, forced labor, traffic in persons and exploitation of prostitutes, stateless persons, refugees, the nationality of married women, political rights of women, minimum age of marriage, consent to marriage, and the freedom of association and of collective bargaining.

Human rights are received into the Israeli legal system like international treaties. That is to say that they are not binding as laws unless they are specifically enacted by the Knesset; however, any norm of customary international law which is internationally recognized as such is deemed to be part of the Israeli legal system as long as it is not incompatible with the statutory laws of Israel. In any case, the Israeli laws will always be interpreted by the courts as conforming with international law, unless otherwise explicitly stated. In this light, Israeli laws have repeatedly been amended so as to conform with international treaties to which Israel is a signatory.

CIVIL AND POLITICAL RIGHTS AND EMERGENCY MEASURES

The security plight of Israel hardly needs to be discussed. Many perceive Israel as a garrison-state whose characteristics, according to Harold Lasswell, should be the withholding of information, an atmosphere of suspicion, decline of the press and of public opinion, weakening of the political parties and parliament, and decline of civil executives and of the court. What is stunning about

Israel is that despite its state of siege, despite its being surrounded on all sides (except Egypt since 1979) by virulent and powerful enemies bent on its destruction, and its control over a large Arab population, most of Lasswell's characteristics are hardly noticeable in the day-to-day conduct of Israeli affairs: the press is critical, the political system is vigorous, no political liberties were repealed, and democracy thrives as in any Western country. Even the emergency measures adopted and applied are surprisingly mild, compared to similar situations in other countries.

In principle, emergency measures are inconsistent with civil rights because they put limitations thereupon. However, since those limitations are recognized as such in liberal democracies, their temporary nature is *eo ipso* implied. The Universal Declaration of Human Rights and the International Covenant on Civil and Political Rights recognize that civil rights cannot be incompatible with the security needs of the state. Therefore, emergency measures must be enacted and carried out only in the context of safeguarding state security and public safety. However, in Israel, because of the sensitivities of the Arab-Israeli conflict and of the Arab minority living in Israel proper, emergency measures, especially when activated against the Arab population are bound to acquire political overtones. Within this scope lie most of the abridgments of civil rights in Israel.

Land and Property Rights

Between the years 1948 and 1963, most of the areas inhabited by Israeli Arabs were administered by military government, which limited their freedom of movement, occasionally decreed expropriation of their lands for public needs, ordered administrative arrests, and controlled many aspects of their lives as security circumstances warranted. Land requisitions, perhaps more than any other infringements, have become the cause célèbre, in the Arab and world media, due to several factors. First, because Arabs in Israel have been, for the most part, settled on the land, any confiscation, even when intended for public well-being (building roads or developing the infrastructure—all subject to due compensation according to the universally applied law in Israel), produces an uproar. The Land Day, which has been commemorated annually by the Arabs in Israel since 1976, illustrates the bitterness and sense of frustration and exploitation that many of them entertain vis-à-vis Israel. The fact that, as a whole, their losses have been compensated and offset in other ways, such as the tremendous pace of development in their villages, industrialization, and progress in education, health care, and welfare under the state of Israel, hardly is of consolation to them. As one of them aptly put it: "Now that our stomachs are full, it is time to worry about our spiritual and emotional needs." Those needs are often couched in "national" terms, hence the politicization of the human rights issue and the no-win situation in which Israel often finds itself.

Second, the Arab and Bedouin clusters of settlement in the Galilee and the Negev, respectively, happen to be located in, or in close proximity to, the hilly and desert areas of the country, the only areas available as training grounds to Israel's army and air force. Confiscation of land for military purposes with which the Arabs have, understandably, little sympathy, further increases their fury against the Israeli policy of land requisition. And finally, for many elements of the Israeli-Arab community, who are interested to boost their nationalistic, often anti-Israeli, sentiments, land confiscation came as no small bonanza to rally Arab masses, and no shrewd politician would pass that opportunity up. The Israeli Arabs' sense of loss has not been assuaged subsequent to the abrogation of the military government in 1963. On the contrary, that abrogation proved to them that the entire device had been unjustified in the first place. In the 1970s those sentiments were awakened anew when the Israeli government initiated a drive to ''Judaize'' the Galilee, that is, to implant new Jewish settlements in the heartland of the Arab-settled areas, even when this was done on government-owned land. In general, the abolition of the military government did not eliminate the frictions and tensions regarding land ownership. This, coupled with the surging Palestinian identity among some Israeli Arabs, has perpetuated the subjective perception of discrimination and has increased the degree of politicization of this otherwise purely human rights issue.

In addition to ongoing tensions and recriminations regarding land ownership and expropriation, there are some notorious cases in Israel where Arabs, former inhabitants of border area villages, or owners of other property which was taken over by the state or the Jewish population during the heat of the Israeli War of Independence (1948), have claimed their right to go back to their villages or regain possession of their property. This issue has become more acute since Israel's occupation of the West Bank and the Gaza District in 1967, where many of the former owners of the said property are now residing. Quite often, Arabs across the ''Green Line'' (that is, the line of demarcation between Israel proper and its post–1967 administered territories) came over to Israel and knocked on the doors of their previous homes, only to find that they had been occupied by others.

On security grounds, successive Israeli governments have claimed that resettlement of long-abandoned Arab villages in close proximity to hostile borders might constitute a threat to Israel, both because of the well-founded suspicion that the Arabs in Israel might side with their neighboring Arab brethren in case of renewed hostilities, and of the Israeli reluctance to expose its military deployment along the borders to potentially hostile Arab scrutiny.

Private property, such as houses, lands, businesses, and frozen bank accounts which belonged to former Arab residents of Palestine, now refugees outside Israel, has been under the control of a government-appointed trustee pending a final settlement of this issue. The problem has become highly political inasmuch as pressures from WOJAC (the World Organization of Jews from Arab Countries) tied it to the issue of Jewish property (estimated at several billions of dollars) left behind when more than 600,000 Jewish refugees escaped from Arab lands and found refuge in Israel during the 1950s and 1960s. That property has been requisitioned by the Arab governments concerned. The Israeli government now claims that in the context of a comprehensive political settlement between Israel and the Arabs, a *quid pro quo* account settling ought to be worked out to satisfy the material claims of both parties. Until then, they say, exactly as the Arab governments, from Morocco to Iraq and from the Yemen to Syria, are holding on to Jewish property, so will Israel keep its control over Palestinian refugee funds and property.

The right to property has yet another aspect to it. Formally, any Israeli citizen may purchase and own property anywhere. In practice, however, most of the land in Israel belongs to the Land Authority, a government agency, and most Israelis who own property or cultivate their land are actually doing so on lease from the government. There are many exceptions to this rule: private developers often buy land from the Land Authority for either building purposes or private farming, and most of the lands in Arab villages are privately owned. However, when Arab villagers want to expand their houses or the built-up area of their neighborhoods to meet their demographic growth, they often clash with the Land Authority which finds its property encroached upon.

In practice, there also exists a dark side to the universal right of property. Prospective buyers of property in predominantly Jewish-orthodox areas might come under the scrutiny of the majority and be denied the right to buy, or to take possession of their property, on the grounds that they do not meet the religious requirements of the neighborhood (complete standstill on Sabbath and Jewish festivals and the like). What is worse, cases of harassment and even violence have been reported against nonreligious tenants of property, or against community centers and other public facilities in religious neighborhoods, where-upon the nonreligious are constrained to cede their rights when their lives become untenable. Similarly, Arabs were denied the right to property in Jewish neigh-borhoods (and the other way around), and some who did take possession of property in a nonhospitable neighborhood were forced to give it up. Harassment of nonreligious tenants or passersby on the Sabbath, like the denial of their right to free access to their property or to public places and thoroughfares, has led to numerous violent clashes between religious and nonreligious Jews, and in some cases between Jews and Arabs.

Equality before the Law

Formally, all Israeli citizens are liable to the same rights and duties, but in practice the Arabs in Israel are subject to one major exemption: the military service, by virtue of the Minister of Defense's authority to exempt from the service individuals on various grounds. The rationale behind this major deviation from the principle of universal conscription is clear: one cannot expose Israeli Arabs to warfare against their families across the border. But military service being one of the major rites of passage into adult Israeli society, the exemption creates *ipso facto* a crucial partition between young Israeli Jews, who intensely experience their national commitment to the country through their military service, and their Arab fellow citizens, who remain torn between their country (Israel) and their people (the Arabs).

Israeli-Arab citizens, who may perhaps feel relieved by this significant exemption, nevertheless grieve over the loss of the benefits which accrue to veterans of the Israeli Defense Forces, such as loans for housing and job opportunities. Moreover, although they accept, for the most part, the rationale behind their exemption, they also realize the deep gap that separates them, as a result, from their Jewish age-group.

Exemption from the military has not been exclusively the realm of the Arabs in Israel, nor do all Arabs refrain in practice from serving in various forms. For on the one hand, extremely orthodox Jews, who elect to devote their lives to religious study, and many young Jewish women who object to service on religious grounds, are also subject to the same exemption from the military by the Minister of Defense, and suffer the same consequences as the Arabs; but on the other hand, minority groups, such as the Druze and the Circassians, have been serving in the military on a regular basis, and other Arabs, mainly Bedouins, do volunteer to the military or the border police. Suggestions have been advanced over the years to substitute "national service" of a civilian nature for military service, for those who benefit from the exemption, but they were only partly applied to religious Jewish women, and not universally to Arabs and all the rest.

The Office of the Prime Minister's Adviser for Arab Affairs, which for years has regulated and coordinated government policy toward the Arabs of Israel, is seen by many Arabs as an indication of the inequality between Arabs and Jews. This inequality begins with the very fact that the Arab is born into a minority group which harbors a sense of frustration, bitterness, and humiliation born from the knowledge that they used to be the predominant majority in Palestine but are now confined to a minority role, that their culture and language used to be universal but now are second to the Hebrew language and the Jewish culture of the majority. Arabs in Israel receive state-supervised education, like all Israelis, but theirs is in Arabic and puts more emphasis on Arab culture and history and on the Islamic faith and heritage than on Jewish history and the modern Israeli-Jewish culture. Jewish education strives to focus on Jewish and Zionist symbols and puts loyalty and devotion to the Jewish state as a primary educational goal, but for Arabs in Israel these symbols are irrelevant, sometimes even humiliating and reprehensible. The holidays of Israel (either religious or national) are irrelevant at best, irritating and insulting at worst, to many Arabs in Israel. How can they feel equal if on such basic issues as national symbols and national holidays they cannot be on a par with their Jewish compatriots?

From this rather uncomfortable situation stem other inequities of which the Arabs of Israel perceive themselves the chronic victims: their Arab education, although it is of their choice, does not put them on a basis of equality with Jewish students when it comes to admissions to Israeli universities, especially in the competitive departments. And when they graduate from universities, entire sectors of the Israeli economy, administration and bureaucracy, to say nothing of the defense establishment, are closed to them: they cannot work in any security-related institution, policy-making office, or industrial plant. This is a particularly severe problem because, for example, the Statistics Bureau, some sectors of the economy, the foreign service, major industrial complexes, and a good deal of the government bureaucracy do in fact handle classified information which the authorities deem too risky to share with the Arab citizens of Israel.

The Right to Participate in Government

The Basic Law imparts to all Israelis over the age of eighteen the right to vote, and Section 4 of the Knesset Election Law of 1969 provides freedom to any political group to submit a list of candidates to run for the legislature. In theory, there is no prohibition on any Arab member of the Knesset to become a minister in the government or a member of any of the parliamentary committees. In effect, Arabs in Israel make use of their right to vote and to elect their representatives, either to the national political parties or to parties of their own making. However, notwithstanding the freedom of political organization, it is not permitted in Israel to form an organization whose aim is to dismantle the state. In the 1950s such an Arab group (al-Ard), was banned from running for the Knesset, and the ban was upheld by the Supreme Court. To the Arabs concerned this was an encroachment on their civil rights, but for the Israeli authorities it was a supreme act of self-defense against internal subversion. In the elections of 1984, two new parties were banned by the Elections Committee, one (Jewish) on the grounds that it was racist (Kahane's List) and one (Arab) because of its putative community of ideas with the Palestinian Liberation Organization, which is perceived in Israel as bent on Israel's destruction. However, the Supreme Court reversed these two decisions of the public committee and allowed both lists to run, arguing that the freedom of organization was indivisible. As a result, the Knesset adopted a new law in 1985 banning any political party which either denied the right of Israel to exist or promoted racism and hatred. It remains to be seen how these new laws will affect the electorate, the parties running for elections, and the makeup of the next Knesset.

For reasons of security, no Arab has served, since the inception of the state of Israel, either as a member of government or of the secretive Foreign Affairs and Security Committee of the Knesset. In the civil service, Arabs were recruited and attained high positions in the court system, education, and other services, but it is for the most part in the Arab sector of the economy and society that they are employed (Arab schools, Arab district courts, Arab hospitals, and the like). All in all, due to the reasons elaborated upon previously, educated Arabs in Israel get fewer job opportunities than do their Jewish compatriots, and they usually turn to the professions (doctors, lawyers, teachers, writers, journalists, and local or national politics).

The Right to Nationality

The Israeli Nationality Act of 1952 (amended in 1968 and 1971) grants Israeli nationality by birth, naturalization, or under the Law of Return (1950). The latter specifically grants the right of citizenship to Jews "returning" to Israel from the Diaspora (the Jewish Dispersion around the world). From the law-makers' point of view, Israel was established expressly for the purpose of af-fording Jews, as a people, a state of their own on the land of their ancestors. In this view, Jews are a nation, not only a faith, hence their natural and historical right to return to the land from which their forefathers had been forcibly exiled, and the obligation of their homeland to absorb them as equal citizens, exactly as the United States or France has the duty to give shelter to its nationals. However, despite that fact that no extra rights are given to the Jews as citizens, compared with their non-Jewish compatriots, the positive discrimination in grant-ing them citizenship has aroused claims that this is a discriminatory measure against the Arabs.

Those who hold this view assert that Arabs who had been born in Palestine had much more of a right to become Israeli citizens, if they chose to, than Jews who were born in Europe, the United States, or any country for that matter, and whose ancestry had nothing to do with Israel. Many Arabs (and some Jews too) contend that Judaism is merely a faith, a claim which finds credence in the fact that most Jews have always elected to live in the Diaspora rather than in the Jewish state. Therefore, they regard Israel's discriminatory law of citizenship as "racist." However, the reality is that Israel was reborn as a Jewish state which recognizes and protects by law the right of the minorities to live freely in its midst as long as they conform with the laws of the land. The state is democratic and *pluralistic*, and its character and policies are determined by the majority of its cit-izenry. Under the circumstances, this arrangement provides the only viable solu-tion to the contradictory Jews and Arabs in Israel. This and other issues of controversy between Jews and Arabs in Palestine will perhaps be conclusively resolved in the context of a political settlement whereby the Arabs in Israel, as part of the Palestinian people, might benefit from the establishment of a Palestin-ian-Jordanian state of which they may become citizens even if they elect to con-tinue to dwell in Israel as permanent residents.

The Right to Cultural Heritage

Israeli law provides that all government notices, laws, and ordinances, in-cluding money bills, be issued in Hebrew and Arabic. The Arabs in Israel are entitled to their own curriculum in Arabic and have equal rights in matriculation examinations and in admissions to Israeli universities. In fact, due to their exemption from military service, they are able to implement the right of higher education sooner than their Jewish compatriots who have to serve first (three years for men and two years for women) and to study later. Nevertheless, some

Arabs interpret their separate education as a deliberate *de facto* educational apartheid calculated, they say, to keep their standards of scholarly achievement inferior to Israeli norms. They complain about the compulsory courses in Hebrew language and literature, Jewish history, and the like which they are not particularly eager to learn. The fact that there is a discrimination in reverse in admissions to universities, to allow more Arabs to pursue academic studies, and that the Arabic language is compulsory in Jewish schools, does not detract from Arab perceptions of discrimination against their heritage. Even the Bureau of Arab Affairs at the Prime Minister's Office and the Information Center for Arab Affairs in the Ministry of Education, which were created to intensify the pace of integration of the Arabs into Israeli society, are considered by some Arabs either as proof of Israel's designs to perpetuate their separation from mainstream Israel or, paradoxically, as the ultimate evidence of its scheming to obliterate their separate heritage.

These and other recriminations, in themselves understandable for any minority group which feels displaced and second-rated by the majority host-culture, are all the more so in an Israel which is immersed in and preoccupied by its conflict with the Arab world. The fact that by and large the Arabs of all creeds in Israel are able to maintain their heritage, and can enjoy the protection of the state through its statutory and customary laws and court system, seems to be the only reasonable, if imperfect, response to these grievances.

Other Abridgments of Civil Rights

The Press Ordinance, dating back to British mandatory rule in Palestine, specifies the qualifications needed by the editors of newspapers to obtain permission to publish their papers and magazines. The Minister of the Interior in Israel retains the discretion to suspend the publication of a newspaper or a magazine if he/she believes that it is likely to endanger the public peace. The argument is that while freedom of expression is a principle most intimately connected with the democratic process, the maintenance of the security of the state requires the limitation of that freedom to some degree and under certain conditions, lest the state would be handicapped in the conduct of its affairs. However, unlike other countries (Britain during World War II) which have imposed censorship of the press in defense matters only on a temporary basis, Israel is in a permanent state of hostilities with its Arab neighbors and is thus constrained to maintain a mandatory and permanent censorship, in security matters, on all written and electronic media and books relating to military affairs.

Other restrictions on the absolute freedom of expression apply to cinema shows and performances where questions of defamation of individuals and accepted moral conventions are considered during the preview of films and performances by a state-appointed, but independent-minded, public board.

The High Court in Israel often intervenes to uphold freedom of the press, as it interferes, in the absence of a Bill of Rights, in upholding freedom of movement, of religious worship and religious belief, the freedom to determine one's own and one's children's ethnic affiliation, and likewise matters of civil rights. In its decisions of this sort, the High Court embraces the premise that these and similar freedoms are characteristic of a modern democracy based on the rule of law and therefore are inherent in Israel's legal system. However, the courts in Israel also hold that statutory law must prevail whenever postulated freedoms are incompatible with it. For example, should nonreligious individuals reject the jurisdiction of religious courts in matters of marriage and divorce, on the grounds that ancient religious law is discriminatory and outdated, the civil courts would uphold the strength of statutory law which places jurisdiction in these matters under religious courts, despite the perceived breach of the basic freedom of religion or the claim of religious coercion. Similarly, in spite of the statutory law of women's equal rights (1961), which accords women full equality in all matters of law, an express reservation is provided by the law to save the prevalence of religious laws in matters of marriage and divorce, even though they might be deemed discriminatory.

ECONOMIC AND SOCIAL RIGHTS

Israel is basically a liberal democracy, with a well-established system of social and economic welfare, guaranteed under law. The right to work, get medical care, marry, raise a family, go on vacation, travel, and benefit from social security, and the protection from disease, crime, joblessness, deprivation, and other calamities are all taken as a matter of course. Any citizen who feels deprived of these rights can petition either the High Court of Justice, whose character as the watchdog of Israel's Civil Rights has been already discussed; or the State Comptroller, who is entitled, by law, to look into the workings of all government- and state-supported institutions and make sure that the rights of individuals are upheld; or to internal ombudsmen in practically all government departments and state-supported institutions.

The right to work is assured to all citizens. Employment offices are run by the government in all towns and cities to match employers and job hunters, free of charge. An unemployment allocation is granted by the state (social security) to the unemployed who fail to find a job. A minimum salary, computed in terms of a set percentage of the average salary in Israel, is guaranteed by law. Each employee is ensured of two to four weeks of paid vacation and sick leave, and tenure after eleven months of employment. Temporary workers who are not considered for tenure have to be officially dismissed at the end of their work term and rehired ad infinitum.

In most Israeli institutions and enterprises, fringe benefits of all sorts have become entrenched as part of the remuneration for work, such as bonuses, presents on high holidays, and studying at the employer's expense. Fringe benefits are sometimes channeled via "Employees Committees," which enjoy a strong backing of the all-powerful Trade Union Organization (Histadrut) in Israel.

The Histadrut bargains collectively for most of Israel's workers with the government and private employers, ensures salary hikes, bonuses of all sorts, cost-of-living allowances, and the diversification of fringe-benefits (car and telephone allowances, grants for rest-house, vacations, funds for sabbaticals, and the like).

In Israel, medical insurance, which is virtually universal, is practiced through membership in "Sick-Funds." The largest (Kupat Cholim) belongs to the Histadrut and encompasses well over 80 percent of Israel's workers. Workers pay a nominal fee monthly, which is supplemented by the employer and subsidized by the Israeli government. Other private sick-funds operate similarly for non-members of the trade unions. Medical care covers clinics, laboratories, hospitalization (unlimited), surgery, and all treatments, except for dental care.

Social security was established in Israel in the 1950s and provides protection for the old, the sick, the disabled, large families, the handicapped and the deprived. The old get monthly pensions set by law and seasonally updated to match the cost of living; the sick get their salaries from social security beyond the thirty days covered by their employer under law; the permanently handicapped or disabled receive living allowances and exemptions from taxes (on cars and appliances); mothers get an allowance to cover the expenses of baby-bearing; large families, from the third child on are entitled to a special allowance commensurate with the number of children in the family. Social security also covers the difference between one's income and the minimum salary in cases of those underemployed and provides for other emergencies such as work and traffic accidents. Everyone employed in Israel pays a nominal fee monthly, which is supplemented by one's employer, and that ensures one's lifetime benefit from the system.

HUMAN RIGHTS AND THE ADMINISTERED TERRITORIES

All the aforementioned abridgments of civil rights in Israel proper, especially those regarding Israeli Arabs, acquire a manifold world resonance when it comes to the territories occupied by Israel since June 1967, namely, the West Bank and Gaza (in Israeli parlance, Judea, Samaria, and the Gaza District), the Golan Heights, and Sinai (until it was returned to Egypt under the peace treaty in 1982). Naturally, the human rights issue in the administered territories is essentially different from what has been happening in Israel proper, if only for the single reason that those territories have not become part of Israel (except for East Jerusalem), and the Israeli legal system has not been extended to them (except for the Golan Heights, where the original population had, for the most part, escaped to the Syrian hinterland during the 1967 war). These territories are ruled by military government or varieties thereof ("civil administration") and ruled by decree since no local legislature exists to enact new laws. In conformity with the relevant rules of international law, there cannot be an administrative vacuum in the occupied territories, and the Israeli military commander is empowered to make the law. However, the Israeli High Court of Justice has decreed that some of the activities of the Israeli administration in the territories are subject to the same criteria of judicial control as those prevalent in Israel, and the High Court has been supervising the administration of justice in those territories since 1968. The Israeli settlers in the territories are subject to a military law which is very similar to the Israeli law, and in any case they are directly subject to the Israeli legal system.

This maze of legal systems is further complicated by the fact that the Jordanian legal system, which had obtained in the territories prior to 1967, still prevails as a source of authority and enactment, and that the principles of international law in occupied territories must be taken into consideration by the Israeli military government in matters of administration and of the judiciary. Israel has indeed stated from the very outset of its occupation of the territories that it would abide by The Hague Regulations and the Geneva Conventions governing occupied enemy territory, as a matter of principle, even though it did not see itself necessarily bound to do so, due to the much disputed question of whether the territories were "occupied," "liberated," or merely "administered" by Israel. Be it as it may, the Israeli military governor took over all legal authority in the territories upon the completion of hostilities in June 1967. But he also declared that the legal system that had prevailed prior to the Israeli occupation would continue to be valid as long as, and to the extent that, it did not stand in contradiction to military decrees to be issued as the Israeli military government wore on.

All these legal safeguards should have created a bearable situation for both the occupiers and the occupied. However, due to the longer than foreseen Israeli presence in the territories, which to some Israelis is neither an occupation nor a temporary one, the dynamics of occupation have set in which dictate the behavior and responses of the occupied and the occupying power alike. The pace of the establishment of new Israeli settlements (over one hundred now), and the ideological motivation of some of the settlers who regard themselves as the legal owners of the land, have indeed created a situation of *de facto* annexation of the territories to Israel, which to some observers seems irreversible. The economic interdependence between Israel and the territories that has crystallized over the years certainly adds to the sense of permanence of the Israeli presence, both in the eyes of many Israelis, who view this either as a right or as a security necessity, and of many Arabs, who either accept the situation with resignation or consider the chances to reverse it as increasingly dim.

The end result is a growing discrepancy between what Israel perceives as a relatively liberal, under the circumstances, administration of the territories, and what the Arabs regard as an oppressive instrument to enforce Israeli rule and to provide the backup for a creeping annexation. For regardless of the merits or demerits of the Israeli presence in the West Bank and Gaza, it is evident that the population regards itself as occupied against its will and therefore oppressed, persecuted, and exploited. As such, it views itself as entitled, indeed duty-bound, to resist occupation by demonstrations, disruptions of public order, strikes, acts of violence and wanton terror, all as legitimate means to struggle against the unwanted occupiers. Thus, by the nature of things, any Israeli action to preserve order, which is incumbent upon any administration, is interpreted by the Arabs as an act of repression. When Israel interfered to democratize the mayoral elections in the West Bank, it was accused of eliminating the traditional local social structures; when it struck passages of hatred against the Jews from local textbooks, it was condemned for obliterating Arab culture; when it undertook archaeological digs in the Old City of Jerusalem, it was accused of undermining the Muslim religious places; when it temporarily closed down colleges where disturbances, acts of incitement and terror, had erupted, it was accused of oppressing academic freedom; and when it blew up houses belonging to convicted terrorists and where stockpiles of weapons and explosives were found, "barbaric acts" were imputed to it; when it arrested children who were trained and instigated to throw rocks and Molotov cocktails at innocent Israeli passersby, it was accused of wanton cruelty; and when it banned local leaders who were instigating disturbances and unrest, it was charged with purposely depriving, by exile, the local population of its leadership. And so on, a long list of no-win situations.

However, viewed from the prism of international law and the conventional norms of conduct of occupying powers, the maintenance of law and order, as decreed by the military governor, is one of his primary responsibilities. Within those constraints, and given the dynamics of occupation discussed above, it is rather extraordinary how relative peace and order prevail in the territories at a relatively low cost in terms of abridgments of human rights. Indeed, the record shows not only a relative peace and quiet most of the time, in a place which could be teeming with terror, unrest, and even civil disobedience, but also an impressive system of safeguards which ensures the basic rights of the occupied Arab population, occasional deviations notwithstanding. And the two sides of the equation are not unrelated.

First and foremost, the inhabitants of the occupied territories can appeal to the Israeli High Court of Justice. This legal recourse, which apparently has no precedent or parallel in other occupations, puts the occupied population on a par with the citizens of the occupying power as far as their expectations of the administration of justice are concerned. This means that when an Israeli branch of government, civil or military, is deemed to have encroached upon the rights of an individual in the territories, he or she can petition the Court to restore the status quo until the case is heard before the Court. Admittedly, not all cases of this sort, which are by nature quite numerous in a state of occupation, are submitted by the Arabs to the High Court of Israel. But this is not because there are no excesses of power on the part of the Israeli administration, or because the High Court lacks the jurisdiction to deal with them, but essentially because terror and even murder are resorted to by some extremists in the territories to discourage "collaboration" with the Israeli court system.

Still, the record of the High Court shows an abundance of petitions from the Arabs in the territories against their military governors. It is the conclusion of some eminent jurists in Israel and abroad that the very existence of the High

Court's jurisdiction in the territories, and its character as an exacting watchdog, have contributed most effectively to the self-restraint which the military governors are imposing on themselves in ever-increasing measure.[3]

Second, two boards were established by the military government to provide relief to the population of the territories in view of the fact that, according to international law, the officials of the occupying power cannot be prosecuted before the local courts. Those boards deal with claims for compensation for injury caused to residents of the region by members of the Israeli Army and with appeals against decisions and orders of the military government.

Third, the local administrative and court systems in the territories were left almost intact by the military government. This was consistent with Israel's policy not to interfere with the local judicial system or with any other sphere of life, for that matter, to the extent possible, unless security considerations were directly involved. Thus, the local administration essentially continues to operate as it had under the Jordanians, while the Israeli professional personnel supervise the various domains of civil administration (agriculture, health, education, public works, and the like). Military courts were established in addition to the local court system, in accordance with Article 66 of the Fourth Geneva Convention, to deal with security violations. In the military courts the rules of evidence obtaining in Israeli courts are applied, which are based on common law, except that according to the Israeli system, which is applied in the territories, no accused may be convicted solely on the strength of his own confession. This reservation removes all possible suspicions that the accused may be confessing a crime he or she did not actually commit. The rights of the accused in the military courts are further protected by an order (Concerning the Closing of Files, 1980) which empowers certain officials of the military government to stay the case if no public interest would be served by the proceedings or if evidence in the case is deemed insufficient.

Fourth, a strict differentiation is maintained by the occupying power between public and private property. The military government adopted the limitations of The Hague Regulations, which enable the occupying power to make use of private property, or to limit the owner's use of it, only for reasons of public welfare and of military necessity. The Israeli Army also requires that such requisition be approved by the Chief of the General Staff; that compensation be paid to the owner; that preference be given to public over private land for the purposes of military installations; that fallow and rocky land take precedence over arable land; and that in case of requisition of private land, advance notice be given to the owners to enable them to collect their harvest prior to the military takeover.

The same rules apply when a new Israeli settlement is founded, when deemed necessary for security reasons. Such requisition orders were repeatedly upheld by the Israeli Supreme Court, when challenging petitions from Arab owners were submitted for its scrutiny. In other cases, notably Elon Moreh (1978), the Court did not allow the building of a settlement on private land that had been requisitioned for training purposes in 1970, and the settlement was dismantled since the Court was not convinced that the security considerations behind the confiscation were justified. Since that verdict was pronounced, the Israeli military administration has consistently refrained from allowing the erection of new settlements on private land. This is only one example of the role of the Supreme Court in restricting excesses of the military government and enforcing the rule of law.

Fifth, the Israeli military administration has promoted commerce, industry, agriculture, and other areas of economic activity, while refraining from interfering, to the extent possible, with the existing economic infrastructure. Thus, it has pursued a rather liberal economic policy, allowing the free flow of goods from the territories to Jordan and the adjoining Arab countries (the "Open Bridges"), and removing tax and custom barriers between itself and the territories, thus encouraging the movement of people and goods in both directions. Unemployment in the territories has been reduced by permitting Arab workers to partake in the Israeli labor market, and many of them were trained by Israel in such skills as construction, carpentry, the tourist industry, handicrafts, and the like.

The military government has also been providing funds for the upkeep of most educational institutions, and has created some twenty-six new vocational training centers for the local population. Six institutions for higher learning were established, where none existed before, and the total number of schools has increased by a third under the Israeli military government. Whereas the population in the territories has increased by only 20 percent under Israeli rule, the number of school students has increased by 80 percent. Dramatic advances have also been made in the areas of agricultural production, health services (including the availability of Israeli facilities to many patients from the territories), electrification, waterworks, roads, and the like. In terms of the right to service and of the general quality of life, which is one of the fundamental human rights in any society, the Israeli military rule cannot be said to have worsened the existing standards in the territories upon the Israeli takeover. Quite the contrary, many aspects of the day-to-day life have markedly improved.

All these safeguards and improvements, and the usually liberal response of the Israeli military government to the needs of the population do not, however, detract one iota from the Arabs' feeling of oppression under occupation. Quite the reverse. The far more oppressive regime of the Hashemite House in the West Bank in the pre–1967 period seems to have generated a far less violent response among the Palestinians than has Israeli rule today, and certainly far less criticism by world media and international bodies than we have been recently witnessing. Paradoxically, it seems that under a relatively liberal government, where safeguards are anchored in law, where legal institutions play the watchdog, where the authorities cannot act with unbridled brutality, and where world media can operate freely and are attentive to the grievances of the population, one can expect a higher propensity for demonstrations, disturbances and clamoring for civil rights. For the payoffs in such cases are high and the risks relatively low. Most of the grievances, when regarded from the viewpoint of the population, would generally seem justified, for one tends to identify with the underdogs and to criticize the occupying power.

Under Israeli rule these grievances usually center around security measures which the military government takes in order to meet its responsibilities as the authority in charge of public safety and order. The security measures adopted by the Israeli military government in the West Bank are based on Jordanian legislation which includes the same emergency rules inherited in Israel proper from the British Mandate. For example, Article 112 of the Regulations empowers the military governor to deport persons for reasons of security. Some of those Arabs deported by Israel have boasted, upon their arrival in Jordan, of their subversive activities against Israel while in the West Bank, and they were rewarded for their services to the Arab cause by promotion to high positions in the Jordanian government. For Israel, deportation was a legal course of action to take against instigators of public unrest, but for Palestinian Arabs and their supporters, any deportation spells oppression and the uprooting of people from their families and environment.

The military governor, though empowered by international law to restrict political freedoms, including the right of assembly, freedom of speech, and the display of hostile emblems, has in fact resorted to the practice of allowing them, either subject to permits (in the case of gatherings or demonstrations) or to a limitation that prohibits hostile incitement and propaganda which can disturb the public order. Censorship of the press applies only to security matters, as in Israel proper, or with regard to passages which explicitly incite hatred and disorder. But again, viewed from the Arabs' point of view, this is oppression of free expression all the same.

CONCLUSION

An intricate web of statutory laws, customary laws, and traditional moral injunctions and inhibitions places the Jewish state in a relatively high spot among nations with regard to its respect of human rights. However, due to the heterogeneous composition of Israeli society, to the presence among the Jewish majority of a sizable Arab minority, to the protracted rule of Israel in the territories since 1967, to its ongoing state of war with most of its neighboring Arab countries, and to its being a state in the making, some abridgments of human rights seem practically inevitable even if morally unjustifiable.

The courts in Israel strive to strike a fair balance whenever statutory law may conflict with the principle of nondiscrimination or other fundamental human rights. Thus, even though Israel does not have a Bill of Rights, and statutory laws may not cover as yet all aspects of human rights, the fact that fundamental freedoms and liberties are recognized and enforced by the Judiciary ensures redress whenever abridgments of human rights occur. On one instance the court expressly said,

We are proud of the freedom of opinion and the freedom of association and the absence of discrimination that are found in Israel, and we regard with disdain and contempt such regimes as those of our enemies where only one party is allowed . . . or where all governmental power is concentrated in the hands of a dictator or a military junta. When the exigencies of a war which our enemies may force upon us so require, the Israeli legislature will know how to authorize the proper bodies to take all necessary defensive actions, and not only on the battlefield; but any measure which is contrary to law, or which is taken without due authorization, and which may adversely affect any civil rights, is illegal and will not be upheld by any judge in Israel.[4]

As to the occupied territories, as long as Israel holds them, it is bound to be confronted with inevitable infringements of human rights. For if peace and quiet were kept, namely, if the Arabs had reconciled themselves to what they regard as occupation, Israel would have had no reason to abridge anybody's human rights. The long periods of almost absolute quiet in the territories indicate that this is the case. However, it is in the nature of things that the occupied should resist and that the occupiers should use coercion to curtail disturbances. The challenge to Israel would be to maintain law and order with the minimum disruption to the lives of the inhabitants and the minimum encroachment on their civil rights, pending a solution of that sore and complicated issue. In so doing, Israel should avoid pushing the Arabs down the pit while it is attempting to reach the peak itself.

NOTES

1. H. H. Cohn, *Human Rights in Jewish Law* (New York: Ktav Publishers, 1984) 23. We are grateful to Justice Cohn for having kindly agreed to go over the original manuscript and correct many points of fact and interpretation. He also made available to us some of his many writings on this matter from which we drew extensively by reason of the immense authority of the author in this domain. We remain, however, solely responsible for the views expressed in this article and for any mistakes and misinterpretations or misjudgments which may have remained uncorrected.

2. Quoted by H. H. Cohn, "Comparative Law and International Protection of Human Rights," *Israel Reports to the IX International Congress of Comparative Law* (Jerusalem, 1982), 270.

3. See the Report of the Israeli Section of the International Commission of Jurists, Tel-Aviv, 1981, the Introduction, pp. 10–11. Much of the material for this section is based on this report.

4. Quoted by Cohn, "Comparative Law," 270.

SUGGESTED READINGS

Cohn, H. H. *Human Rights in Jewish Law*. New York: Ktav Publishers, 1984.
Cohn, H. H. "Comparative Law and International Protection of Human Rights" (sec.

IV A 2), *Israeli Reports to the IX International Congress of Comparative Law*. Jerusalem, 1982, pp. 263–75.

Cohn, H. H. "On the Meaning of Human Dignity." *Israel Yearbook on Human Rights* vol. 13, 1983, pp. 226–51.

Eidelberg, P. "On Moles and Men: The Case of the Jewish Underground." *Morasha*, no. 12. (Winter 1985).

"Israel and Occupied Territories." *Amnesty International Report, 1984* (for the period Jan.- Dec. 1983) (London: Amnesty International Publications, 1984), pp. 340–45.

Judea, Samaria and the Gaza District, a Sixteen-Year Survey (1967–1983). State of Israel, the Ministry of Defence, Nov. 1983.

The Judicial and Administrative System. The Association for Civil Rights in Israel, No. 1, 1985, (in Hebrew).

Levine, E. *Terrorism, Human Rights and Emergency Legislation in Democratic Countries*, A.C.J.S., 1981, Annual Meeting, Philadelphia, Pennsylvania.

The Rule of Law in the Areas Administered by Israel. Israel National Section of the International Commission of Jurists, 1981.

Shamgar, M. "The Observance of International Law in the Administered Territories." *Rights in Warfare* (1971) pp. 262, 266.

Werblowsky, Z. "On Religion and Human Rights with Reference to the Jewish Tradition." *Comprendre* 47–48 (1981–1983): 175–83.

9

JAMAICA

Evelyne Huber Stephens and John D. Stephens

Studying human rights in Jamaica is interesting because the Jamaican case constitutes one of the rare instances of stable democracy in the Third World, having survived severe strains since the mid-seventies.[1] It provides the opportunity to investigate the development of human rights in the context of high levels of social and political conflict but of formally democratic political institutions. An analysis of the Jamaican experience illustrates the interdependence of progress in political, civil, economic, social, and cultural rights, and it highlights the importance of nongovernmental as well as governmental violations of these rights.

Attempting to adopt a baseline in order to assess the human rights record of various Jamaican governments, particularly in the post-independence (1962) period, we follow Rhoda Howard in rejecting an absolute standard, such as the UN declaration, or the situation in the developed democracies, or Jamaica in the colonial period.[2] Rather, we attempt to assess what was objectively possible given the constraints of the development of the Jamaican political economy in historical perspective. Such an approach obviously involves an evaluation by the analyst of what *might have been possible* given the historical and structural constraints. In the Jamaican case, such an evaluation is greatly facilitated by the differing development models pursued by successive governments. Thus, within a given range some important alternatives were actually attempted in the same country, which makes our analysis less speculative.

We begin by briefly outlining the development of human rights in Jamaica in the context of the political and economic development of the country. We proceed to analyze the country's (and various governments') records in political and civil rights and then economic, social, and cultural rights. Our emphasis is not on the mere cataloging of successes and failures but rather on the explanation of the reasons behind those successes and failures. We conclude with some observations on the interdependence of the various categories of human rights and on the importance of protection against nongovernmental as well as governmental abuses of human rights.

HISTORICAL BACKGROUND

Jamaica under British rule in the pre-emancipation period was essentially a "pure plantation economy" and society.[3] African slave labor produced sugar for export to Great Britain; and virtually everything the society consumed, including large amounts of foodstuffs, was imported. Essentially, governmental power was exercised by the local elite, as the governor made only occasional use of his veto power. Property and tax qualifications for voting and standing for election ensured that the wealthy white planters dominated the elected assembly.

After emancipation in 1838, the decline in the sugar industry combined with the diversification of society, i.e., the emergence of a brown middle class of small and medium farmers, merchants, teachers, and ministers, in addition to the black lower classes of small farmers and wage workers, raised fears among the white planter elite that their power would decline and that the local assembly might eventually be penetrated by colored people. The Morant Bay Rebellion of 1865, a reaction of black farmers to their desperate economic situation which was partly due to their complete lack of political and civil rights, intensified these fears to the point of causing the assembly to bring Jamaica under Crown Colony rule. Under Crown Colony rule, all governmental power was concentrated in the hands of the governor. Only elite strata, less than 6 percent of the population, had any political rights at all, but even their elected representatives had only advisory functions.

After 1865 the decline of sugar continued and the cultivation of bananas increased in importance. Since bananas can be produced profitably on relatively small plots, this strengthened the position of medium farmers. Also, trade and commerce grew in the expanding urban areas. Thus, social diversification proceeded; immigrant Middle Eastern groups became urban traders and small businessmen, indentured laborers continued to be imported from India, and a stratum of fairly prosperous medium farmers emerged. Not surprisingly, the enjoyment of civil rights was class-specific and, since class was intimately tied to color, also color-specific. The administration of justice was reformed, which meant a slow improvement for the brown middle classes, but the large mass of black peasants and laborers remained for all practical purposes excluded from protection through the judicial system against abuses by members of the middle and upper classes. The extreme case of deprivation of any civil rights, of course, were the indentured Indian laborers. An important civil right with economic implications was granted to the working class with the legalization of unions in 1919, but strike legislation remained extremely restrictive.[4] As far as economic, social, and cultural rights were concerned, the colonial government made no significant efforts to promote and protect them. Sanitation, housing, and educational opportunities for the lower classes remained exceedingly poor, and all official cultural norms and values remained exclusively British.

The impetus to political change came from the labor rebellions of 1935 and 1938, which gave birth to the nationalist movement. These labor rebellions were part of a Caribbean-wide phenomenon, which was a reaction to the economic hardships experienced in the region in the wake of the Depression. The Jamaica Workers and Tradesmen Union and one of its most vocal and charismatic leaders, Alexander Bustamante, played an important role in these disturbances, which resulted in a significant growth and strengthening of the Jamaican labor movement.[5] In September 1938 the People's National Party (PNP) was formed, under the leadership of Norman Washington Manley, to organize political pressure on behalf of the demands for social reform and political change.[6] By 1940 the PNP had committed itself to the achievement of self-government and the construction of a social order of a Fabian socialist variety, characterized by social ownership of production in key sectors of the economy, social equality, and political democracy.

Originally, Bustamante and the PNP leadership were mutually supportive, and it appeared that they would be able to weld labor and the middle class into a strong reformist nationalist alliance. However, after setting up his own union, the Bustamante Industrial Trade Union (BITU), and having himself made president general of the union for life in its constitution,[7] Bustamante broke with the PNP in 1942 and set up his own political party, the Jamaica Labour Party (JLP). This split induced the PNP to build up a labor base of its own through the Trade Union Council (TUC) and thus gave rise to the two party/union blocs which have dominated Jamaican politics ever since. The two parties have alternated in power in a two-term rhythm since the first elections with universal suffrage in 1944, the JLP winning in 1944 and 1949, the PNP in 1955 and 1959, the JLP again in 1962 and 1967, the PNP in 1972 and 1976, and finally the JLP in 1980 and 1983.

In response to the labor unrest, the Colonial Office set up a commission to report on the situation and make suggestions for improvements. This report was so damaging to the colonial administration that its full contents were not published until after World War II. The main recommendations made were to establish a welfare fund, to encourage industrialization, which before had been deliberately discouraged, and to allow for certain changes in the system of government toward greater local participation. Subsequently, the political rights of Jamaicans were slowly expanded. After long negotiations, the Constitution of 1944 was adopted, which allowed for a lower house elected on the basis of universal suffrage but left ultimate power in the hands of the governor. Full internal self-government was granted with the introduction of cabinet government in 1957. In 1958 Jamaica joined the Federation of the West Indies, but withdrew from the Federation in 1961. Pressures for full independence then mounted.

The Independence Constitution of 1962 set up a political system modeled very closely after the British one.[8] However, as we will discuss below, political practice did not fully conform to this formal legal model; electoral abuses, such as gerrymandering, ballot box stuffing, manipulation of electoral lists, as well as political violence, infringed on the political rights of Jamaicans. The Constitution did include a traditional bill of rights protecting citizens against the arbitrary use of state power but omitting obligations to positive government action in protecting social, economic, and cultural rights. The question of inclusion of the right to own property among the fundamental human rights was very controversial; eventually, the influence of representatives of capitalist interests prevailed to have it included,[9] with the provision that in case of expropriation the courts were to decide on the adequacy of compensation. This clause was to become a significant obstacle to the pursuit of policies expanding economic rights of the lower classes by the PNP government in the seventies, insofar as it made any large-scale land reform prohibitively expensive.

Though some progress in economic rights was made after independence with the introduction of a National Insurance System, the prevailing economic policy orientation in the fifties and sixties hurt rather than helped large parts of the Jamaican lower classes. The governments put exclusive emphasis on economic growth based on industrialization by invitation of foreign capital.[10] Thus, the Jamaican economy remained highly open and dependent and suffered the negative effects characteristic of such a growth pattern, namely, marginalization of significant sectors of the rural and urban population, growing unemployment, and inequality.[11] Socially and culturally, British standards, which were also the standards of the local upper class, remained dominant.

During the fifties and early sixties, both parties shared similar policy orientations. After the 1952 purge of the PNP left, the party put aside socialism and ideology in general and accepted the prevailing orthodoxy concerning strategies for economic development based on foreign investment.[12] Also, there was to a certain extent a sociological convergence between the two parties, insofar as they developed a truly cross-class base, the PNP strengthening its labor base and the JLP making inroads into the middle class, in particular attracting professionals to leadership positions. Nevertheless, some of the initial basic differences persisted; the JLP remained stronger among the small farmers and unskilled workers, particularly in rural areas, and it received support from the more conservative sections of the capitalist class, whereas the PNP remained stronger among the middle class and skilled workers and received support from more liberal capitalists.

During the sixties the parties began to differ in their reactions to the challenges emerging as a result of the detrimental effects of the dependent growth model. These challenges took the form of social protest, two spontaneous riots with racial overtones in 1965 and 1968,[13] and the emergence of radical political groups. The JLP government blamed these challenges on "subversive agitators" and countered them with repression, such as the banning of books, popular songs, and politically suspect people, and the confiscation of passports. The PNP, on the other hand, started to rethink the whole economic development model. With the support of Norman W. Manley, younger radical members were gaining influence in the party, and the 1967 Party Conference called for significant structural reforms. Under Michael Manley, then, who had followed his father as party leader in 1969 and won the 1972 election, the new PNP government started to promote a fundamental reorientation of the development model in a democratic socialist direction.

The central features of this democratic socialist model were increased economic self-reliance, creation of a mixed economy with the state sector playing the leading role, lessening of social inequalities through economic redistribution and social inclusion, deepening of political democracy through popular organization and mobilization for participation in decision making at all levels, and the pursuit of a foreign policy of nonalignment and Third World solidarity in the struggle for a New International Economic Order.[14] Clearly, these new policy directions implied an expansion and strengthening of every category of human rights. Political rights were expanded through the lowering of the voting age to eighteen and through a party-building process which increased grass-roots participation in decision making in the party as well as voter turnout. Fairness in the exercise of political rights was strengthened through the 1979 interparty agreement on electoral reform. Civil rights were extended to new groups, such as through the Status of Children Act which put illegitimate children (the norm among the lower classes) on equal legal footing with children from a marriage; and efforts were made to give more meaning to freedom of the press by creating a more pluralistic media structure through the transfer of a radio station to a variety of popular organizations, such as trade unions, churches, cooperative organizations, etc. The protection of economic rights was promoted, for instance, through jobs programs, minimum wage legislation, equal pay for equal work, compulsory recognition of trade unions, land lease programs, and the establishment of cooperatives on government-owned sugar estates. Social rights were extended through free secondary schooling, an adult literacy program, public housing construction, and improvement of rural health services. Finally, cultural rights were extended through encouragement of and material support for indigenous cultural expressions with partly African roots in music (reggae), dance, painting, and sculpture, and through deliberate emphasis on the national heritage of struggles for freedom and social justice, symbolized by Jamaica's national heroes.

Whereas the political mobilization process and the emphasis on indigenous cultural expression and national heritage had a profound effect on the consciousness and assertiveness of the black Jamaican lower classes, the PNP's efforts in implementing its reform policies and thus expanding and protecting human rights were only in part successful, particularly in economic rights and, to a certain extent, in civil rights, because the seventies were characterized by severe economic difficulties as well as an increase in criminal and political violence. Serious economic difficulties first confronted the government in 1973; after a short-lived improvement due to the imposition of a new levy on bauxite production in 1974 which increased Jamaica's revenue from the industry sevenfold, the need for stringent austerity policies arose in 1975, and by the end of 1976 the country faced a full-blown balance of payments crisis.[15] The PNP's second term was dominated first by the debate about possible alternatives to concluding an International Monetary Fund (IMF) agreement and then by the hardships brought on by very harsh IMF-imposed austerity policies. The recession and consequent deterioration of living standards induced by these austerity policies caused a regression in the protection of economic rights of the majority of the Jamaican population, and led to a rapid erosion of the government's political support base and ultimately its loss in the 1980 elections.

The rise in criminal and political violence in the seventies induced the government to impose certain restrictions on civil rights, most of them temporary. Political violence, mainly to intimidate supporters of the rival party around election time, had a long tradition in Jamaica, and it assumed a very dangerous character with the introduction of gun warfare between rival political gangs in Edward Seaga's West Kingston district in the mid-sixties.[16] From then on, gun violence remained a permanent feature of Jamaican political campaigns, and it was connected to the rise in criminal gun violence insofar as guns given out to political thugs often ended up being used for criminal purposes. In 1976 political gun violence assumed unprecedented proportions and an outright terrorist character, claiming many totally uninvolved victims. Thus, the government imposed a State of Emergency, for which it originally received general support from all organized forces, including business associations, with the notable exception of the opposition JLP. In fact, a poll conducted at the time showed that more than 80 percent of respondents in the corporate area and in parish towns supported its extension.[17] Under the State of Emergency, which remained in force from June 1976 well into 1977, several civil liberties were suspended, through provisions for preventive detention, bans on demonstrations, and censorship of statements inciting to violence.

An upsurge of criminal violence in 1973, which profoundly frightened the society because of the publicity given by the conservative *Daily Gleaner* (the country's major—and at times the only—daily paper) to a series of killings of prominent citizens, brought pressure on the government to take tough measures to bring the violence under control. In response, the government established a special Gun Court to administer extremely stringent legislation on the prosecution of gun crimes. Subsequently, certain provisions in this legislation were challenged as unconstitutional and had to be modified.

In the eighties, the new JLP government under Edward Seaga, who had waged a relentless opposition campaign aimed at delegitimizing the PNP government at home and abroad, returned to the traditional dependent capitalist model. Thus, it further restricted economic rights of the Jamaican lower classes by assigning priority to middle-class consumer imports and committing itself to deregulation of imports under an agreement with the World Bank, and thus incurring severe pressures for further devaluations. Not only did this model sacrifice equity and satisfaction of basic human needs, but it did not even produce significant economic growth, despite substantial support from the World Bank and the U.S. government for Seaga's structural adjustment policies and his emphasis on private sector-led development. Under the impact of ever more stringent austerity policies, which followed the short-lived 1981 spending spree based on foreign borrowing, the JLP rapidly lost political support.

Ironically, this loss of support led Seaga, who had made the issue of human rights and electoral reform the centerpieces of his opposition campaign in the seventies, to break the interparty agreement on electoral reform and call snap elections in late 1983. He knew that the massive devaluation to be introduced at the end of the year would cause a further drastic deterioration of popular living standards and thus of his political support. Thus, he hoped to take advantage of the support in Jamaica for the Grenada invasion by whipping up anti-leftist sentiment, raising the specter that similar events could happen in Jamaica, and calling parliamentary elections immediately. The PNP boycotted these elections on the grounds that they violated the interparty agreement and the integrity of the electoral process, as they were held on the basis of the old voter lists which disenfranchised all those who had come of voting age between 1980 and 1983. Consequently, the JLP won all sixty seats in the lower house and Jamaica at present (October 1986) lacks a parliamentary opposition.

CIVIL AND POLITICAL RIGHTS

Jamaica is a democratic country whose constitution guarantees all basic civil and political rights. With some important exceptions analyzed below, these rights are realized in practice. Given that few Third World countries are democracies, it is incumbent on us to begin our analysis with an account of what social conditions led to the development of democracy in Jamaica. To anyone familiar with Barrington Moore's work on the subject, the plantation origins of modern Jamaica would seem to predict quite another outcome. The brutal suppression of the Morant Bay Rebellion in 1865 by the plantocracy shows that there was potential for development in an authoritarian direction. From an examination of Jamaican history, it becomes apparent that more than one factor prevented forming a coalition of landlords, a politically dependent bourgeoisie, and a strong state, which Moore shows is fatal to the development of democracy.[18]

At two points in modern Jamaican history, challenges from the lower classes have occurred which, in other countries, might have led to a modern form of authoritarianism. The first was the labor rebellion of the thirties. By this time, several social and economic developments had occurred which reduced the chances of the development of an authoritarian coalition. First, after emancipation, an independent, small-holding peasant class began to develop, mainly in the hilly interior. This development was considerably accelerated by the decline of sugar and the rise of bananas as Jamaica's main export, since bananas, as noted above, can be efficiently grown on small plots. The number of large estates fell drastically in this period to one-third their previous number, though this occurred in part through consolidation, increasing the size of the remaining estates. Second, some of the largest estates passed into the ownership of foreign corporations (Tate and Lyle and United Fruit). Both of these developments weakened the economic power and potential political clout of the domestic planter class. Third, a growing commercial bourgeoisie developed independently of the plantocracy. Its ranks were filled primarily by the new ethnic minority immigrants: Lebanese, Syrians, and Jews. Thus, the kinship linkage between the landed class and the nascent bourgeoisie was weaker than in, say, Chile.[19]

Fourth, and most critically, the state and coercive forces were controlled by the British colonial masters in this period. The advisory Legislative Council was dominated by the plantocracy, and the governor generally ruled in their interests. But the colonial power served as a brake on the exploitative objectives of the landholders. It is doubtful if the local oligarchs would have ever abolished slavery without being forced to by outside edict (or by internal rebellion). And given their chronic difficulties in recruiting labor in the post-slavery period, it seems very likely that the plantocrats would have resorted to more coercive methods of labor control. But even if they had maintained their economic dominance up to the time of the 1938 labor rebellion, they could not have chosen the path of repression at that point, simply because the choice was not theirs to make. The class and political alignments in Britain, which pointed to constitutional decolonization, the introduction of universal suffrage, and the institutionalization of the labor movement,[20] were more important for the path chosen than the domestic alignments in Jamaica.

By the time the Manley government came to power, the growth of tourism, bauxite mining and alumina processing, and manufacturing had led to a further differentiation of the class structure, strengthening the bourgeoisie and expanding the working class and the lumpen proletariat. Moreover, and perhaps most important, the labor movement had laid deep roots in the society. These class structural and organizational aspects of Jamaican society in general go far in explaining why democracy endured in most of the Caribbean societies whereas it did not in Britain's former African colonies. In the context of a higher degree of autonomous social organization, it is more difficult for government elites to introduce repressive policies. In the Jamaican case, the decline of sugar after 1965 and the exit of the foreign corporations, leaving the old sugar estates in the hands of the government, meant that by 1972 the old plantocracy was a minor political force. Thus, the dominant class configuration in Jamaica was quite different from that in Chile, and different in ways important for the survival of democracy when it came under severe strain in the seventies. Namely, the anti-democratic opposition against Allende, rooted in the coalition of the landed class and the bourgeoisie, had no counterpart in Jamaica.

Finally, one has to question whether the security forces in Jamaica had the firepower and manpower to carry out a coup had they so desired. With a total force of less than 1,500 and a ground force of around 1,000, the Jamaica Defense Force alone is certainly too small for such a task, and the police force, though perhaps large enough at 6,000, is too indisciplined. As for mentality, the officers' outlook is influenced by the Sandhurst training of the top officers and thus is conservative and anti-communist, but there is no coherent school of thought parallel to the Latin American "new professionalism."[21] The general middle-class outlook of the security forces did lead them to turn against the Manley government, and the actions of the forces definitely aided the JLP and hurt the PNP in the 1980 election campaign. Still, an authoritarian takeover planned and carried out by the security forces at the present level of strength and discipline is quite unlikely. Having a security establishment of limited size is one factor in explaining the survival of political democracy in most of the English-speaking Caribbean and in Costa Rica.

As a result of political democracy and the factors that contributed to it, in particular the strength of the trade union movement, Jamaica's record on political and civil rights has been good by Third World standards. However, as indicated in the historical outline, there have been recurrent abuses even after the full installation of political democracy. The record of the JLP government from 1962 to 1972 was marred by censorship of literature and music, confiscation of passports, and ejection of Commonwealth citizens deemed subversive by the government, such as University of the West Indies lecturer Walter Rodney. The JLP government's reaction to the Black Power movement stimulated the most intensive period of repression, but repression was by no means absent earlier in this period of JLP rule. The immediate cause of this repression was primarily the conservative JLP's fears of radical currents, but the reaction was also rooted socially in the fears of the light-skinned upper middle class and white upper class of mobilization of the black masses of the country. This civil and political repression was intimately connected to, indeed, impossible to separate from, cultural repression of expression of black identity such as the Rastafari religion and reggae music. The JLP government ended its tenure in office with a denial of political rights to thousands of Jamaicans as it conducted the 1972 elections on outdated voter lists, which prevented all those citizens between 21 and 23 years of age from voting. This group of citizens was expected to be heavily PNP, an expectation borne out by post-election polls.[22] Gerrymandering also continued in this election.[23]

The advent of the PNP government of Michael Manley led to a lifting of these repressive measures and, in fact, a positive encouragement of the cultural streams just mentioned. Equally important—and a point often ignored in the human rights literature—through the policies already referred to, the Manley government created conditions which led to a significant expansion of the exercise of political and civil rights formally guaranteed in the Jamaican constitution. The government accomplished this by initiating policies which stimulated cultural inclusion, by providing the economic and social resources to lower-income Jamaicans through its redistributive programs, by widening the range of legitimate ideological positions through its own ideological self-definition, and by the party's own successful attempt at political mobilization.[24]

In terms of legal changes affecting political rights, the PNP government updated the voter lists, extended the right to vote to eighteen- to twenty-year-olds, and redrew electoral districts so that the outcome in seat distribution would more closely reflect the outcome of the popular vote. Electoral corruption, however, continued. Carl Stone estimates that two or three seats in the 1976 election may have been won due to corrupt electoral practices, and the courts did overturn the outcome in one district as a result of a JLP petition.[25] Though this hardly meant that the PNP "stole the election," as the JLP later charged (the PNP won forty-seven of sixty seats),[26] it did nonetheless represent a significant denial of the right of representation to the voters of that district (or those districts).

A path-breaking step in this area was the JLP-PNP agreement of August 1979 to reform the electoral system with the ultimate goal of eliminating the possibility of electoral corruption stemming from manipulation of voter lists, multiple voting and voter impersonation, and gerrymandering. The entire electoral machinery (development and verification of voter lists, drawing electoral boundaries, appointment of electoral officials, etc.) was put in the hands of a seven-member electoral committee with two members chosen by each of the parties and the remaining three chosen by agreement or the Governor General.[27] Due to time pressures, the committee had to scrap its plan to issue photo voter identification cards for the 1980 elections, but otherwise the procedures it developed governed the elections, and these were the fairest elections in Jamaican history.

During this period the JLP did make charges of massive violations of human rights by the PNP government. Indeed, "human rights" was one of the main themes of JLP opposition during the PNP's second term, and not accidentally, Carter's term of office in the United States. But even before the 1976 election, the JLP began to make the charge that the party repeated most insistently through the next few years: that the State of Emergency had been corruptly used by the PNP to suppress the JLP. The party later added the charge that the abuse of the State of Emergency had been part of the PNP's plot to steal the 1976 election. Still later, charges were leveled that the PNP government was using the police to harass supporters of the JLP, a case in point being the forcible ejection of JLP supporters from a public housing project in the Rema area of the Kingston ghetto. Finally, the usual (in Jamaica) charges that the government was corruptly using the state machinery to award jobs, housing, and contracts to its own supporters were intensified.

These charges (other than those relating to the dispensing of patronage) rested on little hard evidence, though they were not totally baseless. Essentially, the PNP did not improve greatly on past practice in these areas. We have already dealt with electoral abuses where, despite the demonstrated instances of corruption in the 1976 election, the movement was generally in a positive direction. The charges of patronage in the awarding of government contracts, jobs, and housing were true and perhaps could be termed a more serious violation of the rights of political outgroups than in the past, if only because the quantity of these benefits grew with the growth of government programs. At the JLP's insistence, the PNP government put together commissions headed by impartial jurists to study the charges surrounding the Rema incident and the corrupt use of the State of Emergency. In both cases, the government was absolved of the charges.[28]

Before moving on to persistent problems in civil and political rights, it is necessary that we mention the only area in which the PNP introduced and passed legislation that clearly constricted civil rights: the Gun Court Law, which regulated all crimes involving firearms. Under this law, anyone arrested for any firearms violation, including the unlicensed possession of a single bullet, would be jailed without bail until the trial. The trial would not be public. If convicted, the person would receive a sentence of indefinite detention at hard labor, with release given only at the discretion of a special review board. The provision of mandatory sentences of indefinite detention was ruled unconstitutional by the Privy Council. The provision was replaced by a mandatory life sentence for more serious offenses (i.e. not simple illegal possession of firearms, but including any crime committed with the use of a firearm).

Clearly, the Gun Court legislation has to be seen against the already mentioned chronic problems of Jamaican society which became serious in the sixties and escalated in the seventies. Violent street crime and political violence, particularly at election time, are the central and most visible manifestations of these problems, but they are intimately connected to a whole syndrome of political and economic phenomena at the very core of the Jamaican political and economic system which involve violations of human rights by both governmental and nongovernmental forces. Picking a starting point in analyzing this syndrome is essentially arbitrary, but for the purposes here it is convenient to begin with the most obvious governmental violation of human rights: police brutality. The Jamaican press constantly carries stories describing incidents in which, for instance, several policemen corner a man who then attacks them with a knife (or even a screwdriver), and the police subsequently shoot him. Ghetto residents constantly complain of indiscriminate harassment and brutality by the police. Ghetto supporters of the party in opposition allege not only harassment but also political murder by the police. The PNP in the eighties charged that an "Eradication Squad" had been assembled with the task of killing its more militant ghetto supporters, and the JLP made similar charges in the seventies, as in the case of the Greenbay Massacre and the killing of JLP militant Claudius Massop.[29]

The social source of police brutality is relatively clear. While some police attitudes may be traced to the colonial legacy of subject (rather than citizen) relations with the authorities, most police excesses can be linked to a defensive reaction to the rising levels of street crime and political violence. By the late seventies, both common criminals and political thugs in the Kingston area were armed to an unprecedented degree, often including sophisticated automatic weapons such as M16s, and there were several incidents where police stations were attacked with machine guns, a situation which led to a virtual siege mentality among the security forces.

Another factor which contributed to the trigger-happy behavior of the police was the frequency with which the gun criminals were acquitted in court because witnesses did not show up to testify after having appeared at the initial hearing or police questioning. The witnesses were frequently intimidated by friends of the accused.[30] As a consequence, the courts could not convict known criminal gunmen, and the police began to take matters into their own hands. From a civil rights point of view the murder of a known criminal is bad enough, yet worse is the fact that, as a popular reggae song laments, "sometime dem make mistake and kill an innocent one."

This same situation leads to occasional outbursts of vigilante justice on the part of citizens in the urban areas. For slightly different reasons, vigilante behavior occurs even more frequently in rural areas. Here, the frequency of crop and livestock theft and the inability of the police to control it leads to spontaneous citizen action, which in the case of livestock theft is often killing by stoning.

The increase in street crime, crop and livestock theft, and, along with other factors, political thuggery, is clearly and obviously related to the growth in unemployment and inequality in the sixties and, after a brief period of progress in the early seventies, again in the late seventies and eighties. Thus, police brutality and nongovernmental violation of civil rights in the form of witness intimidation and vigilantism are intimately connected to the economic and social rights situation.

In the case of political violence, which reached its peak in the 1980 election campaign in which 300 to 400 people were killed, the additional explanatory factor (to unemployment and inequality) is the clientelistic character of the political system. The prospect of patronage jobs and housing in a situation of great material scarcity is the key motivating factor behind political violence which began with fist fighting and rock and bottle throwing, escalating to gun warfare in the mid-sixties and to automatic weapons by the late seventies. The objective of the patronage-seeking thugs is to ensure their party's dominance in a given territorial area through voter intimidation, voter impersonation, and ballot box stuffing, all obvious violations of citizens' political rights. In some ghetto areas, it is virtually impossible to register a vote other than for the party dominant in the area. For instance, in the 1980 election the JLP candidate in West Kingston, Edward Seaga, received more votes in a number of polling divisions than there were voters on the list.[31] The intensely competitive political situation and the promise of patronage have also been the prime source of electoral corruption (gerrymandering, voter list manipulation, encouragement of voter impersonation) at higher levels in the party system.

As we initially pointed out, there have been contradictory trends in political and civil rights in the seventies. On the one hand, at the grass-roots level, political violence, voter intimidation, witness intimidation, and so on increased up to the

1980 election. On the other hand, at the legal and governmental level the trend has been in a positive direction, culminating in the electoral agreement of 1979, which is supposed to be eventually entrenched in the constitution. The improvements at the official level are, at least in part, a direct result of the escalating political violence, as politicians from both parties have increasingly perceived the situation to be out of control.

Before we move on to an analysis of economic, social, and cultural rights, we should make some mention of the recent significant setbacks for political rights. According to the interparty electoral agreement, no new general elections were to be held after the 1980 election until new voter lists were drawn up and photograph and thumbprint identification cards were issued to every voter. However, as mentioned previously, when the Seaga government experienced a temporary (as subsequent events made abundantly clear) surge of popularity in the wake of the Grenada invasion, it called snap elections for December 1983 before the new system was in place, using the outdated 1980 voter list and no photo identification, which resulted in the PNP boycott of the election. Indeed, polls released subsequently indicate that the PNP would have won by a comfortable margin (despite the temporary increase in support for the government) on updated voter lists due to the party's substantial lead among young voters, but would have lost by a narrow margin among voters on the 1980 list.[32] In April 1985 the Seaga government, again trailing badly in the polls, attempted to massively reduce the number of Parish Council seats, necessitating the redrawing of constituency boundaries, apparently in order to delay the Parish Council election, which was constitutionally required no later than June 1985. But since the government was forced to retreat due to public outcry, and since the new voter registration system was now in place, signs seemed to indicate that the 1983 election debacle was only a temporary setback for Jamaican democracy.

ECONOMIC, SOCIAL, AND CULTURAL RIGHTS

Expansion and protection of economic, social, and cultural rights did not really become a central political issue until the seventies. Under colonial rule, power relations in Jamaican society were clearly inimical to any efforts in this direction. It was not until the outbreak of the severe labor unrest of 1935 and 1938 that the Colonial Office seriously concerned itself with economic and social conditions in Jamaica. Even then, regardless of the investigating commission's extremely negative report, concrete efforts and material support to improve the situation of the Jamaican lower classes remained very limited. The main changes resulting from the unrest and the commission's report concerned the gradual extension of political rights to Jamaicans.

The gradual transition to self-government, of course, greatly increased the importance of the role played by the political parties. Given the highly competitive two-party situation and the cross-class base of both parties, patronage became a major instrument for tying supporters to their party. Government jobs and housing constituted patronage for the poor; and government contracts and appointments to a variety of boards, patronage for the rich. This meant that it was highly advantageous for the parties in power to hand out economic benefits on a particularistic basis, more so than spreading governmental resources in an attempt to expand economic and social rights on a universalistic basis to all citizens.

As mentioned above, the economic development model pursued by both parties in the fifties and sixties was concentrated on growth led by foreign investment, primarily in bauxite and tourism, as suggested in the writings of the economist W. Arthur Lewis.[33] Aside from the dispensation of patronage, improvement of the economic situation of the mass of the population was left to the assumed trickle-down effect. Several reasons account for this undisputed pursuit of dependent growth. First of all, Lewis's model, though adapted to local conditions, was in complete correspondence with the dominant Western social science paradigm of development at the time. Theories of economic development and modernization developed and taught at U.S. and British universities, where most of the Jamaican elite were educated, held that only diffusion of Western technology and models of organization and infusion of Western capital would set Third World countries on a path of permanent development.[34] Second, competing paradigms and strategies of development, particularly those rooted in Marxist or other critical paradigms, lacked legitimacy among the power holders in the Jamaican system. Up to 1957, Jamaica was still essentially under colonial rule, which obviously left no room for experiments with strategies coming out of a decidedly leftist bent. Furthermore, the Cold War had an impact on Jamaica, contributing indirectly to the purge of the PNP left in 1952 and discrediting socialist ideas to the extent that the PNP abandoned even its mild Fabian socialist stance. Third, since both parties had a cross-class base and the labor movement was split into two rival blocs, there was no strong force promoting a class analysis of society and a class-based development strategy. The radical groups emerging in the sixties lacked a mass base and thus the power to become politically influential. Fourth, the negative effects of the dependent growth model were not immediately apparent; it took the growing social inequality and social unrest of the mid-sixties to stimulate an intense examination of these effects, and the major critical academic studies were not completed until the late sixties and early seventies.

On the face of it, the performance of the Jamaican economy in the fifties and sixties was very strong. Real gross domestic product (GDP) grew at an average annual rate of 7 percent in this period (4.4 percent per capita), manufacturing increased to 13 percent of GDP, mining to 14 percent of GDP and 50 percent of merchandise exports, and tourism to roughly 10 percent of GDP and over 25 percent of gross foreign exchange earnings, while agriculture declined to 7 percent of GDP and 35 percent of merchandise exports.[35] However, between 1960 and 1972, unemployment increased from 13.5 percent to 23.2 percent.[36] Furthermore, Jamaican income distribution in the fifties was one of the most unequal in the world,[37] and the growth of unemployment along with the increase in per capita income cannot but have worsened the situation.

One of the most obvious results of this growth pattern was that the Kingston ghettos sprawled in the plains at the same time as comfortable new middle-class housing developments sprang up in more elevated areas and the rich built ostentatious mansions on the surrounding hills, most of them in full view of the ghetto dwellers. Under such conditions, the poor did not need to read Marx to feel relative deprivation. If one further takes into account the close correspondence between race and class, one can appreciate both the explosive potential that caused the outbreak of the 1965 and 1968 riots and the threat felt by the lighter skinned, Chinese, and white upper middle and upper classes when the riots occurred. The 1965 riots were sparked by an incident between a Chinese businessman and a black employee, and they were heavily directed against business property, much of it Chinese, in downtown Kingston. The 1968 riots were sparked by the government's refusal to permit reentry to Walter Rodney, a leading thinker of the Black Power movement. Thus, questions of black challenges to dominant cultural norms and values became intertwined with questions of power and fears about loss of economic privileges by the upper middle and upper classes. Accordingly, conservative forces in the society strongly supported the JLP government's repressive measures and continued to emphasize the inferiority of non-British/non-Western cultural norms and values.

In discussing the reorientation of the development model in the seventies with its new emphasis on economic, social, and cultural rights, three questions impose themselves: (1) What were the major reasons accounting for this attempt? (2) What were the factors which allowed it to be pursued successfully between 1972 and 1976? (3) What were the reasons for its demise from 1977 on?

The reasons for the PNP's attempt to pursue a democratic socialist development model can be found in the tensions and intense social pressure produced by the dependent capitalist model on the one hand, and in the commitments and leadership qualities of Michael Manley on the other hand.[38] Two of Manley's central concerns were genuine independence (i.e., reduction of foreign economic control) for Jamaica and social equality for Jamaica's citizens. He was convinced that in order to achieve these goals his party had to strengthen itself organizationally and to recommit itself to its original socialist orientation. Thus, soon after the 1972 election victory, he initiated the processes of party-building and mobilization and of ideological self-definition. At the same time, his government started to introduce a whole set of social and economic policies designed to help the lower classes and to strengthen the state sector to facilitate the exercise of more public control over the economy. Despite considerable internal resistance against the process of ideological self-definition from more conservative party leaders, Manley's persuasive powers swung the majority of the leadership behind the official declaration of the party's commitment to democratic socialism, which was made in 1974.

What made the successful pursuit of redistributive policies designed to satisfy the basic human needs of the Jamaican lower classes possible were the extra resources which the government managed to extract from society through policies such as the property tax and from the bauxite industry through the levy. Politically, the implementation of these policies was facilitated by the party-building and political mobilization process initiated by the PNP, which increased the weight of the lower classes in the balance of power in Jamaican society. The extra resources were used—to an excessive amount, one might argue, given the investment needs of the public sector implied by the democratic socialist development model[39]—for job creation, the financing of free secondary education, housing construction, subsidies on basic foodstuffs, loans to small farmers, etc. The changing political constellation manifested itself in the 1976 election; voter turnout had increased from 58 percent in 1972 to 71 percent, and the PNP won decisively due to an increase in support among the lower classes which made up for its losses among the middle and upper classes. Thus, more Jamaicans were exercising their political rights, and a majority was supporting the government and party which had made the social, economic, and cultural elevation of the lower classes a priority. The policies of social and cultural inclusion, such as the minimum wage for domestic help, the Status of Children Act, the use of reggae music at political rallies, and the honoring of leaders of slave and black lower-class rebellions as national heroes had increased the assertiveness of the lower classes and their awareness of their potential weight in the political process, which worked in conjunction with the PNP's party-building efforts to stimulate greater political participation.

However, despite the strong popular support for its policies demonstrated in the 1976 election, the government found itself unable to continue these policies in its second term, or even to protect the gains made by the lower classes previously. The reason for this was the severe balance of payments crisis of late 1976 and its consequences in the form of two consecutive agreements with the IMF. The crisis was the result of long-term trends (the chronic balance of trade deficit, the end of the investment cycle in the bauxite industry,[40] import price inflation since 1973, oil price increases) and short-term precipitating factors of an economic (steep decline in world sugar prices in 1974, decline in bauxite demand in 1975–1976) and a political nature (capital flight, decline in tourism due to an adverse press campaign in the United States).[41] Furthermore, the government itself contributed to these economic difficulties, though by omission rather than commission. If it had used more of the resources available for investment in projects to increase self-reliance (e.g., food production, use of local raw materials for manufacturing) and to diversify export products and markets, it might have been able to alleviate the foreign exchange shortage and thus possibly reject the IMF agreements.[42] Given the severity of the crisis confronted in 1976, however, the government decided that it was politically impossible to reject an IMF agreement and to adopt a non-IMF emergency production plan which had been elaborated with Manley's support by a team of economists from the University of the West Indies in less than three months of frantic work and which would have entailed significant import restrictions and dislocations in the manufacturing sector.

The austerity policies imposed by the IMF agreements, particularly the combination of devaluation, wage restraint, and cutbacks in government subsidies imposed in 1978, which rolled back Jamaican living standards by one-third in a single year, not only demoralized the PNP and its supporters, but also deprived the government of any room for maneuver to continue or even just protect its reform policies. The prescribed budget cutbacks left the government without the necessary resources, and the IMF's demands for a "favorable business climate" prevented the further pursuit of reform policies aimed at a redistribution of power, such as workers' participation in decision making in enterprises, even though these policies wouldn't have involved any financial costs to the government. The economic hardships brought on by these austerity policies caused a rapid crumbling of the government's popular support base, which—together with the government's loss of room for maneuver—put it on the defensive and made it vulnerable to the aggressive opposition campaign. The JLP and the *Gleaner* blamed the whole economic crisis on "PNP mismanagement" and raised the specter of a communist conspiracy supported by the PNP left, trying to take advantage of the crisis to first take over the PNP and then the whole country. Endless repetitions of such allegations, together with the promises of restoration of business confidence, economic growth, and "jingling in your pockets" by a new JLP government, could not fail but find receptive ears at home and abroad. Foreign lenders and investors became more and more reluctant to deal with the Jamaican government, and the voters, tired of the economic decline, the uncertainty, the political tension, and the violence of the 1980 campaign, gave an overwhelming victory to the JLP in the election.

The JLP's and Seaga's victory in the 1980 election, then, was rooted in the economic failures of the Manley government and thus indirectly in the prescriptions of the IMF and the international economic situation and the government's own neglect of policies which might have saved it from having to go to the IMF in the first place. The JLP's effective propaganda that PNP "mismanagement" was virtually the sole cause of the economic woes of the country (as well as the relentless attacks on the government's alleged communist sympathies) led to a widespread perception, at least in the middle and upper classes, that Seaga could make good on his promise to restore economic prosperity by providing good economic management and returning to a private sector-led model of economic growth, which would restore the confidence of domestic and international investors and lenders and lead to new capital inflows from these sources.

It is not quite accurate to say that the Seaga government wanted to restore the situation that existed in the sixties of pure trickle-down economics and cultural exclusion. The JLP leadership was essentially willing to maintain the social programs of the Manley government insofar as that was economically possible, in part because the mobilization of the Jamaican lower classes under the Manley government made any move to abolish them politically very difficult, and in part because most of the leadership genuinely believed in them.[43] Moreover, the rhetoric about reliance on private sector investment, which was aimed at Washington, was not realized in practice and was probably not even desired by the government. And, finally, Seaga had always been interested in promoting indigenous Jamaican culture, so rollback in this area never occurred.

International lenders did respond favorably to the government's economic and political profile, as did the Reagan administration, in the latter case with unprecedented economic aid. But international economic conditions were no longer the same as in the fifties and sixties; foreign and domestic investors did not come through and growth was far below target, being virtually nil in 1983 and 1984. The massive borrowing, the World Bank structural adjustment loans, and the IMF agreement then forced Seaga to embark on severe austerity policies; devaluation (from $1.80 to U.S. $1 to $5.50) in 1983–1985, massive cuts in government expenditures and so on which resulted in privations of the Jamaican masses that far exceeded those imposed in the worst years of the Manley government. Thus, the real villain insofar as social and economic rights of the Seaga period are concerned, like the latter part of the Manley period, was not the government but the IMF and its one-sided, recession-inducing austerity policies. Tragically, but not surprisingly, given the record of virtually every other Third World country under IMF-imposed austerity plans, the Fund's measures and the suffering they have caused have not resulted in the promised private sector-led growth.

CONCLUSION

The most obvious implication of the Jamaican experience for the ongoing debate on human rights is the support it provides for the contention that political and civil rights and economic, social, and cultural rights are interdependent. The egalitarian and cultural inclusionary policies of the Manley government clearly increased the ability of the Jamaican lower classes to participate in the political and social life of the country. This is not to say, of course, that the existence of democracy and associated civil rights was irrelevant before the advent of the Manley government. On the contrary, it was the democratic process that brought the government to power in the first place, and it was the existence of civil and democratic liberties that allowed the political mobilization which sustained the social and economic reform process. It was a case of interdependence and not one-way dependence of civil and political rights on economic, social, and cultural rights.

A second point we have emphasized is the symbiosis of governmental and nongovernmental violation of human rights. The interrelationship of the excesses of the security forces, vigilantism, predatory crime, criminal violence, and political violence is a striking feature of the Jamaican situation. The importance of organized but nongovernmental violations of human rights (in the Jamaican case, witness intimidation, voter intimidation, ballot box stuffing, etc.) is a neglected feature in most discussions of human rights. Indeed, the opposition JLP bears a large part of the responsibility for the escalating political violence in the mid and late seventies. Even if it did not, in fact, actually direct its supporters into violent activities, its vicious destabilization and delegitimization campaign created a climate in which this was likely to happen.[44]

Finally, we have argued that insofar as economic and social rights are in large part a result of the particular economic model pursued by a government, the human rights situation in countries under IMF-imposed austerity plans is partly the responsibility of the IMF itself. The Fund's policies are not neutral, scientific sets of prescriptions, but rather policies about which politicians and social scientists can and do argue with regard to their efficacy and effectiveness.[45] The IMF has chosen to impose one set of policies among a range of alternatives and has to bear the responsibilities for the human rights outcome of that choice.

In choosing a framework for an assessment of the quality of human rights in Jamaica, one would certainly want to opt for some relevant possible state of affairs. Thus, rather than taking an ideal state as frame of reference, or the Western industrial democracies, or colonialism, it seems more relevant to take different regimes operating within the same structural context but promoting different development models and to compare their human rights records. Furthermore, a dynamic analysis, investigating progress and regress in the protection of human rights, seems more enlightening than a static comparison.

In the Jamaican context, the comparison between the JLP's dependent capitalist model and the PNP's democratic socialist model clearly reveals a stronger commitment and more effective policies for promotion of human rights in the latter. With the exception of the restrictions on civil rights imposed with the Gun Court and the State of Emergency, and the persistent problems of police brutality and of nongovernmental abuses of human rights through crime and political violence, significant progress in all categories of human rights was made between 1972 and 1976. In contrast, the dependent capitalist model not only neglected social and economic rights, but the JLP's repressive actions in the sixties caused by the desire to protect the model and those social groups benefiting from it against the challenges from those marginalized by it, as well as the electoral manipulations in 1972 and 1983, also violated civil and political rights. However, the PNP's record in handling the persistent problems of police brutality, weaknesses in the judicial system, and criminal and political violence was not much better than the JLP's.

Yet, between 1977 and 1980, the democratic socialist model was unable to maintain the progress in human rights; on the contrary, it suffered considerable setbacks in economic rights as a direct result of the IMF-imposed austerity policies. Critics of the PNP and of the democratic socialist model might argue that these setbacks prove that the whole attempt was doomed to failure, that the improvements achieved in the first term were due to profligate spending on the part of the government which led directly to the economic crisis and ensuing hardships, and consequently that the entire progress in human rights was illusory.

This critique is mistaken on two points. First, much of the progress in the noneconomic areas persisted in the PNP's second term, such as political mobilization and participation, and social and cultural inclusion. Second, it is much too simplistic to lay the entire blame for the balance of payments crisis, which forced the government to accept the IMF programs, on the government's economic policies. The central reasons for the crisis lay in the extreme openness and dependence of the Jamaican economy and in negative trends in the world economy. What the government can be blamed for is neglecting preventive and corrective policies which might have mitigated the severity of the crisis. Such preventive and corrective policies would have entailed greater state sector investment to reduce the import dependence of the Jamaican economy and to diversify exports, which in turn would have required diversion of a certain amount of resources from distributive expenditures to capital investment, but by no means a total abandonment of the former. None of the other elements of the democratic socialist development model and thus the progress in human rights would have required modification.

The setbacks during the second term under the IMF policies bring us back to the points raised previously about the IMF as a supra-governmental force having negative effects on human rights. Whereas we are not arguing that the IMF as an institution is deliberately violating the human rights of a majority of the population in developing countries, we are making the point that such violations are an inherent part of the "development" model imposed by the IMF.[46] Thus, the IMF serves as an essential systemic (in the international system, that is) constraint on the ability of Third World governments to pursue development models which do promote an extension of economic rights to the poorer sectors of their population.

The following final observations should be made concerning a frame of reference for the assessment of human rights. One can ask whether there are any policies which the governments could have reasonably and realistically pursued within the framework of their respective development models to improve the human rights situation. In the Jamaican case, two areas can be pointed to: patronage and political violence. Neither party has made a sustained effort to reduce the importance of patronage in the Jamaican political system and thus the incentive for political intimidation and violence. When in opposition, both parties have complained about victimization of their supporters, but when in power both have insisted on rewarding their supporters and expanding their political base through patronage. The National Housing Trust established by the PNP with its system of allocating houses through a lottery is the only significant action in the right direction. As for political violence, not only can one blame the governments for lack of resolute action to stop it, but it is well known that high-ranking politicians in both parties have been directly involved in organizing the passing out of guns to their supporters, particularly politicians whose constituencies include ghetto areas. Certainly, it should be possible for party (and government) leaderships to identify and ostracize those responsible—at the risk, of course, of losing their particular districts.

To end on a note of caution, one has to recognize that some of our foregoing reflections and arguments might be distorted in a self-serving fashion by governments or their ideological supporters to justify abuses of human rights. First, if it is acknowledged that opposition forces can be responsible for the instigation of nongovernmental abuses of human rights, this argument can be, and indeed in a variety of countries has been, used as a pretext to justify repression of the opposition. Second, if it is admitted that international factors, including policies imposed by the IMF, can be obstacles to the realization of economic and social rights, this argument can be, and has been, used by governments to abdicate their own responsibilities to work towards improvements in these areas.

Third, if it is accepted that the assessment of human rights records of Third World countries depends on one's judgment of what would have been objectively possible, it seems unavoidable that there will be disagreements among social scientists (and obviously politicians) in their assessments of these records, given that there are intense debates in the social science community about the desirability and viability of different models of socioeconomic development. Taken to its extreme, this argument, of course, can again be misconstrued by politicians and their apologists to maintain that assessments of human rights records are entirely subjective statements expressing the ideological views of the observers. Fortunately, it is certainly not true that social science is pure ideology; the range of debate can be narrowed substantially by strict adherence to rigorous methodological procedures and standards of evidence, and by efforts of social scientists to be open about their own values and frames of reference. Moreover, social science disagreements apply more to options for the protection of social, economic, and cultural than of civic and political rights; the record of Third World governments with respect to the latter is in most cases relatively easy to assess.

NOTES

1. The research on which this paper is based was part of a larger project on lessons from the Jamaican case for the viability of development models combining growth, equity, and democracy in countries at intermediate levels of dependent capitalist development. The field research was assisted by a grant from the Joint Committee on Latin American Studies of the American Council of Learned Societies and the Social Science Research Council and by a Fulbright Research Award for the American Republics. It was carried out while the authors were Visiting Research Fellows at the Institute for Social and Economic Research at the University of the West Indies at Mona, Jamaica. All of these institutions deserve thanks for their support, but none of them bears any responsibility for the opinions expressed here.

2. Rhoda Howard, "Evaluating Human Rights in Africa: Some Problems of Implicit Comparisons," *Human Rights Quarterly* 6, no. 2 (May 1984): 160–179.

3. Lloyd Best, "A Model of Pure Plantation Economy," *Social and Economic Studies* 17 (September 1968): 283–326.

4. Ralph Gonsalves, "The Trade Union Movement in Jamaica: Its Growth and Some Resultant Problems," in *Essays on Power and Change in Jamaica*, ed. Carl Stone and Aggrey Brown (Kingston: Jamaica Publishing House, 1977).

5. See Ken Post, *Strike the Iron: A Colony at War: Jamaica 1939–45* (The Hague: Martinus Nijhoff, 1983), for a very detailed and well-documented analysis of the period 1939–1945. George E. Eaton, *Alexander Bustamante and Modern Jamaica* (Kingston: Kingston Publishers Ltd., 1975), offers an analysis of Bustamante and his role in Jamaican politics. Trevor Munroe, *The Politics of Constitutional Decolonization: Jamaica 1944– 1962* (Mona, Jamaica: Institute for Social and Economic Research, University of the West Indies, 1972), analyzes the process of constitutional decolonization.

6. For Norman W. Manley's political views, which were crucial in shaping the orientation of the PNP, see Rex Nettleford, ed., *Manley and the New Jamaica* (London: Longman Caribbean Ltd., 1971).

7. Eaton, *Alexander Bustamante*, 72.

8. Munroe, *The Politics*, 149–52.

9. Ibid., 156–62.

10. For analyses of the Jamaican economy in this period, see Owen Jefferson, *The Post-war Economic Development of Jamaica* (Mona, Jamaica: Institute for Social and Economic Research, University of the West Indies, 1972), and Norman Girvan, *Foreign Capital and Economic Underdevelopment in Jamaica* (Mona, Jamaica: Institute for Social and Economic Research, University of the West Indies, 1971).

11. See, e.g., Fernando Henrique Cardoso, "Associated Dependent Development: Theoretical Implications," in *Authoritarian Brazil*, ed. Alfred C. Stepan (New Haven, Conn.: Yale University Press, 1973); Charles K. Wilber and James H. Weaver, "Patterns of Dependency: Income Distribution and the History of Underdevelopment," in *The Political Economy of Development and Underdevelopment*, ed. Charles K. Wilber, 2d ed. (New York: Random House, 1979); Peter Evans and Michael Timberlake, "Dependence, Inequality and the Growth of the Tertiary: A Comparative Analysis of Less Developed Countries," *American Sociological Review* 45, no. 3 (1980): 531–51.

12. On the purge of the PNP left, see Munroe, *The Politics*, 79–80; and Eaton, *Alexander Bustamante*, 135–50.

13. Terry Lacey, *Violence and Politics in Jamaica 1960–70* (Manchester: Manchester University Press, 1977), 86–87; 94–99.

14. A short treatment of the PNP's democratic socialist experience is given in Evelyn Huber Stephens and John D. Stephens, "Democratic Socialism in Dependent Capitalism: An Analysis of the Manley Government in Jamaica," *Politics and Society* 12, no. 3 (1983): 373–411; a more detailed analysis is offered in Evelyne Huber Stephens and John D. Stephens *Democratic Socialism in Jamaica: The Political Movement and Social Transformation in Dependent Capitalism* (London, Macmillan; and Princeton, N.J.: Princeton University Press, 1986).

15. Norman Girvan, Richard Bernal, and Wesley Hughes, "The IMF and the Third World: The Case of Jamaica," *Development Dialogue* 2 (1980): 113–55.

16. Lacey, *Violence and Politics*, 89–94.

17. Carl Stone, *Democracy and Clientelism in Jamaica* (New Brunswick, N.J.: Transaction Books, 1980), 174.

18. Barrington Moore, *The Social Origins of Dictatorship and Democracy* (Boston:

Beacon Press, 1966). The importance of states' capacity for repression for the political outcome, a hidden variable in Moore's argument, is highlighted in Theda Skocpol, "A Critical Review of Barrington Moore's Social Origins of Dictatorship and Democracy," *Politics and Society* 2, no. 1 (1973): 1–34.

19. Maurice Zeitlin et al., "Class Segments: Agrarian Property and Political Leadership in the Capitalist Class of Chile," *American Sociological Review* 41, no. 6 (1976): 1006–1029.

20. This same process occurred everywhere in the British West Indies. Domestic forces primarily influenced the speed at which it happened.

21. For a discussion of the concept of the new professionalism and an analysis of it as a factor in Latin American politics, see Alfred C. Stepan, "The New Professionalism of Internal Warfare and Military Role Expansion," in *Authoritarian Brazil*, ed. Alfred C. Stepan (New Haven, Conn.: Yale University Press, 1973). The concept denotes a military role expansion into social, economic, and political matters, growing out of a concern with internal security and a perception on the military's part that a military government would be better suited to implement changes in those areas necessary to guarantee internal security than civilian governments.

22. Carl Stone, *Electoral Behavior and Public Opinion in Jamaica* (Mona, Jamaica: Institute for Social and Economic Research, University of the West Indies, 1974), 21–32.

23. Gerrymandering actually influenced the outcome of the 1969 Parish Council elections. The PNP garnered 51.3 percent of the vote, but won only the Kingston–St. Andrew area and five other councils compared to seven for the JLP. The PNP won the popular vote in St. Elizabeth and Manchester, but lost in council seats (*Public Opinion*, March 21, 1969). Gerrymandering along with the other corrupt electoral practices described in the text may also have influenced the outcome of the 1967 election, which was very close.

24. For details on these policies, see Stephens and Stephens, *Democratic Socialism*.

25. Stone, *Democracy and Clientelism*, 160.

26. See Stephens and Stephens, *Democratic Socialism*, for an analysis of the charge of corruption in the 1976 election.

27. See G. E. Mills, "Electoral Reform in Jamaica," *Parliamentarian* 62, no. 2 (1981): 97–104, for a discussion of the electoral reform.

28. *Jamaica Daily Gleaner*, July 26, 1978 and August 24–29, 1981.

29. It is relatively clear that the police do harass the militants of the party out of power. The question is whether they do this at the request of the government or not. Another possibility is that their preference is to harass both groups, but avoid the supporters of the government for fear of reprisal. It should be pointed out here that the security forces departed from this general pattern from late 1979 to the 1980 election, when PNP activists were the main object of abuse.

30. See, e.g., *Jamaica Daily Gleaner*, May 27, 1975.

31. Director of Elections, *General Election 1980, Report* (Kingston: Director of Elections, 1981), 29–32.

32. *Jamaica Weekly Gleaner*, January 30, 1984.

33. W. Arthur Lewis, *The Theory of Economic Growth* (London: George Allen & Unwin, 1955), and "The Industrialization of the British West Indies," *Caribbean Economic Review* 2 (1950): 1–61.

34. Whereas Lewis's prescriptions were in accordance with the thrust of the modern-

ization paradigm dominant in sociology and political science, they went against the neo-classical orthodoxy and the doctrine of comparative advantage which were still dominant in his own field of economics. Asserting that the West Indies must industrialize, and behind protective walls where necessary, clearly violated the latter.

35. Jefferson, *Post-war Economic Development*, 42–46; Department of Statistics, *National Income and Product 1972* (Kingston: Department of Statistics, 1973), 44–45.

36. Jefferson, *Post-war Economic Development*, 27; National Planning Agency, *Economic and Social Survey Jamaica* (Kingston: National Planning Agency, various years).

37. Irma Adelman and Cynthia Taft Morris, *Economic Growth and Social Equity in Developing Countries* (Stanford, Cal.: Stanford University Press, 1973).

38. A good exposition of Michael Manley's values and political analysis is offered in Michael Manley, *The Politics of Change* (Washington, D.C.: Howard University Press, 1975).

39. See Stephens and Stephens, *Democratic Socialism*, 270–319, for a development of this argument.

40. The five transnational corporations operating the Jamaican bauxite industry (Alcan, Alcoa, Kaiser, Reynolds, and Revere) had just completed major investments in new facilities in Jamaica and, due to their worldwide source diversification strategies, had no further investment plans of significance for Jamaica for the seventies. For further analysis of the Jamaican bauxite industry, see Evelyne Huber Stephens and John D. Stephens, "Bauxite and Democratic Socialism in Jamaica," in *States versus Markets in the World System*, ed. Peter Evans et al. (Beverly Hills: Sage Publications, 1985).

41. Girvan, Bernal, and Hughes, "The IMF."

42. Stephens and Stephens, *Democratic Socialism*, 270–319.

43. Evelyne Huber Stephens and John D. Stephens, "The Transition to Mass Parties and Ideological Politics: The Jamaican Experience Since 1972," *Comparative Political Studies* (Winter 1987).

44. Political scientist, pollster, and columnist Carl Stone, who has carefully maintained a nonparty partisan stance, has commented a number of times in his columns in the *Gleaner* in the past few years on the difference in the character of the PNP's and JLP's opposition tactics and the impact this has had on the degree of social tranquility in the early eighties as compared to the late seventies.

45. For an early critique of the IMF, see Cheryl Payer, *The Debt Trap: The International Monetary Fund and the Third World* (New York: Monthly Review Press, 1974); Roberto Frenkel and Guillermo O'Donnell, "The 'Stabilization Programs' of the International Monetary Fund and Their Internal Impact," in *Capitalism and the State in U.S.–Latin American Relations*, ed. Richard Fagen (Stanford, Cal.: Stanford University Press, 1979); and Rosemary Thorp and Laurence Whitehead, eds., *Inflation and Stabilization in Latin America* (London: Macmillan, 1979), present excellent case studies of the rationale and effects of IMF policies in a variety of Latin American countries. Girvan, Bernal, and Hughes, "The IMF," provide a cogent critique of IMF policies in the Jamaican case; Richard Feinberg and Valeriana Kallab, eds., *Adjustment Crisis in the Third World* (New Brunswick, N.J.: Transaction Books, 1984), present a number of critical discussions of the IMF and suggestions for alternatives.

46. To understand this "model" one has to understand the IMF's function as protector of an open flow of goods and capital in the world economy and a "financial policeman" of the world in the sense of giving the red or green light to the international financial community. A government refusing to accept an IMF agreement will find all sources of

finance closed and suffer significant disruptions in trade, which in turn, given the highly open and import-dependent character of most Third World economies, create internal shortages and disruptions in production.

SUGGESTED READINGS

America's Watch. *Human Rights in Jamaica*. New York: America's Watch, 1986.

Davies, Omar. "An Analysis of the Management of the Jamaican Economy: 1972–1985." *Social and Economic Studies* 35 (March 1986), 73–110.

Girvan, Norman. *Foreign Capital and Economic Underdevelopment in Jamaica*. Mona, Jamaica: Institute for Social and Economic Research, University of the West Indies, 1971.

Girvan, Norman. "Prospects for Jamaica's Political Economy." Kingston, Jamaica: Friedrich Ebert Stiftung, 1986.

Girvan, Norman, Richard Bernal, and Wesley Hughes. "The IMF and the Third World: The Case of Jamaica." *Development Dialogue* 2 (1980): 113–55.

Kaufman, Michael. *Jamaica under Manley: Dilemmas of Socialism and Democracy*. Westport, Conn.: Lawrence Hill, 1985.

Lacey, Terry. *Violence and Politics in Jamaica 1960–1970*. Manchester: Manchester University Press, 1977.

Manley, Michael. *The Politics of Change*. Washington, D.C.: Howard University Press, 1975.

———. *Jamaica: Struggle in the Periphery*. Oxford: Third World Media Ltd., 1982.

Nettleford, Rex. *Mirror, Mirror: Identity, Race and Protest in Jamaica*. Kingston: Collins & Sangster, 1970.

Stephens, Evelyne Huber, and John D. Stephens. *Democratic Socialism in Jamaica: The Political Movement and Social Transformation in Dependent Capitalism*. Princeton, N.J.: Princeton University Press; London: Macmillan, 1986.

Stone, Carl. *Democracy and Clientelism in Jamaica*. New Brunswick, N.J.: Transaction Books, 1980.

Stone, Carl, and Aggrey Brown, eds. *Essays on Power and Change in Jamaica*. Kingston: Jamaica Publishing House, 1977.

Stone, Carl, and Aggrey Brown, eds. *Perspectives on Jamaica in the Seventies*. Kingston: Jamaica Publishing House, 1981.

10

JAPAN

Lawrence W. Beer

CULTURAL AND HISTORICAL BACKGROUND

This chapter is about human rights in Japan; it is informed by an understanding of constitutional development in Japan and the needs of comparative human rights studies, which requires explanation. Since around 1600 Japan has passed through three major transformations in the system of social values giving legitimacy to law and government; below, I term these transformations "constitutional revolutions," of which the latest has institutionalized human rights since 1945. This approach takes cognizance of two obstacles to the development of comparative human rights and to multicultural communication about human rights.

First, law and social science writers in the United States are not often explicit about their own cultural and philosophical presuppositions regarding human rights. This seems to parallel a tendency not to learn about or take seriously the starting points and social foundations of their counterparts in the non-Western world, to the detriment of accurate intercultural communication about human rights.

I take as the essential presupposition intellectually justifying human rights concerns in whatever culture, and making human rights studies more than a trivial pursuit, that every human being is equally possessed of enormous, inherent value simply by reason of being a person, a human, and that this judgment gives coherence and sense to argumentation attributing "rights" to humans deserving of public and private, official and societal respect.[1] Such explicit mention seems especially important when one is communicating with counterparts in a country with profoundly different traditional presuppositions about state, society, and law, in which attribution of such value and rights to individual humans would have been radically unorthodox, even unimaginable, in the past, but which now accepts the human rights assumption as in a dialectical symbiosis or struggle with different aspects of traditional philosophy and value. It is important to know where the Japanese are coming from, to realize that their human rights understandings and problems do not arise from American history, and that an American, or even more broadly "Western," form of individualism is not an important ingredient of a persuasive understanding of human rights, as one looks at Japan's contemporary institutionalization of human rights.

Second, there has been insufficient attention to interdisciplinary approaches which ease achievement of a primary goal of human rights studies: maximizing multicultural communication (i.e., directed not at readers within one's own culture or within one's own and the foreign country studied, but at readers in *many* cultures) by minimizing misunderstandings about national contexts and issues therein. Part of the problem is that many American human rights scholars tend to write about foreign systems only for an American audience and/or as if the foreign matrix of human rights law and social culture is essentially the same as that of the United States. To write for the multicultural audience of interested, English-reading humans of today and the future is much more difficult, but necessary.

What needs communicating across cultures and is often most difficult to convey is how human rights principles find incarnation or rejection in different national cultural contexts. For cross-cultural human rights studies the highest priority is integrated and sensitive interdisciplinary communication of starkly contrasting philosophical and religious foundations along with sometimes subtle elements of culture affecting human rights. Ideological lines are not so blurred as to obstruct mutual vision of human rights problems across borders; but the tendency to ignore or to deal very cursorily with the relevance to human rights in Asia, for example, of Islam, Confucianism, Buddhism, and various systems of patron-client relationship and kingship[2] colors American perceptions of the region. Misunderstandings across cultures do not arise so much about facts or human rights documents or particulars—such as the unacceptability of torture or a straightforward government closure of an independent newspaper or a stolen election—but about perceptions rooted in history and social culture. These seem best conveyed multiculturally in this very brief analysis of Japan, if the technical language of law, social science, and theory is avoided.

History and social culture are critical determinants of the status and context of human rights in many countries, but especially in an ancient, stable, and homogeneous country such as Japan. Social foundations in history are the primary focus of this essay, rather than details of sociopolitics, formal law, or theory.

Japan's "Constitutional Revolutions"

Japan's human rights experience can be understood in terms of three "constitutional revolutions": the Tokugawa Revolution (1603–1868), the Meiji Revolution (1868–1945), and the postwar Revolution of Freedom (1945–1986 and continuing). Such "constitutional revolutions" have involved a fundamental shift in legitimized constitutional values, the basic public values which are diffused in a society over time by laws, administrative actions, judicial decisions, and education by the family, schools, religious bodies, and mass media, or by analogous institutional means in times and places where one or more of the above is not present.

The Tokugawa Revolution brought peace and permanent national unity after centuries of feudal warfare; the Tokugawa family's leaders, called *Shōgun*, gave unprecedented sociolegal power and legitimacy to a mix of feudal values (e.g., loyalty to one's lord; adherence to duty attendant upon status as a noble or commoner) and neo-Confucian values (e.g., a class system and male-dominated family ethics). The Meiji Revolution permeated society with the primacy of the emperor as a quasi-divine Shinto value in a modern unitary state and with a modern legal system derived from the continental European civil law tradition. The present Revolution of Freedom began in late 1945 and continues on the basis of constitutional and legal recognition of the equally transcendent value of each person, popular sovereignty,[3] and a melding of European, Japanese, and American approaches to legal interpretation and state theory.

In each succeeding age a contrasting set of governmental institutions and rule systems has given expression to a dominant constitutional value radically different from that underlying the earlier era. Unlike the processes of constitutional development in the United States and Europe, present ideas and institutions in Japan did not emerge as refinements or as adaptive mutations under revolutionary pressures of premodern thought and practice. Japan had no tradition of literary, philosophical, or legal reflection on "the rights of a Japanese" counterpart to "the rights of an Englishman" so important to early Americans, let alone a universalist notion of "human rights." As in other non-Western countries, concepts of human rights and constitutionalism came suddenly in the torrent of Western thought when European and American imperialism imposed themselves on the scene.

Beginning in 1854, after centuries of officially enforced isolation, Japan was subordinated to unequal treaties with Western powers. First the United States, then Great Britain, Russia, and France, forced Japan open to trade and diplomatic relations. One aspect of Japan's uniquely successful response to this challenge over the decades that followed was to explore the intellectual and institutional wellsprings of Western power in legal ideas and constitutional systems. By 1900 Japan had developed a new legal system within the continental European civil law tradition and a constitution for a centralized monarchical state with a parliament and, as a benevolent gift of the emperor to his subjects, provisions for individual rights under the law.

At this point, Japan was freed of unequal treaties, thus achieving a principal goal behind its adoption of a Westernized legal system acceptable to Western imperialists. With her defeat of China (1894–1895) and Russia (1904–1905) in war, Japan moved into the small circle of major international powers. Unlike most non-Western peoples, the Japanese have experienced fully independent legal development since that time, with the constitutionally critical exception of the postwar Allied Occupation of under seven years (1945–1952). Both in the decades after 1854 and in 1945, conscious official choices in favor of discontinuity, not evolutionary change within an existing constitutional tradition, ushered in the revolution.

The Sociopolitical Context

Words for "rights" (*kenri*) and for "human rights" (*jinken*) inhering in the individual as a person are of nineteenth-century origin; as in other areas of law, Japanese invented entirely new legal language in East Asian ideographs as they puzzled their way through the corpus of Western politico-legal thought, a remarkable achievement in creative and technical linguistics. However, there were consciousness and some enjoyment of individual rights in traditional and pre–1945 modern Japanese society which provided the social foundation for current human rights in Japan. Some traditional perceptions and social structures, in modified form, still affect the way human rights are exercised, protected, promoted, and violated in Japan today.[4]

In the Tokugawa Period the place of one's family in the stratified social hierarchy determined one's duties and responsibilities. Along with the imperial court, the feudal lords and their knight retainers (*samurai*) were in the place of privilege, followed by farmers, craftsmen, and merchants, in that order. (Below them, and considered not quite human, were outcastes in occupations such as butchery and execution, taboo under Buddhism; their descendants, called *burakumin*, still suffer at times from lingering discrimination.) The *samurai* and commoners lived under separate rule systems. Each feudal house had its rules; the "feudal federal law" of the Tokugawa central government applied only to certain types of disputes and to such matters as armament restrictions and compulsory feudal lord (*daimyō*) residence part of each year in the shogunal capital, Edo (Tokyo). The duties incumbent on a *samurai* were more stringent, on balance, than the law and custom of commoner villages. It was more the rigorous spirit of *samurai* ethics and rules than the relaxed village approach which characterized the modern law of the land during the Meiji Period until 1945.

The notion that all individuals have equal rights under law without reference to the status hierarchy would have seemed unnatural to many in Tokugawa Japan, and freedom of speech, particularly vis-à-vis superiors, was in general repugnant to mores and even to language usage. For example, the Japanese language and bowing system had (and retain, with democratic modifications in meaning) many levels of politeness, which one could finely tune, for any given interpersonal encounter, to the proper degree of deference, formality, or familiarity. (Exquisite sensitivity to individual ranking continues, but there is no longer an elaborate, rigid class system, in law or social practice.)

Choice and responsibilities were defined in terms of duties, or obligations, not rights. However, a "reciprocal duty consciousness" functioned as a type of individual rights consciousness in both egalitarian and hierarchical settings. One's sense of duty normally carried with it, even in relations with superiors, at least a modest expectation that the other recognized a duty to reciprocate, if not in equal measure at least with humane condescension. Furthermore, in the villages, where Japanese lived most of their community lives in relatively autonomous separation from the manor life of the aristocracy, a communal egalitarianism reigned among those of the same class with respect for seniority and other grounds for social hierarchy. These polarities are integrated within Japanese democratic understandings of human rights today.

What commoners sought, even in times of rebellion, was not power or change of regime or social order, but appropriately benevolent response to need from neo-Confucian feudal leaders, that to which they were entitled by "right" under universal *dōri* (natural justice, reason). As a member of a family and of the village community and as one who participated in landholding rights, the individual experienced his/her dignity and sociolegal value. Well-established local means existed for "vindicating" or "protecting" individual rights in the villages, but not in the form of modern institutions. These attitudes and means represented recognition of rights of humans, as conceived within this insular nation. Modern rights mechanisms and policies, especially since 1945, have given transcultural scope as "human rights" to traditional understandings of rights, while retaining within a democratic structure preferred perennial approaches to problem solving.

More often than not, the traditional remedies left little gap between what the individual wanted as just treatment and the results of dispute resolution procedures. As today, both government and society preferred private conciliation of disputes; but unlike today, the Tokugawa government could reluctantly force parties to resolve their conflicts if local processes failed.[5] Mutual concession and persuasion with the help of a respected, perhaps prestigious third local party was—and today still is—seen as the best approach to dispute resolution, though human rights are now also enforceable in court.

In 1889, decades of remaking the sociopolitical order and studying alternative Western models of law and constitution culminated in the Constitution of the Empire of Japan. Able oligarchs from the ruling class themselves eliminated the feudal system and the Tokugawa class structure on which neo-Confucian and feudal duties had been based. All subjects except members of the imperial house and a very small peerage became equal under Westernized law. Duties remained the critical emphasis in law and society, but the idea of equal rights under democratic law also began to spread widely and become an integral part of modern Japanese legal thought. However, an emperor-centered statism was dominant until 1945.

The Meiji Restoration of 1868 had begun a process of changing the emperor from a perennial but powerless presence, who was required to assent to and thus legitimize the rule of each *Shōgun*, into the locus of sovereignty in a modern state. Reaching into ancient history and mythology for precedent and justification, the Meiji leaders claimed to be "restoring" the emperor to primacy of governmental place and made the duty of loyalty to him as embodiment of the state the ultimate consideration for all subjects. Thus, all true Japanese were expected to subordinate personal and family rights to the wishes of national leaders who spoke in the name of the benevolent, quasi-mystical leader of ''the divine land,'' Japan. Note that this mode of political thought was not traditional, but came to pervade the system in modern times through compulsory education, official pronouncements steeped in ideological rhetoric, mass media control, and modern authoritarian techniques of administration and policing.

The early decades of the Meiji Period were full of ferment. By the mid–1930s, however, Japan's system of controlling thought and behavior was among the most thorough and sophisticated ever developed by a large nation-state. As modern technology and Westernized law and administration took hold, repression capabilities increased. The nadir for human rights came during the period of ultranationalist militarism in the wake of the Great Depression, 1930 to 1945. As before 1868 and after 1945, the emperor himself did not exercise governmental power, but hovered in a golden cloud above the land of the rising sun and above politics. Others ruled in the emperor's name.[6] After its inception in 1890, the Diet, Japan's parliament, grew in power over time. However, 1925, the year that brought universal manhood suffrage, also saw passage of the repressive Peace Preservation Law and a progressive tightening of authoritarian controls.

After World War II, the aura surrounding the emperor and those who had denied rights in his name quickly disappeared among a deeply disillusioned people, and the constitutional object under law for loyalty and a sense of duty became the individual person. In behavioral terms, the relocation of authority in the individual citizen as a member of the national community by the American Occupation and the emergence of democratic leaders led to a sudden expansion and legitimation of human rights. But Japan is a profoundly group-oriented society, so the status of many human rights since 1945 can only be grasped when seen in terms of Japan's distinctive ''groupism,'' based on *nationally* shared values and social structure, not, as in so many other countries, on concern about the rights of a specific ethnic, religious, or racial grouping.[7]

Individuals in any society not at war commonly enjoy or are denied their rights within local, stable webs of law, custom, and interpersonal relations with family, individual or group associates, and community, and not as individuals artificially abstracted from social life as in some discussions of rights and in- dividualism. In Japan the adversarial individualism of some American legal thought and practice seems out of balance and less friendly to human rights than a nonindividualist emphasis on the group. To an important extent, a Japanese wants and experiences fulfillment, identity, and the enjoyment or denial of rights as a long-term member of a nonfamilial, face-to-face group. The primary group is often a workplace group which functions as a modern analogy of the Tokugawa village; the context may be a village, a company, a government agency office, a student organization, an academic department, a professional or artistic group- ing, or a political party faction. One does not enter or leave a group easily or often; it provides a satisfying community life and, among other benefits, concern for each member's rights.[8] "Mutualism," not individualism, is the rule and seems more consonant with a human rights theory grounded in the equal dignity of all.

Since 1945 the autonomy of the individual and the nuclear family in the sociopolitical structure has increased markedly in this densely urban society; loyalty to the company, for example, has gradually ceased to be such a preemptive consideration. However, the tendency to identify one's own interests and rights with those of one's group and to lend it loyalty transcending family obligations is still a trait sharply distinguishing Japan from China, Korea, and some other nations rooted in familism. Human rights protection depends on mutualism within a group more than individualism vis-à-vis the state.

Such social sources of rights deserve more stress in human rights theory and in analysis of foreign cultures. A few examples involving free speech and decision making may give a hint of the Japanese understanding of human rights of expression and participation. In group discussion and decision making and in other contexts, the leader's authority is generally more limited than, for example, in the United States, China, or Korea. Commonly, extensive consultation of all in-group members is essential to building the consensus that confers high legitimacy in Japan's democracy. To properly honor human rights to political participation, for example, an elected official should resort to the less democratic majority principle only reluctantly.

Traditionally, Japanese culture has frowned on individual assertiveness about one's own rights as egotistical and inconsiderate of others. Group assertiveness, however, is fundamental to the politico-legal system. If the individual's public assertion of his/her rights—the patterns are found among men and women, old and young—is not made alone and with independent self-reliance, but as a member of an in-group enjoying the consensus support of the group and relying upon the group's solidarity behind the rights of a member, then that is deemed praiseworthy and natural by the group, even if such assertion may be patently contrary to the group's interests. A very sharp sense of in-group rights to expression, the in-group's concern for its members, and the individual's right to speak out within the group and as a group member gives human rights special strengths regarding freedoms of assembly, association, and public demonstrations. Free-spirited but peaceful and colorful street demonstrations of advocacy and protest are a major feature of Japan's post–1945 democracy. On the other hand, should a member too vocally dissent *after* a consensus is reached by a group, he/she may be disciplined or, in serious cases, painfully ostracized.

The status of free speech depends primarily on the individual's relations with a group and its quasi-parental leader (*oyabun*) within a system of diffuse obligations, loyalty, and felt mutuality with respect to individual rights, and depends less on relations with government, the law, or the community at large. The in-group's relations with the community affect its freedom more than government and law. As an in-group member, the otherwise hesitant individual may become an aggressive advocate for personal or group rights, even in myopic disregard for the rights of an "outsider" (*autosaidah*) individual or group, an "assertive groupism" analogous to repugnant extremes of individualist rights assertion in the United States.

In sum, the cultural context of human rights is characterized by a mingling of right and duty, loyalty and freedom, group and individual, hierarchy and equality in a society no longer mentally or legally subject to traditional feudalism, authoritarian government, or the emperor. With its emphasis on consensus decision making, conciliatory dispute resolution, and loyalty to in-group beyond the family or government, Japan might be called a "communitarian feudal democracy" in which individual human rights often blend into group rights, and vice versa. Mutual, reciprocal consciousness of rights and duties toward group colleagues gives cohesive power to the human rights support system under the Constitution of Japan.

CONSTITUTIONAL GUARANTEES AND HUMAN RIGHTS

Before the 1948 United Nations Universal Declaration of Human Rights, the 1947 Constitution of Japan (*Nihonkoku Kempō*), which has never been amended,[9] set forth a comprehensive view of human rights in Chapter 3, Articles 11 to 40 and in Article 97.[10] This enumeration was written for the most part by such "Occupationnaires" as Charles Kades and Beate Sirota and embodied their view of which human rights were appropriate to an American as of 1946. (Paradoxically, American women have yet to enjoy rights given Japanese women at that time.) Based on popular sovereignty and Article 13's insistence that "All of the people shall be respected as individuals," Article 11 recognizes human rights as "eternal and inviolate," while Article 97 sees these rights as "fruits of the age-old struggle to be free . . . conferred upon this and future generations in trust, to be held for all time inviolate."[11] Individual rights are to be "the supreme consideration in legislation and in other governmental affairs" as long as they are consonant with "the public welfare" (Articles 12 and 13). The Supreme Court has defined the public welfare as "the maintenance of public order and respect for the fundamental human rights of the individual." The constitutional revolution after World War II brought not only unequivocal constitutional guarantees of a wide array of human rights, but for the first time a protective and promotive system of laws and institutions.

The Constitution was instigated by a U.S.-dominated Allied Occupation (1945–1952), but is still supported by an overwhelming majority of Japanese citizens; it established the Diet as "the supreme organ of State power" based on the people's exercise of their sovereignty with universal suffrage. Women were given the right to vote for the first time; the age of qualification to vote is twenty. The House of Representatives is the primary locus of legislative authority, but the weaker upper house, the House of Councillors, has powers essentially of delay and modification. The prime minister is elected by parliament and is primus inter pares in a cabinet collectively responsible to the Diet.

Perhaps the most troublesome constitutional issue has been mal-apportionment, especially of the 511 seats in the House of Representatives. The discrepancy between some election districts in the value of a vote has exceeded three-to-one. The Supreme Court (in 1983 and 1985) has found this unconstitutional, violating the Article 14 guarantee of equal human rights under the law. The leading political parties have been very slow to adopt significant reform, but made progress in 1986 by reallocating seven seats and adding one seat to severely underrepresented districts, without impact on election results. [12]

For decades, and to some Japanese analysts still, there has been a vital connection between human rights and pacifism and their opposites, repression and militarism. Therefore, major rearmament is opposed in part out of fear that it would augur a return to militaristic repression. The most distinctive characteristic of the Constitution is Article 9, the world's only pacifist provision limiting in fact as well as word the level of armament well below that proportionate to Japan's great economic and technological prowess. [13] In dramatic contrast to its earlier militarism, Japan's international behavior since 1945, even in the face of provocation, has been remarkably peaceable.

Of great importance to post–1945 human rights has been the Supreme Court, an independent branch of government for the first time, with administrative and rule-making power over all other courts, and with full judicial review powers. [14] The independence of judges in deciding cases has been a treasured ideal of the bench since the late nineteenth century, but the court's jurisdiction was severely limited before World War II in human rights cases. The Supreme Court is now composed of fifteen justices who sit, except in relatively few legal and constitutional cases, as three Petty Benches (*Shōhōtei*) of five.

The law provides for about 2,700 judges in all. The number actually deciding cases for over 120 million citizens is, however, closer to 1,600, resulting in excessively heavy case loads in many courts. Virtually all new judges, prosecutors, and lawyers are products of the Supreme Court's Legal Training and Research Institute, the only rough equivalent of a postgraduate American law school. Each year only about 500 out of approximately 30,000 who take the National Law Examination are admitted; virtually all are socialized to high valuation of human rights, but few become judges and fewer still attorneys (*bengoshi*; analogous to the British barrister) interested in human rights cases. On the other hand, many thousands emerge each year from undergraduate "faculties of law" where all study human rights under law, with comparative attention to European and American law.

Police and prosecutors are highly professionalized. Relatively few Japanese are motivated to commit crimes of violence or theft. Crime rates are relatively low, and case clearance rates excellent. As in the majority of democratic systems, trial is by judges, not jury. Almost all brought to trial are convicted (over 99 percent), but as in other civil law systems, prosecutors possess quasi-judicial powers of disposition and only reluctantly take a case to court.[15] Moreover, of those convicted, only a few ever serve prison sentences. The nation's criminal justice and penal systems effectively employ alternative sentences, including dismissal of cases on penological grounds, suspension of prosecution, delayed execution of sentence, and make use of some 20,000 lay volunteer probation personnel who assist with rehabilitation and reintegration into the community.

Among a people cowed by the thought of police and other pervasive police repression during the militaristic period, one now generally finds friendly trust in the well-trained and helpful neighborhood police. Political demonstrations, on local, national, and international issues, are a major feature of Japanese democracy; the special "mobile police" (Kidōtai) have an envied record of effective nonviolent crowd control.[16] Police brutality is rare.

A number of lay systems serve human rights in Japan. One is the Civil Liberties Commissioners (Jinken Yogo Iin, literally, human rights protectors, or commissioners), some 12,000 unpaid men and women meticulously chosen by local and national process from among respected local citizens for commitment to human rights ideals and other unexceptionable criteria.[17] Each year these commissioners, drawn from many walks of life, deal with over 350,000 varied complaints and problems (both civil and criminal in nature) at the grass-roots level, using conciliatory methods and referring cases beyond their competence to other agencies. Although, or perhaps in part because, they have no coercive authority, they often provide at the grass-roots level quick, cheap, and satisfying remedies without appeal to more cumbersome legal mechanisms. They hold three-year, renewable appointments under the Justice Ministry, which reimburses them for out-of-pocket expenses incurred in casework or by attendance at compulsory commissioner training conferences. In addition, they assist the schools with annual human rights essay and poster contests, and with local and national observances of Human Rights Day (December 10) and Human Rights Week.

Another lay human rights operative is the Local Administrative Counselor (Gyōsei Sōdan Iin, literally, administrative consultant) appointed by the Administrative Management Agency to listen with impartiality to citizen grievances against government officials. While the commissioner system began in 1948, the counselors date from 1961. In 1965, 3,605 counselors handled 55,547 cases, but by 1982, the numbers had increased to 4,789 and almost 200,000 complaints. The average age of these men and women is sixty-one. In cooperation with the aggrieved party and relevant administrators, they generally work effectively to set things right by conciliation, corrective action, and/or fuller information.

Most human rights in the Constitution's comprehensive list have been found justiciable by Japanese courts; they are not merely glowing principles. Here I can offer only the briefest comments on specific human rights, grouped into categories commonly used by Japan's constitutional lawyers.

1. Equality of rights under the law. Article 14 bans "discrimination in political, economic, or social relations because of race, creed, sex, social status, or family origin," as well as inherited honors and an aristocracy. Article 24

recognizes "the equal rights of husband and wife" in all matters. Article 1–2 of the Civil Code makes "the dignity of individuals and the essential equality of the sexes" the governing interpretative principle of private law.[18] In practice— and in contrast to a sometimes coercive earlier tradition of arranged marriages— choice of marriage partner is now usually quite free. Women's equal rights to property and education are fully honored in the sociolegal system; and women's voting rates have been higher than men's. However, remarkably few women are inclined to pursue or are encouraged to seek management positions or electoral office (especially in governmental units closest to home). Opinion studies suggest that women more than men are opposed to other women in elective positions. There is also a genuine lack of interest in public office on the part of most women, a preference that may offend the sensibilities of many Americans, but which challenges the assumptions that certain occupational preferences are essential to a mature human rights system, and that high educational attainment leads women to desire political power in the form of governmental positions.

As in the United States and many other countries, women have suffered considerable discrimination in compensation and opportunities for advancement to management positions when they have opted for certain business careers; but, considerably more than American women, they have enjoyed prestige and social power as wives, mothers, and keepers of the family purse. In the mid–1980s most worked after their schooling until marriage at around age twenty-four, while over half returned to employment, usually part-time, after their children entered elementary school.

A major human rights legislative event of 1985 was the June Diet ratification of the Convention on the Elimination of All Forms of Discrimination against Women after a new Labor Standards Law removed special benefits, such as menstrual leaves, while more clearly than hitherto prohibiting differential treatment of men and women with respect to conditions of employment and advancement. According to critics, penal sanctions for management violations are too weak and some protective measures should have been retained. The Diet action, however, was on balance a noteworthy achievement in human rights law. Anti-discrimination amendments to the Nationality Law, while affecting only thousands, initiated the important right of a Japanese wife of a foreigner to establish a family register (*koseki*) and the right to Japanese citizenship at birth for their children; until then only illegitimate children of Japanese wives and children with a Japanese father and foreign mother were citizens from birth.

Japan is one of the most homogeneous large nations. Minority problems affect relatively few, and do not compare in severity with those of minorities in the United States and other countries. Furthermore, government and private efforts have ameliorated discrimination in recent decades.[19] Men and women have been equally discriminatory towards the following: the *dōwa* or *burakumin*, between 1.5 and 2.5 million ethnic Japanese descended from the occupational outcastes of Tokugawa times;[20] some 670,000 ethnic Koreans, many without full citizenship status, who remain by choice from Japan's pre–1945 possession of the

Korean peninsula;[21] about 50,000 ethnic Chinese; roughly one million Okinawans, identifiable by accent, who regained citizenship with the reversion of the Ryukyu Islands from the United States in 1972; a few thousand Vietnam War refugees; a very small proto-Caucasian group, the Ainu, the remains in Hokkaido of a virtually assimilated minority; the atom bomb victims (*hibakusha*) of August 1945, and their descendants, whose possible contamination makes them undesirable marriage partners in many eyes; and offspring of Japanese women and foreigners (U.S. military personnel in most cases) who have been left without fatherly care and support. (Japan shares this latter problem with Korea and Vietnam.)[22] Rights problems arise much more from customary biases than from official policy or law. On balance, and in comparison with other countries, East and West, discrimination problems are generally not acute, and perhaps most noteworthy in the case of Koreans, *burakumin*, and mixed-blood children.

2. *Economic freedoms and property rights (Articles 22 and 29)*. Japanese enjoy, in law and in fact, the freedoms to choose their occupations, to engage in business, and to hold and use property within limits "in conformity with the public welfare." According to survey research, voters prefer a pragmatically capitalist welfare state which apparently emphasizes the value of socioeconomic equality more than the United States does. The human property right is recognized, but not exaggerated. Although a rich mixture of various Marxist and capitalist views blends in society, neither state nor society is systematically ideological.

3. *Rights related to the quality of socioeconomic life (shakaiken)*, such as the rights to social welfare assistance, social medicine, compulsory education (Article 26), and "minimum standards of wholesome and cultured living" (Article 25) are enjoyed in good measure. Japan's living standards are the highest in Asia, and by most measures comparable to those in the United States and the more prosperous European countries. Problems of disparity in wealth and poverty are not severe. The life expectancy of 80.2 for women and 74.5 for men in 1984 was the highest in the industrialized world and second only to Iceland among all nations; thus, policy adjustments for an aging society are a central concern.[23] Medical and dental care is generally of very high quality and available to all, through a blend of private and low-cost government-supported delivery systems; in remote areas the Red Cross hospitals play a major role.

Although the formidable language barrier impedes public awareness abroad of its educational achievements, Japan has virtually 100 percent literacy and one of the world's leading systems of education. Japanese have a constitutional right to free compulsory education through junior high school, but 94 percent go on to senior high school where only 4 percent drop out before graduation. Over 40 percent go on to some form of tertiary institution; in 1985, about 400,000 were enrolled in junior colleges (90 percent women), while close to two million were in four-year university programs (23 percent women), 45,105 in M.A. programs (14 percent women) and 20,857 working for doctoral degrees (12 percent women).[24] A critical issue in reform debates is the unhealthy pressures put on young people by preparations for entrance examinations of the best universities: how can the fiercely competitive system be moderated without losing its radical merit-orientation? Family, particularly maternal, pressures on children are often extreme, as career and family success can ride on the exam outcome. A noteworthy rights problem of the 1980s was groupistic physical abuse of teachers and other students by precollegiate campus gangs, in part a reaction to these severe childhood pressures.

Workers have protected rights to work under laws which set reasonable conditions of wages, hours, rest, and working environment (Article 27), and "to organize and to bargain and act collectively" (Article 28).[25] The union movement is large and vigorous, but union members are more oriented toward their local enterprise than to solidarity with other unions in their craft across the nation, or even across the street. The right to strike and the freedom of expression of public employees (*kōmuin*), not private employees, have been significantly limited by laws, administrative rules, and judicial decisions, but large numbers of public monopoly corporation workers came under less restrictive law with the mid–1980s privatization of such industries as tobacco production and telecommunications. In laws and judicial decisions no distinctions have been recognized between ministry positions and jobs in a government-operated business (e.g., tobacco) or in the degree of restraint appropriate to a vice minister, a middle-level administrator, or a chauffeur or janitor; a mailman has been punished for putting up peaceful election posters during his leisure time.

4. *The right to participate in election politics (sanseiken)* by standing as a candidate, campaigning, or voting (Article 15) has been routinely honored. Moreover, Article 44 prohibits any discrimination (see Article 14 also) in connection with a person's candidacy and election to office.

5. *Procedural rights (Articles 31 to 40).* In general terms, Japanese law guarantees a full array of procedural rights, through the triad of professionalized and democratic judges, prosecutors, and police described earlier. Article 31 sets the tone: "No person shall be deprived of life or liberty, nor shall any other criminal penalty be imposed, except according to procedure established by law." Other articles set further limits on what law may provide. Most suspects confess voluntarily anyway; but special care is needed during diligent official questioning to guard against a legally unwarranted readiness to cooperate on the part of detained suspects. Judicial decisions have set strict limits on inducements to confess (such as offering a cup of tea or cigarette), and confession alone is not an allowable basis for conviction. A "speedy trial" is generally provided in criminal cases, though a few political trials have dragged on for many years.[26]

Procedural rights have been key to the status of civil liberties, because political activists, especially in the less settled 1945–1960 period, have tested often the considerable tolerance of the public and the democratic professionalism of police, and because the courts have in response had to refine standards protective of both freedom and order, with due sensitivity to the legacy of prewar repression.

6. *Rights and freedoms of the spirit (seishinteki jiyūken).* These human rights,

generally honored in practice, include the freedom of thought, conscience (Article 19), religion (Article 20), expression (Article 21), professional academic activity (Article 23; the first such provision), and the right to choose occupation and place of residence (Article 22), all within the bounds of and with the expressed civic duty to further "the public welfare" (Articles 12 and 13), that is, public order and human rights. To a closed, repressed, ultranationalist, and militarist society just devastated by war, the preparatory actions of the Occupation, with Japanese cooperation or compliance, and these provisions initiated a quite dramatic increase of freedom and respect for the individual. The status of *all* human rights, political, economic, procedural, and sociocultural, was altered decisively. A society relatively closed in 1945 began a long process of opening, a continuing constitutional revolution.

Of these rights, freedom of expression seems the most demanding test of healthy constitutional democracy in any country. Article 21 proclaims: "Freedom of assembly and association as well as speech, press and all other forms of expression are guaranteed. 2. No censorship shall be maintained, nor shall the secrecy of any means of communication be violated."

Two subsectors of freedom of expression seem most critical to the whole edifice of human rights in Japan.[27] First, mass media freedom is critical because the media, especially the press, is one of the most extensive and technically proficient systems in the world and the only major national, reasonably coherent and organized center of democratic power counterbalancing the government on behalf of a broad range of citizens. Of all Japan's institutions, only the Constitution itself and the court system enjoy stronger public confidence than the newspapers and TV news (political parties and the Diet have the lowest level of support).[28] Very high quality national newspapers are easily available to all and serve as a major voice for information and education on human rights issues arising at home and abroad. Second, the freedoms of assembly and association are of special importance because these freedoms are central in a groupistic political culture whose responsiveness to human rights questions is dependent upon assertive groupism on behalf of concrete interests, and group expressions of outrage at injustice or at what elements of the public perceive to be wrong-headed policies. In Japan freedom is not an unachieved goal or a vulnerable new right, but part of the context taken for granted in daily life by citizen advocates.

CONCLUSION

From Japan's earliest recorded existence until 1945, history divided into only two ages, the mythical age before the emperor and the everlasting imperial age.[29] This dichotomy provided the mental context for viewing the individual and the state and dominated the modern framework for official thinking about human rights till 1945. The constitutional revolution since then has shattered the underlying view that legitimate acts are those approved by the emperor himself or (most often) someone ruling in his stead; government was thus *above* the people. This fact and the passionate loyalty and sense of national duty behind Japan's war effort shed light on the continuing political sensitivity of disputes about freedom and school textbook treatments of the emperor. The paradox of Japan is that sometimes tempestuously convoluted emotions and thoughts about imperial Shinto coexist with a rights protection and promotion system of such well-institutionalized strength that the enjoyment of many human rights may seem boringly routine. A single example, wending its way through the courts for over twenty years, brings home these themes and may serve as a vehicle for conclusion.

From 1965 until today, Saburo Ienaga, a noted intellectual historian and left-inclined scholar, has challenged in court, with some success, the Education Ministry's suggestions and sometimes insistence that he modify his textbook treatment of the earliest history of the emperor institution.[30] Ienaga's popular high school text has claimed (1) that all Japan's earliest Shinto mythological writings were motivated solely by a desire to legitimate imperial control over the people; (2) that workers and farmers were the makers of history more than well-known emperors and feudal figures; and (3) that Japan used the Russo-Japanese Neutrality Pact of the early 1940s to strengthen its strategic position for the advance into Southern Asia. More broadly, Professor Ienaga and other authors of social studies textbooks have been at least uneasy and sometimes furious about what they see as the ministry examiners' tendency to downplay Japan's pre–1945 aggressions and the domestic pains of war and repression. In 1982, China, Korea, and other victims of Japan's assertive nationalism earlier in this century joined with internal critics insisting that Japan's certified textbooks and history teachers not gloss over the unpleasant past. To other Asians as to Japanese, militarism in service to the emperor has meant disregard for human rights.

Although a rightist minority would like to revise the Constitution and "restore" the emperor and his military power, the specter of the past, centered around an imperial institution hostile to human rights, has in fact been fading away for the majority of Japanese. They have come to assume a new constitutional framework in which the emperor and the military have receded far into a politically powerless background while popular sovereignty and human rights loom large in the forefront. Symbolic of the Japan of the present and probable future, the Council on Education, reexamining the entire ethos and structure of Japan's postwar system, took as the dominant theme of its June 1985 interim report the need to impress upon youth ever more effectively "the dignity of the individual."[31] How irrational, immoral, even repugnant, such an emphasis would have seemed fifty years ago; how obviously correct a concern for the individual's and group's human rights today.

NOTES

1. Lawrence Ward Beer, *Freedom of Expression in Japan: A Study in Comparative Law, Politics, and Society* (Tokyo: Kodansha International, 1984; New York: Harper & Row, 1985), chap. 1.

2. Beer, *Freedom*, chap. 3; Lawrence Ward Beer, ed., *Constitutionalism in Asia: Asian Views of the American Influence* (Berkeley: University of California Press, 1979); Lucian W. Pye, *Asian Power and Politics* (Cambridge: Harvard University Press, 1985).

3. Beer, *Freedom*, chap. 2.

4. Beer, *Freedom*, chap. 3.

5. Dan Fenno Henderson, *Conciliation and Japanese Law: Tokugawa and Modern* (Seattle: University of Washington Press, 1965); Herbert Bix, *Peasant Protest in Japan, 1590–1884* (New Haven: Yale University Press, 1986).

6. David A. Titus, *Palace and Politics in Prewar Japan* (New York: Columbia University Press, 1974).

7. Beer, *Freedom*, 71–85.

8. Lawrence W. Beer, "Group Rights and Individual Rights in Japan," *Asian Survey* 21 (April 1981): 437.

9. The amendment procedures in Article 96 require passage by a two-thirds majority in each house of the Diet, and ratification by a majority of those voting in a special election called by the Diet. Constitution of Japan (*Nihonkoku Kempō*), 1947, in Hiroshi Itoh and Lawrence W. Beer, *The Constitutional Case Law of Japan: Selected Supreme Court Decisions, 1961–1970* (Seattle: University of Washington Press, 1978), 268. Japan's Constitution is now one of about twenty out of 165 single-document constitutions in the world which date from as early as the 1940s; over one hundred constitutions have been adopted since 1970 in this unprecedented era of institution-making and revisions. Data provided by Albert P. Blaustein, Rutgers University Law School, Camden, New Jersey, 1986.

10. Itoh and Beer, *Constitutional Case Law*, 256.

11. Itoh and Beer, *Constitutional Case Law*, 258–59.

12. Lawrence W. Beer, "Japan's Constitutional System and Its Judicial Interpretation," *Law in Japan* 17 (1984): 36–39.

13. Beer, "Constitutional System," 11–13, 22–23.

14. For judicial decisions on human rights since 1947, see Beer, "Constitutional System," 21–40, and *Freedom*, 161–392; Itoh and Beer, *Constitutional Case Law*; and John M. Maki, *Court and Constitution in Japan* (Seattle: University of Washington Press, 1964).

15. B. J. George, Jr., "Discretionary Authority of Public Prosecutors in Japan," *Law in Japan* 17 (1984): 42.

16. David H. Bayley, *Forces of Order: Police Behavior in Japan and the United States* (Berkeley: University of California Press, 1976); Beer, *Freedom*, 144–46 and 173–75.

17. Lawrence W. Beer, "Human Rights Commissioners (*Jinken Yogo Iin*) and Lay Protection of Human Rights in Japan" (International Ombudsman Institute, Occasional Paper no. 31, October 1985, Alberta, Canada).

18. Civil Code (*Mimpō*), Law No. 89, 1896, as amended, translated in *EHS Law Bulletin, Series II*, No. 2100, Tokyo, 1962. Constitutional provisions are quoted from Itoh and Beer, *Constitutional Case Law*, 256–59. Concerning the 1985 convention ratification, see *Japan Times Weekly*, May and June 1985.

19. Lawrence W. Beer and C. G. Weeramantry, "Human Rights in Japan: Some Protections and Problems," *Universal Human Rights* (now *Human Rights Quarterly*) 1, no. 3 (1979): 1; Ronald Brown, "Japanese Approaches to Equal Rights for Women," *Law in Japan* 12 (1979): 112.

20. Frank Upham, "Ten Years of Affirmative Action for Japanese *Burakumin*," *Law in Japan* 13 (1980): 39, and "Instrumental Violence and Social Change: The *Buraku Liberation League* and the Tactic of 'Denunciation Struggle,' " *Law in Japan* 17 (1984): 185.

21. Yuji Iwasawa, "Legal Treatment of Koreans in Japan: The Impact of International Human Rights Law on Japanese Law," *Human Rights Quarterly* 8 (May 1986): 131; Changsoo Lee and George deVos, *Koreans in Japan* (Berkeley: University of California Press, 1981).

22. William R. Burkhardt, "Institutional Barriers, Marginality, and Adaptation among the American-Japanese Mixed Bloods in Japan," *Journal of Asian Studies* 27 (May 1983): 533; Douglas Sanders, "The Ainu as an Indigenous Population" (Unpublished paper, Faculty of Law, University of British Columbia, Vancouver, June 22, 1983). Until a remedial 1982 law, foreign scholars were not allowed to hold a regular faculty position in public universities, though many have been employed in the much more numerous private tertiary institutions.

23. Michio Nagai, "Planning for a Rapidly Aging Society," *Look Japan* 32 (June 10, 1986): 6; William E. Steslicke, "National Health Policy in Japan," *Bulletin of the Institute of Public Health* (Tokyo) 31 (1982): 1.

24. Ministry of Education, Japan, *Mombu Tōkei Yōran* (Education Statistics), Tokyo, May 1985.

25. Beer, *Freedom*, 205, 220–39.

26. Beer, *Freedom*, 176; on the bribery trials of former Prime Minister Kakuei Tanaka, a long and continuing case, see *Japan Times*, 1979–1986.

27. For a comprehensive study of freedom of expression in Japan, see Beer, *Freedom*.

28. James S. Marshall, "Japan's Successor Generation: Their Values and Attitudes," Office of Research, U.S. Information Agency, Washington, D.C., June 1985, 17.

29. John S. Brownlee, ed., *History in the Service of the Japanese Nation* (Toronto: Toronto University–York University Joint Centre on Modern East Asia, 1983), 1.

30. Beer, *Freedom*, 248–80; and *Japan Times Weekly*, February 8, 1986, 8.

31. *Mainichi Daily News* (Tokyo), June 12, 1985.

SUGGESTED READINGS

Few scholars outside Japan write about human rights in Japan. The best source of reliable articles in English is *Law in Japan*, School of Law, University of Washington, Seattle, WA 98105.

Bayley, David H. *Forces of Order: Police Behavior in Japan and the United States.* Berkeley: University of California Press, 1976.

Beer, Lawrence Ward. *Freedom of Expression in Japan: A Study in Comparative Law, Politics, and Society.* Tokyo and New York: Kodansha–Harper & Row, 1985.

———. "Human Rights Commissioners (*Jinken Yogo Iin*) and Lay Protection of Human Rights in Japan." International Ombudsman Institute, Occasional Paper no. 31 (October 1985), Alberta, Canada.

———. "Japan's Constitutional System and Its Judicial Interpretation." *Law in Japan* 17 (1984): 7–41.

———. "Group Rights and Individual Rights in Japan." *Asian Survey* 21 (April 1981): 437.

Beer, Lawrence Ward and C. G. Weeramantry. "Human Rights in Japan: Some Protections and Problems." *Universal Human Rights* 1 (September-October 1979): 1–41.

Brown, Ronald. "Japanese Approaches to Equal Rights for Women." *Law in Japan* 12 (1979): 112.

George, B. J., Jr. "Discretionary Authority of Public Prosecutors in Japan." *Law in Japan* 17 (1984): 42.

Itoh, Hiroshi and Lawrence Ward Beer. *The Constitutional Case Law of Japan: Selected Supreme Court Decisions, 1961–1970.* Seattle: University of Washington Press, 1978.

Iwasawa, Yuji. "Legal Treatment of Koreans in Japan: The Impact of International Human Rights Law on Japanese Law." *Human Rights Quarterly* 8 (May 1986): 131.

Maki, John M. *Court and Constitution in Japan.* Seattle: University of Washington Press, 1964.

Upham, Frank K. "Instrumental Violence and Social Change: The *Buraku* Liberation League and the Tactic of 'Denunciation Struggle.' " *Law in Japan* 17 (1984): 185.

————. "Ten Years of Affirmative Action for Japanese *Burakumin*." *Law in Japan* 13 (1980): 39.

11

LEBANON

Douglas duCharme

In an order of the day sent to all the Palestinian fighters and Palestine Liberation Organization (PLO) offices in Beirut during the Israeli siege of August 1982, Yasser Arafat quoted the Old Testament. "For the violence done to Lebanon is going to overwhelm you," read the quotation from Habakkuk 2.17, "so will the slaughter of terrified beasts, for you have shed men's blood and ravished the country, the city and all who live in it."

The violence done to Lebanon, the violence *of* Lebanon, has indeed become overwhelming. In the shorthand of the world's headlines Beirut has been equated with chaos, and the past decade of Lebanese history has become synonymous with a new barbarity. The nature of the divisions which have split the country's communities into more than a dozen conflicting loyalties are hardly any more confusing than the strange alliances which suddenly take shape, only to pass just as quickly into obscurity.

Despairing of ever conveying the true nature of the conflict in all of its political-baroque intricacies, the news media, with a few remarkable exceptions, has long since resorted to "victim reporting"—another car bomb, another massacre, another night of shelling. However, after a time, this kind of reporting numbs the sensibilities of even the most astute observers of the Lebanese tragedy. After all, nothing looks like a Lebanese corpse so much as another Lebanese corpse. The violence seems at times to delight in its own endless variation, and all the more so when, to all sane appearance, it betrays an utter lack of cause or direction.

In this savage context any study of the human rights situation in Lebanon may seem to be little more than, in a characteristically Arabic turn of phrase, "baking stones"—a fruitless exercise undertaken for the sake of appearance.[1] However, this is not the case. The basic sources of the Lebanese conflict, and of the human rights abuses which have resulted, are in fact a microcosm wherein we find represented a wide array of tensions, pressures, ideologies, and interferences which are seen elsewhere throughout the world in less concentrated dosages.

Therefore, despite the complex nature of the task, it is important to sketch out the essential components of the conflict which has engulfed Lebanon since 1975, at a cost of at least 125,000 lives. Any subsequent assessment of the human rights record in Lebanon must rely on this prior step.

This is not a topic easily observed and reported on from afar. Numerous naive editorials and books testify to that. Neither is it a topic that yearns for partisan treatment. Enough one-sided, hopelessly distorted pamphlets and publications abound to have made that point clear. The present study is authored by what the editors of this volume have termed an "activist"; the author recently returned from a year (1985–1986) spent primarily in south Lebanon and Beirut working with relief and reconstruction programs. A number of the assessments made within this study derive from many, often difficult, conversations held informally throughout Lebanon.

HISTORICAL BACKGROUND

Looking back on the early years of the civil war, Gregoire Haddad, a Greek Catholic bishop in Beirut, reflected somewhat irreverently that "The fighting was between Palestinians and Lebanese, no, it is between Christians and Moslems. No, it is between Left and Right. No it is between Israel and the Palestinians on Lebanese soil. No, it is between International Imperialism and Zionism on the one hand and the neighboring states on the other."[2]

The tendency to reduce the sources of the Lebanese conflict to one, or at most two, factors is a temptation to which many observers have fallen victim. However, these interpretations can be dangerously misleading, especially when they foster one-sided analyses of the human rights situation which has resulted from the years of conflict. They also betray a serious lack of understanding of Lebanon's history, and of the distinctive balances of its political system.

Human rights, universal though the declarations may be, cannot be assessed in isolation, but must be known in their political, economic, and social context if they are to be appreciated in a credible and persuasive way. Further, an analysis of human rights in the context of a civil conflict depends very much on a clear understanding of the conflict itself.

Lebanon achieved independence in 1943 after more than two decades of French mandatory rule and, before that, four centuries of Ottoman rule. Prior to 1920 "Lebanon" referred to Mount Lebanon alone, the refuge of two communities which had faced religious persecution elsewhere—the Maronite Christians, who arrived from northern Syria in the ninth century, and the Druze Moslems, who arrived from Egypt in the tenth century. These two communities, fiercely jealous of their independence, managed nevertheless to coexist in amicable fashion until the balance was upset during the nineteenth century in favor of the Maronites. This was due in part to the special relationship which the Maronites had already begun to establish with France. The clashes which erupted between the communities during the early summer of 1860 resulted in the killing of more than

12,000 Christians in the Druze areas of the mountain. One hundred thousand were left homeless. While non-Maronite Christians were also victims of the struggle, the memory of this defeat entered the collective consciousness of the Maronite community as a never-ending wrong, which would never be allowed to happen again. Peace was restored to the area after the clashes by the intervention of a multinational force led by France.

In the aftermath of the events of 1860 the system of minority representation within the Ottoman Empire, known as the millet system, became formalized. Through a system of decentralization each religious minority, or millet, was administered by its own religious leaders who in turn had official representation at the Sultan's court in Istanbul. In particular this clarified the semiautonomous status of Mount Lebanon within the empire, and led to fifty years of prosperity.

With the defeat of the Ottomans in 1918, the worst fears of predominantly Moslem Syria, and the greatest hopes of Maronite Lebanon, were realized with the handing over of the Syrian Mandate, including Mount Lebanon, to France. This was done despite the fact that, as the U.S.-sponsored King-Crane Commission discovered in 1920, "the feeling of the Arabs of the East is particularly against the French."[3] A Maronite delegation, led by the Patriarch, had lobbied hard in Versailles for France to be named as the mandatory power. Remarking on the Balkanization of the Middle East entailed by the Sykes-Picot Agreement of 1916,[4] one commentator on the Lebanese situation states simply that "Most of the modern problems of the Middle East, including the Arab-Israeli wars and the Lebanese conflict, stem directly from the decision to divide Syria and distribute the pieces between Britain and France."[5]

Indeed one of the first acts of the French mandatory powers was to form Greater Lebanon by adding to the mountain the adjacent coastal territories belonging to Syria. As David McDowall notes, "It was like introducing a Trojan horse into the body politic of Mount Lebanon"[6] in that the population of these regions was overwhelmingly Moslem. Neither did its inhabitants share the tradition of independence which the Maronites and Druzes so jealously protected. Their identity tended to lie with their co-religionists elsewhere in the Arab world, whether Sunni or Shi'ite Moslem or Orthodox Christian. Economically, the coastal regions with their busy ports of Tripoli, Beirut, Sidon, and Tyre were linked firmly with the hinterlands of Syria.

As a result, Lebanon's present population of approximately 3.5 million is divided among seventeen officially recognized minority groups. Within Lebanon there is not one resident who cannot truthfully claim to belong to a minority group. The major groups, ethnic and religious, include Maronite Christians; Greek Orthodox and Greek Catholics; Armenian Orthodox and Armenian Catholics; Sunni, Shi'ite, and Druze Moslems; Kurds, Assyrians, and Palestinians. Precise population statistics for each group are unavailable, since the last official Lebanese census was taken in 1932. While one's bonds of loyalty are grounded in kinship and religion throughout the Middle East, this is particularly true in Lebanon where the conflicting aspirations and fears of these minorities, confined within this small, mountainous, and rapidly urbanizing area, are clearly a key factor in the Lebanese conflict.

In formal terms Lebanon is considered a confessional democracy. It operates on the basis of a political system which is, in essence, an adaptation of the millet system. Known as the National Pact, this balancing act has remained unwritten and essentially informal. It allocates positions in government to different groups in proportion to their standing in the 1932 census. As a result, Lebanon's Christians have enjoyed the political and economic advantage in the country since independence. Representation in the Chamber of Deputies is divided between Christians and Moslems on a 6:5 ratio. As well, the president is always a Maronite Christian, the prime minister a Sunni Moslem, and the speaker of the Chamber of Deputies a Shi'ite Moslem. The intent of the National Pact, in the minds of many, was to lead to the elimination of sectarianism which, according to Riad al Sulh, one of those who framed the National Pact, "is an obstacle to national progress, impeding the representation of the Lebanese population."[7] However, in reality the National Pact institutionalized the need for confessional balance and made it virtually inconceivable for Lebanon to move away from a sectarian-based political life. Therefore, the day-to-day governing of Lebanon came to depend on a precarious balance of power among the dominant groups, and on a degree of cooperation and compromise among the traditional leadership elites of these groups, especially in times of social and political tension.

A further complication surfaces when demographic changes since the 1932 census are taken into account. At that time Christians were in the majority (52 percent), and Maronites were the largest single group (29 percent). This is no longer the case, and the realization of that fact has kept any subsequent census from being taken. Today's Moslem majority is dominated by the Shi'ite population which now accounts for as much as one-third of the population, and has therefore succeeded the Maronites as the largest single group.[8] The fact that the system of political participation has yet to be altered to reflect this demographic shift has caused widespread internal tensions, and frustration on the part of underrepresented constituencies. It has also meant that the political system has remained unreceptive to emergent political forces.

Lebanon's community of minorities consists not only of Lebanese groups. About one million non-Lebanese now live in the country, among whom the largest group are the Palestinians, numbering some 400,000. A majority of these Palestinians were born in Lebanon, or have lived there since 1948 when they fled from their homes in Palestine during the first Arab-Israeli war. One-third of the Palestinians live in the twelve refugee camps scattered throughout the country under the administration of the UN Relief and Works Agency (UNRWA). Their presence in Lebanon is strongly resented by many Lebanese Christians because, for one thing, they are predominantly Sunni Moslems and therefore threaten to further upset the country's confessional balance. In addition, the influence of the Palestinian resistance has had a radicalizing impact on the activities of discontented groups within Lebanon. Palestinian commando attacks into Israel from south Lebanon also turned that region into a free-fire zone throughout the 1970s, with Israeli retaliation aimed as much at Lebanese civilian and economic targets as at Palestinian commando bases, in an effort to pressure the Lebanese government into restraining the activities of the fighters. One spectacular example of this kind of retaliation came on December 28, 1968, when Israeli troops landed by helicopter at Beirut International Airport and blew up thirteen civilian airliners of Lebanon's Middle East Airlines. Eventually the clashes in the south of Lebanon crippled the region economically, and resulted in the displacement of 40 percent of its largely Shi'ite population into the shantytowns of the "Belt of Misery" which traversed Beirut's southern suburbs.[9]

With its arbitrary boundaries, Lebanon has been called an "artificial" nation, or at best a "nation in formation." As with many other modern countries which find themselves in similar postcolonial conditions this fact is reflected in the economic sphere. Lebanon's economy is service-oriented and concentrated in Beirut and a few other coastal centers. The present-day pattern was set into place by the destruction of the productive capacity of the Lebanese economy through Western trade in the nineteenth century.[10] This led to a weak industrial and manufacturing sector, backward agricultural methods, and a pattern of investment in which capital was largely channeled into nonproductive areas such as import-export, transit, and retail. Examples of economic mismanagement by the government are legion, and include such mega-project failures as the Litani River project.[11] The economic infrastructure, such as the roads, ports, and railways, is chronically insufficient for the demand, and thoroughly below standard, causing a terrific loss of potential. Estimates also suggest that a quarter of Lebanon's working-age male population is now employed outside of Lebanon, whether in the Gulf oil fields, or in the west. Émigré remittances have made a major contribution to the survival of the Lebanese economy, and to its appearance, even well into the war, of relative prosperity. Yet not surprisingly Lebanon's laissez-faire economy has led to gross inequalities in economic development, and in the distribution of wealth in the country. Such socioeconomic cleavages have in turn reinforced certain religious divisions.

Lebanon's dependence on external economic factors is indicative of its widespread susceptibility to foreign influence and pressure. Compounding this inclination is the naive tendency of Lebanese governments and communities to court the favor of this or that foreign power. More often than not this has had pathetic, if not tragic, results, particularly with respect to the United States.[12]

Due to its Western leanings and its Christian leadership, Lebanon's role in the Arab world has never been clear or straightforward. During the sixties Beirut's camps, and its Belt of Misery, provided fertile ground for numerous ideologies and radical movements whose origins lay elsewhere in the Middle East. Lebanon's open society provided increasing opportunity for other Arab states to pursue their vendettas outside their own borders. With the rise of Islamic fundamentalism in the Middle East both before and after the Iranian revolution in 1979 a new factor was added to the role of Lebanon as a proxy battlefield.

Leading the foreign interests in Lebanon have been the two armies of occupation, Syria and Israel. In April 1976 after the first round of fighting in Lebanon, Syria intervened under an Arab League mandate to preserve the status quo. Twenty-five thousand Syrian troops remain in Lebanon under this arrangement, mostly in the eastern part of the country. For its part, Israel's second occupation of Lebanon, in 1982, was largely withdrawn by June 1985. (Israel's first invasion, in March 1978, was halted by the protests of U.S. President Carter, after it had killed 2,000 and left 250,000 displaced.) However, it retains a presence in a twenty-five kilometer so-called security zone along the border inside Lebanon, where it generally works through its own Lebanese militia, the South Lebanon Army. In the same area there are also some four thousand UN troops from six nations serving with the UN Interim Force in Lebanon (UNIFIL).

Apart from the physical presence of these many foreign, often conflicting, factions on Lebanese soil, Lebanon has also become the focus for some of the more elaborate intelligence networks and conspiracy theories of modern times with regard to ongoing U.S., French, Soviet, Israeli, Iranian, and others' activities in the country. The novel *The Little Drummer Girl*, by John Le Carré, is a fictional indication of some of the kinds of activities which inevitably transpire as a result. Lebanon has also spawned a healthy arms market involving nations as diverse as the United States, the Soviet Union, Israel, Ghana, France, Czechoslovakia, South Africa, and Iran.[13]

The tragedy of so much foreign meddling in Lebanon is that while outside interference increased the pressures which eventually led to civil war, it is generally felt that peace, when it comes, will also have its origins outside Lebanon, whether in Damascus, Washington, Paris, or elsewhere. At present the Lebanese government can only assert its sovereignty over about ten square kilometers of Lebanese territory.

In the context of the above general overview, it can now be reiterated that it is a dangerous oversimplification to say that the civil conflict which began in Lebanon in 1975 is simply between Christians and Moslems. The fighting has not been along strictly sectarian lines, nor over religious issues. Nor is it entirely accurate, or even helpful, to speak solely in terms of a single conflict taking place in Lebanon. Within this country, which can fit into one quarter of Switzerland, there exist not one, but three conflicts, which are being fought simultaneously. The distinct sources of each of these conflicts provide invaluable clues to the nature of the human rights abuses which have resulted. These three conflicts can be identified as follows:

1. The Lebanese Civil War. This is a conflict among minorities, a significant number of whom are seeking a redesign of the political system based on the deconfessionalization of Lebanon. This would allow all sectors of society, regardless of religious affiliation, an equal say in government and a more equitable share in the economy. Others who find that their rights are well safeguarded by the present arrangement fear that any change in the system would put that status at risk.

2. The Palestinian Revolution. Lebanon has been a keystone in the development of the Palestinian resistance, having hosted the PLO headquarters from 1970 to 1982. The logic of revolution can, however, be expected to come into conflict with the logic of state, as it did in Lebanon. Specifically, the Palestinian cause in Lebanon aggravated the existing discord between Lebanese nationalism and Arab nationalism within the country. The former reflected the tradition of independence of Mount Lebanon and was hostile to the Palestinians. The latter reflected the broader Arab-Syrian identification of many other groups in the population and was relatively sympathetic to the Palestinians. By their very presence, the Palestinians forced the issue of this conflict of nationalisms in Lebanon and thereby became the spark which is generally understood to have ignited the war. On April 13, 1975, a group of (Christian) Phalangist militiamen ambushed a busload of Palestinians as it passed through a Beirut suburb, killing twenty-seven. The resulting clashes quickly engulfed the entire country.

3. The International Conflict. A comment made by Foreign Minister Yitzhak Shamir in 1982 goes not only for Israel but also for Syria and, in varying degrees, for the United States, France, the Soviet Union, and others. At the time of his country's invasion of Lebanon, Shamir affirmed that Israel ''is fighting its own war on the soil of Lebanon—it is defending its own security from within the 'Land of the Cedars'!''[14] Numerous battles of a less obvious nature have been fought in Lebanon, often using Lebanese combatants. The Iran-Iraq war, tensions between Syria and Iraq, Syria and Jordan, Israel and Syria, and the United States and Iran have all been reflected in clashes which have taken place in Lebanon. Militias receive financial backing from first one, and then another, and then yet another Arab, East-bloc, or West-bloc sponsor. It has gradually become apparent that it is in the common interests of many otherwise hostile parties to keep the Lebanese pot well stirred, as a matter of convenience.

Thus, there are three wars being fought at once by the same group of combatants. It is no wonder that it has become confusing. Clearly, though, the nature of these conflicts, when seen in distinction from one another, has direct implications for the situation of human rights in Lebanon. Minority tensions, vying nationalist ideologies, and a lack of clear sovereignty over much of its own territory make for a potent mixture. Strangely, it is a subject which human rights observers have largely ignored.

HUMAN RIGHTS AND THE LEBANESE CONFLICT

The fact that the conflict has been framed in terms of a struggle between different perceptions of the ideal modern Lebanese state carries significance for analysis of the human rights situation. As one Arab historian has noted, the essential difference is whether Lebanon should be viewed as ''the western frontier of the Arab East'' or ''the eastern frontier of the Christian West.''[15] Without abandoning the universal nature of the human rights accorded to all people in the Universal Declaration of Human Rights, it is worth noting that the actual implementation of the universal standards in societies where Islam is the predominant faith continues to provide us with long and complex sources of debate. This may be particularly true in Lebanon where the Christian and Moslem traditions exist in particularly close proximity to one another, as the quotation above suggests. Thorny as this problem of cultural implementation may be, it can nevertheless be largely set aside for the purposes of this discussion. The reason for this is because, of all the Arab states in the Middle East, the process of individuation is most advanced in Lebanon. The politicization of even the most isolated villages over the past two decades, and the tradition of an entrepreneurial, laissez-faire economy have ensured that the vast majority of Lebanese think of themselves as individuals, though in the context of strong kinship and community loyalties. With this digression in mind, it is now possible to consider the human rights situation in Lebanon, first as it stood before the war, and then in the context of the civil war since 1975.

The Prewar Situation

A brief review of the human rights situation in Lebanon before the war is useful, for it provides links between the condition of human rights at that time and the outbreak of fighting in 1975. It also shows that while the situation worsened considerably after the start of the war, there were nevertheless hints during the prewar decades of what could be expected.

The political setting was structured by the National Pact, which has remained unwritten and therefore prone to violations, particularly by the Maronites, to whom it gave the greatest influence in the affairs of the country. Any objections to such violations have had little recourse, since the Pact is no more than an informal agreement. This lack of any amending mechanism within the loosely conceived political system ensured that, eventually, more radical options for reform would be sought.

When it worked, the political system provided for a kind of representation through public elections to the Chamber of Deputies held every six years. Suffrage was universal from age twenty-one. The electoral system was based on multimember constituencies with the seats in each constituency allotted to the different communities according to their numbers, on the 6:5 ratio. Therefore, in the constituency of Aley, east of Beirut, the electors would return two Maronite deputies, two Druze, and one Greek Orthodox. The electorate voted for a candidate for each seat, with, in this case, only Maronite, Druze, and Greek Orthodox candidates allowed to stand.

In practice, the political life of nearly every Lebanese constituency was controlled by the chieftain of the dominant community. Known as the za'im, this feudal lord figure continues to control community life, in even the smallest details, to the present time. In each minority community these chieftains were more powerful than the government. The names of the major families are well known; the Gemayels and the Chamouns (Maronite), the Jumblatts and the

Arslans (Druze), the Karamis and the Solhs (Sunni), and so on. The *za'im*'s role became incorporated into the political system, providing national leadership and regional cohesion. Inevitably communities elected deputies who were widely known to be on the *za'im*'s slate of candidates. In such conditions, vote buying was widespread and quite open. The CIA was widely known to have financed Camille Chamoun's candidates in the 1957 elections.[16]

Such a system obviously did little for the prestige or the strength of the parliament. It was a system in which a prime minister (Sunni) could, after being forced to resign, return to his stronghold and hand out rifles to his supporters, as Rashid Solh did in May 1975. It was an atmosphere which ensured that, while the Chamber of Deputies was formally the legislature, it did not legislate. Bills were prepared by the government and sent to the Chamber to be passed. Between 1950 and 1966, for example, the Chamber did not reject a single one of the 384 bills brought before it.[17] In comparison to the *za'im*-client relationship, the national political system was ineffectual. One of the major problems preventing any evolution away from the power of the chieftains was, however, the government's insistence that the electorate be registered in their home town or village rather than the city where they might have been living for years. As a result they again faced the same choice of *za'im*-backed candidates. Without personal wealth or financial backing it was impossible to stand for election, and as a result there has never been a working-class deputy in Lebanon.

Given the confessional nature of the political system, national parties with coherent political programs were almost nonexistent. Ideas continually succumbed to religion, ancestry, wealth, and charisma in a system which depended on bargains and alliances at every level. The closest thing to a political party in the formal sense was the Phalangist party controlled by the Gemayel family, which in the 1972 election gained seven deputies out of a total of ninety-nine. At least 60 percent of the deputies have not belonged to parties since independence. The relationship between a *za'im* and his client is simpler, and rarely involves the complex question of principle. This fact permitted Suleiman Franjieh, a suspected murderer and chieftain of the northern Maronite town of Zghorta, to be elected president in 1970. During the 1970 election itself, Franjieh's supporters brandished their revolvers in parliament when it appeared that the speaker was disputing Franjieh's electoral victory.

Since the confessional 6:5 ratio applied to the civil service as well, it was a contributing factor to the corrupt practices of the bureaucracy. Bribery of government workers was generally the only way to get anything done, from obtaining a building permit to getting an overseas line for a telephone call. Competence was less important than whom one knew in obtaining a government job.

The Lebanese version of democracy, while it lasted, was superficial at best. As one Lebanese scholar has said, "the system was built for a liberal, mercantile epoch, not for an ideological or revolutionary one."[18] Or, in the words of Kamal Jumblatt, himself a Druze chieftain, though one who was apparently willing to reform the system, Lebanon "lived too long on foggy liberalism without laws or frontiers, without moral or human restraints.''[19] That ''arrogant alliance of money and the feudal system''[20] which formed Lebanon's political club turned Lebanon's serious political problems into a game of jostling notables, more interested in their own wealth and prestige than in the state of their frail country. In the end, then, the political system prior to the war was not representative of the people's interests and needs. Nor was it able to undertake any serious political or economic strategies which would have put the country on a firmer footing.

It was, however, characteristic of Lebanon that civil liberties were generally respected, especially in the cities. Beirut was known to have the freest and most active press in the Middle East. Dissidents from numerous Middle Eastern states could be found in the cafés expressing their views. Freedom of association and of peaceful assembly were respected, unless one incurred the wrath of one's opponents, which often resulted in armed clashes given the politicized atmosphere of the time. There was freedom of movement throughout the country, though the tendency for communities to concentrate themselves in distinct areas meant that one rarely had cause to travel outside one's home region.

Little has been written concerning the adequacy of the Lebanese legal system. It is, however, worth noting that a person's religion could affect which law courts he might be tried in, since each confession had its own legal systems and courts which were separate from the civil courts. A Sunni Moslem would therefore be tried according to the Koranic law, Sharia.

Depending on the nature of the crime alleged to have been committed by an individual, the person may well have had more to fear from the swift justice of the community. Moral offenses such as rape could well result in a woman's male relatives hunting down the suspect and exacting justice on the spot—often death. It was unlikely that the matter would ever be protested by the family of the executed individual, in view of community norms.

The code of revenge, shared by Christian and Moslem communities alike, could in some cases attain exaggerated proportions. One example of this behavior also illustrates the fact that violent divisions within Lebanese society have, as often as not, involved conflict between members of the same sect, in this case Maronite Christians. It concerns the killing of former President Franjieh's son, Tony, by Phalangist party leader Pierre Gemayel's son Bashir (or more specifically, by members of Bashir's forces under orders) in June 1978. Thirty-four people were killed in the attack on the Franjieh house near Zghorta. Within two months the best estimates scored 342 reprisal killings of Phalangist followers and their families, or ten to one for every victim in the original attack. Ostensibly to control Christian infighting, Syrian forces bombarded East Beirut for three months beginning in July of that year (Suleiman Franjieh had been a personal friend of Syrian President Assad since the late fifties). On the first anniversary of Tony Franjieh's death, Pierre Gemayel barely escaped an assassination attempt. On February 23, 1980, a bomb meant for Bashir Gemayel killed his two-year-old daughter and five staff. Suspicions remain concerning who was behind Bashir's own assassination on September 14, 1982, coming just days before he was to be sworn into office as the new Lebanese president. While this illustration occurred after the start of the war, it was largely unconnected to the broader conflict. Instead it reflects the long-standing approach to communal justice and revenge which has repeatedly undermined the efficacy of the Lebanese legal system.

In keeping with its democratic appearance, prewar Lebanon also had the appearance of prosperity. Certainly the fashionable parts of Beirut were resplendent with material affluence. As well, Lebanon's per capita income was higher than that of any Asian country apart from Kuwait, Israel, Singapore, and Japan, and of any African country apart from South Africa and Libya.[21] One survey of Beirut households, which admittedly included neither the shantytowns nor the Palestinian camps, indicated that a majority possessed a refrigerator, a television, and a washing machine, with nearly half also owning a camera, a car, and a record player.[22] The country's literacy rate, which was approximately 80 percent, was the highest in the Arab world. In addition, malaria and smallpox had been completely eradicated. Lebanon could even boast of having the best airline in the region.

As was noted earlier, Lebanon's prosperity was based on a service-oriented economy—primarily trade, banking, and tourism. The government pursued a rigorous free-trade policy in the interests of the commercial lobby, despite the fact that it prevented many industrial ventures from ever getting off the ground.[23] If there was a market for something in Lebanon it was imported, even if Lebanese manufacturers were struggling to produce a similar product. Nevertheless, some industrial expansion did occur in the years prior to the war, but nearly all of it occurred in close proximity to Beirut. Overall economic growth was 7 percent per annum through the fifties, and only slightly lower in the following decade. However, industry grew by only 5 percent per annum, and agriculture by just over 3 percent, which was, in both cases, worse than in Syria.[24] In 1960 only 12 percent of the gross national product (GNP) was produced by small industry, and only 18 percent by agriculture although the latter employed 60 percent of the population.[25]

A useful illustration of the effect of Lebanon's laissez-faire economic tradition is provided by the prodigious building boom which propelled the development of Beirut. Transforming the city of 1.5 million inhabitants in a thirty-year period, the process went ahead without any planning whatsoever. Individuals were free to build anything they wanted wherever they could buy the land. In the words of a former governor of Beirut, "every notion of town planning . . . is destroyed by the pressure of individualism."[26] Over half the houses in west Beirut were destroyed, and nearly all the gardens built upon, leaving only rare examples of Ottoman architecture, and almost no green space outside the grounds of the American University.

The cost of this wild redevelopment was high, especially in human terms. The population of Beirut increased tenfold between the 1930s and the outbreak of the civil war, but the city area had only grown to less than three times the size of its 1900 boundaries. As a result Beirut became seriously overcrowded, cramming nearly half the population of the country onto its restricted peninsula of land. Nine out of ten residents of the city lived in apartment blocks, 80 percent of them built since 1945. In many districts of Beirut these apartment blocks stood practically back to back.

With profit motive the only guideline, luxury flats and office buildings predominated as developers went for a quick return on their investments. Public buildings such as hospitals, libraries, and schools were ignored. Of greater concern, however, was the lack of cheap housing. In 1965, under pressure from labor unions, the Chamber of Deputies passed a law ordering the construction of 4,000 low-cost housing units, but typically the project was never completed.[27] Therefore, the thousands of poor migrants who lived in shantytowns near the airport on the southern edge of the city remained where they were, though it was illegal, and the government did nothing about moving them.

What was in fact happening in all of this was the transformation of Lebanon from "an agrarian republic into an extended city state," which one Lebanese historian calls "the most important event in Lebanese history after 1920."[28] By the mid-seventies only 39 percent of Lebanon's population could still be described as rural, and in this rapidly urbanizing society 43 percent of the population was under sixteen years of age.[29] The social and political consequences, obvious as they may be, went unnoticed by the government.

Throughout these years of uncontrolled growth and rapid social transformation, the economic inequalities in the country, which had always existed, became glaring discrepancies. By 1960, 4 percent of the population disposed of 32 percent of the GNP. The less wealthy half of the population enjoyed only 18 percent, or just over half of what the top 4 percent absorbed.[30] This disparity, which to some degree cut across all sects in the society, tended to follow geographic divisions. The areas of the Akkar in the north, the Jabal 'Amil in the south, and the Beqaa Valley in the east compared poorly to Greater Beirut and the mountain. In 1960 the annual per capita income in Beirut was U.S. $803 compared to only U.S. $151 in the south. The mountain, with 29 percent of the population, had 39 percent of the schools, while the south with 19 percent of the population had only 15 percent of the schools. In the Akkar region there was not a single doctor for a population of 200,000.[31] In these predominantly rural areas agricultural production had stagnated. Even in the mid-sixties the governor of the south complained that 200 villages in his region had no running water, that half the children received no education, and that none of the 445 villages had electricity. By the beginning of the war most of this had improved, though the standard of rural housing remained low, with over half lacking bathroom facilities, and more than one-third still lacking running water.[32]

Although taxation could have been used to reduce these inequalities, and to encourage rural development, it was in fact a means of increasing inequalities. The government raised most of its funds through indirect taxation which hit everyone, rather than through direct taxation which could have been aimed at the wealthier citizens. Only 10 percent of the government's revenues came through income tax, due to low rates and widespread evasion. Development programs, when they were formulated at all, were largely ignored by the government. A Planning Board and a Ministry of General Planning, both set up in the mid-fifties, received little attention. Development plans put forward in 1958 and 1965 were never implemented apart from one or two token projects. A National Development Bank was legislated in 1962 but not set up until 1973. Nor was the social welfare system effective. Founded in 1963, the National Social Security System was very primitive, and in any case it excluded half the population.[33]

Resistance to development schemes, and to any more equitable distribution of the nation's wealth, faced automatic opposition from the commercial lobby and the political bosses. In effect Lebanon was privately run. The public sector was almost nonexistent. The majority of the country's schools were in private hands, with the public schools being noticeably inferior. Similarly, the country's 20 public hospitals were inferior to its 123 private ones. While Beirut had the best medical facilities in the Middle East, only one of its 48 hospitals was public, the rest being priced out of the range of the less wealthy members of society.[34] As a former Minister of Municipal and Rural Affairs once admitted, "Medical treatment is beyond the means of the poorest class."[35] Indeed, as one observer notes, "Practically nothing ever happened in Lebanon, no measures taken, no reforms made, unless somebody, somewhere, was going to make a profit out of it."[36] It is no wonder that, as ex-president Chehab (1958–1964) once said, "If the rich continue to maintain their privileges at everybody else's expense in this way, there will be a social revolution in Lebanon."[37]

The economic and social disparity was nowhere as glaring as in Beirut's Belt of Misery. This shantytown, on the southern reaches of the city, was home to at least 250,000 urban poor, many of them Shi'ites displaced from the south due to fighting between Israel and the Palestinians during the early 1970s. In the middle of the slums were the two sprawling Palestinian camps of Sabra-Chatilla and Burj al Barajneh. Here the mortality rate was two to three times higher than the national average.[38] Many of the concrete block and corrugated iron homes lacked running water or toilets. Many of these people had been agricultural workers, often driven from their land in the south by the government's neglect of agriculture as well as by the hostilities. They were unskilled. They picked up occasional odd jobs, being paid on a daily basis, and had no work security. Unemployment benefits were nonexistent. Needless to say, the people of this part of Beirut had no input into the political process and remained unrepresented in the political system. Many of them, apart from the Shi'ites, had no political rights anyway since they were Palestinians, Kurds, and Syrians. It should be noted that while there were Christian poor in Lebanon, they did not face such extreme poverty, nor were they as alienated from the political processes in the country.

To conclude this discussion of the human rights situation in Lebanon prior to the civil war, a brief note on the situation faced by the Palestinians in Lebanon is appropriate. Whereas in Jordan the refugees were given citizenship, and in Syria, though not citizens, they could enter the army and government service, in Lebanon the Palestinians were regarded as neither nationals nor foreigners but as nonnationals. They were barred from the government and the military, and in general their children were not admitted into Lebanese state schools. Most of Lebanon's Palestinians had been farmers from Galilee, but it was difficult for them to find agricultural work in Lebanon, given the prevailing state of poor agricultural development. Lebanese authorities often refused to give the refugees work permits, which meant that employers felt justified in paying them low wages. Sixty percent of the refugee workers were paid on a daily basis and therefore lacked any job security. Few were permanently employed, with a large majority getting by on seasonal or part-time work.[39]

As nonstatus residents of Lebanon the Palestinians had no political or legal rights within the Lebanese system. Freedom of movement outside Lebanon was inhibited by the need to obtain a special travel document for Palestinians (in lieu of a passport), which would generally expire within three to six months. Incidents of social degradation and humiliation were common, and, combined with harassment from police and security forces, made the Palestinians' nonstatus condition woefully apparent to them.

In sum, then, the human rights situation in Lebanon prior to 1975 was worthy of serious concern. This is particularly frustrating when one realizes the wasted potential, given Lebanon's relative economic prosperity and the rudiments of a representative democratic system.

Consequences of the War

In considering the prewar situation it has been possible, and appropriate, to sketch out the conditions in broad terms. This is no longer possible once one moves into the post–1975 period. Given the brutal conditions of the war, human rights statistics are difficult to obtain and often impossible to verify. Examples of systematic human rights abuses tend to be anecdotal, coming in most cases from news correspondents or diplomatic sources. Still, it is possible to begin with some general observations on the situation.

To begin with, political rights disappeared with the effective collapse of the government at the outset of hostilities. The last election was in 1972, though the Chamber of Deputies continues to dutifully elect a new president every six years. The government became totally powerless with the dissolution of the army in 1976, and again in 1984 (after the army had been briefly reunited). Effective power lies in the hands of the numerous militias which have carved up the country between them. This is true even in Christian East Beirut where one might have expected the president, a Maronite, to have sustained a certain degree of authority. Ironically, in some ways the relationship between the militias and members of the communities in areas they control, which largely parallels the traditional *za'im*-client relationship, is more effective at serving the people's day-to-day needs than the peacetime government ever had been. However, there are no longer any political rights with the collapse of the political system, the rule of the militias being arbitrary at best.

Similarly, the legal system can no longer be said to function, although a few quasi-legal procedures can still take place, mainly concerning family law and commercial dealings. Once again, what legal system exists is administered by the militias. This is undertaken in a rather arbitrary manner, with public execution a common result of privately held "trials." One of the early events of the war was the storming of Beirut's prisons by the militias, setting free some 1,346 prisoners. All the prison records were burned. PLO commandos later captured the central police headquarters and made off with all the archives. Militias, themselves the perpetrators of the vast majority of crime in the country, from robbery to the drug trade, are clearly in no position to protect the legal rights of Lebanon's citizens, even to a nominal degree.

Civil liberties, once the pride of Lebanese society, have been effectively curtailed in the spirit of suspicion and fear which prevails. The print media have remained surprisingly active, despite occasional attacks on their offices and staff. The war, which has succeeded in polarizing opinion throughout the country, has, however, also affected the ability of the press to report events objectively. This polarization of Lebanese society consists of a subtle restriction of individual opinions, thought, and conscience. It is, for example, no longer possible for a Christian to publicly express sympathy for the Palestinians. It is now almost impossible for a Moslem to maintain close Christian friends, and vice versa. Because this polarization has also meant the increased physical separation of communities on the ground, it has tended to restrict freedom of residence and freedom of movement—it just is not safe to live and move outside one's communal heartland. Freedom of religion may well be restricted if one is in a part of the country where the other main religious tradition (Christian or Moslem) is in the majority.

A vast array of basic human rights are violated simply by the day-to-day conditions of open warfare. The right to life is an obvious example. The war has so far claimed some 125,000 lives, according to local estimates, of which the vast majority have been noncombatants. The situation of daily indiscriminate terror which prevails in many parts of the country, but especially in Beirut, is equivalent to a massive case of cruel, degrading, and inhuman treatment, as the psychological condition of much of Lebanese society bears grim witness. Random shellings, widespread population displacements, and the tactics of modern urban warfare result in continuous arbitrary interference with family and home. The war has resulted in the displacement of about 600,000 people, many of whom have faced multiple displacements. Estimates suggest that 65,000 housing units have been totally destroyed since the beginning of the war. UN statistics indicate that the prewar emigration rate of 10,000 per year (already high) has quintupled since 1976.[40]

Economic and social rights have been particularly eroded by the conditions of war. The standard of living of most Lebanese residents has been significantly reduced in the face of an unemployment rate of 40 percent, an inflation rate approaching 200 percent,[41] and a drop in the value of currency from three Lebanese pounds to the U.S. dollar in early 1984 to 45 Lebanese pounds to the U.S. dollar by mid-1986. The education of individual Lebanese people has become increasingly difficult to complete given the wartime disruptions. Medical and social services, which were never sufficient, have been strained to the breaking point by the overwhelming number of people who have been permanently disabled by injuries sustained in the war. Finally, any participation in community life and culture has had to cease in the prevailing atmosphere of tension and anxiety where basic survival uses up all available energy.

While it is hardly surprising that a state of civil war would severely restrict the human rights of individual noncombatants, this broad sketch of the situation which has existed in Lebanon since 1975 may be useful in expressing that impact with greater clarity. The general situation established, it is now appropriate to consider a number of more specific aspects of the human rights situation. These will be discussed in terms of the primary perpetrators of human rights abuses in Lebanon: the Lebanese government, the militias, the Syrian Army, and the Israeli Defense Forces.

The Lebanese Government

It has already been stated that the Lebanese government holds little effective control over most of the country. However, governments and individuals around the world continue to press for the return of Lebanon's sovereignty. As a result, it is important to consider the human rights record of the Lebanese authorities at those times when they have possessed effective control over parts of the country, particularly in Beirut from September 1982 to February 1984. On November 9, 1982, the Chamber of Deputies voted to extend emergency powers to President Gemayel, allowing him to rule by decree for six months. This was later extended to September 1983. During this period the government was largely in control of the Greater Beirut area.

An immediate result of the extension of control was the arrest and detention of at least two thousand persons by the Lebanese army. Hundreds more simply disappeared.[42] Those who were detained were said to have not had their papers in order, but the motivation for their arrest seems in reality to have been political. Arrests were conducted without warrants. The conditions of detention were far below standard—the cells were overcrowded, mattresses were few, there was no toilet access, and the food was poor. Press reports spoke of beatings during interrogation, of deaths in prison, of several hundred persons deported to the Beqaa Valley or expelled from the country. The prisoners could receive no visitors, and even the International Committee of the Red Cross (ICRC) was not permitted access. Most of the detainees were Lebanese and Palestinian Moslems. After international protests, conditions were improved, and several hundred detainees were released. Nevertheless, arrests continued at a rate of five to ten per day well into 1983. By 1985 Amnesty International and the ICRC estimated that about 300 detainees remained in confinement.[43]

At the same time the government turned its attention to the Belt of Misery shantytowns which had been devastated by the Israeli invasion. Its residents had since occupied abandoned apartments throughout the city and had set up a strip of huts along the beach south of the city. Government authorities began to evict the squatters and to bulldoze the shantytowns. A wave of local resistance and international concern halted the operation. However, in July 1983 the authorities again tried to clear out these areas, and there were several armed clashes with Shi'ite militiamen. The government had made no provision for alternate housing for the people it was displacing. The vast majority of the tens of thousands of people affected by this policy had nowhere else to go. The government's harsh yet ineffective attempt to deal with this housing problem caused it to lose what little credibility it may still have had among the poor.

An obstacle to the government's ability to administer the law effectively and to respond to the vital needs of the people at this time was the relationship between the government and the Phalangist party. This resulted in numerous partisan actions. One example is that, following the prompt disarming of Moslem and leftist militias in west Beirut in the fall of 1982, it took some months before the authorities even attempted to disarm the Phalangist and other rightist militias in the eastern sector of the city. Similar in its partisan appearance was the government's failure to prosecute any of those Phalangist militiamen who directed and carried out the massacre of Palestinian civilians in September 1982 at the Sabra and Chatilla refugee camps in Beirut. This was despite the fact that the identities of all the main perpetrators were well known. The treatment of Palestinians in general by Lebanese authorities, such as the practice of refusing them work permits, the deportation of those whose papers are said to be not in order, and the refusal to renew travel documents for Palestinians from Lebanon currently residing overseas, all reflect the Phalangists' resistance to the presence of Palestinians in Lebanon more than any official government policy.

In general, even the limited information available indicated that the Lebanese authorities, when they have had control over sectors of the country, have acted in a partisan manner with a clear disregard for the people under their authority.

The Militias

A list of the militias which are currently active in Lebanon would cover several pages. However, most of these are small, insignificant groups caught up in the general atmosphere of violence and extremism. For the most part it is sufficient to consider the activities of the dominant militia groups: the Shi'ite Amal, the Druze Popular Socialist party (PSP), and the Christian Lebanese Forces. Between them, these three paramilitary organizations control vast areas of Lebanon. Together they have some 45,000 men (and a few hundred women) under arms. They are equipped with heavy artillery, tanks, armored personnel carriers, and other tools of modern warfare such as the AK–47 Kalashnikov and M16 assault rifles. In Greater Beirut, Mount Lebanon, the Chouf Mountains southeast of Beirut, and south Lebanon, they are the only existing forces of authority. Their actions therefore have direct impact on the majority of Lebanon's residents.

In general, the behavior of the militias flagrantly disregards the rights of civilians, ranging from small annoyances to gross and systematic violations of the most fundamental rights. All conventions concerning the conduct of war are similarly disregarded in the most extreme manner. Although militia leaders regularly express deep regret over the behavior of their fighters, it is clear that given the structure of these paramilitary organizations and the conditions of the war that is being fought, the militia leaders are in no position to bring their fighters under control.

Many of the systematic abuses of human rights by militias are brought about by the standard operating procedures common to the Lebanese conflict. A case in point would be the extensive network of checkpoints by which all movement within and between militia-controlled zones is monitored. Some of these are fairly permanent installations, while others, known as "flying checkpoints," can turn up anywhere at anytime. At each checkpoint vehicles are stopped while the identity of all the passengers is verified. Since identity papers in Lebanon state not only a person's nationality and place of residence but also his/her religion, this is a thorough process. Further questioning can also follow, as well as, in some cases, intimidation of a vehicle's occupants. It is not unusual for occupants to be removed by force, often leaving their possessions or luggage behind, and to have their vehicle commandeered by militia members. Those vehicles are not generally returned. In other cases, occupants are dragged out of their vehicles as other cars wait in line, and shot, if the militiamen at the checkpoint consider them to be from an opposition community. This extreme type of activity occurs in particular during periods of tension along the Green Line separating East and West Beirut.

These situations can become particularly brutal if attacks occur which are felt to be worthy of retaliation, usually without warning. The brutal ax killing of four Phalangist militiamen near a Beirut Palestinian camp early on the morning of December 6, 1975, is an example of this behavior. Hundreds of the victims' fellow militiamen set up checkpoints throughout the downtown sector of Beirut, and when Moslems were found, they were shot instantly. Within hours more than two hundred Lebanese Moslem civilians were dead. Ten years later, during the summers of 1985 and 1986, the same scenarios were being acted out, now in the context of the "War of the Camps" between the Shi'ite Amal militia and the Palestinians of Sabra-Chatilla and Burj al Barajneh camps in West Beirut. Palestinians were chased from their cars at checkpoints along the coastal highway south of Beirut, and along the streets of Beirut itself, and were shot.[44] Bodies of victims were generally then collected and dumped at the morgue of the American University Hospital in West Beirut.

Checkpoints have been the mainstay for another common form of militia behavior—kidnapping. The origins of this hostage-taking tactic are now lost. However, in the course of the war thousands of people have been abducted, often from their cars. In some cases release has later been arranged. In cases where the perpetrators of a kidnapping can be traced, a direct offer of cash ransom has sometimes been effective. Occasionally an exchange has occurred between militias holding members of each other's community. Depending on the state of tensions in the country, kidnap victims may eventually be killed, their bodies dumped in a conspicuous location. It is estimated that at least ten thousand Lebanese residents have disappeared in this manner since 1975 and have not been seen since. It is not known how many kidnap victims remain in the custody of the militias. In April 1983 the Maronite Patriarch, who had been asked to help in obtaining the release of some fifteen hundred missing persons who were known to have been abducted by the Lebanese Forces, stated after some inquiries into the situation, "There is no more anything to negotiate about," acknowledging that those held had been killed.[45] In general, if release cannot be arranged quickly, within one or two days, the likelihood of eventual release becomes reduced. A nonsectarian Committee of Relatives of the Detained, Kidnapped and Disappeared Persons was formed in November 1982. It is active in pressuring for the release of missing persons and in publicizing the situation. It has, however, succeeded in gaining the release of only a very few persons.

At certain points in the war the brutality practiced by the militias has reached the level of mass killings. In January 1976 the Phalangist militia attacked one of the remaining Moslem population centers in what had become East Beirut. A slum district near the ports, populated mostly by Shi'ites, it was known as Karantina. Its 30,000 residents had been recently joined by some Palestinian fighters with the result that the Phalangists decided to eradicate these elements. There was little resistance, except from the small unit of Palestinians. Yet in three days one thousand people were estimated to have been killed. Stories of unarmed men being gunned down by the dozen were prevalent.[46]

Two days later the Palestinians and their allies from the Lebanese leftist militias overran the Maronite stronghold of Damour, twenty kilometers south of Beirut. Entire families were gunned down and their homes looted and dynamited. Out of the population of 20,000, estimates indicate that about 200 were killed.[47] The rest fled, and Damour became home to a number of Karantina's refugees, along with a large number of Palestinians.

Six months later, during the summer of 1976, Christian militias surrounded the Palestinian camp of Tal Zaater, the last Palestinian stronghold in East Beirut. Although a surrender could have been negotiated, as the ICRC was trying to do, a fifty-two–day siege resulted, the toll of which was 2,000 killed. The massacre of Palestinian civilians by Lebanese Forces militiamen at Sabra-Chatilla camp in September 1982 is now well-known, largely due to Israeli complicity. Estimates of the toll there range from five hundred to two thousand killed. The actual numbers will never be known.

The Wars of the Camps in West Beirut during the summers of 1985 and 1986 have produced similar reports of mass killings. In this case Shi'ite Amal militiamen sought to dislodge the Palestinian fighters in the camps near the airport. Reports state that 650 people were killed during the fighting in 1985, with about half that number killed during the 1986 hostilities. Reports of massacres of civilians were numerous.[48] When Gaza Hospital was overrun by Amal militiamen, thirty people were shot, some of them in their hospital beds. In another instance a refrigerator truck containing the bodies of fifty-five men was left outside the American University Hospital. Several of the victims had been shot at point-blank range. All were later identified as Palestinians.[49] Some fifteen Amal prisoners were also shot by their Palestinian captors.

The militias behave in a similar manner when clashes break out between previously allied groups. On July 7, 1980, the Phalangists attacked their allies, the National Liberal party's Tiger militia, to force them into the unified command of the Lebanese Forces militia. During the day of fighting at least 150 people were killed. People were thrown out of upper-story windows and shot as they plummeted to the ground. Several people, including some women and children, were shot while swimming in a seaside pool. About forty-five Pakistani dockworkers who got in the way were used as target practice by the crazed fighters.[50]

Even within individual militias human rights are ignored. Disobedient fighters can be shot on the spot. Anyone suspected of contacts with the enemy is similarly executed.[51] Many of the fighters are only in their early teens. Drugs, especially hashish, are widely used by fighters. In some cases hashish is distributed by lieutenants to their units. Any attempt by fighters to leave their militia has serious, sometimes fatal, consequences. The level of despair among some fighters has led to games of Russian roulette in which dozens of fighters have shot themselves in the head when the odds caught up with them.[52]

Clearly, then, the militias, which control much of the situation in Lebanon, are guilty of a sustained pattern of gross and systematic human rights abuses. However, it is almost impossible to change this situation for the better due to the irregular nature of the militias and the general social chaos which their activities have spawned. There is little basis from which to bring pressure to bear on them to significantly change their activities.

The Forces of Occupation—Syria and Israel

Because Syria and Israel are sovereign states with regular armies, their activities in Lebanon have been much easier to assess. As a result, much more has been written about the impact of their occupations on the human rights of Lebanese residents. Therefore, it will be sufficient to consider simply the issues of greatest concern.

The legitimacy of the presence of Syrian forces in eastern Lebanon has become questionable since its mandate as a peacekeeping force was not extended by the Arab League Summit at Fez, Morocco, in 1982. Syrian withdrawal was to have been subsequently achieved through negotiation. Syrian involvement in the Lebanese conflict at many levels is well known, though its precise nature and extent cannot usually be identified. In cases in which it has armed and supported certain groups which it favors, it has clearly fueled further hostilities, at the expense of Lebanese civilians.

Troop indiscipline in the Syrian army has often led to attacks on civilians at Syrian checkpoints. Syrian soldiers have been guilty of robbery, car theft, and extortion in demanding protection money from local residents. Cases of abduction and detention without charge or trial have been frequent, though the exact number of detainees is unknown.[53] Syrian soldiers often seize homes for accommodation. The property of any who oppose Syrian presence or policy may be destroyed. Syrian involvement in opposing Yasser Arafat's leadership of the PLO has fueled conflicts in Tripoli and in the Beqaa Valley. The armed presence of Libyan and Iranian forces in the Beqaa Valley, which entered through Syria, has further undermined Lebanese sovereignty and has been a source of interference in the life of Lebanon's Shi'ite community as these forces seek to advance Libyan and Iranian regional interests from a Lebanese base.

Following its 1982 invasion Israel deployed some 100,000 troops in Lebanon. After its substantial withdrawal, completed in June 1985, it maintains fewer than one thousand troops in a 25-kilometer wide "security zone" along the border inside Lebanon. Most of the security duties inside the zone are pursued by members of the Israeli-sponsored South Lebanon Army, which is largely Christian, though it has some Shi'ite fighters as well.

The brutal tactics of the June 1982 invasion, including the month-long siege of West Beirut, have been widely denounced. The best estimates indicate that the invasion, and the siege of Beirut, had by the beginning of September 1982 resulted in 18,000 dead and 30,000 wounded, of which 90 percent were civilians.[54] The high proportion of civilian casualties was a result of Israeli tactics, which sought to minimize Israeli military casualties, and its use of U.S. cluster bombs and phosphorus shells.

Following the invasion, Israeli cleanup operations in southern Lebanon resulted in further demolition of property and the detention of over ten thousand Palestinians and Lebanese Shi'ites. These detainees were mostly held at Ansar, in a makeshift prison compound.[55] Soon after the invasion, large quantities of Israeli agricultural produce and manufactured goods began to enter Lebanon, threatening the fragile Lebanese economy, especially its devastated agricultural sector. Lebanese goods may not enter Israel. Israeli forces also began arming, and encouraging the proliferation and operation of, militia groups in areas under its control. This sponsored numerous conflicts once Israel withdrew from those territories, the most serious one being the Chouf Mountain war of September 1983, in which the Lebanese Forces were defeated by the Druze PSP militia at the cost of about a thousand lives, mostly civilian.

Despite its pullback in 1985, the Israelis continued to hold over a thousand prisoners, mostly Lebanese Shi'ites. In violation of international law these were transported into Israel and held there for some months. After the hijacking of a Trans World Airlines airliner in June 1985, pressure was placed on the United

States to quietly urge Israel to release the illegally held detainees, this being the main demand of the hijackers. Denying that the hijacking had had any effect on the decision, Israeli authorities released the detainees in groups of a few hundred at a time during the month following the end of the hijacking.

Raids against Palestinian targets in southern Lebanon have resumed since Israel's withdrawal. Attacks by Lebanese groups on Israeli and Southern Lebanese Army (SLA) targets in the security zone result in brutal search and seizure operations, property destruction, and displacements. In one case, on February 21, 1986, the entire population of the village of Shakra was subjected to torture and harassment by SLA fighters as Israeli soldiers stood by. The SLA's men drove nails into people's ears, whipped people with barbed wire, and applied electric shock to people's heads. This came in the wake of an attack which had killed two Israeli soldiers near the village.[56] Random shellings of Shi'ite villages in the zone are conducted on a daily basis. UN soldiers have been known to wave UN flags to dissuade the SLA from firing at villagers as they plow their fields.[57] The activities of Israel and the SLA show a complete disregard for the efforts of the UNIFIL troops to keep the peace in the area. Clashes are not uncommon, resulting on occasion in the death of UN troops.

CONCLUSION

Lebanon is a tortured and fragmented country, whose agonies are a microcosm of the social and political troubles of the modern world. Its dilemmas should therefore give us all pause for thought, and its mistakes should give rise to careful study. As for the future, the overwhelming litany of killing and destruction does not hold out much promise for the near future. As long as the fighting goes on, the human rights tragedy will be perpetuated. A few lines from Baudelaire's "Les Fleurs du Mal" sum up that tragedy, and its impact on the life of the Lebanese people:

> I am the wound and the knife!
> I am the blow and the cheek!
> I am the limbs and the wheel—
> The victim and the executioner!

However, the most fitting conclusion to this study is provided by Lebanon's own literary genius, Khalil Gibran. In 1934, long before the present conflict, Gibran composed the following lines in his book *The Garden of the Prophet*:

> Pity the nation that is full of beliefs and empty of religion.
> Pity the nation that wears a cloth it does not weave, eats a bread it does not
> harvest, and drinks a wine that flows not from its own wine press . . .
> Pity the nation that raises not its voice save when it walks in a funeral, boasts
> not except among its ruins, and will rebel not save when its neck is laid
> between the sword and the block.

Pity the nation whose statesman is a fox, whose philosopher is a juggler, and
   whose art is the art of patching and mimicking . . .
Pity the nation divided into fragments, each fragment deeming itself a nation.

NOTES

1. In fact, only one previous publication exists on the subject of human rights in
Lebanon, undoubtedly for this reason. It is a report published in 1983 by the American
Friends Service Committee's Advisory Committee on Human Rights in Lebanon entitled
"Lebanon: Toward Legal Order and Respect for Human Rights." The emphasis in the
report is on Israeli violations within Lebanese territory, although the report also contains
sections on the Syrian-controlled zone and on the Lebanese government–administered
area. The Israeli invasion of Lebanon in June 1982 heightened interest in human rights
in Lebanon for a time, but since the 1985 Israeli withdrawal into a southern "security
zone," attention has once more shifted away from Lebanon itself.

2. As quoted in Jonathan Randal, *The Tragedy of Lebanon: Christian Warlords,
Israeli Adventurers and American Bunglers* (London: Hogarth Press, 1984), 60.

3. See the relevant excerpts of the King-Crane Commission Report in George An-
tonius, *The Arab Awakening: The Story of the Arab National Movement* (Beirut: Khayats
Press, 1983), 443–58.

4. This agreement, between the foreign ministers of Britain and France respectively,
attenuated earlier support for Arab independence in the wake of the Ottoman Empire's
decline. It retained some provision for an independent Arab state, or confederation of
states, but made it clear that there would be large British and French spheres of influence.
The Sykes-Picot Agreement therefore laid the groundwork for colonial interference in
the Middle East between the two world wars. Uneasiness with this arrangement between
the great powers turned into indignation with the declaration by Lord Balfour in 1917
that Britain favored the establishment of "a national home for the Jewish people" in
Palestine.

5. David Gilmour, *Lebanon: The Fractured Country* (New York: St. Martin's Press,
1984), 63.

6. David McDowall, *Lebanon: A Conflict of Minorities* (London: Minority Rights
Group, 1983), 10.

7. Michael C. Hudson, *The Precarious Republic: Modernization in Lebanon* (New
York: Random House, 1968), 44.

8. The best estimate of the current population figures is found in McDowall, *Lebanon*,
9.

9. McDowall, *Lebanon*, 13.

10. See Paul Saba, "The Creation of the Lebanese Economy," in *Essays on the Crisis
in Lebanon*, ed. Roger C. Owen (London: Ithaca Press, 1976), 24–28.

11. The Litani River project involved the construction of a dam on the Litani River
in southern Lebanon. The dam was to produce electricity and provide water for an
extensive irrigation scheme which would rehabilitate the agricultural sector in the south.
The dam was built, and electricity produced, but the irrigation scheme was never
implemented.

12. Examples of this state of affairs are traced in detail in Wilbur Crane Eveland,
Ropes of Sand—America's Failure in the Middle East (New York: W. W. Norton, 1980).
Numerous anecdotes can also be found in Randal, *Tragedy of Lebanon*, in a chapter

entitled "The Offhand Americans." A typical incident recounted by Randal (156–57) concerns the outrage of Lebanon's President Franjieh when, upon arriving in New York to address the UN General Assembly in 1974, his luggage was sniffed at by dogs of the U.S. Bureau of Dangerous Drugs who were checking for hashish. Arabs tend to find dogs disgusting, and this incident sparked an embarrassing diplomatic scene.

13. Randal, *Tragedy of Lebanon*, 76.

14. Ibid., 234.

15. Labib Zuwiyya Yamek, *The Syrian Social Nationalist Party* (Cambridge: Harvard Middle Eastern Monograph Studies, 1966), 36.

16. See Eveland, *Ropes of Sand*, 250–57.

17. Ralph E. Crow, "Parliament in the Lebanese Political System," in *Legislatures in Developmental Perspective*, ed. Allan Kornberg and Lloyd D. Musolf (Durham: Duke University Press, 1970), 294.

18. Elie Adib Salem, "Lebanon's Political Maze: The Search for Peace in a Turbulent Land," *Middle East Journal* 33, no. 4 (Autumn 1979): 450.

19. Kamal Jumblatt, *I Speak for Lebanon* (London: Zed Press, 1982), 48.

20. Phrase used by Georges Naccache, quoted in David C. Gordon, *Lebanon: The Fragmented Nation* (London: Croom Helm, 1980), 101.

21. Gilmour, *Lebanon*, 5.

22. George T. Murray, *Lebanon: The New Future* (Beirut: Thomson Rizk Press, 1974), 206.

23. Gilmour, *Lebanon*, 6.

24. McDowall, *Lebanon*, 14.

25. Gordon, *Lebanon*, 62. It should be noted that the problem of increasingly dated statistics is faced by every author seeking to write about Lebanon. The last census was in 1932, and the latest comprehensive socioeconomic statistics date from the early 1960s. As a result I make sparing use of this data in order to simply highlight basic socioeconomic realities which led up to the conflict, and which are generally understood to have remained largely unchanged to this day.

26. Halim Said Abu-Izzedin, ed., *Lebanon and Its Provinces: A Study by the Governors of Five Provinces* (Beirut: Khayats Press, 1963), 105.

27. Gilmour, *Lebanon*, 9.

28. A. H. Hourani, "Lebanon: From Feudalism to Modern State," *Middle Eastern Studies* 2, no. 3 (April 1966): 263.

29. McDowall, *Lebanon*, 13.

30. Roger C. Owen, "The Political Economy of Grand Liban, 1920–1970" in *Essays on the Crisis in Lebanon*, ed. Roger C. Owen, 28.

31. Gordon, *Lebanon*, 66.

32. Murray, *Lebanon*, 65.

33. Michael Wall, "The Tightrope Country: A Survey of Lebanon," *Economist*, 26 January 1974.

34. Gilmour, *Lebanon*, 18.

35. Abu-Izzedin, *Lebanon and Its Provinces*, 114.

36. Gilmour, *Lebanon*, 12.

37. Quoted in Jumblatt, *I Speak for Lebanon*, 49.

38. Eric Rouleau, *Le Monde*, 23 September 1975.

39. Bassem Sirhan, "Palestinian Refugee Camp Life in Lebanon," *Journal of Palestine Studies* 14 (Winter 1975): 101.

40. Randal, *Tragedy of Lebanon*, 259.

41. "Economic Outlook Grim," *Daily Star* (Beirut), 30 December 1985, 6.

42. American Friends' Service Committee (AFSC), "Lebanon: Toward Legal Order and Respect for Human Rights" (Philadelphia: AFSC, August 1983), 33. See also Martha Salper, "Lebanese Missing: Still No News," *Israel and Palestine Political Report 116* (June-July 1985), 15.

43. *Amnesty International Report 1985* (London: Amnesty International Publications, 1985), 234–36.

44. International Centre for Information on Palestinian and Lebanese Prisoners, Deportees and Missing Persons (ICIPLP), "Report on the War in the Palestinian Camps of Beirut" (Paris: ICIPLP, July 1985), 34–35.

45. AFSC, "Toward Legal Order," 40.

46. Randal, *Tragedy of Lebanon*, 88–90.

47. Ibid., 23, 90.

48. See ICIPLP, "The War in the Camps," 13–43. See also "Not Massacres, Annihilation," *Israel and Palestine Political Report 114* (June 1985).

49. *Le Monde*, 28 May 1985; *Sunday Times* 26 May 1985, cited in ICIPLP, "The War in the Camps," 21.

50. Randal, *Tragedy of Lebanon*, 135–37.

51. See "Public Execution Draws 1000 in Beirut," Associated Press, 31 July 1986.

52. Rod Nordland, "Playing the Death Game," *Newsweek*, 30 December 1985, 29.

53. AFSC, "Toward Legal Order," 7–11.

54. *L'Orient Le Jour* (Beirut), 2 September 1982.

55. AFSC, "Toward Legal Order," 23–27.

56. See news item in *Israel and Palestine Political Report 122* (March 1986), 23.

57. See news item in *Israel and Palestine Political Report 121* (February 1986), 19.

SUGGESTED READINGS

Gilmour, David. *Lebanon: The Fractured Country*. New York: St. Martin's Press, 1984.

Gordon, David C. *The Republic of Lebanon—Nation in Jeopardy*. London: Croom Helm, 1983.

Hirst, David. *The Gun and the Olive Branch: The Roots of Violence in the Middle East*. London: Faber and Faber, 1977.

Hourani, A. H. *Syria and Lebanon: A Political Essay*. Oxford: Oxford University Press, 1946.

Hudson, Michael C. *The Precarious Republic: Modernization in Lebanon*. New York: Random House, 1968.

Owen, Roger C., ed. *Essays on the Crisis in Lebanon*. London: Ithaca Press, 1976.

Randal, Jonathan. *The Tragedy of Lebanon: Christian Warlords, Israeli Adventurers and American Bunglers*. London: Hogarth Press, 1984.

Salibi, K. S. *Crossroads to Civil War: Lebanon 1958–1976*. London: Ithaca Press, 1976.

———. *The Modern History of Lebanon*. London: Weidenfeld and Nicholson, 1965.

Wright, Robin. *Sacred Rage: The Crusade of Modern Islam*. New York: Simon and Schuster, 1985.

12

NICARAGUA

Catherine Gander

The subject of human rights in Nicaragua has generated international controversy from the time the revolutionary government took power in July 1979. Accusations that Nicaragua was "totalitarian" and "repressive" were countered with claims that a "grass-roots democracy" was being forged there.

This chapter will focus on the revolution, which was the most significant landmark in the evolution of human rights in Nicaragua, and include material up to July 1986, and in some selected instances, the early fall of 1986. It is based on publications by international human rights organizations, American scholars and journalists, Nicaraguan governmental and private sources, and information gathered by the author during her four and a half years in Nicaragua.

The war against 15,000 armed "counterrevolutionaries," or *contras*, had serious repercussions on human rights. This chapter will examine the Nicaraguan state's human rights practices, although mention will also be made of violations by the *contras*.

It is difficult to provide a relatively durable evaluation of human rights in a country undergoing revolutionary transformation. Economic, political, and social relations change very quickly, in comparison to more "stable" systems that have evolved gradually over a century or two.

The Nicaraguan revolution took human rights beyond the conventional categories defined in the Universal Declaration of Human Rights and sought to promote popular participation on all levels. This process of empowerment and consciousness raising is essential for the advancement of human rights in the broadest sense.

HISTORICAL BACKGROUND

The Somoza family ruled Nicaragua virtually uninterrupted for forty-three years, which were characterized by constant violations of human rights. A movement called the Sandinista National Liberation Front (FSLN) was founded in 1961 to organize resistance to the dictatorship. In an effort to curb growing support for the guerrillas, the country's armed forces, or National Guard, increasingly terrorized the citizenry.[1] International human rights organizations, including the Inter-American Commission on Human Rights (IACHR) of the Organization of American States (OAS), strongly criticized the Somoza regime for its generalized practices of arbitrary arrest, disappearance, torture, group massacre, indiscriminate bombing of the civilian population, and grave restrictions on freedom of expression and assembly.[2] The economic exploitation and political repression existing under Anastasio Somoza Debayle led to a full-fledged insurrection that ousted the dictator in July 1979.

The new government's provisional Constitution, in effect since August 1979, ratified Nicaragua's adherence to the 1949 Geneva Conventions, the United Nations' Universal Declaration of Human Rights and International Covenants and the OAS's American Convention on Human Rights. In April 1985, Nicaragua signed the UN Convention against Torture and Other Cruel, Inhuman or Degrading Treatment or Punishment. This commitment to international human rights conventions was tentatively reaffirmed in February 1986, in the first draft of the new Constitution. The document also specified comprehensive social, family, political, property, and economic rights that would be guaranteed.

Human rights in revolutionary Nicaragua were monitored by two main domestic agencies.[3] A private organization, the Permanent Commission on Human Rights (CPDH), published a monthly bulletin criticizing human rights practices. Its relations with the government were often tense. While lamenting the lack of official cooperation with the CPDH, Americas Watch reported in 1984 that the CPDH was able to "function effectively in Nicaragua."[4] The CPDH had more international projection than the pro-government National Commission for the Protection and Promotion of Human Rights (CNPPDH). Despite the fact that each organization had a political bias, their presence contributed in some measure to the defense of human rights in Nicaragua.[5]

Personal, Legal Rights

The new government quickly took steps to guarantee personal and legal rights. It abolished the death penalty and prevented widespread mistreatment of the 8,000 members of Somoza's National Guard who had been captured. The penitentiary system initiated what Americas Watch referred to as a "humane" rehabilitation process, which included open prison farms, technical training, and work programs.[6]

As the war against anti-Sandinista insurgents escalated, however, certain restrictions were placed on legal rights. Beginning in March 1982, the government imposed a "national state of emergency," although exceptional measures were not always implemented with the same stringency. Habeas corpus was in effect except for people arrested for security or war-related crimes. These prisoners were sometimes held incommunicado for several weeks under inadequate conditions and subjected to harsh interrogation techniques.[7] They were then tried by special tribunals. International human rights groups objected to these courts, saying they were partial and did not permit an independent appeal process. According to the March 1986 Americas Watch report, some 3,200 of the more than 7,000 prisoners in Nicaragua were charged with security-related offenses (including the more than 2,000 former guardsmen still serving sentences).[8]

Compared to other Latin American countries, Nicaragua's record was quite good in the category of "integrity of person." Human rights organizations generally concurred that the Nicaraguan government did not have a "systematic practice of forced disappearances, extrajudicial killings or torture,"[9] although isolated abuses did occur. Amnesty International wrote in March 1986 that it had "received some reports of torture, arbitrary killings and unacknowledged detention carried out by military personnel in remote areas undergoing armed conflict. However, the organization also received information on the public trial and imprisonment of military personnel found responsible for such abuses."[10] By early 1986 some 600 former members of Sandinista military or security forces were serving sentences on charges ranging from robbery and rape to murder.[11]

In addition to prosecuting those guilty of violations, the government took other steps to guarantee legal rights. For example, from December 1983 onward, amnesty was granted to *contras* who laid down their arms. By April 1986, 1,500 *contras* had turned themselves in and resumed civilian life.[12]

Civil Rights

After July 1979, the serious restrictions Somoza had placed on civil liberties were abolished. Nicaraguans' freedom was curtailed somewhat by the war, however. The emergency measures included press censorship on matters relating to national security and limitations on the right to assemble and freedom of movement. The exceptional measures did not, in themselves, violate international human rights charters for a country at war.

Two civil liberties attracted most attention—the freedoms of religion and expression. In its first seven years, the Nicaraguan government expelled a dozen foreign priests accused of actively supporting the *contras*, and stated that the religious would be allowed to return when the war ended. Authorities called other priests in for questioning and periodically clamped down on Catholic radio stations and publications. Neither the priests nor radio stations were sanctioned for their religious beliefs, however, but for their political practices or their transgression of existing laws.

The Roman Catholic Church continued to be one of the major social and political forces in the country. Many religious observers contended that the principal problem facing the Church was not persecution by the state, but rather a fundamental split within the Church itself. The polemic between the traditional, hierarchical view of Christianity and "liberation theology" was occurring in several Catholic countries throughout the world. Nicaraguans who chose the new model Church found that many Christian values were embodied in the revolution.[13]

The extent of press censorship varied considerably from the time it was first imposed. The opposition newspaper *La Prensa* was frequently censored for articles not strictly within the realm of national security, as defined by the emergency legislation. While criticizing the sometimes arbitrary censorship, Americas Watch reported that "what *La Prensa* was actually allowed to publish was the harshest criticism of its own government that could be read in any newspaper in Central America during 1985."[14] Media analyst John Spicer Nichols wrote, "Despite assertions by President Reagan, IAPA and others that the control of the Nicaraguan media was virtually totalitarian, the diversity of ownership and opinion was unusual for a Third World country, particularly one at war."[15]

Freedom of expression was further limited, however, as the war escalated. In June 1986 the Nicaraguan government shut down *La Prensa* indefinitely, alleging that the newspaper's editorial line defended the Reagan administration's policy and the U.S.-backed *contra* war. The communiqué on the closure indicated that *La Prensa* could resume publication once U.S. aggression against Nicaragua ceased.

According to Amnesty International, civil and political rights were abused by the Nicaraguan government's periodic "intimidation and harassment" of opposition political figures.[16] Some U.S. journalists contended that the only dissidents who could speak out in Nicaragua were members of the Catholic hierarchy. Shirley Christian wrote:

The opposition that remained inside the country—business and farm groups, traditional political parties, media, labor federations—was repressed, broken, confiscated, censored or otherwise lost ground. All of this served to thrust the Church hierarchy into a more visible and active role in opposing Sandinista measures, whether they touched directly on the Church or not.[17]

Other analysts thought the opposition had considerable freedom of expression. Richard Fagen found that

Professional and business associations in deep disagreement with government policy meet openly and protest loudly. Opposition political parties, although not able to mobilize wide popular support, are nevertheless active and vocal. The opposition trade-union movement is small but vigorous. The Catholic Church, some of whose members are supportive of the Sandinista revolution and some of whom are in opposition, continues as a major cultural and political force. . . . And certainly in the streets, markets, churches, bars, and buses of the country one hears plenty of openly voiced complaints and criticisms—hardly what one would expect in a "totalitarian" society.[18]

The Sandinista government was charged with violating the human rights of the Miskito Indians, a group of about 70,000 living in small communities in northeastern Nicaragua. In 1981–82, Sandinistas committed abuses ranging from racism to arbitrary arrest, physical mistreatment of prisoners, murder, and the alleged disappearance of some seventy Miskitos, at least one of whom turned up later. Americas Watch and other organizations concluded that these isolated actions did not reflect official policy, but criticized the government for not immediately investigating the charges made against it.

The Nicaraguan government acknowledged, and worked to rectify, violations perpetrated in the early years of the revolution. It began paying monthly stipends to 99 families of Miskitos who had disappeared or were killed in 1981 or 1982. In December 1983, the government released all Miskito prisoners who had been detained on security-related charges. From then on, few indigenous people were arrested or held in custody. Americas Watch reported that in January 1986, "fewer than ten" Miskitos were in jail.[19] By the same date, a few hundred Miskito former combatants had returned to civilian life in Nicaragua, under the 1983 amnesty. In 1985, Americas Watch noted that Sandinista treatment of the Miskitos had improved "dramatically" since 1982[20] and that "for the past two years, the most serious abuses of Miskitos' rights have been committed by the *contra* groups."[21]

One of the main efforts to redress past wrongs came in May 1985, when the Nicaraguan government announced that 8,500 Miskitos who had been moved in 1982 from the Río Coco to settlements further south, could return to their communities of origin. By January 1986 some 14,800 Miskito and Sumu Indians, who had been living in Nicaragua and Honduras, returned to the Río Coco. However, in response to widespread, unsubstantiated rumors that the Sandinistas were planning to invade the villages and force people to camps inland, 12,000 Miskitos followed *contra* leaders across the Río Coco into Honduras in April 1986.[22]

The Sandinistas demonstrated their concern for indigenous rights by seeking to grant the Atlantic region relative autonomy. Beginning in June 1985, a special governmental commission and representatives of each ethnic group on the Atlantic coast worked to draft an autonomy statute to be incorporated into the new Constitution. Analysts said that if the draft under consideration at this writing were passed, Nicaragua's legislation on indigenous rights would be exemplary in Latin America.[23]

Political Rights

Under Somoza, only two political parties, the Liberals and the Conservatives, were legal, and nominally "competed" in prearranged elections. True opposition parties were brutally repressed. The majority of citizens who voted did so out of tradition, or coercion.

To foster participatory democracy, the new government immediately tackled illiteracy and promoted a variety of grass-roots organizations. In the months preceding the November 1984 elections, emergency restrictions on the freedoms of assembly, expression, and movement were eased. A massive civic education program helped citizens understand the electoral process. International observer teams found the elections to be free and democratic.[24] As a result of a system of proportional representation that deliberately favored minority parties, dissident parties of the right and left won a third of the seats in the newly formed National Assembly. With the exception of three parties that had abstained from the electoral race, the opposition played an active role in preparing the first draft of the new Constitution.[25]

Subsistence Rights

The Somoza government grossly abused the Nicaraguan people's economic and social rights. From 60 to 70 percent of the population lived in extreme poverty.[26] By July 1979, 1 percent of landowners had usurped nearly half the land, leaving 60 percent of small farmers without enough land to survive.[27]

In addition to this legacy, the insurrection against Somoza left 50,000 dead,[28] 100,000 wounded, and 200,000 families homeless, out of a total population of 2.7 million.[29] The National Guard bombed many manufacturing and agricultural processing plants and destroyed key crops. Somoza left the country bankrupt and saddled with a $1.6 billion foreign debt.[30]

Despite the obstacles it faced, the Sandinista government did more in its first four years to improve the social welfare of the Nicaraguan people than had been done in forty-three years of dictatorship. The revolution's efforts to promote subsistence rights won international acclaim from bodies such as the World Health Organization.

Increased production and government subsidies of basic grains led to a 30 percent increment in per capita consumption of corn, beans, and rice by 1982.[31] Because Nicaragua is primarily an agricultural country, agrarian reform was one of the key programs to redistribute wealth. As of February 1986, 68 percent of all peasant families had received individual or collective land titles.[32] New and longtime landowners benefited from technical assistance, agricultural inputs, and credit.

The first years of revolution also brought low-income housing projects, subsidized public transport, and the extension of basic services like potable water and electricity to the country's most remote areas. New health programs, particularly in the area of preventive medicine, were highly successful. As a result of a nationwide vaccination campaign, polio was reduced from 101 cases in 1979 to none in 1982.[33] The infant mortality rate was reduced from 121 per 1,000 in 1978 to 90 per 1,000 in 1983.[34] Health care centers were built throughout the country, giving more than 70 percent of the population regular medical attention, as opposed to 28 percent under Somoza.[35]

As the war of attrition waged by the *contras* intensified, however, the government had to cut back record-high public spending on health, education, and social welfare. By 1985 half the national budget was destined for defense.

According to the UN Economic Commission for Latin America (ECLA), from 1980 to 1984 the material damage and production losses due to the war totaled $380 million, equaling Nicaragua's export earnings for 1984.[36] Official Nicaraguan figures tallied the war's total cost at $2.8 billion by late 1986.[37] Tens of thousands of farms were abandoned as families fled the fighting. By June 1986 the war had claimed 16,416 lives. Another 12,600 civilians and soldiers had been either wounded, kidnapped, or captured by the *contras*.[38]

The war curbed efforts to improve living standards and to reform land tenancy. Average per capita consumption of basics like food and clothing was 20 percent lower in 1984 than in 1982.[39] Thousands of acres of staple and export crops either were burnt by the *contras* or could not be harvested because of threats against migrant workers. The resulting loss in export earnings meant the country had less ability to import products essential to its economic and social development. The *contras* murdered dozens of Ministry of Agriculture specialists and attacked many cooperatives and state farms. By the end of 1985, ninety-eight medical workers had been killed,[40] and fifty health centers had been forced to close.[41] This left a quarter of the population living in the war zones without regular medical attention[42] and greatly hindered the preventive health campaigns the Sandinistas had implemented.

Economic Rights

Under Somoza's Labor Code, workers could join only plant-based unions, which were repressed when they got too militant. At Somoza's defeat, there were 133 unions with a membership of just over 27,000. By December 1983 this number had grown to 1,103 unions with over 233,000 members.[43] Five of the eleven trade union federations that existed were affiliated with opposition political parties of the right and left.

With the economic difficulties it faced upon taking power, the government could not grant substantial increases in real wages, so it tried to shore up social wages. Workers' rights were promoted through training and job creation programs and the enforcement of minimum wage laws and occupational health and safety standards. The number of people covered by social security quintupled from 1979 to 1985, to include more than 90 percent of urban workers and their dependents.[44]

The state of emergency first implemented in 1982 suspended the right to strike, and wage increases did not keep up with inflation.[45] Thousands of men were called up to fight, and thousands more farmers and agricultural workers were killed or kidnapped by the *contras*. This loss of labor power led to decreased production and productivity. Another direct result of the war was the cancellation of all new social security and welfare programs. From 1985 onward, available resources were channeled to assist the estimated 250,000 people who had to relocate away from the fighting.[46]

Social, Cultural Rights

In the category of social and cultural rights, the revolution brought important changes to Nicaragua. Education became the right of every citizen, rather than the privilege it had been under Somoza. By 1985 more than 1,450 new primary and high schools had been built, 95 percent of them in the countryside.[47] The number of teachers, and school enrollment at all levels, more than doubled, to the point where nearly half the Nicaraguan population was studying.[48] Private schools, the majority Roman Catholic, received substantial financial support from the government.

The revolution made health and education inviolable national priorities. However, the economic constraints resulting from the war and U.S. sanctions against Nicaragua forced the government to freeze the 1985 education budget. Some 240 schools in war zones were closed or destroyed, leaving 35,000 primary and adult education students unattended.[49] By late 1985 the *contras* had killed 170 rural teachers and kidnapped another 133.[50] Given the *contras'* hatred of any public employee, it could be assumed that they had also killed many of the missing teachers.

CURRENT HUMAN RIGHTS CONTEXT

Economic Factors

Economic, military, and ideological factors must be considered in an analysis of human rights in Nicaragua. One of the Nicaraguan government's main economic limitations was underdevelopment, in that it lacked material and trained human resources with which to promote national development and improve the country's standard of living. On top of this existing poverty, the Somoza regime's policies exacerbated economic disparity and social injustice. The country's economy was devastated by the insurrection and burdened by a disproportionate foreign debt, as mentioned earlier.

Despite this black economic legacy, the new government reactivated the country relatively quickly. Although the Nicaraguan economy fared well by regional standards from 1980 to 1983,[51] the crisis affecting Central America eventually engulfed Nicaragua as well. The region's problems were caused in part by the deterioration of its terms of trade, spiraling foreign debt payments, capital flight, and the growing military tension. The crisis was accompanied by widespread unemployment and inflation. Unlike other governments in the region, however, Nicaraguan authorities tried to mitigate the effect on the poor, by changing import regulations to favor basic goods, subsidizing many commodities and transportation, and providing social services free. As the situation worsened, though, and Nicaragua was subjected to other external constraints, it became harder to defend citizens' economic and subsistence rights.[52]

To add to these obstacles, the U.S. government began in 1981 to apply economic sanctions. These measures were particularly damaging because Nicaragua's economy had traditionally been very dependent on the United States. Bilateral aid was cut off, and trade was continually reduced until the May 1985 imposition of a total economic blockade against Nicaragua. The Reagan administration also applied pressure on international financial institutions to block all loans to Nicaragua, and on private U.S. banks and corporations not to extend credit to, or invest in, Nicaragua. From 1981 to 1984, Nicaragua lost $423 million in bilateral and multilateral loans.[53] In attempting to justify U.S. sanctions, however, the National Security Council wrote in May 1985: "Depressed economic conditions in Nicaragua were, of course, due to disastrous economic policies adopted by the Sandinistas, and not to any actions by the U.S."[54]

The U.S. government allocated millions of dollars annually to finance a war of attrition against Nicaragua.[55] Nicaragua's economy was hindered by *contra* attacks on infrastructure, including the tele-communications system, ports, and oil pipelines. The country's productive capacity was impaired by the destruction of vehicles, co-ops, crops, etc. This economic warfare violated several international laws governing commerce, navigation, and economic rights between states.[56]

Military Factors

The war created exceptional circumstances in Nicaragua. When the life of a nation is threatened, the International Covenant on Civil and Political Rights allows the state to limit most of the rights defined in the treaty "to the extent strictly required by the exigencies of the situation" (Article 4). Many human rights groups considered that the war warranted extraordinary measures and that Nicaragua's emergency legislation complied with international guidelines.

Emergency restrictions, however, were sometimes applied in an arbitrary and abusive way. The fact that Nicaragua was under attack could not serve to justify human rights violations or to dismiss the revolution's inability to deal with several fundamental problems. Nor should the war have been used for pathos. Rather than being pitied, Nicaraguans were to be admired for what they achieved under difficult circumstances. The war helped to unite citizens in the face of adversity and to deepen the sense of nationalism that had been evolving gradually since 1979.

Ideological Factors

The Nicaraguan government had a definite political will to promote human rights in the broadest sense. It was relatively open to admitting its human rights violations and frequently took steps to prosecute offenders and rectify erroneous policies.

One of the revolution's objectives was to effect deep changes in economic, political, and social relations. It had a commitment to guarantee the rights of the country's poor majority, rather than those of a privileged minority. To achieve this, political power had to be transferred to those who had previously been oppressed.

At the same time, however, the government reaffirmed its alliance with the middle class and bourgeoisie, which played a vital role in the country's "mixed economy." Sectors of the bourgeoisie that had expected to take control when Somoza fell realized instead that their political clout was diminishing as the revolution advanced. Large-scale private owners and members of the Catholic hierarchy, among others, portrayed their relative loss of social and political power as a "violation of human rights."[57]

Nicaragua's model would appear to have had inherent contradictions between giving priority to the basic needs of the majority and promoting a mixed economy dominated by a minority of private producers. It was difficult to pursue a policy of "national unity," whereby the expectations and aspirations of all social classes would be fulfilled. Inevitably, the collective well-being conflicted at times with minority interests, and extremely limited resources had to be rationed.[58] It would be simplistic, however, to conclude that the poor majority automatically prevailed. The government struggled to maintain a delicate balance of power. In reference to the Sandinista agrarian reform, analyst Joseph Collins wrote:

> It does not assume that the individual's self interest must, on principle, be quashed in order to serve the community. The urgent question for Sandinista leaders is not how to stifle individual self-interest but how to build economic structures in which people do not have to choose between themselves and community needs, in which people can serve both simultaneously.[59]

Putting Human Rights in Perspective

U.S. President Reagan characterized Nicaragua as a "totalitarian dungeon" where a "communist reign of terror prevails."[60] The "Sandinista dictatorship"

> has done what communist dictatorships do: created a repressive state security and secret police organization assisted by Soviet, East German and Cuban advisers—harassed and in many cases expunged the political opposition and rendered the democratic freedoms of speech, press and assembly, punishable by officially sanctioned harassment, and imprisonment or death.[61]

The Nicaraguan government's human rights record must be put in perspective. Human rights, religious, labor, and other organizations repeatedly dismissed the Reagan administration's allegations against the Sandinistas as grossly exaggerated and misleading. Many of the most serious charges made by Reagan and top U.S. officials were proven to be totally false. Amnesty International, Americas Watch, Pax Christi International, and the IACHR concluded that the human rights situation improved dramatically after Somoza was overthrown[62] and that the majority of violations that occurred were not instigated, or condoned, by the government.

The Nicaraguan revolution raised questions about the rights of a nation, or people, confronting another, in this case far more powerful, nation. Every people should have the right to choose their leaders and define their own destiny. The United States violated the Nicaraguan people's fundamental right of self-determination and national sovereignty by striving to oust their recognized government.[63]

After twenty-six months of proceedings, the World Court ruled in June 1986 that the United States had breached international law by supporting the *contra* war. The World Court called on the U.S. government to immediately halt all anti-Sandinista military activities and to pay reparations to Nicaragua, as did the UN General Assembly a few months later. The Reagan administration refused to recognize the Court's jurisdiction in the case. In its war against Nicaragua, the United States transgressed numerous international treaties and domestic U.S. laws, although it continued to demand that Nicaragua adhere strictly to international law.[64]

This "double standard" was also apparent in the way the U.S. government viewed human rights in different Central American countries. Several North American organizations pointed out that Nicaragua was harshly criticized for isolated human rights violations, while little was said about "massive and systematic" abuses in El Salvador and Guatemala.[65] Unlike authorities in the rest of Central America, the Nicaraguan government respected its citizens' "integrity of person." There were no death squads in Nicaragua. In El Salvador and Guatemala, thousands of priests, nuns, lay leaders, and others were killed by government-sanctioned paramilitary groups. The Christian lay workers who died in Nicaragua were killed by the *contras*. The Nicaraguan government was striving to redress its worst human rights performance, in relation to the Miskito Indians. Human rights activists considered that the treatment of indigenous peoples in Nicaragua bore "no comparison whatever with the genocidal policies of Guatemala."[66]

To be "universal," human rights standards must not be applied unevenly or arbitrarily. The same criteria must be used in each case. A striking example of "seeing no evil" when it was politically convenient was the U.S. government's backing of the *contras*. American legal, human rights, and religious groups documented hundreds of human rights violations perpetrated by the *contras*. Members of the Nicaraguan Democratic Force (FDN), operating in the northwest of the country, brutally tortured and killed unarmed civilians, including children and young women who were raped and mutilated. Particular cruelty was shown toward community leaders who had helped implement health, education, and agricultural programs, although many ambushes and murders were indiscriminate. Hundreds of civilians were kidnapped as a form of forced recruitment by the FDN, which also had the practice of summarily executing prisoners.[67]

Through its support of the *contras*, the U.S. government contributed directly to the suffering of innocent Nicaraguans and violated their right to life, health, education, etc. The Reagan administration could not justify prolonging the war if it were truly concerned about human rights. Americas Watch wrote:

Far from being the "moral center" of U.S. foreign policy toward Nicaragua, the human rights issue has been utilized in the service of a foreign policy that seeks to advance other interests.

Allegations of human rights abuse have become a major focus of the Administration's campaign to overthrow the Nicaraguan government. Such a concerted campaign to use human rights in justifying military action is without precedent in U.S.–Latin American relations, and its effect is an unprecedented debasement of the human rights cause.[68]

Many human rights activists and politicians found that U.S. policy had actually been counterproductive. "The harsh rhetoric of the Reagan Administration and its continued support for the 'contras' . . . has had disastrous consequences for human rights in Nicaragua," concluded the Lawyers' Committee for International Human Rights.[69] This and other groups advocated working critically with Nicaragua's existing authorities to ensure that human rights were respected and conditions improved. Since 1979 the Nicaraguan government has been very open to receiving international human rights delegations. Americas Watch, the IACHR, and the Lawyers' Committee for International Human Rights praised the government's efforts to implement their recommendations.

The final element needed to put Nicaragua's human rights situation in perspective is the process of empowerment and popular participation that accelerated from 1979 on.

EMPOWERMENT, POPULAR PARTICIPATION, AND HUMAN RIGHTS

Analysts often confine their discussion of human rights in Nicaragua to the parameters of the ongoing debate over alleged abuses, thus overlooking a unique dimension of Nicaragua's human rights practices. Efforts to promote basic rights in Nicaragua transcended conventional civil and political rights, or economic, social, and cultural rights, in and of themselves, to encompass a process of empowering people to take increasing control of their lives.

A country's progress in human rights is directly related to its level of political participation. Nations in which the majority of the population is excluded from any degree of power are more apt to transgress rights than those wherein people take an active part in decision making and can fight for their rights. Democratization seldom occurs in a trickle-down fashion, in which the nation's leaders voluntarily cede basic rights.

The form that participatory democracy assumes in each country is determined by the particularities of each people's historical struggle. Nicaraguans had little tradition of organized, popular participation. Fearing repression, they tended to resign themselves to impotence. Beginning in the early 1960s, however, the FSLN worked to consolidate the widespread discontent that existed, and people slowly came to realize that together they wielded enough power to overthrow the hated dictatorship.

But, as Nicaraguans were fond of saying, defeating Somoza was easier than rebuilding the country. One of the foundations of "national reconstruction" was the revolution's commitment to grass-roots participation. The new government relied initially on the organizations that had arisen during the insurrection, including the women's association, the youth federation, Christian base communities, neighborhood committees, and the farmworkers' union. People were organized by sectors to defend common interests.

This popular participation was essential for the promotion of economic, social, cultural, and political rights. Despite Nicaragua's extreme shortage of material resources, it was able to make significant advances in areas such as health and education because hundreds of thousands of citizens volunteered their labor.

The examples cited below reflect the nascent participation of sectors that supported the revolution. They are not indicative of the whole Nicaraguan population, since tens of thousands of people were represented through nonrevolutionary business, professional, or producers' associations, political parties, labor unions, and church groups. Other Nicaraguans did not belong to any organization.

The following types of participation all afford some degree of political and ideological power, and form part of the process to foster participatory democracy. Education is one of the best examples of the empowerment of Nicaraguans. Over the space of five months in 1980, 85,000 young volunteers worked to reduce the illiteracy rate from the over 50 percent level inherited from Somoza to 13 percent. Following the "Literacy Crusade," some 160,000 adults attended daily classes in 19,000 "popular education collectives" in factories, neighborhoods, and rural communities throughout the country.[70] In many cases, grass-roots organizations were able to build upon the basics provided by the adult education program and offer courses to develop higher technical skills.

Nicaragua's literacy process focused on teaching students to examine their reality critically, seeking the causes of, and solutions to, their problems. Repressive regimes do not tend to promote literacy, because it is a powerful consciousness-raising tool. Literacy is a prerequisite for people to be able to fully exercise all their rights. The Nicaraguan government assigned top priority to literacy, precisely because it sought to prepare the way for ever greater popular participation.[71]

Neighborhood associations, known as Sandinista Defense Committees, or CDSs, were designed to be the broadest form of participation. By 1984 more than half a million Nicaraguans from diverse social sectors took part in CDS activities.[72] One of the CDSs' main tasks was to distribute basic products at subsidized prices. The CDSs worked to ensure their neighborhoods had adequate housing, electricity, potable water, garbage disposal, etc. Volunteers recruited and trained by the CDSs were responsible for the success of health campaigns, adult education classes, and local crime prevention.

Specifically in the area of community health, 80,000 members of the CDSs and other grass-roots organizations vaccinated children against polio and measles; cleaned up neighborhoods to reduce outbreaks of malaria, dengue fever, and other diseases; and briefed residents on basic hygiene. The volunteers achieved impressive results, as illustrated by the statistics noted above, including a 25 percent reduction in infant mortality in five years.

As well as allowing citizens to take an ever greater part in matters affecting them, the CDSs were supposed to convey people's concerns and grievances to the state. As we shall see in the next section, however, this objective was not always fully met.

The Nicaraguan people played a vital role in national defense. In the case of all-out war, hundreds of thousands of citizens[73] trained as militia units would have been largely responsible for the defense of their neighborhoods and work-places. The members of many agricultural cooperatives located in war zones worked with their rifles over their shoulders, to defend themselves against *contra* attacks. This was also the case with several of the more than 20,000 volunteers who went out from the cities each year to pick coffee.

The fact that militia members received military training and arms reflected the government's confidence that the people would not turn against it. Opinion polls taken up until September 1986 revealed that citizens' strong criticism of the country's economic policy did not necessarily undermine their political support of the government, or the FSLN.[74] Despite serious grievances, most Nicaraguans would have fought to defend what they considered to be concrete achievements of the revolution.[75]

Through neighborhood and workplace committees and schools, Nicaraguans also received extensive training in civil defense. To be prepared for natural disaster or war, they learned how to fight fires, clear away ruins, guarantee food and medical supplies, administer first aid, and construct air-raid shelters.

There was growing citizen participation in the country's formal political process. Nearly half the seats in the Council of State, the co-legislative body formed in 1980, were held by direct representatives of the grass-roots organizations.[76] The 1984 national elections were possible because 40,000 volunteers handled everything from voter registration to ballot counting. The electoral process was an unprecedented lesson for Nicaraguans in civic duty and participation.

This experience was deepened in 1985–1986, when twenty-four grass-roots organizations took part in drafting the new Constitution. The consultation was then broadened to encompass 100,000 citizens, who evaluated and criticized the draft in a series of public forums throughout the country. Concurrent with the national debate, thousands of Atlantic coast residents were consulted about an autonomy statute to be incorporated into the Constitution. Despite the reticence of some citizens, especially the coastal peoples, to get involved in this process, the "constitutional literacy campaign"[77] granted Nicaraguans an unprecedented role in determining the nation's political system.

The revolution also democratized cultural life. The Somoza regime promoted only a narrow range of cultural activities catering to a minority of the population, while repressing grass-roots expression. American values and life-styles were emulated. From 1979 on, Nicaraguans were striving to rediscover and promote traditional, indigenous values. Popular cultural participation was fomented through nationwide workshops and through initiatives such as the peasant theatre groups that were formed in many rural communities.[78]

Grass-roots organizations channeled the popular creativity released by the revolution. Instead of allowing themselves to be overcome by the country's material difficulties and the war, the Nicaraguan people responded with ingenuity and determination. When the United States stopped exports to Nicaragua, factory workers designed and fabricated many necessary replacement parts. Peasants revived traditional techniques for homemade soap when the commercial variety was no longer available, and substituted herbal remedies for scarce imported medicines.

ANALYSIS OF POPULAR PARTICIPATION

The Nicaraguan government did not espouse the view of human rights purported by many Third World planners—that civil rights and political participation could be fostered only after a certain level of development had been attained. Nor did the Nicaraguan experience fit the thesis that revolutions sacrifice liberty for equality.[79] Is liberty not served by teaching an illiterate farmer to read and giving him land? He is thus freed from ignorance and from dependence on a rapacious landowner. Liberty and equality were sought through the incipient process of empowerment.

Participatory democracy in Nicaragua was not centered on political parties or ballots cast once every few years during elections. Grass-roots participation was not confined to conventional democratic parameters, because it had the potential to radically change power relations.

This is not to say that the popular classes alone would determine Nicaragua's future. Participation had to be as eclectic and complex as was the revolutionary process itself. The government's commitment to a "mixed economy" and "national unity" sometimes meant giving priority to the economic and political participation of the middle classes and bourgeoisie.

Agricultural policy was an example of an uneasy balance between bourgeois and peasant participation. The first six years of agrarian reform tended to favor large landowners, by granting them extensive production facilities and guarantees. The government obliged peasants to abandon lands occupied since the fall of Somoza, and work either on state farms or cooperatives. Peasant associations became increasingly militant, however, until they forced the government in mid–1985 to reverse its policy and distribute more land to individual, small farmers.[80]

In times of crisis, the government limited popular participation and demands, in order to protect broader class interests. Members of grass-roots organizations had to make real sacrifices. Unions were asked to accept prolonged wage freezes, while prices soared. The women's organization, AMNLAE, assigned top priority to support work for the war effort, thus relegating its struggle for women's rights.[81] Given their focus on the country's military and economic defense, and their serious material limitations, grass-roots organizations were often unable to adequately address the specific concerns of the sectors they represented. This, in turn, undermined their credibility.

Popular participation was somewhat restricted by the lack of a clear division of authority and functions between the grass-roots organizations and the FSLN party. Many popular associations were headed by FSLN militants who would sometimes pass along decisions made by the party, without first having consulted the rank and file. Communications thus became top-down, rather than two-way. This made it more difficult for grass-roots organizations to develop internal democracy and promote a broad, pluralistic range of interests.

The CDSs were criticized for merely conveying FSLN directives, rather than fulfilling their original objective of serving as the basic units of participatory democracy. In many instances, the CDS leadership was not really in touch with its constituents. In late 1985, efforts were undertaken to convert the CDSs into true agents of community development, which would respond to local needs rather than party instructions. As part of the reorientation, CDS coordinators would no longer be chosen for their declared political views but for their proven community involvement. This would help eliminate another of the problems the CDSs themselves had strongly condemned—that of opportunistic CDS coordinators abusing power and acting arbitrarily.[82]

According to analyst Luis Hector Serra, there was another flaw of the grass-roots organizations:

In that context of ever-greater aggressions in 1983 and 1984, the dividing line between opposition and counterrevolution, between those sectors that dissented with some aspects of the revolutionary process and those identified with the intervention forces, became increasingly difficult to perceive. This polarization led some leaders of the OPs [popular organizations] to develop Manichean attitudes that identified any criticism or dissidence as "counterrevolutionary." The belligerent climate, characterized by the constant death of young people and innocent women and children, led certain OPs to use force to stop the publicity activities of the opposition, such as those carried out by church leaders. These attitudes were justified in the eyes of the conscientious revolutionary sectors but were incomprehensible to, or condemned by, confused and politically backward sectors. Accordingly, they had a negative effect on the image of the grass-roots organizations, on the incorporation of these same people into the OPs, and on frank and open criticism within the grass-roots organizations.[83]

Incidents between Sandinista supporters and opposition groups were frequently picked up, and magnified, by the U.S. press. Shirley Christian, of the *Miami Herald*, said the CDSs were one of the driving forces behind the *turbas*, or "mobs of Sandinista militants" who were "periodically turned loose" to harass or attack opposition leaders.[84] Critics contended that instead of promoting popular participation, grass-roots organizations, and in particular the CDSs, served as instruments of Sandinista control and repression. Nicaraguan "exile" Jorge Alaniz wrote, "The CDSs represent one of the pillars of FSLN power over the people."[85]

Serra pointed out, however, that many of the charges made against the popular organizations responded to domestic political interests:

The grass-roots organizations were the target of an adverse propaganda campaign by the small bourgeois parties and certain religious sectors. These groups, which had shared power with the Somoza family, perceived the growing process of organization and participation of the OPs as an inadmissible insubordination on the part of the "inferior classes." Ecclesiastical figures such as some Catholic bishops prohibited the clergy and their parishioners from participating in the grass-roots organizations, to which they referred in their sermons as "communist mobs."[86]

The grass-roots organizations had trouble maintaining a constant level of citizen involvement. They were best able to mobilize people during "critical" periods, such as the weeks following the U.S. invasion of Grenada in October 1983. In many regions of the country, the war served as a catalyst to foment political, social, economic, and defense activities. Statistics showed that participation in adult education, health campaigns, and so forth was highest in areas directly affected by the war.[87] The mobilization of men to the war-front also propelled women into nontraditional jobs and roles, granting them a new confidence with which to demand their rights.

Popular participation in Nicaragua was limited to some degree by the country's lack of democratic tradition. The Somoza dictatorship fomented libertinage and individualism. The revolution began to try to make citizens aware of their rights and duties in society, and to get them to think and act in an organized, collective fashion.

It would take a long time for Nicaragua to overcome its weak democratic heritage. Political involvement and consciousness were still very uneven after seven years of revolution. On the Atlantic coast particularly, deep-rooted apathy and distrust of the political process inhibited people from taking part fully in consultations about regional autonomy. At the same time, however, Nicaraguans had come a long way since 1979. The active participation of 100,000 people in nationwide consultations about the new Constitution demonstrated how much political consciousness had progressed. Even the FSLN was not expecting such an outstanding citizen response.

One of the most difficult tasks ahead in the consolidation of "participatory democracy'' would be to determine its very nature and parameters. Nicaragua was in the midst of a dynamic process of experimenting, changing, and rejecting, in its search for a unique formula of participation that would incorporate the class interests present in its model of revolution.

Part of this debate over how to define participation in Nicaragua revolved around the drafting of the new Constitution. Some opposition members of the National Assembly favored the concept of "representative democracy," which usually refers to liberal political systems, while many Sandinista representatives advocated the term "popular democracy," usually associated with socialism. The draft Constitution was, in a sense, a compromise. It included the innovative term "participatory democracy," as well as "representative democracy." The differences manifested were more than merely semantic. They reflected conflicting views of the nature of democracy, and participation, in Nicaragua.

The Nicaraguan revolution was attempting to go beyond populist formulas, in which paternalistic leaders would cede a small quota of power to create the appearance of popular control. From 1979 on, citizens gained a significant dose of human dignity, which constituted an important first step in ensuring that they would fight for their rights in the broadest sense. Even the poorest, humblest Nicaraguans were beginning to exercise their right, and their duty, to speak out.

The Sandinista government realized that participation would be effective only if citizens developed a critical consciousness. Rather than suppressing criticism, as Somoza had done, the Sandinistas sought to channel it in a systematic and constructive way. One of the most frequent and vigorous demands by peasants and workers was to play a greater role in economic decision making.

Government leaders addressed citizens' questions and concerns in a variety of ways, including weekly televised forums known as "Face the People," and daily radio programs. The call-in radio show "Contact 6–20," which was not subject to government censorship, had the largest audience of any mass medium in the country. In its first two years (1984–1986) "Contact 6–20" received 33,000 calls, most of which were from disgruntled citizens complaining about problems such as inadequate health care or housing in a particular neighborhood, or denouncing some negligent public employee.[88] The radio thus provided one of the most effective channels through which Nicaraguans could criticize their government.

The popular input encouraged by the Sandinistas often got sidetracked by bureaucracy or inexperience. Also, it was not always easy for government and party officials to stimulate and assimilate criticism and self-criticism. As we saw earlier, one example of policy changes as a direct result of grass-roots pressure was the reorientation of the agrarian reform program.

Nicaraguans have rectified many initial errors and planted the seeds of participatory democracy, although they still face many obstacles. Citizens will have to overcome the apathy and sense of political impotence dating from the Somoza days, and gain the skills and experience necessary to take increasing control of their lives. Only after a few decades will it be possible to evaluate the concrete results of efforts to create mechanisms of participation, to empower people and get them maximally involved in decision making.

CONCLUSION

Nicaragua was neither a "second Cuba" nor "another communist country." The Nicaraguan revolution arose from a unique historical struggle, and it must be evaluated for its own faults and merits. The Nicaraguan government had to meet international human rights standards and be criticized for the violations it committed. At the same time, however, credit has to be given where due for improvements in human rights. After the fall of the repressive Somoza regime, Nicaragua made considerable progress in civil, political, economic, and social rights. Many of the shortcomings that persisted were caused, or exacerbated, by the war of attrition confronting Nicaragua.

Putting the situation in perspective, international organizations and human rights activists tended to conclude that the most serious human rights violations in Nicaragua were isolated incidents, not government policy. Nicaraguan authorities had the political will to respect human rights and worked to rectify abuses. Going beyond conventional human rights, the revolution was quite successful in its efforts to increase grass-roots participation and power, the real basis for the long-term respect for, and promotion of, human rights.

NOTES

1. For further information about the repressive practices of the U.S.-trained National Guard, see George Black, *Triumph of the People: The Sandinista Revolution in Nicaragua* (London: Zed Press, 1981); and Richard Millet, *Guardians of the Dynasty* (New York: Orbis, 1977).

2. Inter-American Commission on Human Rights, *Report on the Situation of Human Rights in Nicaragua* (OEA/ser. L/V/II.45/doc. 16 rev. 1, 1978).

3. According to Americas Watch, in addition to the two human rights groups per se, other organizations in Nicaragua also monitored human rights practices. The Moravian Church's Association of Jurists followed closely the situation of Miskito Indians, while the International Committee of the Red Cross maintained a program of visiting prisons, tracing missing persons, and assisting displaced people. Americas Watch, *Human Rights in Nicaragua. Reagan, Rhetoric and Reality* (New York: Americas Watch Committee, 1985), 47.

4. Americas Watch, *Human Rights in Nicaragua* (New York: Americas Watch Committee, 1984), 42.

5. The CPDH had a political interest in exaggerating its charges against the government. Americas Watch indicated that it had been unable to verify all of the CPDH figures for torture, disappearances, deaths, etc. The Reagan administration often further inflated CPDH figures in offering "proof" of Sandinista repression. The CNPPDH sought to defend the revolution and was therefore sometimes not rigorous enough in its criticism. However, the CNPPDH was a useful ombudsman in particular cases, especially in relation to Miskito detainees.

6. Americas Watch, *Human Rights in Nicaragua 1985–1986* (New York: Americas Watch Committee, 1986), 42.

7. Amnesty International discussed these techniques in its report *Nicaragua. The Human Rights Record* (London: Amnesty International, 1986), 19–23.

8. Another 3,200 of the 7,000 were common criminal offenders. Americas Watch, *Human Rights* (1986), 41.

9. Americas Watch, *Reagan, Rhetoric*, 3.

10. Amnesty International, *Human Rights Record*, 1.

11. Americas Watch, *Human Rights* (1986), 41.

12. "Contras Seeking Amnesty in Nicaragua; Returnees Describe Life with the Contras," *Update* 5, no. 14 (April 10, 1986): 1.

13. The evolution of the Church-state and traditional Church–liberation theology conflicts is covered in detail in several issues of *Update* and *Envío*.

An ardent critic of the Sandinistas, Humberto Belli, argued that Nicaragua's "Marxist-Leninist" government was determined to eradicate religion. See *Nicaragua: Christians Under Fire* (Garden City, Mich.: Puebla Institute, 1984).

14. Americas Watch, *Human Rights* (1986), 47.

15. John Spicer Nichols, "The Media" in *Nicaragua: The First Five Years*, ed. Thomas W. Walker (New York: Praeger, 1985), 192. Nichols also said that the "editorial function" of *La Prensa* was clearly to "overthrow the existing political order." He contrasted that with U.S. media, wherein criticism "is seen as a means of maintaining the existing political system in functional balance. . . . Most people would be hard pressed to think of a daily newspaper in the United States that openly advocates a change in the country's form of government" (p. 187).

16. Amnesty International, *Human Rights Record*, 12.

17. Shirley Christian, *Nicaragua. Revolution in the Family* (New York: Random House, 1985), 265.

18. Richard Fagen, "The Nicaraguan Crisis," in *The Nicaraguan Reader*, ed. Peter Rosset and John Vandermeer (New York: Grove Press, 1983), 31.

19. Americas Watch, *Human Rights* (1986), 66.

20. Americas Watch, *Reagan, Rhetoric*, 53.

21. Ibid., 55.

22. For an analysis of the April 1986 exodus of 12,000 Miskitos, see Americas Watch, *With the Miskitos in Honduras* (New York: Americas Watch Committee, 1986); "Miskitos on the Río Coco. Whose Political Football Are They?" *Envío*, no. 59 (May 1986).

23. "Autonomy for the Atlantic Coast," *Envío*, no. 45 (March 1985), 3b. Several issues of *Envío* and *Update* contain useful information about autonomy and other events on the Atlantic Coast.

Bernard Nietschmann was one of the most outspoken critics of Sandinista policy toward the Miskitos. He contended that the Nicaraguan government was guilty of "widespread, systematic and arbitrary abuses." *Statement Before the Organization of American States Inter-American Commission on Human Rights, on the Situation of the Indians in Nicaragua* (Washington, D.C.: Indian Law Resource Center, 1983).

Other reports concluded that the Nicaraguan government gradually improved its treatment of the Miskitos, after a poor start. In addition to *Reagan, Rhetoric*, see Americas Watch, *Human Rights* (1986), and *The Miskitos in Nicaragua 1981–4* (New York: Americas Watch Committee, 1984); Center for Research and Documentation of the Atlantic

Coast (CIDCA), *Trabil Nani. Historical Background and Current Situation on the Atlantic Coast of Nicaragua* (New York: Riverside Church Disarmament Project, 1984).

24. For observer team reports on the elections, see Latin American Studies Association (LASA), *The Electoral Process in Nicaragua: Domestic and International Influences* (Austin: LASA, 1984); National Lawyers' Guild (NLG), *Nicaragua: An Eye-Witness Report on the Electoral Process* (Chicago: NLG, 1984); Inter-Church Committee on Human Rights in Latin America (ICCHRLA), *Nicaragua 1984: Democracy, Elections and War* (Toronto: ICCHRLA, 1984).

Robert Leiken and Shirley Christian, among others, disagreed with many of the observer team findings. The two Americans contended that opposition parties did not have any chance to campaign, given FSLN control of state security, the army and militias, the media, and grass-roots organizations. Leiken contended that many Nicaraguans had voted out of fear and that the FSLN inflated and manipulated election results. Leiken also wrote that opposition parties exercised no power in the new National Assembly, which just served to "mechanically endorse Sandinista policy." See Robert Leiken, "The Nicaraguan Tangle," *New York Review of Books*, December 5, 1985.

25. For information on the constitutional process, consult *Envío* and *Update* from September 1985 on.

26. Statistic provided in private communication by Thomas W. Walker, author and editor of several books on Nicaragua (see suggested readings).

27. Joseph Collins, *What Difference Could a Revolution Make? Food and Farming in the New Nicaragua* (San Francisco: Food First, 1982), 2.

28. David Halperin and Richard Garfield, "Developments in Health Care in Nicaragua," in *Nicaraguan Reader*, ed. Rosset and Vandermeer, 340.

29. EPICA, "The Somoza Legacy: Economic Bankruptcy," in *Nicaraguan Reader*, ed. Rosset and Vandermeer, 299.

30. For a good summary of the costs of the insurrection and of the Somoza legacy, see Michael E. Conroy, "Economic Legacy and Policies," in *First Five Years*, ed. Walker.

31. Collins, *What Difference*, 4.

32. "Agrarian Reform Undergoes Change in Nicaragua," *Update* 5, no. 4 (February 7, 1986): 2. After seven years of revolution, President Daniel Ortega reported that Nicaragua had given peasants nearly five million acres of land. In their history, four of the other Central American governments together had distributed less than three and a half million acres. See "De Esteli a Nueva York," *Envío*, no. 62 (August 1986), 12a.

33. Thomas John Bossert, "Health Policy," in *First Five Years*, ed. Walker, 356.

34. Thomas W. Walker, *Nicaragua. The Land of Sandino* (Boulder, Col.: Westview Press, 1986), 90.

35. Halperin and Garfield, "Developments," 341.

36. ECLA data cited in "The Economic Costs of the Contra War," *Update* 4, no. 31 (October 10, 1985): 1–2.

37. Nicaraguan President Daniel Ortega gave this total for the "direct and indirect" costs of the war in a speech on November 8, 1986. Cited in the Mexican newspaper *Excelsior*, November 9, 1986, 9-A.

38. Casualty figures were given in a speech by President Ortega on June 27, 1986. According to Ortega, more than 12,100 of the 16,416 killed in the war were *contras*. Cited in "Vencer Guerra con la Guerra," *Envío*, no. 61 (June 1986), 14a.

As with any war situation, it was difficult to verify figures on casualties and material losses. The government's casualty figures were very different from those released by the *contras*. In its 1985 World Court case against the United States, the Nicaraguan government provided the names of 3,886 civilians and soldiers who had been killed in the first three years of war, and another 4,731 who had been wounded.

39. "The Economic Costs of the Contra War: Nicaragua's Case Before the World Court," *Envío*, no. 51 (September 1985), 10b.

40. "Literacy Programs Continue in Nicaragua Despite Contra Attacks," *Update* 5, no. 2 (January 24, 1986): 2.

41. "Economic Costs," *Update*, 7.

42. Ibid.

43. "Nicaragua's Trade Unions," *Update* 3, no. 30 (September 6, 1984): 1.

44. Instituto Nicaraguense de Seguridad Social y Bienestar (INSSBI), *Informe sobre Cinco Años de Revolución* (Managua, Nicaragua: INSSBI, 1984), 9. Some critics would not agree that the Nicaraguan government sought to promote worker and union rights. U.S. "labor activist" Sam Leiken wrote: "When centralizing efforts failed, the Sandinistas used state power to penalize unions unwilling to affiliate with them, to organize disruptive factions, and ultimately to jail opposition union leaders. I was told of death threats, beatings, police raids on union headquarters, military conscription of union dissidents, and blacklisting." See "Labor Under Siege," *New Republic*, October 8, 1984, 18.

45. *Envío*, no. 51 (September 1985), reported that workers' real wages fell by up to 50 percent between 1982 and 1984 (p. 10b), and that in the first few months of 1985, the price of basic goods went up 300 to 400 percent, while wages only increased 150 percent (p. 14c).

46. "Agrarian Reform," *Update*, 3.

47. "Education in the Midst of Poverty," *Envío*, no. 48 (June 1985), 2c.

48. Ibid.

49. "Economic Costs," *Update*, 7.

50. "Education in Poverty," *Envío* no. 48 (June 1985), 4c.

51. See Conroy, "Economic Legacy," for a good evaluation of the government's economic policies and performance.

52. For further information on the external pressures on Nicaragua's economy, see Sylvia Maxfield and Richard Stahler-Sholk, "External Constraints," in *First Five Years*, ed. Walker.

53. "Economic Costs," *Update*, 4.

54. National Security Council, "Nicaragua Sanctions: Sandinista Responsibility for Their Economic Failures" (Memorandum, May 18, 1985). Cited in "A Survival Economy," *Envío* no. 52 (October 1985), 1b.

55. From 1979 to 1984 the U.S. government provided the *contras* with more than $400 million in "covert aid," according to U.S. press reports published in August 1986. Cited in "De Esteli a Nueva York," *Envío*, 2a. In mid–1986, the U.S. Congress approved an additional $100 million in *contra* aid, and the U.S. media reported that the CIA would channel another $400 million to the anti-Sandinistas. The $500 million total equaled about half of Nicaragua's annual budget. Cited in "Vencer Guerra con la Guerra," *Envío*, 10a. The *contras* also received millions of dollars annually from private sources in the United States and Latin America, and at the close of 1986 the U.S. government admitted as well that American officials were involved in channeling the proceeds of arms sales to Iran to the *contras*.

56. The economic measures taken by the United States against Nicaragua are detailed in Maxfield and Stahler-Sholk, "External Constraints," in Walker, *First Five Years*, 258–59. See also Marlene Dixon, *Reagan's Central America Policy: A New Somoza for Nicaragua* (San Francisco: Institute for the Study of Militarism and Economic Crisis, 1984), 29–31; and numerous issues of *Update*.

57. In examining the mixed economy, Conroy, "Economic Legacy" in Walker, *First Five Years*, 236, wrote that

those who had benefitted under the laissez faire policies of the Somoza era could [not] have been expected to accept the "changes in the rules of the game" that were embodied in the design of the new Nicaraguan society. The changes embodied in the new society were, in fact, "totalitarian" for them. They had lost significant elements of their opportunity to produce and trade without government intervention. They had also lost much of the political influence that they enjoyed when power was closely associated with personal wealth.

58. The "collective well-being" would include programs to promote "social justice," i.e., to improve the lot of the formerly exploited majority, such as social services and welfare, agrarian reform, etc. An example of "minority interests" would be efforts by the middle and upper classes to retain their traditional level of consumption of luxury goods despite the country's drastic shortage of foreign exchange.

59. Collins, *What Difference*, 142.

60. President Reagan, "Central America: Defending Our Vital Interests" (Presidential Address before a joint session of Congress on April 27, 1983).

61. President Reagan, "Text of Remarks by the President at the Nicaraguan Refugee Fund Dinner" (White House press release, April 15, 1985).

62. Collins, *What Difference*, 147.

63. Many of those interviewed by the author in Nicaragua stressed that the revolution was the first period in Nicaragua's history during which its people, united as a nation, defended their right to self-determination and national sovereignty. Under Somoza, Nicaraguans did not take pride in their national history or identity. The war against the *contras* accelerated the formation of a sense of national identity or consciousness. The revolution was helping to forge a nation. This view was expressed by, among others, Fr. Fernando Cardenal, Minister of Education, interview with the author, Managua, Nicaragua, June 1985, and María López Vigil, researcher, Instituto Histórico Centroamericano, Managua, Nicaragua, June 1985, interview with the author.

64. Dixon, *A New Somoza*, 57–61, provides a thorough list of international laws broken by the Reagan administration's policy toward Nicaragua.

65. ICCHRLA, *Democracy, Elections*, 14.

66. Ibid.

67. Several reports document gross human rights violations by the *contras*. These include Americas Watch, *Human Rights* (1986); Reed Brody, *Attacks by the Nicaraguan 'Contras' on the Civilian Population of Nicaragua* (Boston: South End Press, 1985); many issues of *Update* and *Envío*; and *Witness for Peace Newsletter* (515 Broadway, Santa Cruz, CA 95060). See also the *Report of Donald T. Fox and Michael J. Glennon to the International Human Rights Law Group and the Washington Office on Latin America concerning Abuses against Civilians by Counterrevolutionaries Operating in Nicaragua* (Washington: Washington Office on Latin America, 1985).

In late 1985 the newly formed umbrella *contra* organization, the United Nicaraguan Opposition (UNO), set up a human rights commission to investigate violations by *contras* and improve their image in Nicaragua and the United States. At this writing, the commission had proved relatively ineffective in curbing *contra* atrocities. See Americas Watch, *Human Rights* (1986), 86–125; Aryeh Neier, "Contra Justice," *New York Review of Books*, May 29, 1986, 50–51; "Contra Atrocities August 1985-February 1986," *Update* 5, no. 5 (February 21, 1986); "Contra Atrocities Continue," *Update* 4, no. 29 (September 25, 1985).

68. Americas Watch, *Reagan, Rhetoric*, 2. For a summary of how the Reagan administration manipulated the human rights issue, consult "The Politics of Human Rights Reporting on Nicaragua," *Envío*, no. 60 (June 1986).

69. Lawyers Committee for International Human Rights, *Nicaragua: Revolutionary Justice. A Report on Human Rights and the Judicial System* (New York: Lawyers Committee, 1985), 152.

70. Luis Hector Serra, "The Grass-Roots Organizations," in *First Five Years*, ed. Walker, 71.

71. For accounts of the literacy campaign, see Valerie Miller, *Between Struggle and Hope: The Nicaraguan Literacy Crusade* (Boulder, Col.: Westview Press, 1985), and Sheryl Hirshon, *And Also Teach Them to Read* (Westport, Conn.: Lawrence Hill, 1983). Deborah Barndt, "Popular Education," in *First Five Years*, ed. Walker, offers a good overview of popular education.

72. Serra, "Grass-Roots," 66.

73. Serra, ibid., 75, said that "by the end of 1983, there were approximately 300,000 members" of the militia. Shirley Christian, writing in 1985, estimated there were "60,000 in the active militia, plus tens of thousands of other people who had been given some degree of military training." Christian, *Revolution Family*, 351.

74. "Crisis Económica: Lenta Transición A Un Modelo de Sobrevivencia Popular," *Envío*, no. 63 (September 1986), 11b.

75. Some U.S. journalists would disagree, pointing to allegedly high rates of draft evasion and desertion as signs that young people were not willing to die for the revolution. Robert Leiken went so far as to charge that unpopular Sandinista policies drove people to take up arms against them. See "The Battle for Nicaragua," *New York Review of Books*, March 13, 1986.

76. The National Assembly, elected in November 1984, was based on a system of proportional representation. Some leftist critics within Nicaragua and abroad claimed that electing representatives from political parties, rather than grass-roots organizations, would undermine the more direct popular input that had been achieved in the Council of State, formed in 1980. They considered the parliament voted in by the 1984 elections to be a step backward for popular power.

77. Term used by Fr. Alvaro Arguello, director of International Relations for the National Assembly, cited in "Nicaragua's Constitution," *Update* 5, no. 5 (January 31, 1986), 4.

78. Culture's role in the revolution is examined in Kent Johnson, "Nicaraguan Culture. Unleashing Creativity," *NACLA* 19, no. 5 (September-October 1985); and Chris Brookes, *Now We Know the Difference: The People of Nicaragua* (Toronto: NC Press, 1984).

Some critics said the Sandinista government imposed its line on the arts in Nicaragua. See Chris Hedges, "Revolution Art—Sandinistas want culture to be a tool of the state," *Dallas Morning News*, May 6, 1985.

79. Mario Vargas Llosa, a well-known Peruvian novelist and proponent of the thesis that liberty and equality are potentially incompatible in a revolutionary context, wrote

Tragically, liberty and equality are harsh antagonists. At the heels of a revolution, there is a temptation to establish social justice by sacrificing individual freedom; conversely, a desire to safeguard liberty can lead to further exploitation and unspeakable inequality. Real progress depends on achieving a tense equilibrium between the two ideals. No socialist revolution has yet achieved that balance. In Nicaragua," *New York Times Magazine*, April 28, 1985, sec. 6.

80. For additional information, see "The Nicaraguan Peasantry Gives New Direction to Agrarian Reform," *Envío*, no. 51 (September 1985); "Agrarian Reform," *Update*; "Reactions to Agrarian Reform Modification in Nicaragua," *Update* 5, no. 20 (May 21, 1986).

81. Women's rights are discussed in Jane Deighton, Rossana Horsley, Sarah Stewart, and Cathy Cain, *Sweet Ramparts. Women in Revolutionary Nicaragua* (London: War on Want, 1983); Maxine Molyneux, "Women," in *First Five Years*, ed. Walker; and Catherine Gander, "Nicaraguan Women at War," *Canadian Dimension* 19, no. 6 (January-February 1986), 20, no. 1 (March 1986), and 20, no. 3 (May 1986).

82. The FSLN and CDS leadership considered the arbitrary conduct of some CDS coordinators a problem serious enough to warrant a major evaluation beginning in October 1982. As a result, a number of CDS coordinators were removed from their positions. The strong criticism made of the CDSs by FSLN leader Bayardo Arce can be found on pp. 61–63 of *Nicaragua: The Sandinista People's Revolution* (New York: Pathfinder Press, 1985).

83. Serra, "Grass-Roots," 82. Serra's chapter provides a good summary of the "contradictions and limitations" of grass-roots participation.

84. Christian, *Revolution Family*, 294.

85. Jorge Alaniz, *Nicaragua. Una Revolución Reaccionaria* (Panama: Kosmos, 1985), 60.

86. Serra, "Grass-Roots," 82.

87. While this was generally true, the war did not necessarily have a uniform impact on the process of conscientization. There were some areas, in the midst of the fighting, where people were terrified to get involved in anything, for fear it would cost them their lives. In other isolated places, the *contras* received some support from peasant farmers, for any of several reasons.

88. Information on "Contact 6–20" is from "La Prensa: Post-Mortem a un Suicidio," *Envío*, no. 62 (August 1986), 14c.

SUGGESTED READINGS

Americas Watch. *Human Rights in Nicaragua: Reagan, Rhetoric and Reality*. New York: Americas Watch, 1985.

———. *Human Rights in Nicaragua 1985–1986*. New York: Americas Watch, 1986.

Black, George. *Triumph of the People: The Sandinista Revolution in Nicaragua*. London: Zed Press, 1981.

Booth, John A. *The End and the Beginning: The Nicaraguan Revolution*. 2d ed. Boulder, Col.: Westview Press, 1985.

Christian, Shirley. *Nicaragua: Revolution in the Family*. New York: Random House, 1985.

Collins, Joseph. *Nicaragua: What Difference Could a Revolution Make? Food and Farming in the New Nicaragua*. 2d ed., rev. San Francisco: Institute for Food and Development Policy, 1985.

Rosset, Peter and John Vandermeer, eds. *The Nicaraguan Reader. Documents of a Revolution Under Fire*. New York: Grove Press, 1983.

Walker, Thomas W. *Nicaragua: The Land of Sandino*. 2d ed., rev. Boulder, Col.: Westview Press, 1986.

————, ed. *Nicaragua: The First Five Years*. New York: Praeger, 1985.

————, ed. *Reagan vs. the Sandinistas. The Undeclared War on Nicaragua*. Boulder, Col.: Westview Press, 1987.

Periodicals

Envío, published monthly by the Instituto Histórico Centroamericano, Managua, Nicaragua. Distributed in the United States by publishers of *Update*.

Update, published weekly by the Central American Historical Institute, Georgetown University, Washington, D.C.

13

THE PHILIPPINES

Richard Pierre Claude

Martial law came to the Republic of the Philippines in 1972 and in one percussive blow shattered the traditions of Asia's first democracy. In the ensuing and prolonged constitutional crisis the Philippines increasingly appeared to the world as a country failing in its quest for constitutional legitimacy, national self-respect, and economic growth. Beneath the stories and struggles of the leading actors in this drama—the Marcos and Romualdez families, the courts, the military, the electoral system, the church, the American masters of the past—lies the suffering of those most deeply injured by political misadventure, common citizens, largely unobserved by the outside world, yet victims of daily human rights violations on a vast scale.

HISTORICAL BACKGROUND

Like other Third World countries with the burdens of a colonial past, the twentieth-century Philippines is engaged in a struggle for national self-respect and political identity. Handicapped by the birth defect of an American-imposed constitution, Filipino leaders have tried time and again to reorder constitutional arrangements by the supposed standards of nationalistic priorities. But time and again, constitutional surgery has been fouled by corruption, trickery, and fraud. The result has been that a prime requisite for political development—regime legitimacy—has rarely been achieved in the Philippines.

The United States occupied the Philippines after the decimation of the Spanish fleet in 1898 in Manila Bay by Admiral Dewey. Spain ceded the islands to the USA under the terms of the Treaty of Paris (1898) which ended the Spanish-American War. Insurrection against the United States, led by the revolutionary leader Emilio Aguinaldo, broke out in 1899.[1] This state of hostilities, an important reference point in nationalist ideology, is referred to by Filipinos as the Philippine-American War (1899–1902).

From the outset, American administration of the islands was said to be temporary and to have as its goal the development of institutions which would foster free and democratic rule. In 1935, under the terms of the Tydings-McDuffie Act, the Philippines became a self-governing Commonwealth.[2] According to American enabling legislation, the constitution had to be "republican"; and it could go into effect only if the president of the United States certified that it conformed to the conditions of the statute. Convention delegates, largely products of the American system of education, took care to avoid any radical departure from the constitutional system of the United States. The United States and the Philippines pressed plans forward toward independence after World War II, which was achieved on July 4, 1946, when the political framework became that of the American-style Constitution, including a strong Bill of Rights.

In this framework, an open and competitive political system developed dominated by two parties, the Nationalists and the Liberals. They flourished in a civil libertarian environment, but they competed largely on the basis of experience and abilities of candidates rather than upon formal party platforms. Marcos, a Nationalist, first won election to the presidency in 1965, followed by a second four-year term.

The second Marcos term was marred by widespread unrest and demonstrations. On the evening of August 21, 1971, a rally gathered in the Plaza Miranda, the "Hyde Park of the Philippines." Featured speakers were to be eight official senatorial candidates of the opposition Liberal party. All the major Liberal leaders except Senator Benigno S. Aquino, Jr., were on the platform when two fragmentation grenades exploded among them. Opposition leaders were seriously injured, and dozens of spectators were either maimed or killed. Thereupon, the president announced the suspension of the writ of habeas corpus, and the National Bureau of Investigation rounded up "suspects."

Comparison of the Plaza Miranda bombing to the Weimar firing of the Bundestag—a trumped-up emergency to justify a power grab—has been based upon the fact that no suspect has ever been convicted for the crimes resulting in death and injury at Plaza Miranda.[3] Moreover, Senator Aquino, the only major Liberal standing for interim election who was not among the Plaza Miranda victims, was ordered arrested for aiding insurrection by personal command of his bitter enemy, Ferdinand Marcos, and condemned to death, a fate which he met unofficially in 1983.[4]

According to President Marcos in his book *Notes on a New Society*, by 1972 "anarchy had taken over from the local police as well as the constabulary who were prevented from undertaking any initiative by both political interference as well as corruption."[5] Against the background of this presidential perception, martial law was proclaimed on September 21, 1972. Solicitor General Mendoza, speaking with enthusiasm about this development, said, "The proclamation of martial law restored order in society. Among other things it enabled the new Constitutional Convention, which since convening on June 1, 1971, had been deeply mired in political wranglings, to finish its work."[6] Because the old

Constitution forbade presidential service "for more than eight years," Marcos's term was to expire in 1973. With little more than a final year left he declared martial law and called into operation a new Constitution clumsily engineered to allow him to stay in office indefinitely.[7]

The origins of the new Constitution were spoiled by procedural defects and Supreme Court ambiguity in according it legitimacy. Examples of these "birth defects" abound, but a few may serve to illustrate.

The Constitutional Convention of 1971, convened before martial law, was thereafter purged of Marcos critics and allowed to continue. By a series of decrees under martial law, Marcos forced the convention to approve changes permitting him to become prime minister as well as president and to remain in office indefinitely. Delegates were asked to accept the new arrangement or by their negative votes deny themselves and their constituents representation in the new assembly.[8]

For popular ratification of the new Constitution, Marcos called a formal plebiscite on January 15, 1973. The people were to consider its provisions under the terms of a period of free discussion. During that time, opponents of the new charter were to be authorized the use of the media. As interpreted by then-Senator Raul S. Manglapus, "When it became evident that opposition to the new constitution was so strong that no amount of manipulation could possibly bring a 'yes vote,' President Marcos suddenly announced the postponement of the plebiscite 'to February or March,' and stopped the privilege of discussion, charging opponents with making use of free speech to circulate subversive ideas."[9] Indeed, there was no referendum, although in January some hastily marshaled "Barangays"—"Citizens Assemblies"—were convened in scattered areas. Official photographers were present at each meeting to record votes taken by a show of hands on the question: "Do you approve of the New Constitution?" By the end of the month, the adoption of the new Constitution was announced by Presidential Proclamation 1102 entitled "The Ratification of the Filipino People of the Constitution Proposed by the 1971 Constitutional Convention." The document was publicly heralded as a harkening back to the anti-American plan of government advocated by Emilio Aguinaldo in 1900.

In 1973 Josue Javellana and other citizen-voters filed a "class suit," asking the Supreme Court to declare Proclamation 1102 null and void.[10] Four justices held that it was in force by virtue of popular acquiescence; four abstained on the basis that they could not ascertain whether the people had accepted the Constitution; and two voted that the proposed charter was not in force. In the context of such ambiguity, the Court nevertheless concluded, "there is no further judicial obstacle to the New Constitution being considered in force and effect." National heritage was thus traded for the proverbial mess of pottage.

EMERGENCY MEASURES VERSUS CIVIL AND POLITICAL RIGHTS

The suspension of habeas corpus and the imposition of martial law were the first steps on a slippery slope leading to the end of democracy and the death of rule of law as the protector of human rights in the Philippines. In 1977 the International Commission of Jurists (ICJ) noted that the Supreme Court ruling in the *Javellana Case* lent legality to President Marcos's initial proclamations. But the ICJ report concluded that the "present Government is now employing the power granted to it by the Constitution, not primarily to protect the nation, . . . but rather to perpetuate the personal power of the military to control Philippine society."[11] They also noted that the very judicial review which gave some semblance of constitutional legitimacy to the government was itself compromised by making the continued tenure of Supreme Court justices depend on the whim of the president.

During the course of martial law (1972–1981), the Philippines had no free press, no free elections for representatives, no union organizing, and fear and disarray among vestigial opposition political groups.[12] Virtually all partisan opponents of Marcos were jailed at one time or another. Amnesty International estimated that during the first three years of martial law, over 50,000 persons were arrested under emergency regulations, many of whom were tortured and almost all of whom were detained without charge or trial.[13] Presidential decrees curtailed the rights of assembly, association, and expression, and suspended the writ of habeas corpus. All of these actions were justified as the requisites of martial law, transformed by Proclamation 1102, in the words of President Marcos, into "martial law with a smiling face."

The indefinite suspension of the writ of habeas corpus and the consequent lack of outside judicial scrutiny set in motion the rapid decline of all human rights. The absence of this basic legal check (whereby police detention of a person must be promptly justified by law before an independent judge) led to a situation in which police under executive authority and the military had an individual under their absolute authority. Proclamation 1102 thrust Philippine police, constabulary, and military forces into taking on political control and government responsibility.

International human rights groups continued to monitor conditions in the Republic of the Philippines, despite the fact that President Marcos formally lifted the state of martial law on January 17, 1981, upon issuing Proclamation 2045. In so doing, he said that the government had "significantly defused the dangers of subversion, sedition and rebellion." Nevertheless, political corruption and human rights abuses continued unabated. Moreover, Marcos thwarted political opponents in their efforts to reestablish party competition.

The 1983 assassination of President Marcos's strong political rival, Senator Benigno Aquino, insulted Filipino sensibilities and shocked opinion worldwide. The government's Agrava Commission, with one dissent, concluded that the murder at the Manila airport was committed by the military. In a report on his murder and on human rights in the Philippines, the Canada-Asia Working Group presented its views to the 40th Session of the United Nations Commission on Human Rights. It said:

A shot that rang at the tarmac of the Manila International Airport on the afternoon of August 21, 1983, was heard not only throughout the Philippines but also in many parts of the globe. The slaying of [the] prominent Filipino politician . . . made the world look at the escalating violations of human rights in the Philippines. . . . While the Aquino murder has grabbed headlines, similar executions have been unpublicized. . . . [T]here are many nameless Aquinos.[14]

The Canadian report detailed the increasing reliance in the 1980s upon "salvaging," the perverse military term for murdering political undesirables, "saving on the costs of following judicial procedures." The Canadians acknowledged that the military explained these murders as results of "armed encounters" with subversive adherents of the New Peoples Army (NPA) and other guerrilla groups, when in fact the human rights group's report found frequently "the victims were unarmed civilians." According to the Canada-Asia Working Group, many of the killings they investigated were barbarous. For example, "Elizer and Jessie Pasay were beheaded by the para-military 'Lost Command', a group under retired Colonel Carlos Lademora. . . . Seven unidentified persons were butchered in Mindanao. . . . Other cases of beheading and death by torture can be documented."

After lifting martial law, President Marcos retained extensive emergency powers, among them the power to arrest and detain anyone suspected of crimes against national security. Such Presidential Commitment Orders (PCOs) continued the suspension of habeas corpus because national security detainees could be held by military and police agencies indefinitely without reference to civil judicial authorities.[15] A year and a half after the 1981 lifting of martial law, over 1,100 persons had been or were detained under PCOs, according to Amnesty International.[16]

In 1983 a campaign against the use of PCOs enlisted the vocal support of labor and human rights groups, jurists, clergy, and the Catholic Bishops Conference of the Philippines, which denounced the PCOs as "immoral." On August 5, 1983, Marcos announced the abolition of the PCO and its replacement by the Preventive Detention Action (PDA).[17] The late Benigno Aquino quipped that this was the same dog with a different collar. Habeas corpus remained suspended under PDA, except that unlike PCO, a review procedure within a year was to accompany a Preventive Detention Action. Even so, the president could countermand the recommendation of such a review.

The PDA was abused systematically. That was the conclusion presented to the UN Commission on Human Rights in 1984 in a report by a Filipino group, Task Force Detainees–Philippines. It detailed the ever-increasing scope of human rights violations in the island country. Despite the legal shift from PCOs to PDAs, arrests in 1981 numbered 1,377; 1,911 in 1982; 2,088 in 1983; 3,038 in 1984. Also escalating were extrajudicial killings: 321 in 1981; 210 in 1982; 368 in 1983; and in 1984 such "salvaging" cases numbered 445. In 1983 alone, the Task Force Detainees also documented torture cases (644), massacre victims (163), and strafing victims (102).[18]

Task Force Detainees placed responsibility on the Marcos regime for this record of human tragedy and abuses. They claimed that the Philippines Constabulary, the military, and paramilitary groups such as the Integrated Civilian Home Defense Force were the instigators for the great majority of slayings and human rights violations. The Integrated Civilian Home Defense Forces consisted of 75,000 armed but poorly trained recruits, and it was loosely affiliated under Marcos with irregular military-type forces.[19] The massive expansion of the scope and operations of the military forces intermixed military and police functions and greatly increased the government's ability to intervene in the lives of ordinary citizens.[20]

Although Pentagon officials in the United States said that they saw no apparent external threat to the Philippines and that the guerrilla forces of the NPA do not appear to receive foreign arms or assistance, nevertheless, the U.S. has substantially paid for the gigantic Philippines military apparatus. The Reagan administration in 1985 pledged to continue to provide $900 million over five years in exchange for American use of Clark Field and Subic Bay bases in the Philippines. Unfortunately, U.S. military aid can be and was used by the Marcos regime against the Filipino people.[21] For example, the Philippine Constabulary was integrated into the command structure of the armed forces; in practice, there was little distinction between the armed forces and police operatives with respect to internal suppression. Under Marcos, U.S. Congressman Tony Hall said in 1985, "there is no guarantee that . . . [American military aid] will not be sent for use by the Philippine Constabulary in perpetrating human rights violations upon the Filipino people."[22] That year Jaime Cardinal Sin, Archbishop of Manila, put the same point more simply: "The United States should stop sending military aid to the Philippines because it only goes to slaughter Filipinos."[23]

The militarization of Philippine society strengthened executive power at the same time that judicial authority continued to weaken and decay. A study in 1985 of the judiciary by a group of Filipino lawyers, businessmen, and clergy concluded that judges are underpaid, understaffed, and "under attack on grounds of lack of integrity, inefficiency and incompetence."[24] The deterioration of the legal system was obvious at all levels. Its debilitation partly explained continued post–martial law human rights abuses. A weakened court and bar constituted one of the tragic legacies of the twenty-year rule of President Ferdinand Marcos. For example, the Supreme Court in key cases testing PCO and PDA arrests generally rubber-stamped Marcos policies that imprisoned citizens without charges in the various detention centers around the country. In a preventive detention ruling insensible to disgrace, the Court abdicated its authority by saying it could "ill afford to assume the authority to check or reverse or supplant presidential actions."[25]

The judiciary and legal system in the Philippines traditionally had been burdened by funding problems. For example, trials often are slowed by numerous postponements. Lawyers are induced to postponements because they are paid on a "per appearance" basis for courtroom activity. Court-appointed lawyers for the poor are not paid at all, and they often try to put off their cases for as long as possible.

Moreover, under Marcos the use of political influence in trials was sometimes devoid of subtlety. On April 3, 1985, a lawyer affiliated with the Free Legal Assistance Group (FLAG), Romaflo Taojo, was murdered in the course of his work defending persons in cases where human rights were involved. The same month, two other FLAG lawyers, Romeo Astudillo and Alberto Benisa, who live in Abra Province, were arrested under PDA authority. According to a report by the Lawyers Committee for Human Rights, "The judge responsible for the case allegedly told the two lawyers that the fiscal [prosecutor] threatened him if he acquitted the two."[26] Lawyers Committee contacts say that the two—officers of the Human Rights Organization of Northern Luzon—were arrested because they had been successful in defending clients falsely charged with subversion.

Justice was also denied through failure to carry out prompt and impartial inquiries into serious allegations of human rights violations and to punish those implicated when allegations were well attested.[27] In 1985, Defense Under Secretary Jose Crisols said that the backlog and large number of pending and unresolved investigations into civilian complaints against the military was partly owing to "witnesses' fear for their lives if they testified against soldiers."[28]

According to the study of the Philippine courts in the last year of the Marcos regime, the root problem was structural: the lack of checks and balances on the power of the president. "The inevitable consequence is to make everyone, especially the judiciary, subservient to the will of the chief executive," the report explained. It concluded: "Once a judge bends the law to please those in positions of power, soon enough he will bend the law to suit himself or whomever he wishes to please."[29]

In analyzing the origins of such flagrant human rights abuses as torture and the defects in the administration of justice, groups such as Amnesty International and the International Commission of Jurists tend to emphasize proximate causal factors. For example, they agree that the worst mistreatment often grows out of the conditions inherent in the helplessness of incommunicado detention, immediately after arrest and before the detainee is permitted access to legal counsel or family.[30] Filipino lawyers, such as those linked to Task Force Detainees, agree, but they also insist on probing more deeply into causal explanations for what otherwise appears to be senselessly inhumane treatment. For example, Joker Arroyo, a distinguished Filipino human rights lawyer, insists on a larger perspective. He argues: "The historical reality reveals that the variety and ubiquity of torture is inevitable in an unjust social dispensation. It is convenient in the pursuit of conformity and submission and . . . is a symptom of structural violence."[31]

SOCIAL AND ECONOMIC RIGHTS

Moving from civil rights failings to socioeconomic rights, the picture, as suggested by Attorney Arroyo, is that of an "unjust social dispensation" marked by inequities and deprivation. This assessment was the premise for a World Bank evaluation of Filipino conditions in 1980. It stressed the irony that Marcos had rationalized civil liberties derogations as the sacrifice needed to achieve economic gains. But this justification for dictatorship was vacuous, according to the World Bank analysis.

While poverty is generally a politically sensitive subject, it is even more sensitive in the Philippines than in most of our borrowing countries. First, the skewedness of income distribution is worse in the Philippines than elsewhere in the region, and is exceeded only in Latin America. Secondly, whereas military-dominated government in, for example, Thailand or Korea, has been justified on the basis of credible external threats, martial law in the Philippines has been justified considerably on the basis of its benefits for the poor.[32]

For a Western-dominated body such as the World Bank, known for evading the links between economics and politics, such a statement is particularly telling.

According to a study conducted in 1984 by economists at the University of the Philippines, the national income distribution gap between the rich and the poor widened during the years of martial law. For example, the poorest 60 percent of Filipino households, which had received only 25 percent of total national income in 1971, saw their share drop to 22.4 percent in 1979. Simultaneously, the richest 10 percent of the population increased their share of total income from 37.1 percent to 41.7 percent.[33] The situation did not improve after martial law was lifted. To make matters worse, the Filipino economists found that by 1985 their country had become the only non-Communist country in Asia with a negative growth rate.[34] From 1984 to 1985 the gross national product fell between 4 and 5 percent in real terms. Unemployment also worsened. In 1985 over three million people—or 15 percent of a total labor force of 20.6 million—were out of work. When the inflation rate reached 50 percent in 1985, over half of the work force was either unemployed or underemployed. At the same time, the average employed laborer could not expect to earn over $60 per month. Nationwide, nearly four out of five people in the Philippines were said to be living below the poverty line.[35]

Article 25 of the Universal Declaration of Human Rights states that "Everyone has the right to a standard of living adequate for the health and well-being of himself and of his family, including food, clothing, housing and medical care and necessary social services." These are government responsibilities. That 47 percent of the Filipino population is without safe drinking water and 27 percent are anemic are facts attributable to inadequate government policy and programs. That four million slum dwellers and squatters congregate in Metro-Manila and other urban centers is a mark of failed housing policy.[36]

In the context of basic human needs, the Philippines' major positive achievement lies in an educational system which has in recent years provided almost universal elementary education, with a consequent high literacy rate. Adult literacy increased from 72 percent in 1960 to 89 percent in the mid–1980s.[37] But the Philippines is a country where people are both literate and malnourished. Where food needs are concerned, a World Bank report on poverty in the Philippines concluded in 1979: "Measured by caloric consumption, the level of nutrition in the Philippines is well below income predicted levels when compared with most of the Southeast Asian countries."[38] In 1978 about 54 percent of one- to six-year-old children were malnourished. Most poignantly, malnutrition among infants and nursing mothers is reflected in the fact that about sixty infants out of one thousand die before the age of twelve months.[39] Health care, nutrition, and food needs are directly affected by private sector activity, but government policy slighting rural over urban medical needs, politicizing health delivery services, and encouraging the displacement of cash crops in favor of the expansion of multinational agribusiness are clearly public sector policies antithetical to basic needs and economic rights of the Filipino people.

Health care in the Philippines suffers from problems of maldistribution and misordered priorities. The Philippine National Economic and Development Authority reported in 1983 that over half of all fifty-five million Filipinos live in rural areas where preventable diseases such as pneumonia and tuberculosis account for 43 percent of total deaths. Nutritional deficiencies, gastroenteritis and comparable communicable diseases weigh especially heavily upon children, who make up nearly 25 percent of total deaths in the country, according to government statistics.[40] In an analysis of development and human rights, A. Caesar Espiritu of the University of the Philippines lamented in 1978 that the government typically spent three dollars per capita for health compared to eight dollars per capita for the military.[41]

In 1983 a human rights fact-finding mission to the Philippines was organized by the American Association for the Advancement of Science (AAAS) and the American Committee for Human Rights. They documented the finding that human rights abuses impede the development of badly needed primary care services, especially in rural areas. For example, large-scale problems sometimes developed as a consequence of the forced relocation of tens of thousands of farmers and rural dwellers under a program of "strategic hamleting"—officially defended as necessary to protect civilians from armed clashes between the military and insurgents. The AAAS reported, for example, "Infant deaths in the hamleted area of San Vincente rose significantly in the first year following the forced relocation of [20,000] farmers in the region."[42]

The AAAS mission sought to assess the problems health professionals face, especially in rural areas, given the prevailing human rights situation. Under Marcos rules, failure by medical personnel to report gunshot wounds to the military was a serious offense. Being an "informer" was equally intimidating to health workers when it elicited reprisals from the NPA, Muslim separatists, or other armed dissident groups. Clearly in Filipino rural areas, physicians, nurses, and village paramedics connected with private, community-based health care programs were providing services to the civilian population under trying conditions. The AAAS study concluded that such health professionals should receive the full protection of Common Article 3 of the Geneva Convention of August 12, 1949, which maintains that all parties in an armed conflict should allow doctors and health personnel to provide relief to the civilian population without intimidation and on a basis of political neutrality.

In 1985, 119 doctors, nurses, and other health workers from all over the southern Filipino island of Mindanao attended a convention and organized a Health Alliance (HEAL). They passed a resolution calling for the repeal of Presidential Decree 169, which provides that any health worker who treats persons injured under "suspicious circumstances should report to the military authorities."[43] They also criticized governmental lack of support for rural medicine and community-based health programs in favor of the Marcos-sponsored showcase Heart Hospital in Manila, pointing out that the incidence of heart disease is relatively low in the Philippines. In a very broadly framed Declaration of Principles, the HEAL Assembly said misplaced medical and health priorities are rooted in

foreign domination of our economics, political and social structures, resulting in International Monetary Fund and World Bank dictation of the Philippine economy, the unlimited entry of foreign capital and the remittance of profits by industries, 705 of which are foreign-owned; increasing concentration of land ownership and land used by multinational corporations and a few local landlords; sham agrarian reform; anti-democratic laws such as PCO and PDA depriving freedom of speech, dissent and right to life; intensifying militarization with increasing incidence of arbitrary and illegal searches, hamleting, arrests, detentions, "salvaging," and massacres; and exploitation of labor through inhuman working conditions and repressive laws such as . . . (those) denying workers in vital industries their right to strike and to unionize.[44]

Institutional politicization has become widespread when a professional health group adopts a statement reflecting such deep distrust and alienation.

THE ECONOMIC CRISIS

Why should a group such as HEAL spotlight the impact on the domestic economy of international financial institutions as among the problems at the root of the country's inability to meet basic human needs? To the casual Western observer, such a claim might seem abstract or strained at best, or ideologically motivated and disingenuous at worst. But to Filipinos in the 1980s the statement became commonplace. It reflected widely shared views on economic failings.[45]

Historically, the Marcos regime had been a good citizen among countries in the lending program of the International Monetary Fund (IMF). Since 1972 the country had been under one variety or another of IMF "stabilization."[46] For example, a prescribed policy of "export led growth" displaced both small farmers and tribal peoples.[47] This took on the aspects of a human rights issue when such displacement arbitrarily involved land transfers by government fiat to agrobusinesses. Such action took land out of production of food for local consumption in favor of coconut, sugar, and pineapples for export.[48]

Two members of the British Parliamentary Human Rights Group visited the Philippines in 1983 to investigate the conditions in a British government–financed development project: the Guthrie palm oil and rubber plantations in Mindanao. Alf Dubs and Colin Moynihan, both members of Parliament, reported that paramilitary groups (Lost Command)—with the blessing of the military—had been intimidating, harassing, and even murdering people in the countryside. They said that the government's commitment to large-scale projects and its dependence on the inflow of foreign capital meant that agro-industrial projects competed for land with small farmers, reinforcing economic inequalities.[49] Thus the British report illuminates the reason why the view developed and spread among Filipinos that the "cures" of the international financial institutions and even foreign aid programs sometimes rendered their country too dependent on export markets.[50] By 1986 the external debt of the Philippines exceeded $25 billion, with multiple billions owed to such U.S. institutions as Citicorp and Manufacturers Hanover Bank.

In 1985 a U.S. Senate Select Committee on Intelligence issued a "Situation Report" on the Philippines. It avoided criticizing the policies of international financial institutions affecting the Filipino economy. Instead, it strongly emphasized the culpability of the Marcos regime in undermining the economy:

Political and economic power are monopolized at the top by a small oligarchy, while at the bottom the mass of Filipinos live in poverty without real input into the political process. A few favored Marcos cronies have been given control of large agricultural and industrial monopolies that dominate the economy. They retain their favored position by demonstrations of loyalty to the President and financial support for his political machine. Political corruption and human rights abuses, particularly by the Armed Forces, have fueled popular resentment.[51]

The effectiveness of IMF and foreign aid strategies for economic growth in the Philippines as well as the security of creditor-banks had been compromised over the years by the development of a class of "presidential cronies" who amassed colossal personal fortunes.[52] One example among many involved Herminio Disini (whose wife is a Romualdez cousin of Imelda Marcos). Disini enjoyed a massive government financial bailout when his tobacco and mining cartels began to fail in 1981. A college "fraternity brother" of Marcos, Roberto Benedicto, became a multimillionaire based on the sugar monopoly he controlled as chairman of Philsucom, authorized by law "to act as the single buying and selling agency of sugar." On September 4, 1984, the Reagan administration signaled diplomatic distance from Marcos by supporting a "no vote" for a World

Bank loan to the Philippines. The position of the U.S. Treasury Department on the matter was that the granting of an agricultural loan to facilitate purchase of fertilizers in the Philippines should be conditioned on breaking the monopolies in the sugar and coconut sectors.[53]

After the Aquino assassination in 1983, diplomatic loyalty to Marcos waned on the part of the United States. In addition, personal loyalties of Filipino millionaires toward Marcos also ebbed. The *New York Times* reported evidence of this in terms of $2 million per day flight of capital from the country.[54] Moreover, the declining business confidence in the regime was apparent in a statement issued in November 1983 by the presidents of the Philippines, the Filipino-Chinese, American, Australian, European, and Japanese Chambers of Commerce that called for reforms to reinstate investor confidence.[55] They specified the need for the clear designation of a presidential successor, freedom of the press, an independent and honest judiciary, restoration of constitutional rights, and an end to pervasive militarization. They averred that political rights help to support economic growth.

Responding to domestic criticism, President Marcos blamed business people for "economic sabotage," and on November 13, 1984, he ordered criminal charges against thirty-three executives for "smuggling" and "hiding their dollars abroad." Replying to criticisms from abroad, President Marcos explained:

Reforms, they keep telling me about reforms. . . . The error of the human rightists is that they think political (rights) are the only rights we have to take care of. But our historical experience dictates that we also think of economic rights. And when at times this clashes with other human rights . . . well, it is a matter of judgment.[56]

Marcos's revealing view exposes to examination the proposition that economic goals are more effectively secured by sacrificing political rights in favor of material plenty.[57] This is a dubious proposition, but it is widely shared as the self-serving support for dictators, commissars, and authoritarian regimes worldwide. Unfortunately, in the Philippines, choosing between bread and freedom has proved a strategy for securing neither.

One reason why economic gains do not add up to an acceptable alternative to civil and political rights was ably stated by a University of the Philippines School of Economics report issued in 1985. Titled "Towards Recovery and Sustainable Growth," it asserted as fundamental that the exercise of individual rights such as freedom of expression, freedom to organize, the access to information by citizens, etc., are themselves "economically valuable as channels of information by which to determine peoples' evolving preferences and behavior."[58] In other words, the economists recognized that civil and economic rights are intertwined and mutually reinforcing. Justification for trade-offs between the two categories of rights is too often couched in deception whereby the gainers are not the common people but self-serving power holders.

THE ELECTORAL CRISIS

By 1986 President Ferdinand Marcos had managed to maneuver his island country into the dangerous intersection of social, economic, and political crisis. First, the crisis of institutional integrity grew out of the fact that the key social institutions—law, health services, education, labor, and the military—were overly politicized. Institutional crisis is palpable when people perceive a crooked and caviling judiciary and a deprofessionalized military led by sadists and sycophants. Second, the economic crisis was fouled by corruption and cronyism at the highest levels, international dependency, and crushing inequities and poverty at the grass roots. An economic crisis is apparent when people view the government as the main obstacle to financial and material survival. Third, the crisis of political legitimacy involved doubts about the government's command of authority, brought into question by the Aquino assassination, the growth of NPA insurgency, the adverse World Bank vote, cool Reagan diplomacy, and international human rights criticism from all quarters. Since the third crisis pained Marcos more directly than the others, he chose to deal with it first, reckoning that regime legitimacy would be shored up by an election for the presidency and vice presidency. He calculated cynically and wrongly that the crisis of legitimacy could be resolved by a managed exercise in electoral democracy.

On November 4, 1985, during a live interview on American television, Ferdinand Marcos announced his intention to hold a "snap" election "to erase doubts regarding the popularity of my administration." Three weeks later the Philippines National Assembly approved presidential and vice presidential elections for February 7, 1986, and the electoral race thereby commenced. The widow of slain opposition leader Benigno Aquino—Corazon Aquino—and Salvador Laurel, initially appeared to be political rivals. The prospect of Aquino and Laurel running for office separately prompted Cardinal Sin to appeal to them "to think of the greater interest of the country." In early December Aquino and Laurel announced that they had agreed on a joint ticket to oppose Ferdinand Marcos. A reluctant contestant, Aquino premised her candidacy on the ability of her partisans to gather the signatured petition of one million supporters. Aquino and Laurel agreed to stand together as candidates of the United (Nationalist) Democratic Organization (UNIDO).

Serious debate on public issues was not the hallmark of the campaign. In most of his political speeches, Marcos emphasized that Aquino was not sufficiently experienced to deal with economic problems, military insurgency, or international problems. The UNIDO candidate responded by admitting that she had no experience "in cheating, stealing, lying, and assassinating political opponents." Throughout the campaign, Aquino attracted more sizable and enthusiastic crowds than Marcos in every part of the country except in Marcos strongholds in the north. The UNIDO ticket coalesced around a "minimum program" demanding (1) the restructuring of the constitution to ensure "checks and balances" in government; (2) the guarantee of press freedoms; (3) the elimination of corruption; (4) the release of all political prisoners; and (5) the willingness to respect current agreements regarding U.S. bases in the Philippines—due to expire in 1991. Aquino specified that her government would thereafter "keep its options open" regarding American military bases in the Philippines.[59]

In terms of Aquino-Laurel support, significant signals came from both military and church sectors. For example, on January 7, 1986, fifteen military officers of the Reform the Armed Forces of the Philippines Movement announced plans promising to support "honest, clean, free and fair" elections. The officers announced opposition to any effort to "resort to despicable activities such as vote-buying and the unscrupulous use of the Armed Forces of the Philippines, integrated national police personnel and hired goons." They also said soldiers should disobey any "illegal orders" they might receive which were contrary to the electoral code. On January 19, Cardinal Sin issued a pastoral letter complaining of "many signs that show a very sinister plot by some people and groups to frustrate the honest and orderly expression of people's genuine will." He also denounced undue pressure exerted on "helpless government employees to make them work for certain candidates," and he warned people to resist "intimidation and bribes."

Despite NPA and other guerrilla groups involved in boycotting the elections, NPA leaders announced that they would not interfere with the elections, and indeed the NPA was less active during the election campaign. Of the fifty-one people killed in election-related incidents, a majority of those who died were opposition workers whose deaths were linked to the excesses of Marcos partisans.

The National Citizens' Movement for Free Elections (Namfrel), an independent elections monitoring group, reported many irregularities and acts of violence throughout the country on election day. For example, a Namfrel member was murdered while trying to guard ballot boxes. On the morning of February 8, when vote-counting delays developed at the official National Committee on Elections (Comelec), international observer teams and UNIDO spokespersons became convinced that fraud was being carried out. This was attested by a group of computer operators at the Comelec headquarters who dramatically and tearfully walked out of their job sites complaining of discrepancies between voting figures which they were registering favoring Aquino and the aggregate totals recorded favoring Marcos.

Several teams of outside elections observers attended the Philippine electoral contest of 1986. The co-leaders of the most internationally diverse such group were Misael Pastrana, former president of Columbia, and John Hume, a member of the British and European Parliaments from Northern Ireland. They concluded that the election of February 7 was not conducted in a free and fair manner. They set out the belief that the government of Ferdinand Marcos and Comelec "bear responsibility for this failure." Moreover, they concluded that the February 15 National Assembly proclamation naming Ferdinand Marcos and Arturo Tolentino to be winners of the elections was invalid because the Assembly "ignored explicit provisions of the Philippine Electoral Code requiring that tampered ballots be set aside during the final counting process.'' Although the International Observer Delegation detailed numerous pieces of ''smoking gun'' evidence pointing to debased voting rights, they also insisted on the positive significance of the landmark election: ''We observed millions of Filipinos who were committed to making the electoral process work. Principally because of their commitment, the election succeeded in providing a vehicle through which the national will of the Philippines was ultimately expressed.''[60]

On February 21, Defense Minister Juan Ponce Enrile and Deputy Chief of Staff Lt. General Fidel Ramos staged a remarkable rebellion against President Marcos. From their retreat position at Camp Aguinaldo, they announced that they no longer considered Marcos to be a legitimate ruler and that Aquino had been cheated of victory in the February 7 election. The same day General Ramos joined troops loyal to him at Camp Crame, the national police headquarters. Potentially bloody crisis was averted by widespread and massive popular action. In response to a radio summons from Cardinal Sin to protect the rebels, thousands of people—dramatically headed up by nuns and priests urging non-violence—poured onto the streets to form a human shield around the rebel military bases. This imposing direct action protection of the rebels was hailed by Corazon Aquino as ''people power.''

In a state of confusing irony, both Marcos and Aquino were formally sworn in as president in rival ceremonies on February 25. By that evening, however, increasing military defections to the Aquino forces, demonstrations of mass popular support for her, and imminent U.S. recognition of Corazon Aquino as president persuaded Marcos to step down and leave the country.

Within days after her inauguration, President Aquino ordered the release of political prisoners and restored the writ of habeas corpus, giving protection against arrest without charges. On March 25 she abolished the National Assembly—''to cut out the cancer in our political system''—and announced a temporary ''Freedom Constitution,'' retaining the 1973 Bill of Rights.[61] Aquino announced that she would exercise all legislative powers until a new constitution could be written and submitted to popular referendum. This proclamation amounted to a declaration of a revolutionary government, though that title was avoided. According to the proclamation of March 25, the aims of the Aquino regime were described as reorganizing the government, restoring democracy, reviving the economy, recovering ill-gotten Marcos and crony wealth, protecting basic rights, eliminating corruption, and establishing civilian supremacy over the military.

In a meeting with an Australian delegation of the International Democratic Union, President Corazon Aquino spoke of the need for a ''national refresher course'' on the workings of democracy. ''Our people,'' she said, ''have to unlearn what Marcos taught them about politics and government.''[62] She stressed that her government, committed to human rights and due process, would never resort to Marcos-style legal shortcuts for convenience.

In keeping with this commitment, the president issued Presidential Memorandum No. 27 in July 1986, requiring the teaching of human rights at all levels of education. In an adjoining memorandum, she stated that the study of human rights would become "an integrated and indispensable part" of military and police training. The memorandum specified that the continuance in office of all police and military enforcement personnel "shall depend on their successfully completing the courses offered" under the human rights education program.[63]

The Constitutional Commission charged with writing a new plan of government also took human rights and human rights education seriously. Following the president's lead, the forty-eight-member commission adopted for the proposed constitution a section saying, "The State shall enforce the teaching of human rights in all levels of education, as well as in non-formal training to persons and institutions tasked to enforce and guarantee the observance and protection of human rights."

The prospective Bill of Rights also contains strong protective provisions against abuses of personal security. The charter strictly prohibits the practice of "hamleting" or arbitrary arrests by the military in the absence of a lawful order of a court or as provided by law. In the same vein, the use of safe houses or secret detention centers is outlawed. The Bill of Rights provides that "No torture, force, violence, threat, intimidation or any other means which violates the free will shall be used" against any person under criminal investigation. The charter also bans the use of "physical, psychological or degrading punishment against any prisoner or detainee or the use of substantial or inadequate penal facilities under sub-human conditions." It instructs the future National Legislature to provide penal and civil sanctions for human rights offenders, as well as "compensation and rehabilitation of victims of torture or similar practices, and of their families." The new Bill of Rights also abolishes the death penalty, except for "heinous crimes" as provided by law, and converts to life imprisonment those who already face capital punishment (numbering about 650).[64]

One section of the proposed new constitution is devoted to social justice "to enhance the inalienable right to dignity." Several provisions deal with land distribution and labor policy, agrarian and natural resource reform, problems of the urban poor and housing, education, women, indigenous people, and "the people's right to health." Health care is to be promoted through a comprehensive program that "shall make essential goods and social services available to all citizens at affordable cost, with priority for the needs of the disadvantaged, sick, women and children, aged and disabled."

Among the beneficiaries of the proposed constitution are groups that monitor civil rights. In addition to guarantees of freedom of expression and association, the constitution provides the "right to information on matters of public concern," including access to "government research data used as the basis for policy development." In an apparent recognition of the February Revolution, the constitution states:

In the pursuit of the ends of Social Justice, the State shall respect the independence and the role of people's organizations as a principal means of empowering the people to pursue and protect through peaceful means their legitimate and collective interests and aspirations.

The State shall respect the right of the people and their organizations to effective and reasonable participation at all levels of social, political and economic decision-making, and shall ensure adequate consultation mechanisms for such participation.

CONCLUSION

As the Philippines begins anew in the late 1980s to lay a constitutional foundation for human rights and social order, it is appropriate to cite the words of Salvador P. Lopez, member with Eleanor Roosevelt of the Drafting Committee for the Universal Declaration of Human Rights and onetime president of the University of the Philippines:

The central problem of constitutionalism in our contemporary society is whether or not the Constitution remains an efficient instrument for the moderation of conflict within society. There are two aspects of this problem. One is the regulation of freedom in order to prevent anarchy. The other is the limitation of power in order to prevent tyranny.[65]

In the post-Marcos era, the Aquino-Laurel administration has premised its rule on respect for human rights and a return to constitutional government. That is a solid, not a sentimental, basis on which to rest a political system. The role that human rights play in undergirding the legitimacy of a political regime was clearly underestimated by Ferdinand Marcos. He relied on militarily supported coercive measures to effect political stability as if police cannons could substitute for civic conscience. He ignored and belittled the ethically based consensual tenets of human rights. The history and demise of the Marcos regime illustrate the basic wisdom of the Preamble of the Universal Declaration of Human Rights: "... it is essential, if man is not to be compelled to have recourse, as a last resort, to rebellion against tyranny and oppression, that human rights should be protected by the rule of law."

NOTES

1. Salvador P. Lopez, "The Colonial Relationship," in *The United States and the Philippines*, ed. Frank Golay (Englewood Cliffs, N.J.: Prentice-Hall, 1966).

2. United States, *Statutes at Large*, "Philippines Independence Act," 48, 459 (1934).

3. Salvador P. Lopez, "The Philippines under Martial Law," *The Dillingham Lecture Series, East West Center* (Quezon City: University of the Philippines Press, 1974), 4.

4. Fred Poole and Max Vanzi, "An Ultimate Act of Terror, The Death of the Dictator's Rival," *Revolution in the Philippines* (New York: McGraw-Hill, 1984), 1–10.

5. Ferdinand Marcos, *Notes on a New Society* (Manila: Government Printing Office, 1973), 19.

6. Estelito P. Mendoza, Introduction, *Martial Law and the New Society in the Philippines*, 2d ed. (Manila: Supreme Court of the Philippines, 1976), 4–5.

7. Stephen Shalom, *The United States and the Philippines: A Study of Neocolonialism* (Philadelphia: Institute for the Study of Human Issues, 1981), 168–71.

8. Harry P. Gideonese, "The Philippines: Speaking Frankly," *Freedom at Issue* 4 (March-April 1973): 11.

9. Raul S. Manglapus, "Philippine Martial Law: The Truth and the Fiction," *Freedom at Issue* 4 (July-August 1973): 18–23.

10. Philippines, *Javellana v. Executive Secretary*, 50 SCRA 30 (1973).

11. William T. Butler, John P. Humphrey, and G. E. Bisson, *The Decline of Democracy in the Philippines* (Geneva: International Commission of Jurists, 1977), 46. For an earlier Filipino assessment, see Civil Liberties Union of the Philippines, *The State of the Nation after Three Years of Martial Law* (Manila: Philippines Civil Liberties Union, September 21, 1975).

12. "The Philippines Press: What Are the Boundaries of Freedom?" *Business Day*, February 25, 1983, 12.

13. Amnesty International, *Report of the Amnesty International Mission to the Republic of the Philippines, 1975* (London: Amnesty International, 1976).

14. Canada-Asia Working Group, *Submission to the 40th Session of the United Nations Commission on Human Rights: Philippines 1983* (Toronto: Canada-Asia Working Group, 1984), p. 8.

15. Philippines, "Presidential Letter of Instruction No. 1125" (May 9, 1981).

16. Amnesty International, *Report of an Amnesty International Mission to the Republic of the Philippines, 1982* (London: Amnesty International, 1982).

17. Philippines, "Presidential Decree No. 1877" (August 5, 1983).

18. Task Force Detainees–Philippines, *Human Rights Situation and Militarization in the Philippines: Trends and Analysis 1984, Report to the United Nations Commission on Human Rights, 41st Session, 1985* (Manila: Association of Major Religious Superiors, 1985), Tables 1 and 11.

19. Lawyers Committee for Human Rights, *The Philippines: A Country in Crisis* (New York: Lawyers Committee for Human Rights, 1983), 20–23.

20. Jim Zwick, "Militarization in the Philippines: From Consolidation to Crisis," *Philippines Research Bulletin* (Durham, N.C., Philippines Information and Research Center, Fall-Spring 1984–1985), pp. 5–6.

21. Lawyers Committee for Human Rights, *"Salvaging" Democracy, Human Rights in the Philippines* (New York: Lawyers Committee for Human Rights, 1985), 20–41.

22. House of Representatives, Congressman Tony Hall, "Statement in Support of Cutting Military Aid to the Philippines," *Congressional Record*, 98th Cong., 2d sess., 1984, 130, H3587.

23. "Statement of U.S. Church Leaders and the Church Coalition for Human Rights in the Philippines," *PHIDOC, Philippine Information and Documentation* (Washington, D.C.: Church Coalition for Human Rights in the Philippines, 1985), 5.

24. Anthony Spaeth, "Philippines Judiciary Has Been Turned into a Shambles during the Marcos Era," *Wall Street Journal*, July 12, 1985.

25. Philippines, *Garcia-Padilla v. Ponce Enrile*, G.R.No. 61388, 1983.

26. "The Philippines: Lawyers under Attack," *LCHR Bulletin* 5, no. 2 (1985): 4.

27. R. Scott Greathead, *Human Rights Advocacy in the Philippines: A Report on a Mission of Inquiry* (New York: Association of the Bar of the City of New York, 1985). See also Anti-Slavery Society, "The Chico River Basin Development Project," *The*

Philippines, Authoritarian Government, Multinationals and Ancestral Lands, Indigeneous Peoples and Development Series: 1 (London: Anti-Slavery Society, 1983), 102–112.

28. Amnesty International USA, "Testimony Presented before the Subcommittee on Human Rights and International Organization of the Foreign Affairs Committee of the U.S. House of Representatives," 97th Congress, 1st sess., September 22, 1983.

29. Spaeth, "Philippines Judiciary."

30. Lawyers Committee, *The Philippines*, 44.

31. Joker Arroyo, "The History, Causes and Remedies of Torture," *MAG Bulletin* (Manila, Medical Action Group) 1, no. 4 (March 17, 1985): 15.

32. World Bank, "Philippines—Working Level Draft Country Program Paper" (Washington, D.C.: World Bank, August 29, 1980), 17.

33. Reported by Pete Carey, Katherine Ellison, and Lewis M. Simons, "How Top Filipinos Hide Fortunes Overseas," *San Jose Mercury News* June 23, 1985, 20A. The Pulitzer Prize–winning article focused on "capital flight" to the United States from wealthy Filipinos. "It is illegal, and every once in awhile, there'll be fines and confiscations," said the San Francisco lawyer who represented Filipinos in 1985 and who insisted on anonymity. "But if the Philippine government really did anything about this, they'd be indicting all their own officials. They're the biggest offenders."

34. U.S. Senate, Staff Report, "The Philippines: A Situation Report," Senate Select Committee on Intelligence, 99th Cong., 1st sess., November 1, 1985, 14.

35. Ibid.

36. Church Coalition for Human Rights in the Philippines, "Fact Sheet on the Philippines" (Washington, D.C.: Church Coalition for Human Rights in the Philippines, 1984).

37. Ibid.

38. "The Confidential First-Draft Version," *World Bank Philippines Poverty Report* (Washington, D.C.: Congress Task Force and Counterspy Magazine, 1980), 22.

39. Ibid., p. 24; see also Alicia de la Paz, "A Second Look at the Philippine Health Statistics," *Medical Action Group Magazine* 3, no. 1 (January-March 1986): 22–27. More recent World Bank figures are slightly lower. See appendix 2 below.

40. Disease Intelligence Center, *Philippines Health Statistics* (Manila: National Economic and Development Authority, 1983).

41. A. Caesar Espiritu, "Keeping Human Life Human," *Development, Human Rights and Rule of Law*, International Commission of Jurists (Oxford: Pergamon Press, 1981), 176–77.

42. American Association for the Advancement of Science, *Report of a Fact-Finding Mission to the Philippines* (Washington, D.C.: American Association for the Advancement of Science, 1983), 4.

43. Veritas, "Calls for Repeal of PD 169," *MAG Bulletin* 1, no. 4 (March 17, 1985), 12–13.

44. Ibid., 13.

45. Gerald Sussman, David O'Connor, and Charles Lindsey, "Philippines 1984: The Political Economy of a Dying Dictatorship," *Philippines Research Bulletin* (Durham, N.C.: Philippines Information and Research Center, (Summer, 1984); 1–3.

46. Jim Browning, "Inside Story: The Philippines and the IMF," *Asian Wall Street Journal*, August 15, 1979, 1.

47. "Export-Oriented Development," *The Philippines*, Anti-Slavery Society, 137–39.

48. "The Corporate Farming Programme," ibid., 142–44.

298   Richard Pierre Claude

49. Parliamentary Human Rights Group, "The CED and Minanzo: Report of a Visit to the Philippines by Alf Dubs, M.P. and Colin Moynihan, M.P., 21 September–October 10, 1983" (Unpublished).

50. Guy Sacerdoti and Philip Bowring, "Marx, Mao and Marcos," *Far Eastern Economic Review*, November 21, 1985, 52–62.

51. U.S. Senate, Staff Report, "The Philippines," 1.

52. Ninez Cacho-Olivares, "Those Who Have the Most of What is There to Have," *Business Day* (17th Anniversary Special Report on "Crisis of Leadership" February 27, 1984, 17; see also Eduardo Lachica, "Philippines Agrees to Change Cartels, Gets IMF Accord," *Wall Street Journal*, November 18, 1985, 35.

53. "IMF Stops Loans to Philippines," *Washington Post*, October 31, 1985, p. A22.

54. "Bankers Say Marcos Must Act Soon," *New York Times*, October 29, 1983, p. 38.

55. "Marcos Blames Businessmen for Economic Crisis," *Washington Post*, November 11, 1983, p. A20.

56. "Embattled President Comes Out Fighting," *South*, no. 56 (Wellington, New Zealand) June 1985, 20.

57. Robert E. Goodin, "The Development-Rights Trade-Off: Some Unwarranted Economic and Political Assumptions," *Universal Human Rights* 1 (April-June 1979): 31–42.

58. Florian A. Alburo, Dante B. Canlas, Emmanuel S. de Dios, et al., "Towards Recovery and Sustainable Growth" (Quezon City: University of the Philippines, 1985), 4.

59. *New York Times*, January 4, 1986.

60. International Observer Delegation, *"A Path to Democratic Renewal,"* A Report on the February 7 Presidential Election in the Philippines (Washington, D.C.: National Democratic Institute for International Affairs, National Republican Institute for International Affairs, 1986).

61. Philippines, Presidential Proclamation 3, "Declaring a New Policy to Implement the Reforms Mandated by the People, Protecting their Basic Rights, Adopting a Provisional Constitution, and Providing for an Orderly Transition to a Government under a New Constitution" (Manila, March 25, 1986).

62. *Manila Bulletin*, 1 August 1986, 1.

63. Presidential Memorandum No. 20, "Education of Arresting and Investigating Personnel on Human Rights," and Presidential Memorandum No. 27, "Human Rights Education at All Levels" (Manila: Malacenany, 4 July 1986).

64. Interview by the author with Commissioner Edmundo Garcia, 1 August 1986.

65. Salvador P. Lopez, "University of the Philippines President's Keynote Address" (Quezon City: University of the Philippines Law Center, Series on the 1973 Constitution, December 3, 1973).

SUGGESTED READINGS

Averch, Harvey A. *The Matrix of Policy in the Philippines*. Princeton: Princeton University Press, 1971.

George, Thayil J. S. *Revolt in Mindanao: The Rise of Islam in Philippine Politics*. New York: Oxford University Press, 1980.

Claude, Richard P., and Eric Stover. *The February Revolution: Health Professionals in the Philippines and the Protection of Human Rights.* Washington, D.C.: American Academy for the Advancement of Science, 1986.

Hill, Gerald N. *Aquino Assassination: The True Story and Analysis of the Assassination of Philippine Senator Benigno S. Aquino, Jr.* Sonoma, Calif.: Hilltop Publishing Co., 1983.

International Bank for Reconstruction. *The Philippines: Priorities and Prospects for Development.* Washington, D.C.: World Bank, 1976.

Kerkvliet, Benedict J. *The Huk Rebellion: A Study of Peasant Rebellion in the Philippines* Berkeley: University of California Press, 1977.

Kessler, Richard. *The Politics of Rebellion in the Philippines.* New York: Praeger, 1987.

McCoy, Alfred W. *Priests on Trial.* New York: Penguin Books, 1984.

Manglapus, Raul S. *Philippines; The Silenced Democracy.* Maryknoll, N.Y.: Orbis Books, 1976.

May, Glenn Anthony. *Social Engineering in the Philippines: The Aims, Execution, and Support of American Colonial Policy 1900–1913.* Westport, Conn.: Greenwood Press, 1980.

Poole, Frederick K. *Revolution in the Philippines: The United States in a Hall of Cracked Mirrors.* New York: McGraw-Hill, 1984.

Rosenberg, David A. *Marcos and Martial Law in the Philippines.* Ithaca, N.Y.: Cornell University Press, 1979.

Shalom, Stephen. *The United States and the Philippines: A Study of Neocolonialism.* Philadelphia: Institute for the Studies of Human Issues, 1981.

Stanley, Peter W., ed. *Reappraising an Empire: New Perspectives on Philippines and American History.* Cambridge, Mass.: Harvard University Press, 1984.

14

POLAND

Stefania Szlek Miller

Human rights as defined by United Nations declarations and covenants and by the 1975 Helsinki Agreement are in principle accepted by the Polish government, the influential Roman Catholic Church, and mass social movements such as the now-outlawed Solidarity Union. Differences center on the meaning and application of these rights, and the state's violation of them in the name of "socialism" and national security. The objective of this chapter will be to explain briefly the historical, ideological, and religious justifications of human rights in Poland, and to define the major contentious issues concerning civil, political, economic, social, and cultural rights. It will be argued that international declarations and agreements concerning human rights serve important functions in communist systems such as Poland. First, they define common norms that transcend ideological, philosophical, and religious perspectives. Second, they serve as reference points for opposition groups who demand that their government adhere to principles that it champions in international forums.

In developing this thesis, the chapter will examine the following topics: (1) the historical heritage and the events that led to the establishment of the Polish People's Republic as a communist system; (2) post–1945 constitutional guarantees and state policies pertaining to human rights; (3) opposition to the state's interpretation and implementation of rights and the major demands of societal groups, including the now-outlawed Solidarity Trade Union; and (4) the post–1981 period and the government's reaction to international and domestic criticisms of its violation of certain human rights.

HISTORICAL BACKGROUND

A brief chronology of Polish history is necessary in order to define factors that are pertinent to an analysis of the contemporary situation. Poland as a political entity came into existence in A.D. 966, and prior to the eighteenth century occupied a prominent position in Europe. As a result of changes in the European balance of power and domestic weakness, Poland was partitioned in the late eighteenth century by its neighbors, Russia, Prussia, and Austria. From 1795 to 1918 the Polish state virtually ceased to exist, and it was during this period that modern Polish nationalism developed and found expression in the concept of national self-determination.[1]

The goal of state sovereignty was realized in the aftermath of World War I with the establishment of the Second Polish Commonwealth. Its turbulent life was short-lived and was marked by authoritarian rule from 1926 to the 1939 invasion and occupation of the country by Nazi Germany and the Soviet Union. In 1941 Germany invaded the Soviet Union and occupied the whole of Poland until Nazi forces were driven out by Soviet troops. In the post–World War II period, the Polish People's Republic was established as a communist system within the Soviet Union's sphere of interest.

From this brief outline, several factors stand out. First is the determination of the nation to survive following the disappearance of the Polish state during the extended partition period. The goal of national self-determination and state sovereignty was achieved in the brief twenty-year period between the two world wars. As a result of World War II, Poland's sovereignty is limited by its alliance with the Soviet Union. To what extent the Polish government voluntarily agrees to follow policies made in Moscow, or has to acquiesce to Soviet dictates, cannot be definitively answered.[2] The fact remains that the Polish People's Republic is dependent on the Soviet Union, and Poland's post–1945 record on human rights must be assessed within that context.

Another important feature of Poland's historical heritage is the lack of experience in living under democratic institutions based on civil liberties. This has to be qualified to some extent, in that Poles take pride in having one of the oldest libertarian traditions in Europe prior to the partition period. Statutes such as the 1430 Charter *Neminem Captivabimus*, granting habeas corpus to the landed gentry, and the sixteenth- and seventeenth-century Acts of Religious Toleration are significant documents in the history of human rights even if the record of actual implementation was primarily of benefit to the upper strata of society.[3] The concern for rule of law and civil liberties could have provided a basis for Poland's development into a modern liberal democratic society. That possibility, however, was thwarted by the partition of the Polish state in the late eighteenth century and the administration of the three separate sectors by the autocratic regimes of the partitioning powers. The recollection of Poland's contribution to progressive traditions, nevertheless, serves as a symbol and inspiration in the contemporary context.[4] Poland's Western cultural traditions, moreover, contrast to the more autocratic and despotic ones of Poland's eastern neighbor.[5]

Neither the libertarian tradition of the past nor the Poles' achievement of self-determination following World War I, however, was an adequate foundation for social integration and human rights in the Second Commonwealth. Polish nationalism and claims to historical territories were in conflict with the aspirations of minority groups who constituted almost one-third of Poland's interwar population.[6] Polish interests were also in conflict with those of neighboring states and peoples. The attempt to establish a liberal democratic system of rule modeled on the institutions of the French Third Republic also failed. While the country did not degenerate to fascism, it was, nevertheless, under authoritarian rule for most of its short-lived existence.[7]

To be fair, the Second Polish Commonwealth faced enormous problems of forging a community and an economic and political infrastructure out of the three separate sectors that were under the extended jurisdiction of the former partitioning powers. Wartime losses and the unstable international situation, especially the Great Depression and the emergence of fascist regimes, aggravated the situation. Poland in 1921, moreover, was largely an agrarian society with 74 percent of the 27.2 million population earning a living from agriculture.[8] This sector, moreover, remained inefficient and primitive in that the vast majority of peasants lacked capital to modernize their small holdings; prices of industrial goods, moreover, remained high relative to agricultural products. These problems were augmented by the further fragmentation of peasant holdings as a result of population growth (the population of Poland in 1939 was 34,849,000). It is estimated that eight million persons could have left the countryside in 1939 with no adverse effect on agriculture production.[9]

Shortage of capital and the unstable economic and political situation, domestic and international, also impeded industrial growth and social welfare measures. Indicators of the level of underdevelopment are that life expectancy in 1931 for men and women was 48.2 and 51.4 respectively,[10] and despite the introduction of compulsory primary education in 1919, that only 70 percent of the population could read and write.[11] The Second Commonwealth was thus not noted for its enhancement of individual civil and political rights or of minority rights; it also did not provide a base for the realization of social and economic ones. This interwar experience is important in that it provides a point of reference for communist leaders in demonstrating the progressive achievements of post–1945 socialist development (discussed below).

Of recent events, the tragic experience of World War II continues to have a profound bearing on the human rights issue. The genocide of millions of human beings by the Nazis more than any other factor led to the heightened international concern for human rights and to commitments to safeguard them. For Poles, regardless of their ideological or political orientation, Nazi wartime atrocities are etched in the collective memory. The brutal statistics are that during the six years of the war, over six million Polish citizens perished, half of them Jews.[12] There are in addition painful questions concerning the complicity in wartime crimes by people who were themselves victims of Nazi occupation or who ignored the evidence of genocide because of fear or the pursuit of military wartime objectives. These complex questions cannot be addressed here; they apply to all peoples and states.[13] We still know too little about this most inhumane period; and for Poles, bitter memories remain not only of the atrocities committed by the Nazis, but also of the 1939 Soviet invasion and occupation, and the subsequent "liberation" of Poland by Soviet forces.[14]

World War II also set in motion the chain of events that led to the radical transformation of the Polish nation. As a result of Allied agreements, and the military and political situation at the end of the war, Poland's pre–1939 boundaries were altered with territorial gains in the West assumed from defeated Germany, and territorial losses in the East taken by the Soviet Union. War losses, postwar repatriation, and the transfer and expulsion of peoples living in territories that were altered by political agreements also had a dramatic effect on the demographic profile of the reconstituted Polish state.[15] Compared to the interwar period when ethnic Poles, defined in terms of linguistic criteria, constituted only two-thirds of the population and the treatment of minorities, especially Ukrainians, Jews, Byelorussians, and Germans, posed serious problems concerning the realization of civil and minority rights, post–1945 Polish society is almost 99 percent homogeneous in ethnic composition;[16] in terms of religious affiliation some 90 percent of the population describes itself as Roman Catholic.[17]

The religious affiliation of the population helps to explain the influential position of the Roman Catholic Church in contemporary Poland, a factor that is very important in defining the major contentious human rights issues. The role of Christianity and specifically the Roman Catholic Church is an integral feature of Poland's development from its inception in A.D. 966 to the present.[18] The religious conception of man in relation to a transcendental order, moreover, is one of the major justifying theories of human rights. It assumes that rights are given by God and are thus inherent to the human person. This conception is accepted in principle by Catholics who constitute the vast majority of the present population, and it stands in opposition to the Polish government's official dialectical-materialist Marxist interpretation. The Church in addition is the leading conservative body in opposing, on human rights principles, the norms and patterns of behavior of modern industrial society (discussed below).

The task of rebuilding postwar Poland and of transforming society from a largely agrarian to an industrial one was assumed by Polish communist leaders backed by the Soviet Union. The communist model of political, economic, and social development was also patterned on that of the first communist state. One of its main characteristics is the adoption of Marxism-Leninism as an official ideology.[19] It serves as the justifying theory of socialist policies and practices including the area concerned with human rights. It legitimizes the monopoly of power of the Polish United Workers' Party (PUWP) to realize the goals of socialism, which involve the rapid modernization of society based on state-owned industrial enterprises and government control over other aspects of economic and social life.

HUMAN RIGHTS IN THE POLISH PEOPLE'S REPUBLIC

The Polish government supports international declarations and covenants on human rights and has committed itself to guaranteeing the rights of citizens in conformity with international standards. The government takes particular pride in having provided the material conditions for the realization of economic and social rights. This includes state programs that provide citizens with full employment, universal education, and medical and other social welfare services. The government further claims that these rights as well as civil and political ones are extended without discrimination based on "sex, birth, education, profession, nationality, race, religion and social origin, and position."[20]

The government's interpretation of the meaning of human rights, however, is based on the official ideology of the state, that is, Marxism-Leninism. From that perspective, it is assumed that the concept of "inherent human rights" is a meaningless principle so long as exploiting classes defined in relation to the means of production exist, and so long as the material base for the fulfillment of human needs is not adequately developed.[21] Poland thus supports the position of other communist states in denouncing Western liberal guarantees of civil and political rights as abstract principles without genuine meaning, by virtue of the inequalities and injustices associated with capitalism. The priority given to economic and social rights is further reflected in the communist states' support of the "Group of 77's" demands for economic development as a necessary precondition for the realization of human rights.[22]

A brief analysis of the Polish Constitution illustrates this interpretation and reveals the problems associated with it. The Polish Constitution does not premise citizen's rights on "the inherent dignity" and "the equal and inalienable rights" of the human person, as enunciated in international documents on human rights. The preamble defines the historical development of Poland in its struggle to realize the "great ideals of socialism." That the realization of citizens' rights is dependent on progress in this aim is explicitly stated in the first article of the chapter outlining the Fundamental Rights and Duties of Citizens: "The Polish People's Republic in consolidating and multiplying the gains of the working people, strengthens and extends the rights and freedoms of citizens." The latter, moreover, is linked to citizens' fulfillment of "duties" to the state and to socialist development.[23]

This conception of human rights thus seriously qualifies, if not undermines, the "inalienable" nature of rights as defined in international documents. It makes human rights dependent on the state's interpretation and enforcement of rights and duties of citizens as defined by PUWP, whose monopoly of power in the state is also enshrined in the Constitution[24] and is asserted in practice based on the Soviet model. It is a conception of human rights that views their full realization only in the ultimate communist society, as envisaged by Karl Marx. It is assumed that at this stage the necessary material and social conditions will be present to lead to the "withering away" of the state and the full emancipation of man from exploitation and from material deprivation. Up to that point, paradoxically, the role of the state is perceived by contemporary communist ideologues to become stronger in promoting the interest of citizens and in defending socialism from international and domestic enemies.[25]

This interpretation has served to justify Warsaw Bloc intervention in the domestic affairs of a socialist state, such as Czechoslovakia in 1968.[26] It was used as a justification for the declaration of martial law in Poland on December 13, 1981, and the subsequent outlawing of the Solidarity Trade Union. Under normal circumstances, constitutional provisions concerning citizens' rights and duties are also subject to abuse by the state, especially as a means of suppressing opposition to the government or its policies. A person accused of "anti-state" or "anti-socialist" activities can be imprisoned if indicted by judicial process, which is not independent from political power and is in fact an extension of it. Opponents and dissenters can have their rights restricted by being denied work in their profession while being obligated to accept a menial job based on the citizen's duty to work. Other sanctions may include restrictions concerning adequate housing and social services and the denial of a passport to travel abroad. In comparison to some other countries, Poland has, however, been spared the widespread and violent terror directed at citizens by the state apparatus, and this applies even to the martial law period.[27]

The issue is not that citizens should not be expected to fulfill duties or responsibilities; that is an essential feature of any civil society. The problem is that state and party officials in the Polish communist system are not genuinely accountable to citizens. Rights concerning freedom of speech, press, assembly, and association are restricted by the state's interpretation of them, based on the assumption that only the PUWP has a right to rule. Party membership, moreover, is restricted to a very small proportion, less than 10 percent, of the population,[28] and is not open to citizens who do not espouse the Marxist-Leninist worldview. By definition, this excludes citizens who have the constitutional right of freedom of religion and conscience but who are denied access to the ruling party and a free choice in the nomination of candidates and the election of public officials[29] because of their non-Marxist-Leninist beliefs. For example, adherents of Catholicism, who constitute the vast majority of the population, cannot become members of the ruling party. Since party membership is required for other major state positions such as in the judiciary and the socialized economic sector, the vast majority of the population is also denied full enjoyment of other constitutional guarantees of rights. Societal discontent concerning the preferential treatment and privileges accorded party members in hiring and access to material advantages such as housing was particularly manifested during the Solidarity period.[30]

The other major problem concerning the state's interpretation of human rights is the conception that economic development is a necessary precondition for their realization. State officials, for instance, point with pride to the impressive achievements of post–1945 socialist development under the leading role of the PUWP. On the thirtieth anniversary of the establishment of the Polish People's Republic, the official *Handbook* reported the following impressive indicators of socioeconomic modernization and of the population's increasing welfare standards. In 1974, 54.1 percent of the population lived in urban centers as compared to 27.4 percent in 1931; 72.9 percent earned their livelihoods outside agriculture in 1974 compared to 40 percent in 1931. Life expectancy for men and women increased to 67.8 and 74.6 respectively in 1974 compared to 48.2 and 51.4 in 1931.[31] The *Handbook* also reports:

A gauge of the economic growth rate in People's Poland is provided by the fact that the national income increased 6 times over between 1951 and 1975, as compared with a three- or four-fold increase in the world as a whole. Per capita national income in Poland increased over six-fold as compared with the pre-war period. Between 1947 and 1974, Poland's national assets increased 2.6 times over and her productive assets increased 3.5 times over.[32]

Other statistics concerning the progress achieved in increasing the living standard, educational, medical, and other social welfare measures are equally impressive and serve to support the Polish authorities' claims of providing the material and social conditions for the fulfillment of rights guaranteed under the Constitution.

In the mid–70s, moreover, Polish analysts were optimistic that the superiority of the communist model of development via-à-vis the capitalist one would continue to be demonstrated:

In 1980, Poland will be an entirely different country from what it was ten years before. The seventies will give it a place among the economically highly developed countries of the world. Today it may be reckoned that in 1980 the national per capita income will amount to $3500 (in 1975 prices). This will not yet be the level of the world's top countries, but it should be remembered that not so long ago Poland was twenty to thirty years behind them. Now that distance is rapidly shrinking and the prospect of Poland's joining the world club of rich and highly developed countries is becoming increasingly visible.[33]

The emergence of Solidarity in 1980 indeed did mark a radical change in the country, but not in the way anticipated in the above quotation. The accelerated growth rate of the Polish economy in the early 1970s was in large measure paid for by credits from Western countries. Mismanagement and poor planning of the economy, as well as the deteriorating international economic and political situation, resulted in the dramatic decline of Poland's growth.[34] This is reflected in the following statistics from UN sources: Poland's gross domestic product/ net material product increased from 31,217 (millions of U.S. dollars) in 1970 to 67,756 in 1975. It declined to 59,991 in 1980. The per capita income figures for the same period are 960 (U.S. dollars); in 1970; 1992 in 1975; and 1686 in 1980.[35]

Setting aside the poor economic performance in the latter half of the 1970s, the problem remains that Poland is not a rich developed country. Even if it were a rich country, it would not necessarily mean that human rights would be realized so long as the ruling party insists on its monopoly to rule and to represent the people, without at the same time being accountable to them. The poor economic performance also reveals the fallacy of premising a ruling party's legitimacy on ever-increasing growth and promises of perpetual improvements in the living standard. The latter merely fuels unrealistic expectations of a society still undergoing the transition from a rural to an urban and industrial one. When these promises could not be fulfilled, moreover, blame centered on the incompetence of state officials, who in turn could not motivate frustrated citizens to greater productivity and sacrifice. The economic policies of the 1970s also had the effect of burdening the country with an extremely heavy foreign debt, amounting to some $30 billion (U.S.) in 1985.[36]

Consequently, opposition to state policies accelerated in the later half of the 1970s. Not only was the state's position on human rights criticized, but the opposition also focused on the central problem, i.e., the monopoly of power by the party that claims to represent all citizens but refuses to be accountable to them.

OPPOSITION TO STATE POLICIES

As in other East European societies, the communist model of socialism clashes with the national, cultural, and religious values of the population. In Poland, this conflict is polarized by the fact that communist ideology and practices are associated with alien values and foreign domination. The ethnic and religious homogeneity of the post–1945 population reinforces Polish nationalist values and also does not allow for a divide-and-rule policy based on ethnic, religious, or linguistic differentiation. The state's attempts to eradicate religious beliefs and to inculcate Marxist-Leninist values through state-controlled education, media, and other means of socialization have not been effective. The vast majority of the population continues to identify with certain Catholic beliefs both for nationalistic and religious reasons. Both traditions in turn are nurtured by the Roman Catholic Church, which retains a strong institutional network in society, one that is augmented by its transnational connections to the Vatican and other institutions outside of the communist bloc.[37]

At the same time, it must be acknowledged that the Church has its own corporate values and interests to pursue and that these do not necessarily coincide with or reflect all the values or norms of the populace, including those who espouse Catholicism. The Roman Catholic Church's position on the sanctity and the procreative function of marriage, and its defense of the inalienable rights of the human embryo, for instance, set the Church in opposition to the state's relatively liberal laws pertaining to civil marriage, divorce, birth control, and abortion.[38] Considering the religious affiliation of the vast majority of the population, one might expect the Church's teachings to be reflected in behavior patterns. Yet statistics reveal that the abortion and divorce rates in Poland, particularly in urban centers, do not differ significantly from those in other industrial societies.[39] Survey data of Polish women's attitudes concerning employment (women constitute 42 percent of the Polish labor force), abortion, and contraception appear to reinforce the conclusion that there is a correlation between family structure and norms and modern industrial society, irrespective of type of political system. D. Peter Mazur, for instance, notes, "The educational level of women, together with the rural-urban dimension as its correlate, reinforce and strengthen the association found to exist between family disorganization, i.e., divorce, and pregnancy interruption."[40] And despite the Church's emphasis on the traditional family and on the important role of the mother as nurturer, the entrance of women, including mothers, into the labor force is a feature of modern Polish society that is encouraged by state policies aimed to assure women the right to work and to equal rights with men. The problems associated with gender issues such as the extra heavy burden on women carrying the tasks of "mother, worker, and citizen," moreover, are not peculiar to Poland and are evident in other industrial societies.

Despite the above qualifications that the Church's position cannot be equated with all the values or norms of the vast majority who espouse Catholicism, the Church's influential position is, nevertheless, readily evident, and is, moreover, acknowledged by Polish political officials.[41] Its existence as a relatively autonomous organization represents one of the major deviations of the Polish model of socialism.

Other sectors in Polish society have also provided significant counterchecks to standard communist ideology and practices, modeled on that of the Soviet Union. The agricultural sector remains predominantly in private holdings, reflecting farmers' successful resistance to the state-collectivist model of agricultural production. Industrial workers' and intellectuals' dissatisfaction with the government's economic, social, and cultural policies has been manifested by recurring work stoppages, demonstrations, and petitions. The circulation of information and views that have not been approved or censored by the state is another effective means of challenging official assertions concerning socialist reality and achievements.[42]

The common denominator that has facilitated the process of aggregating various societal demands and interests into a coherent set of demands is the human rights issue. References to international declarations and agreements on human rights serve this purpose. They define principles that transcend ideological, philosophical, and religious differences. The latter perspectives color the interpretation of human rights but also define important bases of agreement. In Poland this has facilitated the process of uniting people of various perspectives and of directing opposition from indiscriminate anti-communist positions to a position that does not negate the positive achievements of post–1945 social and economic development but does insist that benefits accruing from development should be distributed without discrimination and that civil and political rights should be respected. The Polish government's use of international documents and debates to legitimize its record and achievements on human rights, especially in comparison to capitalist systems, also legitimizes citizens' use of them to hold the government accountable for infringing on rights that it supports in its declarations. The state's use of human rights for legitimization and propaganda purposes can by the same logic be turned against the state. A brief examination of opposition to the government's proposed amendments to the Polish Constitution in the mid–1970s and of the Solidarity movement in 1980–1981 will serve to demonstrate this process as well as to define the major issues.

At issue in the mid–1970s controversy was the government's intent of enshrining in the Polish Constitution the three major principles that were and continue to be at the foundation of the communist system in practice: (1) the monopoly of power by the PUWP to build socialism; (2) the linkage of citizens' rights to duties to the state; and (3) Poland's alliance with the Soviet Union.[43] For the PUWP, the codification of the above tenets serves to legitimize its power and its interpretation of socialist development as well as to define Poland's special attachment to the Soviet Union and the socialist camp. In addition, the codification brings the Polish Constitution in line with other socialist states.[44]

To what extent this process involves pressure from the Soviet Union cannot be answered. The maintenance of power by the PUWP is dependent on Soviet support, and in that sense Soviet and Polish ruling elites' interests coincide. The fact that the Polish government decided to press for constitutional amendments in the year that the 1975 Helsinki Agreement was signed is also relevant. Constitutional legality is important for internal as well as external legitimization purposes. The concern for legality, however, is more than just an issue of form. It is central to the conception of rule of law that both the Polish government and societal opposition advocate as an essential feature of civilized society based on human rights.

For the Church hierarchy, the proposed 1975 amendments afforded yet another opportunity to challenge the state's ideological and power premises. Arguing that the enshrinement of the party's monopoly of power would constitutionally relegate Catholics and non-Marxists in general, to the role of second-class citizens, the Church hierarchy stressed: "Parliament should be assembled by free elections and should be the guardian of all civil rights and duties." The episcopate also demanded an "independent judicial system and civil service," as well as "free trade unions." Consistent with the Church's transcendental conception of human rights, the episcopate also stressed that certain civil rights are "indispensable" and may not be conditional on the fulfillment of duties. These include the right of life, including the life of the unborn fetus; the rights of the family as a primary unit of society; and the "freedom of the Church and the individual's freedom of conscience and of religious practice both public and private."[45]

Petitions signed by intellectuals paralleled the Church's concerns regarding the linkage of rights to duties, especially since both rights and duties would be subject to interpretation and implementation by a government that is not accountable or responsible to the electorate. Petitioners thus demanded the "right to nominate and vote for representatives according to the accepted democratic principles of free elections. The courts must be assured of their independence from the executive power, and the highest legislative power must effectively be given to Parliament."[46]

The intellectuals' protest also paralleled the Church's concerns regarding the constitutional enshrinement of Poland's alliances with the Soviet Union and the world socialist system. Stressing that these treaty obligations were not at issue, one of the protest documents noted that their incorporation "to the rank of a fundamental constitutional principle is universally acknowledged as a limitation of a country's sovereignty."[47]

The primary difference between the Church's and the intellectuals' respective positions was that the latter expressed their demands for specific civil liberties in more universal terms reflecting the pluralist makeup of intellectual groups constituted of people of various philosophical as well as religious perspectives. The freedoms that were stressed by intellectuals focused on the following: freedom of conscience and religious practice (the latter to apply to "all denominational groups"); freedom of work (including the "freedom to choose" one's own "trade representation which is independent of both state and Party"); freedom of speech and exchange of information (this includes the abolition of "preventive censorship" and the establishment of regulations of publishing as defined by law and due process); and freedom in education (the reassertion of the autonomy of academic institutions in the "selection of teaching staff and subjects for study").[48]

The common foundation that linked both categories of opposition, Church and intellectuals, was the justification of human rights with reference to Polish national traditions and international documents and agreements on human rights. The Polish episcopate stated: "In so far as human rights are concerned, our society understands them in the spirit of its national tradition of respect for the freedom of the individual and for the Declaration of Human Rights, reaffirmed at the Conference in Helsinki."[49] References to the latter as well as the UN Charter were also asserted in defense of the nation's right to self-determination.

The effect of these protests on the government's proposed constitutional amendments was negligible in terms of the substantive principles that were incorporated into the Polish Constitution in 1976. The mid–1970s constitutional debate is, nevertheless, important in revealing the major points of contention between the government and opposition groups in Polish society. In contrast to the state's Marxist-Leninist interpretation of rights and duties of citizens and its stress on socialist development as a precondition for the realization of rights, especially social and economic ones, the opposition stressed that human rights are "inalienable." Without denying the importance of economic and social rights, the opposition focused on fundamental civil liberties and political rights. The latter are essential for the realization of equitable social and economic rights without discrimination based on political, philosophical, or religious beliefs. Without civil liberties and political rights, citizens are subject to abuse and to arbitrary rule or oppression. Even the most humanitarian Constitution, of course, is no defense against arbitrary rule backed by force, but it would at least deny oppression legitimacy. For the same reason, the Church and intellectuals opposed the codification of Poland's alliance with the Soviet Union.

The opposition's conception of inalienable and indivisible human rights is embedded in international covenants on human rights, a factor that explains the opposition's reference to international documents in support of its case. The opposition's demands, moreover, serve to discredit the Polish government's claims of promoting citizens' rights without discrimination and of representing the will of society.

The complex period beginning with the August 1980 workers' strikes and the emergence of Solidarity further demonstrates the importance of the issues raised during the mid-1970s constitutional controversy. The similarity between the demands of Solidarity and those articulated in the mid-1970s is not surprising given the universal nature of the issues and the fact that Solidarity sought and received advice and guidance from intellectuals as well as the Church.[50] What the Solidarity period revealed was the depth of societal support for human rights and the government's unwillingness or inability to reconcile societal demands with its conception of communism and power interests.

Justifying their Twenty-one Demands[51] with reference to the International Labor Organization (ILO), the Gdansk strikers in August 1980 demanded the right to form trade unions independent of the state and the PUWP, as well as the right to strike. Recognizing that these rights would be meaningless without access to communication, the striking workers also demanded: "Freedom of speech, the press and publications, guaranteed under the Constitution of the Polish People's Republic, is to be observed, and thus independent publishing houses should not be repressed, and all denominations should have access to the mass media." In addition, the strikers demanded the abolition of special privileges and benefits "enjoyed by the Citizens' Militia, the security service and the party apparatus" and the selection of leading public servants "on the principle of qualifications, and not of party affiliation." Other demands included basic wage increases and the linkage of wages to increase in the cost of living; Saturdays free of work; improvement in food supply, housing, medical services, and disability payments; and the extension of paid maternity leaves to three years (from seventeen weeks). Stating that the socioeconomic situation of the country had reached crisis proportions, the strikers demanded the publication of information in order to enable all citizens to participate in the discussion on the program for reforms.[52]

In conceding to the strikers' major demands at the end of August 1980, government officials expected to circumvent the new trade union's autonomy by insisting that it had to be bound by the Polish Constitution (as amended in 1976), and this included the tenet legitimizing PUWP's monopoly of power in developing socialism and in defining state interests.[53] What was apparently not anticipated at that time was the phenomenal societal support for the new trade union, Solidarity. Some ten million working men and women out of a total labor force of fourteen million joined the union. Solidarity, moreover, served as a model for and protector of other groups seeking to exert their right to form autonomous associations. Solidarity thus represented the broadest cross section of Polish society, a fact that gave the new union and other associations, such as Rural Solidarity, strength in pressing to maintain their independence from party control and fueled societal demands for fundamental reforms. Party officials, on the other hand, were not prepared to concede to Solidarity's demands if these threatened the basic tenets of the communist system.

The impasse between the two sides was evident in the results of the July 1981 PUWP Congress and the October 1981 Solidarity Congress of Delegations.[54] While the party congress did address societal grievances and demands, communist leaders were not prepared to institute the type of fundamental changes that would allow for the existence of autonomous associations, especially an association that represented the very constituency that the party purported to represent, i.e., the vast majority of the working population. Such fundamental changes would require genuine civil liberties and political rights, and if instituted would undoubtedly result in the loss of power and control by PUWP. The latter was not prepared to take that step and was probably also unable to do so without incurring Soviet bloc intervention.[55]

Solidarity's Program, on the other hand, demanded the full range of civil, political, economic, and social rights. This document, in fact, reflects the principles and tenets of the two UN Covenants on Human Rights. Solidarity's Program, moreover, was justified with reference to "national traditions," "Christian ethics," and the "workers' and democratic traditions of the labor world." While Solidarity explicitly denied any attempts to form a political party, its Program, nevertheless, asserted the demand for free elections based on genuine political rights. It boldly proclaimed the intention to

seek both to transform the structure of the state and to create and support independent and self-governing institutions in all spheres of social life. Only such a direction of changes will ensure the agreement of public life's organization with the needs of the human being, society's ambitions and the Poles' national aspirations. These changes are also necessary to overcome the economic crisis. We regard pluralism, democratization of the state and the opportunity to make full use of constitutional freedoms as the basic guarantee that the working people's toil and sacrifices will not be once again wasted.[56]

The unacceptability of this program from the perspective of PUWP and of Poland's socialist allies was registered with the imposition of martial law on December 13, 1981, and the suspension and subsequent outlawing of Solidarity.

POST–1981 DEVELOPMENTS

The imposition of martial law itself was justified on human rights terms. In his address to the UN General Assembly, the Minister of Foreign Affairs, Stefan Olszowski, reconfirmed his government's official justification with reference to Article 4 of the International Covenant on Civil and Political Rights, which was "to divert the exceptionally serious danger threatening the nation and the state, as well as to create conditions for an effective protection of Poland's sovereignty and independence." He added: "For the price of the provisional application of the extraordinary measures, Poland avoided a civil war. We ourselves know how high a price it is but it is not the highest price; a mass-scale loss of the basic human right—the right to live."[57]

The implications of this justification are that Solidarity and its demands posed a threat to the socialist system, as indeed Solidarity had by challenging the ruling party's right to rule and to impose its interpretation of socialism on society. Second, there is the clear implication that had the Polish government not reacted with drastic measures, Poland's socialist allies, led by the Soviet Union, would have intervened, as they had done in Czechoslovakia in 1968. It was assumed that Warsaw bloc military intervention in Poland would have been violently resisted by the population. With some justification as it turned out, it was assumed that there would be less resistance to the imposition of martial law by Polish forces.

The swiftness and efficient manner in which the "state of war" was implemented facilitated the Polish regime's objectives of reasserting its control with a minimum of violence. The internment of potential resistance leaders, including most of the high-ranking Solidarity officials as well as dissidents, and the suspension of civil liberties and of organizations such as Solidarity were effective measures in imposing the regime's will on society. An indicator of this is that by December 19, 1982, the authorities were sufficiently confident in their ability to maintain order to suspend certain emergency measures. By July 22, 1983, martial law was lifted and a general amnesty was granted to most of the people interned.

The actual record of human rights violations during the nineteen-month martial law period is not and may never be fully known. An investigation begun in 1982 by the UN Commission on Human Rights concluded in its 1984 report[58] that at least five Polish citizens died as a result of clashes between demonstrators and the police during that period, a figure that is disputed as too low by other sources.[59] The UN Commission also reported that significant progress had been achieved in the release of political prisoners: as of February 18, 1984, 281 people were still detained compared to 1,500 on January 4, 1983. In general, the UN Commission was positive in its conclusion that the lifting of martial law and the amnesty had "produced conditions favourable to a reconciliation between different sectors of Polish society." In expressing concern about some of the other legislative measures introduced during this period, the report concluded that the

UN investigators were impressed with the "spirit of moderation" of Polish government officials.[60]

The legislative acts referred to by the UN Commission have an important bearing on future human rights questions in Poland. The Polish Constitution, for instance, was amended to strengthen provisions pertaining to the imposition of extraordinary measures. In addition to state of war and martial law, a third category was added, the "state of emergency" which can be implemented "if the internal security of the State is in jeopardy, or in cases of natural disaster" (Amendment to Article 33 of Polish Constitution, approved on July 20, 1983). The Polish parliament on July 21, 1983, also approved temporary special legal regulations to deal with socioeconomic problems. These included restrictions on workers' rights to change employment and provisions to increase working hours up to forty-six hours a week if deemed necessary to realize important economic tasks. On July 28, 1983, changes to the penal code provided for penalties of up to three years imprisonment for "whoever participates in a union of which the existence, structure or purpose remains secret from the state organs or which was dissolved or the legalization of which has been refused."[61] The latter law is particularly directed against the Solidarity Trade Union, which was suspended with the imposition of martial law and outlawed on October 8, 1982, with the passage of a new Trade Union Act.[62]

The above measures are aimed to maintain state control over society. The fact that the UN Commission was impressed with the government's "spirit of moderation" concerning the above measures misses the most important point, which is that citizens' rights are totally dependent on the government's interpretation of them in relation to its objectives of maintaining its rule and its understanding of "socialist" order. The ILO addressed this fundamental issue in its investigation of the Polish government's treatment of the Solidarity Trade Union and the state's 1982 Trade Union Act. In its conclusion, the ILO report asserted:

The essential point is that the principal consequence of the cancellation of the registration of the trade unions and of the absence of all possibility of establishing similar ones was to deprive the workers of the right to join the existing unions which had been freely and lawfully set up since 1980, and thus of joining organizations of their own choosing. It has to be concluded that the Act of 8 October 1982, by pronouncing the dissolution of the trade unions, infringed the guarantees provided for by Article 2 of Convention No. 87 [ILO] respecting the free choice of organizations....[63]

The ILO report in its detailed study of the Polish government violations of workers' rights also concluded that the 1982 Trade Union Act unduly restricted the right of workers to exercise the right to collective bargaining, including the right to strike.[64]

The Polish government's response to the investigations and criticisms by international bodies is instructive. Defending its record of human rights, the Polish government accused the UN Commission on Human Rights and the ILO of interfering in the internal affairs of a sovereign state. The Polish government consequently refused to cooperate with the ILO in its investigations and retaliated against the ILO's charges of the Polish government's violation of labor conventions by declaring Poland's intent to leave that specialized agency.[65] In its response to the United States' and other NATO allies' sanctions against Poland, the Polish government accused Western states of subversion in interfering in Poland's domestic affairs and of moral hypocrisy.[66] Defending legislative acts to obligate citizens to work, General Wojciech Jaruzelski, the leader of the PUWP, drew unfavorable comparisons to Western systems. Defending the anti-parasite law with reference to human rights under socialism, Jaruzelski declared:

On the one hand it is a violation of human rights to force somebody to work. On the other hand, failure to force somebody to work is non-fulfillment of a requirement of democracy. . . . This is what socialism is all about. . . . This is not understood by even a representative of a very rich country [U.S. congressman], where unemployment is one of the most painful plagues and one of the most serious violations of human rights—the right of man to work. Just like terrorism, murder, crimes of all sorts, homicide, robbery, rape are a violation of the right of man to personal safety. After all the crime rate in the USA is 9 or 10 times higher than in Poland; while in a number of West European countries it is 3 or 4 times higher. I am not claiming that in this respect the situation in our country is good. We consider that it is necessary to fight crime and we shall do so, but in this respect, too, human rights are better protected.[67]

From the above, it is obvious that human rights is a political issue, subject to interpretation by states representing different ideological or philosophical foundations. Given the state sovereignty principle, zealously guarded by all governments, especially those accused of violating largely unenforceable international norms, the promotion of human rights into positive legal rights remains within the domestic jurisdiction of the state. That function in turn is dependent on a government's willingness and capacity to respond to the human rights demands of its citizenry.

The fact that governments are forced to justify their domestic and external policies with reference to human rights by nature of the power struggle among rival systems is not without significance. International declarations, debates, and polemics on this issue have been instrumental in raising citizens' consciousness of human rights, in aggregating people in support of a human rights program, and in providing legitimacy for their demands vis-à-vis governments. These functions are evident in the Polish case. The vitality of the debate on human rights as reflected by the Church's and intellectuals' concerns over the constitutional debate, and the mass support accorded to Solidarity and its efforts to win concessions from the government in the sphere of civil, political, economic, and social rights, demonstrate the importance of these issues to citizens. The Polish government's ongoing efforts to justify its actions with reference to human rights is also an indicator that the issue will remain an important one.

NOTES

1. Peter Brock, "Polish Nationalism," in *Nationalism in Eastern Europe*, P. F. Sugar and I. J. Lederer (Seattle: University of Washington Press, 1969). For a discussion of Polish history, including the contemporary post–1945 period, see Norman Davies, *God's Playground: A History of Poland*, 2 vols. (New York: Columbia University Press, 1982); R. F. Leslie, ed., *The History of Poland since 1863* (Cambridge: Cambridge University Press, 1980); M. K. Dziewanowski, *Poland in the 20th Century* (New York: Columbia University Press, 1977); and *Poland: A Handbook* (Warsaw: Interpress Publishers, 1977). The latter reference book was issued to commemorate the thirtieth anniversary of the Polish People's Republic and represents the government's official position.

2. This is acknowledged by Western scholars (see reference to Davies, Leslie, and Dziewanowski in note 1) as well as official Polish sources such as *Poland: A Handbook* (1977). The emphasis of the latter is on the voluntary nature and the positive aspects of Poland's linkage to the Soviet Union and other socialist countries; the former sources, on the other hand, stress the constraints placed on Poland's sovereignty by the Soviet Union. Societal opposition in Poland to the state's circumvented sovereignty within the Soviet bloc will be discussed below.

3. See Krystyna M. Olszer, ed., *For Your Freedom and Ours: Polish Progressive Spirit from the 14th Century to the Present*, 2d ed. (New York: F. Ungar, 1981), especially 13–52, and see Janusz Tazbir, *A State Without Stakes: Polish Religious Toleration in the Sixteenth and Seventeenth Centuries* (New York: Twayne, 1973).

4. Solidarity's Program, adopted by the First National Congress on October 7, 1981, refers to "national traditions" as one of the sources of inspiration for Solidarity's demands. See "Program of the Independent Self Governing Trade Union: Solidarnosc," trans. Polish Workers Solidarity Committee (Toronto, Canada); hereafter referred to as Solidarity's Program. Also see Stan Persky and Henry Flam, eds., *The Solidarity Sourcebook* (Vancouver: New Star Books, 1982), 205–225.

5. See W. Bienkowski, "Open Letter to the Authorities of the Polish People's Republic on the Normalization of Relations with the Soviet Union," in *Dissent in Poland: Reports and Documents in Translation, 1975–1977* (London: Veritas Foundation Press, 1977), 38–43. (Documents compiled by Association of Polish Students and Graduates in Exile, London.)

6. According to the 1931 Polish Census, which defined nationality on linguistic criteria, Poles constituted 69 percent of the population; Ukrainians, Jews, and Byelorussians constituted 15, 8.5, and 4.7 percent respectively. See Davies, *God's Playground*, 2: 404–410.

7. An indicator of the political fragmentation prior to the 1926 takeover of power by Marshal Jozef Pilsudski is that in 1925 there were ninety-two registered political parties, of which thirty-two were represented in the Polish parliament (*Sejm*). Between 1918 and Pilsudski's coup in 1926, there were fourteen different cabinets. See Leslie, *The History*, p. 147.

8. Davies, *God's Playground*, 2: 406.

9. Leslie, *The History*, 200.

10. *Poland: A Handbook*, 127.

11. Leslie, *The History*, 148.

12. *Poland: A Handbook*, 91–96, 126.

13. For an account of Poles who helped Jews during World War II, see Wladyslaw Bartoszewski and Zofia Lewinowna, *Ten jes z ojczyzny mojej* (Cracow: Znak, 1969).

14. Official directives of the Polish censorship office prohibit the discussion of Soviet atrocities, such as the 1940 massacre of 8,000 Polish officers in the Katyn forest by Soviet troops. See J. L. Curry, ed. and trans., *The Black Book of Polish Censorship* (New York: Vintage Books, 1984), 338–45.

15. According to the 1946 Census, the population was 23,930,000, a decline of some eleven million compared to the 1939 figure of 34,849,000. Aside from six million killed during the war, the other five million were either incorporated to territories in the USSR or expelled from Poland's post–1945 Western territories. *Poland: A Handbook*, 126.

16. *Poland: A Handbook*, 137.

17. *The Europa Year Book 1984: A World Survey* (London: Europa Publications, 1984), 1:724. Official Polish government-approved sources do not provide data about religious affiliation in that post–1945 census forms do not ask questions concerning religion. Data concerning church structure and number of clergy are available in *Poland: A Handbook*, 215–21.

18. See Stefania S. Miller, "Church and Catholic Opposition in the Polish Communist System," in *Solidarity: The Origins and Implications of Polish Trade Unions*, ed. A. Jain (Baton Rouge, La.: Oracle Press, 1983), 115–48.

19. For a discussion of the main features, see Stephen White, "What Is a Communist System?" *Studies in Comparative Communism* 16, no. 4 (Winter 1983): 247–63.

20. Article 67(2) of the Constitution of the Polish People's Republic of July 22, 1952 (As Amended), in *The Constitutions of the Communist World*, ed. W. B. Simons (Alphen aan den Rijn, The Netherlands: Sijthoff & Noordhoff, 1980); hereafter referred to as the Polish Constitution. Post–1981 amendments to the Constitution will be discussed in the last section of this chapter.

21. See documents in W. Laqueur and B. Rubin, eds., *The Human Rights Reader* (New York: New American Library, 1979), 171–89. Also see *ABC of Dialectical and Historical Materialism* (Moscow: Progress, 1978), 479–507.

22. Jack Donnelly, "Recent Trends in UN Human Rights Activity: Description and Polemic," *International Organization* 35, no. 4 (Autumn 1981): 633–55.

23. Polish Constitution, chap. 8.

24. Article 3(1) of the Polish Constitution states, "The leading political force of society in the building of socialism is the Polish United Workers' Party." Two other political parties, the United Peasant party and the Democratic party, are also recognized, but they are subordinated to the dominant role of PUWP.

25. See *ABC of Dialectical*, 402–412.

26. See documents in R. A. Remington, ed., *Winter in Prague* (Cambridge, Mass.: M.I.T. Press, 1969), 299–323.

27. Discussed in the last section of this chapter.

28. As of December 31, 1982, PUWP membership was 2,327,349, a 20 percent decline since 1978. Total population of Poland in 1982 was 36.6 million. See R. F. Starr, ed., *Yearbook on International Communist Affairs, 1984* (Stanford, Calif.: Hoover Press, 1984), 343.

29. For a discussion of the electoral process, see R. F. Staar, *Communist Regimes in Eastern Europe*, 4th ed. (Stanford, Calif.: Hoover Press, 1982), 157–59.

30. "Nomenklatura" lists of major posts and of cadres who are entitled to occupy them are a means of social control by the ruling party. In Poland it is estimated that there

are some 150,000 to 300,000 major positions that require PUWP approval. For a discussion of this process and the opposition to it during the Solidarity period, see Takayuki Ito, "Controversy over Nomenklatura in Poland," *Acta Slavica Iaponica*, Vol. 1 (Sapporo, Japan: 1983), 57–103.

31. *Poland: A Handbook*, 127–30.

32. Ibid., 226.

33. Ibid., 613.

34. For an analysis of the origins of the economic problems, see Z. M. Fallenbuchl, "The Polish Economy since August 1980," *Canadian Slavonic Papers* 25, no. 3 (September 1983): 361–79.

35. *National Accounts Statistics: Analysis of Main Aggregates, 1982*, vol. 2 (New York: United Nations, 1985), 11.

36. Editorial, *Polish Perspectives* (Warsaw) 28, no. 3 (Summer 1985): 3.

37. See Miller, "Church and Catholic Opposition."

38. D. Peter Mazur, "Women in Contemporary Poland," in *Women in Eastern Europe and the Soviet Union*, ed. Tova Yedlin (New York: Praeger, 1980).

39. Ibid.; also see C. Tietze, *Induced Abortion: A World Review, 1981*, 4th ed. (A Population Council Fact Book. New York: The Population Council, 1981).

40. Mazur, "Women," 236.

41. See Miller, "Church and Catholic Opposition," and Adam Piekarski, *The Church in Poland* (Warsaw: Interpress, 1978).

42. See White, "What Is a Communist System?" for deviations from the standard communist model.

43. For a more detailed account of the constitutional debate, see Miller, "Church and Catholic Opposition."

44. See Simons, *The Constitutions of the Communist World*.

45. Quotations from the episcopate's March 1976 letter in *Dissent in Poland*, 20–23.

46. "Letter of 14," in Ibid., 15–17.

47. "Manifesto of the 59," in Ibid., 12–15; also "Memorandum of the 101," Ibid., 17–18.

48. Ibid., 13–14.

49. Ibid., 20–21.

50. See A. Kemp-Welch, trans. *The Birth of Solidarity: The Gdansk Negotiations 1980* (London: Macmillan Press, 1983), and Peter Raina, *Poland 1981: Towards Social Renewal* (London: George Allen & Unwin, 1985). For a discussion of the influence of Catholic social thought on Solidarity's program, see Stefania Szlek Miller, "Catholic Personalism and Pluralist Democracy in Poland," *Canadian Slavonic Papers* 25, no. 3 (September 1983): 425–39.

51. Solidarity's Program, 8–9; also see Kemp-Welch, *The Birth of Solidarity*, for the full text of negotiations between the Polish government and strikers at the Gdansk shipyard in 1980.

52. Ibid.

53. Article 2 of "The Agreement" signed by Strike Committee and Government Commission, August 31, 1980; see Kemp-Welch, 168–79.

54. Documents and commentary in Raina, *Poland 1981*, 229–53 and 319–90.

55. For a discussion of the international dimension, see Adam Bromke, *Poland: The Protracted Crisis* (Oakville, Canada: Mosaic Press, 1983), and by the same author,

Eastern Europe in the Aftermath of Solidarity (New York: Columbia University Press, 1985).

56. Solidarity's Program, 25.

57. Stefan Olszowski's Address to the 37th Session of the UN General Assembly, in *Documents and Materials*, no. 18 (Warsaw: Ministry of Foreign Affairs, 1982), 4–5.

58. UN Commission on Human Rights, "Question of the Violation of Human Rights. ...Report on the Situation in Poland" (Fortieth Session, 1 March, 1984), UN doc. E/CN.4/1984/26; hereafter cited as CHR Report on Poland.

59. The Polish Helsinki Watch Committee identified fifty victims who died "as a result of police action" between 1981 and 1983; four others "died in mysterious circumstances suggestive of foul play on the part of police." See "Fatal Victims of Martial Law" and "The Helsinki Committee in Poland: Memorandum to the Human Rights Commission of the United Nations," in *Poland Watch*, no. 6 (1984), 22–30 and 137–69. Also see Polish Helsinki Watch Committee, *Poland Under Martial Law* (Eng. ed. by U.S. Helsinki Watch Committee, 1983).

60. CHR Report on Poland, 11.

61. Ibid., 7–8, 11.

62. "Model Statute of a Trade Union," in *Documents and Materials*, no. 18 (1982).

63. International Labour Office, *Official Bulletin: Special Supplement 67: Series B* (ILO: 1984), 131.

64. Ibid., 143–47.

65. Ibid., Annex 1.

66. *Documents and Materials*, no. 10/33 (Warsaw, Ministry of Foreign Affairs, 1983), 16–26.

67. Ibid., 25.

SUGGESTED READINGS

Bromke, Adam. *Eastern Europe in the Aftermath of Solidarity.* East European Monographs, No. 183. New York: Columbia University Press, 1985.

Curry, J. L., ed. and trans. *The Black Book of Polish Censorship.* New York: Vintage Books, 1984.

Davies, N. *God's Playground: A History of Poland.* 2 vols. New York: Columbia University Press, 1982.

International Labour Office. *Official Bulletin: Special Supplement* [Report on Poland]. Vol. 67, Series B (1984).

Jain, A., ed. *Solidarity: The Origins and Implications of Polish Trade Unions.* Baton Rouge, La.: Oracle Press, 1983.

Kemp-Welch, A., trans. *The Birth of Solidarity: The Gdansk Negotiations 1980.* London: Macmillan Press, 1983.

Leslie, R. E. *The History of Poland since 1863.* Cambridge: Cambridge University Press, 1980.

Persky, Stan and Henry Flam, eds. *The Solidarity Sourcebook.* Vancouver: New Star Books, 1982.

Poland: A Handbook. Warsaw: Interpress Publishers, 1977.

Polish Helsinki Watch Committee. *Poland Under Martial Law: A Report on Human Rights*. New York: Helsinki Watch, 1983.

Raina, P. *Poland 1981: Towards Social Renewal*. London: George Allen & Unwin, 1985.

Yedlin, Tova, ed. *Women in Eastern Europe and the Soviet Union*. New York: Praeger, 1980.

15

SENEGAL

Martin A. Klein

In the center of Dakar, there are a large number of vendors selling a wide range of newspapers and magazines. There is generally a section of the table or an umbrella to which are attached local publications printed on newsprint or cheap paper. Some of them are published by Muslim groups. Many are Marxist-Leninist. All of them are printed locally and all regularly take issue with government policies. The range of viewpoints and the vigor of the local press mark Senegal as one of the freest and most open societies in Africa. The major restraints on freedom of the press are the standard laws of libel and the funds needed to print.

Many Senegalese would be reluctant to give so much credit to the current regime. Abdoulaye Bathily is one. Bathily has been arrested six times, most recently in 1985. On one occasion, he was forcibly placed in the army along with a group of his comrades in the student movement. Bathily's case underlines both the liberties available in Senegal and the limits to those liberties. Bathily is a professor of history at the University of Dakar. He is also the leader of a Marxist-Leninist opposition party, which campaigned openly during the elections of 1983. He is free to say what he wishes because the regime is not threatened, but he and his comrades know well that those freedoms could be removed.[1]

HISTORICAL BACKGROUND

Senegal was France's original colony in Africa. From its coastal cities, known as the Four Communes, a military and economic penetration of the interior began. Dakar was for over half a century the capital of French West Africa and its most important port. Though ethnic conflict exists, it is more subdued than elsewhere in Africa, in large part because of a common culture. The five largest ethnic groups in Senegal resemble each other, and those who move to city or town generally learn Wolof, the language of the most numerous, and fit into Wolof urban life.

The most important element of this shared culture is Islam, a religion that first took root in Senegal over eight hundred years ago and claims over 85 percent of Senegalese as adherents.[2] Senegalese Islam is dominated by several religious fraternities, of which the most important politically is the Mourides, a purely Senegalese religious order, which places importance on work and the submission of disciples to religious guides, known as marabouts. Among the Mourides and in rival religious orders, these marabouts control significant agricultural production and commerce and tend as a result to be quite conservative. They have not sought power for themselves, but have used their substantial following to elect friends. From 1948 to his retirement in 1980, Léopold Sédar Senghor, a Catholic, was able to command the support of most marabouts because he could protect their interests. Most important, they understood that a Catholic president would never attack their interests. Religious conflict has thus not been a problem. In the past, the most important threat the marabouts faced was from young Muslim intellectuals, hostile not to Islam but to maraboutic power. In recent years, these reformers have been outflanked by a newer and more intolerant group, called integrists, who call for the enforcement of Muslim law. So far, neither group has made much headway, and most observers think that in the absence of a real social base, they are not likely to do so.

Since the middle of the nineteenth century, when the Atlantic slave trade ended, Senegal's peanuts have been the most important export from France's African colonies. Senegal is, however, a poor place, an area of sandy soils and uncertain rainfall. Its importance came more from its location than from its wealth. Like its neighbors in the Sahel belt of West Africa, it has experienced regular droughts since 1968 and has had difficulty finding new sources of income. There has been some industrialization, but not enough to compensate for drought or low peanut prices on the world market. Only fish and phosphate exports have seen much growth since independence.

There are a number of reasons why Senegal is such a free place. First, there is a long tradition of modern politics, longer and more important than anywhere else in Africa. The Four Communes elected a member of the French Chamber of Deputies from 1872. They also had a local legislative council with more authority than any other such body in Black Africa, and municipal councils which operated under French law.[3] Disagreements over the question of citizenship were resolved during World War I when Senegal's black deputy, Blaise Diagne, persuaded the French Chamber to recognize those born in the Four Communes as citizens. Though this right was not extended to the interior, the existence of a body of African citizens and a corps of elected officials operated to minimize the arbitrariness that characterized colonial rule elsewhere. As citizens, those born in the Four Communes were immune from arbitrary arrest, could say or write what they wished, and had the vote. If accused of crimes, they were tried in French courts with the same procedural protections they would have had in France itself. Elections in Senegal were hotly contested and open, though often corrupt. The press was free and lively, and public issues were debated by it. Senegalese were accustomed to rights similar to those known in Europe.[4]

In much of Africa, Western institutions did not take root because they were not tried. In Senegal, they took deep root. The rest of French West Africa was subject to a law code known as the *indigénat*, under which an administrator could arbitrarily jail subjects for crimes as trivial as disrespect. Forced labor was widely used, and the individual subject had no way to protest against the whims of the local French administrator or his African underlings. By contrast, in Senegal, the existence of elected institutions meant that the administration was accountable. Public letter writers could articulate the grievances of the illiterate. Lawyers often represented the poor. Cases of arbitrary action could be discussed in the Conseil Général or in the local press.[5] Accountability was a significant check on arbitrariness. It meant that freedoms not available in Guinea and the Ivory Coast were taken for granted in Dakar.

The second reason for the degree of freedom in Senegal is its large bourgeoisie. It was the capital of French West Africa and is today a favored location for embassies and the offices of international agencies. Though literacy in French was only about 10 percent at independence in 1960, there was by African standards a large bureaucratic class and a significant intellectual elite. Senegalese staffed a large part of the bureaucracy of French West Africa. This group has expanded dramatically since independence. In 1985 almost 50 percent of school-age children were in school and university enrollments had risen sharply.[6] In 1980 Senegal had over 13,500 students in university-level institutions.[7] The general level of training had improved across the society. This has permitted a significant development of the civil service, the professional classes, the arts, the academy, and the business community. Senegal has seen a dramatic growth in the number of all kinds of professionals.

The only restraint on the development of this class has been money. Senegal is basically a poor country. Gross national product per capita (GNP) in 1985 was $440 a year. Rural incomes run about one-seventh of urban incomes.[8] Until recently the World Bank ranked Senegal among the "lower middle income" rather than among the very poor, "low income economies," but by 1984 it had fallen into this group of the world's three dozen poorest countries. This steady slide is largely the result of a decline in per capita income at a rate of almost 0.5 percent per year since 1965, a decline caused largely by intermittent drought and declining peanut prices.[9] In spite of even worse than stagnant economic conditions, the new middle class seeks a better standard of living, though often on limited salaries. There are not many Mercedes on the streets, but there are a lot of Toyotas, Fiats, and motorbikes, and Dakar shops display a wide range of stereo equipment. This growing class is well-educated. Many of them have studied in France. The maintenance of a free and open society is important to them. My limited contacts with the military suggest that even the officer corps of the army is a part of this bourgeoisie. They are well-educated, well-spoken, and very professional.

A third reason why Senegal is so free is that until 1980 it was dominated by Léopold Sédar Senghor.[10] A poet and grammarian who once taught Latin and Greek in a French lycée, Senghor was always sensitive to both European public opinion and to the values of the European democratic tradition. In practice, he did not always behave as a democrat, but his style favored pluralism. During the first years of independence, Senegalese leadership divided into two factions, one that looked to Senghor and the other to his handpicked prime minister, Mamadou Dia. They were members of the same party, but favored different policies. Dia and his faction had a clearer view of development problems and where they wanted to go, but Dia's political style was to identify allies and reinforce them. Senghor's was always to encourage rivalries so that he could more effectively play groups off against each other. Thus, in every town in Senegal, there were inevitably two clans, and if one got wiped out, a new rival would appear.[11] Dia always wanted to know who his man was. He would then channel resources through his supporters to strengthen them. In some ways, Senghor's approach was less attractive, but it did establish multipolar norms loosely analogous to Western pluralism. Senegalese "clan" politics was marked by constant conflict, but elimination was rare and there was a regular circulation of elites.

In 1962 a group of threatened politicians, all of them from Dia's own party, brought a motion of censure against Dia in the National Assembly. When Dia became convinced that he was going to fall, he arrested four of the organizers of the opposition and tried to carry out what his opponents saw as a coup d'état. The army sided with Senghor; Dia failed and was arrested with a number of his collaborators. The trial set important precedents. It was before a special tribunal, but it was open, and Dia was allowed to make his case. Dia's defense was essentially that members of his own party had no right to introduce a motion of censure and that he was acting constitutionally.[12] The case set another precedent. Dia and his collaborators were sent to prison. No one was executed. In fact, no one has ever been executed in Senegal for political crimes. And in 1974, when Dia was released, he returned to public life. For a number of years, he put out what was probably the best of the opposition journals and, in 1983, was the leader of a minor opposition political party. In 1962, after Dia fell, many of his protégés were purged, but most speedily moved back into the system, including Abdou Diouf, who peacefully succeeded Senghor as president in 1980.

POLITICAL CENTRALIZATION AND SOCIAL TENSIONS

Once Dia and his supporters were in prison, Senghor moved in directions very similar to those followed during the same period elsewhere in Africa.[13] In 1963 a new constitution set up a strong presidential system and a single-slate winner-take-all National Assembly. This meant that one party would control all of the seats. It made it difficult for an opposition party to get a toehold in the government or to use the National Assembly as a forum. In effect, it guaranteed Senghor's Union Progressiste Sénégalais (UPS) control of the National Assembly, but in doing so, made the Assembly unimportant. Furthermore, fraud in the 1963 elections guaranteed the defeat of the opposition. There were then two opposition parties. The Bloc des Masses Sénégalaises joined with the UPS just before the 1963 elections, but only over the heated objections of the Bloc's leader, Cheikh Anta Diop, who was outvoted by his own executive. The popular Diop, a cultural nationalist with family links to key marabouts, wanted to contest the 1963 elections. Diop then spent almost twenty years first looking for a party, and then, after he found one, getting government recognition for it.

The second opposition party, the Parti du Régroupement Africain-Sénégal (PRA), contested the elections vigorously. Supported by Diop and backers of Dia, the PRA had large rallies in the cities but was defeated in an election marked by massive vote fraud and election-day violence. The government claimed 94.2 percent of the vote, clearly an exaggeration of their actual support. In 1966 PRA also merged with the UPS and a number of PRA leaders became cabinet ministers. A third opposition party, the communist Parti Africain d'Indépendence (PAI) had been banned at independence. Thus, by 1966 Senghor had firm control over party and government. He had created a single-party system simply by banning one opposition party and absorbing the others. This was not a party-state, but there was only one party. It had been done with no bloodshed and few arrests.

The decade that followed was to sorely try Senghor's liberal image. Blocked in the political arena, opposition appeared in the social arena. Peasants, workers, students, and merchants all protested against a government they found increasingly alien. The peasants may well have had the most substantial grievances. They were being squeezed both by natural disasters and government policies. A series of drought years, the first in 1966 and 1968, have now troubled this area for a generation. At the same time, Senegal had to deal with the end of French subsidies for peanuts, subsidies that dated to the Depression of the 1930s and protected peasants from the vagaries of the world market. This meant a sharp drop in prices and thus a sharp drop in peasant incomes. By 1968 peasants increasingly found themselves heavily in debt and without the income to pay those debts. They responded by shifting land from peanuts to millet, by refusing to borrow for fertilizer and for new equipment, and by refusing to pay debts. A sharp drop in fertilizer purchases came in 1969, and 1970, a good year for rainfall, saw a peanut harvest about half that of 1965.[14]

These events, called the "malaise paysan," were a disaster economically but not as threatening politically as what the students and workers did. The government could simply ride out peasant opposition, though peasants in the 1970s found a spokesman, the new leader of the Mourides, who used his influence on several occasions to get debts forgiven and producer prices raised. Workers and students, however, were clustered in the cities, where governments rise and fall.

In 1968, just after the student rising in Paris, students in Dakar went out on strike over a decision to cut scholarships. Within weeks, the Union National des Travailleurs Sénégalais (UNTS), the national union federation, also went out on strike. There were student strikes again in 1969 and 1971. The 1971 strike was linked to protests against the visit of French President Georges Pompidou, a high school comrade of Senghor's. In effect, they were against Senghor's pro-French policies. The government was threatened by the fact that the strikes extended down into the high schools and, thus, into every important town in the country. Senegalese businessmen were also unhappy about the foreign domination of the economy. In 1968 the Union des Groupements Économiques du Sénégal (UNIGES) was formed by businessmen unhappy about the government's friendship with French and local Lebanese economic interests.

The government generally responded to these social disturbances with a combination of concession, coercion, and co-optation. In May 1968 workers were bitter about policies that had frozen wages since 1961 and reduced real income. When the UNTS went on strike, the government arrested militant leaders, dissolved the UNTS, and encouraged the creation of a rival union federation, the Confédération Nationale des Travailleurs Sénégalais (CNTS). Three years later, the Labor Code was amended to restrict the right to strike. At the same time, the government raised the minimum wage and made efforts to co-opt labor leaders into the political system. Similarly, they dealt with the businessmen by forming a rival organization, the Conseil Fédéral des Groupements Économiques du Sénégal (COFEGES). At the same time, they increased credit for Senegalese businessmen and encouraged the Senegalization of key sectors of the economy. In 1970 the two business groups merged.

The restlessness of the working class was probably the government's greatest fear, but the students were the spark that could ignite other grievances. While the government made concessions to students in 1968, especially on fellowships and Africanization of the university, the years of social conflict saw increasingly strong action against students. On several occasions the police or the army invaded the campus and made massive arrests. The university was restructured to give the government tighter control. The major student union, the Union Démocratique des Étudiants Sénégalais, was banned, and the university was closed several times. In 1969 and again in 1971, student leaders were placed in the army, where one of them was killed in a clash with Portuguese troops on the Guinea border. Finally, after the 1971 strike, forty-nine students were excluded from the university. Those from other countries were sent home. The exclusion process extended down into the high schools, where many student leaders were barred from further education. This ban also meant that they would not be sponsored for scholarships abroad. For some excellent students, it meant the end of their education. It was during this period that most of Abdoulaye Bathily's arrests took place. He was picked up at least twice in attacks on the university and was arrested several times because he was the leader of the student union.

A few of the abler students survived the ban. Friends helped Bathily find a fellowship to study in Great Britain, where he eventually completed a doctorate. He returned to Dakar as a member of the university faculty. Similarly, Iba der Thiam, the leader of the militant teachers union, was accused of complicity in the bombing of the French cultural center in 1971. It is unlikely that there was any evidence to tie him to the act. He took his exams under police guard, but then was allowed to go to France, where he wrote the *aggrégation*, a prestigious examination that has no equivalent in the English-speaking world. He too then returned as a member of the history faculty and is now minister of education. These cases once again show Senegal's flexibility, but the opportunities open to a few leaders were not available to others. Exclusion of militant students from the university probably broke the back of student protests, at least for a time. Students have, however, remained strongly opposed to the government.

POLITICAL RIGHTS

During the early 1970s Senegal seemed to be moving hesitantly but remorselessly down the path of autocracy, but having established his authority and that of the party, Senghor began to move in the other direction. In 1970 he revised the constitution to restore the office of the prime minister. This took much of the burden of daily administration off his shoulders. In 1974 Mamadou Dia and other political prisoners were released. Later the same year the formation of an opposition party, the Parti Démocratique Sénégalais (PDS), under the leadership of liberal lawyer Abdoulaye Wade, was approved. Within a few years, Senegal tried to move toward a system in which there were first two, then three, authorized opposition parties, each with its assigned position in the political spectrum.[15] There was thus to be a Marxist-Leninist party, a position assigned to the once-banned but now anemic PAI, and a liberal democratic party, a position assigned to Wade's PDS. Senghor opted for social democracy and the UPS accordingly became the Parti Socialiste. A fourth party, conservative and traditionalist, was also eventually approved, but the government refused to register the Rassemblement National Démocratique (RND) of Cheikh Anta Diop. Most observers at the time considered Diop the most popular opposition leader. Ironically, in 1983, when he finally had a chance to contest an election, he chose not to do so, largely because the Mouride leadership refused to support him.

Senghor also did away with the all-or-nothing system in favor of proportional representation. In 1978 the PDS received eighteen seats with a little over 18 percent of the vote. Since then, the National Assembly has been an increasingly vigorous forum for debate and is often televised. In 1980 Senghor resigned, the first African president to retire while in good health and in full control of the government. The new president, Abdou Diouf, moved quickly to authorize anyone to organize a political party. The first new party to register was Cheikh Anta Diop's RND. The 1983 elections were contested by eight of the fourteen registered parties, though only five ran candidates for the presidency. More than half of the parties represent different Marxist-Leninist tendencies, but there is also a clustering of center-left parties and one conservative traditionalist party.

Thus, Abdou Diouf's Senegal operates in many ways like a liberal democracy. There is no prior censorship of the printed word. Speech, expression, assembly, and association are all free. People can organize what they wish, can write and say what they wish. Only in 1986 did the government bring in a press law that makes it possible to suspend publications not "abiding by ethics." As of July 1986 this law had not been used. The arena of debate in Dakar is a lively one, and even government-controlled media like the party newspaper, Le Soleil, and the television are open to a certain amount of dissent. Opposition parties do not get "equal time," nor do they find many advertisers willing to risk government displeasure by placing ads in opposition papers. The freedom is there, but within certain clear limitations.

The major limitation is that opposition political parties can compete in elections, but they cannot win. During the 1983 election, the most revolutionary parties freely campaigned in both rural and urban areas and were allocated time on television and radio. To the best of my knowledge, there was no harassment of opposition parties, even in rural areas.[16] There is little doubt that the government would have prevailed without fraud or coercion. Diouf was at the time enjoying a honeymoon with the intellectuals, largely because of the opening up of the political system. He seemed much more popular than Senghor had been. Nevertheless, on election day there was massive fraud. Electors did not need identification to vote. The ballot was not secret and irregularities were common. The result was a sweeping victory for Diouf's Socialist party, which took almost 80 percent of the votes in the legislative elections and over 83 percent in the presidential election. Only two of the opposition parties won seats in the Assembly, and total opposition strength declined to nine. Abdoulaye Wade's centrist PDS remained the major opposition party, but with less strength in the assembly. It is not clear what Diouf wanted, but the party hierarchy clearly was not going to take risks. Diouf was in many ways the loser. In relying on fraud, he lost the respect of many who expected more of him. I am also convinced that a stronger opposition in the National Assembly would have strengthened Diouf's hand in dealing with his own party. For example, the electoral law, which permitted fraud by not requiring identification, has not been changed. It is doubtful whether the next election will be any more honest than the last one.

FREEDOM OF EXPRESSION

There is no censorship in Senegal, though the regime's position in this area was tried by Senghor's relationship with novelist and filmmaker Ousmane Sembene. Sembene is the author of God's Bits of Wood, a passionate novel of working-class conflict, and the producer of a series of films which are biting social commentaries. The best known are Xala and Mandabi. Senghor and Sembene disagree radically on political questions and seem to dislike each other.

In spite of this, Sembene has had public money for his films and was not troubled by the state until he made *Ceddo* in 1977. *Ceddo* was denied a license, supposedly because of a disagreement on Wolof orthography, but probably because of its harsh picture of Senegal's marabouts. After Senghor retired, the film was eventually given its license, but by this time, many Senegalese had seen it and it created little fuss. Government support for Sembene and other film producers was partly an effort to create a film industry, but also undoubtedly an effort to shape that industry. Sembene, however, is irrepressible and probably incorruptible. Senghor also used to subsidize the publication of books, which forced often hostile writers and academics to apply to him for assistance. It is not clear whether this made the would-be clients more docile. It must have been a great disappointment to Senghor the poet and intellectual that his philosophical and cultural ideas had little support in his own country. Both the university and the arts community have been centers of opposition to Senghor and to the regime almost from the day of independence.

The absence of censorship did produce one amusing incident. In 1984 the French satirical weekly, *Le Canard Enchaîné*, published a story which suggested that Abdou Diouf's daughter, Fabienne, was involved in irregular import dealings. Without any review procedure, the newspaper was on the streets before anyone in the Ministry of Information knew about the story. As soon as it was read, an official in the Ministry hurried out to buy up all extant copies. By the time the day was over, photocopy machines all over the city had reproduced the story many times over; it was being sold on the streets, and was being passed from hand to hand. Censorship in Senegal has always been a bit absurd. From time to time, sales of *Le Monde* have been suspended, but so many members of Senegal's elite have subscriptions to it and other important French publications that censorship has always been a way of ensuring publicity.

HUMAN RIGHTS AND THE SYSTEM OF JUSTICE

Senegal seems a model of freedom of expression. Policing and law enforcement do not always, however, show the same respect for human rights. To be sure, no one in Senegal has ever been executed for a political crime, but detainees have been beaten in prison. Invasions of the university and handling of demonstrations have often been quite rough. The criminal code prohibits physical abuse, torture, and degrading treatment. Most observer groups think Senegal has been reasonably scrupulous except for occasional excesses in interrogation.[17]

The one disturbing case involves a separatist movement from the Casamance, the southernmost region of the country. Physically separated and culturally distinct—it was exposed to Islam late and lacked the hierarchical social and political structures of the rest of Senegal—the lower Casamance has always felt itself another country from Senegal and has been responsive to autonomists or separatist appeals. Riots in the Casamance in December 1982 led to the arrest of 148 persons. Preventive detention is permitted only when there is a threat of civil disturbance. In this case, there were continued disturbances, which justified holding the detainees. Eventually, 105 were tried, and in January 1986, 32 were convicted.[18] Many accused the police of torture and degrading treatment in prison. They charged beating, electric shocks, and in one case, mistreatment leading to an abortion.[19] Such a deviation from Senegalese norms probably reflects, first, the fact that the people of the Casamance are outside the dominant political community, and second, the fear that separatism in the Casamance would jeopardize hopes of eventually integrating into some kind of political and economic union the Gambia, an English-speaking country of about 600,000 people surrounded by Senegal.

ECONOMIC RIGHTS

In some ways the greatest limitation on human rights is an economic one. Human rights in Senegal have been very dependent on the ability of the state to provide a modern life-style for a growing elite. Those who own their Fiats are not likely to become a radical force, but the system cannot continue to absorb new people without economic growth. Furthermore, the people who have paid for this modern life-style are the peasants, workers, and fishermen. Human rights manifestos since World War II have increasingly spoken of freedom from want and the rights of peoples to a decent living. What is decent varies from place to place, but it is certain that many Senegalese are poor. Distribution of food has limited the impact of disastrous droughts, but even in the best years, most Senegalese peasants know a "hungry season" when their diet is short of both needed calories and vital proteins. In 1985 average daily caloric intake in Senegal was a little under 2,400 calories.[20] This is about what nutritionists recommend as a minimum, but some get more than the average and some get less. Few starve, but for most Senegalese, both in town and in the country, subsistence is achieved with difficulty.

They do have most of the commonly considered economic rights. People have the right to seek work, to own property, to organize, and to move. The right to strike was for a while severely limited, but liberalization in the late 1970s extended both to trade union organization and to the right to strike. From 1976, the government permitted the organization of unions not affiliated with the CNTS. The right to strike was subject to proper advance notification, but this requirement has not prevented strikes. The most important of the new unions has been SUDES, the teachers' union (Syndicat Unique et Démocrate des Enseignants de Sénégal). Grouping teachers from primary school up through university, it was for several years a more important center of opposition than any of the political parties. A series of teachers' strikes in 1979 led President Abdou Diouf to call a States-General of Education to review educational policy shortly after his inauguration in January 1981. The government could not meet many of the economic demands of the teachers, but it committed itself to phasing out foreign teachers, greater use of national languages, universal primary education, and a more practical curriculum.

There has been some social progress. Life expectancy went from 37 in 1957 to over 40 in 1965. In 1983 it was 44 for men and 47 for women.[21] The difference came largely from a drop in infant and child death. For children under age 1, mortality dropped from 172 per thousand in 1965 to 140 in 1983. For children from 1 to 4, it dropped from 42 to 28. Access to schools, to medical personnel, and to hospital beds increased significantly. In 1965 there were over 21,000 persons per doctor. In 1980 the figure was under 14,000.[22]

In the rural sector we see both the strengths of Senegal's commitment to human rights and its limitations. In the late 1960s there was an interesting experiment with peasant self-expression called Radio Paysanne. The idea, which originated with UNESCO, was to use the radio to stimulate community development. The program devoted several hours a week to dealing with peasant questions and complaints. The planners of the exercise were not aware how deep peasant grievances ran, and when this effort produced constant expressions of hostility to government policy, it was cancelled.[23] This means that at the national level, peasants have difficulty getting heard. Even at the local level, they are subject to greater coercion than city-dwellers, if only because rights cannot easily be guaranteed in the countryside. The traditional chiefs are gone. Now, local authority is exercised by a modern trained cadre of bureaucrats. They hold office not by hereditary right, as under the colonial regime, but as a result of education and training. Though they speak the language of human rights, they are often tempted to use strong-arm methods when they have problems, for example, with the collection of taxes or monies owed to cooperatives. The major issue was for many years the repayment by peasants of loans for the purchase of agricultural machinery. From time to time local administrators were removed or censured for using force to make peasants repay.

Development policy under Senghor centered on the creation of cooperatives and of a marketing board for peanuts. The cooperatives were very much government organisms. They were the major channel for rural credit, and they handled the major cash crop, peanuts. These peanuts were in turn sold to the marketing board. The original idea of the marketing board was to reduce fluctuations in price, but the effect has largely been to skim off a part of what has been a very thin surplus.[24] Peasants have often been hostile to the system, preferring when possible to sell their crops in the Gambia. Though the governing party is called the Socialist party, Diouf's government, pushed by the International Monetary Fund (IMF) and major aid donors, has made a strong commitment to a free market economy. The peanut marketing board has been dissolved, and major development projects have been redesigned to allow more room for local initiative. The removal of restraints seems to have been accompanied by a flowering of peasant initiative. Local groups are moving into new crops and developing projects to attract the wide range of nongovernmental aid organizations operating within Senegal. There is thus increasing economic freedom linked to the political liberalism of the technocrats around Diouf.

The expansion of the free market has, however, been accompanied by the withdrawal of the government from important development activities. The government is no longer providing seed advances, something the colonial government started during the first years of the twentieth century. It is also not providing credit for fertilizers, pesticides, and agricultural machinery. The result has been a process of technological regression. Fewer and fewer peasants are using plows, seeders, or fertilizer. Faced by increasing stagnation in a peasant sector unable to pay for its own modernization, Senegal is increasingly turning to private capital. In the Senegal river area, the completion of the Ndama dam has led to the expropriation of lands soon to be increased in value by irrigation and the award of these lands to outsiders, many of them powerful Wolof marabouts. Diouf's free market policies could backfire if their effect is only to increase the gap between the rich and the poor in rural areas.

This policy has been furthered by an economic stabilization plan imposed by the IMF. Like many Third World countries, Senegal borrowed heavily and not always wisely when the world economy was growing and was caught out when prices dropped. Its problems were compounded by high oil prices, low prices for peanuts on the world market, and intermittent drought. It was forced to accept an IMF austerity plan in 1980. This plan foundered on two bad harvests, which reduced exports and increased the public debt. Thus, Senegal found itself forced to accept an even tighter plan, which involves drastic cuts in public expenditure, in particular, a hiring freeze, higher food prices, and the sale or closing of money-losing parastatals (government-owned enterprises). Embassies abroad have been closed, and expenditures have been tightly controlled. One result has been increasing unemployment among university graduates, even in programs like medicine, which led to guaranteed employment up to 1984. Graduates of the École Normale Supérieure, the secondary schoolteachers college, were also guaranteed jobs, but that is no longer true. Bad as the situation is for university graduates, it is worse for school-leavers. Crime is increasing as younger males become frustrated with the absence of opportunity.

It is this economic stagnation that restricts the government and threatens the human rights situation. In 1985 a coalition of five opposition parties, the Alliance Démocratique Sénégalaise, was formed with Abdoulaye Bathily as chairman. In August they planned a demonstration in opposition to apartheid. The planned demonstration was denied authorization, probably because the proposed line of march went past the largest market in the city. The government seems to have feared that the demonstration might grow into something larger. The opposition decided to go ahead with its plans. When they did so, Bathily, Abdoulaye Wade of the PDS, and a series of opposition leaders were arrested. They were detained and charged, but all were released when a judge found that there was no case against them. It was Bathily's sixth arrest. Even after he was released, his phone line was disconnected and friends abroad were unable to call in. The minister of justice responsible for the arrests was fired as a result of his actions. The incident was a brief one, but it made clear that human rights are still rather fragile. It is quite probable that the real reason for the government's nervousness was social tensions exacerbated by the IMF's austerity plan. Young people are growing bitter as they face an uncertain future. In 1984 there was a long student strike in Dakar which failed in part because the government had nothing to give students worried about their future. The government is no longer committed to hiring either graduates of the medical school or of the teachers college. Even those groups who once felt secure no longer do so.

CONCLUSION

Bathily is only one of several able opposition leaders. In many countries, any one of them would be dead or in exile. Senegal can tolerate Bathily, Wade, and Cheikh Anta Diop only so long as it can maintain stability and guarantee most groups within the society a secure, if not comfortable, existence. Senegal's greatest accomplishment has been to build a relatively free society in a stagnant economy. Whether that free society can indefinitely stand the strains of a stagnant economy remains to be seen. The rights enjoyed by Senegalese are fragile both because the government can take back much of what it has given and because social tensions could erode the progress that has been made. The men who run Senegal seem to be committed to human rights, a commitment that reflects the values of their society and of their social class. They have also, however, been men concerned with creating a new political order and with holding on to power.

Human rights are always fragile. A quarter century of Senegalese history underlines that. Power has its temptations. Those who have power can often convince themselves that they must put aside first principles in order to keep power or to prevent disorder. As Senegal's rulers have grown more sure of themselves, they have made greater concessions, and yet, when the situation demands it, those concessions can be withdrawn. For the moment, Senegal is one of the freest societies in Africa. Clearly, most Senegalese would like to keep it that way.

NOTES

I would like to thank Abdoulaye Bathily, Samba Ka, and Donal Cruise O'Brien for their comments on an earlier version of this article.

1. Kaye Whiteman, "Senegal. The Problems of Opposition," *West Africa* 3570 (1986): 238–39.

2. Vincent Monteil, *L'Islam Noir* (Paris: Editions du Seuil, 1964); Jean Copans, *Les Marabouts de l'Arachide* (Paris: Le Sycomore, 1980); Christian Coulon, *Le marabout et le Prince. Islam et pouvoir au Sénégal* (Paris: Pedone, 1981).

3. H. O. Idowu, "Assimilation in Nineteenth Century Senegal," *Cahiers d'Études Africaines* 9 (1969): 194–218; H. O. Idowu, "The Establishment of Elective Institutions

in Senegal, 1869–1880," *Journal of African History* 9 (1969): 261–77; G. Wesley Johnson. *The Emergence of Black Politics in Senegal: The Struggle for Power in the Four Communes 1900–1920* (Stanford: Stanford University Press, 1971).

4. Johnson, *Emergence*.

5. Martin A. Klein, *Islam and Imperialism in Senegal, Sine-Saloum 1847–1914* (Stanford: Stanford University Press, 1968), 214–16.

6. The World Bank *World Development Report*, (New York 1985), Table 25, p. 222.

7. *United Nations Statistical Yearbook* (New York: United Nations), 1982.

8. *Economist Intelligence Unit*.

9. *Economist Intelligence Unit*; *World Development Report, 1986* (Washington, D.C.: World Bank, 1986).

10. Irving L. Markowitz, *Léopold Sédar Senghor and the Politics of Negritude* (New York: Atheneum, 1969); Jacques Hymans. *Léopold Sédar Senghor. An intellectual biography* (Edinburgh: Edinburgh University Press, 1971).

11. Jonathan Barker, "Political Factionalism in Senegal," *Canadian Journal of African Studies* 7 (1973): 287–303; Clement Cottingham, "Political Consolidation and Centre-Local Relations in Senegal," *Canadian Journal of African Studies* 4 (1970): 101–120.

12. The major actors in the 1962 drama are mostly retired and, in some cases, still anxious to justify their behavior. As a result, a debate has begun in press and memoirs about what actually happened.

13. Pierre Biarnes, *L'Afrique aux africains: 20 ans d'independence en Afrique Noire Francophone* (Paris: Armand Colin, 1980); Sheldon Gellar, *Animation Rurale and Rural Development: The Experience of Senegal* (Ithaca: Cornell Rural Development Committee, 1980).

14. Sheldon Gellar, *Annimation Rurale*; Donal Cruise O'Brien, "Ruling Class and Peasantry in Senegal, 1960–1976," in *The Political Economy of Underdevelopment: Dependence in Senegal*, ed. Rita Cruise O'Brien (Beverly Hills: Sage, 1979); Edward J. Schumacher, *Politics, Bureaucracy and Rural Development in Senegal* (Berkeley: University of California Press, 1975).

15. Ibrahima Fall, *Sous-dévelopement et démocratie multipartisme. L'expérience sénégalaise* (Dakar: Nouvelles Editions Africaines, 1977).

16. Donal B. Cruise O'Brien, "Senegal's Elections. What went wrong?" *West Africa* 3423, 21 March 1983.

17. Amnesty International, *Annual Reports*; U.S. State Department, *Country Reports on Human Rights for 1983*.

18. *Africa Contemporary Record*, 16 (1985): B540–542.

19. These charges were made in an opposition paper, *Fagaru*, January 14, 1986, and April 15, 1986.

20. *World Development Report*, 1985, Table 24, 220.

21. *World Development Report*, 1985, Table 23, 218.

22. *World Development Report*, 1985, Table 23, 218 and Table 24, 220.

23. Cruise O'Brien, "Ruling Class," p. 221.

24. Schumacher, *Politics* Chap. 4–8; Cruise O'Brien, "Ruling Class," pp. 218–25.

SUGGESTED READINGS

Biarnes, Pierre. *L'Afrique aux africains: 20 ans d'indépendance en Afrique Noire Francophone*. Paris: Armand Colin, 1980.

Copans, Jean. *Les Marabouts de l'Arachide, la confrérie mouride et les paysans du Sénégal*. Paris: Le Sycomore, 1980.

Coulon, Christian. *Le marabout et le Prince. Islam et pouvoir au Sénégal*. Paris: Pedone, 1981.

Cruise O'Brien, Donal. *Saints and Politicians: Essays in the Organization of a Senegalese Peasant Society*. London: Cambridge University Press, 1975.

Cruise O'Brien, Rita, ed. *The Political Economy of Underdevelopment: Dependence in Senegal*. Beverly Hills: Sage, 1979.

Dia, Mamadou. *Mémoire d'un Militant du Tiers Monde*. Paris: Publisud, 1985.

Diagne, Pathe. *Senegal: Crise Économique et Sociale et Devenir de la Démocratie*. Dakar: Sankore, 1984.

Fall, Ibrahima. *Sous-développement et démocratie multipartisme. L'experience sénégalaise*. Dakar: Nouvelles Editions Africaines, 1977.

Gellar, Sheldon. *Senegal. An African Nation Between Islam and the West*. Boulder, Col.: Westview Press, 1982.

Idowu, H. O. "Assimilation in Nineteenth Century Senegal." *Cahiers d'Études Africaines* 9 (1969): 194–218.

Markowitz, Irving L. *Léopold Sédar Senghor and the Politics of Negritude*. New York: Atheneum, 1969.

Schumacher, Edward J. *Politics, Bureaucracy and Rural Development in Senegal*. Berkeley: University of California Press, 1975.

16

SOUTH AFRICA

Frederick Johnstone

South Africa is one of the worst cases of human rights violation in the world today. The majority of its people have been thoroughly deprived of basic human rights by a system of racial domination which has been in place for a long time and which is still very much in existence today. While no country has a perfect human rights record, the South African system is a gross and extreme violation of human rights, which has been universally condemned for its constitutional and institutional denial of rights on the basis of race. In a world in which international consensus is rare, it is a significant fact that there is not a single country anywhere which approves of this system.

Defining the human rights problem in South Africa is thus initially a fairly simple matter. It is the racial system, which is, in its structure and consequences, a fundamental violation of all basic human rights. But this system is a human rights problem in different ways. And as a complex problem, it has correspondingly complex implications for social change and for human rights.

The concern here, therefore, is first of all to give a concise account of the main elements of the human rights problem in South Africa. How and why did the racial system develop, and what of current trends? In what ways is it a system of human rightlessness, for what reasons and with what consequences? I shall then conclude with some discussion of the complexity of the problem in relation to different approaches to social justice and to the future outlook for human rights in South Africa.

THE RACIAL SYSTEM: DOMINATION, EXPLOITATION, AND REPRESSION

What exists in South Africa today is a system of white supremacy, in which a minority of about 5 million whites (15 percent of the population) dominates a majority of about 28 million blacks (85 percent of the population). The black population is made up of an African majority (about 24 million, 74 percent of the population), and a small group of Coloureds (about 2.8 million, 9 percent of the population) and of Asians (about a million, 3 percent of the population). This system is ultimately the result of the colonial conquest and settlement of Africa by European peoples equipped with superior military and economic power and propelled by the acquisitive commerce of early capitalism. In South Africa this process occurred between the seventeenth and nineteenth centuries. The often-debated question of "who was where first" is irrelevant to the question of what actually happened between whites and blacks. What happened was that whites subjugated blacks and gradually established a system of white supremacy. The development of the diamond and gold mining industries in the late nineteenth century launched South Africa into a process of industrialization and modernization which has produced the most advanced economy and the most modernized society in Africa. So, too, was the racial system modernized, as the whites consolidated their power and harnessed the system to the modern economy. A system of "segregation" was formalized after World War I, and this was continued and further modernized as "apartheid" after World War II.[1]

Apartheid was thus simply a new stage of an older system. South Africa's white population has been divided into two main groups—the English and the Afrikaners (descendants of the original Dutch settlers). Historically, the Afrikaners were a more economically and culturally insecure group than the English, and Afrikaner nationalism developed in resistance to English power, British imperialism, and the threat of black power. Its strategy was to use political power and the state to further Afrikaner economic and cultural interests. It was already doing this in the 1920s and 1930s, but the Nationalists (the Afrikaner political party) finally won a majority government in 1948 with their ideology of apartheid (an Afrikaner word meaning "separateness").[2] Responding to white fears about the integration possibilities of postwar urbanization, apartheid was a promise to retain and extend white supremacy. This is precisely what the new government did during the 1950s and 1960s, efficiently and ruthlessly. Racial domination was modernized; the economy boomed; resistance was smashed. However, growing internal and external pressures for change during the 1970s and 1980s (notably an explosion of black unrest in 1976) led to a new reformism by the Botha government (in power since 1978). This has combined some limited reform with continuing apartheid and repression. But this "neo-apartheid" has not succeeded in defusing these pressures, which have since 1984 reached a quite unprecedented level, and may well augur some kind of more fundamental change.[3]

Why all this happened in South Africa, and what it signifies, have been a matter of much debate. The conventional view for a long time was that this was essentially a cultural problem of racism and nationalism, generated by South Africa's ethnic diversity, but increasingly obsolete in South Africa's modern capitalist economy. For this liberal view, the problem was that the state had been taken over by racist-nationalist Afrikaners, whose apartheid program was intent on preserving the traditional system of white supremacy. This was, however, impossible in an advanced economy, for capitalism and industrialism were "color blind" and universalistic, incompatible with (and thus subversive of) an "archaic" and ascriptive racial system. The "rational economy" was thus undermining the "irrational polity." Economic integration was "making nonsense of apartheid." Economic growth would mean political liberalization, and was thus to be encouraged by all means, including foreign investment.[4]

This liberal view of South Africa's "race relations" problem reached its peak in the economic boom of the 1960s. The paradox of the 1960s, however, was that South Africa's impressive economic growth had been accompanied not by liberalization but by intensification of racial domination. This paradox did not go unnoticed. In fact, it gave rise to a whole new way of looking at South Africa. Perhaps this was not so paradoxical after all, it was now argued. Perhaps what it meant was that capitalism and racial domination were actually quite compatible. More than that, perhaps, it meant that racial discrimination had been and still was highly beneficial for capitalist profits, as a means of intensifying the control and exploitation of black labor.[5] Racial domination thus came to be seen not as some kind of irrational cultural invasion of an innocent and progressive economic system, but rather as an exploitative tool for different white class interests in this system. The basic rationale of racial discrimination, it was now argued, was the super-exploitation of black labor.[6] And apartheid, far from being an archaic antithesis of modern times, was actually a pragmatic modernization of domination and exploitation.[7]

This class analysis of racial domination (as developed in the 1970s and 1980s) has thus provided us with a fuller picture of South African development.[8] While the old liberal view recognized the problem of domination, the new class analysis linked this to the problem of exploitation, and these are the two key aspects of the racial system as a human rights problem. Political domination it has certainly been. But this has not simply been some kind of free-floating by-product of cultural forces. It has had basic economic dimensions.

South African development is thus essentially a story of domination and exploitation. But it is, as well, a story of resistance and repression. The racial system has always been rejected and opposed by its victims, and the institutional violation of human rights has been accompanied by a more active abuse of human rights in the government's historic and continuing repression of this resistance.

This, then, is our main concern here: the human rights problem in South Africa as a problem of domination, exploitation, and repression. While it is generally correct to equate South Africa's human rights problem with the "racial system," to understand this so-called racial problem we need to know about its substantive elements in their historical and contemporary context.

DOMINATION: WHITE POWER AND BLACK RIGHTLESSNESS

The human rights problem in South Africa is first of all an issue of civil and political rights. The racial system has been a massive violation of the basic rights of individuals to participate freely in society as equals before the law. Political domination through a racial franchise is the most serious and obvious aspect of this restriction of civil freedoms. But as a sweeping system of discrimination and segregation, apartheid has curtailed such freedoms in many other areas as well.

Whites getting power over blacks first of all involved excluding blacks from basic political rights. But in dividing up political power unequally along racial lines, the whites went one step further and divided up the land as well. What thus occurred in South Africa is not just a racialization of human rights but a territorialization of racial rights. Racial domination has meant a fusion of vertical and horizontal forms of racial discrimination, in which whites have monopolized both political power and physical territory.

The vertical/political side of this has been the formal exclusion of blacks from the political system. As white settlers conquered and settled South Africa, they curtailed black political rights, and blacks were excluded from the franchise by the constitution when South Africa became a self-governing dominion in 1910 (with the exception of limited franchise rights for Africans and Coloreds in the Cape Province, which were abolished in 1936/1960 and the 1950s respectively).[9] This has continued up to the present. Apartheid is a system of white political supremacy based on the constitutional denial of the franchise to the black majority.

The horizontal/territorial side has been the attachment of racial rights to territory through a double system of racial segregation: a macro/territorial division of South Africa into different racial areas, and a micro/residential segregation of racial groups living and working within the white areas. With its monopoly of political power in the new Union of South Africa, the white group set about defining most of South Africa as a "white area." The white minority generously gave itself exclusive ownership of 87 percent of the land, while "reserving" the rest for the African majority. This territorial division was supplemented by a system of residential segregation, limiting black rights of residence, movement, property, work, and local government within the urban areas. Territorial separation was formalized by the 1913 Natives Land Act and the 1936 Natives Trust and Land Act, and residential segregation by the 1923 Natives Urban Areas Act. This segregation system included measures to enforce it, known as the pass laws, which controlled black movement to, from, and within the white areas. The pass laws restricted the right of blacks to remain in urban areas without employment, forced blacks to carry identification documents known as passes, and subjected blacks to penal sanctions for pass offenses. This all amounted to the most complex system of segregation and internal movement control in the modern world. The Urban Areas Act alone has justly been described as "one of the most complex pieces of control legislation ever devised anywhere."[10]

This distinctive combination of political-cum-territorial discrimination was revitalized and relegitimized by apartheid after 1948, both structurally and ideologically. Structurally, as a use of power to structure power, apartheid meant a further curtailment of basic civil rights, through a general consolidation of discrimination and segregation. This vigorous recommitment to white supremacy was immediately symbolized by hard-line measures which, among other things, enforced the official classification of all individuals by racial group (the 1950 Population Registration Act), criminalized interracial marriage and sex (the 1949 Prohibition of Mixed Marriages Act and the 1957 Immorality Act), tightened up on social segregation and movement control (the 1950 Group Areas Act, the 1953 Reservation of Separate Amenities Act, the 1952 Bantu Abolition of Passes and Coordination of Documents Act), and criminalized political opposition to the system (the 1950 Suppression of Communism Act).

Ideologically, apartheid set out to relegitimize racial domination in terms more acceptable to a now decolonizing world that was more concerned with human rights and democracy. The old system of segregation, insofar as it ever had to be justified in an era of colonialism and racism, was rather passively accompanied by paternalistic ideas of trusteeship. Apartheid was a more dynamic attempt to redefine human rightlessness as social justice, by redefining the old "segregation" as "separate development," by redefining (through the 1959 Promotion of Bantu Self-Government Act) the old "Reserves" as "Bantustans" and "ethnic homelands" on the way to "self-determination" and "independence," and by thus positively redefining the problem of black rightlessness in the white areas as an issue of black rights in the black areas. Apartheid has thus been a kind of Orwellian project of denying human rights in the name of human rights.

Far from being an archaic throwback to traditionalism, apartheid was thus a pragmatic attempt to adapt and justify the old system in the more modern postwar world. This process of pragmatic domination has, in the 1970s and 1980s, been continued by a neo-apartheid strategy that, while making certain concessions, has maintained the basic structure of political domination. The Botha government's constitutional reforms of 1983–1984 (which gave some limited and separate parliamentary representation to Indians and Coloureds) made no change whatsoever to the constitutional status of the African majority. And although the government is continuing to announce certain political reforms, as long as these do not include enfranchising the African majority, the basic apartheid system of domination remains in place. And Africans were further excluded politically by being deprived of South African citizenship. As part of the separate development strategy, the 1970 Black Homelands Citizenship Act defined "homeland independence" as entailing loss of South African citizenship, and by 1983, with the "independence" of four "homelands," about nine million blacks had been thus decitizenized into "foreign aliens."

In this distinctive fusion of vertical and horizontal forms of discrimination, apartheid has meant the systematic and extreme curtailment of basic civil and political rights. Apartheid is a gross violation of the rights of individuals to participate fully and freely in society as equals before the law. In its constitutional exclusion of the black majority from political rights, it is an outright and explicit system of political domination—what one human rights analyst has referred to as "a pigmentocracy in which all political power is vested in a white oligarchy."[11] But this is merely one part of the many-sided "law of apartheid," in which "the individual's political, social and economic status in society is dependent on the racial group . . . to which he belongs."[12]

EXPLOITATION: WHITE WEALTH AND BLACK POVERTY

Black civil and political rightlessness has had important socioeconomic functions and consequences. As a system of domination, the racial system has been targeted against black workers in particular. And this systematic violation of black labor rights has, in turn, produced a pattern of white wealth and black poverty which is in itself an affront to social justice.

What developed in South Africa was a labor-repressive economy, in which powerful white class interests used racial discrimination not only to make blacks workers but also to make black workers highly exploitable. Segregation had already racialized the class structure, by denying blacks ownership and commercial rights in most of South Africa, thus forcing blacks into employee rather than employer roles. But racial discrimination was also used to keep black labor cheap by curbing black labor rights (both horizontally, over movement, and vertically, over trade unions).

By restricting the free movement of blacks and denying many of them permanent residence rights outside the reserves, segregation and the pass laws led to a migrant labor system which helped to depress black wages and to exclude black families from the benefits of the white economy. Employers benefited from the weak bargaining power of a transitory and insecure labor force kept under tight control by the pass laws, as well as from the contribution of the subsistence economy of the reserves to the social costs of black labor. Developed on a large scale first, and for these reasons, by the mining companies, the migrant labor system became more widely generalized by the famous doctrine of Stallardism (after the then Minister of Native Affairs, and in terms of which the 1923 Urban Areas Act was justified), that blacks should only be allowed in the urban areas on a temporary basis as workers for whites.[13] A major thrust of apartheid was to reinforce this basic idea in the more complex postwar economy, by tightening up the whole "influx control" system (as the pass laws came to be called) and pushing ahead with "separate development." This has meant, since 1960, about 10 million influx control arrests, the forcible resettlement of about 3.5 million "surplus" (i.e., nonworking) black residents in the white areas to the homelands, and a black labor force in the white areas which is still, in the 1980s, about 50 percent migrant labor of one kind or another.[14]

But the cheapness of black labor was most directly secured by restricting the trade union rights of black workers. Most significant here was the criminalization of black strikes (by the Master and Servant Laws, which subjected black workers to penal sanctions for breach of contract) and the exclusion of black workers from basic trade union rights in the legal industrial relations system established from the 1920s onwards (notably by the Industrial Conciliation Act of 1924, as further amended since 1948).

Increasing pressures for change in the 1970s, notably the resurgence of black labor unrest as of 1973, generated certain labor reforms. The recommendations, at the end of the 1970s, of two important commissions on labor issues, one dealing with the more vertical side of discrimination (the Wiehahn Commission on trade union and employment rights) and the other dealing with the more horizontal side (the Riekert Commission on movement and residence rights), led to some liberalization of the residence and bargaining rights of urban black workers, as part of the Botha government's neo-apartheid strategy of stabilization through limited reform. Thus black trade unions were given the right to participate in the legal industrial relations system.

But the violation of black labor rights has continued despite such legal reforms, because the latter have not been accompanied by a more general liberalization of civil and political rights, and because of the continuing repression of black trade unionism in practice. As the International Labour Organization (ILO) has pointed out about South Africa, "freedom of association . . . is not established by mere legislative change; if it is to be genuine it must be accompanied by the will to allow it to function and by the removal of constraints."[15] But instead, there has been a continuing "use of police and penal sanctions in labor disputes," with the police being called into black labor disputes on an average of about once every two days during the first half of the 1980s.[16] Union leaders have been arrested (and some have died in detention); union meetings have been banned or curtailed under various sweeping security laws; black workers have been charged with illegal striking and have been fired and deported.[17] And this repression reflects the wider fact that, as the ILO has observed, the labor reforms "have not changed the apartheid system, with its widespread effects on the labor and social fields; they merely occur within it."[18] The ILO has thus concluded that "trade unionism in South Africa is not allowed to function in accordance with the principles of genuine freedom of association. The government continues, on the one hand, . . . to create an impression of normal labor administration whilst, on the other, employing security and other non-labor legislation to supervise and harass both unions and their members."[19] Likewise, the April 1986 abolition of the pass laws in favor of a policy of "orderly urbanization" seemed, in keeping with neo-apartheid strategy, to be leading simply to more indirect and less overtly discriminatory movement control rather than to genuine freedom of movement.

South Africa's black workers have thus historically been denied basic trade union and movement rights, and they remain highly exploitable despite recent neo-apartheid reforms. This labor-repressive system has greatly strengthened the power of whites over blacks in the distribution of wealth. It thus underlies, and is most clearly visible in, another distinctive feature of the apartheid system: white wealth and black poverty.

This economic inequality stems directly from the labor market, in the form of low black wages and high black unemployment, and more indirectly from a racialized welfare state and a racialized class structure, which have channeled most public spending to whites and confined most blacks to lower-class positions.

A super-exploitable black labor force has meant that black wages have always been very low, both absolutely and relative to white earnings, and have been kept low over long periods of time. Thus, for example, the real wages of black workers in the gold mines in the 1960s were no higher than in 1910.[20] While the unrest of the 1970s did lead to certain wage improvements (such as a tripling of black mine wages), such gains have been of minor significance. In the first place, the rate of improvement has been very slow. The ILO, which has systematically monitored the racial inequality of income in South Africa in recent years, has calculated that between 1970 and 1983 black wages as a percentage of white wages grew at an average annual rate of only about one percent, and that at this rate it would take about one hundred years to close the racial wage gap.[21] Second, not all blacks receive wages. A major problem in South Africa is the very high level of black unemployment, recently estimated at over four million (between a third and a half of the black labor force).[22]

The problem of low black wages and high black unemployment has been compounded by the highly unequal government spending of the "apartheid welfare state." The South African government's per capita spending on health, education, and welfare has been far higher for the white minority than for the black majority. Thus in the 1984–1985 budget allocation for child welfare payments, about R80 million of the total R210 million went to whites as compared to R7 million for Africans in the white areas.[23] And decitizenization has disentitled "homeland citizens" to South African unemployment insurance. The ILO has thus concluded that the South African welfare system makes "little or no contribution to the alleviation of black poverty."[24]

Government spending in South Africa's segregated education system has been notoriously inequitable. For decades, most of the annual education budget has gone to white education, and average per pupil spending has thus always been much higher for whites than for blacks. Thus in the education budget for 1984–1985, about 50 percent was allocated to the white minority, and per capita educational spending for whites was about seven times higher than for Africans (R1,654 as compared to R234).[25] It is a well-established fact that black educational facilities and opportunities are grossly inferior to those of the white minority. Thus the pupil-teacher ratio in 1984 was 41:1 for Africans as compared to 19:1 for whites.[26]

This educational apartheid, as combined with direct discrimination in employment itself, has had serious structural consequences for black educational and occupational attainment. It has confined blacks to low positions within the class system. In the early 1980s, according to South Africa's own National Manpower Commission, about 85 percent of the black population had received no education beyond primary school as compared to only 2 percent of the white population.[27] In 1983, 51 percent of African school-leavers were illiterate or semiliterate, and it is estimated that about 70 percent of adult Africans in South Africa are illiterate.[28] And there is a correspondingly unequal distribution of the racial groups in South Africa's occupational structure, with virtually no blacks in higher-level positions and virtually no whites in lower-level positions.[29]

While reproduced by educational apartheid, this racialized occupational structure also reflects nearly a century of racial discrimination in employment. Beginning with the mining revolution at the turn of the century, white workers, in response to black labor competition and white racism, secured a "job color bar" keeping blacks out of skilled work, which was entrenched in law and generalized throughout the economy.[30] While this statutory discrimination was abolished in 1979 (with the exception of the mining industry), decades of such discrimination in employment have racialized the occupational structure, and informal discrimination still persists. Thus it is forecast that by 1987, 70 percent of apprentices will still be white and only 7 percent African, and the ILO has concluded that at the current rate of black apprenticeship, it would take about a century to close this occupational gap.[31] And the basic point remains that educational discrimination continues to racialize the class structure despite the abolition of statutory discrimination in employment.

This extreme violation of black educational and employment rights has thus had very serious structural consequences. Educational and occupational apartheid has effectively reproduced racial inequality within the class structure itself, with all the distributive consequences implied by that. This racialization of the occupational structure has meant the "classization" of racial inequality, such that the problems of black poverty and black unemployment now become independently caused by low class position in itself, irrespective of the persistence or abolition of statutory racial discrimination.

In these various direct and indirect ways, then, apartheid has meant a very unequal distribution of wealth. For the whites, it has meant one of the highest average living standards in the world. At the end of the 1970s, 64 percent of national income went to the white 15 percent of the population, while 26 percent went to the African 74 percent of the population.[32] In 1984 the whites enjoyed an average household income which, at R1,834 per month, was nearly seven times higher than the average African monthly household income of R273, and in 1980 African per capita income was only 10 percent of white per capita income.[33] For white business it has meant high profits, with average net profits in the early 1980s considerably higher than those in the Western democracies.[34] For white farmers it has meant American-level incomes, rising during the last decade, as compared to lower real wages for black farm workers in 1980 than in 1960.[35] And for blacks it has meant poverty. That black poverty is a serious and growing problem has recently been confirmed by the largest and most thorough inquiry ever made in South Africa into this issue—the Second Carnegie Inquiry into Poverty and Development in Southern Africa. Its major finding was that, in the words of its director, "there is poverty all over South Africa" and that "it is really in the rural areas that it is most acute."[36] Its research estimated that by 1980, 81 percent of black families in the homelands (about nine million people) still fell below the national "minimum living level," and that the percentage of destitute homeland families, receiving no income of any kind, had increased to 13 percent (from 5 percent in 1960).[37]

The human reality of this economic inequality and black poverty is one of enormous human suffering, as babies and children die from or are stunted by acute malnutrition; as millions of blacks lack food, water, clothing, and shelter in Africa's most advanced economy; and as black families are forced to endure the separations and torments of South Africa's oppressive migrant labor system.[38] One quarter of all African wives are separated from their husbands; one-third of African children under the age of fourteen are victims of severe malnutrition; and the African infant mortality rate is one of the highest in the world (80 per 1,000 live births in 1982 as compared to 13 for whites, and estimated to be as high as 30–50 percent in some rural areas).[39]

Economically, apartheid has thus meant wealth for whites and poverty for blacks. It is a systematic violation not only of the civil and political rights of blacks but also of their social and economic rights—of their labor, educational, employment, and subsistence rights. It has kept black labor cheap, and it has ensured that the benefits of economic growth have gone to the white minority at the expense of the black majority. And this is what the racial system was essentially designed to do. The whites did not seize power by accident, nor have they resisted giving it up for so long because of anxieties about "ethnic identity." The whites have used power to pursue privilege. Domination has been geared to exploitation.

REPRESSION: STATE COERCION OF HUMAN RIGHTS STRUGGLES

This system of domination and exploitation was never simply accepted by South Africa's blacks. As it evolved, so too did formal and informal kinds of resistance to it, both from blacks and from some whites as well. This resistance was met with repression rather than reform. This repression of human rights struggles continues unabated in South Africa today, and constitutes a significant human rights problem in itself, as civilians have been arrested, imprisoned, tortured, and killed for attempting to exercise basic rights of political expression.

South African history has been an intensifying cycle of resistance and repression, in which each has produced more of the other. Resistance developed gradually during the early decades of the twentieth century. The exclusion of blacks from political and labor rights in the new Union of South Africa of 1910 led to the formation of the South African Native National Congress (now known as the African National Congress, or ANC, the main opposition movement, banned since 1960), to unite blacks in a struggle for a democratic society. It also led to sporadic black labor unrest in the workplace and black protests against such hated symbols of the system as the pass laws. The Congress remained rather ineffectual for various reasons, such as its commitment to gradualist liberal ideas of moral persuasion rather than to more militant and socialist ideas of direct action and revolutionary struggle. But the political balance began to change during and after World War II, as a younger generation of black leaders turned to more radical ideas and tactics, at a time of intensifying urban-industrial change and class conflict (e.g., the 1946 mine workers strike) and growing international emphasis on democracy and human rights.[40]

Apartheid was in part a response to this changing political situation, and in turn generated a new cycle of resistance and repression. Apartheid gave new teeth to "state security." Yet nationalist and socialist resistance increased during the 1950s and early 1960s, with the rise of an interracial Congress movement and growing civilian unrest. Government repression, as symbolized in particular by the Sharpeville massacre of 1960 (in which sixty-nine peaceful black protesters were shot by police), led to underground revolutionary resistance. But this was also smashed by the government, and resistance leaders, like ANC leader Nelson Mandela, were sentenced to life imprisonment. The 1970s saw a resurgence of resistance, which now took less conventional and less controllable forms (such as grass-roots worker and student activism, and a cultural "black consciousness" movement). This was effective enough to generate the neo-apartheid reforms. But the very limited nature of these reforms, together with continued repression, has further intensified this resistance, leading to the current phase of unrest (which began in 1984, in protest against the constitutional reforms which excluded Africans) and which is the most serious challenge yet made to white supremacy in South Africa.

As a human rights problem, apartheid is thus, in addition to everything else, a police state system. Apartheid has meant the deployment and enforcement of what are probably the most sweeping state security measures anywhere in the world. Like other parts of apartheid, these have become so extensive and complex as to defy any simple account. Foremost among these are the 1950 Suppression of Communism Act, the 1960 Unlawful Organizations Act, the 1962 General Law Amendment Act, the 1967 Terrorism Act, and the 1982 Internal Security Act. These have defined communism, terrorism, subversion, and treason in such sweeping ways as to criminalize virtually any kind of opposition to the system, including peaceful protest and dissent. And the South African government has used this power ruthlessly in the last thirty years to suppress attempts to change the system.[41]

This repression has taken various forms. It has meant a continuing process of political detention: the arrest and imprisonment of leadership figures in the resistance movement for "political subversion" as very broadly defined by the various security laws, notably the 1982 Internal Security Act.[42] Between 1961 and 1981 nearly 5,000 people were convicted of political offenses. And the unrest since 1984 has been accompanied by a new wave of political arrests, notably of leaders of the United Democratic Front (a loose federation of opposition groups which is now the main unbanned opposition movement in South

Africa) and of black trade unions. Over 1,000 activists were detained in 1984, and over 1,300 in the first two weeks of the seven-month state of emergency declared in July 1985 (leading Amnesty International to conclude that "the scale of detentions under the state of emergency is staggering").[43] And over 10,000 such arrests were made during another state of emergency declared in June 1986 (the tenth anniversary of the 1976 student uprising in the black township of Soweto).

It has also meant the persecution and violent suppression of popular protest and labor unrest. Public meetings have been banned, and peaceful protesters have been shot and killed, and detained without trial, by the police and by the army (which as of 1984 has been performing police functions of social control). Over five hundred blacks were killed in the 1976 unrest. The more recent massacres at Uitenhage in March 1985 (twenty blacks killed), and Mamelodi in November 1985 (twelve blacks killed), are merely the more dramatic instances of what is in reality a continuing daily process of state terror designed to crush and intimidate public popular opposition to apartheid.

And it has meant the torture and murder of prisoners. There have been widespread and well-substantiated allegations of physical and psychological ill-treatment of prisoners. The United Nations has repeatedly found "numerous instances of prolonged and intensive interrogation, sometimes by successive teams of interrogators and sometimes for periods extending over several days . . . involving methods of torture relating to physical and psychological abuse."[44] Likewise Amnesty International has found "considerable evidence to show that political detainees in South Africa have commonly been tortured and physically assaulted," and that "methods of torture and ill-treatment have reportedly included electric shocks, hooding and partial suffocation, beatings, pulling of hair from the body, sleep deprivation and exposure to severe cold."[45] A number of such detainees, such as Black Consciousness student leader Steve Biko, white activist Neil Agget, and black trade unionist Andries Raditsela, have died while in police custody in circumstances which undoubtedly point to such torture. South Africa also has the highest rate of state executions in the world, with over one thousand people hanged since 1968, virtually all blacks.

This ongoing repression of human rights struggles is thus another important dimension of the human rights problem in South Africa. As a systematic violation of human rights, apartheid has generated an intensifying dialectic of resistance and repression, in which human rights have been even further abused by direct and indirect forms of state terror. This repression has increased since 1984 in response to a new escalation of resistance provoked by the meaninglessness of neo-apartheid reforms. Neo-apartheid has been a pragmatic attempt to reconstitute domination in a less coercive form in new historical conditions in which the mass of the people can less easily be kept in line by the old hard-line methods. But these methods are still very much in use, and since 1984 hundreds of blacks, including children and babies, have been shot to death by the white forces of law and order.

LIBERATION: THE FUTURE OF HUMAN RIGHTS IN SOUTH AFRICA

These, then, are the basic elements of the human rights problem in South Africa: domination, exploitation, repression. The whole social system is in itself a fundamental violation of human rights, as also is the continuing repression of efforts to change it.

There can be no doubt, therefore, about the existence of an extreme human rights problem in South Africa. This is reflected in the universal international condemnation of apartheid and in the leading role played by the United Nations in defining and attacking apartheid as a gross violation of the UN's Universal Declaration of Human Rights. The United Nations has condemned apartheid as a "slavery-like practice" (a form of "collective or group slavery" denying freedom to a whole group of people) and as a "genocidal crime against humanity" (because of its destructive effects on black people), and it has taken a variety of actions against apartheid, including its International Convention on the Suppression and Punishment of the Crime of Apartheid (adopted in 1973 and signed by eighty-seven states by 1986).[46]

But this human rights problem is complex in its theoretical and political implications. For if, as we have observed, its dimensions are indeed both civil-political and socioeconomic, what this essentially means is that the human rights problem in South Africa is partly a civil rights problem and partly a class problem. These are distinctly different kinds of problems, which are differently significant for different theoretical and political viewpoints about human rights and social justice. A liberal approach is more concerned with the civil rights problem, while a socialist approach is more concerned with the class problem. And these different kinds of problems imply different kinds of solutions. A civil rights problem is in principle resolved through an extension of civil rights and the abolition of discrimination. A class problem is in principle resolved by reduction of unacceptable kinds and levels of economic inequality. These problems and solutions are irreducible to each other. The liberal solution, with its equal rights to be unequal, does not in itself resolve the class problem, while the socialist solution, with its trade-offs of freedom for equality, does not necessarily eliminate civil rights problems. Liberation from domination and liberation from poverty do not mean the same thing and do not necessarily imply each other.

Since, as we have seen, apartheid is so obviously a problem of racial discrimination, it is not surprising that the liberal view of it as a civil rights problem has widely prevailed and is still unquestionably relevant today. Social injustice is seen to mean racial domination as a problem of civil discrimination and political unfreedom, which requires a democratic extension of civil and political rights to all people. While this view has tended to neglect the class dimensions of the problem, it has become more rather than less relevant with the current reformism of South African capitalism. For insofar as capitalism increasingly disengages from apartheid (as big business is tending to do, e.g., its 1985 meeting with

ANC leaders in Zambia), this in principle means that demanding an end to racial domination is no longer synonymous with attacking capitalism. As a deracializing capitalism gets "on side," national liberation ceases to imply revolutionary socialism.

Yet as we have seen, the problem is also one of exploitation and poverty, and these are part of a discrimination-induced but no longer discrimination-dependent class problem of extreme socioeconomic inequality, which cannot be resolved merely by eliminating racial discrimination. Social injustice in South Africa is not now simply a problem of current racial discrimination. It is also a problem of the negative class consequences of past discrimination, which have left most blacks at the bottom of a very unequal class structure which is now itself a major cause of black poverty and unemployment. A liberal extension of civil and political rights would not in itself do much about this Brazilian aspect of the human rights problem in South Africa. This extreme economic inequality thus ensures the continuing relevance of the socialist approach to human rights and of Marxist ideas about South Africa, which are fundamentally concerned with class issues and economic justice.

Defining and resolving the human rights problem in South Africa is thus ultimately a matter not of the facts but rather of value priorities and political philosophy. And perhaps the key issue for the future of human rights in South Africa will be how the underlying tension between these equally relevant yet different approaches to social justice will be resolved. But to speak of their difference is not to imply their incompatibility. On the contrary, they are certainly compatible, in the form of Western social democracy. How this tension will work itself out in post-apartheid South Africa—whether in such social democratic compromise or in a more extreme and revolutionary way—remains to be seen. But this will not be a completely arbitrary process. It will reflect South Africa's particular historical realities. These realities do have some revolutionary potential, notably the slow pace of change in relation to increasingly militant demands and the severe problems of black poverty. And it must be noted that whatever limited reform has been achieved so far stems far more from the real threat of revolution as expressed in militant internal and international confrontations with apartheid than from the peaceful persuasion tactics of the "constructive engagement" policy pursued by Western governments. Yet there is, I would argue here, more of a basis for a social democratic future in post-apartheid South Africa than is sometimes recognized. This is because of South Africa's advanced economic and political development, and the historic fusion of liberal and socialist themes in the resistance movement itself.

A century of industrial development has left South Africa with a highly advanced economy, capable of generating relatively high mass living standards and of subsidizing welfare state reforms. And in a world increasingly disillusioned with the inefficiencies of state socialist economics, South Africa's advanced capitalism (its exploitative history and current problems notwithstanding) may come to be seen by the majority (just as it has in the West) as something of an asset for the efficient production of consumer goods and redistributable wealth. All of this has social democratic possibilities, along the lines of some kind of mixed economy (even if, in all likelihood, this only finally materializes in response to more revolutionary pressures of change), as also does the capitalist culture which has accompanied this economy and in some ways shaped the people.

South Africa's political system may also have certain social democratic implications for the future. A long history of British parliamentary and constitutional development has left South Africa with an institutionally quite advanced (though discriminatory) political and judicial system, and one which, apart from the racial franchise, is structured along classically liberal lines. This may, after apartheid, and if the people are given a choice, also be retained as something of an asset, by a majority disinclined to exchange it for a one-party state system. If so, this would be conducive to a pluralistic Western politics, something which is not ruled out simply by the fact of South Africa's much emphasized ethnic diversity, as the evidence of ethnic compromise in the West may remind us.

Another significant political aspect of South Africa is the historic fusion of democratic and socialist struggle. On the one hand, racial inequality has meant that historically the resistance movement has mainly been a civil rights movement. On the other hand, in response to the obvious class dimensions of the racial system and to the growing influence of white socialists, this nationalist democratic movement came to include some socialist concerns about economic justice. Thus the Freedom Charter (drawn up by the Congress movement in 1955 and still the basic opposition manifesto) is characterized by a distinctively social democratic blend of liberal democratic principles (akin to the American Declaration of Independence) with more socialist ideas that "the people shall share in the country's wealth," "the land shall be shared among those who work it," and "there shall be work and security." This historic mix of liberal and socialist concerns about social justice may well, for the future, foster a social democratic politics, even if continuing repression and slow reform provoke revolutionary rather than reformist means of change.

South Africa is thus a particularly ambiguous and unusual "revolutionary situation," characteristic of an economically and politically advanced nation, in which the combination of political and economic forms of oppression has generated a corresponding fusion of liberal and socialist themes in a resistance movement which thus paradoxically combines a revolutionary rhetoric of change with a more social democratic vision of the future. The real possibility of revolutionary means of change does not in itself imply the necessity or likelihood of revolutionary socialist ends (as the revolutionary origins of Western liberal democracy may remind us). Nor does the extreme class problem in South Africa necessarily imply this, as some would argue. For such problems are amenable to social democratic and not just revolutionary socialist solutions. And the fact is that the ANC, while influenced by the left, is not a revolutionary socialist movement. For post-apartheid South Africa, it is committed to free elections, a mixed economy, and social reform.

If we can assume that the escalating resistance will eventually end apartheid once and for all, then a critical question over the long term becomes the extent to which progress can occur in a manner least costly to the various kinds of human rights that are differently emphasized by liberal and socialist views. Extreme violations of human rights in highly polarized social systems have historically generated correspondingly extreme revolutionary solutions, which have ended up becoming serious human rights problems in themselves. And it has sometimes been said that to combine liberal and socialist concerns about human rights and social justice is a luxury that the social democratic West can talk about but that the rest of the world cannot afford. Yet South Africa may be an exception to all this. South Africa has had a long and painful history. But what this history may ultimately mean is that this combination is something which South Africa can indeed afford.

NOTES

1. For historical background, see Rodney Davenport, *South Africa: A Modern History* (London: Macmillan, 1978). On the modernization of racial domination, see Martin Legassick, "Gold, Agriculture and Secondary Industry in South Africa 1885–1970: From Periphery to Sub-metropole as a Forced Labour System," in *The Roots of Rural Poverty in Central and Southern Africa*, ed. Robin Palmer and Neil Parsons (London: Heinemann, 1977).

2. On Afrikaner nationalism, see Dunbar Moodie, *The Rise of Afrikanerdom: Power, Apartheid and the Afrikaner Civil Religion* (Berkeley: University of California Press, 1975); Dan O'Meara, *Volkskapitalisme: Class, Capital and Ideology in the Development of Afrikaner Nationalism, 1934–48* (Johannesburg: Ravan Press, 1983); and Heribert Adam and Hermann Giliomee, *Ethnic Power Mobilized: Can South Africa Change?* (New Haven: Yale University Press, 1979).

3. On the contemporary situation and neo-apartheid, see John Saul and Stephen Gelb, *The Crisis in South Africa: Class Defence, Class Revolution*, 2d ed. (New York: Monthly Review Press, 1986); Heribert Adam and Kogila Moodley, *South Africa after Apartheid: Dismantling Racial Domination* (Berkeley: University of California Press, 1986); and South African Institute of Race Relations (SAIRR), *Annual Surveys of Race Relations in South Africa* (Johannesburg: SAIRR, annual), hereafter referred to as SAIRR, *Annual Survey*.

4. See, for example, M. C. O'Dowd, "The Stages of Economic Growth and the Future of South Africa," in *South Africa: Economic Growth and Political Change*, ed. Adrian Leftwich (London: Allison and Busby, 1974); Ralph Horwitz, *The Political Economy of South Africa* (London: Weidenfeld and Nicolson, 1967).

5. Frederick Johnstone, "White Prosperity and White Supremacy in South Africa Today," *African Affairs* 69 (April 1970): 125–40.

6. For a systematic exposition of this view, see Frederick Johnstone, *Class, Race*

and Gold: A Study of Class Relations and Racial Discrimination in South Africa (London: Routledge and Kegan Paul, 1976).

7. On apartheid as a pragmatic modernization of domination, see Johnstone, "White Prosperity"; and Heribert Adam, *Modernizing Racial Domination: The Dynamics of South African Politics* (Berkeley: University of California Press, 1971).

8. For an overview of this new school of work, see Frederick Johnstone, " 'Most Painful to Our Hearts': South Africa Through the Eyes of the New School," *Canadian Journal of African Studies* 16 (1982): 5–26.

9. On the historical background of the constitution and the franchise, see Leonard Thompson, *The Unification of South Africa, 1902–10* (Oxford: Clarendon Press, 1960); and Davenport, *South Africa.*

10. Davenport, *South Africa,* 340. On the development of segregation, see Davenport.

11. John Dugard, *Human Rights and the South African Legal Order* (Princeton: Princeton University Press, 1978), 7.

12. Ibid., 4.

13. On the migrant labor system, see Francis Wilson, *Migrant Labour in South Africa* (Johannesburg: SPROCAS, 1972); and Harold Wolpe, "Capitalism and Cheap Labour Power in South Africa: From Segregation to Apartheid," *Economy and Society* 1 (1972): 425–456.

14. Surplus Peoples Project (SPP), *Forced Removals in South Africa* (Cape Town: SPP, 1983), 1: xxv; International Defence and Aid Fund (IDAF), *Apartheid: The Facts* (London: IDAF, 1983), 41. On influx control and forcible resettlement, see also IDAF, "Removals and Apartheid: The Enforced Relocation of Black People in South Africa" (Briefing Paper no. 5, 1982); and Amnesty International, *South Africa: Imprisonment under the Pass Laws* (New York: Amnesty International, 1986).

15. ILO, *Special Report 1983,* 14. On these and other aspects of labor and apartheid, see in particular the excellent annual reports of the International Labour Organization, which monitors labor developments in South Africa in relation to the ILO's labor rights conventions. *Special Reports of the Director General concerning the Application of the Declaration concerning the Policy of Apartheid in the Republic of South Africa* (Geneva: ILO), here referred to as ILO, *Special Report.* See also the important periodical *South African Labour Bulletin.*

16. ILO, *Special Report 1984,* 12.

17. On the repression of black trade unionism in South Africa today, see ILO, *Special Report 1983,* 11; ILO, *Special Report 1984,* 12–14; ILO, *Special Report 1985,* 3–16; SAIRR, *Annual Survey 1984,* 318–21; *South Africa Labour Bulletin*; and *Focus on Political Repression in Southern Africa* (IDAF, periodical), here referred to as IDAF, *Focus.*

18. ILO, *Special Report 1984,* 3.

19. ILO, *Special Report 1985,* 16.

20. Francis Wilson, *Labour in the South African Gold Mines, 1911–69* (Cambridge: Cambridge University Press, 1972).

21. ILO, *Special Report 1983,* 26; ILO, *Special Report 1984,* 31–2; ILO, *Special Report 1985,* 36; ILO, *Special Report 1986,* 32.

22. ILO, *Special Report 1983,* 27–29; ILO, *Special Report 1985,* 45; ILO, *Special Report 1986,* 41; *Manchester Guardian Weekly,* Sept. 21, 1986, 7.

23. SAIRR, *Annual Survey 1984,* 729.

24. ILO, *Special Report 1985,* 60.

25. SAIRR, *Annual Survey 1984*, 647–48; ILO, *Special Report 1984*, 28–30.

26. SAIRR, *Annual Survey 1984*, 650.

27. ILO, *Special Report 1983*, 20.

28. SAIRR, *Annual Survey 1984*, 662. On education and poverty in South Africa, see Bill Nasson, "Ambiguous hope: Education and poverty," *Social Dynamics* 10 (1984): 1–19.

29. SAIRR, *Annual Survey 1984*, 248–49. According to the government's 1984 Manpower Survey of the South African labor force (excluding agricultural and domestic workers, and artisans and apprentices), in the category of managerial/executive/administrative there were 170,491 whites and 2,860 Africans, and in the category of laborers there were 1,003,162 Africans and 858 whites (Ibid.).

30. On the historical development of the job color bar, see Johnstone, *Class, Race and Gold*; and Robert Davies, *Capital, State and White Labour in South Africa 1910–60* (Brighton, England: Harvester, 1979).

31. SAIRR, *Annual Survey 1984*, 250; ILO, *Special Report 1984*, 21; ILO, *Special Report 1985*, 40.

32. SAIRR, *Annual Survey 1978*, 161.

33. SAIRR, *Annual Survey 1984*, 241–42.

34. ILO, *Special Report 1985*, 18–19, 38.

35. ILO, *Special Report 1983*, 25. See also Anti-Slavery Society for the Protection of Human Rights (ASSPHR), *Child Labour in South Africa* (London: ASSPHR, 1983); and Alan Cook *Akin to Slavery: Prison Labour in South Africa* (London: IDAF, 1982).

36. Francis Wilson, "South African poverty: Major issues," *Social Dynamics* 10 (1984); 62. For more detailed information on the poverty problem, see the 306 research papers prepared for this inquiry and available from the University of Cape Town, School of Economics, Southern Africa Research and Development Unit (SALDRU), as well as other SALDRU research papers.

37. Ibid.; SAIRR, *Annual Survey 1984*, 568.

38. On black malnutrition, infant mortality, and health problems in South Africa, see Aziza Seedat, *Crippling a Nation: Health in Apartheid South Africa* (London: IDAF, 1984); and Carnegie research papers.

39. SAIRR, *Annual Survey 1984*, 723–24; Sedat, *Crippling a Nation*, 9; Wilson, "South African Poverty," 63; United Nations, *The Effect of the Policy of Apartheid on Black Women and Children in South Africa* (Report E/CN.4/1497, 1983).

40. On resistance and repression in the first half of the twentieth century, see Jack Simons and Ray Simons, *Class and Colour in South Africa, 1850–1950* (London: IDAF, 1983 reprint).

41. For detailed accounts of South Africa's complex state security system, and of recent and current resistance and repression in South Africa, see in particular the IDAF periodical *Focus*.

42. The 1982 Internal Security Act consolidated twenty-eight previous state security laws, widened the definition of terrorism, and extended the discretionary powers of the government and the police, notably in its notorious Sections 28 and 29, permitting preventive detention without trial and the indefinite interrogation of uncharged detainees held incommunicado. Most of the recent detentions have been made under this act. These powers were further extended during the June 1986 state of emergency.

43. Amnesty International, "Situation of Human Rights in South Africa" (Bulletin AFR 53/64/85, Aug. 1985), 3; Amnesty International, "Detentions under the state of

emergency" (Bulletin AFR 53/57/85, Aug. 1985); SAIRR, *Annual Survey 1984, 756; IDAF, Focus* 60 (Sept. 1985). Since the unrest of 1976, there has been a general ban on outdoor meetings, which has been supplemented by more specific bans on meetings, individuals, groups, and publications.

44. United Nations, Commission on Human Rights, *Violations of Human Rights in South Africa* (Report E/CN.4/1985/8, 1985), 35–36. On the torture and maltreatment of prisoners in South Africa, see this and other UN reports; Amnesty International reports; SAIRR, *Annual Survey 1984*, 766–68; and IDAF, *Focus*, various issues.

45. Amnesty International, "Situation of Human Rights," 2; SAIRR, *Annual Survey 1984*, 768–70.

46. On the UN condemnation of apartheid as a slavery-like practice, see United Nations, Sub-Commission on the Prevention of Discrimination and the Protection of Minorities, *Report on Slavery*, 1984, chap. 6, and other UN reports (e.g., *Apartheid as a Collective Form of Slavery*, Report E/CN.4/1413, 1981). On the UN condemnation of apartheid as a "practice bordering on genocide," see United Nations, Commission on Human Rights, *Violations of Human Rights in Southern Africa* (Report E/CN.4/1985/14, 1985), 7–23, and other reports of the UN Commission on Human Rights. On UN actions, see IDAF, *Apartheid*, 86–87; and UN reports on apartheid.

SUGGESTED READINGS

Adam, Heribert and Kogila Moodley. *South Africa after Apartheid: Dismantling Racial Domination*. Berkeley: University of California Press, 1986.

Benjamin, Anne. *Part of My Soul: Winnie Mandela*. Harmondsworth: Penguin, 1985.

Benson, Mary. *Nelson Mandela*. Harmondsworth: Penguin, 1986.

Davenport, Rodney. *South Africa: A Modern History*. London: Macmillan, 1978.

Dugard, John. *Human Rights and the South African Legal Order*. Princeton: Princeton University Press, 1978.

International Defence and Aid Fund. *Apartheid: The Facts*. London: IDAF, 1983.

———. *Children under Apartheid*. London: IDAF, 1980.

———. *Women under Apartheid*. London: IDAF, 1981.

International Labor Organization. *Special Report to the Director General on Labour and Apartheid in South Africa*. Geneva: ILO, annual.

South African Institute of Race Relations. *Annual Survey of Race Relations in South Africa*. Johannesburg: SAIRR, annual.

Saul, John and Stephen Gelb. *The Crisis in South Africa: Class Defence, Class Revolution*. 2d ed. New York: Monthly Review Press, 1986.

Simons, Jack and Ray Simons. *Class and Colour in South Africa, 1850–1950*. London: IDAF, 1983.

17

SPAIN

Thomas D. Lancaster and James Larry Taulbee

The transition of Spain to a liberal democracy following the death of General Francisco Franco in November 1975 stands as one of the more remarkable feats of modern political development. Through essentially nonviolent and nonrevolutionary means, a liberal democratic political system replaced a repressive, authoritarian regime. Spain's political transformation demonstrates that it is possible to establish a democratic system, with all the values such a systems entails, in a country with rather shallow democratic roots.[1]

Human rights form a central consideration in this nonrevolutionary transformation to democracy. The Franco regime had little concern or respect for human rights. In contrast, the record of democratic Spain up to now, while not perfect, demonstrates a firm commitment to the fundamental principles of individual liberty. Progress in the protection of human rights stands high on the list of positive consequences of the country's regime change. Most important, the concern for, and commitment to, human rights appears not as a short-term phenomenon but as an integral part of contemporary Spanish political life. Democratic Spain has taken many essential steps toward institutionalizing procedures to guard against human rights abuses.

HISTORICAL BACKGROUND: THE FRANCO ERA

The roots of Francisco Franco's dictatorship (1939–1975) lay in the breakdown of civil order in 1936. Radical factionalism within the Second Republic (1931–1939) had attenuated, if not totally neutralized, the government's ability to function effectively. In response to widespread disorder, a group of younger senior military officers attempted to seize control. They had hoped to duplicate the 1923 bloodless coup of General Primo de Rivera. Instead, the action began a bloody three-year civil war.

Both the rebellious Nationalists and the Republicans fought the Civil War with great brutality. No precise figures on casualties exist but Hugh Thomas estimates battle deaths alone, for both sides, at 285,000.[2] As in many civil wars, civilian casualties equaled or exceeded the military's. Another 300,000 to 350,000 people identified with the Republican cause fled into exile. The enormous human and economic toll fueled not only the vengeance exacted against Republican sympathizers but the determination by Francoists that no one should forget lest it happen again.

Under Franco, Spain evolved through three different phases. The first, a period of political consolidation, extended from the end of the Civil War to the early 1950s. Ruthless repression, international isolation, and hard economic conditions characterized this era. Totally unconcerned with its image abroad—in fact using the overt hostility of democratic governments as an excuse for its excesses—the government systematically sought to eliminate all opposition through repression, exile, and execution. After World War II, accurately perceived or not, the Allied states found in the Franco regime a living reminder of a Fascist ideology that had cost a great deal in blood to defeat. This perception served to reinforce the isolation of Spain from the main currents of European and world politics. Estimates of reliable observers placed the number of political prisoners at 250,000 in the 1940s.[3]

After the defeat of the Republican forces, much of the historic opposition (socialists, republicans, anarchists, Basque and Catalan nationalists) fled into exile and eventually became cut off from direct struggle within Spain. Many communists, however, remained and even managed to sustain a minor guerrilla war from 1944 to 1948. Some socialist enclaves survived in the Basque provinces and the mining districts of Asturias: members of the illegal labor union Confederación Nacional de Trabajo (CNT) managed to mount occasional attacks against the government, and nationalist sentiment surfaced from time to time in Catalonia and the Basque provinces. Still, by 1953 the historic opposition ceased to exist as an effective political reality within Spain itself.

The second phase began in the early 1950s following U.S. recognition of the Franco government and the establishment of military bases there. During this time the regime attempted some cosmetic changes in an effort to gain international acceptability. The third stage began in 1960–1961 with an economic liberalization that marked the beginning of the move to the economic modernization which produced Spain's "economic miracle." This stage ended with the energy crisis shortly before Franco's death. Despite more liberal economic policies, the political essence of the regime remained unchanged. To suppress opposition the government readily resorted to violence, often killing demonstrators and marchers. The 1969 crackdown on unauthorized political activity, which included innumerable arrests and trials of workers, students, Basque militants and priests, furnished a vivid illustration of the fact that economic liberalization had not engendered a corresponding political tolerance.[4]

In theory, the rights of Spaniards were guaranteed by a series of Fundamental Laws issued over a twenty-eight–year period, culminating in the Organic Law of 1967. Each of the Fundamental Laws contained declarations of rights. In practice, however, rights were severely circumscribed by ordinary legislation and discretionary procedures. For example, the 1945 Fuero de los Españoles (Charter of the Spanish People) contained a formal guarantee of civil rights, but these were contingent upon the prior and superior claims of security and internal order by the state. Individuals could exercise these rights provided the result did not undermine the "fundamental principles of the State," or the national, spiritual, or social unity of Spain. All laws, including the Fundamental Laws, could be suspended by decree. None placed constraints on Franco's authority and power. As lawgiver and guardian, he stood above the "constitution."

Franco served as both head of state and prime minister until 1967 when he made Mariano Navarro Rubio premier. He had absolute power to appoint other ministers who served at his pleasure although all governments were coalitions in which Franco carefully balanced the competing interests supporting his regime: the army, the Falange (later transformed into the Movimiento Nacional), and in the early years, the Catholic Church.

From Franco's personal adherence to the puritan morality of the conservative Church came a rather amorphous ideal of a *Rechstaat (Estado de derecho)*, a rule of peace and order exemplified by the watchwords "Por la Patria, el Pan y la Justicia" (for country, bread, and justice). The political expression of this was the idea of "organic democracy," which assumes that individuals exist only as members of several natural communities—the family, the *sindicato* (work), the municipality, and the nation—in which they share common experiences. Supporters of the Franco regime often compared the virtues of "organic democracy" to the defects of "inorganic" or liberal democracy as demonstrated in Spain's ill-fated Second Republic. Article 8 of the 1942 Fundamental Law establishing the Cortes provided that:

The representative character of the political system is the basic principle of our public institutions. The participation of the people in the legislative and other functions of general interest shall be implemented through the family, the municipality and the trade union (syndicates) and other organically representative bodies recognized by law for this purpose. *Any political organization whatever outside this representative system shall be deemed illegal.* (emphasis added)

The Cortes, nominally the national legislature, was not a true representative body. Its members were either elected or appointed by the various syndicates, municipalities, professional associations, or Franco himself.[5] The body had very limited power to influence the government. The members could not initiate legislation, seriously debate the merits of government proposals, or offer substantive amendments to laws proposed by the government.

Roman Catholicism was established as the official religion of the state. Other faiths could exist only under "effective legal guidance." The Church and the government both had the right of censorship.[6] Laws were expected to conform to Catholic dogma. Civil marriages, divorce, and abortion were absolutely prohibited. Church-state relations soured, however, toward the end of Franco's tenure, particularly when the Vatican began to favor the rights of minorities and free trade unionism and openly criticized censorship and the overt manipulation of information.

The first of the Fundamental Laws, the Fuero de Trabajo, gave workers extensive *individual* rights and benefits. It guaranteed each man the right to a job with a salary sufficient to maintain a family and working conditions in keeping with "Christian dignity." The guarantee of employment was of paramount importance because it substituted for the legal right to form trade unions. In theory, the syndicate—the vertically organized state-supported union—wedded owners and workers in a common enterprise, obviating the need for an intermediary organization to guard collective rights. Workers could not unionize, demonstrate, or engage in any form of worker resistance such as slowdowns, sitdowns, or strikes. Strikes were criminal offenses against the sovereign power of the state and carried heavy sanctions under the law.

Early on, the regime systematically suppressed the historic unions and moved harshly against any manifestation of new clandestine attempts to organize. During the 1940s and 1950s, labor unrest was rare. When work actions did occur, the government easily dealt with them through arrests, limited concessions, and some changes in local administrators.[7] The Barcelona transport boycott and strike in 1951, disturbances in the Basque provinces over the cost of living in 1956, and the walkout of miners in Asturias in 1958 all gained national attention, but the small scale of Spanish industry combined with government control of the media and communications networks kept most disturbances localized.

The syndicate's economic system favored employers in that wages were kept low. Employers also sought to evade regulations by not registering workers because of the difficulty of shedding labor, the high cost of dismissal, and the burden of social security payments.[8] The job security provided by law locked employers into labor-intensive methods, inhibiting modernization. In comparison with other West European workers, Spanish workmen suffered from sweatshop conditions, inadequate pensions, and woeful public medical services. Unemployment insurance covered only half of the work force.

The employment of women was extremely limited. Consistent with conservative Catholicism, the place of a woman was at home, caring for her family. Those seeking work outside the home found themselves limited to traditional women's occupations: charity, domestic service, cultural activities, health, and education.

Under Franco, the media served the state. Every publication, every film script, every radio and television broadcast, except those of the Catholic Church, was subject to prior censorship. The state regulated the number and conditions of publications, took an integral part in the appointment of the managerial personnel in all publishing institutions, even those privately owned, and regulated the journalistic profession by licensing its members. Until 1958, only one school of journalism operated in the entire country.[9] The official news agency, EFE, controlled the distribution of all news, including that from foreign countries. The censorship of the press reflected the suppression of civil rights. The government could mount public attacks on individuals through the media, while denying the target a right of reply.

The abolition of prior censorship in 1966 changed the relationship between the various media and the government. The new law did not liberalize the standards governing publication, but instead gave rise to what came to be known as "publish and be damned." Over the next nine years several newspapers and magazines were closed down. These included the progressive magazine *Triunfo* in June 1971 and the newspaper *Madrid* in November of the same year. In the case of *Madrid*, the government appropriated the assets of the paper and destroyed the building where it was published.

To summarize, considerations of human rights had little role in Francoist Spain. In terms of its treatment of prisoners, the question of torture, and the violent suppression of strikes and demonstrations, "the Francoists had never balked at violations of the human rights supposedly enshrined in the Fundamental Laws."[10] One noteworthy set of abuses concerned the manner in which several headline-making executions were carried out. Selected "enemies of Spain"— regional extremists, communists, and anarchists—were subjected to a barbaric method of execution through strangulation known as *garrote vil*. For example, in 1963, *garrote vil* ended the lives of two anarchists, Francisco Granados Gata and Joaquín Delegado Martínez, following their rapid trial for a bombing incident at the Madrid police headquarters. In 1974 two Catalan anarchists, accused of killing members of various Spanish security forces, were also executed by this barbaric method after Franco refused to commute their sentences.[11]

Despite the severe international criticism, executions continued in Spain until Franco's death. The last occurred in late September 1975, only a few months before the Caudillo died. The cabinet met at that time to consider a possible reprieve for eleven people awaiting execution—three Basques and eight members of the Frente Revolucionario Antifascista Patriotica (FRAP). Five of the sentences were upheld, and over the objections of the Pope and the revulsion expressed by many political observers within Spain, the dying regime demonstrated its brutality by carrying out the executions on September 27.

In any authoritarian regime, the denial of political rights, incidences of torture, arbitrary arrest, or other forms of brutality may make headlines, but less dramatic actions taken at relatively low levels of the administrative bureaucracy can also seriously impair an individual's exercise of rights, particularly in the absence of any independent forum of appeal or concept of due process. In authoritarian Spain, an individual citizen had no right to petition the government directly, only through the appropriate organic groups which presumably acted to protect the interests of all their members. Individuals who ran afoul of the government suffered arbitrary discrimination with respect to entrance into schools or trades for themselves or their children, denial or withdrawal of work permits and licenses, eviction from housing or a thousand other petty persecutions.

By rigidly controlling the rights of association and free speech, the Franco regime effectively controlled opposition. Meetings of more than twenty persons had to have explicit government sanction. Even after permission, an agent of the government could attend the meeting and dissolve it if he disapproved. All unauthorized public meetings, with the exception of Catholic ceremonies and meetings held by legitimately established associations in accordance with their statutes, were strictly prohibited. Masonic, communist, and anarchist organizations were outlawed. With the exception of those sponsored by the Catholic Church, all organizations had to be approved by the Ministry of the Interior. The limits on the rights of speech and assembly outside of syndicates or church groups, and the absolute control of all media forms, made organization of a broad-based public opposition difficult.

Transition to Democracy

With the Law of Succession in 1947, Franco declared Spain a kingdom. He nevertheless resisted pressure to designate a king. Franco distrusted and disliked Don Juan, the son of Alfonso XIII, the king who left the Spanish throne in 1930. Franco struck a bargain with Don Juan whereby Juan Carlos, Don Juan's son, would be educated in Spain with the expectation that Juan Carlos would become Franco's successor. Not until 1969, however, when Juan Carlos swore fidelity to Franco and the Principles of the Movement did the dictator officially recognize him and complete the provisions of the Law of Succession. Even then, Franco gave Juan Carlos little more than ceremonial duties within the government.

When he assumed power shortly after Franco's death, Juan Carlos was an unknown quantity with limited political experience. Opponents referred to him cynically as "Juan the Brief." Initially the king drew his advisers from the old-line Francoists, but he rapidly moved to consolidate his position by replacing these with his own people. In doing so, he skipped over an entire political generation to appoint individuals closer to his own age. In retrospect, the most important of these appointments was that of a relatively unknown leader in the Movimiento named Adolfo Suárez as prime minister in 1976. Together, Juan Carlos and Adolfo Suárez spurred the effort that produced the democratic constitution of 1978, with the king using his position as Franco's chosen heir to offset the open discontent of the military and internal security forces. The king and his advisers walked a tightrope between those who naively argued for a total break, *ruptura*, moderates who favored *reforma*, and those who defended the old order. Progress never came fast enough for political skeptics and always too quickly for defenders of the old order.

Considering Franco's long tenure, the restraints of the old regime crumbled quickly following his death in 1975. The rapid transition becomes all the more remarkable given the level of internal violence, particularly by Basque separatist organizations, in the period between Franco's death and the attempted military coup in February 1981. Also remarkable is the fact that important elements of the state apparatus—the military, the judiciary, and the internal security forces—were still staffed and managed by individuals who owed their professional careers to the old regime. The ongoing problem in the transition to a stable liberal democracy became instilling different standards of conduct, different operational philosophies, in government agencies that essentially continued into the new era with little change.

The case that best demonstrates how quickly the restraints of the old regime crumbled involved Santiago Carrillo, the head of the Spanish Communist party (PCE). Without permission, Carrillo returned from exile in December 1976, before the formal legalization of political parties, and held a press conference in Madrid. The transition government of Adolfo Suárez did arrest and detain him for a few days but then released him and permitted him to remain in Spain. His presence caused great difficulties in the transition because the willingness of the transition regime government to legalize the PCE became the sine qua non, the criterion by which the seriousness of the commitment to democracy was judged even by leaders of more moderate movements. Yet legitimizing the PCE would intensify opposition from defenders of the old order and enhance the risk of a coup by the military. In a courageous move by Suárez, the Spanish Communist party was legalized on April 9, 1977, concluding this process for all political parties. The king, as he would do again in 1981, faced down military dissidents by reminding them of their oath to support him as king, chief of the armed forces, and symbol of the unity of Spain.[12]

Treatment of the press offers an excellent example of the overlap between the old and the new. Not only attitudes but often legislation still on the books gave rise to conflict, given that all laws of the Franco regime remained in force until they were explictly removed, updated, or replaced. The 1978 Constitution guarantees freedom of the press, but to a great extent the press operates in a legal vacuum. The 1966 Press Law as amended in 1977 still technically controls the media, although many provisions may be of dubious legality under the 1978 Constitution. Many laws still protect the Church and the military. Presumably through the transition, the government operated on the vague guideline that no journalistic endeavor should undermine the establishment of democracy.[13]

Three prominent cases in 1980 illustrate this point. First, the civil courts tried Juan Luis Cebrián, editor of *El Pais*, for "disrespect to the courts" and sentenced him to two months in prison, suspended because it was a first offense, and a fine. Second, the military charged Pilar Miro, a director and producer, with "disrespect to the military" because of a film about an incident in the 1930s. The film, *Crimen de Cuenca*, allegedly portrayed the Civil Guard in a defamatory way. Eventually the film was cleared after an extensive legal battle and overt government intervention. Third, the military again moved to charge Miguel Angel Aguilar, editor of Madrid's *Diario 16*, with disrespect for the armed forces after the paper published a story alleging coup plotting in the military. The case never came to trial.

HUMAN RIGHTS AND THE DEMOCRATIC CONSTITUTION OF 1978

The Form of Government

Following general elections in March 1977, the first since 1936, the Cortes set out to draft a new constitution.[14] The final document reflects in spirit and form the impact of liberal democratic principles. The new Constitution abolishes the death penalty except for certain military offenses in time of war and explicitly forbids the use of torture or cruel and inhuman punishment. It guarantees the "right to life," the right to "physical and moral integrity," and the rights of honor, personal and family privacy, and identity. In sum, the rhetoric and substantive provisions of the Constitution stand in close proximity to that of the Universal Declaration of Human Rights and other major international human rights instruments.

More important than words, however, are the mechanisms for implementation and the remedies available to redress injuries. Indeed, the section of the 1978 Constitution which defines fundamental rights cannot be the subject of constitutional litigation unless the concepts, rights, or articles themselves have been elaborated and specified in an organic law. In many respects, the fundamental rights guaranteed by the new Constitution are little different from those contained in the 1945 Charter of the Spanish People. To understand the extent of the transformation, we must examine contemporary institutions and their performances.

Antonio López Pina highlights five fundamental areas of the constitution, all of which are related to the question of human rights: the form of government, the problem of sovereignty, the territorial organization of the state, church-state relations, and the economic system.[15]

The Constitution of 1978 declares Spain's form of government to be a parliamentary democracy with a constitutional monarch. The political Left compromised on the monarchical aspect by not insisting on a republican form of government. In exchange, the political Right did not push to make the monarch the chief executive, instead giving him mostly symbolic duties. In this manner, the Right partly avoided the normal interpretation of republicanism in Spain, associated not only with individual liberties and political rights but also with such social revolutionary tendencies as land redistribution, radical federalism, and anti-clericalism.

The Constitution follows in most respects the basic model of a continental parliamentary form of government. The Cortes, consisting of the Chamber of Deputies and the Senate, forms the legislative body. Its essential functions are the exercise of legislative power, the approval of budgets, and the control of government action. The executive—the cabinet headed by the prime minister—is ultimately accountable to the parliament, and directly responsible to the Chamber of Deputies, with an absolute majority of the members of the Chamber needed to censure it.

The 1978 Constitution clearly places sovereignty with the Spanish people: powers of the state clearly emanate from the people. In the Spanish case, an important implication of popular sovereignty is the subordination of the military to a democratically elected government. While the king is the commander in chief of the armed forces (Article 62), the "Government directs domestic and foreign policy, civil and military administration as well as the defense of the State" (Article 97). This military-civilian relationship, with the elected government's clear legal and leadership dominance, is essential to a long-term improvement of Spain's record on human rights given the country's long history of military intervention into political affairs.

The Constitution of 1978 also addresses the question of the state's territorial organization. Article 2 asserts the "indissoluble unity of the Spanish nation," a point fundamentally important to the Francoists and all centralists and rightists. This same article, however, also breaks sharply with the past in that it simultaneously recognizes and guarantees "the right to self-government of the nationalities and regions" of Spain, specifically mentioning Catalonia, the Basque country, and Galicia as "nationalities." Seventeen regional governments share administrative and political power with the national and municipal governments, having been granted some powers via different procedures outlined in the Constitution. Many on both sides, however, were left unsatisfied. The Partido Nacionalista Vasco (PNV), for example, sought a constitution giving precedence to the Basques' right to self-government instead of the principle of national sovereignty.[16] Many ex-Francoists and other conservatives and centralists felt that the granting of regional autonomy fragmented the unity of the Spanish state.

Church-state affairs comprise another important element of the Constitution of 1978 that affects human rights. Historically, republican anti-clerical tendencies have sharply conflicted in Spain with the nation, Church, and government of the Franco regime. Initially in the Franco regime, the Catholic Church was given an important and often monopolistic role in Spanish social and political life. Particularly during the early years of the Franco regime, the Church's central role in daily life often left the rights of non-Catholics unprotected. The 1978 Constitution, however, guarantees free exercise of religion. No faith is to be established as an "official" religion of the state. This does not mean, however, that the Catholic Church does not remain in a privileged position. Church control and influence within the Spanish educational system means the Church still receives large subsidies from the state.

The Constitution does not clearly resolve questions regarding the country's economic order. The political balance of the drafting body itself and the intense controversies such economic questions aroused forced a compromise that left a very ambiguous framework for future policy-making. Constitutional clauses dealing with the economy recognize both free market and planned economies despite their inherent contradictions. On one hand, the Spanish Constitution recognizes "the right to private property and inheritance," with the stipulation that seizure by the state is justified only if it serves the public utility or social interest. In such cases, the Constitution also stipulates that proper compensation must be paid in accordance with the law. On the other hand, the Constitution allows for public sector monopolies, state intervention into companies economically central to the public interest, and the state's right to plan general economic activity. Future legislation will undoubtedly have to clarify these ambiguities. The Spanish economy, nevertheless, remains mixed, with primary reliance on private initiative and market mechanisms.

In sum, the Spanish Constitution of 1978 established a broad framework for governance, generally held to be a vast improvement over the Franco regime, particularly with regard to the protection of individual rights and freedoms. The Constitution's text with its guarantee of basic liberties was approved in a referendum in December 1978 by 87.8 percent of the people voting; 7.9 percent voted against it and 4.3 percent cast blank or null ballots. In all, 67.7 percent of Spain's 26.6 million eligible voters cast ballots. The extreme Left and Right did not support the democratic framework; and given their concern for decentralization, the Catalan and Basque nationalists wavered in their support, partly accounting for the relatively low turnout during the referendum.

Social and Civil Rights

The 1978 Constitution outlines a number of social and civil "rights" in rather ambiguous language, referring sometimes to rights and at others to "guiding principles."[17] In context, these rights, though ultimately concerned with the well-being of individual citizens, initially imply a set of positive duties for those in public office. While ambiguous in reference, the *tone* of the document clearly projects the expectation that these "rights" will be reflected in positive organic legislation by emphasizing the duties of the state, through its elected officials, to promote the defense of such rights.

For example, the Constitution of 1978 legitimized the law on unionization of April 1, 1977, in recognizing the right to unionize freely as distinct from the general right of association. In contrast to the obligatory syndicate system of the Franco regime, the Constitution goes to great lengths to spell out an individual right to work, free from compulsory union membership. Everyone has the right to establish a union, to choose the union they wish to join, to participate in union activity, or to choose *not* to participate *or* join. Thus, the provisions attempt to balance the social liberty of professional association with the personal right of independent choice.

The Constitution of 1978 also outlines certain social and civil rights in which it explicitly uses the word *right*, albeit in an imprecise manner. As with many other rights spelled out in the Constitution, each of these must be actualized by organic legislation. Thus, the actual content and full definition of the guarantee of these rights will depend on future legislation and judicial decisions. The tone of the Constitution, nevertheless, clearly encourages the government to promote social and economic progress, the equitable distribution of regional and personal income, economic stability, and full employment. In this last area, the liberal economic nature of the Constitution should be noted. The right to work does not carry with it a guarantee of a job. It does obligate the state to maintain economic conditions consonant with full employment and, in periods of recession, to provide unemployment insurance and other forms of social assistance.[18] These benefits can generate concrete legal claims by individuals against the government. Related to the question of individual choice, the Constitution also prohibits any limitation on access to professions beyond reasonable and fair licensing standards based upon expertise.

Much of Spain's social welfare coverage was already in place under the Franco regime. Particularly in workers' compensation, unemployment benefits, and health care, the Francoist authoritarian system provided remarkably broad protection for individuals. In line with its corporatist philosophy, the Francoist state was concerned for individual social welfare in a rather paternalistic fashion. Despite abuses regarding other individual rights, the Franco system had already institutionalized a rather extensive social welfare system when the transition to democracy began. Spain's current social welfare system is not out of line with other West European systems. In recent years it has been the subject of much debate in terms of reform—primarily in order to increase its efficiency and to fill some gaps in coverage. But such debate in democratic Spain has been one of quality, not a call for the creation of such a welfare system.

The Constitution also prohibits discrimination of any kind on the basis of sex. Along these same lines, Spain ratified the Convention on the Political Rights of Women in 1984. In 1983 the government set up the Women's Institute with a mission to research the situation of women in Spain and, in conjunction with other ministries, to sponsor programs and legislation to correct the social, judicial, and economic inequalities that still exist. The Institute has a broad mandate to address all issues and areas that concern women. These range from practical difficulties (employers are under no legal obligation to announce jobs for open competition) to questions of sexist language, treatment of women in the media, and bias in the interpretation and application of the laws.

The Women's Institute has achieved some remarkable advances. A 1985 law permits women to have abortions if giving birth would threaten their physical and mental health. Over the past two years the problem of battered women has gained prominence. Centers for battered women have been established in major cities, and the Civil Guard has voluntarily extended its support to the Women's Institute in the implementation of its educational program for battered women.[19] Still, as in many other societies, narrowing the gap between the goal and the reality will entail considerable efforts, even with the support of the government.

Judicial Institutions

One of the major institutional developments in post-Franco Spain has been in the judiciary. The Spanish legal system, like most others in Europe, is essentially a civil law system.[20] The only major source of non–civil law derives from the Catholic Church and from distinct regional legal traditions. Except for infrequent yet highly publicized abuses, the Franco regime did not heavily politicize Spain's ordinary courts.

Spain's transition to democracy brought at least three major changes in the legal system that bear directly on the treatment of human rights. First, Spanish military courts have historically been an instrument for oppression of potential civilian political opposition. The most severe derogation of individual rights involved broad grants of jurisdiction to the military to try civilians in courts-martial.[21] The Franco regime relied heavily on such special courts for much of the repression that occurred through the legal system, and often extended the jurisdiction of the military courts to include many acts considered offensive to the government. This authority extended to any action that cast aspersions on any aspect of military "honor," including anti-military statements in the press, support for regional separation, and armed robbery; other acts deemed anti-nationalistic and anti-Francoist were often tried in these military courts. Civilian courts had no power of review over military justice. Between 1955 and 1958, 40 percent of the defendants in military trials were civilians. This figure dropped to 22 percent between 1963 and 1966 with the creation of the Court of Public Order.[22]

Nevertheless, the Franco regime continued to reflect its military mentality in governing during its struggle for survival beginning in 1969. The government could decree the military mobilization of any workers on strike, as it did with the 3,800 Madrid metro workers on strike in 1970.[23] Such a decree subjected them to the threat of court-martial for mutiny. The new Constitution, however, limits "the exercise of military jurisdiction strictly within military limits."[24] In addition, the 1981 code of military justice prohibits the charging or trying of civilians by military courts and provides for the civilian review of military court decisions. The system met its first severe test in the court-martial of the leaders of the February 1981 coup attempt. The military court meted out relatively mild sentences to the conspirators. Much to the shock of most Spaniards, many of these sentences were subsequently upgraded by the civilian court which reviewed the verdicts.[25]

A second fundamental change in the Spanish legal system regarding human rights is the Constitutional Court. The creation of the Constitutional Court follows the post–World War II trend in several European countries of creating special courts with some powers of judicial review in an attempt to deal with the issue of the constitutionality of government status and actions. As an autonomous institution, this twelve-member body hears three types of cases. First, and most important, are cases involving the constitutionality of the statutes, organic laws, and general laws of the Spanish Parliament, the laws of the Autonomous Communities, and executive acts with legal force such as decree-laws.[26] Second, the Constitutional Court resolves conflicts of power between the different state institutions and bodies. This area is particularly important in Spain's current democratic system with its creation of seventeen regionally based Autonomous Communities. Third, and directly related to the protection of human rights against administrative abuse, the Constitutional Court hears *amparo* appeals. Consistent with Spain's Republican Constitution of 1931 and those in Latin American countries such as Venezuela and Mexico, which drew on Hispanic legal tradition, the *amparo* appeal permits redress for an abuse of power or a violation of guaranteed rights; an "act or decree authorizing the abuse was contrary to the constitution."[27] In other words, an *amparo* appeal simply asks that a law not be applied in a particular case. It does not challenge the constitutionality of a statute, but protects against a law's application. It does not constitute an action against the law itself. Central to our consideration here, "the amparo appeal is key to the system of guarantees of constitutionality that established fundamental individual rights and liberties, seeking to protect against the violation of rights recognized in Articles 14 through 29 of the 1978 Constitution and objections of conscience."[28]

The third major institutional creation in the Constitution of 1978 that directly affects defense of human rights is the Defender of the People. This ombudsman-like creation has as its primary raison d'être the protection of the fundamental rights and liberties guaranteed to the Spanish under the 1978 Constitution. The Defender of the People seeks to protect these rights against intrusion by administrative and legislative activities, including laws passed by Parliament. As an administrative watchdog, the Defender has open access to all public administrative offices in order to obtain information concerning any potential abuses of administrative power against an individual or group. The Defender is appointed by, and ultimately accountable to, the Spanish Parliament, but remains highly autonomous.

The Defender's powers and instruments for protecting individual rights are quite strong. Following his investigation into possible abuse, he can recommend changes to administrative authorities and bureaucrats. If ignored, the Public Defender can then bring the issue to the attention of the appropriate minister and, as a last resort, to the Parliament itself. In another area, the Defender of the People has the power of the Constitutional Court behind him. He can place before the Court *amparo* appeals and appeals of unconstitutionality. This power is particularly important for the defense of human rights in democratic Spain since it permits the Defender to respond to the concerns of individual citizens.

The Constitution also provides that "citizens may participate in the administration of justice through the institution of the jury in the manner that the law may determine for certain criminal trials, and in the usual and traditional courts.'' While such citizen participation in the judiciary system has not been implemented through an organic law, legislation to create a jury system has been proposed. Some magistrates oppose the plan because they fear juries would hamper terrorist trials. Individual participation in the more political aspects of the Spanish system has not, however, been as limited.

Political Participation

The right to open and free participation in political and governmental affairs is basic to most definitions of human rights. The freedom to support or to criticize one's leadership both formally, through established structures and procedures, and informally is fundamental to basic tenets of individual political rights. Under Franco, political participation was severely restricted; hence increased political participation has been a logical and natural consequence of Spain's transition to democracy. The replacement of authoritarian norms with liberal democratic ones has meant increased political participation at many levels. Three such levels will be considered here as indicators of this increased participation: formal electoral participation, informal political participation at the mass level, and elite activity.

Meeting the criteria of individual rights in Western democracies, suffrage in Spain is universal, direct, equal, and secret. While common in a comparative perspective, such electoral participation in democratic Spain is a significant break with the past since the Francoist corporative voting excluded most of the Spanish population from voting. The voting age was initially set at twenty-one and has since been lowered to eighteen.

Spanish citizens have been inundated with opportunities to participate formally in the new democracy. Besides local elections and those for regional governments, four national elections and three referenda have been held. General elections were held in 1977, 1979, 1982, and 1986. Referenda were held in 1976 on the Law of Political Reform, in 1978 on the Constitution, and 1986 on the question of NATO membership. In all of these elections, turnout has been quite high, ranging from 67.1 percent in the 1979 election to 80.2 in the 1982 election.

The Constitution recognizes political parties as the basic mechanism reflecting political pluralism. The Constitution does not restrict their existence, except in that all parties must respect Spain's constitution and its laws and be internally democratic themselves. Furthermore, Article 9.2 stresses the duty of public authorities to facilitate participation. Elections must be held at every level of government—local, regional, and national—at least every four years. The Constitution also grants the right to run for national office to all citizens over eighteen years of age, establishes public control of all state mass media, and recognizes the right to vote of all Spanish citizens living outside the country.

Political participation and involvement at the mass level can take numerous forms. Individual citizens can participate in party activities, contribute money to a political cause, contact governmental officials, engage in community activities, etc. Little systematic research has been done, however, utilizing such indicators. Survey evidence measuring frequency of political discussion as an indicator of political participation suggests that, in comparison to citizens of other major West European countries, Spaniards engage less frequently in political discussions.[29] The Franco regime's long period of systematic depoliticization and banning of political dissent helps explain this low level of political discussion. However, the survey also reveals that younger Spaniards engage in political discussions no less frequently than their fellow Europeans. This suggests that the gradual replacement through time of the older depoliticized Spaniards will add to Spain's increasing legitimacy as a pluralistic democratic regime.

Women's participation at the elite level in Spain tends to be fairly limited. Of the 350 seats in the Chamber of Deputies, 21 were held by women after the 1977 election, and 19 following the 1979 balloting. There were 645 female candidates in 1977 (out of a total of 4,692) and 1,290 in 1979 (out of 6,996). With most of the women candidates on ultra-leftist party lists, "The number of women candidates presented by the parties seems to be inversely proportional to their chances of winning."[30] Several charges of discrimination against women were made in protest of the machismo within their parties. Some women, such as the socialist deputy for Madrid, Carlota Bustelo, resigned their seats in Parliament.

Organized Labor

The Spanish Constitution of 1978 grants the right to strike while not permitting lockouts. The right to strike is recognized as the workers' means to defend their interests. Similarly, contained within the right to unionize is the right to collective labor negotiations between the representatives of the workers and owners. The Workers' Statute also recognizes the right of the unions, federations, or confederations, and the employers associations to form part of the negotiating commissions.

Two major trade union federations dominate the Spanish labor movement. The Communist-oriented Workers Commissions (CCOO) laid the foundation during the Franco period for democratic Spain's free labor movement.[31] The CCOO began in the late 1950s following reforms in the labor law that permitted collective bargaining and the election of factory committees to represent the workers' interests. The CCOO formed permanent bodies to represent the workers, drawing much of its leadership from the PCE. Workers Commissions proliferated at the firm level throughout the 1960s. The CCOO grew strong enough to influence governmental policy, becoming a major anti-Francoist force by 1967. Overt labor activity came to a halt, however, in 1967 when the Francoist Supreme Court declared the Workers' Commissions illegal and a decree-law ceased collective bargaining. The Franco regime then began a systematic campaign of repression against the CCOO which continued until Franco's death. Nevertheless, given its rapid growth, the CCOO had by then established a strong organizational base.

The General Workers Union (UGT), on the other hand, has long been a central party of the Spanish labor movement. Formed in 1888 as a moderate socialist union, the UGT grew rapidly during the period immediately prior to World War I. Along with the anarcho-syndicalist National Confederation of Workers (CNT), the UGT dominated the Spanish labor movement during the Second Republic. This, of course, led to the extreme hostility toward it during the Franco regime which prevented the rebuilding of its organizational base. The UGT thus remained largely inactive during the early Franco regime. The UGT, along with other labor organizations like the CNT, the Basque STV, and the Catalan SOCC, remained secondary to the CCOO throughout the Franco period. Thus, Franco's death left the CCOO in a much better organizational position than any of the other unions. The first syndical elections of 1978 reflected the disparity. The UGT won only 22 percent of the delegates compared to the CCOO's 34 percent. In more recent union elections, however, the UGT has outpolled the CCOO.

Several factors work against a strong union influence in Spain in comparison to other West European countries.[32] First, less than 20 percent of Spanish workers belong to a union, making the movement intrinsically weaker than in other industrialized European countries. Second, the continued division of the union movement in two large federations—the UGT and the CCOO—makes united action by the labor movement difficult. Third, Spain's extremely high unemployment of over 20 percent leaves the unions very little leverage in using the strike as a weapon. Finally, Spain's generally conservative and depoliticized working class does not provide an easy recruitment ground for a more powerful and militant union movement.

Nevertheless, oganized labor has been at the center of policy-making in contemporary Spain. Labor, along with management and the government, has signed a series of agreements that have aided the transition to democracy as well as giving considerable policy guidance for the future. The Moncloa Pacts of 1977, the Basic Interconfederal Accord in 1979, the Framework Interconfederal Accord in 1980, the National Accord on Employment in 1981, and the Economic and Social Accord in 1984 have ensured labor peace in critical times. The nonrevolutionary nature of the transition to democracy can, in part, be attributed to the moderate demands placed on the system by organized labor. The important trade-off for the labor movement, of course, has been its continued recognition and legitimacy and the institutionalization of the right of the Spanish working class to organize collectively. The organized labor movement in Spain now enjoys the same basic rights and privileges afforded to workers in other Western liberal democratic nations.

The Regional Question

Spain is a multinational political system.[33] Besides Castile, the central part of Spain that has generally dominated Spain politically, this political system includes historical-social-linguistic regions such as the Basque country, Catalonia, Galicia, and Valencia and Andalucia. These areas have periodically pushed for either independence or some form of autonomy. While strong unitary rule from Madrid has been the norm, decentralization has occurred in Spain during democratic periods. This was the case during the Second Republic of 1931–1939 and the current constitutional monarchy.

The Franco regime implemented its philosophy of "national unity" by returning Spain to centralized rule from Madrid. Immediately following the Civil War and upon coming to power, Franco revoked the autonomy granted by the government of the Second Republic to Euskadi (the Basque provinces) and Catalonia. The public use of all regional languages such as Basque and Catalan was declared illegal. Schools instructed only in Castillan. All forms of regional, political, cultural, and ethnic associations were banned. All political decision making was centralized in Madrid. The Basques were particularly sensitive to this centralization given the disregard for their centuries-old *forales*, or local laws.

The rift between Franco and the Basques had deep roots. Given their traditionally deep Catholic beliefs and their concern for self-determination, the Basques were caught between siding with either the Nationalists or the Republicans at the beginning of the Civil War. Ultimately, most individual Basques and their political organizations cast their lot with the Republicans. For example, the Basque National party (PNV), the largest and oldest Basque party, supported the Republic. During the Civil War, the Nationalists were responsible for numerous atrocities, among them the destruction of Guernica through an indiscriminate air attack and the summary execution of fourteen Basque nationalist priests. Throughout Franco's tenure, the Basque provinces were the only section of the country not completely pacified.

Until the late 1950s, protests and violence were sporadic. In 1958 a Basque terrorist organization, Euskadi Ta Askatusuna (ETA—Basque Fatherland and Freedom), began a program of violence, a war of "national liberation," directed at forcing the Spanish state to grant it total independence. The level of violence became such that in 1968 the police became a virtual permanent army of occupation operating under a continuing state of emergency.[34] The resulting resentment of the general population only led to increased support for ETA's cause. Franco's frequent declaration of a "state of exception" in response to unrest in the Basque country permitted the government to exercise emergency powers there. Such political repression highlighted the Franco regime's "token respect for the rhetorical guarantees of civil liberties enshrined in the Francoist constitution."[35]

The 1978 Constitution established a legal framework for the return of decentralization and home rule. Despite a rather cumbersome process for devolving power, much progress was made in this area between December 1978 and February 1981. Catalonia, the Basque country excluding Navarra, and Galicia obtained autonomous status. The February 1981 coup attempt slowed the decentralization momentum, but by early 1983 the current seventeen Autonomous Communities had statutes approved.

Autonomous statutes and regional legislatures exist, but Spain has by no means become a federal structure or seen a major transfer of power from Madrid to the regions.[36] Educational policy remains a source of much tension and uncertainty. Major questions about regional financing and other problems remain. While slow, some progress in decentralization has occurred. In the Basque Autonomous Community, steps toward policy implementation have involved internal governmental organization, law enforcement, financing, budgets, taxation, communications, and energy.[37] The Basque language, Euskera, now has special status as a distinctive regional language, sharing co-official status with Castillan. Bilingualism continues as the Basque government's eventual policy goal. Regional elections have become almost routine. Spain's policy toward its peripheral nations, particularly the Basques, should therefore receive mixed reviews at this time. Other factors such as terrorism continue to plague Spain's record on human rights and threaten the entire process of devolution of power from Madrid.

Since before Franco's death, government responses to ETA violence have brought the greatest number of alleged violations of human rights. Throughout the transition period, the overall level of violence within Spain, and in particular in the Basque provinces, may have provided the most tangible motive for the attempted coup in 1981. During 1980, 121 people died as a result of various acts of terrorism. In one week in early May 1980, eight people including a prominent general were killed, and General Valenzuela, head of the king's military household, barely escaped an assassination attempt. Influential members of the military had grave doubts about the capacity and willingness of democratic institutions to deal with the problem.

After the 1981 coup attempt, the level of violence dropped below that of the late 1970s. It nevertheless continues as a very serious problem, particularly in the Basque provinces.[38] Targets have generally been restricted to military personnel, members of the security forces, governmental officials, or members of the business community who ignore demands made on them. More recently, ETA has assassinated some former members who had accepted the government's offer of amnesty. To add to the problem, radical separatist movements have recently surfaced in both Catalonia and the Canary Islands.

In an effort to curb the violence, the government passed in 1981 a tough anti-terrorist statute. The law suspends certain constitutional guarantees and criminal justice procedures for individuals charged with terrorist activity. With the consent of a judge, prisoners charged with committing, aiding, or abetting terrorism can be held up to ten days incommunicado; their homes may be searched, their mail opened, and their telephones tapped. Until 1985 prisoners had no right to legal counsel during the period of detention. The amended statute provides for the presence of legal counsel during interrogation, although the attorney may not confer with the prisoner privately until the police declare the interrogation finished. Prisoners do not have the right to choose their own legal counsel, nor do they have the right to an independent medical examination. Responsibility for appointing counsel lies with the various regional bar associations.

The supervising judge may ask for reports on treatment and must review the suspension periodically to decide if it may continue. The government must report to Parliament every three months on the application of the law. During the first nine months of 1985, police arrested 393 persons under the law. This compares with 849 during 1984 and 691 in 1983.[39]

The 1981 law also sought to curb all dealings with terrorists. *Egin*, the organ of Herri Batasuna, the political arm of ETA, has suffered frequent fines and threats of closings. The touchiness of the government on the subject of terrorism extends to other publications as well. This is illustrated by the case of Javier Vinader, a reporter for the magazine *Interviu*. In 1982 Vinader wrote a story based on information gained from the police about right-wing activities directed against ETA in the Basque country. After publication of the story, ETA assassinated two of the individuals named in the story. Vinader was prosecuted under the 1981 anti-terrorism statute, found guilty of aiding and abetting the assassinations, and sentenced to two years in prison. While the case was on appeal, he jumped bail and fled to London. Vinader returned to Madrid in February 1984 and was arrested. His appeals were rejected by the courts. Amnesty International directed an appeal to the government for Vinader's release on the basis that the imprisonment violated the right to free expression. The government released Vinader in March 1984.[40]

Some human rights activists have criticized the 1981 anti-terrorist law as a serious departure from human rights principles. In particular, Amnesty International has criticized the use of incommunicado detention because the practice breeds opportunities for abuse. In their view, the judiciary, particularly in ETA cases, has not been diligent in carrying out its supervisory responsibilities.[41] The government will not likely yield on this point because it believes the law necessary to cope successfully with ETA. All of the cases of possible abuse cited in the 1985 Amnesty International Report and the 1985 State Department Country Report to the Congress involve ETA members.

ETA activists regularly claim political persecution, but constitutional guarantees of individual rights have normally been respected in practice. All ETA members currently detained have either been convicted of, or are awaiting trial in connection with, ordinary crimes. Occasionally the police have overreacted to ETA activity with zealous searches of neighborhoods. For example, in a 1983 search for a kidnapped Madrid banker, police restricted access to and from the area and inspected dwellings for over two days. Questions still remain about the blanket application of the anti-terrorism statute to large groups of citizens.

The 1980 Amnesty International Report cited fourteen cases of maltreatment or torture of prisoners. Of these, the most prominent concerned José Ignacio Arregui, an ETA member who died of pneumonia. In response to accusations of torture while Ignacio was held incommunicado under an earlier anti-terrorist law, the government began an investigation that resulted in charges against several officials in the case. In the aftermath of the 1981 coup attempt, the charges were quietly dropped.

Another widely publicized case occurred in May 1981. Immediately after the ETA's attempted assassination of General Valenzuela, head of the king's military household, the Civil Guard arrested three youths from Santander in Almeria. Officers of the Civil Guard in sworn statements claimed the three died as the car in which they were riding went out of control after a struggle between the three and their captors. The physical evidence did not support the testimony and a special prosecutor was named. Eventually, the colonel in charge of their transportation to Madrid was prosecuted along with three others for failure to carry out his duty, but the charges were not upheld.

We must distinguish between earlier and later cases. These events indicate that under elected governments maltreatment has not been condoned, though judicial procedures have not always resolved the cases to the satisfaction of critics. The most important fact concerns the willingness to investigate reports of police misconduct. In the 1983–1985 period, investigations resulted in punishment for thirty members of various security forces for mistreatment of prisoners.[42]

As noted above, members of ETA routinely accuse the government of abuses. A recent case is that of Mikel Zabalza, a prisoner who died subsequent to his arrest in December 1985. The government claimed he drowned during an escape attempt. An autopsy observed by an independent medical team found no evidence of torture, but Amnesty International, because of the issue of incommunicado detention, has raised questions about government policy. The same holds true for José María Olarra and his brothers, arrested and questioned because of their ETA connections.[43]

At present, apart from ETA accusations, Spain has no "prisoners of conscience." The last case to qualify was possibly that of Albert Boadella, director of the *El Joglars* Mime groups, considered by some a political prisoner. Boadella, released on July 22, 1979, had been imprisoned by a military court for a play, *La Torna*, about a civilian immigrant condemned to death by a court-martial in 1974. The military had accused Boadella of insulting the honor of the military. Post-Franco governments have made several offers of amnesty, and the 1983 reform of the penal law concerning pretrial detention resulted in the release of many prisoners incarcerated pending trial because the "speedy trial" provisions of the new law could not be satisfied.

International Organizations

Spain ratified the Constitution of the European Commission of Human Rights in 1978 and thus became a member of the Commission, which is a subdivision of the Council of Europe. Individual Spaniards have not availed themselves of this international mechanism for addressing questions of human rights. Through 1983, no Spaniard had brought an action before the court despite the fact that

Spain has a member judge, Eduardo Garcia de Enterria, on it.[44] Various Spanish governments have permitted investigative groups to enter the country, openly tour, and report on the status of human rights. Amnesty International reports that the government is accessible and generally responsive to inquiries and requests from them.[45] The government established an Office of Human Rights in the Ministry of Foreign Affairs in late 1983 to maintain relations with international human rights organizations.

Spain is an active member of many international human rights organizations. Of the twenty-one multilateral treaties listed in the latest State Department compendium of relevant materials, Spain had signed and ratified seventeen, including the International Covenant on Civil and Political Rights, the Optional Protocol to the International Covenant on Civil and Political Rights, and the Genocide Convention.[46] In terms of acceptance of the obligations contained in these treaties, the only reservations deal either with the terms under which disputes may be submitted to the International Court of Justice or with preserving special relationships with other Spanish-speaking countries established by prior treaty obligations.

CONCLUSION

Human rights remain a problem for Spain as well as for all countries of the world. Spain's major concern is political terrorism in the Basque country, the government's efforts to control and eliminate it, and the rights of the citizens of this and other peripheral nations that form Spain. Charges of governmental support of anti-terrorist violence and allegations of mistreatment and even torture of persons allegedly connected with terrorist activities continue to be heard. Violent terrorist acts against hundreds of individuals in Spain by many groups, but especially the Basque separatist group ETA, make many citizens fearful, even though the targets have generally been police and military personnel. Both, however, revolve around an ongoing political tension stemming from ethnic nationalism in Spain. Policy disputes concerning language usage, cultural rights, and social identity stem squarely from the larger questions of political self-determination and nation-state status for Spain's ethnic nationals, particularly the Basques.

Respect for human rights in Spain has nevertheless improved dramatically with the country's transformation from an authoritarian regime under Francisco Franco to the current liberal, parliamentary democracy. Voter participation is high. Basic individual liberties such as the freedoms of speech, press, religion, assembly, movement, and participation in political affairs are fundamental to the system. Furthermore, and most important for long-term prospects, Spain's liberal democratic system has created institutions which seek to provide basic protection for these freedoms. The country's system of courts, particularly the recent creation of the Constitutional Court, suggest an institutional mechanism through which accusations of violations of human rights may be addressed. Other judicial institutions like the ombudsman-like Defender of the People are also positive developments in this area.

The most important indicator, however, of the progress Spain has made and will continue to make in human rights is the very success of its democracy. Spain's transition to democracy appears at this time as a permanent change in the direction of its political history. The country's move away from authoritarian rule brought it squarely and permanently in line with the much better developed democratic traditions of its other European neighbors. The dismantling of the previous regime was accomplished in a nonviolent and nonrevolutionary manner, thus leaving little life-threatening animosity or motives for revenge, as was the case following the Spanish Civil War. The maneuvering to transform the system and instill democratic principles occurred at the elite level, permitting the necessary time and compromise that must accompany any such long-term solution. But most important, despite the fact that the country's elite tended to set the course for the country's democratic development, adherence to democratic principles, norms, and procedures appears to have taken root rather quickly at the mass level. The average Spanish citizen seems to have accepted the principles of liberal democracy, and all that entails, including the defense of basic individual rights. The wide acceptance of democratic principles will be the best guarantor of the long-term status of human rights in this Iberian country.

NOTES

1. Richard Herr, *Spain* (Englewood Cliffs, N.J.: Prentice-Hall, 1971); Stanley G. Payne, *A History of Spain and Portugal: in Two Volumes* (Madison: University of Wisconsin Press, 1973). Little scholarly work has focused specifically on the military dictatorship of Miguel Primo de Rivera. On the Second Republic, see Gabriel Jackson, *The Spanish Republic and the Civil War: 1931–1939* (Princeton: Princeton University Press, 1965). The literature on the Spanish Civil War is voluminous. See, for example, Hugh Thomas, *The Spanish Civil War*, rev. ed. (New York: Harper & Row, 1977). On the Franco period, see Charles W. Anderson, *The Political Economy of Modern Spain* (Madison: University of Wisconsin Press,1970); Richard Gunther, *Public Policy in a No-Party State* (Berkeley: University of California Press, 1980). On the transition to democracy, see Raymond Carr and Juan P. Fusi, *Spain: Dictatorship to Democracy* (London: Allen & Unwin, 1979); John F. Coverdale, *The Political Transformation of Spain after Franco* (New York: Praeger, 1979); José Maravall, *Transition to Democracy in Spain* (New York: St. Martin's Press, 1982); Thomas D. Lancaster and Gary Prevost, eds., *Politics and Change in Spain* (New York: Praeger, 1985); Paul Preston, *The Triumph of Democracy in Spain* (London: Methuen, 1986); Richard Gunther, Giacomo Sani, and Goldie Shabad, *Spain After Franco: The Making of a Competitive Party System* (Berkeley: University of California Press, 1986); Peter McDonough, Samuel H. Barnes, and Antonio López Pina, "The Growth of Democratic Legitimacy in Spain," *American Political Science Review* 80 (1986): 735–60.

2. Hugh Thomas, *The Spanish Civil War* (New York: Harper & Row, 1961), estimates that 175,000 of these were on the Republican side, 110,000 on the Nationalist.

3. Coverdale, 13. Others have estimated the diaspora at 400,000. See Robert Graham,

Spain: Change of a Nation (London: Michael Joseph, 1984), 35. Graham notes that battle deaths and exiles comprised 3 percent of Spain's 1936 population of twenty-six million.

4. Preston, 22.

5. Juan J. Linz, "Legislatures in Organic Statist-Authoritarian Regimes—The Case of Spain," in *Legislatures in Development: Dynamics of Change in New and Old States*, ed. Joel Smith and Lloyd D. Musolf (Durham, N.C.: Duke University Press, 1979).

6. In one notable instance the Church censors banned Garcia Serrano's *La fiel de infantería* after the novel had won a national literary prize.

7. Graham, 124.

8. Graham estimates that 35 percent of the workers in the shoe industry were not registered (127).

9. Juan A. Giner, "Journalists, Mass Media and Public Opinion in Spain: 1938–1982," in *The Press and the Rebirth of Iberian Democracy*, ed. Kenneth A. Maxwell (Westport, Conn.: Greenwood Press, 1983).

10. Preston, 120.

11. Quoted in Preston, 60.

12. Fusi and Carr, 220.

13. Graham, 246.

14. On the drafting and contents of Spain's Constitution of 1978, see Antonio López Pina, "Shaping the Constitution," in *Spain at the Polls, 1977, 1979, and 1982*, ed. Howard R. Penniman and Eusebio M. Mujal-León (Durham, N.C.: Duke University Press and American Enterprise Institute, 1985); Richard Gunther, "Constitutional Change in Contemporary Spain," in *Redesigning the State: The Politics of Constitutional Change in Industrial Nations*, ed. Keith Banting and Richard Simeon (Toronto: University of Toronto Press, 1984); Richard Gunther and Roger Blough, "Religious Conflict and Consensus in Spain: A Tale of Two Constitutions," *World Affairs* 143 (Spring 1981), 366–412; and Andrea R. Bonime, "The Spanish State Structure: Constitution Making and the Creation of the New State," in *Politics and Change in Spain*, ed. Thomas D. Lancaster and Gary Prevost (New York: Praeger, 1985).

15. López Pina, "Shaping the Constitution," 35. The following relies on his discussion, 35–42.

16. López Pina, 38.

17. For commentary on Spain's Constitution of 1978, see Enrique Sánchez Goyanes, *El sistema constitucional español* (Madrid: Paraninfo, 1981); Jose Belmonte, *La Constitución: texto y contexto* (Madrid: Prensa Española, 1979); Luis Sanchez Agesta, *Sistema político de la constitución española de 1978*, 3d ed. (Madrid: Nacional, 1984).

18. The Constitution requires the maintenance of a public system of Social Security that guarantees sufficient assistance and social aid during situations of special need in times of unemployment (Article 41). Similar references are made to the right to health protection. The Constitution also encourages promotion and access to culture, the promotion of scientific and technical investigation (Article 44); the right to personal development in a healthy environment (Article 45); the conservation and promotion of works of historical, cultural, and artistic value (Article 46); the right to adequate and dignified housing (Article 47); the promotion of conditions facilitating participation of youth in political, social, economic, and cultural development (Article 48); the policy of prevention, treatment, and rehabilitation and integration of the physically, sensorially, and mentally handicapped (Article 49); and the guarantee of economic sufficiency for the elderly (Article 50). All of these, of course, require legislative action to implement them.

19. Department of State, "Country Reports on Human Rights Practices for 1985" (Report Submitted to the Committee on Foreign Affairs House of Representatives and the Committee on Foreign Relations U.S. Senate, February 1986).

20. The following section relies heavily on Thomas D. Lancaster and Micheal W. Giles, "Spain," in *Legal Traditions and Systems: An International Handbook*, ed. Alan N. Katz (New York: Greenwood Press, 1986).

21. Lancaster and Giles, 365.

22. Lancaster and Giles, 365.

23. Paul Preston, *The Triumph of Democracy in Spain* (London: Methuen, 1986), 26.

24. Title 6, Article 117: 3.

25. The Court of Public Order, created in 1963 with the support of the military, is the other Francoist special court which merits mention. Constituted as a response to the criticism over use of the military courts to try civilians, these courts had jurisdiction over cases involving subversion, broadly defined, and illegal propaganda. The Court of Public Order, a patently political court, became a focal point of protest against the system's abuses of human rights toward the end of the Franco regime. These abuses became so blatant, and the cries of protest so loud, that in 1970 the Spanish bar unprecedentedly called for its dissolution. The 1978 Constitution eliminated the Court of Public Order. See J. J. Toharia, "The Spanish Judiciary: A Sociological Study" (Ph.D. diss., Yale University, 1974), 400–404.

26. Lancaster and Giles, 367.

27. W. W. Pierson and F. G. Gil, *Governments of Latin America* (New York: McGraw-Hill, 1957), 291.

28. Lancaster and Giles, 369. See also J. L. Garcia Ruiz, *El recurso de amparo en el Derecho español* (Madrid: Editora Nacional, 1980); and V. Gimeno Sendra, "Naturaleza juridica y objeto procesal del recurso de amparo," *Revista Española de Derecho Constitucional* 6 (1982).

29. Thomas D. Lancaster and Michael S. Lewis-Beck, "The Spanish Voter: Tradition, Economics, Ideology," *Journal of Politics* 48 (1986): 648–74.

30. Jorge de Esteban and Luis López Guerra, "Electoral Rules and Candidate Selection," in *Spain at the Polls*, ed. Penniman and Mugal-León, 66.

31. On the labor movement during the Franco regime, see José Maravall, *Dictatorship and Political Dissent: Workers and Students in Franco's Spain* (London: 1979); and John Amsden, *Collective Bargaining and Class Conflict in Spain* (London: Weidenfeld and Nicolson, 1972).

32. On the labor movement during the transition, see Victor Pérez Dias, *Clase obrera, partidos y sindicatos* (Madrid: Fundación del Instituto Nacional de Industria, 1979); Robert M. Fishman, "The Labor Movement in Spain: From Authoritarianism to Democracy," *Comparative Politics* 14 (1982): 281–305; and Gary Prevost, "Change and Continuity and the Spanish Labor Movement," *West European Politics* 7 (January 1984), 80–94.

33. See Juan J. Linz and Amando de Miguel, "Within-National Differences and Comparison: the Eight Spains," in *Comparing Nations*, ed. Richard L. Merritt and Stein Rokkan (New Haven: Yale University Press, 1966).

34. Carr and Fusi, 160.

35. Preston, 14. The Burgos Trials of 1970 focused world attention on the Franco regime's crusade against Basque nationalist aspirations and the regime's general repressive nature. The trials' legal pretext was the Law on Banditry and Terrorism applied against sixteen defendants. These show trials drew international attention to Franco's persecution

of the Basques. They also demonstrated the Franco regime's insensitivity to the worldwide revulsion they provoked. See Preston, 32–35, for details.

36. This discussion relies on Thomas D. Lancaster, "Comparative Nationalism: the Basques in Spain and France" (paper presented at the European Consortium for Political Research's Joint Sessions of Workshops, Barcelona, Spain, March 25–30, 1985), 9.

37. Robert P. Clark, "Madrid and the Ethnic Homelands: Is Consociational Democracy Possible in Post-Franco Spain?" in *Politics and Change in Spain*, ed. Lancaster and Prevost, 82–83.

38. From 1978 to 1982 violence caused 390 deaths. In 1983 there were 38, 27 in 1984, and 49 during the first nine months of 1985.

39. State Department Report, 1985.

40. Amnesty International, *Spain: The Question of Torture*, Documents Exchanged by Amnesty International and the Government of Spain (London: Amnesty International Publications, 1985).

41. Amnesty International, 28.

42. State Department Report, 1985.

43. Amnesty International, 15.

44. Information from Council of Europe, *Yearbook of the European Convention on Human Rights*, (Dordrecht, Netherlands: Martinus Nijhoff, annual) which lists all cases heard by the Commission.

45. Amnesty International.

46. Of those treaties not signed by Spain, two involve statelessness and two concern questions relating to the administration of criminal justice.

SUGGESTED READINGS

Barnes, Samuel H., Peter McDonough, and Antonio López Pina. "The Development of Partisanship in New Democracies: The Case of Spain." *American Journal of Political Science* 29 (1985): 695–720.

Graham, Robert. *Spain: Change of a Nation*. London: Michael Joseph, 1984.

Gunther, Richard, Giacomo Sani, and Goldie Shabad. *Spain After Franco: The Making of a Competitive Party System*. Berkeley: University of California Press, 1986.

Lancaster, Thomas D. "Economics, Democracy, and Spanish Elections." *Political Behavior* 6 (1984): 353–67.

Lancaster, Thomas D. and Michael W. Giles. "Spain." In *Legal Traditions and Systems: An International Handbook*. Ed. Alan N. Katz. New York: Greenwood Press, 1986.

Lancaster, Thomas D. and Michael S. Lewis-Beck. "The Spanish Voter: Tradition, Economics, Ideology." *Journal of Politics* 48 (1986): 648–74.

Lancaster, Thomas D. and Gary Prevost, eds. *Politics and Change in Spain*. New York: Praeger, 1985.

Maravall, José. *The Transition to Democracy in Spain*. New York: St. Martin's Press, 1982.

McDonough, Peter, Samuel H. Barnes, and Antonio López Pina. "The Spanish Public in Political Transition." *British Journal of Political Science* 11 (1981): 49–79.

———. "The Growth of Democratic Legitimacy in Spain." *American Political Science Review* 80 (September 1986): 735–60.

Mujal-León, Eusebio. *Communism and Political Change in Spain*. Bloomington: Indiana University Press, 1983.

Penniman, Howard R. and Eusebio M. Mujal-León, eds. *Spain at the Polls, 1977, 1979, and 1982*. Durham, N.C.: Duke University Press and American Enterprise Institute, 1985.

Preston, Paul. *The Triumph of Democracy in Spain*. London: Methuen, 1986.

18

UGANDA

Edward Kannyo

At the end of January 1986, the guerrilla forces of the National Resistance Movement (NRM) defeated the Uganda National Liberation Army (UNLA) forces of the incumbent military regime and quickly proceeded to take control of the entire country. For the fifth time since the attainment of political independence from the British in 1962, Uganda had undergone a major political change.

Previously, the country had experienced a civilian constitutional coup (1966); a classical military coup (1971); a successful foreign invasion backed by armed Ugandan insurgents (1978–1979); and another military coup of the classical type in July 1985. Between 1981 and 1985, Uganda was involved in a bitter struggle between guerrilla forces and the military and paramilitary forces of the Obote regime. By the end of 1985 the conflict had developed into a full-fledged civil war pitting the rapidly expanding National Resistance Army (NRA)—the armed wing of the NRM—against the crumbling UNLA, which had overthrown the Obote regime earlier in July.

The upheavals that have punctuated Uganda's politics since 1962 have been accompanied by an escalating spiral of instability, violence, and socioeconomic disintegration which has led to some of the grossest forms of human rights violations experienced anywhere in the world in recent decades. Possibly hundreds of thousands of Ugandans have perished over the last fifteen years as a direct or indirect result of the violence, and others have been forced to flee the country.[1]

Political instability and violence have led to the disruption of economic institutions and of administrative and welfare services, and have had other negative effects leading to a drastic decline in the living conditions of the majority of the population. This decline was most remarkable during the eight-year reign of the Amin regime.[2]

The majority of African states have been subject to different degrees of political and socioeconomic tensions and conflict arising out of the struggle for control of the state and the attendant access to economic and other resources among the politico-administrative and military elites, competition for economic resources between the different social groups, and the disintegration of traditional social groups and their normative value systems. Nevertheless, in most cases, a degree of political and social stability has been achieved through regimes founded on the basis of authoritarian civilian-military coalitions of various types.

These coalitions have been cemented by a combination of factors including economic rewards to followers and clients; ethnic or other types of communal loyalties; ideological or programmatic considerations and external support based on ideological, economic, and strategic factors. What is remarkable about Uganda is the fact that none of these factors or any combination of them has been able to ensure political stability and orderly government. It is to the analysis of this rather unique experience that this chapter addresses itself.

HISTORICAL BACKGROUND

Whatever the philosophical justification for its existence, the state as an institution is, in the final analysis, based on the threat of the use of force to sustain itself and the prevailing socioeconomic order. However, while force is crucial, no stable state owes its survival solely to force. A far more important factor is the public acceptance of the legitimacy of the state and the socioeconomic and legal order expressed, promoted and reinforced by its political, economic, social, and cultural institutions.[3] Once this legitimacy is lost, tyranny, revolution, or anarchy must ensue. For many years in Uganda there have been manifestations of each of these possibilities.

The roots of political and social instability in Uganda lie in the fragmentation of the polity at the time of the attainment of political independence in 1962. This fragmentation is traceable to political, administrative, economic, and cultural processes which developed during the colonial regime.

Like virtually all other African states, Uganda is a creation of the nineteenth-century European colonial expansion. It encloses dozens of cultural and linguistic groups which had previously lived independently of each other. Within the space of sixty years, they were arbitrarily brought under one politico-administrative system.

The colonial regime was a bureaucratic authoritarian system and did not provide for full-fledged political participation by the indigenous peoples at the national level. In Uganda, meaningful African political participation was restricted to local administrative levels which varied in size and form of government.

The kingdoms of Buganda, Bunyoro, Ankole, and Toro enjoyed higher degrees of administrative autonomy than the other parts of the colony. Among the kingdoms, Buganda stood out through its greater size, its greater administrative autonomy and, more particularly, its attachment to the "1900 Agreement" signed with the British government which provided for a high degree of political autonomy and was regarded as a covenant by the Buganda government, and the resultant special consideration which the colonial regime always showed to the Buganda monarchy.[4]

The restriction of effective African political participation to local levels during the colonial regime was compounded by the uneven socioeconomic development of the country. Buganda took the lead in the development of modern education, commerce, and the cultivation and marketing of export cash crops. The relative lag of the other parts of the country, compounded by the desire of important segments of the political elites in Buganda to seek independence outside the colonial territorial framework, as decolonization looked imminent, led to resentment on the part of political leaders from other areas which must on balance be considered as having been an obstacle to the evolution of strong national political leadership on the eve of political independence.[5]

Another major colonial legacy has been rivalry based on conflict between Protestant and Roman Catholic political elites. This rivalry originated in the late nineteenth-century struggles between the French (Catholic) and English (Protestant) Christian missionaries, backed by their respective countries, for control of the kingdom of Buganda, which became the nucleus and heart of the future Uganda. It was reinforced by the dominant role which the missionaries came to play in the provision of primary and secondary education for their followers. When national political parties were formed in the 1950s, they came to reflect these religious rivalries. Thus, the Democratic party (DP) was identified with Roman Catholic elites who sought to redress their discriminatory underrepresentation in national and local administrative bodies, while the Uganda People's Congress (UPC) was, though to a lesser degree than was the case with respect to the DP and Catholicism, identified with the Protestant elites who sought to preserve their overrepresentation.

In the period immediately before and after the attainment of political independence, the major claims articulated by the contending political parties and groups involved the institutional character of the postcolonial state, that is, unitarism vs. federalism and the closely related issue of the terms on which Buganda would be incorporated in an independent Uganda; the redress of socioeconomic inequalities between regions and districts; and the representation of different religious groups in elite political and administrative positions. The resultant pattern of politics was extremely complex.

Broadly speaking, in the period 1961–1966, politics revolved around the overlapping and yet conflictual relationships between (1) the two major political parties, the UPC and the DP; (2) the four kingdoms of Buganda, Bunyoro, Toro, and Ankole; (3) the district of Busoga, whose dominant elites wanted to convert it to a kingdom; and (4) the other districts of the country which did not have monarchical institutions and comprised the majority of the population of the country. The dominant elites in these various institutions competed for power and influence at certain times and over certain issues and collaborated at other times and over other issues. The same pattern applied within the institutions themselves.

The four kingdoms were united in their determination to preserve their monarchical institutions and a certain degree of political autonomy. However, in the period leading up to the political independence of the country, the leaders of Bunyoro, Toro, and Ankole would often join with the leaders from other political groups to oppose any attempts on the part of Buganda to secede from the country or to acquire any status which exceeded their own. In addition, Bunyoro had a direct quarrel with Buganda over some border territories which the British had transferred from Bunyoro to Buganda at the beginning of the colonial regime.

The elites in Busoga sought to convert their district into a monarchical unit and to emulate the institutions of the Buganda and Bunyoro kingdoms, with which the region shared important cultural and historical links. As for the rest of the districts in the country, the main goal was to maintain as much parity of status as possible with the kingdom areas.

It was against this complex background that the UPC and the DP competed for control of the postcolonial state. Both parties were united in their desire to preserve the inherited state in its colonial boundaries. In spite of some rhetorical ideological disputes within the UPC between 1964 and 1966, there were no serious class ideological differences between the two parties. The best one can say is that the UPC contained more people who espoused a more radical interpretation of African nationalism and who advocated a more neutralist foreign policy posture than the DP. However, these individuals were far from being dominant within the party.[6] Both parties were compelled to make compromises with the strong prevailing ethno-cultural sentiments.

The two most contentious issues which the political leaders faced at the time of independence were the degree of autonomy which would be enjoyed by the Kingdom of Buganda and the other kingdoms and the question of who would be head of state. The 1962 Independence Constitution provided for a complex political structure granting a high degree of regional autonomy for Buganda, lesser autonomy for the kingdoms of Bunyoro, Toro, and Ankole, and even lesser autonomy for the "Territory" of Busoga. The rest of the country had a unitary relationship with the central government.

As had happened in other former British colonies, when Uganda became independent, the British monarch became the head of state and was represented in that ceremonial position by a governor-general who, in this as in other cases, was the last British governor. However, it was clear that this was a temporary arrangement and within a year, the question of who would replace the governor-general arose. This was an emotional issue for the various political groups. As George W. Kanyeihamba has recalled:

While there was agreement on this change the problem was to find the right candidate. The kingdoms would not accept a commoner to occupy the important position of Head of State and thereby become, in importance, greater than their Kings. Buganda went further, no one even if he be King, could be Head of State unless he was the Kabaka [King] of Buganda Himself. The non-kingdoms districts were not silent either. Unused to the regions of Kings they would not accept one of them to be Head of their Independent State.[7]

A compromise solution was found. The head of state would be chosen from among the traditional rulers. However, in order to satisfy the nonkingdom areas, the position of "constitutional head," a type of surrogate king, was created for these districts. Any one of these leaders would be eligible for the position of head of state. The head of state was to be known as "president." There was also to be a vice president, and both offices were to be held for a term of five years and were to be elected by the National Assembly on a secret ballot.

The *Kabaka* of Buganda became the head of state and the *Kyabazinga* (king) of Busoga (who was also the UPC vice president) became vice president of Uganda. To quote Kanyeihamba again: "The Baganda were jubilant, the other Kings happy and the rest of the country satisfied for now there was a possibility that each region was in a position to produce a President."[8]

It is almost certain that this solution would have failed eventually. The replacement of the *Kabaka* of Buganda as head of state, which would have been demanded to give a chance to another ruler, would have been strongly resisted in Buganda. Moreover, the creation of nontraditional "king surrogates" outside the kingdom areas was not universally popular and had given rise to conflicts within some districts.

The first government of independent Uganda was a coalition between the UPC and the Buganda-based and monarchist *Kabaka Yekka* (KY) movement. However, by 1966 disagreements between the two organizations had led to the termination of the alliance. Defections from the DP and KY had enabled the UPC to form a government on its own. At the same time, the consolidation of a parliamentary majority by the UPC coincided with, and was apparently closely connected with, a plan by Obote's opponents within the party to remove him and his supporters through defeat in the party or parliament.

Between 1964 and 1966 two factions within the ruling party emerged, and as the struggle for control of the state intensified, they inexorably moved toward a major clash. One faction was headed by the leader of the UPC and the prime minister, Milton Obote. This faction was identified with a more anti-monarchist and hard-line position on the Buganda–Central Government question and a more neutralist foreign policy stance. The opposing faction, led by party secretary-general Grace Ibingira, who was also a senior cabinet member, was regarded as being more accommodative toward the country's monarchical institutions, more moderate in its attitudes towards the role of the Buganda state within Uganda, and more sympathetic to the West in the sphere of foreign relations.

In early 1966 Milton Obote used the army and police to carry out a swift strike against his intra-party opposition. Grace Ibingira and four allies—all senior party and cabinet ministers—were arrested at a cabinet meeting and were eventually imprisoned for nearly five years without trial, on charges of having plotted to overthrow the government by force.

The intra-party conflict had strong regional-ethnic undertones. Ibingira and the principal members of his faction were from the southern parts of the country, while Obote and most, though not all, of his key supporters were from the northern parts. Even more significant, the police and army which Obote used to strike against his opponents had been overwhelmingly recruited from the northern parts of the country. It is generally accepted that Obote largely owed his success in the intra-party struggle to the fact that the military identified with him on an ethno-regional basis and remained loyal to him.[9]

After arresting his opponents, Obote suspended the 1962 Constitution. He then removed the *Kabaka* of Buganda from the office of ceremonial president, which he had occupied since 1963 simultaneously with his role as *Kabaka* and as part of the bargain which had brought about the coalition between the UPC and the KY. Obote himself took over the presidency in an executive capacity. What had taken place was a civilian constitutional coup with the support of the army.

The *Kabaka* left the official presidential residence and retired to his palace on the outskirts of Kampala, but took political and legal steps together with the Buganda government to challenge Obote's constitutional coup. Obote claimed that the *Kabaka* planned to use violent means to challenge him and that the *Kabaka* had participated in plots against him even before 1966. The *Kabaka* denied those charges. In May, Obote ordered the army, then under the command of a certain Major-General Idi Amin, to attack the *Kabaka*'s palace, allegedly to search for arms which Obote later claimed were being distributed to the *Kabaka*'s supporters. In the ensuing battle, which caused a large but unspecified number of casualties, the palace was shelled, and the *Kabaka* barely escaped with his life. He eventually made his way to Britain where in 1969 he died a destitute exile.

Immediately after the confrontation, a state of emergency was declared in the Buganda region and many people were arrested. An undetermined number of civilians were killed in isolated attacks by soldiers in different parts of the region. In 1967 Obote introduced a new constitution which abolished the monarchical institutions in the entire country, abolished federalism, and concentrated power in his hands as executive president. Parliament, whose five-year term would have expired in 1967, was extended for another five years without a referendum or any other form of popular consultation. Clearly, the country had moved from a liberal polity towards an authoritarian regime based essentially on the loyalty of the military to the regime. In 1969, following an attempt on Obote's life, the opposition DP was banned and the country became effectively a one-party state.

The overthrow of the Buganda monarchy, the imposition of a state of emergency whose provisions were used to imprison hundreds of people without trial, and a pervasive atmosphere of police-military intimidation created bitterness and extreme hostility, especially in the Buganda region. Although Buganda represented only 20–25 percent of the country's total population, the strategic location of the region—which contains the country's capital city, the international airport, and the main cultural and socioeconomic institutions—meant that the hostility of the majority of the Buganda population translated into political vulnerability for the regime, which could be exploited by other opponents as well.

Opposition to the regime was not necessarily confined to Buganda. Although most of the DP parliamentary opposition had defected to the regime for a number of reasons, possibly including political conviction and the hopes of ministerial appointments, there was little clear indication that those who had voted for them had changed their loyalties. The Catholic-Protestant political division remained strong in many parts of the country. Even within the UPC, factional conflict had only been suppressed, not resolved, following the 1966 constitutional coup and the suppression of intra-party opposition. Obote was not able to evolve a viable political formula for noncoercive government.[10]

In 1969, following the attempt on Obote's life, the state of emergency was extended to the whole country. Between 1966 and 1971, approximately 570 people were listed in the *Uganda Gazette* as having been arrested under the provisions of the Emergency Regulations.[11]

Since 1966, control of the military has been central to the exercise of political power in Uganda. At the same time, military loyalty has been primarily predicated on the creation of a core of officers and soldiers whose support can be more or less expected in the long run on the basis of common ethnic or regional identity with the leader. Thus, politicized ethnicity and militarism have been twin features of Uganda's political life since independence.

POLITICAL CONFLICT, ETHNICITY AND MILITARISM

Right from the time of the attainment of political independence, some Ugandan political leaders expressed concern about the ethnic composition of the army and its potential implications for the exercise of political power. Later, the use of the military to determine the outcome of political conflict, the deterioration of discipline, and the harassment of civilians were to become important causes of human rights violations in the country.

The military organization that was bequeathed by the departing British colonial administrators, in the form of one infantry battalion, was predominantly recruited from the northern parts of the country, which were also economically the most underdeveloped and represented less than 25 percent of the country's total population. According to what the minister of defense told the National Assembly in 1968, within the northern region, recruitment into the army had been concentrated in East Acholi and West Nile and Madi. In the police force, the bulk of the recruits were from West Acholi and Teso (in the northeast).[12]

The ethno-regional composition of the army was one of the subjects of the intra-party conflict in the 1964–1966 period.[13] Obote and his key supporters managed to maintain the regional imbalance in the military which worked to their advantage.

From 1966, the perception that there was a close link between the ethnic composition of the army and the exercise of political power became more pronounced. In 1967 B. Byanyima, an opposition member, told the National Assembly: "Already, especially in Kingdom areas and in Bantu [i.e., southern] areas, it is a common saying that Obote is now able to pass his measures through this Parliament because he has got Uganda Troops which are predominantly Nilotic (i.e., northern)."[14]

Occasionally, politicians from those areas that were underrepresented in the military spoke out in favor of an adjustment to bring out more balanced representation. Thus in the debate on the proposals for the 1967 Constitution, E.M.K. Mulira, a member from Buganda, suggested that "in order to avoid dictatorship from one Region, our Army should reflect the unity we are talking about by having in the Army people from all Regions each of which have its own quota either on a district level or on a regional basis."[15]

The growing prominence of the army, its increasing use for partisan political purposes by the regime, and its growing indiscipline reflected in, among other things, harassment of civilians, were questioned in the National Assembly from time to time. In 1967 H. M. Luande, an independent member of the opposition, told the National Assembly that the public were wondering if the country was under military government, and complained that the army and police were being misused in a partisan manner.[16] A. A. Nekyon, an independent-minded member of the UPC, complained that party officials who should have been organizing the party had been transferred to the security forces, "which means in fact, that the party is out of power without knowing that it is not in power and the Security Forces are, in fact, in power without knowing that they are in power."[17] In 1969 J. H. Obonyo, a DP member, complained that a military contingent had been used in the arrest of fellow opposition member A. K. Mayanja.[18]

The attitudes of some leading officials in government, as expressed in public statements, are likely to have encouraged the military to think of itself as a crucial actor in a brutal political contest in which ethnic identity was a major consideration. In 1967, in response to a complaint by a member from Buganda concerning the fact that when dealing with civilians, soldiers sometimes inquired about their ethnic identities, F. K. Onama, the minister of defense, sought to justify the practice by saying that in 1966, this type of inquiry would have enabled the soldiers to know whether or not the individual in question supported the *Kabaka* and the Buganda government in their confrontation with the Obote government.[19] When the same member complained about the general harassment of civilians, the minister replied: "When security forces go on an operation, I cannot be responsible for the way they conduct their arrest."[20]

The fact that the military basis of the Obote regime ultimately lay in the ethnic composition of the bulk of the army did not mean that this ethnic composition was the sole basis of the regime or that all its support came from the northern part of the country. As was indicated above, political cleavages had always been patterned by religious differences, among other factors, and since these differences did not coincide with but rather crisscrossed ethno-regional divisions, the issues were never entirely framed in ethnic or religious terms. The respective weights of ethnicity, religion, or mere personal ambition fluctuated with time, place, and the specific issues at hand.

There were undoubtedly many people who felt that the forcible abolition of the Buganda monarchy and of the political autonomy of the region would lead to the elimination of the region's perceived privileged status. Thus, continuing resentment of Buganda's status and role achieved during the colonial regime would have translated into support for the Obote regime even outside his home region.[21] Others might have felt that unitarism and authoritarianism were necessary to achieve national unity and progress.

In January 1971 Idi Amin led a military coup while Obote was attending a Commonwealth Summit Conference in Singapore. The exact circumstances of the estrangement between the two men who had supported and rewarded each other with political power and status since 1966 are not entirely clear. Each of them has given self-serving accounts. One can surmise, though, that as the military increasingly became the basis of Obote's continued tenure in office, Amin's megalomania and capriciousness might have begun to come out and alarm Obote. At the same time, the latter's increasing political insecurity appears to have driven him to rely more heavily on officers from his own Lango district of the northern region. Idi Amin reacted to this development by placing soldiers from his own West Nile area in key positions in the army. Thus the demon of ethnicity began to affect relations within the army itself.[22]

Large-scale political killings began immediately after the 1971 coup within the military, when substantial numbers of soldiers and officers from Obote's home area of Lango and the closely related area of Acholi were murdered because of attempts to resist the coup or because of presumed loyalty to the deposed regime. Amin feared that they might constitute a fifth column in case of an attempted countercoup by Obote and his partisans. Many other soldiers from these areas fled the country and eventually joined Obote and his supporters in exile in Tanzania.

In the beginning, the Amin regime had some degree of support among broad segments of the population. Eventually, however, it came to rely on a combination of narrow-based ethno-regional and religious foundations. As a reputed member of the Kakwa group originating in West Nile, Amin was able to mobilize support from the large number of soldiers who originated from this area. As a Muslim, he attracted support from the Nubians, who constituted a significant proportion of noncommissioned officers and soldiers. Nubians are Muslim descendants of mercenaries who entered Uganda at the end of the nineteenth century in the service of the Egyptian and later British colonial administrations. Originally recruited from the southern and possibly parts of the northern Sudan, they have acquired an Islamic and Arab-influenced culture which gives them a distinct identity. Military service has been a traditional career among them.[23]

Throughout its existence, the Amin regime never made any serious effort to seek popular support or legitimation. There were elections in 1973 for the posts of local chiefs, but soldiers and other clients of the regime eventually were appointed to replace the elected chiefs. The electoral exercise was never again tried by Amin; the regime rested on naked, undisguised force. The country was divided into provinces which were put under governors appointed from the army. A number of them acquired notoriety for their brutal and sadistic caprices. One of them, Abdalla Nasur, was captured following the downfall of the regime in 1979, tried, and sentenced to death for murder.

In contrast to the situation which developed in the post-Amin period, soldiers were apparently responsible for fewer murders than the two notorious murder squads of the regime: the State Research Bureau and the Public Safety Unit. Within the army, the Military Police was responsible for a lot of the murders and other atrocities. The total number of murder victims has been estimated as low as 12,000–30,000[24] to upwards of 500,000.[25]

Given the circumstances of the killings during the Amin regime, the lower figure seems to be more plausible. It is well-known that large-scale killings of civilians did not begin until the end of 1972, when Obote's supporters launched an abortive invasion to restore him to power. Since Amin was overthrown in early 1979, the period during which the large-scale killings took place did not exceed seven years. The higher estimate of 500,000 would suggest an annual rate of some 70,000. However, the majority of killings were carried out by hit squads using selective methods; there were no large-scale disposal techniques comparable to the crematoria of the Nazis. It should also be recalled that in fact the majority of victims were chosen on the basis of capricious and often personal reasons having to do with the desire to seize their possessions or to settle private scores. For these reasons, one must doubt the plausibility of the higher estimates. In any case, though, the number of direct deaths was high, and most human rights were regularly violated.

THE MILITARY, POLITICS AND VIOLENCE IN THE POST-AMIN PERIOD

Following an armed incursion into northwestern Tanzania in late 1978 by Amin's army that caused tremendous havoc to lives and property, the Tanzanian army launched a successful counterattack which was transformed into a war culminating in the disintegration of Amin's army and his flight into exile. This event set the stage for the struggle for power among a motley collection of Ugandan exile political groups. They had gathered in Tanzania in April 1979 under the sponsorship of the Tanzanian government and formed the Uganda

National Liberation Front (UNLF) under the chairmanship of Yusuf Lule, a former academic who was regarded as essentially nonpolitical. He formed the first post-Amin government in April but was removed from leadership after barely two months.[26]

Lule was replaced by Godfrey Binaisa, a former attorney-general under the first Obote government who had, however, broken with Obote. He too was removed through a military coup arranged in collaboration with Obote's civilian supporters in June 1980. The new regime, which styled itself the Military Commission of the National Liberation Front, led the country until December 1980, when it organized elections resulting in the declaration of Obote's UPC as the victors and thus ushering in his second regime.

In the struggle for control of the state in the period 1979–1981, three major groupings stood out: the resurrected UPC of Milton Obote, the equally resurrected DP, and two new small parties, the Uganda Patriotic Movement (UPM) and the Conservative party (CP). As had happened in the 1960s, the ethno-regional composition of the army turned out to be crucial for the outcome of the struggle.

When the 1971 coup occurred, hundreds of Acholi and Lango soldiers had succeeded in escaping from the country and eventually ended up in Tanzania where Obote had taken refuge. They had participated in the abortive 1972 invasion which had been designed to restore Obote to power. In 1979 when the Tanzanian army routed Amin's forces, the Tanzanians had been accompanied by some one thousand armed Ugandan exiles organized as the Uganda National Liberation Army (UNLA).[27] The core of this force was made up of officers and men who had fled following the 1971 coup and therefore reflected the heavy Acholi and Lango northern representation of the pre–1971 army.

In the period 1979–1980, the UNLA had been expanded through licit and illicit recruitment of soldiers, particularly from Acholi and Lango. In May 1980 the UNLA had helped Obote's UPC supporters to overthrow Binaisa. The Tanzanian army, whose government clearly supported Obote's ambition to regain power and which was then the only effective and dominant force in the country, stood aside, or actually helped the putschists consolidate their control by mounting roadblocks and searching cars for arms.

The Military Commission, which was in effect the armed wing of the UPC, made preparations for the holding of elections which had been promised for December 1980. Before they were actually held, the regime took controversial measures which cast serious doubt on the validity of the impending elections. The chief justice of the country was summarily dismissed without explanation, and over a dozen district administrators who would have acted as returning officers were also summarily dismissed. It was clear that their loyalty to the UPC was suspect. In addition, it is widely believed that the actual vote results were altered in key constituencies to give a victory to the UPC.[28]

In December 1980 Milton Obote once again became president of Uganda, and Paulo Muwanga, who had been the head of the Military Commission regime, became vice-president and minister of defense. The volley of gunfire discharged by soldiers in celebration of the UPC "victory" was an eloquent testimony of the continuing key role of the army in Uganda's politics.

Army killings of civilians had been suspected in 1979 when scores of people in and around Kampala were gunned down under circumstances which were often obscure. On June 14, 1980, soldiers murdered some fifteen people during a tense period when former president Yusuf Lule was expected to come back and lead the electoral opposition to the UPC. All the victims were presumed to be opponents of the UPC.

Following the disputed return to power of Obote and his UPC, militant opponents organized the Uganda Freedom Movement (UFM) and the National Resistance Movement (NRM), guerrilla movements which concentrated their activities in Buganda. That both movements found ready support in this area is undoubtedly due to the solid opposition and hostility which Obote and the UPC had reaped since the violent 1966 overthrow of the Buganda monarchy and the 1962 Constitution. That at least some close associates of Obote came to give up any hopes of reconciliation with Buganda was demonstrated by the head of the pre–1971 political intelligence and security General Service Department and Obote's kinsman, Akena Adoko, when he suggested that the country's capital should be moved elsewhere as long as it continued to be surrounded by "enemies" who would continue to do everything to wipe out the government.[29]

In the northwest of the country, former soldiers of the Amin army also organized to resist the Obote regime. Army operations against these guerrilla movements were the occasion for large-scale killings and massacres of civilians, looting, rapes, and other atrocities in Buganda and West Nile. By 1984 some 300,000 people had fled from the West Nile region alone.[30] The number of displaced in the regions north of the capital was estimated at 150,000; between 100,000 and 500,000 people were estimated to have died violently since 1979.[31] As in the case of deaths during the Amin regime, these statistics are based more on guesswork than systematic calculation.

Not all the victims of violence and repression died at the hands of the army. Many people were arrested, tortured, and killed by the civilian National Security Agency (NASA), officials of the UPC, or both jointly.[32] In 1982 and 1983, UPC officials, chiefs, party Youth Wingers and the police Special Force evicted some 75,000 members of the Banyarwanda ethnic group from their homes and properties in Ankole in the southwest of the country. Some of them lost their lives; most lost their property and were compelled to flee to Rwanda or to refugee camps in Uganda.[33] The Banyarwanda were widely believed to support the opposition DP. There had also been conflicts between the Banyarwanda, most of whom were pastoral refugees from Rwanda, and indigenous agriculturalists.

The overthrow of the Amin regime through the successful invasion of the country by Tanzanian forces was a precedent that created a certain degree of controversy in inter-African politics. An equally important precedent—at least in East African politics—was the participation of armed Ugandan dissidents in the overthrow of the regime. For the first time in the region it was demonstrated that the monopoly of arms that keeps authoritarian regimes in power can be challenged and possibly even broken. Following the disputed 1980 Uganda general elections, the political groups that organized guerrilla forces to challenge the second Obote regime sought to apply this lesson.

The guerrilla forces started out with only a small number of combatants, although this was compensated for by the strong support which they enjoyed in the strategic Buganda region around the capital. As the struggle escalated, government forces quickly resorted to indiscriminate killings of civilians, devastation of villages suspected of harboring or even merely supporting guerrillas, raping, looting, and other atrocities. The fact that the army was heavily recruited from the northern and northeastern parts of the country, and the near-total absence of soldiers from Buganda, accentuated the ethno-regional undertone of the struggle.

In spite of the horrendous price paid by civilians in lives and property lost, support for the guerrillas persisted. The Obote regime lacked any meaningful strategy to win "the hearts and minds" and thus failed to destroy the insurgency. Increasing army indiscipline threatened not only those suspected of supporting guerrillas but every civilian—including the regime's own supporters. In addition, the guerrillas gained in support, combat experience, and equipment as they increasingly defeated government offensives and captured weapons.

By 1985 persistent casualties at the hands of the guerrillas combined with generalized political repression and corruption had led to dissension within the ruling UPC and, most significantly, within the army. Some politicians and officers began to seriously consider the possibility of some kind of reconciliation with the NRM, which was by now the only major guerrilla force confronting the regime. Eventually, the intra-regime and intra-army conflict took the form of an ethnic conflict between the officers and men from Acholi, who once again had come to form the single largest contingent, and the Lango soldiers who were associated with the uncompromising stance of their ethnic kinsman, Milton Obote. Conflict over the guerrilla war was intertwined with competition for control of the army command and the political power that would accrue from such control.

The coup of July 1985 was in some ways reminiscent of the 1971 coup. Obote was accused of ethnic favoritism which supposedly benefited his Lango kinsmen. The Military Council regime that emerged was dominated by officers from Acholi associated with some officers from West Nile, and it formed a coalition civilian government including the DP, the UPM, the CP, and even elements from the UPC of the ousted Obote.

Efforts on the part of the Military Council to bring the NRM into the coalition government and the ruling military body as a junior partner were resisted by the latter, and the cease-fire which had been put into force shortly after the July coup soon broke down. As the fighting in the western and Buganda regions intensified in the last five months of 1985 and demonstrated the growing strength of the NRM, the Military Council was compelled to make more political concessions involving greater power for the NRM in a projected coalition regime.

The UNLA troops had followed their capture of Kampala in the July coup by widespread looting of businesses and some private homes. Their discipline was to decline even further as the war with the NRM intensified. Murders, rapes, kidnapping of women and girls, and theft of civilian property caused untold losses and suffering, especially in Buganda between July 1985 and February 1986. The NRM's growing strength and the continuing army atrocities against the civilians persuaded the guerrilla movement to undertake an all-out campaign against the UNLA which culminated in the capture of Kampala and the overthrow of the Military Council regime at the end of January 1986.

With the victory of the NRA, the ethnic and regional basis of the Uganda army fundamentally changed for the first time since 1962. The overwhelming majority of NRA soldiers were recruited from Buganda and the western parts of the country. Between July 1985 and February 1986, a fair number of soldiers with origins in the northern part of the country were captured or defected to the NRA and were incorporated. Nevertheless, for the moment, the majority of the new Uganda army are recruited from the southern parts of the country where the majority of the country's population lives.

While the form which the struggle for political power in Uganda has taken has been strongly defined by religion and—more recently—strong ethnic identity, the substance of the struggle has always been control of the state for purposes of determining public policy and, increasingly, access to and control of economic resources and privileges. Political power has increasingly translated into direct access to the means to accumulate wealth for the power holders, their relatives, clients, and followers. Public cynicism about politics and politicians has grown in proportion to the use of state power for private gain. One of the consequences of this development has been the fact that those who have not had direct access to the levers of power have used whatever other means they have had, including violence, to seize wealth from the public and private domains. This development has aggravated violations of human rights.

THE STRUGGLE FOR CONTROL OF ECONOMIC RESOURCES

As in the other postcolonial states, on the eve of political independence control of political power in Uganda was perceived primarily in terms of the redress of imbalances in the distribution of resources among different social groups and geographical regions. In terms of race relations, there was generalized resentment of control of economic wealth by the non-Africans, particularly the Indo-Pakistanis, that is, immigrants or descendants of immigrants from the Indian subcontinent. Feelings against them were sometimes expressed in strong language. In 1962 A. Y. Lobidra, a member from West Nile, told the National Assembly:

There is nothing worse we have ever inherited from the British Government than the Asians. We shall ever be sick and we shall have only Africans to produce and they will hold the silver spoon in the mouth of the Asians and they will eat. They will be spoon-fed while we starve. Kampala is their Calcutta the second, Jinja is another Bombay second, go to Mbale, it is another Delhi second. We have no towns in Uganda. We have only got Indians everywhere you go in every Uganda town.[34]

Ten years later, Idi Amin was to expel the Indo-Pakistani merchant community—some 80,000 of them—including those who had become Uganda citizens, seize their properties, and distribute them to indigenous army officers, political clients, and other ethnic African citizens. It was the first act of massive economic dispossession by a Ugandan government in the postcolonial history of the country. The rights of citizenship and the rights of private property were breached at the same time. Exactly ten years later, the same fate was to befall the Banyarwanda of western Uganda.

It is very plausible that such subsequent phenomena as looting of private businesses and homes following the downfall of the Amin regime in 1979 and the Obote regime in 1985 and sporadically at various times, demolition of private homes and theft of roofs and other housing material, and the ransom of travelers by soldiers stemmed from the gradual erosion of respect for private property and the legitimacy of the means for its acquisition. These processes started with the expulsion of the Indo-Pakistanis and were accelerated by the escalating spiral of violence and the deterioration of public security institutions, especially the police force.

Within the majority African population, the distribution of socioeconomic resources was uneven. There were strong feelings among people from other regions about the fact that the colonial distribution of roads, schools, hospitals, and other amenities had been concentrated to a substantial degree in Buganda. Many politicians from other regions expressed the desire to redress this imbalance. Shortly after the attainment of independence, E. Y. Lakidi, a member of the National Assembly from Acholi in the north of the country, suggested a "solution" to the problem of inadequate developmental resources from the perspective of regional distribution. He told the National Assembly:

We know the four regions involved. The most backward region is the North, followed by the West, then the East, and Buganda is the most wealthy nation. I would like, Mr. Speaker, if there is any money at all, the North should get a bigger share; the West should get the next share, and Buganda go without. This should continue, Mr. Speaker, for some time so that we bring up these two regions, the West and the North, to the level of Buganda and the East; and after that, Mr. Speaker, the money should be shared out equally.[35]

This suggestion was strongly opposed by J. W. Kiwanuka, a member from Buganda, who argued that more than 60 percent of the country's revenues came from Buganda.[36]

Sometimes, discontent was expressed at the level of the district rather than the region. In 1962 M. A. Okelo, a member from West Nile, stated: "(W)e are sick and tired of being told that West Nile is too far away, that West Nile is only good as a source of labour. We are tired of this. We must be given our fair share. If the government thinks that we are not part and parcel of Uganda, we must be told now so that we have a second thought."[37]

While politicians made demands for the distribution of economic resources in the name of group interests, they did not neglect their personal interests. They used access to state power and influence to obtain loans to start businesses and acquire directorships of companies and partnerships with rich members of the Indo-Pakistani community. During a discussion of programs to launch more Africans into the field of commerce, J.S.L. Zake, minister of education, told the National Assembly:

And of course I want to say that the best way of earning a living is when you can know exactly what you have earned that day, or what you have lost or what you have been cheated out of and that is business. Therefore, I would like to call upon all the people, including the hon. Members here, to go into business, to go and trade—(*Hear Hear!*)—to go and sell. . . .[38]

From time to time, the propriety and wisdom of the use of public positions to accumulate wealth were questioned by some of the politicians themselves. In 1967 M. A. Okelo, an opposition member, told the National Assembly:

Sir, some people accuse religion and tribalism of being the cause of instability in this country but I say no. The real cause of instability in the country is over-eating by some human beings. . . . You come across one man being an M.P. [member of parliament], and at the same time being a member of Central [i.e., East African] Legislative Assembly, he is also the chairman of the local council, or he is Assistant Director of a firm, he owns a school and all the rest of it. He eats several times a day from the national dish. . . .[39]

Between 1969 and the 1971 coup, Obote introduced the "Move to the Left," a series of measures which were ostensibly designed to move the country towards a more socialistic kind of society. However, since the most important members of his regime were among those who had amassed wealth in the period following the acquisition of independence, there was a lot of skepticism about the seriousness of the measures.[40]

In the course of the Amin regime, those who controlled the state and their clients exploited it to enrich themselves in a much more ruthless way than had happened before. Combined with mismanagement and the disruption of the economy, the policies or absence of policies on the part of the regime resulted in the impoverishment of many and contributed to the erosion of the legitimacy of state institutions.

In the first place, within a relatively short time, members and clients of the regime acceded to enormous wealth through the seizure of the businesses of the expelled Indo-Pakistani community in 1972 and the direct appropriation of monies from the national treasury.[41] Second, the use of violence and illegal means to acquire wealth by members and clients of the regime vitiated the notion of the state as the upholder of the rule of law and the defender of the public interest. Soldiers and policemen engaged directly or indirectly in armed robbery, and the average citizen was left virtually defenseless. As Aidan Southall has pointed out, soldiers and prison staff were ordered to join the police in fighting *kondoism* (armed robbery), "but since the latter often appeared in military kit with army weapons, some seemed to be playing a double role."[42]

A third and related development was the severe deterioration in the living conditions of the majority of the population. This was due to the combined effects of the atrophy of the preexisting commercial network following the expulsion of the Indo-Pakistani commercial class; the attrition of productive activities due to the shortage of foreign exchange for spare parts and the flight of skilled manpower; the neglect of administrative and social services and the overall decay of the country's modern socioeconomic infrastructure. Workers on fixed incomes were probably hit hardest; it has been estimated that by 1978, the real minimum wage in the country was 20 percent of its 1970–1971 level.[43]

The economic conditions which prevailed during the Amin regime led to the development of the phenomenon of *magendoism*; a concept with no accurate English translation that covers legal and illegal speculation involving the purchase and sale of public and private goods and services.[44] *Magendoism* naturally favored those who had the best access to the state or its agents. Thus economic necessity, enterprise, and illegality met under the shelter of arbitrary state power.

By and large, the processes and methods of economic competition which arose during the Amin regime were carried over into the post-Amin period. An observer writing in 1984 had the following to say about conditions under the second Obote regime: "Generally, bribe-taking and allocations to favourites and family are widespread; the visible wealth of government appointees and the inner coterie (which extends to tribes-mates and favoured girl friends) is quite astonishing."[45]

Predictably, not having direct access to the national treasury or patronage, the soldiers of the post-Amin regime used their guns to enrich themselves or to keep up with the escalating cost of living. Roadblocks, ostensibly set up to check guerrillas, were used as "toll stations." Houses were invaded and looted of all valuables, sometimes including tin roofs, wooden doors, and window frames.[46] The pattern continued after the July 27, 1985, coup until the destruction of the UNLA in January 1986.

THE EXTERNAL DIMENSION

The Ugandan state is a small, underdeveloped participant in the world economy.[47] Colonial rule has left a legacy of close economic, political, and cultural ties with Britain and other Western capitalist states. Following the acquisition of political independence, the Obote government sought to diversify the country's political and economic links and entered into various forms of relations with the United States, West Germany, the Soviet Union, China, Israel, and other states.[48]

Direct foreign involvement in Uganda's politics was not conspicuous until the 1971 coup. Strong circumstantial and anecdotal evidence indicates that the British and Israeli governments at the very least encouraged Amin to carry out his coup and probably played an even more active role in the putsch.[49]

By 1971 the British government was disenchanted with Obote, particularly his vocal oppposition to its policies in Southern Africa, which he criticized for being too accommodative of the racist regimes, and his nationalization of British and other foreign assets within the framework of his "Move to the Left." As far as the Israeli government was concerned, following a long period in which Israel enjoyed good and close relations with Uganda, Obote's gradual shift of policies toward the more radical and anti-imperialist camp of the Third World in the late 1960s appeared to threaten its political interests.

Both countries initially enjoyed close relations with Idi Amin. However, he suddenly shifted allegiances and embraced the radical Arab states, particularly Libya, and expelled the Israelis from Uganda. His relations with the British also deteriorated following the expulsion of the Indo-Pakistani community, many of whom, as holders of British passports, ended up as refugees in Britain. Nevertheless, British firms continued to supply the regime and the country in general with a variety of commodities up to the very end.

Uganda-Soviet relations had been initiated during the Obote regime. The Soviet Union was involved in the training of air force pilots and was involved in other assistance programs. In spite of Amin's initial flirtation with the more conservative African and non-African regimes, the Soviet Union maintained its Uganda connection and eventually came to be heavily involved in the supply of weapons and the provision of military training.[50] Soviet leaders most probably realized that Amin was incapable of grasping dialectical materialism. Nevertheless, they most likely hoped that training would provide them with good connections with a new generation of army officers who might one day take over and establish a friendly regime.

Amin played on his nominal Islamic faith and was able to attract financial and political support from Libya, Saudi Arabia, and a number of other Arab countries. These regimes were particularly encouraged by Amin's adoption of a militant anti-Zionist stance.

As long as he was not perceived to be pursuing "communist" policies or as being subservient to the Soviet Union, Amin was not actively opposed in the West. It was not until shortly before his downfall, for instance, that the U.S. Congress, in the face of initial opposition by the Carter administration, imposed an embargo against the import of Uganda coffee, which contributed virtually all the foreign exchange that the Amin regime was receiving by the end of the 1970s.[51]

In 1972 and 1979 Libya intervened to support Amin through the dispatch of combat troops and military equipment when exile forces crossed over from

Tanzania with the intention of overthrowing the regime. On the second occasion, the assistance did not save the regime from defeat.

Between 1971 and 1979 as many as four thousand Southern Sudanese are reported to have joined the Uganda army and provided one of the strong bases of support for the regime. During the last years of the Amin regime, an undetermined number of Palestinian agents are reported to have provided intelligence and bodyguard assistance to the dictator.

A more massive form of foreign intervention occurred on the heels of the Tanzania-Uganda war when some forty thousand Tanzanian troops entered the country and overthrew the Amin regime. Many of them stayed on, and for the next two to three years after 1979, they provided the only serious protection for the administrations which succeeded in office until 1981.

Tanzania had given Obote shelter and political support during his exile. He had enjoyed good relations with Julius Nyerere in the 1960s and had appeared to be moving in the same socialistic ideological direction as Tanzania with his "Move to the Left" before the 1971 coup. The effective conquest and occupation of the country by Tanzanian troops gave Nyerere considerable leverage which was used to support Obote and his UPC in the post-Amin struggle for power in Uganda. During their brief tenure as president of Uganda, both Lule and Binaisa were summoned on several occasions to Tanzania by Nyerere to discuss complaints made by Obote or his supporters.[52] It is also arguable that the 1980 coup which led to the creation of the pro-UPC Military Commission regime would not have taken place if Nyerere had opposed it.

The second Obote regime enjoyed important foreign military support in the form of training facilities within the country and abroad from a broad array of states, notably Tanzania, Britain, North Korea, the United States, and several Commonwealth states. As in the case of the Amin regime, commercial and ideological interests combined to explain the involvement of this heterogeneous group of states.

Tanzania sought to help a loyal friend whose political stance was close to that of Nyerere. Britain still retained important economic interests in Uganda and perceived Obote as the man who could restore stability and economic rehabilitation. The North Koreans probably sought political and economic openings which would help them in their competition with South Korea. And the United States stayed in touch to counter any possible moves towards the Soviet bloc.

The anti-Obote guerrillas who started their campaign in 1981 received some support from Libya, apparently still smarting from the defeat and deaths of many members of their expeditionary force which had vainly flown to the aid of Amin in 1979. The guerrillas sought assistance wherever they could get it.

The abortive mediatory role that President Moi of Kenya played during the talks between NRM and the military regime which replaced the Obote regime in 1985 further highlighted the extent to which external forces had come to exercise direct influence in Ugandan politics. The final outcome of the struggle was, however, decided on the Ugandan battlefields.

CONCLUSION

Over the last fifteen years, Uganda has acquired the unenviable reputation of having one of the worst human rights records in the entire world. Large-scale killings of innocent people, looting, raping, imprisonment of political opponents, and other atrocities have characterized the political and social life of the country during this period. A succession of governments and leaders have up to now failed to ameliorate these conditions.

The failure of Uganda's political elites to create a consensual polity is attributable to a number of interrelated factors: the political fragmentation of the state that was bequeathed by the colonial regime; the breakdown of the constitutional regime based on the Independence Constitution of 1962, the subsequent use of violence to impose an alternative arrangement, and the rule of a faction of the political elite; the rise of an ethnically defined military as an increasingly important participant in the struggle for political power; the use of the state in an increasingly direct manner for self-enrichment on the part of the power holders; and the erosion of the legitimacy of state institutions and respect for the rule of law, leading to loss of respect for life itself.

The evolution of human rights conditions in Uganda has been strongly influenced by the intrusion of foreign political and economic interests. Different regimes and political groups have sought to enhance their chances in the struggle for power by entering into mutually beneficial arrangements with these interests. It is in the concatenation of internal and external historical, political, economic, and social forces that the roots of Uganda's tragedy must be traced.

Following the seizure of the capital in January 1986, the NRM formed a broad-based government incorporating representatives of the DP, the UPC, the UPM, and the CP. The new national army—the National Resistance Army—showed itself to be a far more disciplined force than anything Ugandans had seen since 1966. In addition, its composition reflected the ethnic composition of the entire country much more closely than had been the case since 1962.

Partisan political activities were put on hold for the next couple of years while the country settled down. In the meantime, the NRM program called for the formation of grass-roots village committees to form the basis of a new form of government designed to cut through the religious and ethno-regional cleavages associated with the traditional political parties.

Whether Uganda will turn a new page after so many years of bitter strife cannot be predicted at this stage. However, most observers agree that the wide support that the NRM apparently (1986) enjoyed, their record of discipline and austerity, and the clear desire of the Ugandans to pull back from the disastrous history of the past two decades augured well for the future.[53]

NOTES

1. Amnesty International, *Political Killings by Governments* (London: Amnesty International, 1983), 44–49; Amnesty International, *Torture in the Eighties* (London: Am-

nesty International, 1984), 130–33; Amnesty International–USA, "Uganda: Evidence of Torture" (Mimeographed, New York, 1985); Minority Rights Group, *Uganda and Sudan*, Report no. 66 (London: Minority Rights Group, 1985); U.S. Committee for Refugees, *Human Rights in Uganda, the Reasons for Refugees* (Washington, D.C.: American Council for Nationalities Service, 1985).

2. Commonwealth Secretariat, *The Rehabilitation of the Economy of Uganda, a Report by a Commonwealth Team of Experts*, vol. 1 (London: Commonwealth Secretariat, 1979); G. K. Helleiner, "Economic Collapse and Rehabilitation in Uganda," *Rural Africana* 11 (1981): 27–35; S. P. Heyneman, "Education During a Period of Austerity: Uganda, 1971–1981," *Comparative Education Review* 27 (1983): 403–413; Cole P. Dodge and Paul Wiebe, eds., *Crisis in Uganda, The Breakdown of Health Services* (Oxford: Pergamon Press, 1985).

3. Ralph Miliband, *The State in Capitalist Society* (London: Weidenfeld and Nicolson, 1969): 179–264.

4. The *Kabaka* (king) of Buganda was the only ruler accorded the honorific "His Highness." See D. Anthony Low and R. Cranford Pratt, *Buganda and British Overrule* (London: Oxford University Press, 1960).

5. Cf. Ali A. Mazrui, "Privilege and Protest as Integrative Factors: The Case of Buganda's Status in Uganda," in *Protest and Power in Black Africa*, ed. Robert I. Rotberg and Ali A. Mazrui (New York: Oxford University Press, 1970), 1072–87; David E. Apter, *The Political Kingdom in Uganda* (Princeton, N.J.: Princeton University Press, 1967); Tarsis B. Kabwegyere, *The Politics of State Formation* (Nairobi, Kenya: East African Literature Bureau, 1974); Nelson Kasfir, *The Shrinking Political Arena* (Berkeley: University of California Press, 1976); Samwiri R. Karugire, *A Political History of Uganda* (Nairobi, Kenya: East African Literature Bureau, 1980); Grace S. Ibingira, *The Forging of an African Nation* (New York: Viking Press, 1973).

6. Cf. Mahmood Mamdani, *Politics and Class Formation in Uganda* (New York: Monthly Review Press, 1976), 189–227.

7. George W. Kanyeihamba, *Constitutional Law and Government in Uganda* (Nairobi, Kenya: East African Literature Bureau, 1975), 67.

8. Ibid., 68.

9. A.G.G. Gingyera-Pinycwa, *Apolo Milton Obote and His Times* (New York: NOK Publishers, 1978), 246.

10. J. Cartwright, *Political Leadership in Africa* (London: Croom Helm, 1983), 237–42.

11. The regulations empowered the government to imprison individuals without recourse to the courts of law. The statistics compiled from the *Gazette* do not give an accurate picture of the extent to which this device was used for purposes of political repression. According to the 1967 Constitution, Article 21.6b, the government was required to publish in the official *Gazette* notification of the detention of persons after not more than twenty-eight days of incarceration. However, it is quite conceivable that some detainees were, in practice, imprisoned for less than twenty-eight days. Such prisoners would not appear in the *Gazette*. On the other hand, there were a few people, including some aliens, who were imprisoned under the Emergency Regulations on suspicion of involvement in nonpolitical criminal activities. See *Uganda Gazette*, vols. 59–64 (1966–1971).

12. Uganda, *Parliamentary Debates, Second Series*, vol. 81: 2906.

13. Grace Ibingira, *African Upheavals Since Independence* (Boulder, Col.: Westview Press, 1980), 81–90 passim.

14. Uganda, *Parliamentary Debates*, vol. 73: 750.

15. Uganda, *Parliamentary Debates*, vol. 72: 503.

16. Uganda, *Parliamentary Debates*, vol. 61: 254.

17. Uganda, *Parliamentary Debates*, vol. 72: 477.

18. Uganda, *Parliamentary Debates*, vol. 91: 1205.

19. Uganda, *Parliamentary Debates*, vol. 61: 249.

20. Uganda, *Parliamentary Debates*, vol. 70: 2088.

21. Mazrui, "Privilege and Protest."

22. Samuel Decalo, *Coups and Army Rule in Africa* (New Haven, Conn.: Yale University Press, 1976), 208–211.

23. P. Woodward, "Ambiguous Amin," *African Affairs* 77 (1978): 153–64.

24. Jan J. Jorgensen, *Uganda, A Modern History* (London: Croom Helm, 1981), 315.

25. International Commission of Jurists, *Uganda and Human Rights* (Geneva: International Commission of Jurists, 1977).

26. Cherry Gertzel, "Uganda After Amin: The Continuing Search for Leadership and Control," *African Affairs* 79 (1980): 461–89.

27. Tony Avirgan and Martha Honey, *War in Uganda* (Dar es Salaam, Tanzania: Tanzania Publishing House, 1981), 72–75.

28. *Africa Confidential*, 22, 15 (1981).

29. Akena Adoko, *From Obote to Obote* (New Delhi, India: Vikas Publishing House, 1983), 333.

30. Jeff Crisp, "National Security, Human Rights and Population Displacements, Luwero District, Uganda," *Review of African Political Economy* 27/28 (1984): 164–74.

31. U.S. Committee for Refugees, *Human Rights in Uganda*.

32. Amnesty International–USA, "Uganda: Evidence of Torture."

33. U.S. Committee for Refugees, *Human Rights in Uganda*, 17–20.

34. Uganda, *Parliamentary Debates*, vol. 4: 794.

35. Uganda, *Parliamentary Debates*, vol. 1: 118–19.

36. Uganda, *Parliamentary Debates*, vol. 2: 254.

37. Ibid., 446.

38. Uganda, *Parliamentary Debates*, vol. 87: 60.

39. Uganda, *Parliamentary Debates*, vol. 71: 149.

40. James H. Mittleman, *Ideology and Politics in Uganda* (Ithaca, N.Y.: Cornell University Press, 1975), 12–167; Irving Gershenberg, "Slouching Towards Socialism: Obote's Uganda," *African Studies Review* 15 (1972): 79–95; T. Aasland, *On the Move-To-The-Left in Uganda, 1969–1971*, Research Report No. 26 (Uppsala: Scandinavian Institute of African Studies, 1974), 38–49.

41. J. W. Harbeson and D. Rothchild, "Rehabilitation and Rural Development in Uganda," *Rural Africana* 11 (1981): 6.

42. Aidan Southall, "Social Disorganization in Uganda: Before, During and After Amin," *Journal of Modern African Studies* 18 (1980): 642.

43. Helleiner, "Economic Collapse and Rehabilitation," 29.

44. Nelson Kasfir, "State, *Magendo*, and Class Formation in Uganda," *Journal of Commonwealth and Comparative Politics* 21 (1983): 84–103.

45. A Correspondent, "Uganda: the Pearl of Africa Loses its Lustre," *World Today* 40 (1984): 218.

46. Nelson Kasfir, "Uganda's Uncertain Quest for Recovery," *Current History* 84 (1985): 172 passim.

47. Dan W. Nabudere, *Imperialism and Revolution in Uganda* (London: Onyx Press; Dar es Salaam, Tanzania: Tanzania Publishing House, 1980).

48. Mahmood Mamdani, *Imperialism and Fascism in Uganda* (Trenton, N.J.: Africa World Press, 1984).

49. Avirgan and Honey, *War in Uganda*, 10.

50. Gad W. Toko, *Intervention in Uganda*, Occasional Working Paper Series, No. 1 (Pittsburgh, Penn.: University Center for International Studies, University of Pittsburgh, 1979).

51. "Prepared Statement of William C. Harrop, Deputy Assistant Secretary of State for African Affairs," in United States Government, United States Senate, *Uganda: The Human Rights Situation, Hearings Before the Subcommittee on Foreign Economic Policy of the Committee on Foreign Relations, Ninety-Fifth Congress, June 15, 21, 26, 1978* (Washington, D.C.: U.S. Government Printing Office, 1978), 126–29.

52. Avirgan and Honey, *War in Uganda*, 197–214.

53. United States Committee for Refugees, "Human Rights in Uganda: A Season of Hope for Its Refugees and Displaced Persons" (Mimeographed, May 1986).

SUGGESTED READINGS

Apter, David E. *The Political Kingdom in Uganda.* Princeton, N.J.: Princeton University Press, 1967.

Ibingira, Grace. *The Forging of an African Nation.* New York: Viking Press, 1976.

Kabaka of Buganda. *Desecration of My Kingdom.* London: Constable, 1967.

Karugire, Samwiri R. *A Political History of Uganda.* Nairobi: East African Literature Bureau, 1980.

Kasfir, Nelson. *The Shrinking Political Arena.* Berkeley: University of California Press, 1976.

Kyemba, Henry. *A State of Blood.* New York: Grosset and Dunlap, 1977.

Low, D. Anthony. *The Mind of Buganda.* London: Heinemann Educational Books, 1971.

Mamdani, Mahmood. *Politics and Class Formation in Uganda.* New York: Monthly Review Press, 1976.

Southall, Aidan. "Social Disorganization in Uganda: Before, During and After Amin." *Journal of Modern African Studies* 18 (1980): 627–656.

Uzoigwe, G. N., ed. *Uganda, the Dilemma of Nationhood.* New York: NOK Publishers, 1982.

19

THE UNION OF SOVIET SOCIALIST REPUBLICS

David Kowalewski

When dealing with human rights in the USSR, Winston Churchill's observation that the Soviet Union is a riddle wrapped in a mystery inside an enigma is only partly applicable. That Soviet authorities systematically violate the rights embodied in the Universal Declaration on Human Rights on a wide scale is beyond dispute. Although the human rights performance of the USSR may seem positively admirable when compared with the brutalities inflicted on citizens by regimes such as those in El Salvador and Guatemala, it falls far short of the performance of the industrialized western democracies.

Ascertaining the reasons for this repression, however, presents a number of difficulties. Several theories can be adduced to shed light on Soviet violations—all of them with some merit but all of them with serious problems as well. The present essay recounts Soviet performance along a broad array of guaranteed citizen rights, then attempts to bring some theoretical analysis to bear on the problem.[1]

ECONOMIC RIGHTS

Since the Russian Revolution, the Soviet regime has unquestionably registered substantial gains in providing citizens with basic material needs. Indeed, it regards the fulfillment of economic rights as a necessary precondition for the meaningful exercise of political and civil rights.[2] Although critics unjustifiably compare Soviet fulfillment of economic rights with that in advanced capitalist countries (but justifiably ask, Was Stalin really necessary?), compared with the Tsarist period the material needs of the Soviet people are certainly more fulfilled. Yet even in the arena of economic welfare the USSR is not beyond some reproach.

The right to work, for example, is guaranteed by the Soviet Constitution and mass unemployment is nonexistent. On the other hand, citizens lack the "right not to work" as well, being subject to criminal prosecution as "parasites."

While this measure undoubtedly discourages a luxury class of social drones feeding off the hard labor of the citizenry, it occasionally serves as a political weapon against dissent. Because dissidents are frequently fired from their jobs and have difficulty finding subsequent employment from KGB-leery employers, they then become targets of perfectly legal recriminations.

The recent policy of Party First Secretary Mikhail Gorbachev, moreover, to "accelerate" the economy by reducing the overmanning of enterprises seems a harbinger of future unemployment problems. For example, up to 70,000 scientific jobs will be displaced as a result of a new incentive pay system introduced at the beginning of 1986. Modernization displaced over 700,000 industrial workers in 1985. Although retirement and a shrinking work force will account for many redundant slots, the process will generate substantial disruption. Further, the right to work is being made increasingly conditional on job performance as "rationalization" proceeds apace. Many workers will have to resettle in less hospitable parts of the country, with possible adverse health effects.[3]

The Soviet health system provides free medical care to all Soviet citizens. Cases of infectious disease continue to decline.[4] Other indicators, however, suggest that tremendous health achievements may be in a process of reversal. Average life expectancy for both men and women actually dropped from 70 years in 1971–72 to 69 years in 1985–86. Undoubtedly part of the reason is the alarming growth of alcoholism and drug abuse, which Soviet authorities have taken measures to correct. Infant mortality has risen from an all-time low of 22.9 deaths per 1000 live births in 1971 to 26.0 in 1985. Much of the problem can be traced to the poor working conditions, low morale, and inadequate training of medical personnel, whose status ranks far lower than that of their Western counterparts. No doctors are on duty in Soviet maternity homes at night—only nurses. Pediatric training has lost ground to other specialties. Maternity homes are often criticized for unsanitary conditions and overcrowding. Soviet doctors are evaluated on fulfilling the "plan," which measures quantity of patients rather than quality of treatment. Over half of doctors' time is spent filling out forms.[5]

Yet most disturbing is the regular internment of political dissidents in mental hospitals. Too much evidence is available to take seriously the Soviet official contention that the "patients" are truly "sick." Internment serves a number of political purposes: delegitimation of dissent as insanity, avoidance of a public trial, indeterminacy of length of confinement, terrorization of actual and potential dissidents, and a public image of humanitarianism. Soviet "psychiatrists" are seen coming to hospitals wearing their KGB uniforms. Patients are told they will be "cured" if they renounce their beliefs. Some Soviet psychiatrists (and many Western ones) have condemned the confinements as purely political. Formerly incarcerated dissidents who have emigrated to the West and volunteered to undergo examination show no signs of mental illness.

Soviet citizens are guaranteed pensions for old age, disability, and loss of breadwinner. Yet allotments often are insufficient and result in officially admitted "underprovisioning." Although old age pensions were raised in 1985, they still fall below what some Western economists consider the poverty threshold in the USSR.[6]

Soviet authorities have also taken measures to enhance fulfillment of the right to shelter. Soviet apartments have grown in size in the last two decades, helping to alleviate the crowding problem. Shoddy construction, however, in the harsh conditions of Soviet winters, cannot be called an insignificant shortcoming. Although the Soviet regime denies the existence of homeless people in the USSR, "street people" or *brodyagi*, many of them alcoholics, do exist. Since provision of facilities would contradict the regime's anti-alcoholism campaigns, such people must find shelter wherever they can.[7]

Rather miserable performance has characterized Soviet provision of care for the disabled. In a Soviet version of the American "invalids' rights" movement, a number of citizens have petitioned and protested at Soviet offices against bureaucratic "benign neglect" and demanded better facilities, equipment, and accommodations for their special medical problems. Perhaps because of their public outspokenness, and the regime's pride in fulfilling economic rights, their efforts have been met with harassment, surveillance, and threats.

SOCIAL AND CULTURAL RIGHTS

Soviet performance with respect to social rights presents a far more mixed picture. Achievements in guaranteeing citizens an education are evidenced by universal literacy and remarkable gains in science and technology. Labor unions representing worker interests before employers are active and generally their voices must be considered by enterprise managers. However, when workers try to press for their interests autonomously, outside of officially sanctioned structures, repression of varying sorts is predictable. Independent union members are subjected to intimidation and often sent off to Siberian labor camps. Unofficial, spontaneous worker protest, in the form of numerous wildcat strikes and demonstrations, is also met with state disapproval, albeit belatedly. A common pattern is evident in underground literature (*samizdat*) reports: workers suddenly walk off the job and often march through town shouting slogans and displaying banners; Party officials quickly arrive and negotiate with the strikers; strike demands are usually fulfilled, at least in part, and workers return to their jobs; a few weeks or months later the strike leaders are fired or arrested and some of the gains are reversed.[8]

Rights to religious belief and expression are systematically violated in the context of official "state atheism" (*gosateism*), especially against those bodies who collectively catechize their young, publicly engage in mass expressions of belief, or otherwise refuse to accept the restrictions of official structures. Repression varies, however, with denomination. Russian Orthodoxy generally enjoys more privileges, while religions connected with non-Russian nations (e.g., Ukrainian Catholics) or foreign countries (Jehovah's Witnesses) experience special persecution.[9]

The "double burden" of Soviet women—obligations to housework as well as job in order to ensure a minimum standard of living—has been protested by a number of Leningrad citizens, for which they have incurred the wrath of the KGB. Along with the heavily male-dominated decision-making structure of polity and economy, these phenomena cast serious doubt on official commitment to sexual equality.

The right of family integrity is frequently violated, again especially against groups with foreign links. Children are occasionally separated from dissident Baptist parents because of the latter's "pernicious influence." Jewish families are occasionally split between those who have emigrated and those who have been refused visas ("refusedniki") or have been incarcerated in labor camps for their public dissent. Soviet citizens who have married foreigners have great difficulty rejoining their spouses abroad and have agitated for reunification through their "Divided Families Group." In the latter case, Soviet authorities have recently made certain concessions "on an individual-case basis."

Cultural workers are severely circumscribed by heavy state censorship in the form of "socialist realism" canons. Unorthodox music groups are also harassed. In 1984 the leader of the Christian rock group "Trumpet Call," Valery Barinov, was sentenced to almost three years in a labor camp. The burgeoning volume of underground poetry and other literary forms, as well as unofficial art exhibits on Soviet streets and in private apartments, indicate the frustration of the cultural intelligentsia at obstacles to the display of their works to a mass audience.[10]

Social and cultural discrimination is often the lot of non-Russian peoples who constitute one-half of the Soviet population. Ethnographic societies face harassment and intimidation, histories are censored and rewritten, cemeteries are bulldozed, and heavy pressure is exerted to learn and speak Russian. Day-to-day popular prejudice, occasionally fanned by official media organs, is most often faced by Jews (referred to as "kikes" by many members of the security organs and popular militias) and Germans ("fascists"), for reasons of history and foreign contacts. Perhaps for these reasons these two nationalities have developed the strongest dissident movements for emigration, for which the activists have usually been incarcerated.[11]

CIVIL AND POLITICAL RIGHTS

The USSR has received greatest criticism for its performance in the field of civil and political rights. As suggested above, these rights have clearly lower priority than others among Soviet officialdom. Although the population enjoys considerable participatory opportunities and legal guarantees within the framework of Party-sanctioned structures, their rights outside these confines are virtually nonexistent. Incipient political parties are quickly crushed by the KGB. Most street demonstrations are harassed or broken up by police, volunteer militias, KGB operatives, and army troops. Suspected dissidents are subject to heavy surveillance (including electronic surveillance and wiretapping), harassments, street provocation, anonymous threats, loss of jobs, confiscation of correspondence, and searches.

Political prisoners in the Soviet Union number about 10,000. Although Soviet courts have received some international acclaim in the realm of non-political cases, political dissidents receive far less open and fair treatment from judicial organs. Pre-trial legal norms are routinely violated and dissidents insist that all political cases are directed by the KGB. Courtrooms are often filled with state-mobilized supporters of the regime, while family members are frequently forbidden to attend the proceedings. In only a tiny fraction of such cases are defendants released without incarceration or given minor fines. All others are sentenced to prisons and labor camps.[12]

Conditions of incarceration have been justifiably condemned around the world. Political prisoners are usually malnourished, undergo beatings, and suffer occasional torture. In special "pressure cells," criminal prisoners are specially selected to beat and torture their cellmates. Sessions in such cells have at times resulted in disabilities and even death.[13] In psychiatric hospitals inmates are routinely beaten and forced to take mind-altering drugs. A number of prisoners have prematurely died because of poor health deriving from harsh living conditions or have committed suicide.[14]

HUMAN RIGHTS ORGANIZATIONS

Numerous collectivities of Soviet citizens have arisen in the past few decades to protest these violations of human rights.[15] The major groupings and the fates of their members deserve a brief description. (For a more complete listing see Table 1.)

Formed in May 1969 in Moscow, the Action Group for the Defense of Human Rights in the USSR was the first unofficial organization in the Soviet Union to concern itself with all human rights violations against all segments of the population. Throughout its existence, the Group released statements and appeals in defense of rights, beginning with a 1969 letter to the United Nations Commission on Human Rights protesting judicial and psychiatric repression in the USSR. Original members of the group included citizens of various political and religious beliefs from Moscow, Leningrad, Tashkent, Kharkov, and Kiev. Since its inception, the Group has been the subject of repression continuing up to the present. All fifteen founders have either been imprisoned or forced to emigrate.

A year later the Committee for Human Rights in the USSR was formed by physicists Andrei Sakharov, Valery Chalidze, and Andrei Tverdokhlebov as a formal non-political association in accordance with Soviet law. Its aim was to investigate the problems of human rights in the USSR in light of the Universal Declaration. It sought cooperation with the state and offered consultative assistance to organs of the government. It also expressed a willingness to work with international social, scientific, and other non-governmental organizations. The Committee offered assistance to persons engaged in creative research into

Table 1
Major Human Rights Groups in the USSR

Group	Date of Founding	Rights Defended
Action Group for Periodic Seminars on the History and Culture of the Jewish People	1982	Ethnic
Action Group for the Defense of Human Rights in the USSR	1969	General
Action Group to Defend the Rights of the Disabled in the USSR	1978	Social/Economic
Adventist Group for Legal Struggle and Investigation of Facts concerning the Persecution of Believers in the USSR	N/A	Religious
All-Union Coordinating Committee of Soviet Jews	1969	Ethnic
Amnesty International—USSR	1977	Social/Economic
Association of Free Trade Unions of Workers in the USSR	1973	General
Christian Seminar on the Problems of Religious Renaissance	Mid–1970s	Religious
Chronicle of Current Events	1968	General
Committee for Human Rights in the USSR	1970	General
Committee of Jewish Veterans for Emigration	N/A	Ethnic
Committees for Emigration of the Association of Citizens of German Nationality	N/A	Ethnic
Conceptualists	1975	Artistic
Council of Relatives of Prisoners of Evangelical Christian-Baptists	1964	Religious
Elections 79	1979	Political
Express-Information—Bulletin "V"	1978	General
Fraternal Council of Christians of Evangelical-Pentecostal Faith	1979	Religious
Free Interprofessional Association of Workers	1978	Social/Economic
Free Library	1976	Intellectual
Fund to Aid the Evangelical Christian-Pentecostals of Russia	1980	Religious
Good Will Group	1984	Political

Group for the Defense of the Rights of Evangelical Christian-Pentecostals	1980	Religious
Group of Separated Families	1982	Social
Group—73	1973	General
Group to Establish Trust between the USSR and USA	1982	Political
Herald of the Movement for the Defense of Rights	1983	General
In Defense of Economic Freedoms	1978	Economic
Independent Initiative	1982	Political
Initiative Group of Communists, Komso-mol Members, and Non-Party People of German Nationality	1965	Ethnic
Initiative Groups for Cooperation with the Party and Government in Solving the Cri-mean Tatar Nationalities Problem	1956	Ethnic
Jewish Independent University	1980	Ethnic
Mariya	1980	Social
Political Diary	1964	Political
Public Committee for the Right to Emi-grate from the USSR	1979	Political
Public Group to Promote the Observance of the Helsinki Accords in the USSR	1976	General
Public Group to Promote the Observance of the Helsinki Accords in the Mordovian Camps	1979	General
Russian Social Fund for Assistance to Political Prisoners and Their Families	1974	General
Society of Israeli-Soviet Friendship	1979	Ethnic
Temporary Organizing Committee for the Return of the Meskhetian People to the Homeland	1963	Ethnic
Trumpet Call	1980s	Cultural/Religious
Voronezh Helsinki Committee	N/A	General
Woman and Russia	1979	Social
Working Commission to Investigate the Use of Psychiatry for Political Purposes	1977	Political

Source: From author's compilation in Human Rights Internet, ed., *Human Rights Directory: Eastern Europe and the USSR* (Cambridge, Mass.: HRI, Harvard University). Groups include those with all-Union membership or aims; smaller groups with narrower constituencies or interests are omitted. Items in italics refer to major serial publications devoted to human rights issues whose editorial board is largely anonymous; many minor publications with only one or a few issues are excluded.

the theoretical aspects of human rights and in the study of the specific nature of this question in a socialist society. In August 1971 the group was officially associated with the International League for Human Rights in Strasbourg, becoming the first independent association in the Soviet Union to receive membership in an international organization. It also became a member of the International Institute of Law in Strasbourg. In October 1973 the group issued its last collective document. Occasional joint appeals by Sakharov and other members, signing as individuals, have been issued.

In November 1973 Andrei Tverdokhlebov and Valentin Turchin formed the Moscow chapter of Amnesty International–USSR and requested formal registration with the AI Secretariat. The group was officially accepted as an affiliate chapter by AI in September 1974. Consistent with AI bylaws, the chapter was assigned to work for the release of prisoners of conscience outside their own country, in this case Spain, Yugoslavia, and Sri Lanka. Membership soon increased to twenty with representation of many nationalities. Tverdokhlebov published the journal *Amnesty International* and by 1975 some four issues had appeared. In 1982 the group also published three issues of a *Bulletin* containing information on human rights violations. Soviet authorities cracked down on the group in August 1974 with a search of Tverdokhlebov's apartment, from which the chapter's archives were confiscated. The homes of several members were searched in connection with the case. These actions resulted in protests from the AI Secretariat to Party Secretary Leonid Brezhnev. In the following years, several members were imprisoned.

The Russian Social Fund for Assistance to Political Prisoners and Their Families was established in 1974 by Alexander Solzhenitsyn two months after he was expelled from the USSR, in order to render financial assistance to prisoners and their kin. It is financed with the worldwide royalties from his book, *Gulag Archipelago*, which dealt with the labor camp system in the Soviet Union. Various distributors in the USSR take responsibility for allocating the monies. By 1983 the fund was helping 1000 prisoners, without discrimination with respect to religion, nationality, or other affiliation. Several members have been sentenced or forced to emigrate.

In May 1976 the Public Group to Promote the Observance of the Helsinki Accords in the USSR was founded—the first of five such organizations (in Moscow, Ukraine, Georgia, Armenia, and Lithuania). The Group was created to promote observance of the humanitarian provisions of the 1975 Helsinki Final Act. In their first announcement, members announced their intention to collect and forward to the thirty-five signatory nations of the Accords complaints by Soviet citizens concerning violations outlined in the Final Act. The organization received information from hundreds of citizens in both oral and written form and published 195 short documents for the signatory governments. In the winter of 1977 several members were arrested, usually on charges of anti-Soviet agitation and propaganda or conscious dissemination of false information. On 8

September 1982, the Group issued its final document, stating that oppression had forced it to terminate its activities.

Economic and social rights of workers have been defended by the Association of Free Trade Unions of Workers in the USSR, founded in 1977. It is considered to be the first public trade union in the USSR that is independent of official unions. The AFTU was formed by a group of workers, engineers, and technical employees who had been dismissed from work as a result of conflicts with management. The initial members met while addressing complaints to various Moscow officials. Instead of submitting individual complaints, they decided to act collectively with the hope of better results. In November the AFTU appealed to Soviet authorities and foreign media, asking for the creation of an independent commission to investigate the manner in which worker complaints were handled by the Administrative Organs Department of the Central Committee of the Party. In the same year it held a press conference with foreign journalists. In February 1978 the Association requested official recognition from the International Labour Organization and released the group's Statutes as well as a list of 110 candidates for membership. The group's founder, Vladimir Klebanov, was detained by police in December 1978 and incarcerated in a Moscow psychiatric hospital. By 1979 the group was effectively neutralized through harassment, arrests, and psycho-repression.

Another labor organization, the Free Interprofessional Association of Workers, was formed in October 1978 by Evgeny Nikolaev and seven other workers in Moscow to continue and extend the work of the repressed AFTU. By 1983 the group had some ten chapters with about 300 members and 1500 supporters in twenty-one towns and cities. The Association criticized the lack of representation of workers and called for decentralization and rejection of the concentration of power in a few officials' hands. It aimed to defend its members rights in all spheres of their lives within the framework of the Soviet Constitution. The Association has provided members with legal, moral, and financial help via cooperatives for mutual-aid funds, real estate purchase, daycare centers, and barter services. Special working groups were set up to collect information on specific rights. It supported the Polish Solidarity trade union, went on hunger strikes against repressions, and circulated leaflets calling for boycott of voluntary Saturday labor (*subbotniki*). The Association has published over thirty issues of an information bulletin and circulated among themselves transcripts of foreign radio broadcasts about Polish Solidarity. Several members have been sentenced by Soviet authorities.

Economic rights have also been demanded by the Action Group to Defend the Rights of the Disabled in the USSR, formed in 1978 in Moscow by citizens suffering from serious impairment of motor functions. The group's aim is to collect and disseminate information about the disabled, petition for the improvement of social security, seek the creation of an All-Union Society for the Disabled, and improve contacts with international organizations for invalids. There are members from Moscow, Ukraine, Moldavia, and Kazakhstan. Its *Information Bulletin* has documented the poor conditions of invalids in the USSR. The group has been pressured by authorities to disband because of its "illegal" and "anti-Soviet" behavior. Members continue to agitate and the group has recently been accepted as a branch of the International Society of Invalids.

In 1979 the Public Committee for the Right to Emigrate from the USSR was formed to collect and disseminate information on cases of clear violations of the right to leave freely and return to the Soviet Union, to provide assistance to those wishing to emigrate for social, economic, or religious reasons, and to work for a change in present Soviet emigration policy and the adoption of a new and more precise law on the issue. Members have been active in the Russian, Latvian, Estonian, and Byelorussian republics. Several members have been detained by police. In April 1982 Vasily Barats was confined to a mental hospital. Another member, Leonty Timoshchuk, was found killed in the Ternopol region.

In April 1982 five spouses of foreigners now living abroad formed the Group of Separated Families in Moscow to attain reunification. The organization was later joined by seven more individuals. Since then the group has carried out numerous hunger strikes and won a number of individual victories for emigration.

Religious rights have been demanded by several groups, in particular the Council of Relatives of Prisoners of Evangelical Christian-Baptists which was formed in 1964. Its aim has been to monitor and publicize cases of harassment of the church and to petition for a clear policy of non-interference by the state. Since 1971 the group has published a monthly bulletin. Several members have been arrested and sentenced to the camps.

Orthodox believers founded the Christian Committee to Defend the Rights of Believers in the USSR in 1976 and by 1980 had fifteen official members. It declared its intention to collect and distribute information on the situation of religious believers in the USSR, to give legal advice to believers when their civil rights were infringed, to appeal to state institutions concerning the defense of believers' rights, to research the legal and actual position of religion in the USSR, and to assist in putting Soviet legislation on religion into practice. As of 1983 the Committee had published over seventy documents in nine volumes. Its last known statement appealed to the Sixth Assembly of the World Council of Churches to assist in preventing religious persecution in the Soviet Union.

The Working Commission to Investigate the Use of Psychiatry for Political Purposes was formed in 1977 in Moscow by Alexander Podrabinek and four others. Podrabinek's large manuscript, *Punitive Repression*, contributed towards the August 1977 resolution by the Sixth Congress of the International Association of Psychiatrists condemning the Soviet practice of psycho-repression. The Congress also established an investigative committee to look into such abuses worldwide. The Commission's work also contributed in part towards an October 1979 appeal by Amnesty International to Party chief Brezhnev calling for an end to the policy. Over twenty issues of its information bulletin have appeared. It also compiled an index of political prisoners in Soviet mental hospitals (about 200 today) as well as a "black list" of physicians who committed them to the institutions. All known members of the Commission have experienced arrest, imprisonment, or forced emigration.

The Group to Establish Trust between the USSR and USA was formed in 1982 to demand the political right to agitate for disarmament ends. It was the first independent pacifist group to form in the USSR. By 1984 the Group claimed 2000 active supporters organized in nine cities. Its program, generally aimed at creating a four-sided communication system among the governments and peoples of the two countries, proposed the dissolution of NATO and the Warsaw Pact, reduction of conventional weapons, cessation of development of the MX missile, declaration of the Black Sea as a zone of peace and Moscow as a nuclear-free zone, joint Soviet-American space flights, and enhanced cultural exchange. Members have declared their avoidance of the military draft, held press conferences with foreign correspondents, exhibited materials of the American peace movement, produced pacifist posters and badges, and collected signatures on several petitions. The authorities have disconnected members' telephones, blocked off their apartments, and sent several to the camps or mental hospitals. The Group has continued its activities, establishing contacts with a large number of Western pacifist organizations: American Friends Service Committee, Greenpeace International, Mobilization for Survival, European Nuclear Disarmament, and the Dutch Ecumenical Peace Council.

TWO YEARS IN THE LIVES OF SOVIET DISSIDENTS

In light of Western media reports praising the new "openness" (*glasnost'*) of Party Secretary Gorbachev, it may be instructive to survey the human rights scene in more detail since the time of his ascendance to examine the degree to which Western perceptions and public-relations efforts in the USSR fit Soviet dissident realities. The evidence suggests that Gorbachev's reign has much in common with its post-Stalinist predecessors and that overall improvement in the human-rights scene may prove difficult.[16]

Nineteen eighty-five had the makings of a promising year for Soviet dissidents. Gorbachev immediately began an effective purge of the old guard, shook up the propaganda apparatus, and displayed a bright new international image. The *glasnost'* campaign promised a fuller discussion of official malpractices.

In June 1986 a new department for Humanitarian and Cultural Ties, headed by the former chief of the Soviet delegation to the Helsinki Accords meeting on human contacts in Berne, was reported established in the Ministry of Foreign Affairs. This was followed in July, on the eleventh anniversary of the signing of the Accords, by the creation of a Commission on Human Rights Questions, to include intellectuals and workers, which would inform Soviet citizens of their rights.

In the same month Soviet jurists were allowed openly to criticize abuses of administrative law governing additional camp terms for "malicious disobedience to camp authorities,'' under which several political prisoners had been resent-enced. At the same time Moscow television carried a discussion between young Yakuts and Russians which hinted at the problems which gave rise to riots between the two nationalities shortly before in Yakutsk province.

Concessions on human contacts and repatriation have also marked the Gor-bachev era. Merab Kostava, a member of the Georgian Helsinki Group suffering from tuberculosis in the camps, was unexpectedly released. Latvian human rights activist Ints Calitis was allowed to return home shortly thereafter. Dozens of Soviet citizens were permitted to rejoin their families in the United States. Jewish dissident Anatoly Shcharansky was released from camp and emigrated to Israel in an East-West prisoner exchange, after which his close relatives rejoined him abroad. Elena Bonner, wife of exiled dissident Andrei Sakharov, was granted a medical exit visa to the United States. Later her husband was released from internal exile. Fourteen families of Meskhetians, a nation deported from their homes in World War II, were allowed to resettle in Georgia. The level of Jewish emigration rose slightly, from a record low of 904 in 1984 to 1,140 in 1985. Literary figures were allowed somewhat more space in which to operate. At the Sixth Congress of Writers of the Russian Republic, poet Yevgeny Yevtushenko criticized Stalin's collectivization, the banning of genetics and cybernetics, party purges, and curtailments of literary freedom.

Other more ominous signs, however, also appeared. On the anniversary of the Soviet victory over Nazi Germany, Gorbachev praised Stalin's leadership during the war. Although the anniversary served as the occasion for an amnesty of Soviet prisoners, political dissidents were not included.

In July 1985 KGB chief Viktor Chebrikov linked dissent with "outside influ-ence," thereby associating it with treason. At the Ottawa Review Conference on Human Rights, the head of the Soviet delegation, Vsevolod Sofinski, denied that the USSR persecuted citizens for their religious beliefs. At a New York Conference on U.S.-Soviet relations, the head of the Soviet contingent claimed there was no Jewish problem in the USSR.

The right to peaceful assembly has been violated on numerous occasions. On December 10, 1985, anniversary of the signing of the Universal Declaration, a handful of citizens holding their traditional silent demonstration at Pushkin Square in Moscow were arrested for "disturbing public order." A month earlier a group of Soviet Germans was detained and sent back to their homes after demonstrating on Red Square for emigration visas to West Germany. Another group of five Germans was detained in June of the following year while trying to visit the West German embassy in Moscow. A number of demonstrations by Jewish refuseniks, holding signs reading "Let Us Go to Israel," was broken up by police. In August 1986 a handful of refuseniks was detained outside Central Committee headquarters after a hunger-strike demonstration for visas. When in June 1986 two members of the Public Group to Establish Trust between the USSR and USA protested in a Moscow subway against the loss of their jobs, they were detained and placed under house arrest. Two months later a Group member and four Western peace activists were detained for distributing leaflets concerning the effects of radiation arising from the Chernobyl nuclear disaster. In August several Estonians were arrested during marches against the forcible use of military reservists for decontamination work around the Chernobyl plant. The father of draft resister Serafim Evsyukov was placed in a mental hospital in July after demonstrating in Moscow against the conviction of his son. Georgian Helsinki Group member Eduard Gudava was sentenced to four years' imprisonment for displaying a sign in public demanding freedom for his imprisoned brother and fellow Group member Tengis Gudava. In September a group of unofficial Moscow artists who attempted to hold a peaceful exhibit dedicated to peace was broken up by police and KGB agents. The participants were detained and the paintings confiscated.

The ability of Soviet citizens to maintain human contacts within the USSR and abroad was frustrated on numerous occasions. In the Crimea, from which many Tatars seeking repatriation have been evicted, state offices have refused to register marriages if one spouse lives outside the province. In April 1986 officials took her three-year-old son away from peace activist Larisa Chukaeva and gave him to her mother-in-law. In August it was reported that Christian poetess Irina Ratushinskaya, imprisoned in 1983, had not been allowed to see her husband for three years.

The integrity of the person was violated by numerous beatings and, according to dissident reports, murders. *Samizdat* writer Anatoly Marchenko was beaten unconscious in a Perm camp by officials in the fall of 1985. He later died in camp. Dr. Anatoly Koryagin, a consultant to the dissident Working Commission to Investigate the Abuse of Psychiatry for Political Purposes, was subjected to repeated beatings in the camps. Human rights activist Vladimir Albrekht was beaten in camp after refusing to recant his political views. Jewish dissident Boris Gudko was beaten after a demonstration in front of the Moscow Chess Federation in April 1986. In the same month Trust Group member Nikolai Khramov suffered serious physical injuries at the hands of attackers in front of his home. Invalid and former political prisoner Nikolai Pavlov was severely attacked in August by KGB agents after refusing to stop receiving packages from abroad. In August 1985 a member of the Lithuanian Catholic Committee for the Defense of Believers' Rights, Father Vaclovas Stakenas, was violently assaulted by two assailants and then thrown into a pond. A follower of Hare Krishna and his wife were beaten in Sukhumi for distributing religious literature.

In February 1985 Olena Antoniv, an activist in Alexander Solzhenitsyn's Russian Social Fund for Assistance to Political Prisoners and their Families and the wife of former political prisoner Zinovy Krasivsky, died in a mysterious automobile accident in Lvov. One year later a founder of the Lithuanian Catholic Committee, Father Juozas Zdebskis, who had been under surveillance for twenty years and been physically attacked on a number of occasions, was killed when his car smashed into a large milk truck while allegedly trying to pass another vehicle. In official reports the names of the drivers of the other vehicles were not mentioned. According to the underground *Chronicle of the Catholic Church of Lithuania*, the collision was a carefully planned act of official violence.

The resentencing of political prisoners just before their release continued. The hopes of eventual release have been frustrated by application of the "malicious disobedience" article in the Criminal Code. New sentences in the camps and prisons have been handed down to artist Galina Maximova, unofficial trade union member Vsevolod Kuvakin, Orthodox believer Alexander Ogorodnikov, Social Fund distributor Sergei Khodorovich, Baptist pastor Pyotr Rumachik, and Psychiatric Group member Anatoly Koryagin.

Authorities also continued to place dissidents in mental hospitals. Ominously, a new branch of the infamous Serbsky Psychiatric Institute, where many dissidents have been brutalized, was opened in Kiev.

New judicial repressions were experienced across the entire spectrum of dissenters. Nationalists from Lithuania, Estonia, and the Ukraine were incarcerated for their activities. Jews from Riga, Chernovtsi, Poltava, and Odessa were sent to the camps. Authorities cracked down especially hard on Jewish cultural activities. Hebrew teachers in Gorky, Kharkov, and Leningrad were tried and sentenced. One Jewish activist in Moscow was convicted for "stealing books from the synagogue."

In Georgia, two members of the Helsinki Watch Group and the music ensemble "Phantom" who agitated for emigration were arrested in Tbilisi. Another member was beaten on the streets by unknown assailants and told to cease contacts with other members. After experiencing apartment searches in July, Svetlana Kurdianni and Marina Tertsian "disappeared"—Latin American-style. Crimean Tatar activists also believe that Smail Bilyalov, who has not been heard from since August 1984 when he was arrested for supporting the nation's repatriation cause, was also "disappeared."

Religious dissidents also discovered that little had changed under Gorbachev. Several Pentecostals seeking emigration were sentenced to the camps. Two Lutheran believers were convicted in Latvia and Estonia. An Orthodox believer in Riga and a Catholic priest in Novosibirsk were put on trial. Iosyp Terelya, a founder of the Action Group for the Defense of the Rights of Believers and the Church in the Ukraine, was tried and sentenced. In Lithuania, Vladas Lapienis was sentenced for assisting in the publication of the *Chronicle of the Catholic Church of Lithuania* and for writing his camp memoirs. Dissident Baptists were especially repressed. Police broke up prayer meetings and several members of the Committee of Relatives of Prisoners were arrested and sentenced to camp terms. Rumblings among the Muslims of Central Asia were suppressed by authorities. A self-declared mullah was sentenced in Samarkand for holding unofficial religious ceremonies. Three Muslims in Azerbaidzhan were tried for operating an underground religious press. Five Krishna believers were arrested in Kiev, Erevan, and Sukhumi, and two were incarcerated in mental hospitals in Vilnius and Erevan for "Krishna mania." In the Stavropol region ten followers of the sect were convicted for their "links to the Sakharov Committee, the Jewish Movement, and other subversive groups" and for "scaring Soviet citizens with the threat of nuclear war."

Civil rights groups were also decimated by arrests. Muscovite Leonid Volvovsky was arrested for attempting to contact Sakharov. In Moldavia and Kazakhstan, two citizens were interned in psychiatric hospitals for trying to form Helsinki Watch Groups. In Moscow, Kirill Popov was incarcerated for assisting political prisoners with monetary aid. Vladimir Sytinsky, a member of the unofficial Free Interprofessional Association of Workers, was tried in Leningrad.

Pacifist dissenter Vladimir Brodsky was tried in Moscow for "hooliganism." Some thirty peace activists, on their way to a seminar sponsored by the Trust Group, were detained in the capital. Shortly thereafter, two high school students were put in a mental hospital for associating with the group.

In some respects, indeed, conditions for political prisoners have appeared to worsen. Jewish activist Zakhar Zunshain suffers from jaundice; human rights dissident Viktor Grinev from nephritis, ulcers, and pleurisy; Ukrainian Catholic Sofia Balyak from malnutrition; Christian poetess Irina Ratushinskaya from kidney illness, chest pains, and high blood pressure; and Baptist Yakov Ivashchenko from lung infections. In August 1986 Mark Moroz, an invalid and member of the Free Interprofessional Union, died in Chistopol prison after suffering from infections and heart and lung diseases. According to Yosyp Terelya, founder of the Action group for the Defense of the Rights of Believers in Ukraine, sanitary conditions at the Lvov prison are abominable and authorities have taken no action. Particularly notorious is Perm Camp No. 36, known as the "death camp." In an eighteen-month period four Ukrainian prioners of conscience—three Helsinki Group members (Oleksa Tykhy, Yuri Lytvyn, and Vasyl Stus) and Catholic activist Valery Marchenko—have died. Three perished after medical neglect by camp administrators, while Lytvyn committed suicide.

In sum, the Soviet regime appears as distrustful of dissidence as it was when human rights activists began their activities two decades earlier. Given the new regime's extensive shakeup of Party and State bureaucracies, the new repressions can only with difficulty be attributed to Brezhnev-Andropov-Chernenko "holdovers." The systematic repression of activists involved in many human rights dimensions appears to be a conscious policy having much in common with that of Gorbachev's predecessors.

Certainly some real concessions have been made, at least with respect to dissidents well-known abroad. Andrei Sakharov was released from his exile and over 100 prisoners were amnestied. Yet thousands still languish in places of incarceration. One is forced to conclude that, thus far, the new era of "openness" under Gorbachev reflects more symbol than substance. Perhaps the mid–1986 attack on Amnesty International as a front for U.S. and British intelligence services—a charge strongly rejected by the human rights organization—reflects better the actual situation under Gorbachev than the many other optimistic pronouncements in the Soviet media. Only when Soviet reality matches official rhetoric will Amnesty and other human rights observers be only too happy to give the regime a clean bill of humanitarian health.

THEORETICAL PERSPECTIVES

A number of theories have been adduced to explain these rather continuous violations of citizens' rights throughout Russian/Soviet history. These perspectives fall under the general rubrics of political culture, security concerns, communism, and imperialism.

The political culture argument lays stress on the Russian mass belief-system which accords the individual few rights vis-à-vis society. The historical Russian peasant notion that the primary social unit, the *mir* or community, has rights over the individual almost guarantees that individuals and minority groups will be occasionally suppressed for the sake of social harmony. Perhaps not so coincidentally, the Russian word *mir* also means "peace." In a Russian version of the Japanese proverb that "the nail that sticks out gets hammered down," the population has generally accepted and supported strong autocratic Tsars, and later Party First Secretaries, along with their large and authoritarian bureaucracies to enforce public order. Without this repressive state, the Russian nationality quickly degenerates into much-feared anarchy.

The ideological—indeed, quasi-religious—dimension of this national belief-system is the preservation of Orthodoxy—Russian Christian Orthodoxy before 1917 and Marxism-Leninism thereafter. Russians feel uncomfortable without ideological monism; pluralism threatens the harmony of the *mir*. Little surprise should be registered, according to this argument, that political parties have been routinely repressed, or that non-Russians are pressured to assimilate into the Russian nation, under Tsars and Commissars alike. "Autocracy, Orthodoxy, and Nationality" is a continuous thread throughout Russian history because of its positive resonance among the Russian masses.

Regardless of the degree to which Ivan the Terrible resembled Stalin the Terrible, or the *oprichnina* of the former has similarities to the secret police of the latter, considerable problems beset the explanation. Peasant revolts punctuate Russian history and the Revolution of 1917 did gain support from Russian urban workers. And the communist revolution did make a difference—at least with respect to economic and social rights. The communist regime, moreover, has often shown little respect for the Russian cultural heritage, having destroyed Orthodox churches and transformed them into grain storage bins, jailed Russian nationalist groups, and polluted cherished environmental sites. Some of the dissidents repressed today are loyal—even fervent—members of the Communist Party who desire that the leadership fulfill their ideological dreams. Under Stalin's Great Terror, of course, "orthodox" Party members were killed in massive numbers.

National security concerns, according to some observers, are greatly responsible for human rights violations. Having the longest land border in the world to defend, along which reside numerous non-Russian nationalities whose love for Russia is certainly less than perfect, national-security managers are forced to violate the rights of citizens to preserve internal stability and thereby territorial boundary-maintenance. An authoritarian "Fortress Russia" is seen as a function of the numerous land invasions of Russia, dating from the "Tater Yoke" through the Allied Intervention against the 1917 Revolution to the German invasions of World Wars I and II. The U.S. "Star Wars" plan now plagues national security from above. Little wonder, then, that xenophobia is often deemed a Russian hallmark or that contacts with foreign countries are severely circumscribed and controlled. Dissent from within is often connected with subversion from without. Domestic policy toward dissent is a function of foreign-policy nightmares.

The difficulty with this interpretation, however, is that several countries have experienced similar invasions throughout their history yet managed to treat their citizens with far greater respect (e.g., France). Conversely, many gross violators of human rights have far fewer security problems than Russia/USSR (e.g., Indonesia). Thus we must ask, "Why Russia?" Further, the tremendous growth of Soviet military power has yet to lead to substantial structural changes with respect to greater citizen rights.

The theory that communism with its associated political structures is largely responsible for rights violations is based on Marxist-Leninist tenets of the historical inevitability of capitalist collapse and socialist victory. In the interim, a dictatorship of the proletariat is perfectly acceptable. History will vindicate repression. The state exists, in fact, for the very purpose of oppressing bourgeois elements. And certainly other communist regimes, like the Kampuchean Khmer Rouge and the Ethiopian Dergue, have much repression in common with their earlier Soviet counterparts.

Problems arise, however, when one notes that a number of Russian Tsars proved at least as brutal as subsequent Soviet Party First Secretaries. The CPSU has certainly respected economic rights far more than their Tsarist predecessors. Conversely, one can question the degree to which it respects proletarian social rights. From the crushing of the "Workers' Opposition" and numerous proletarian anarchist elements early in Soviet history to the current repression of autonomous union organizations, Soviet authorities reveal that only "controlled workers" have rights. The fact that fulfillment of the economic plan often takes precedence over safe working conditions also suggests that worker welfare is not always the Party *apparat*'s top priority. Soviet treatment of workers' Solidarity in Poland is another case in point. Finally, not all communist regimes curb all rights uniformly; Yugoslavia, for example, allows its citizens greater latitude, especially with respect to travel and contacts abroad.

The imperialism theory suggests that Russian/Soviet authorities violate citizen rights for the sake of greater expansion to "catch up with" and imitate the West and thus attain world-leadership status. The fact that Tsarist Russia saw itself as the "Third Rome," and Soviet Russia views itself as the "center" of socialist internationalism, reveals a sense of ideological missionary arrogance toward dissidents within the Russian nation and toward non-Russians without. Russian imperial authorities tolerate no dissent against the imperial project and demand the unity and sacrifices necessary to carry it out. They superiorize the Russian nation and inferiorize non-Russian ones for the sake of imperial integration and expansion. Suppression of dissent is justified in terms of a higher global good.

The problem, of course, is that other imperial powers have guaranteed the rights of their own nationals far better than Russia (e.g., Great Britain). On the other hand, the economic welfare of non-Russians in the Soviet Empire ranks far higher than that of European colonials (e.g., in Africa). Indeed, Russians have borne considerable economic burdens to raise their internal colonies (the Central Asian Republics in particular) and external clients (e.g., Cuba, Vietnam) from the level of economic misery.

All the above theories shed some light on rights violations yet all are inadequate. To the degree that they can be integrated, such integration involves a multidisciplinary historical-structural approach detailing the conjunctural development of the Soviet polity. Such a comprehensive analysis lies beyond the scope of the present essay.

NOTES

1. For Soviet views on human rights, see Mary Hawkesworth, "Ideological Immunity: The Soviet Response to Human Rights Criticism," *Universal Human Rights* 2, 1 (January-March 1980), pp. 67–84; Roger Hamburg, "American and Soviet Views of Human Rights," *Conflict* 2, 2 (1980), pp. 163–75; and John Evrard, "Human Rights in the Soviet Union," *DePaul Law Review* 29 (1980), pp. 819–68.

2. Eduard Shevardnadze, "Two Worlds—Two Conceptions of Human Rights," *Mirovaya ekonomika i mezhdunarodnye otnosheniya* 1 (January 1986), p. 2.

3. Stanislav Shatalin, "Social Development and Economic Growth," *Kommunist* 14 (September 1986), p. 63.

4. *Narkhoz* (Moscow: 1984), p. 559.

5. For a recent survey, see Aaron Trehub, *Social and Economic Rights in the Soviet Union* (Munich: Radio Liberty Research Bulletin, 29 December 1986).

6. Shatalin, "Social Development," p. 69.

7. Trehub, *Social and Economic Rights*.

8. Betsy Gidwitz, "Labor Unrest in the Soviet Union," *Problems of Communism* 31, 6 (November-December 1982), pp. 25–42; Viktor Haynes and Olga Semyonova, *Workers against the Gulag: The New Opposition in the Soviet Union* (London: Pluto, 1979). On *samizdat* literature see J. Telesin, "Inside Samizdat," *Encounter* (February 1973), pp. 25–34.

9. See the author's "Protest for Religious Rights in the USSR: Characteristics and Consequences," *Russian Review* 39, 4 (October 1980), pp. 426–41; Cretiens de l'est, *Catholics in Soviet-Occupied Lithuania: Faith under Persecution* (El Toro, Calif.: Aid to the Church in Need, 1981); Michael Bourdeaux, *Land of Crosses* (Devon, U.K.: Augustine, 1979); Estonian Evangelical Lutheran Church, *Church in Bondage* (Stockholm: 1979); Commission on Security and Cooperation in Europe, *Religious Rights in*

the Soviet Union and Eastern Europe (Washington, D.C.: U.S. Congress, 1980); Commission on Security and Cooperation in Europe, *On the Right to Emigrate for Religious Reasons: The Case of 10,000 Soviet Evangelical Christians* (Washington, D.C.: U.S. Congress, 1979); Marite Sapiets, *Unknown Homeland* (London: Mowbrays, 1978).

10. See also Irene Lainer, *Human Rights of Scientists in the Soviet Union* (Waltham, Mass.: Soviet Jewry Legal Advocacy Center, 1980).

11. See the author's "National Rights Protest in the Brezhnev Era," *Ethnic and Racial Studies* 4, 2 (April 1981), pp. 175–88; Commission on Security and Cooperation in Europe, *Religious and National Dissent in Lithuania* (Washington, D.C.: U.S. Congress, 1981); Thomas Remeikis, *Opposition to Soviet Rule in Lithuania* (Chicago: Institute of Lithuanian Studies Press, 1980); V. Stanley Vardys, "Human Rights Issues in Estonia, Latvia, and Lithuania," *Journal of Baltic Studies* 12, 3 (Fall 1981), pp. 275–98; Commission on Security and Cooperation in Europe, *Soviet Treatment of Ethnic Groups* (Washington, D.C.: U.S. Congress, 1980); Commission on Security and Cooperation in Europe, *On Human Rights Violations in Ukraine* (Washington, D.C.: U.S. Congress, 1979); Gesellschaft für Menschenrechte, *Deutsche in der UdSSR* (Frankfurt: 1980); Subcommittee on International Organizations, *Human Rights and the Baltic States* (Washington, D.C.: Committee on Foreign Affairs, House of Representatives, 96–1, June 1979).

12. See Committee for the Defense of Soviet Political Prisoners and Ukrainian National Women's League of America, *Women Political Prisoners in the USSR* (New York: 1975).

13. Helsinki Watch, *Ten Years Later: Violations of the Helsinki Accords—August 1985* (Washington, D.C.: 1985), p. 231.

14. Avraham Shifrin, *First Guidebook to Prisons and Concentration Camps of the Soviet Union* (Seewis, Switzerland: Stephanus Edition, 1980).

15. See the author's "Human Rights Protest in the USSR," *Universal Human Rights* 2, 1 (January-March 1980), pp. 5–29; David Powell, "Controlling Dissent in the Soviet Union," *Government and Opposition* 7, 1 (Winter 1972), pp. 85–98; Frederick Bargnoorn, "Soviet Political Doctrine and the Problem of Opposition," *Bucknell Review* 12, 2 (May 1964), pp. 1–29; Edward Corcoran, "Dissension in the Soviet Union: The Group Basis and Dynamics of Internal Opposition," unpublished Ph.D. dissertation, Columbia University, 1977; Joshua Rubinstein, *Soviet Dissidents: Their Struggle for Human Rights* (Boston: Beacon, 1980).

16. See the author's "Soviet Union," in Human Rights Internet, ed., *Human Rights Directory: Eastern Europe and the USSR* (Cambridge, Mass.: Harvard Law School, 1986); the summary is based on several serial publications dealing with Soviet human rights issues: *Chronicle of the Catholic Church of Lithuania, Elta Information Service, Freedom: Russia for Christ, Help and Action Newsletter, Latvian Information Bulletin, Materialy samizdata, Radio Liberty Research Bulletin, Religion in Communist-Dominated Areas, Religion in Communist Lands, Right to Believe, Samizdat Bulletin,* and *Vesti iz SSSR.*

SUGGESTED READINGS

Alexeyeva, Ludmilla. 1977–78. "The Human Rights Movement in the USSR." *Survey* 23, no. 4 (Autumn):72–85.

———. 1985. *Soviet Dissent.* Middletown, Conn.: Wesleyan University Press.

Bloch, Sidney, and Peter Reddaway. 1977. *Psychiatric Terror: How Soviet Psychiatry Is Used to Suppress Dissent.* New York: Basic Books.

Chalidze, Valery. 1972. *Important Aspects of Human Rights in the Soviet Union*. New York: Institute of Human Relations, American Jewish Committee.

Hopkins, Mark. 1983. *Russia's Underground Press: The Chronicle of Current Events*. New York: Praeger.

Kaminskaya, Dina. 1982. *Final Judgement: My Life as a Soviet Defense Attorney*. New York: Simon and Schuster.

Kirk, Irina. 1975. *Profiles in Russian Resistance*. New York: Quadrangle.

Kowalewski, David. 1980. "Human Rights Protest in the USSR.: Statistical Trends for 1965–78." *Universal Human Rights* 2, no. 1 (January-March):5–29.

Shatz, Marshall. 1980. *Soviet Dissent in Historical Perspective*. Cambridge University Press.

Spechler, Dina. 1982. *Permitted Dissent in the USSR*. New York: Praeger.

Tokes, Rudolf. 1975. *Dissent in the USSR*. Baltimore: Johns Hopkins University Press.

20

THE UNITED STATES

Robert Justin Goldstein

Probably no country in world history has ever so completely and consistently stressed human rights in its official ideology as has the United States of America. Thus, in a speech delivered on December 6, 1978, in commemoration of the thirtieth anniversary of the United Nations–sponsored Universal Declaration of Human Rights, President Jimmy Carter declared "Human rights is the soul of our foreign policy, because human rights is the very soul of our sense of nationhood."[1] Even a cursory examination of crucial documents in American history and crucial elements in American patriotic rituals and speeches reveals a repeated and heartfelt stress on such concepts as liberty, justice, and equality. Thus, the Declaration of Independence of July 1776, in which the then British colony announced its independent status (in perhaps the earliest anti-colonial revolution), proclaims as "self-evident" truths that "all men are created equal" and "endowed by their Creator with certain unalienable Rights," including "Life, Liberty and the pursuit of Happiness." Perhaps the most famous monument in the United States is the Statue of Liberty, erected in 1886 in New York Harbor, welcoming immigrants who are widely perceived as fleeing the economic injustices and political tyranny of other countries for the "Land of Freedom." The American national anthem, the "Star Spangled Banner," refers to the United States as the "land of the free." The Pledge of Allegiance, a patriotic ritual performed in many American schoolrooms every day, defines the United States as delivering "liberty and justice for all." All American coins bear the word "liberty" on their face.

This chapter will often stress the ways in which America has failed to fulfill its promise in human rights; a critical look at the American record is required precisely because America's self-proclaimed standards are so high. The *official* American self-identification with the principles of liberty, justice, and equality has probably exceeded that of any other major country in the world, but it seems unlikely that any large, complex, multinational, and multiracial state with the population and geographic spread of the United States could possibly meet the promises of its self-proclaimed standards. Furthermore, the American definition of "human rights" has a curiously narrow aspect to it: the stress is almost invariably on *political* rights such as freedom of speech, press, and assembly, and on *due process* rights such as justice and equality before the courts, all of which are constitutionally enshrined. The American "human rights" definition makes no bow, either in general parlance, constitutional provision, or statute, to anything even approaching the *social and economic rights* proclaimed in the Universal Declaration of Human Rights: "Everyone has the right to a standard of living adequate for the health and well-being of himself and his family, including food, clothing, housing and medical care and necessary social services."

In assessing the American human rights record, both in political and social-economic rights, a great deal depends upon which countries one uses for comparative purposes. Compared to *most* countries (i.e., including the underdeveloped Third World dictatorships which predominate today in the world), the American record looks extremely good, since both American political freedoms and living standards are among the best in the world. Even the millions of poor Americans live far better than do the poor in most countries, as is clearly demonstrated by such key indicators as life expectancy and infant mortality rates. On the other hand, if the United States is compared to other relatively similar countries—i.e., the twenty or so Western industrialized democracies—the record looks much less attractive. The American record in political rights has been repeatedly flawed in the last hundred years by periodic surges of "anti-subversive" hysteria which have significantly contributed to making the United States the only Western industrialized democracy without a functioning socialist party or militant or socialist-oriented trade unions.[2] This absence largely explains a political dialogue which is extraordinarily constricted and almost totally monopolized by an upper-middle-class corporate capitalist perspective, which has helped to create an economic-social human rights record that in terms of distributive equity is perhaps the very worst in the Western industrialized world.

POLITICAL RIGHTS

Periodically since the Revolutionary War (1776–1783), the United States has been swept by outbursts of repressive activity, but the early introduction of universal male suffrage and constitutional guarantees of freedom of the press, assembly, and speech created a far freer climate during the 1780–1870 period than in Europe, where generally the suffrage was restricted to a tiny wealthy fraction of the population, the press was censored, and freedom of assembly and association were highly limited. The earliest of the relatively few and episodic repressive periods before 1870 came in 1798, when the government of President John Adams tried to crush the rise of the first political opposition led by Thomas Jefferson by passing a Sedition Act which outlawed the printing or uttering of "false, scandalous and malicious" statements about the government intended to "defame" the government or bring it into "contempt or disrepute." The prospect that the country might quickly turn into a one-party state ended only when Jefferson beat Adams in the 1800 presidential election, pardoned those convicted under the Sedition Act, and let the law expire. The rights of those advocating abolition of slavery were frequently severely abridged in both North and South during the 1820–1860 period leading up to the Civil War, and during the war itself dissenters again faced widespread repression. Thus, in seeming defiance of the constitutional provision apparently granting only to Congress the right to suspend the writ of habeas corpus, President Abraham Lincoln suspended the writ nationwide in 1862, and subsequently about 25,000 people were arrested and detained in the North without any legal procedures, some on charges as vague as "being a resident of Atlanta, Georgia," or, in one case, of "being a dangerous man."[3]

Following the northern victory during the Civil War (1861–1865), the United States underwent an industrial boom of enormous dimensions, which created in its wake a modern industrial urban labor force. These developments and the slow growth of an organized labor movement that was peripherally under Marxist influence inaugurated a period when repressive outbursts became considerably more frequent. Ironically, just as most European governments were enfranchising the masses and grudgingly and gradually accepting the legitimacy of socialist-oriented trade unions and working-class parties after decades of severe repression,[4] the United States (a country which before 1870 had been extremely tolerant of numerous utopian socialist communities) often treated the growth of an organized labor movement, and subsequently of rather small socialist and communist parties, as intolerable. Thus, the entire period from about 1870 until the Supreme Court's upholding of the constitutionality of the Wagner Act in 1937 (which effectively legalized a broad array of labor-organizing activities about 50 years after similar legislation in Western Europe) was marked by virtual guerrilla warfare between industrial corporations and the developing labor movement, in which government was repeatedly allied with business. The civil liberties of labor union organizers and striking workers were repeatedly trampled upon, and labor's freedoms of speech, assembly, and association, to say nothing of freedom to strike, were repeatedly abridged, frequently in extremely violent ways. This was particularly the case during the periodic depressions and resultant increased labor unrest that struck the United States in 1873–1878, 1882–1886, 1892–1896, 1908, and 1913–1916.

Although the entire labor movement suffered repeatedly from repressive tactics, this was especially the case of radical (i.e., anti-capitalist) unions such as the Western Federation of Miners (flourished 1900–1905), the Industrial Workers of the World (1905–1918), and Communist party unions (1920–1954). Repression was especially intense during critical strikes such as the nationwide Pullman railroad strike of 1894 and the national steel strike of 1919, both of which were largely broken through massive use of police, troops, and arrests of strikers; the collapse of each strike set the labor movement back for about a decade. Many business corporations supplemented governmental coercion of labor with their own privately paid and armed police, amassing huge ammunition depots and arsenals to carry on the struggle. At least 700 were killed and thousands were seriously injured during American labor struggles between 1870 and 1940, a toll exceeding that in any European country save perhaps Russia and Italy.[5] While the violence by no means came solely from the business-governmental coalition, for the most part the fundamental *cause* of violent confrontations was that labor was denied the right to exercise basic freedoms peacefully. As labor historian Jerold S. Auerbach has noted:

Union organization depended on the constitutional freedoms of speech, press and assembly, but employers consistently abridge these rights. Their reliance on espionage, blacklisting, strikebreakers, private police, and ultimately armed violence, nullified the Bill of Rights for those workers who had the temerity to resist their employers' unilateral exercise of power. . . . The Wagner Act, by prohibiting interference with the right to organize, extended First Amendment guarantees . . . to workers who had enjoyed civil liberties if they did at all, solely on their employers' sufferance.[6]

It was only after the Wagner Act was passed in 1935 by Congress and upheld by the Supreme Court in 1937 that labor's rights were protected; not coincidentally, labor union membership exploded from three million to over eight million between 1934 and 1938. By then, repression had virtually destroyed the more radical wings of the labor movement. (Even after passage of the Wagner Act, remaining radical unions were battered into submission during the 1947–1954 McCarthy period.) These historical developments significantly explain the weak, conservative, and largely ineffectual nature of the American labor movement to this day. (In 1985, only 18 percent of American workers were organized, compared to 80 percent or more in most European democracies, although the fact that this percentage has declined since a 1955 peak of 32 percent clearly demonstrates that factors in the American culture aside from repression are involved.) The American labor movement has been essentially absorbed and co-opted into the middle-class corporate capitalist perspective that monopolizes the American political scene, and one major reason for this is that labor has been forcibly taught the lesson that anti-capitalist perspectives are not "acceptable" in the United States.

New targets for those seeking to stifle freedom of expression gradually emerged during the twentieth century with the growth of small but influential radical political movements. These groups have suffered more or less continuous police harassment and have been virtually blocked from gaining mass media exposure to further their ideas, with the worst repression occurring during three major periods: 1917–1920, 1947–1954, and 1967–1972. On the eve of American entry into World War I, the Socialist Party of America (SPA) had emerged as a growing political force with a membership of 100,000, a lively press with a circulation of two million, 1,200 elected officeholders in 340 cities across the country, and strong influence in a number of labor unions. As a result of its strong anti-war stand, the SPA received an astonishing average of 21.6 percent of the vote during municipal elections in 1917. However, shortly after these elections, top SPA officials were arrested across the country under state and federal sedition and espionage acts, particularly the draconian 1918 Federal Sedition Act which outlawed virtually all wartime criticism of the government, including uttering or printing any "disloyal, profane, scurrilous or abusive language about the form of government of the United States." The Industrial Workers of the World (IWW), an increasingly powerful radical labor union, also suffered severe repression, with its entire leadership across the country jailed under trumped-up sedition charges. Altogether, over two thousand Americans were indicted by the federal government alone during the war, solely for verbal or printed opposition to the war; over a hundred persons received jail sentences of ten years or longer for such activities; and a total of 75 newspapers had issues banned from the mail, including virtually the entire SPA and IWW press.[7]

Although the wartime repression severely damaged the SPA and destroyed the IWW, after the war ended in 1918 and repression eased, there was a new radical upsurge in 1919. Following a series of major strikes and unexplained bombings in American cities in 1919, public and elite sentiment for curbing the radical menace culminated in the notorious "Palmer raids" of November 1919 and January 1920, during which about 10,000 "radicals" were rounded up and over 500 were eventually deported under American immigration laws that provided for deportation of aliens solely on the basis of affiliation with organizations deemed to be subversive, regardless of any evidence of personal lawbreaking. The Palmer raids virtually destroyed the newly formed American Communist Party (CP) and drove it underground a few months after its creation as a left-wing split-off from the SPA in 1919.[8]

As the result of a continuing repressive climate, political dissent in the United States lay virtually dormant for ten years after 1920, reviving only with the onset of the Great Depression. The civil liberties climate for radical and have-not groups improved dramatically during the next ten years, as was reflected by the passage of the Wagner Act in 1935. However, after American entry into the war in December 1941, the handful of existing pro-Nazi and pro-Fascist groups were subjected to prosecutions for speech and press offenses, and 110,000 Japanese-Americans were forced to leave their homes on the West Coast and were subsequently incarcerated in detention camps without any charges, evidence, or hearings, under the rising tide of racism and anti-Japanese hysteria which followed the Japanese attack on Pearl Harbor.[9]

One of the results of Depression and the World War II American-Russian alliance was that the CP developed a better public image and was able to revive. By 1945 the CP had about 80,000 members and controlled about 20 percent of the Congress of Industrial Organizations, one of the two major American labor federations. As the Cold War intensified, however, in 1947 President Harry

Truman initiated a series of repressive measures which later developed into what has become known as McCarthyism. All federal employees were subjected to loyalty investigations, often based on vague charges from unknown sources; the top CP leadership was indicted for sedition; communist aliens who had long resided in the United States were subjected to deportation proceedings; and suspect Americans and foreigners such as Negro singer Paul Robeson, movie star Charlie Chaplin, and painter Pablo Picasso were prevented from entering or leaving the country through highly arbitrary government passport restrictions.[10]

Truman's actions, widely publicized congressional "red hunting" hearings, and the repeated charges of communist subversion leveled after 1950 by Senator Joseph McCarthy of Wisconsin and scores of other publicity-hungry congressmen spread waves of fear throughout American life that far exceeded in length and intensity anything experienced in the democratic countries of Western Europe, which were far closer geographically to Russia and whose communist parties were far stronger than the American CP. Loyalty oaths were soon required in order to obtain permits to fish in New York City; to sell insurance or pianos in Washington, D.C.; or to wrestle, barber, or sell junk in Indiana. Those suspected of left-wing sympathies were blacklisted from American movies, radio, and television; were unable to find publishers; and were fired from scores of schools and colleges. The CP, which for better or worse was the most important organization offering a fundamentally critical view of American society, was effectively destroyed.

In 1954 Albert Einstein, who had fled the threat of Nazi tyranny to come to the United States, stated sadly: "If I would be a young man again and had to decide how to make my living, I would not try to become a scientist or scholar or teacher. I would rather choose to be a plumber or peddler in the hope to find that modest degree of independence still available under present circumstances."[11] Another observer of America during the McCarthy period has summed up the general atmosphere:

Nearly everyone learned to be careful, to be anxious, to fear: not to sign a petition, not to join an organization, not to give money, not to be seen with certain books, not to speak your opinions lest someone misinterpret, accuse, inform. Americans were told every horror story of Soviet suppression of free expression and everyone knew that Siberia was the cold and barren place where the Russians sent their dissidents for punishment. Yet all too few Americans realized they were generating their own Siberias in their minds.[12]

While the overt manifestations of McCarthyism declined significantly after the Senate censured him for misconduct in 1954, the lingering effects of this period stifled virtually any serious debate about American domestic problems for the rest of the 1950s and froze American foreign policy in a rigid, militaristic, anti-communist posture that eventually culminated in the Vietnam War.

Another long-term result of the period was the growing autonomy and power of the Federal Bureau of Investigation (FBI), which by the 1960s had become an almost uncontrolled national secret political police agency.[13] Unknown to most Americans, the FBI had been conducting illegal wiretaps and burglaries since the 1940s, and during the Cold War period and after, FBI spying on dissenting political groups mushroomed. Massive files were maintained on such prominent residents as the novelists Ernest Hemingway and John Steinbeck, scientist Albert Einstein, actor Charlie Chaplin, and singer John Lennon. As a result of the rising protests against the Vietnam War after 1965, the activities of the FBI and other intelligence agencies such as the Central Intelligence Agency, the National Security Agency, and Army Intelligence further expanded in response to pressures from Presidents Lyndon Johnson and Richard Nixon, who regarded the anti-war movement as part of a Russian-directed communist plot. The Senate Intelligence Committee reported in 1976 that the intelligence agencies had collected data on hundreds of thousands of Americans "not suspected of criminal activity," including "intimate details of citizens' lives and about their participation in legal and peaceful political activities." FBI activities designed to disrupt radical groups during the 1967–1973 period "often risked and sometimes caused serious emotional, economic or physical damage," the committee reported, and involved violations of "Federal and State statutes prohibiting mail fraud, wire fraud, incitement to violence, sending obscene materials through the mail and extortion."[14]

Ultimately, Republican President Richard M. Nixon was forced to resign in 1974 when it was revealed that presidential operatives had conducted FBI-type operations against the opposition Democratic party. Massive revelations of previously secret intelligence agency activities emerged in the aftermath of Watergate, but aside from assurances from Presidents Gerald Ford, Jimmy Carter, and Ronald Reagan that new executive directives will prevent such actions in the future, there have been no real developments to give serious confidence that the intelligence agencies will not engage in similar activities in some future time of tension. (In fact, Reagan's 1983 executive directive on the intelligence agencies considerably eased restrictions which had been imposed upon them by Ford and Carter.) As one spokesperson for a civil liberties research organization has noted, "All that the executive branch has offered the nation to stand as a bulwark between a history of abuses of secret powers and a future possibility of their return is the facile assertion that Watergate has somehow turned all American officials into automatically honorable men who can again be trusted with vast power."[15]

In summary, repression directed against the labor movement during the 1870–1937 period and against radical political and labor organizations during the post–1870 period significantly contributed to the absence today in the United States of influential radical labor or political organizations. The result is a country in which—although the press is extraordinarily free in theory and restrictions on freedom of speech and assembly are usually episodic and limited in scope—politics, media, and the general culture are to an extraordinary degree (in comparison with Western Europe) dominated by the upper-middle and upper classes; the problems and points of view of millions of poor Americans get little attention; and systematic critiques of flaws in the American capitalist democratic system are almost never aired in the mass media.

Opportunities for peaceful mass action, however, are usually available (though the absence of well-entrenched radical organizations requires each protest movement to be organized from ground zero) and, as was the case with the anti–Vietnam War movement and demands for improving the conditions of women, generally have some impact upon the system if carried on long enough and gaining enough popular support. Furthermore, the existence of reasonably influential organizations such as the American Civil Liberties Union helps to ensure that at least those violations of fundamental rights that come to public attention (i.e., not including those of the intelligence agencies) become the target of criticism. Finally, it must be stressed that despite all the manifold historical flaws in the American political rights record, the American experience, like that of other Western democracies, has been far better than that of most countries. As constitutional law expert Ivo Duchacek has noted: "The freedom of expression, however incomplete it may be in the United States, Britain, Canada, Australia and New Zealand and most European countries, is still separated by an abyss in comparison to the complete suppression of free speech in most of the modern world."[16] In the end, the American political rights record can probably best be fairly assessed as "not good enough" rather than bad. Unfortunately, the same cannot be said for the American record in social and economic rights.

ECONOMIC AND SOCIAL RIGHTS

Except in education, the United States fares poorly when its economic and social rights are compared with those in other industrialized Western democracies. Indeed, the United States is probably the most socially unjust of all such countries. The essence of this injustice can be summarized as follows: (1) per capita income in the United States in terms of real purchasing power is the highest in the world among Western industrialized democracies, yet (2) the United States also has more poverty than most such societies. The reasons for this seeming paradox are that (3) income and wealth are, comparatively, distributed inequitably; (4) American tax policy fails to redistribute income to any significant degree; and (5) American governmental social programs are the least generous in the Western industrialized world.

The best measure of comparative income is generally considered to be real gross domestic product (GDP) per capita, a measure which cross-nationally adjusts income for actual purchasing power in terms of a standard basket of goods. This measure for 1974 and 1982 indicates that the United States is considerably wealthier per capita than any other Western industrialized democracy; for example, for both years over 20 percent above Denmark, Japan, and West Germany and over 30 percent higher than Italy and the United Kingdom.

This aggregate measure of average consumer purchasing power is easily confirmed by data indicating that Americans own more cars, telephones, televisions, radios, etc., per capita than the citizens of any other country. At the same time the United States also has more poverty than most other industrial democracies. Using a standardized definition of poverty as the percentage of the population with an income below two-thirds of the average national income, data for the early 1970s indicates 13 percent of the American population was poor, well above the comparable figure for five other industrialized democracies (11 percent in Canada, 7.5 percent in Britain, and 5 percent or less in Norway, Sweden, and West Germany) and lower only than France (16 percent).[17]

The paradox of greater average wealth in the United States combined with a higher level of poverty reflects an extraordinary maldistribution of wealth. The richest one-half of 1 percent of the population owns about 35 percent of the nation's wealth (including assets like stocks and real estate as well as income), compared to 25 percent in 1963, and the wealthiest 20 percent control 75 percent of all wealth. At the very top, in the mid–1980s an estimated 830,000 households had an average net worth of $1 million and 14 percent of all families were worth over $160,000; in terms of income alone, in 1983 over 37,000 Americans (including 11,526 millionaires) earned more than $500,000, and 14 percent of the population earned over $50,000. In 1984 the 482 wealthiest families and individuals in the United States owned $166 billion in business investments, while figures for 1976 indicate that 45 percent of all corporate stock and 30 percent of all bonds are owned by 1 percent of the population. Data for virtually every sector of the American economy reveals similar concentrations of individual and corporate wealth. For example, in the mid–1980s the largest 1 percent of all farms produced 30 percent of all farm products and earned 60 percent of all farm income, while the largest 100 corporations (out of a total of 200,000 industrial corporations) controlled 52 percent of the nation's industrial assets and the largest 200 companies controlled two-thirds of all industrial sales. At the very bottom, the poorest 25 percent of the American population in the mid–1980s had no assets at all, 23 percent of all households earned less than $10,000, and 34 million Americans (14 percent of the population) were officially classified as impoverished.[18]

Comparisons with other Western industrialized democracies suggest that American income and wealth may be the most maldistributed. Thus, in 1972, the 3.8 percent of all income (i.e., excluding assets) earned by the poorest 20 percent of American households was lower than the figure for every one of nine other Western industrialized states studied (in Canada, for example, the poorest fifth earned 4.3 percent, and in Sweden, 6 percent), while the 44.8 percent of all income received by the richest fifth exceeded six of the other nine countries. The 40 percent of total wealth controlled by the richest 2 percent of Americans exceeded that held by the comparable percentage in three other countries studied in the period around 1970. (For example, in Sweden the top 2 percent controlled less than 25 percent of total wealth, and in West Germany they owned about 32 percent of all wealth.) In 1985 a committee of American Catholic bishops, not a notably radical group, declared that American economic disparities are "among the greatest in the western industrialized world" and are "morally unjustifiable" and in violation of a "minimum standard of distributive justice."[19]

These inequities in the United States could be alleviated by highly progressive tax policies or by generous social welfare programs, but neither exist. Although the most important American tax, the federal income tax, is theoretically highly progressive (supposedly 70 percent of income was taxed at the highest income levels before 1981, and 50 percent thereafter), in fact special provisions that primarily benefit the wealthy riddle the tax system. Further, most other taxes, notably sales and social security taxes and many state income taxes, are either regressive or flat taxes, with the result that the overall impact of American taxation upon the distribution of income is insignificant (after the impact of taxes is calculated, the poorest fifth of the American population fared worse than their counterparts in eight of nine Western industrialized democracies in 1972, while the American wealthiest fifth earned a lesser percentage of total income than only two of their nine counterparts).[20]

Severe cuts in federal social welfare programs that primarily aid the poor—for example, a 28 percent cut in child nutrition programs affecting one million children—coupled with massive federal income tax cuts that especially benefited the rich have further increased economic disparities under the Reagan administration. Thus, according to congressional and independent studies, federal tax and budget policies between 1983 and 1985 cost families earning under $20,000 $20 billion while yielding $135 billion, an average of $7,000, for families earning over $80,000. The typical family earning under $10,000 obtained a $20 tax cut but lost over $400 in income due to program cutbacks, leading to an overall decline of about 8 percent in real disposable income.[21]

The lack of progressivity in the tax structure above all reflects massive loopholes in the federal income tax which primarily benefit the wealthy. For example, special tax preferences granted to those earning so-called capital gains (money made from the sale and transfer of property rather than from salaried work) benefit the average family earning $500,000 an estimated $165,000 a year while yielding less than $150 to the average family earning under $25,000. Due to such tax breaks, in 1982 over 250 Americans with incomes of over $200,000 paid no taxes. Similar tax loopholes, which provide escape routes from the official corporate tax rate of 46 percent, allowed 130 companies to avoid paying any taxes during at least one year between 1981 and 1985, on profits in those years totaling $73 billion.[22]

All of the disparities thus far discussed with regard to poverty and the distribution of wealth in the United States would be relatively unimportant if American social welfare programs designed to aid the poor were generous enough to overcome them, but America maintains what has accurately been called the "cheapest welfare state in the industrialized world." Thus, social spending (excluding education) as a percentage of gross domestic product (GDP) in the United States—about 15 percent in 1981—trails far behind comparable figures for most other Western democracies (e.g., 28 percent in the Netherlands, 25 percent in West Germany, 28 percent in Sweden, and 21 percent in Italy). Social welfare costs in the United States also lag behind those in virtually all comparable countries as a percentage of total budgetary expenditures, amounting to 34 percent of the 1980 American budget compared to 41 percent in Denmark, 45 percent in Sweden, and 50 percent in West Germany. Government transfer programs as a percentage of wages and salaries of the total American labor force amounted to 18.7 percent in the United States in 1977–1979, compared to over 30 percent in Denmark, Norway, Sweden, and West Germany, and over 50 percent in France and the Netherlands.[23]

In general, American social welfare programs have been inadequately funded and so strictly regulated and narrowly targeted to the indigent that millions of Americans in need of help are unable to qualify for bureaucratic reasons or are unwilling to suffer the humiliating stigma associated with being on welfare. Thus in 1970 only half of all American families in the poorest sixth of the population received any government transfer program benefits, compared to 95 percent of the poorest sixth in Sweden and 78 percent in Britain; in 1972 nearly two-thirds of all families earning below the official poverty level received no government cash assistance. Another glaring problem is that while most American social welfare programs are jointly funded by the federal and state governments, the states usually exercise ultimate administrative control, so benefits vary drastically from state to state. For example, in 1976 total average federal-state funding for a poor person in the American south was $784, yet the average for a person in the northeast was $2,425.[24]

Due to such inadequacies, the richest nation in the world continues to have a severe poverty problem, with 14.4 percent of the American population, or 33.7 million people, officially classified as poor in 1984 (defined as having an income of below $10,609 for an urban family of four). In 1984, 22 percent (13.8 million) of all children under eighteen were poor (compared to less than 15 percent in 1970), and about 50 percent of the poor were children. The number and percentage of poor Americans in the 1982–1984 period was the highest since 1964, even though the official poverty level has declined as a percentage of median income from 53 percent to 40 percent between 1959 and 1980.[25]

The most obvious sign of America's failure to solve its poverty problem has been the massive growth in the 1980s of emergency food kitchens and shelters in major American cities designed to provide stop-gap solutions to hunger and homelessness. According to various estimates by government and private organizations, in the mid–1980s between 250,000 and three million Americans lacked any permanent shelter (including 20,000 or more each in New York, Chicago, and Los Angeles), while nationwide only 125,000 emergency shelter beds were available. While perhaps one-third of the homeless—who often end up begging in the streets by day and sleeping on park benches or over sidewalk steam grates by night—are mentally ill, most are simply poor, and increasingly they include functioning adults and families with children.[26]

Clearly, one major reason for this problem is that government housing programs for the homeless and for an estimated 5.6 million American households living in deficient housing have been grossly inadequate. Unlike most other Western industrialized countries, the United States lacks comprehensive government housing policies designed to ensure adequate housing at affordable prices for the entire population. The sprawling, squalid slums that mar most large American cities outstrip the worst housing in England and France and are entirely lacking in Scandinavia, West Germany, Switzerland, and Austria. Most American government efforts in housing have been designed to subsidize, through tax breaks, the ability of the middle and upper classes to purchase homes, with only a small trickle of money devoted to the needs of the poor. In 1982 such tax breaks provided $36 billion for those wealthy enough to own homes (with the greatest subsidies going to those earning the highest incomes and purchasing the costliest homes), while only $5 billion was directed towards housing problems of the poor. The average household with an income of $50,000 gained $3,200 in government housing assistance in 1981, while those earning under $10,000 received an average of $1,353.

The major government program to house the poor has been federal construction of rent-subsidized large housing projects ("public housing"), which have typically been located in rundown central city areas and associated with such high crime rates, social stigma, and general squalor that President Nixon observed that the federal government "has become the biggest slumlord in America." Yet by 1978 only 1.3 million units of public housing existed in the United States, comprising only 1.5 percent of total housing stock, the smallest percentage in any nation in the Western industrialized world (compared to 2.7 percent in the Netherlands, 1.8 percent in West Germany, and 35.1 percent in Britain). Altogether, in 1982 only 3.4 million poor families out of a total of 9 million who qualified for various federal housing programs actually gained any assistance due to lack of funding. This lack, combined with the rising numbers of the poor and decreasing availability of affordable private housing (an estimated 500,000 low-income units have disappeared annually due to demolition, arson, conversion, and other causes), has led to an increase of the median nationwide rent paid as a percentage of income, from 20 percent of income in the 1960s to 27 percent in 1980. Seven million low-income renters paid over 50 percent of income for housing in the early 1980s, and half of the very poorest (those with annual incomes under $3,000) paid over 72 percent for rent, leaving an average of $71 monthly for all other needs.[27]

Aside from homelessness, America's failure to deal adequately with poverty is most clearly indicated by the persistence of hunger. In 1985 the *New York Times* reported, "there are more soup kitchens serving more meals to more people than at any time since the Great Depression," and a panel of doctors and public health experts reported that the United States suffers hunger of "epidemic proportions" affecting twenty million people. Although $18 billion in annual federal food programs—notably the Food Stamp program, which in 1985 provided about twenty million Americans monthly coupons redeemable for food in stores—has largely eliminated the acute malnutrition that was common in the 1960s, as a reporter who traveled the country to investigate hunger in 1985 reported, "everywhere there are families for whom food is an abiding problem," especially as the monthly food stamp allotment is exhausted toward the end of each month, leading to a food crisis that becomes "marginal, if not desperate in the final week or 10 days." According to the Food Research and Action Center, a private research group, food stamp allotments in 1985 provided only 80 percent of the food necessary for poor Americans to adequately feed themselves. American hunger intensified in the 1980s due to high unemployment and cutbacks totaling $12 billion in federal food programs, which took food stamps away from one million recipients (and resulted in the same number of people receiving stamps in 1985 as in 1980 even though five million more Americans were living in poverty in the latter year). In 1986 fifteen million Americans with incomes below the poverty line (and 45 percent of all of those eligible) were not receiving food stamps, largely due to lack of funding and bureaucratic obstacles, although by definition their incomes do not allow adequate diets without assistance.[28]

By far the most important anti-poverty program in the United States is Aid to Families of Dependent Children (AFDC), which in 1980 provided financial assistance to 3.8 million families with 7.6 million children in which the parent or parents are unable to otherwise support their children. In 14 percent of AFDC families (and a nationwide total of 1.2 million households) the heads of households were employed full-time but were still unable to support their families. At the American minimum hourly wage of $3.35, it is possible to work full-time and earn less than $7,000 a year, $3,600 under the 1984 official poverty standard for a family of four. In 1986 the American minimum wage was less than 38 percent of the average private hourly wage, a steady decline from 55 percent in 1968 due to the failure to adjust the minimum wage to keep up with inflation; in contrast, in the Netherlands the minimum wage is pegged at over 70 percent of the average wage. In 1985 fourteen million workers, well over 10 percent of those employed, were earning at or just above the minimum wage.

By any reasonable analysis, AFDC fails to provide adequate support or to aid many who theoretically qualify for it. AFDC has not been adequately adjusted for inflation since 1970, so annual AFDC payments as a percentage of median family income dropped from 23 percent to 17 percent between 1970 and 1979, and the average monthly support for a family of four (in constant 1980 dollars) has fallen 20 percent from $435 in 1970 to $350 in 1980, with the latter figure translating into annual support of $4,200, half the official 1980 poverty level for such a family. The stigma attached to receiving AFDC in the United States and the intense bureaucratic formalities involved in qualifying put up such high barriers that at any given time 47 percent of all women legally entitled to AFDC assistance are receiving no benefits. Finally, since the program is under ultimate state control (although the funding is 54 percent federal), benefits vary wildly from state to state, ranging in 1984 for a family of four from $120 a month in Mississippi to $676 in New York. In states with low benefits like Texas, a reporter found in 1984 that "people on welfare were living right at the lower limit, and sometimes past the limit, of decency, especially with respect to food and medical care."[29]

Other clear indicators of the inadequacy of American social policies and the distortions resulting from the severe maldistribution of wealth in the United States are data concerning infant mortality and life expectancy. Although American spending on medical care consumes over 10 percent of the GNP, and in recent years has generally been at or near the very top among industrialized countries, life expectancy in the United States was exceeded, in some cases by two or more years, by about fifteen other countries in 1981. Infant mortality rates in 1982 ranked seventeenth best in the world (compared to seventh thirty years earlier); even Hong Kong and Singapore had lower infant mortality rates than the United States in 1984. Almost certainly these figures reflect the fact that in the Western industrialized world the United States is the only country lacking systems of comprehensive national health insurance and comprehensive health services and social supports for pregnant women. Although the federal Medicare and Medicaid programs provide health benefits for virtually all elderly Americans and about 50 percent of the nonelderly poor and near poor at a cost of about $100 billion in 1985, about thirty-seven million other Americans lacked any form of medical insurance in 1986 (up from twenty-five million in 1981), with the result that about a million Americans are refused medical treatment each year and five million more fail to seek needed help. Since most Americans who have private insurance obtain it as a job benefit, unemployment frequently also entails loss of insurance.[30]

Among seventy-five countries recently studied by Sheila Kamerman of Columbia University, including all industrialized nations and many developing countries, only the United States lacked comprehensive maternal and infant health programs. While other countries ensure that all pregnant women receive regular medical care, in the United States about 30 percent of pregnant women receive no prenatal care during the first three months of pregnancy; in some cases women in labor have been turned away from hospitals due to inability to pay for care. In the related area of maternity leave, of 118 countries studied by Kamerman, only the United States was found to lack a statutory paid childbirth leave and a job-protected, partially paid child care leave. Such leaves in the United States are totally at the discretion of employers except for women living in the five (out of fifty) states which mandate such leaves. In contrast, in Sweden new mothers are guaranteed 90 percent of pay during a nine-month leave; in Hungary 100 percent of pay is guaranteed for twenty weeks; and in Canada 60 percent of pay is mandated for fifteen weeks.[31]

Unlike most European countries and Canada, the United States also lacks family allowances—payments to all families with children to help pay for child support. A network of state-subsidized day care centers such as that found notably in Scandinavia is also lacking. Indeed—despite a growing need for child care facilities as increasing numbers of mothers have been forced to seek work for economic reasons—in 1985 52 percent of all women with children less than six years old were employed, compared to only 32 percent in 1970; half of the states reduced support for such programs between 1981 and 1986. In Los Angeles alone, a shortage of 264,000 spaces in child care centers was reported in 1986. Nationwide, the average family was forced to pay $3,000 per child in 1985 for child care services where they were available. According to the 1986 report of the Family Policy Panel, a private group of academic, business, and labor leaders, "Most industrialized countries have implemented family policies to accommodate the changing economic and social environment. The U.S. has not."[32]

Although unemployment has tended to be a far more serious problem in the United States than in Western Europe during the post–World War II period (with the major exception of the 1983–1986 period when the United States recovered more quickly from the 1981–1983 recession), American programs are far less generous in payments and far more restrictive in coverage. While unemployment benefits in most West European countries typically provide coverage to 70 percent or more of all unemployed workers and provided 70 percent or more of previous earnings for a family of four, in the United States less than half of all unemployed workers qualify for benefits, and the replacement income for a family of four averaged, in 1985, only 40 percent. In 1983, for example, a congressional research study showed that of the twenty-six million Americans unemployed at some time during that year, only 39 percent ever received any unemployment benefits. While U.S. unemployment benefits generally expire after about twenty-six weeks, in European countries coverage is typically provided for one or more years. While European coverage is generally uniform nationwide, in the United States benefit levels are set by each state and vary radically, yielding $211 a week in West Virginia in 1983 for an unemployed worker yet $84 a week for the same worker living in Indiana. In the last quarter of 1981, the national average weekly check was $111, an annual rate of $5,772 or $3,500 below the 1981 poverty level for an urban family of four.[33]

For those American workers lucky enough to remain employed, the threat of unexpected unemployment is far greater than in most West European countries. American workers can generally be dismissed by private companies without notice, cause, or government restrictions (although some recent court decisions have penalized companies for "unfair" dismissal), whereas in most European countries sudden or arbitrary dismissals are illegal. Dismissals occur so frequently in the United States that although the average 1980 unemployment rate was 7.1 percent, 18.7 percent of the work force was unemployed at some time during the year for one or more weeks, with an average unemployed period of fourteen weeks. In 1980 only 55 percent (sixty-five million) of all those who worked at some time had full-time jobs for the entire year, and they earned 80 percent of all wages, averaging $17,600, while the other fifty-one million workers, including about twenty million part-timers (six million of whom unsuccessfully sought full-time work), earned an average of only $5,400. Largely due to the frequency of part-time work and unemployment, an estimated 25 percent of the population fell below the official poverty line at some point in the 1970s although the rate never exceeded 12.6 percent for any one year. Another area where American workers suffer by comparison with other industrialized democracies is in terms of vacations, with annual holiday days (paid vacation days plus public holidays) averaging twenty-five or less in the United States compared to thirty-five or more in such countries as West Germany, France, the Netherlands, and Sweden.[34]

Two areas of social expenditure where the United States fares well are education and pensions. About 5 percent of GDP was spent for education in 1981, a figure above average among Western democracies; 55 percent of Americans aged twenty to twenty-four attended college in 1979, a rate twice that of most comparable countries. Governmental expenditures for old-age, disability, and survivors benefits constituted about 7 percent of GDP in 1981, a figure typical for other Western democracies.[35]

American social injustices no doubt highly contribute to one "human right" notably deficient in American society—the right to security in one's home and on the streets. Despite the fact that the United States has a higher rate of jailing its citizens than any other industrialized country save South Africa and the Soviet Union, American rates of violent crime far exceed those in other Western industrialized democracies, with the result that over 40 percent of all Americans report they are "afraid to walk alone at night" within a mile of their homes. The rate of homicides and serious assaults in the United States in 1980 exceeded by five to nine times that in most West European countries. In all of Sweden in 1985, there were only 115 murders (in a population of 8.5 million); in New York City alone, there were 1,384 murders (in a population of 7 million). No doubt such high rates of murder are related to the fact that the United States has the laxest gun control laws among all Western democracies, but frustrations caused by the gulf between the poor and the rich and the lack of adequate living conditions among the poor surely play a major role also. Social injustices and the relative paucity of American programs of social and family support are also almost certainly related to a variety of other indicators of high social disintegration in American society. Thus, the America divorce rate is twice that of any West European country, the rate of teenage pregnancy is twice that of any other industrial nation (and continually rising, unlike that of any other developed country in recent years), and the incidence of adolescent alcohol and drug abuse exceeds that of any other country in the world.[36]

THE PLIGHT OF OPPRESSED GROUPS

Social and economic injustices in the United States have not affected all segments of the population equally. Instead, particular groups have suffered especially. In terms of general social and/or economic discrimination, blacks and some other ethnic minorities like Hispanics and American Indians, women, certain occupational categories like agricultural migrant workers, and certain geographic regions like the Appalachian Mountains and many rural areas, especially in the South, have tended to rank particularly high in such indices as poverty and unemployment. Homosexuals have suffered continuing social discrimination, sometimes entailing loss of jobs and apartments. In the space allotted for this chapter, it is not possible to do all of these categories justice. Instead, a lengthy treatment of the situation of American blacks and a brief summary of the situation of American women will have to suffice as representative of a broad variety of groups that have traditionally suffered especially discriminatory treatment in American society.

American Blacks

American society has practiced severe discrimination against American blacks for over three hundred years. This discrimination, and the general issue of black-white relations in the United States, have unquestionably constituted the single worst stain on the American human rights record and the single greatest unsolved domestic problem in American history, significantly responsible for the American Civil War in 1861–1865 and ever since periodically responsible for severe domestic tensions, political conflict, and, in 1919 and 1964–1968, virtual nationwide outbreaks of serious civil disorder.[37]

From the seventeenth century until the passage of the Thirteenth Amendment (1865) to the Constitution at the conclusion of the Civil War, millions of blacks were formally enslaved in the United States (almost entirely in the American South after the Revolutionary War ended in 1783). After being shipped from Africa under conditions so horrible that over 20 percent may have died on the transatlantic journey alone, the slaves were bought and sold like chattel in the American colonies, generally treated with harshness and brutality, denied all legal protections, and subjected to repressive slave codes which denied them most opportunities to become educated or otherwise advance themselves. Although importation of slaves from abroad (but not slavery itself) was outlawed after 1808, by 1860 there were almost four million slaves, almost all of whom were owned by the fewer than 400,000 plantation owners who dominated southern politics, culture, and economics.

The victory of the North in the Civil War resulted in the passage of the constitutional amendments which outlawed slavery, banned voter discrimination based on race, and provided that no state could "deny to any person within its jurisdiction the equal protection of the laws." However, while moral and humanistic objections to *slavery* had been one of the motivating factors leading to the Civil War, even in the North there were few whites who really favored *equality* for blacks. Therefore, these amendments (except for the ban on slavery) became almost meaningless in the South after 1877 when the last federal troops designed to enforce fair treatment for blacks were withdrawn.

The Supreme Court, by its extraordinarily narrow interpretation of the meaning of the Fourteenth Amendment ban on state denial of "equal protection of the laws" to its citizens during the 1880–1945 period, both reflected and reinforced the general national mood of disinterest in the plight of southern blacks after the Civil War. Thus, in the famous 1896 case of *Plessy v. Ferguson*, the court declared that governmentally mandated segregation of the races did not amount to denial of equality as long as "separate but equal" facilities were involved. The court's decision suggested that segregation did not discriminate against blacks any more than it did against whites, and asserted that if the blacks chose to construe enforced separation as stamping them with a "badge of inferiority" this was so "not by reason of anything found in the act, but solely because the colored race chooses to put that construction upon it."

Encouraged by the principles established by the court and by the general disinterest of nonsouthern society in the situation of the blacks, the southern states established in the years after 1877 an apartheid-like system in which blacks were kept very separate indeed, in schools, saloons, parks, circuses, and water fountains (some states even had segregated Bibles for black witnesses to swear upon in courtrooms), but were never granted real equality. By 1930, for example, southern states spent from two to ten times as much on educating each white child as they did for each black child. Through a variety of means of intimidation and legal chicanery, voter discrimination against blacks was practiced throughout the South until the 1960s; thus, in 1956 only 25 percent of blacks of voting age were registered in the South compared to 60 percent for voting-age whites. Most blacks in the South remained economically as well as politically powerless, with incomes far below those of southern whites and with many of them living as sharecroppers constantly indebted to white farmers and store owners. The most disgraceful manifestation of southern intransigence on the race question was the virtual institutionalization of lynching (vigilante murders) of blacks; there were three thousand lynchings in the South between 1883 and 1903, and over one thousand between 1900 and 1917. Increasing numbers of blacks began migrating to northern industrial urban areas during the early twentieth century in hopes of better prospects; while most of the northern states had no formal segregation laws, blacks were still severely discriminated against, particularly in attempting to find jobs and housing. Most blacks could only find housing in northern urban ghettos, and were generally hired only in the most menial and low-paying jobs. Racial tensions in the North periodically burst out into severe disorders, especially during the "red summer" of 1919, when riots broke out in over twenty cities, with the worst outbreak in Chicago, during which 38 persons were killed and 537 injured.

A gradual, indeed glacial, thawing in white attitudes toward blacks took place in American society at the national, if not the southern, level, during the first half of the twentieth century. The pace of change in American society on the racial question stepped up significantly after World War II, and the Supreme Court increasingly reflected—and led—this shift of attitudes. These changes reflected the development of the Cold War, in which the United States was increasingly embarrassed internationally by its treatment of blacks, as it claimed to be leading a worldwide fight for "freedom"; a booming economy, which decreased tensions arising from job competition between blacks and whites; and the power of television, which brought into northern living rooms scenes of often violent discrimination against southern blacks, until then a remote abstraction. The most important blow for racial equality was unquestionably the Supreme Court decision of May 17, 1954, in *Brown v. Board of Education*, which declared that segregation of schools was inherently unequal, thus overturning *Plessy v. Ferguson*. The court held that to separate schoolchildren "from others of similar age and qualifications solely because of their race generates a feeling of inferiority as to their status in the community that may affect their hearts and minds in a way unlikely ever to be undone." The *Brown* decision was followed by a slew of similar decisions striking down state-supported segregation in such public facilities as golf courses, parks, courtrooms, airports, municipal bus systems, and public housing. Civil rights bills were passed by Congress in 1957, 1960, 1964, 1965, 1968, and 1975, which collectively provided substantial new gains for blacks, especially in voting rights. Largely as a result of these laws, the number of southern blacks registered to vote jumped from 1.4 million in 1960 to 4.5 million in 1976 (56 percent of those eligible, compared to 58 percent of southern whites). The 1964 Civil Rights Act also included provisions barring discriminatory hiring by employers or labor unions in large companies and outlawed discrimination in public accommodations affecting interstate commerce such as hotels and restaurants.

The anti-housing discrimination features of the 1968 law have never been effectively enforced, and in retrospect this law can be seen as the high tide of the civil rights victories of the 1960s. After 1963 the civil rights movement became increasingly militant, and beginning with serious disorders in New York City in 1964, the period 1964–1968 was filled with major rioting by blacks in scores of American cities, climaxing in the disorders which occurred in 125 cities in April 1968, following the assassination of black pacifist leader Martin Luther King, Jr., during which 70,000 troops were deployed, 46 people were killed, 3,500 were injured, 20,000 were arrested, and an estimated $45 million in damage was caused. During this same period, violent crimes skyrocketed in the segregated black urban cores of many American cities, and the political result of the "law and order" issue arising from the riots and increasing fear of crime was reflected in the election of Richard Nixon as president in 1968, who ran on a thinly disguised pledge to halt further progress in civil rights. Under the Nixon (1969–1974) and Reagan (1981–00) administrations, federal pressures by the executive, congress, and courts to further establish equal rights for blacks eased dramatically, as did many indexes of black progress.

The situation of American blacks in 1985 had improved immeasurably since the *Brown* decision of 1954, yet the United States still bears a three-hundred-year stigma of basic human injustice in the racial area that has by no means been eradicated. It is not difficult to point to impressive gains for the 12 percent of the American population that is black: the jump in voter registration noted earlier (nationwide 66 percent of blacks and 70 percent of whites were registered in 1984); the over 6,000 black elected local, state, and federal officials in 1985 (including the mayors of such cities as Los Angeles, Detroit, Chicago, Phila-delphia, Cleveland, and Newark) compared to less than 500 elected black officials in 1963; the appointment of the first black members of the Cabinet and the Supreme Court in the 1960s; an increase in the percentage of blacks completing high school from 51 percent to 80 percent between 1964 and 1985 (compared to 84 percent for whites in the latter year), and in the percentage of black college students from 3 percent of the total in 1972 to 10 percent in 1982; an increase in the percentage of black professionals from 2.3 percent to 4.3 percent of the total between 1970 and 1980; an increase in black median family income (in constant 1974 dollars) from $5,200 to $8,000 between 1959 and 1970, and a corresponding drop in the percentage of blacks living in poverty from 55 percent to 33 percent during these same years. The first federal government building ever named for a black, out of a total of 7,200 such structures, was dedicated in 1985.[38]

Unfortunately, there is a much bleaker side to this picture. Although legal discrimination against blacks has disappeared, the legacy of hundreds of years of past discrimination combined with continuing extralegal prejudice and, in some areas, de facto discrimination, has consigned the majority of American blacks to decaying urban ghettos riddled by crime and drugs, where housing, education, and social services are inferior and jobs scarce. Studies have repeat-edly shown that the quality of education in black ghetto areas is inferior to that offered to whites, that massive informal discrimination prevents blacks from renting or buying housing in many areas and that most of the nearly ten million residents of federally financed housing are racially segregated with white facilities far superior in condition and services to those occupied by blacks. Informal discrimination still pervades the rural South, where a reporter found many small towns in 1985 where ''there are bars where blacks know they cannot buy drinks, restaurants in which they cannot eat, motels in which they cannot get a room and golf courses at which they cannot tee off.''[39]

Black economic gains have been stagnant in the post–1974 period and blacks still lag far behind whites economically. Thus, in constant dollars, black median family income declined $1,500 between 1970 and 1984 and, as a percentage of median family white income, decreased from 62 percent to 56 percent (back to the same level as in 1960) during the same period. The average college-educated black in 1983 earned about the same as the average white high school graduate. Despite the increase of black professionals, black urban communities are often drastically underserved, as white professionals are often reluctant to practice there, and in 1980, fewer than 4 percent of all lawyers and doctors were black. Despite recent gains, in 1985 only 2 percent of elected officials were black, as were only 6 percent of journalists and fewer than 1 percent of faculty at predominantly white colleges. In the South, two-thirds of all black workers were employed in 1985 in the three lowest-paid job categories of service workers (e.g., maids), unskilled general laborers, and semiskilled operators (e.g., chauffeurs); only one-third of southern whites held comparable positions. Black unemployment rates have consistently been twice as high as those for whites; thus in February 1986 black unemployment was 14.8 percent, compared to 6.4 percent for whites. Black teenage unemployment rates have typically been at the catastrophic rate of 35 percent or above ever since 1975 (compared to under 20 percent for white teenagers). Many black men have given up even looking for work, with the result that the percentage of adult black males employed has plunged from 74 percent to 55 percent between 1960 and 1982 (comparable figures for white males are 76 percent and 70 percent). In 1984, 33 percent of blacks were living in poverty (the same percentage as in 1970), compared to 12 percent of whites. Blacks were 15 percent of all American children in 1984, yet constituted 32 percent of all poor children, since 47 percent of blacks younger than eighteen (compared to only 17 percent of white children) were living in poverty; for all black children under the age of six the poverty rate was 51 percent, and for blacks under age eighteen living in female-headed households the rate was 70 percent. Blacks born in the United States in 1984 had a life expectancy of five years less than whites, and almost twice as many black children as white children born alive die before the age of one (indeed, in urban slums American black infant mortality rates exceed those of some Third World countries. For example, in poor black neighborhoods of Chicago and Baltimore in 1981 rates were fifty-five to sixty per thousand, compared to the American national average of eleven per thousand and exceeding the national rates for more than two dozen Third World countries, including Sri Lanka, the Philippines, Jamaica, Mexico, Panama, and Taiwan).[40]

Inevitably, poverty and unemployment have been accompanied by family disintegration and high rates of crime, violence, and drug usage in black inner-city ghettos. In 1982, 47 percent of all black families with children under eighteen were headed by women (compared to 15 percent among white families in 1982 and a massive increase among blacks from 8 percent in 1950 and 21 percent in 1960); 57 percent of all black children were born out of wedlock, compared to 12 percent among whites, and black teenage pregnancy rates were twice those of white teenagers (due primarily to higher rates of sexual activity and lower rates of abortion and use of contraception among black teenage females). The black divorce rate is double that of whites, and the percentage of black women over eighteen who are married has plunged from 62 percent to 48 percent between 1970 and 1981. Although blacks constitute only 12 percent of the total population, they fill almost half of the country's jail cells and constitute 40 percent of those awaiting execution. Violence is so prevalent in black ghettos that murder is the leading cause of death among young black males, and homicide rates among all black men are eight times those of white men. These figures indicating high rates of marital failure among blacks and high rates of violence among black men almost certainly reflect rage and frustration especially among black men created by a society which, as Audrey Chapman, a Howard University family therapist, notes, strips them of "having any kind of economic power" and creates a feeling of impotence "in the global sense, in the community and in the family." As James Comer, a Yale University psychiatrist, notes, "In a society where the male is supposed to be the breadwinner, . . . it's a tremendous psychological burden when you don't have a snowball's chance in hell of taking care of your family. One of the defenses is not to care, not to try."[41]

There can be and is no easy answer to a problem which is rooted in three hundred years of history. Yet there is nothing more certain than that the militancy which characterized American blacks during the 1960s will return, sooner or later, unless American public attention and resources can once more be focused on the plight of 12 percent of the American population, and especially the 55 percent of all blacks now living in central city areas. Otherwise, the fire next time will be even worse.

American Women

Virtually all discrimination against women has been eliminated from American legal codes during the last few decades, yet pervasive cultural and social discrimination continues to relegate American women to second-class status. In this respect the status of American women resembles that of women in most other industrialized Western democracies, although the American record on the whole ranks unfavorably with comparable countries. American women are the best educated in the world (61 percent enter college after school, compared to only 22 percent in Western Europe, and, unlike any country in Western Europe more women attend college than do men). Yet despite their better education and the fact that a higher percentage of American women work than do their West European counterparts, they fare worse relative to men economically than do women in most other comparable countries (American women who work full-time earned 64 percent of American male salaries in 1984, compared to earnings ratios exceeding 70 percent in Britain, West Germany, and Austria, and over 80 percent in Italy, France, and Sweden). Whereas wages of women compared to those of men have steadily increased recently in most other similar countries, in the United States the female-male wage ratio remains the same as it was in 1939. Further, the political power of American women trails behind almost all Western countries and many Third World countries (in 1984 only 5 percent of American legislators were women, compared to 10 percent or more in Scandinavia, Austria, West Germany, Switzerland, Australia, and Guyana). Unlike Great Britain, Sri Lanka, Israel, India, Iceland, and Norway, no woman has ever served as American chief executive (or even been nominated for this position by a major party).[42]

The primary obstacles faced by American women are the strong sociocultural matrix of modern western civilization that has traditionally treated them as a secondary partner (or servant) to men in the world's "serious business," and the dominance over the existing political, economic, social, and cultural system by men (for example, women hold fewer than 3 percent of seats on the boards of control of the 1,000 largest U.S. corporations). Thus, a 1986 New York state task force on the judiciary reported that women lawyers were "routinely" treated in a demeaning manner by male judges and attorneys, and that, in general, in the courts, "Women uniquely, disproportionately and with unacceptable frequency must endure a climate of condescension, indifference and hostility." Such treatment has been also typical of American society as a whole. As a result, women have traditionally been either discouraged from working at all or channeled into jobs that have low prestige and poor pay.

While the percentage of the labor force composed of women jumped dramatically, from 33 percent to 44 percent of all workers between 1960 and 1985, as increasing proportions of women have chosen (or been forced for economic reasons) to work, what amounts to sexually based job segregation has continued: of 420 job classifications established by the federal government, only 20 account for 80 percent of all women workers, and these tend to be jobs like secretaries and bank tellers in which 90 percent or more of all workers are women and which pay far less than "male" jobs such as engineers and skilled workers. Although in recent years more women have entered higher paying jobs (for example, between 1960 and 1983 the percentage of women lawyers jumped from 2 percent to 15 percent), the vast majority of women continue to enter low-paying professions (the percentage of women working in retail sales and miscellaneous services increased from 47 percent of all employed women to 51 percent between 1980 and 1986). Fewer than 2 percent of all women earned over $35,000 in 1986, compared to over 15 percent of men. On the other hand, in what has become known as the feminization of poverty, two-thirds of all poor American adults are women, and 35 percent of all families headed by women are impoverished (compared to an overall poverty rate in 1984 of 14 percent); while women are the heads of only 16 percent of all families, they are the heads of 48 percent of all families living in poverty. Male domination of American economics and politics, combined with the traditional American disinclination towards adequate social welfare programs, has contributed to and compounded the economic plight of American women. As previously noted, social support systems common in Europe such as national health insurance, government-subsidized child care programs, and mandated job-protected, paid maternity leaves are lacking in the United States.

CONCLUSION

The American record in civil liberties can be viewed from different angles, like the glass partially filled with water that can be viewed as either half empty or half filled. Clearly the American civil liberties record has deep flaws in it, especially in social and racial justice and toleration of radical political expression, and clearly the record is not as pristine as American ideals are. Yet it must also be remembered that the record would probably not be as good as it is if American ideals were not so high, for they act as a constant standard and a constant challenge. Further, the American record, it should be reiterated, compares favorably with the vast majority of countries in the world today. It is in the nature of idealism that it can rarely be satisfied, and certainly it would be a grave mistake to ever be complacent about individual freedom and dignity. American ideals in civil liberties have had a profound impact upon the world; the future alone can tell whether, in a world of increasing centralization and technological capabilities for governmental control and intrusion in the lives of everyone, American reality can move closer to those ideals.

NOTES

1. *New York Times*, December 7, 1978.

2. In general, see Robert J. Goldstein, *Political Repression in Modern America: From 1870 to the Present* (Cambridge, Mass.: Schenkman, 1978).

3. See James Smith, *Freedom's Fetters: The Alien and Sedition Laws and American Civil Liberties* (Ithaca, N.Y.: Cornell University Press, 1956); Russell Nye, *Fettered Freedom: Civil Liberties and the Slavery Controversy, 1830–1860* (Urbana, Ill.: University of Illinois Press, 1972); Harold Hyman, *To Try Men's Souls: Loyalty Oaths in America* (Berkeley, Cal.: University of California Press, 1960).

4. See Robert J. Goldstein, *Political Repression in Nineteenth Century Europe* (London: Croom Helm, 1983).

5. See, for example, the following: Graham Adams, *The Age of Industrial Violence, 1910–1915* (New York: Columbia University Press, 1966); Jeremy Brecher, *Strike!* (San Francisco: Straight Arrow, 1972); Melvin Dubofsky, *We Shall Be All: A History of the Industrial Workers of the World* (Chicago: Quadrangle, 1969); Almont Lindsay, *The Pullman Strike* (Chicago: University of Chicago Press, 1964); Sidney Lens, *The Labor Wars* (Garden City, N.Y.: Doubleday, 1974); George Suggs, *Colorado's War on Militant Unionism: James H. Peabody and the Western Federation of Miners* (Detroit: Wayne State University Press, 1972); Philip Taft and Philip Ross, "American Labor Violence," in *Violence in America*, ed. Ted Gurr and Hugh D. Graham (New York: Bantam, 1969).

6. Jerold S. Auerbach, "The Depression Decade," in *The Pulse of Freedom*, ed. Alan Reitman (New York: Norton, 1975), 73, 78.

7. See H. C. Peterson and Gilbert Fite, *Opponents of War, 1917–1918* (Madison: University of Wisconsin Press, 1957); James Weinstein, *The Decline of Socialism in America, 1912–1925* (New York: Vintage, 1969); Harry Scheiber, *The Wilson Administration and Civil Liberties* (Ithaca, N.Y.: Cornell University Press, 1960).

8. Robert Murray, *Red Scare: A Study in National Hysteria, 1919–1920* (New York: McGraw-Hill, 1964).

9. Jacobus tenBroek, *Prejudice, War and the Constitution* (Berkeley: University of California Press, 1968).

10. See Irving Howe and Lewis Coser, *The American Communist Party* (New York: Praeger, 1962); David Caute, *The Great Fear: The Anti-Communist Purge Under Truman and Eisenhower* (New York: Simon & Schuster, 1978); Michal Belknap, *Cold War Political Justice: The Smith Act, The Communist Party and American Civil Liberties*

(Westport, Conn.: Greenwood Press, 1977); Eleanor Bontecue, *The Federal Loyalty-Security Program* (Ithaca, N.Y.: Cornell University Press, 1953); Robert Griffith, *The Politics of Fear* (Lexington: University of Kentucky Press, 1970).

11. Quoted in Lawrence Wittner, *Rebels Against War: The American Peace Movement, 1941–1960* (New York: Columbia University Press, 1970), 221.

12. Robert Sklar, Introduction to *The Truman Era* by I. F. Stone (New York: Vintage, 1973), ix.

13. Athan Theoharis, *Spying of Americans: Political Surveillance from Hoover to the Huston Plan* (Philadelphia: Temple University Press, 1978); Frank Donner, *The Age of Surveillance: The Aims and Methods of America's Political Intelligence System* (New York: Vintage, 1981); Morton Halperin et al., *The Lawless State: The Crimes of the U.S. Intelligence Agencies* (New York: Penguin, 1976).

14. U.S. Senate, 94th Congress, 2d Session, *Final Report of the Select Committee to Study Governmental Operations with Respect to Intelligence Operations*, Book II: Intelligence Activities and the Rights of Americans (Report No. 94–755, April 26, 1976) 139, 216.

15. Christine Marwick, "Using Civil Litigation to Protect Constitutional Rights," *First Principles* 1 (April 1976): 3.

16. Ivo Duchacek, *Rights and Liberties in the World Today: Constitutional Promise and Reality* (Santa Barbara, Cal.: ABC-Clio, 1973), 174.

17. *The Economist*: "Nirvana by Numbers," December 24, 1983, "Economic and Financial Indicators," May 12, 1984; George Kurian, *New Book of World Rankings* (New York: Facts on File, 1984), 104; Charles Taylor and David Jodice, *World Handbook of Political and Social Indicators* (New Haven, Conn.: Yale University Press, 1983); Arnold Heidenheimer, Hugh Heclo and Carolyn Adams, *Comparative Public Policy: The Politics of Social Choice in Europe and America* (New York: St. Martin's, 1983), 227; Lester Thurow, "A Surge in Inequality," *Scientific American*, May 1987.

18. Ira Magaziner and Robert Reich, *Minding America's Business* (New York: Harcourt Brace Jovanovich, 1982), 25; *Detroit News*, "Study Says Millionaires Don't Act It," August 26, 1985, p. 11A; *New York Times*: "Agricultural Price Supports Coming Under Sharper Scrutiny," December 5, 1983, 16; "Perception of Wealthy Seen as Challenge to Mondale Tax Plan," September 12, 1984, p. 11; "The Leverage of Our Wealthiest 400," October 11, 1984, p. 27; "Wealthiest Americans Found to Work in Business Fields," March 2, 1986, p. 13; G. William Domhoff, *Who Rules America Now?* (Englewood Cliffs, N.J.: Prentice-Hall, 1983), p. 42; U.S. Department of Commerce, *Statistical Abstract of the United States, 1985* (Washington: Government Printing Office, 1985), 463; Thomas Dye and L. Harmon Zeigler, *The Irony of Democracy* (North Scituate, Mass.: Duxbury, 1978), 95; Edward Greenberg, *The American Political System* (Cambridge, Mass.: Winthrop, 1977), 121–27.

19. U.S. Department of Commerce, *Social Indicators 1976* (Washington: Government Printing Office, 1977), 478; Magaziner and Reich, *Minding America's Business*; *New York Times*: "Perception of Wealthy Seen as Challenge to Mondale Tax Plan," September 12, 1984, 11; "In Four Years, Reagan Changed Basis of the Debate on Domestic Programs," October 25, 1984, 15; Andrew Hacker, "The Coming Welfare Wars," *New York Review of Books*, February 28, 1985; Nicholas Lemann, "The Culture of Poverty," *The Atlantic*, September, 1984.

20. Charles Andrain, *Politics and Economic Policy in Western Democracies* (North

Scituate, Mass.: Duxbury, 1980), 184–85; Greenberg, *The American Political System*, 145; "America Becomes Less Equal," *The New Republic*, February 18, 1985.

21. Sar Levitan, "The Politics of Unemployment," *The New Republic*, September 20, 1982; *New York Times*, "No Way to Balance the Budget," October 23, 1985, p. 23; Nicholas Lemann, "Culture of Poverty," *The Atlantic*, September, 1984.

22. *Detroit Free Press*, "It's Time to Put Fairness in Taxes," September 5, 1985, p. 9A; Greenberg, *The American Political System*, 147–57; *New York Times*, "Keep the Bite on Corporations," March 17, 1986, 21.

23. Organization for Economic Cooperation and Development (OECD), *Social Expenditure, 1960–80* (Paris: OECD, 1985); Michael Harrington, "The Lower Depths," *The New Republic*, June 9, 1982; Magaziner and Reich, *Minding America's Business*, 16; Heidenheimer et al., *Comparative Public Policy*, 202, 204, 211; Kurian, *New Book of World Rankings*, 118.

24. Andrain, *Politics and Economic Policy*, 190; Heidenheimer et al., *Comparative Public Policy*, 224; Howard Leichter and Harrell Rodgers, *American Public Policy in a Comparative Context* (New York: McGraw-Hill, 1984), p. 35.

25. Christopher Jencks, "Have the Poor Been Losing Ground," *New York Review of Books*, May 9, 1985; *Detroit News*, "Study Says Millionaires Don't Act It," August 26, 1985, p. 11A; "Poverty," *The Economist*, September 7, 1985; Leichter and Rodgers, note 24 above, pp. 38–39; James Patterson, *America's Struggle Against Poverty, 1900–1985* (Cambridge, Mass.: Harvard University Press, 1986).

26. *New York Times*: "Warm Season Masks But Doesn't End Problem of Homeless," June 3, 1983, 6; "Homeless in U.S. Put at 250,000," May 2, 1984, 1; "Anguish of the Homeless Outlasts Winter's Cold," April 14, 1985, 6E; "Cuts Seen Leading to Crisis of Homeless," May 22, 1986, 13; Gregg Easterbrook, "Housing: Examining a Media Myth," *The Atlantic*, October, 1983.

27. *New York Times*: "Housing Debate Focuses on Question of U.S. Duty to Poor," May 4, 1985, 1; "Why So Many Are Priced Out of the Market," March 16, 1986, E5; Heidenheimer et al., *Comparative Public Policy*, 88–121; Leichter and Rodgers, *American Public Policy*, 265–91.

28. *New York Times*, "Doctors Find Hunger Is Epidemic in U.S.," February 27, 1985, 8; Physician Task Force on Hunger in America, *Hunger in America: The Growing Epidemic* (Middletown, Conn.: Wesleyan University Press, 1985); J. Larry Brown, "Hunger in the U.S.," *Scientific American*, February, 1987.

29. "Dutch Welfare," *The Economist*, March 3, 1985; Nicholas Lemann, "The Culture of Poverty," *The Atlantic*, September, 1984; Leichter and Rodgers, *American Public Policy*, 39; Greenberg, *The American Political System*, 378; Andrew Hacker, "The Truth About the Underclass," *New York Review of Books*, August 12, 1982; C. Arden Miller, "Infant Mortality in the U.S." *Scientific American*, July, 1985.

30. Magaziner and Reich, *Minding America's Business*, 19; C. Arden Miller, "Infant Mortality in the U.S.," *Scientific American*, July, 1985; "Nirvana by Numbers," *The Economist*, December 24, 1983; *New York Times*: "Harvard Researchers Propose Medicare Overhaul," March 13, 1986, 15; "Poor, Sick and Uninsured," May 30, 1986, 26; Leichter and Rodgers, *American Public Policy*, 64–104; Heidenheimer et al., *Comparative Public Policy*, 52–87; Lester Thurow, "A Surge in Inequality," *Scientific American*, May, 1987.

31. Sheila Kameraman, *Maternity and Parental Benefits and Leaves* (New York:

Columbia University Center for the Social Sciences, 1980); C. Arden Miller, "Infant Mortality in the U.S.," *Scientific American*, July, 1985.

32. *New York Times*: "Experts Debate Impact of Day Care," September 4, 1984, 12; "Job Structure Outmoded, Panel Finds," January 17, 1986, 10; "Child Care and Business," May 6, 1986, 9; "GOP Congresswoman Pushes Aid for Day Care," June 15, 1986, 19; Leichter and Rodgers, *American Public Policy*, 47.

33. U.S. Department of Health and Human Services, *Social Security Programs Throughout the World—1983* (Washington: Government Printing Office, 1984); Magaziner and Reich, *Minding America's Business*, 15; Robert Kuttner, "Getting Off the Dole," *The Atlantic*, September, 1985; *New York Times*: "Record Unemployment Rate," May 9, 1982, 1; "Reform Jobless Benefits," January 23, 1983, EY23; "Economic and Financial Indicators," *The Economist*, March 30, 1985.

34. Magaziner and Reich, *Minding America's Business*, 14, 17; "Part-time Pay for a Full-time Lifestyle," *Detroit Free Press*, December 18, 1983, B1; "Census Report Shows Gains in Education and Housing," *New York Times*, April 20, 1982, 1; Andrew Hacker, "The Truth About the Underclass," *New York Review of Books*, August 12, 1982; "Economic and Financial Indicators," *The Economist*, March 24, 1984.

35. "Nirvana by Numbers," *The Economist*, December 24, 1983; OECD, *Social Expenditure*; Ruth Sivard, *World Military and Social Expenditures 1985* (Washington: World Priorities, 1985).

36. "Nirvana by Numbers," *The Economist*, December 24, 1983; Urie Bronfenbrenner, "Alienation," *Phi Delta Kappan*, February, 1986.

37. Unless otherwise noted, material on blacks is based on such standard sources as Richard Kluger, *Simple Justice* (New York: Vintage, 1976); John Hope Franklin, *From Slavery To Freedom: A History of Black Americans* (New York: Vintage, 1967); Harvard Sitkoff, *The Struggle for Black Equality, 1954–1980* (New York: Hill & Wang, 1981); Kenneth Stampp, *The Peculiar Institution: Slavery in the Ante-Bellum South* (New York: Vintage, 1956); C. Vann Woodward, *The Strange Career of Jim Crow* (New York: Oxford University Press, 1966); and U.S. Department of Commerce, *The Social and Economic Status of the Black Population in the United States: An Historical View, 1790–1978* (Washington: Government Printing Office, [1979?]).

38. "King's Legacy," *Ann Arbor* (Michigan) *News*, January 20, 1986, B1; *New York Times*: "With Gain in S. Carolina, Blacks are on 10 States' High Courts," September 1, 1985, 14; "Minority Enrollment in Colleges is Declining," October 27, 1985, 1.

39. *New York Times*: "Discrimination is Reported in Federal Housing Projects," February 11, 1985, 11; "Across the Rural South, Segregation as Usual," April 27, 1985, 1; "Education of Blacks Assailed," *Detroit News*, March 22, 1985, 1.

40. "Urban League Attacks Reagan," *Detroit News*, January 24, 1986, 6; *New York Times*: "Gap in Income Between the Races," July 18, 1983, 1; "Breakup of Black Family Imperils Gains," November 30, 1983, 1; "Jim Crow is Gone, But White Resistance Remains," April 6, 1985, 1; "Behind Poverty Data," August 29, 1985, 14; "Infant Mortality Rate at Record Low," October 12, 1985, 14; "Blacks Losing Ground, Urban League Asserts," January 23, 1986, 7; "Stagnant Revenue Worrying Editors," April 14, 1986, p. 13; *New York Times Sunday Magazine*, April 27, 1986; *Ann Arbor News*: "King's Legacy," January 20, 1986, B1; "Jobless Rate in U.S. Takes Sudden Jump," March 7, 1986, A1; "America's Underclass," *The Economist*, March 15, 1986; "Increase Reported in Infant Death Rate," *Detroit Free Press*, January 17, 1986, A1; Michael Robin, "Black Baby Deaths," *The Nation*, June 9, 1984.

41. *New York Times*: "Breakup of Black Family Imperils Gains," November 20, 1983, 1; "Black Men More Likely to Serve Time in Prison," July 29, 1985, 7; "U.S. Poverty Rate Dropped," August 28, 1985, 1; "Behind Poverty Data," August 29, 1985, 14; "Churches vs. Teen-Age Births," March 12, 1986, 20; *New York Times Magazine*, June 2, 1985; "America's Underclass," *The Economist*, March 15, 1986; U.S. Department of Commerce, *Social Indicators 1976*, 226–27.

42. The section on women is based primarily on the following sources: Leichter and Rodgers, *American Public Policy*, 105–42; Ruth Sivard, *Women: A World Survey* (Washington, D.C.: World Priorities, 1985); "Why Can't a Woman Be More Like a Woman?" *The Economist*, May 17–23, 1986; "Unequal Work, Unequal Pay," *Scientific American*, March 1986; Andrew Hacker, "Women and Work," *New York Review of Books*, August 14, 1986; *New York Times*: "Sex Bias Found in New York Courts," April 20, 1986, 1; "Feminism's Next Challenge," June 17, 1986, p. 27.

SUGGESTED READINGS

Caute, David. *The Great Fear: The Anti-Communist Purge under Truman and Eisenhower*. New York: Simon & Schuster, 1978.

Donner, Frank. *The Age of Surveillance: The Aims and Methods of America's Political Intelligence System*. New York: Vintage, 1981.

Franklin, John Hope. *From Slavery to Freedom: A History of Negro Americans*. New York: Vintage, 1967.

Gilbert, Dennis, and Joseph Kahl. *The American Class Structure*. Chicago: Dorsey, 1982.

Goldstein, Robert J. *Political Repression in Modern America: From 1870 to the Present*. Cambridge, Mass.: Schenkman Publishing, 1978.

Heidenheimer, Arnold J., Hugh Heclo, and Carolyn Adams. *Comparative Public Policy: The Politics of Social Choice in Europe and America*. New York: St. Martin's, 1983.

Hewlett, Sylvia. *A Lesser Life: The Myth of Women's Liberation in America*. New York: Morrow, 1986.

Kluger, Richard. *Simple Justice: The History of Brown v. Board of Education: Black America's Struggle for Equality*. New York: Vintage, 1976.

Leichter, Howard M., and Harrell Rodgers. *American Public Policy in Comparative Context*. New York: McGraw-Hill, 1984.

Patterson, James T. *America's Struggle Against Poverty, 1900–1985*. Cambridge, Mass.: Harvard University Press, 1986.

Physicians Task Force on Hunger in America. *Hunger in America: The Growing Epidemic*. Middletown, Conn.: Wesleyan University Press, 1985.

Sitkoff, Harvard. *The Struggle for Black Equality, 1954–1980*. New York: Hill & Wang, 1981.

APPENDIXES

Appendix 1 ————————————————

Universal Declaration of Human Rights

————————————————————————————————

UNIVERSAL DECLARATION OF HUMAN RIGHTS, Dec. 10, 1948, U.N.G.A. Res. 217 A (III), U.N. Doc. A/810, at 71 (1948).

Whereas recognition of the inherent dignity and of the equal and inalienable rights of all members of the human family is the foundation of freedom, justice and peace in the world,

Whereas disregard and contempt for human rights have resulted in barbarous acts which have outraged the conscience of mankind, and the advent of a world in which human beings shall enjoy freedom of speech and belief and freedom from fear and want has been proclaimed as the highest aspiration of the common people,

Whereas it is essential, if man is not to be compelled to have recourse, as a last resort, to rebellion against tyranny and oppression, that human rights should be protected by the rule of law,

Whereas it is essential to promote the development of friendly relations between nations,

Whereas the peoples of the United Nations have in the Charter reaffirmed their faith in fundamental human rights, in the dignity and worth of the human person and in the equal rights of men and women and have determined to promote social progress and better standards of life in larger freedom,

Whereas Member States have pledged themselves to achieve, in co-operation with the United Nations, the promotion of universal respect for and observance of human rights and fundamental freedoms,

Whereas a common understanding of these rights and freedoms is of the greatest importance for the full realization of this pledge,

Now, therefore,

The General Assembly

Proclaims this Universal Declaration of Human Rights as a common standard of achievement for all peoples and all nations, to the end that every individual and every organ of society, keeping this Declaration constantly in mind, shall strive by teaching and education to promote respect for these rights and freedoms and by progressive measures, national and international, to secure their universal and effective recognition and observance, both among the peoples of Member States themselves and among the peoples of territories under their jurisdiction.

Article 1. All human beings are born free and equal in dignity and rights. They are endowed with reason and conscience and should act towards one another in a spirit of brotherhood.

Article 2. Everyone is entitled to all the rights and freedoms set forth in this Declaration, without distinction of any kind, such as race, colour, sex, language, religion, political or other opinion, national or social origin, property, birth or other status.

Furthermore, no distinction shall be made on the basis of the political, jurisdictional or international status of the country or territory to which a person belongs, whether it be independent, trust, non-self-governing or under any other limitation of sovereignty.

Article 3. Everyone has the right to life, liberty and the security of person.

Article 4. No one shall be held in slavery or servitude; slavery and the slave trade shall be prohibited in all their forms.

Article 5. No one shall be subjected to torture or to cruel, inhuman or degrading treatment or punishment.

Article 6. Everyone has the right to recognition everywhere as a person before the law.

Article 7. All are equal before the law and are entitled without any discrimination to equal protection of the law. All are entitled to equal protection against any discrimination in violation of this Declaration and against any incitement to such discrimination.

Article 8. Everyone has the right to an effective remedy by the competent national tribunals for acts violating the fundamental rights granted him by the constitution or by law.

Article 9. No one shall be subjected to arbitrary arrest, detention or exile.

Article 10. Everyone is entitled in full equality to a fair and public hearing by an independent and impartial tribunal, in the determination of his rights and obligations and of any criminal charge against him.

Article 11. (1) Everyone charged with a penal offence has the right to be presumed innocent until proved guilty according to law in a public trial at which he has had all the guarantees necessary for his defence.

(2) No one shall be held guilty of any penal offence on account of any act or omission which did not constitute a penal offence, under national or international law, at the time when it was committed. Nor shall a heavier penalty be imposed than the one that was applicable at the time the penal offence was committed.

Article 12. No one shall be subjected to arbitrary interference with his privacy, family, home or correspondence, nor to attacks upon his honour and reputation. Everyone has the right to the protection of the law against such interference or attacks.

Article 13. (1) Everyone has the right to freedom of movement and residence within the borders of each State.

(2) Everyone has the right to leave any country, including his own, and to return to his country.

Article 14. (1) Everyone has the right to seek and to enjoy in other countries asylum from persecution.

(2) This right may not be invoked in the case of prosecutions genuinely arising from nonpolitical crimes or from acts contrary to the purposes and principles of the United Nations.

Article 15. (1) Everyone has the right to a nationality.

(2) No one shall be arbitrarily deprived of his nationality nor denied the right to change his nationality.

Article 16. (1) Men and women of full age, without any limitation due to race, nationality or religion, have the right to marry and to found a family. They are entitled to equal rights as to marriage, during marriage and at its dissolution.

(2) Marriage shall be entered into only with the free and full consent of the intending spouses.

(3) The family is the natural and fundamental group unit of society and is entitled to protection by society and the State.

Article 17. (1) Everyone has the right to own property alone as well as in association with others.

(2) No one shall be arbitrarily deprived of his property.

Article 18. Everyone has the right to freedom of thought, conscience and religion; this right includes freedom to change his religion or belief, and freedom, either alone or in community with others and in public or private, to manifest his religion or belief in teaching, practice, worship and observance.

Article 19. Everyone has the right to freedom of opinion and expression; this right includes freedom to hold opinions without interference and to seek, receive and impart information and ideas through any media and regardless of frontiers.

Article 20. (1) Everyone has the right to freedom of peaceful assembly and association.

(2) No one may be compelled to belong to an association.

Article 21. (1) Everyone has the right to take part in the government of his country, directly or through freely chosen representatives.

(2) Everyone has the right of equal access to public service in his country.

(3) The will of the people shall be the basis of the authority of government; this will shall be expressed in periodic and genuine elections which shall be by universal and equal suffrage and shall be held by secret vote or by equivalent free voting procedures.

Article 22. Everyone, as a member of society, has the right to social security and is entitled to realization, through national effort and international co-operation and in accordance with the organization and resources of each State, of the economic, social and cultural rights indispensable for his dignity and the free development of his personality.

Article 23. (1) Everyone has the right to work, to free choice of employment, to just and favourable conditions of work and to protection against unemployment.

(2) Everyone, without any discrimination, has the right to equal pay for equal work.

(3) Everyone who works has the right to just and favourable remuneration ensuring for himself and his family an existence worthy of human dignity, and supplemented, if necessary, by other means of social protection.

(4) Everyone has the right to form and to join trade unions for the protection of his interests.

Article 24. Everyone has the right to rest and leisure, including reasonable limitation of working hours and periodic holidays with pay.

Article 25. (1) Everyone has the right to a standard of living adequate for the health and well-being of himself and of his family, including food, clothing, housing and medical care and necessary social services, and the right to security in the event of unemployment, sickness, disability, widowhood, old age or other lack of livelihood in circumstances beyond his control.

(2) Motherhood and childhood are entitled to special care and assistance. All children, whether born in or out of wedlock, shall enjoy the same social protection.

Article 26. (1) Everyone has the right to education. Education shall be free, at least in the elementary and fundamental stages. Elementary education shall be compulsory. Technical and professional education shall be made generally available and higher education shall be equally accessible to all on the basis of merit.

(2) Education shall be directed to the full development of the human personality and to the strengthening of respect for human rights and fundamental freedoms. It shall promote understanding, tolerance and friendship among all nations, racial or religious groups, and shall further the activities of the United Nations for the maintenance of peace.

(3) Parents have a prior right to choose the kind of education that shall be given to their children.

Article 27. (1) Everyone has the right freely to participate in the cultural life of the community, to enjoy the arts and to share in scientific advancement and its benefits.

(2) Everyone has the right to the protection of the moral and material interests resulting from any scientific, literary or artistic production of which he is the author.

Article 28. Everyone is entitled to a social and international order in which the rights and freedoms set forth in this Declaration can be fully realized.

Article 29. (1) Everyone has duties to the community in which alone the free and full development of his personality is possible.

(2) In the exercise of his rights and freedoms, everyone shall be subject only to such limitations as are determined by law solely for the purpose of securing due recognition and respect for the rights and freedoms of others and of meeting the just requirements of morality, public order and the general welfare in a democratic society.

(3) These rights and freedoms may in no case be exercised contrary to the purposes and principles of the United Nations.

Article 30. Nothing in this Declaration may be interpreted as implying for any State, group or person any right to engage in any activity or to perform any act aimed at the destruction of any of the rights and freedoms set forth herein.

Appendix 2
Ratification of International Human Rights Instruments

	Genocide[1]	Racial Discrimination[2]	Economic Social[3]	Civil Political[4]	Optional Protocol[4]	Women[5]
Canada	X	X	X	X	X	X
Chile	X	X	X	X		
China	X	X				X
Cuba	X	X				X
El Salvador	X	X	X	X	X	X
India	X	X	X	X		
Israel	X	X				
Jamaica	X	X	X	X	X	X
Japan			X	X		X
Lebanon	X	X	X	X		
Nicaragua	X	X	X	X	X	X
Philippines	X	X	X	X		X
Poland	X	X	X	X		X
Senegal	X	X	X	X	X	X
South Africa						
Spain	X	X	X	X	X	X
Uganda		X				
USSR	X	X	X	X		X
UK	X	X	X	X		
USA						

[1]International Convention on the Prevention and Punishment of the Crime of Genocide (1948), United Nations *Treaty Series* vol. 78, p. 277. Parties as of 31 December 1985.

[2]International Convention on the Elimination of All Forms of Racial Discrimination (1965), United Nations *Treaty Series* vol. 660, p. 195. Parties as of 31 December 1985.

[3]International Covenant on Economic, Social and Cultural Rights (1966), United Nations *Treaty Series* vol. 993, p. 3. Parties as of 31 December 1985.

[4]International Covenant on Civil and Political Rights (1966) and Optional Protocol (1966), United Nations *Treaty Series* vol. 999, p. 171. Parties as of 25 July 1986.

[5]International Convention on the Elimination of All Forms of Discrimination Against Women (1979), United Nations resolution 34/180 of 18 December 1979. Parties as of 23 March 1986.

Appendix 3
Basic Economic and Social Indicators (ca. 1984)

	Population (millions)	GNP per capita $	Avg. annual GNP growth % 1965-1984	Life expectancy	Per capita calories (% of required)	Infant mortality (per 1000)	Population per physician	Population per nurse	Primary school enrollment %
Canada	25	13280	2.4	76	130	6	510	120	103
Chile	12	757	-0.1	70	105	22	950	...	111
China	1029	310	4.5	69	111	36	1730	1670	116
Cuba	10	...	...	75	126	16	600	...	108
El Salvador	5	710	-0.6	65	90	66	3220	...	69
India	749	260	1.6	56	96	90	2610	4670	85
Israel	4	5060	2.7	75	121	14	400	130	96
Jamaica	2	1150	-0.4	73	111	20	...	...	107
Japan	120	10630	4.7	77	113	6	740	210	100
Lebanon	...	...	...	...	...	...	...	...	...
Nicaragua	3	860	-1.5	60	101	70	2290	590	100
Philippines	53	660	2.6	63	104	49	2150	2590	114
Poland	37	2100	1.5	71	127	19	550	...	101
Senegal	6	380	-0.5	46	102	138	13060	1990	53
South Africa	32	2340	1.4	54	118	79	...	...	...
Spain	39	4400	2.7	77	132	10	360	280	111
Uganda	15	230	2.9	51	101	110	22180	2000	57
USSR	275	...	...	67	132	...	260	...	106
UK	56	8570	1.6	74	128	10	680	120	101
USA	237	15390	1.7	76	137	11	500	180	100

Source: *World Development Report 1986*. Washington, D.C.: World Bank, 1986, Annex, Tables 1, 27, 28, 29.

Appendix 4

The Case of Adnan Buyung Nasution

Adnan Buyung Nasution, a prominent Indonesian lawyer, agreed in 1984 to write a chapter on Indonesia for this volume. The following description explains why he had to withdraw from this commitment.

Political opposition in Indonesia is extremely circumscribed, and in 1985 and early 1986 a series of political trials was held arising from the 1984 Tanjung Priok riots and the later bombing of branches of the Bank Central Asia in Jakarta. One of those tried, and convicted in January 1986, was Lieutenant-General H. R. Dharsono, a former Secretary-General of ASEAN (Association of Southeast Asian Nations). Adnan Buyung Nasution was part of Dharsono's defense team. Dharsono was sentenced to ten years simply for signing a petition and attending a meeting. A colleague of Nasution's, who has requested anonymity, sent us the following description of what followed.

While reading his decision, on January 8, 1986, judge Soedijono of the first instance court of Central Jakarta at one point impugned the integrity of the defense counsel for doubting the government's version of the Tanjung Priok incident. Nasution rose to protest, with much attention from a sympathetic audience. When a policeman entered the court room, Nasution shouted and ordered the police out, because they have no authority in the court room.

A month later, judge Soedijono, apparently after having been pressured by the government, sent a report to the Supreme Court accusing Nasution, in effect, of contempt of court. Actually, contempt of court does not exist in Indonesian legal procedure. Nonetheless, on the basis of judge Soedijono's report, the Supreme Court ordered the Chairman of the Central Jakarta Court, judge Subandi, to consider the issue. On March 17, 1986, judge Subandi delivered an "administrative decision" advising the Supreme Court and the Minister of Justice to revoke Nasution's registration as an advocate. This decision came without hearing the arguments of either Nasution or the Indonesian Advocates Association.

The International Commission of Jurists, the Netherlands Order of Advocates, and the American Bar Association protested the case and the "administrative decision" to the Minister of Justice. However, the Jakarta Court of Appeal affirmed the "administrative decision'' and advised the Supreme Court to revoke Nasution's advocate status for six months. At this time (July 1986) the case is waiting the disposition of the Supreme Court and the Minister of Justice.[1]

Dharsono, being quite prominent internationally, was treated substantially better than the other defendants.[2] Similarly, Nasution only had his license to practice revoked for what the court called his "rude interruptions," which amounted to an attempt to get at the truth, plus a quite understandable outburst at the end of a long and tense political show trial. Often, victims of human rights violations in Indonesia and elsewhere fare even worse. A case like this reminds us, in yet another fashion, of the dangers still faced in much of the world in the struggle for human rights.

NOTES

1. For a similar published account, with more detail on the trial, see Lincoln Kaye, "Guilty as Charged," *Far Eastern Economic Review*, January 23, 1986, 10–11; and *Human Rights Forum*, July-September 1985 and January-March 1986.

2. Kaye, "Guilty as Charged," 11.

SELECTED
BIBLIOGRAPHY

Abella, R. S. *Report of the Commission on Equality in Employment.* Ottawa: Ministry of Supply and Services Canada, 1984.

Adam, Heribert and Kogila Moodley. *South Africa after Apartheid: Dismantling Racial Domination.* Berkeley: University of California Press, 1986.

Alston, Philip. "Human Rights and Basic Needs: A Critical Assessment." *Revue des Droits de l'Homme/Human Rights Journal* 12 (1979): 19–68.

———. "International Trade as an Instrument of Positive Human Rights Policy." *Human Rights Quarterly* 4 (Spring 1982): 155–83.

Americas Watch. *Human Rights in Nicaragua: Reagan, Rhetoric and Reality.* New York: Americas Watch, 1985.

———. *Human Rights in Nicaragua 1985–86.* New York: Americas Watch, 1986.

Americas Watch Committee and the American Civil Liberties Union. *Report on Human Rights in El Salvador.* New York: Vintage Books, 1982.

Amnesty International. *China—Violations of Human Rights: Prisoners of Conscience and the Death Penalty in the People's Republic of China.* London: Amnesty International, 1981.

———. *Political Imprisonment in the People's Republic of China.* London: Amnesty International, 1978.

———. *Report.* London: Amnesty International, annual.

Apter, David E. *The Political Kingdom of Uganda.* Princeton: Princeton University Press, 1967.

Arancibia, Jinny, Marcelo Charlin, and Peter Landstreet. *State Repression and Civil Opposition in Chile: 1973–1984.* Toronto: LaMarsh Research Programme on Violence and Conflict Resolution, York University, 1985.

Averch, Harvey A. *The Matrix of Policy in the Philippines.* Princeton: Princeton University Press, 1971.

Baloyra, Enrique. *El Salvador in Transition.* Chapel Hill: University of North Carolina Press, 1982.

Bay, Christian. *Strategies of Political Emancipation.* Notre Dame: University of Notre Dame Press, 1981.

Bayley, David H. *Forces of Order: Police Behavior in Japan and the United States.* Berkeley: University of California Press, 1976.

Beddard, Ralph. *Human Rights in Europe: A Study of the Machinery of Human Rights Protection of the Council of Europe.* 2d ed. London: Sweet and Maxwell, 1980.

Beer, Lawrence Ward. *Freedom of Expression in Japan: A Study in Comparative Law, Politics, and Society.* Tokyo and New York: Kodansha–Harper & Row, 1985.

———. "Group Rights and Individual Rights in Japan." *Asian Survey* 21 (April 1981): 437.

———. "Human Rights Commissioners (*Jinken Yogo Iin*) and Lay Protection of Human Rights in Japan." International Ombudsman Institute, Occasional Paper No. 31. Alberta, Canada, October 1985.

———. "Japan's Constitutional System and Its Judicial Interpretation." *Law in Japan* 17 (1984): 7–41.

Beer, Lawrence Ward and C. G. Weeramantry. "Human Rights in Japan: Some Protections and Problems." *Universal Human Rights* 1 (September-October 1979): 1–41.

Beitz, Charles R. "Human Rights and Social Justice." In *Human Rights and U.S. Foreign Policy.* Ed. Peter G. Brown and Douglas MacLean. Lexington, Mass.: Lexington Books, 1979.

———. *Political Theory and International Relations.* Princeton: Princeton University Press, 1979.

Benditt, Theodore M. *Rights.* Totowa, N.J.: Roman and Littlefield, 1982.

Benjamin, Anne. *Part of My Soul: Winnie Mandela.* Harmondsworth: Penguin, 1985.

Benson, Mary. *Nelson Mandela.* Harmondsworth: Penguin, 1986.

Berger, T. R. *Fragile Freedoms: Human Rights and Dissent in Canada.* rev. ed. Vancouver: Clark, Irwin, 1982.

Bergesen, Helga Ole. "Human Rights—The Property of the Nation-State or a Concern of the International Community? A Study of the Soviet Positions Concerning U.N. Protection of Civil and Political Rights Since 1975." *Cooperation and Conflict* 14 (1979): 239–54.

Biarnes, Pierre. *L'Afrique aux africains: 20 ans d'independence en Afrique Noire Francophone.* Paris: Armand Colin, 1980.

Black, George. *Triumph of the People: The Sandinista Revolution in Nicaragua.* London: Zed Press, 1981.

Black, W. W. *Employment Equality: A Systemic Approach.* Ottawa: Human Rights Research and Education Centre, 1985.

Boler, Jean. "The Mother's Committee of El Salvador: National Human Rights Activists." *Human Rights Quarterly* 7 (November 1985): 541–56.

Bonner, Raymond. *Weakness and Deceit: U.S. Policy in El Salvador.* New York: Times Books, 1984.

Booth, John A. *The End and the Beginning: The Nicaraguan Revolution.* 2d ed. Boulder, Col.: Westview Press, 1985.

Boyer, J. P. *Report of the Parliamentary Committee on Equality Rights.* Ottawa: Queen's Printer for Canada, 1985.

Branson, Margaret Stimman and Judith Torney-Purta, eds. *International Human Rights, Society and the Schools.* Washington, D.C.: National Council for Social Studies, 1982.

Bromke, Adam. *Eastern Europe in the Aftermath of Solidarity.* East European Monographs, No. 183. New York: Columbia University Press, 1985.

Brown, C. G. *Chile Since the Coup: Ten Years of Repression.* New York: Americas Watch, 1983.

Brown, Cynthia, ed. *With Friends Like These. The Americas Watch Report on Human Rights and U.S. Policy in Latin America.* New York: Pantheon Books, 1985.

Brown, Peter G. and Douglas MacLean, eds. *Human Rights and U.S. Foreign Policy.* Lexington, Mass.: Lexington Books, 1979.

Brown, Ronald. "Japanese Approaches to Equal Rights for Women." *Law in Japan* 12 (1979): 112.

Brownlie, Ian, ed. *Basic Documents on Human Rights.* 2d ed. New York: Oxford University Press, 1981.

Buergenthal, Thomas and Robert E. Norris. *Human Rights: The Inter-American System.* 3 vols. Dobbs Ferry, N.Y.: Oceana, 1982–1984 and updates.

Caccia, I. *Charter Bibliography.* Ottawa: Human Rights Research and Education Centre; Saskatoon: Canadian Human Rights Reporter, 1985.

Campbell, Tom. *The Left and Rights.* London: Routledge and Kegan Paul, 1983.

Campbell, Tom, David Goldberg, Sheila McLean, and Tom Mullen, eds. *Human Rights: From Rhetoric to Reality.* New York: Basil Blackwell, 1986.

Carleton, David and Michael Stohl. "The Foreign Policy of Human Rights: Rhetoric and Reality from Jimmy Carter to Ronald Reagan." *Human Rights Quarterly* 7 (May 1985): 205–29.

Carty, Robert. "Miracle or Mirage? A Review of Chile's Economic Model, 1973–1980." *LAWG Letter* 7, no. 5–6 (1982): 2.

Casal, Lourdes, ed. *Caso Padilla: Literatura y revolution en Cuba: Documentos.* Miami: Nuevo Atlatida, 1971.

Caute, David. *The Great Fear: The Anti-Communist Purge under Truman and Eisenhower.* New York: Simon and Schuster, 1978.

Chalidze, Valery. *To Defend These Rights.* New York: Random House, 1974.

Chile: Human Rights and US Policy. Washington, D.C.: Washington Office on Latin America, 1985.

Chkidvadze, V. "Constitution of True Human Rights and Freedoms." *International Affairs* (Moscow) (October 1980): 13–20.

Chomsky, Noam. *Human Rights and American Foreign Policy.* Nottingham: Spokesman Books, 1974.

Chomsky, Noam and Edward S. Herman. "The United States versus Human Rights in the Third World." *Monthly Review* 29 (1977): 22–45.

Christensen, Cheryl. *The Right to Food: How to Guarantee.* New York: Institute for World Order, 1980.

Christian, Shirley. *Nicaragua: Revolution in the Family.* New York: Random House, 1985.

Claude, Richard P., ed. *Comparative Human Rights.* Baltimore: Johns Hopkins University Press, 1976.

Claude, Richard P. and Eric Stover. *The February Revolution: Health Professionals in the Philippines and the Protection of Human Rights.* Washington, D.C.: American Academy for the Advancement of Science, 1986.

Cohen, Roberta. "Human Rights Diplomacy: The Carter Administration and the Southern Cone." *Human Rights Quarterly* 4 (Spring 1982): 212–42.

Cohn, H. H. "Comparative Law and the International Protection of Human Rights." (sec. IV A2). *Israeli Report to the IX International Congress of Comparative Law* (Jerusalem) (1982): 263–75.

———. *Human Rights in Jewish Law.* New York: KTAV, 1984.

———. "On the Meaning of Human Dignity." *Israel Yearbook on Human Rights* 13 (1983): 226–51.

Collins, Joseph. *Nicaragua: What Difference Could a Revolution Make? Food and Farming in Nicaragua.* 2d ed., rev. San Francisco: Institute for Food and Development Policy, 1985.

Colonnese, Louis M., ed. *Human Rights and the Liberation of Man in the Americas.* Notre Dame: University of Notre Dame Press, 1970.

Copans, Jean. *Les Marabouts de l'Arachide, la confrérie mouride et les paysans du Sénégal.* Paris: Le Sycomore, 1980.

Coulon, Christian. *Le Marabout et le Prince. Islam et pouvoir au Sénégal.* Paris: Pedone, 1981.

Coulson, N. J. "The State and the Individual in Islamic Law." *International and Comparative Law Quarterly* 6 (1957): 49–60.

Crahan, Margaret E. *Human Rights and Basic Needs in the Americas.* Washington, D.C.: Georgetown University Press, 1982.

Cranston, Maurice. *What Are Human Rights?* London: Bodley Head, 1973.

Cruise O'Brien, Donal. *Saints and Politicians: Essays in the Organization of a Senegalese Peasant Society.* London: Cambridge University Press, 1975.

Cruise O'Brien, Rita, ed. *The Political Economy of Underdevelopment: Dependence in Senegal.* Beverly Hills: Sage, 1979.

Curry, J. L., ed. and trans. *The Black Book of Polish Censorship.* New York: Vintage, 1984.

Davenport, Rodney. *South Africa: A Modern History.* New York: Macmillan, 1978.

Davies, N. *God's Playground: A History of Poland.* 2 vols. New York: Columbia University Press, 1982.

Davies, Omar. "An Analysis of the Management of the Jamaican Economy: 1972–1985." *Social and Economic Studies* 35 (March 1986): 73–110.

Dia, Mamadou. *Mémoire d'un Militant du Tiers Monde.* Paris: Publisud, 1985.

Dinges, John and Saul Landau. *Assassination on Embassy Row.* New York: Pantheon, 1980.

Dominguez, Jorge I. *Cuba: Order and Revolution.* Cambridge, Mass.: Harvard University, Belknap Press, 1978.

Donnelly, Jack. *The Concept of Human Rights.* New York: St. Martin's Press, 1985.

———. "Human Rights and Development: Complementary or Competing Concerns?" *World Politics* 36 (January 1984): 255–83.

———. "International Human Rights: A Regime Analysis." *International Organization* 40 (Summer 1986): 599–642.

Donner, Frank. *The Age of Surveillance: The Aims and Methods of America's Intelligence System.* New York: Vintage, 1981.

Dowrick, F. E., ed. *Human Rights: Problems, Perspectives, Texts.* Farnborough, England: Saxon House, 1979.

Dugard, John. *Human Rights and the South African Legal Order.* Princeton University Press, 1978.

Dworkin, Ronald. "Liberalism." In *Public and Private Morality*. Ed. Stuart Hampshire. Cambridge: Cambridge University Press, 1978.

―――. *A Matter of Principle*. Cambridge, Mass.: Harvard University Press, 1985.

―――. "Neutrality, Equality and Liberalism." In *Liberalism Reconsidered*. Ed. Douglas MacLean and Claudia Mills. Totowa, N.J.: Rowman and Allanheld, 1983.

―――. *Taking Rights Seriously*. Cambridge: Cambridge University Press, 1977.

Echevaria, Roberto Gonzalez. "Criticism and Literature in Revolutionary Cuba." In *Cuba: Twenty-five Years of Revolution, 1959–1984*. Ed. Sandor Helebsky and John M. Kirk. New York: Praeger, 1985.

Edwards, R. Randle, Louis Henkin, and Andrew J. Nathan. *Human Rights in Contemporary China*. New York: Columbia University Press, 1986.

Egorov, A. G. "Socialism and the Individual—Rights and Freedoms." *Soviet Studies in Philosophy* 18 (Fall 1979): 3–51.

Eidelberg, P. "On Moles and Men: The Case of the Jewish Underground." *Morasha*, no. 12 (Winter 1985).

Ewing, A. C. *The Individual, the State and World Government*. New York: Macmillan, 1947.

Falconer, Alan M., ed. *Understanding Human Rights: An Interdisciplinary and Interfaith Study*. Dublin: Irish School of Economics, 1980.

Falk, Richard. *Human Rights and State Sovereignty*. New York: Holmes and Meier, 1981.

Fall, Ibrahima. *Sous-developpement et democratie mutipartisme. L'experience sénégalaise*. Dakar: Nouvelle Editions Africains, 1977.

Farer, Thomas J. "Human Rights and Human Wrongs: Is the Liberal Model Sufficient?" *Human Rights Quarterly* 7 (May 1985): 189–204.

Fegley, Randall. "The UN Human Rights Commission: The Equatorial Guinea Case." *Human Rights Quarterly* 3 (February 1981): 34–47.

Feinberg, Joel. *Doing and Deserving: Essays in the Theory of Responsibility*. Princeton: Princeton University Press, 1970.

―――. *Rights, Justice and the Bounds of Liberty: Essays in Social Philosophy*. Princeton: Princeton University Press, 1980.

Flathman, Richard E. *Political Obligation*. New York: Atheneum. 1972.

―――. *The Practice of Rights*. Cambridge: Cambridge University Press, 1977.

Forsythe, David P. *Human Rights and World Politics*. Lincoln: University of Nebraska Press, 1983.

―――. "The United Nations and Human Rights, 1945–1985." *Political Science Quarterly* 100 (Summer 1985): 249–70.

Foxley, Alejendro. *Latin American Experiments in Neoconservative Economics*. Berkeley: University of California Press, 1983.

Franco, Jean. "Death Camp Confessions and Resistance to Violence in Latin America." *Socialism and Democracy* no. 2 (Spring-Summer 1986): 5–18.

Franklin, John Hope. *From Slavery to Freedom: A History of Negro Americans*. New York: Vintage, 1967.

Fruhling, Hugo. "Stages of Repression and Legal Strategy for the Defense of Human Rights in Chile, 1973–1980." *Human Rights Quarterly* 5 (November 1983): 510–33.

Fuentes, Carlos. *Latin America at War with the Past*. Montreal: CBC Enterprises, 1985.

Galey, Margaret E. "International Enforcement of Women's Rights." *Human Rights Quarterly* 6 (November 1984): 463–90.

Galtung, Johan and Anders Helge Wirak. "Human Needs and Human Rights: A Theoretical Approach." *Bulletin of Peace Proposals* 8 no. 3 (1977): 251–58.

Gastil, Raymond, et al. *Freedom in the World: Human Rights and Civil Liberties.* Westport, Conn.: Greenwood Press, annual.

Gellar, Sheldon. *Senegal: An African Nation Between Islam and the West.* Boulder, Col.: Westview Press, 1982.

George, B. J., Jr. "Discretionary Authority of Public Prosecutors in Japan." *Law in Japan* 17 (1984): 42.

George, Thayil J. S. *Revolt in Mindanao: The Rise of Islam in Philippine Politics.* New York: Oxford University Press, 1980.

Gewirth, Alan. *Human Rights: Essays on Justification and Applications.* Chicago: University of Chicago Press, 1982.

Gibson, D. *The Law of the Charter: General Principles.* Toronto: Carswell, 1986.

Gilbert, Dennis and Joseph Kahl. *The American Class Structure.* Chicago: Dorsey, 1982.

Gilmour, David. *Lebanon: The Fractured Country.* New York: St. Martin's Press, 1984.

Girvan, Norman. *Foreign Capital and Economic Underdevelopment in Jamaica.* Mona, Jamaica: Institute for Social and Economic Research, University of the West Indies, 1971.

———. *Prospects for Jamaica's Political Economy.* Kingston, Jamaica: Friedrich Ebert Stiftung, 1986.

Girvan, Norman, Richard Bernal, and Wesley Hughes. "The IMF and the Third World: The Case of Jamaica." *Development Dialogue* 2 (1980): 113–55.

Goldstein, Robert Justin. *Political Repression in Modern America: From 1870 to the Present.* Cambridge, Mass.: Schenkman, 1978.

———. *Political Repression in Nineteenth Century Europe.* Totowa, N.J.: Barnes and Noble, 1983.

Goodin, Robert E. "The Development-Rights Trade-Off: Some Unwarranted Political Assumptions." *Universal Human Rights* 1 (April-June 1979): 31–42.

Gordon, David C. *The Republic of Lebanon: Nation in Jeopardy.* London: Croom Helm, 1983.

Haas, Ernst B. *Global Evangelism Rides Again.* Berkeley, Calif.: Institute of International Studies, 1978.

———. *Human Rights and International Action: The Case of Freedom of Association.* Stanford, Calif.: Stanford University Press, 1970.

Hannam, Hurst, ed. *Guide to International Human Rights Practice.* Philadelphia: University of Pennsylvania Press, 1984.

Hart, H. L. A. "Are There Any Natural Rights?" *Philosophical Review* 64 (1955): 175–91.

Heidenheimer, Arnold J., Hugo Heclo, and Carolyn Adams. *Comparative Public Policy: The Politics of Social Choice in Europe and America.* New York: St. Martin's Press, 1983.

Henkin, Louis, ed. *Introduction to the International Bill of Human Rights: The Covenant on Civil and Political Rights.* New York: Columbia University Press, 1981.

———. *The Rights of Man Today.* Boulder, Col.: Westview Press, 1978.

Henle, R. J. "A Catholic View of Human Rights." In *The Philosophy of Human Rights:*

International Perspectives. Ed. Alan S. Rosenbaum. Westport, Conn.: Greenwood Press, 1980: 87–93.

Hersch, Jeanne. "Is the Declaration of Human Rights a Western Concept?" In *Ethics and Social Justice*. Ed. Howard Kiefer and Milton K. Munitz. Albany: State University of New York Press, 1970.

Hevener, Natalie Kaufman. "An Analysis of Gender Based Treaty Law: Contemporary Developments in Historical Perspective." *Human Rights Quarterly* 8 (February 1986): 70–88.

Hewlett, Sylvia Ann. "Human Rights and Economic Realities: Tradeoffs in Historical Perspective." *Political Science Quarterly* 94 (Fall 1979): 419–52.

———. *A Lesser Life: The Myth of Women's Liberation in America*. New York: Morrow, 1986.

Hill, Gerald N. *Aquino Assassination: The True Story and Analysis of the Assassination of Philippine Senator Benigno S. Aquino, Jr.* Sonoma, Calif.: Hilltop, 1983.

Hirscowitz, Marina. "The Marxist Approach." *International Social Science Journal* 17 (1966): 11–21.

Hirst, David. *The Gun and the Olive Branch: The Roots of Violence in the Middle East*. London: Faber & Faber, 1977.

Hoffman, Stanley. *Duties Beyond Borders*. Syracuse, N.Y.: Syracuse University Press, 1981.

Hourani, A. H. *Syria and Lebanon: A Political Essay*. Oxford: Oxford University Press, 1946.

Howard, Rhoda E. "The Full-Belly Thesis: Should Economic Rights Take Priority over Civil and Political Rights?" *Human Rights Quarterly* 5 (November 1983): 467–90.

———. *Human Rights in Commonwealth Africa*. Totowa, N.J.: Rowman and Littlefield, 1986.

Howard, Rhoda E. and Jack Donnelly. "Human Dignity, Human Rights and Political Regimes." *American Political Science Review* 80 (September 1986): 801–17.

Hudson, Michael C. *The Precarious Republic: Modernization in Lebanon*. New York: Random House, 1968.

Human Rights Coalition (Canada), eds. *Take Care: Human Rights in the 80s*. Ottawa: Human Rights Research and Education Centre, 1983.

Ibingira, Grace. *The Forging of an African Nation*. New York: Viking Press, 1976.

Idowu, H. O. "Assimilation in Nineteenth Century Senegal." *Cahiers d'Etudes Africains* 9 (1969): 194–218.

Inter-American Commission on Human Rights. *Sixth Report on the Situation of Political Prisoners in Cuba*. Washington, D.C.: OAS General Secretariat, 1979.

International Bank for Reconstruction and Development. *The Philippines: Priorities and Prospects for Development*. Washington, D.C.: World Bank, 1976.

Internatioinal Defense and Aid Fund (IDAF). *Apartheid: The Facts*. London: IDAF, 1983.

———. *Children Under Apartheid*. London: IDAF, 1980.

———. *Women Under Apartheid*. London: IDAF, 1981.

International Labor Office. *Official Bulletin: Special Supplement* [Report on Poland]. Series B. 67. Geneva: ILO, 1984.

International Labor Organization. *Special Report to the Director General on Labour and Apartheid in South Africa*. Geneva: ILO, annual.

Itoh, Hiroshi and Lawrence Ward Beer. *The Constitutional Case Law of Japan: Selected Supreme Court Decisions, 1961–1970*. Seattle: University of Washington Press, 1978.

Iwasawa, Yuji. "Legal Treatment of Koreans in Japan: The Impact of International Human Rights Law on Japanese Law." *Human Rights Quarterly* 8 (May 1986): 131.

Jacqeney, Theodore. "The Yellow Uniforms of Cuba." *Worldview* 20 (January-February 1977): 4–10.

Jain, A., ed. *Solidarity: The Origins and Implications of Polish Trade Unions*. Baton Rouge, La.: Oracle Press, 1983.

Jhabvala, Farrokh. "The Soviet Bloc's View of the Implementation of Human Rights Accords." *Human Rights Quarterly* 7 (November 1985): 461–91.

Joyce, James Avery. *The New Politics of Human Rights*. London: Macmillan, 1978.

Kabaka of Buganda. *Desecration of My Kingdom*. London: Constable, 1967.

Kamenka, Eugene and Alice Ehr-Soon Tay, eds. *Human Rights*. New York: St. Martin's Press, 1978.

Karugire, Samwiri R. *The Political History of Uganda*. Nairobi: East African Literature Bureau, 1980.

Kasfir, Nelson. *The Shrinking Political Arena*. Berkeley: University of California Press, 1976.

Kaufman, Edy and Patricia Weiss Fagan. "Extrajudicial Executions: An Insight into the Global Dimensions of Human Rights Violation." *Human Rights Quarterly* 3 (Fall 1981): 81–100.

Kaufman, Michael. *Jamaica under Manley: Dilemmas of Socialism and Democracy*. Westport, Conn.: Lawrence Hill, 1985.

Keene, J. *Human Rights in Ontario*. Toronto: Carswell, 1983.

Kemp-Welch, A., trans. *The Birth of Solidarity: The Gdansk Negotiations 1980*. London: Macmillan, 1983.

Kerkvliet, Benedict J. *The Huk Rebellion: The Study of Peasant Rebellion in the Philippines*. Berkeley: University of California Press, 1977.

Kessler, Richard. *The Politics of Rebellion in the Philippines*. New York: Praeger, 1977.

Kluger, Richard. *Simple Justice: The History of Brown v. Board of Education: Black America's Struggle for Equality*. New York: Vintage, 1976.

Kommers, Donald P. and Gilburt D. Loescher, eds. *Human Rights and American Foreign Policy*. Notre Dame: University of Notre Dame Press, 1979.

Konvitz, Milton R., ed. *Judaism and Human Rights*. New York: W. W. Norton, 1972.

Kyemba, Henry. *A State of Blood*. New York: Grosset and Dunlap, 1977.

Lacey, Terry. *Violence and Politics in Jamaica 1960–1970*. Manchester: Manchester University Press, 1977.

Landstreet, Peter and Jorge Nef, eds. *By Reason of Force: Social Science Perspectives on Contemporary Chile*. (in preparation).

Laqueur, Walter and Barry Rubin, eds. *The Human Rights Reader*. Philadelphia: Temple University Press, 1979.

Lauterpacht, Hersch. *International Law and Human Rights*. New York: F. A. Praeger, 1950.

Leichter, Howard M. and Harrell Rodgers. *American Public Policy in Comparative Context*. New York: McGraw-Hill, 1984.

Leslie, R. E. *The History of Poland since 1863*. Cambridge: Cambridge University Press, 1980.

Levine, E. *Terrorism, Human Rights and Emergency Legislation in Democratic Countries.* Philadelphia: A.C.J.S. Annual Meeting, 1981.

Liang, Heng and Judith Shapiro. *After the Nightmare: A Survivor of the Cultural Revolution Reports on China Today.* New York: Alfred A. Knopf, 1986.

Liang, Heng and Judith Shapiro. *Cold Winds, Warm Winds: Intellectual Life in Post-Mao China.* New York: Wesleyan University Press, 1985.

Locke, John. *Two Treatises of Government.* Cambridge: Cambridge University Press, 1967.

Low, D. Anthony. *The Mind of Buganda.* London: Heinemann Educational Books, 1971.

McChesney, R. Allan. "Promoting the General Welfare in a Democratic Society: Balancing Human Rights and Development." *Netherlands International Law Review* 27 (1980).

McCloskey, H. J. "Human Needs, Rights and Political Values." *American Philosophical Quarterly* 13 (1976): 1–11.

———. "Rights." *Philosophical Quarterly* 15 (1965): 115–27.

McCoy, Alfred W. *Priests on Trial.* New York: Penguin Books, 1984.

McDougal, Myres, Harold Lasswell, and Lung-chu Chen. *Human Rights and World Public Order.* New Haven: Yale University Press, 1980.

Machan, Tibor R. *Human Rights and Human Liberties: A Radical Reconsideration of the American Political Tradition.* Chicago: Nelson Hall, 1975.

Maki, John M. *Court and Constitution in Japan.* Seattle: University of Washington Press, 1964.

Mamdani, Mahmood. *Politics and Class Formation in Uganda.* New York: Monthly Review Press, 1976.

Manglapus, Raul S. *Philippines: The Silenced Democracy.* Maryknoll, N.Y.: Orbis Books, 1976.

Manley, Michael. *Jamaica: The Struggle in the Periphery.* Oxford: Third World Media, 1982.

———. *The Politics of Change.* Washington, D.C.: Howard University Press, 1975.

Markowitz, Irving L. *Léopold Sédar Senghor and the Politics of Negritude.* New York: Atheneum. 1969.

Matthews, Robert and Cranford Pratt. "Human Rights and Foreign Policy: Principles and Canadian Practice." *Human Rights Quarterly* 7 (May 1985): 159–88.

May, Glenn Anthony. *Social Engineering in the Philippines: The Aims, Execution and Support of American Colonial Policy 1900–1913.* Westport, Conn.: Greenwood Press, 1980.

Melden, A. I. *Rights and Persons.* Berkeley: University of California Press, 1977.

Meltzer, Milton. *The Human Rights Book.* New York: Farrar, Strauss, Giroux, 1979.

Meron, Theodore, ed. *Human Rights in International Law: Legal and Policy Issues.* Oxford: Clarendon Press, 1984.

Mesa-Lago, Carmelo. *The Economy of Socialist Cuba.* Albuquerque: University of New Mexico Press, 1981.

Meyers, Diana T. *Inalienable Rights: A Defense.* New York: Columbia University Press, 1985.

Montaner, Carlos Alberto. *Secret Report on the Cuban Revolution.* Trans. Eduardo Zayas-Bazan. New Brunswick, N.J.: Transaction Books, 1981.

Montgomery, Tommie Sue. *Revolution in El Salvador: Origins and Evolution.* Boulder, Col.: Westview Press, 1982.

Moore, Barrington, Jr. *Injustice: The Social Bases of Obedience and Revolt*. White Plains, N.Y.: M. E. Sharpe, 1978.

Morse, B. W., ed. *Aboriginal People and the Law: Indians, Metis, and Inuit Rights in Canada*. Ottawa: Carleton University Press, 1985.

Moskowitz, Moses. "Implementing Human Rights: Present Status and Future Prospects." In *Human Rights Thirty Years after the Universal Declaration*. Ed. B. G. Ramcharan. The Hague: Martinus Nijhoff, 1979.

————. *International Concern with Human Rights*. Dobbs Ferry, N.Y.: Oceana Publications, 1974.

Nathan, Andrew. *Chinese Democracy*. New York: Alfred Knopf, 1985.

Neier, Aryeh. "Castro's Victims." *New York Review of Books* 33, no. 12 (July 17, 1986): 28–31.

Nelson, Jack L. and Vera M. Green, eds. *International Human Rights: Contemporary Issues*. Stanfordville, N.Y.: Human Rights Publishing Group, 1980.

Nettleford, Rex. *Mirror, Mirror: Identity, Race and Protest in Jamaica*. Kingston, Jamaica: Collins & Sangster, 1970.

Newburg, Paula R., ed. *The Politics of Human Rights*. New York: New York University Press, 1980.

Nielson, Niels, Jr. *The Crisis of Human Rights: An American Christian Perspective*. Nashville: Thomas Nelson, 1978.

North, Liisa. *Bitter Grounds: Roots of Revolt in El Salvador*. 2d ed. Toronto: Between the Lines, 1985.

Ojo, Olusola and Amadu Sessay. "The OAU and Human Rights: Prospects for the 1980s and Beyond." *Human Rights Quarterly* 8 (February 1986): 89–103.

Owen, Davis. *Human Rights*. New York: Norton, 1978.

Owen, Roger, ed. *Essays on the Crisis in Lebanon*. London: Ithaca Press, 1976.

Pagels, Elaine. "Human Rights: Legitimizing a Recent Concept." *Annals* 442 (1979): 57–62.

Paine, Thomas. *The Rights of Man*. New York: Penguin, 1985.

Patterson, James T. *America's Struggle Against Poverty: 1900–1985*. Cambridge, Mass.: Harvard University Press, 1986.

Paul, Ellen Frankel, Jeffrey Paul, and Fred D. Miller, Jr., eds. *Human Rights*. Oxford: Basil Blackwell (for the Social Philosophy and Policy Center, Bowling Green State University), 1984.

Pennock, J. Roland and John W. Chapman, eds. *Human Rights (Nomos XXIII)*. New York: New York University Press, 1981.

Persky, Stan and Henry Flam, eds. *The Solidarity Source Book*. Vancouver: New Star Books, 1982.

Physicians Task Force on Hunger in America. *Hunger in America: The Growing Epidemic*. Middletown, Conn.: Weslyan University Press, 1985.

Poland: A Handbook. Warsaw: Interpress, 1977.

Polish Helsinki Watch Committee. *Poland Under Martial Law: A Report on Human Rights*. New York: Helsinki Watch, 1983.

Pollis, Adamantia and Peter Schwab, eds. *Human Rights: Cultural and Ideological Perspectives*. New York: Praeger, 1980.

Pollis, Adamantia and Peter Schwab, eds. *Towards a Human Rights Framework*. New York: Praeger, 1982.

Poole, Frederick K. *Revolution in the Philippines: The United States in a Hall of Cracked Mirrors*. New York: McGraw-Hill, 1984.

El presidio politico en Cuba comunista. Miami: Instituto Internacional de Cooperation y Solidaridad Cubana, 1983.

Raina, P. *Poland 1981: Towards Social Renewal*. London: George Allen & Unwin, 1985.

Randal, Jonathan. *The Tragedy of Lebanon: Christian Warlords, Israeli Adventurers and American Bunglers*. London: Hogarth Press, 1984.

Raphael, D. D., ed. *Political Theory and the Rights of Man*. Bloomington: Indiana University Press, 1967.

Reanda, Laura. "Human Rights and Women's Rights: The United Nations Approach." *Human Rights Quarterly* 3 (May 1981): 11–31.

Ritchie, David G. *Natural Rights*. London: Swan Sonnenschein, 1895.

Robertson, A. H. *Human Rights in the World*. 2d ed. New York: St. Martin's Press, 1982.

Rosenberg, David A. *Marcos and Martial Law in the Philippines*. Ithaca: Cornell University Press, 1979.

Rosset, Peter and John Vandermeer. *The Nicaraguan Reader. Documents of a Revolution Under Fire*. New York: Grove Press, 1983.

Rudolf, Jorg-Meinhard. "China's Media: Fitting News to Print." *Problems of Communism* (July 1984).

Ruggie, John Gerhard. "Human Rights and the Future International Community." *Daedalus* 112 (Fall 1983): 93–110.

The Rule of Law in the Areas Administered by Israel. Israel National Section of the International Commission of Jurists, 1981.

Said, Abdul Aziz, ed. *Human Rights and World Order*. New York: Praeger, 1978.

Salibi, K. S. *Crossroads to Civil War: Lebanon 1958–1976*. London: Ithaca Press, 1976.

————. *The Modern History of Lebanon*. London: Weidenfeld and Nicholson, 1965.

Saul, John and Stephen Gelb. *The Crisis in South Africa: Class Defense, Class Revolution*. 2d ed. New York: Monthly Review Press, 1986.

Schumacher, Edward J. *Politics, Bureaucracy, and Rural Development in Senegal*. Berkeley: University of California Press, 1975.

Seymour, James D. *China Rights Annals—1: Human Rights Development in the People's Republic of China from October 1983 through September 1984*. Armonk, N.Y.: M. E. Sharpe, 1985.

————. *The Fifth Modernization: China's Human Rights Movement, 1978–79*. Crugers, N.Y.: Earl Coleman Enterprises, 1980.

Shalom, Stephen. *The United States and the Philippines: Study of Neocolonialism*. Philadelphia: Institute for the Studies of Human Issues, 1981.

Shamgar, M. "The Observance of International Law in the Administered Territories." *Rights in Warfare* (1971): 262, 266.

Shepherd, George W. and Ved P. Nanda, eds. *Human Rights and Third World Development*. Westport, Conn.: Greenwood Press, 1985.

Shue, Henry. *Basic Human Rights: Subsistence, Affluence and US Foreign Policy*. Princeton: Princeton University Press, 1980.

Simons, Jack and Ray Simons. *Class and Colour in South Africa, 1850–1959*. London: IDAF, 1983.

Singer, Peter. "Famine, Affluence and Morality." *Philosophy and Public Affairs* 1 (1972): 229–43.

Sitkoff, Harvard. *The Struggle for Black Equality, 1954–1980*. New York: Hill & Wang, 1980.

Smith, Brian. *The Church and Politics in Chile: A Challenge to Modern Catholicism*. Princeton: Princeton University Press, 1982.

Smith, L., G. Cote-Harper, R. Elliott, and M. Seydegart. *Righting the Balance: Canada's New Equality Rights*. Saskatoon and Vancouver: Canadian Human Rights Reporter, 1986.

Sommerville, John. "Comparison of Soviet and Western Democratic Principles with Special Reference to Human Rights." In *Human Rights: Comments and Interpretations*. UNESCO. London: Allan Wingate, 1949.

Spiegelberg, Herbert. "Human Dignity: A Challenge to Contemporary Philosophy." *Philosophy Forum* 9 (March 1971): 39–64.

South African Institute of Race Relations. *Annual Survey of Race Relations in South Africa*. Johannesburg: SAIRR, annual.

Southall, Aidan. "Social Disorganization in Uganda: Before, During and After Amin." *Journal of Modern African Studies* 18 (December 1980): 627–56.

SPEAHRHEAD: Bulletin of the Society for the Protection of East Asians' Human Rights. PO Box 1212, Cathedral Station, New York, NY 10025.

Special Committee on Participation of Visible Minorities in Canadian Society. *Equality Now*. Ottawa: Queen's Printer for Canada, 1984.

Stacey, Judith. *Patriarchy and Socialist Revolution in China*. Berkeley: University of California Press, 1984.

Stackhouse, Max L. *Creeds, Society and Human Rights: A Study in Three Cultures*. Grand Rapids, Mich.: William B. Eerdmans, 1984.

Stallings, Barbara. *Class Conflict and Economic Development in Chile, 1958–1973*. Stanford: Stanford University Press, 1978.

Stanley, Peter W., ed. *Reappraising an Empire: New Perspectives on Philippine and American History*. Cambridge, Mass.: Harvard University Press, 1984.

Stephens, Evelyne Huber and John D. Stephens. *Democratic Socialism in Jamaica: The Political Movement and Social Transformations in Dependent Capitalism*. Princeton: Princeton University Press; London: Macmillan, 1986.

Stohl, Michael and George A. Lopez, eds. *The State as Terrorist: The Dynamics of Governmental Violence and Repression*. Westport, Conn.: Greenwood Press, 1984.

Stone, Carl. *Democracy and Clientelism in Jamaica*. New Brunswick, N.J.: Transaction Books, 1980.

Stone, Carl and Aggrey Brown, eds. *Essays on Power and Change in Jamaica*. Kingston: Jamaica Publishing House, 1977.

Stone, Carl and Aggrey Brown, eds. *Perspectives on Jamaica in the Seventies*. Kingston: Jamaica Publishing House, 1981.

Sweeney, Jane P. "Promoting Human Rights Through Regional Organizations: Women's Rights in Western Europe." *Human Rights Quarterly* 6 (November 1984): 491–506.

Tarnopolsky, Walter S. *The Canadian Bill of Rights*. 2d ed. Ottawa: Carleton Library (no. 83), 1975.

———. "The Equality Rights of the Canadian Charter of Rights and Freedoms." *Canadian Bar Review* 61 (1983): 242.

———. "The New Canadian Charter of Rights and Freedoms as Compared and Contrasted with the American Bill of Rights." *Human Rights Quarterly* 5 (August 1983): 227–74.

Tarnopolsky, Walter S. and G. A. Beaudoin, eds. *The Canadian Charter of Rights and Freedoms—Commentary*. Toronto: Carswell, 1982.

Tarnopolsky, Walter S. and W. F. Pentney. *Discrimination and the Law*. Don Mills, Ontario: Richard De Boo, 1985.

Thomas, Hugh S., George A. Fauriol, and Juan Carlos Weiss. *The Cuban Revolution: Twenty-five Years Later*. Boulder, Col.: Westview Press, 1984.

Thompson, Kenneth W., ed. *The Moral Imperatives of Human Rights: A World Survey*. Washington, D.C.: University Press of America, 1980.

Tolley, Howard, Jr. "The Concealed Crack in the Citadel: The United Nations Commission on Human Rights' Response to Confidential Communications." *Human Rights Quarterly* 6 (November 1984): 420–62.

———. "Decision-Making at the United Nations Commission on Human Rights, 1979–82." *Human Rights Quarterly* 5 (Winter 1983): 25–57.

———. *The United Nations Commission on Human Rights*. Boulder, Col.: Westview Press, 1987.

UNESCO. *The Birthright of Man*. Paris: UNESCO, 1969.

———. *Human Rights: Comments and Interpretations*. London: Allan Wingate, 1949.

Upham, Frank K. "Instrumental Violence and Social Change: The *Buraku* Liberation League and the Tactic of 'Denunciation Struggle.' " *Law in Japan* 17 (1984): 185.

———. "Ten Years of Affirmative Action for Japanese *Burakumin*." *Law in Japan* 13 (1980): 39.

Uzoigwe, G. N., ed. *Uganda, The Dilemma of Nationhood*. New York: NOK Publishers, 1982.

Valenzuela, Arturo. *The Breakdown of Democratic Regimes: Chile*. Baltimore: Johns Hopkins University Press, 1978.

Valladares, Armando. *Against All Hope: The Prison Memoirs of Armando Valladares*. Trans. Andrew Hurley. New York: Alfred A. Knopf, 1986.

Vallat, Francis, ed. *An Introduction to the Study of Human Rights*. London: Europa Publications, 1972.

Van Dyke, Vernon. *Human Rights. Ethnicity and Discrimination*. Westport, Conn.: Greenwood Press, 1985.

———. *Human Rights. The United States and World Community*. New York: Oxford University Press, 1970.

Vasak, Karel and Philip Alston, eds. *The International Dimensions of Human Rights*. Westport, Conn.: Greenwood Press, 1982.

Vicaria de la Solidaridad: Decimo Ano de Labor, 1985. Santiago: Vicaria de la Solidaridad, 1986.

de Vylder, Stefan. *Chile 1970–73: The Political Economy of the Rise and Fall of the Unidad Popular*. Cambridge: Cambridge University Press, 1977.

Waldron, Jeremy, ed. *Theories of Rights*. Oxford: Oxford University Press, 1984.

Walker, Thomas W. *Nicaragua: The Land of Sandino*. 2d ed., rev. Boulder, Col.: Westview Press, 1986.

———, ed. *Nicaragua: The First Five Years*. New York: Praeger, 1985.

———, ed. *Reagan vs. the Sandinistas. The Undeclared War on Nicaragua*. Boulder, Col.: Westview Press, 1987.

Welch, Claude E. and Ronald I. Meltzer, eds. *Human Rights and Development in Africa*. Albany: State University of New York Press, 1984.

Werblowsky, Z. "On Religion and Human Rights Violations with Reference to the Jewish Tradition." *Comprendre* 47–48 (1981–1983): 175–83.

White, Alan R. *Rights*. Oxford: Clarendon Press, 1984.

Wiarda, Howard J., ed. *Human Rights and US Human Rights Policy*. Washington, D.C.: American Enterprise Institute, 1982.

Wright, Robin. *Sacred Rage: The Crusade of Modern Islam*. New York: Simon and Schuster, 1985.

Xu Wenli. "My Self-Defense." *Index on Censorship* (London) (May 1986): 18–25.

Yedlin, Tova, ed. *Women in Eastern Europe and the Soviet Union*. New York: Praeger, 1980.

INDEX

ABOUT THE CONTRIBUTORS

JINNY ARANCIBIA is a former human rights researcher with the Vicariate of Solidarity, Archdiocese of Santiago, Chile. Her husband was executed in a military trial after the 1973 coup, and she helped found the Association of Relatives of the Politically Executed. She also worked in the national coordination of the activities of that and four other such Associations of Relatives: of the Disappeared, of Political Prisoners, of the Exiled and of the Banished. She is a Research Associate of the Chile Program of the Centre for Research on Latin America and the Caribbean (CERLAC), York University, Toronto, and has written and spoken widely on the Chilean human rights situation. She currently lives in Chile.

MARCELO CHARLIN is a Chilean architect with graduate studies in urban planning in England, completing his doctorate in sociology at York University, Toronto. He has done volunteer work with the Chilean Human Rights Commission in Santiago, and has written and spoken extensively on his country's human rights situation. He is the Coordinator of the Chile Program of the Centre for Research on Latin America and the Caribbean (CERLAC), York University. He also coordinates a major cooperative research project between CERLAC and the Facultad Latinoamericana de Ciencias Sociales (FLACSO), in Chile, where he currently lives.

RICHARD PIERRE CLAUDE is Professor of Government and Politics at the University of Maryland, College Park. He is the Editor of *Comparative Human Rights* and Founding Editor of *Human Rights Quarterly* (both published by the Johns Hopkins University Press). He is the co-editor (with Tom Jabine) of "Statistical Issues in Human Rights," sponsored by the American Association for the Advancement of Science. In 1986 he served on a reviewing team to the Philippines to report on "The Health Professions and Human Rights." He has written several articles on politics in the Philippines. He serves on the Board of Directors of the American Committee for Human Rights and is a member of the Advisory Council of Amnesty International–USA.

JACK DONNELLY is Associate Professor of Political Science at the University of North Carolina at Chapel Hill, where he teaches international relations and political theory. He received his Bachelor's and Master's degrees from George-town University, and a Ph.D. from the University of California, Berkeley. He is the author of *The Concept of Human Rights* (1985) and numerous articles on the theory and practice of human rights. His current research focuses on the theory of political realism and the place of morality in international relations.

DOUGLAS DUCHARME was born in Ottawa, Canada, where he began studies in political science at Carleton University. He completed his Bachelor's degree in political science from University College, University of Toronto. He then earned a Master's degree in theology from Knox College, University of Toronto. A year in Lebanon has been followed by doctoral studies in theology at the University of Toronto. He is also a Staff Associate at the Canadian Council of Churches in Human Rights and International Affairs, with special responsibilities for the Middle East.

CATHERINE GANDER is a writer and researcher based in Mexico City. From January 1981 to July 1985, she lived in Nicaragua. She worked at the Instituto Histórico Centroamericano, an independent information center, and at the Vice-Ministry of Adult Education, and participated in a number of research projects, including a study of religion and ethnic groups in Nicaragua's Atlantic Coast region. Her articles on Nicaragua, the rest of Central America, and Mexico have appeared in several North and Latin American publications. She holds a B.A. from Queen's University, Kingston, and an M.A. in Political Science specializing in Latin American Studies, from the University of Toronto.

ROBERT JUSTIN GOLDSTEIN is Associate Professor of Political Science at Oakland University, Rochester, Michigan. He is the author of *Political Repression in Modern America: From 1870 to the Present* and of *Political Repression in Nineteenth Century Europe* and has published articles in many scholarly and popular outlets, including the *Columbia Human Rights Law Review*, *Comparative Social Research*, the *Nation*, and the *Progressive*.

RHODA E. HOWARD is Professor of Sociology at McMaster University, Hamilton, Ontario, Canada, where she teaches courses on human rights, the political economy of Africa, and social change. She is the author of *Colonialism and Underdevelopment in Ghana* (1978) and *Human Rights in Commonwealth Africa* (1986), as well as many articles on human rights and development in Africa, Canadian refugee policy, and Canadian foreign policy. Her current research is a theoretical study of the linkages between human rights, development, and social change.

FREDERICK JOHNSTONE was born in Montreal, Quebec, grew up in Geneva, Switzerland, and studied at Queen's University in Kingston, Ontario, where he received his B.A. and M.A. degrees, and at Oxford University in England, where he received his Ph.D. His research in and on South Africa led to work which challenged conventional thinking about South Africa and helped to develop an alternative approach. This is part of his wider interest in the comparative study of social development, human rights, and social justice. He is currently Associate Professor of Sociology at Memorial University, St. John's, Newfoundland, Canada.

EDWARD KANNYO, at the time of writing (1986), is Visiting Assistant Professor of Political Science at the University of California, Los Angeles. He obtained his Ph.D. in Political Science from Yale University. He has worked with the International League for Human Rights, the Lawyers' Committee for Human Rights (both based in New York), and the United Nations. He has written articles and contributed essays to publications on politics in Uganda and Zaire, the Organization of African Unity, African international relations, and human rights in Africa.

MARTIN A. KLEIN teaches African history at the University of Toronto. He is a student of the social history of Francophone West Africa. He has written on slavery, peasants, Islam, and colonial administration. His most recent book is *Women and Slavery in Africa*, edited with Claire Robertson. He is now working on a study of slavery and French colonial rule in West Africa.

DAVID KOWALEWSKI teaches Comparative and International Politics at the University of Texas at San Antonio. His works on human rights in the Soviet Union have appeared in *Social Science Quarterly*, *Journal of Politics*, *Sociological Quarterly* and elsewhere.

PETER LANDSTREET, a sociologist, is Deputy Director of the Centre for Research on Latin America and the Caribbean (CERLAC), York University, Toronto. He was the Founder and first Director of CERLAC's Chile Program, is the former Coordinator of York University's undergraduate program in Latin American and Caribbean studies, and helped establish that university's program of graduate studies in the same field. He is the author of *Cuban Population Issues in Historical and Comparative Perspective*, co-author of *Centros Privados de Investigacion en Ciencias Sociales en Chile*, and co-editor of *Human Rights in Latin America and the Caribbean* (forthcoming).

ROBERT ALLAN McCHESNEY is a Research Associate, Human Rights Research and Education Centre, University of Ottawa. He is a barrister in Ontario and the Northwest Territories, where he was Executive Director of legal aid from 1981 to 1983. He has prepared a draft Northwest Territories Human Rights Code and conducted community human rights education in the North and elsewhere. He taught law at the Polytechnic of the South Bank in London, England, during 1978–1980 prior to a research fellowship and "stage" at the Directorate of Human Rights, Council of Europe. His publications discuss human rights in development and foreign policy as well as human rights within Canada.

STEFANIA SZLEK MILLER is a member of the Department of Political Science, McMaster University, Hamilton, Ontario, Canada. She was President of the Canadian Association of Slavists, 1985–1986, and was Guest Editor of the *Canadian Slavonic Papers* special issue on Poland, vol. 25, no. 3 (September 1983). Her publications include an analysis of the role of the Roman Catholic Church and Opposition groups in the Polish political system, and the influence of Catholic social thought on Solidarity's 1981 Program. Her current research is on Canadian Foreign Policy and Human Rights pertaining to the Soviet Bloc.

LIISA LUKKARI NORTH is Associate Professor of Political Science and a Fellow of the Centre for Research on Latin America and the Caribbean (CERLAC), York University. She received a Ph.D. in Political Science at the University of California at Berkeley. She is the author of *Bitter Grounds: The Roots of Revolt in El Salvador* and co-author of *The Peruvian Revolution and the Officers in Power, 1968–1976*; she co-edited *Democracy and Development in Latin America* and has published articles on the military and politics, democratization, and political movements in Latin America.

RHODA RABKIN is a Visiting Fellow in the Latin American Studies Program at Cornell University. She received a B.A. from Cornell and a Ph.D. in Government from Harvard University. Her research specialty is Cuban politics, and she is writing a book on that subject to be published by Praeger Publishers.

BARNETT R. RUBIN is Associate Professor of Political Science at Yale University. He received his Ph.D. from the University of Chicago. In addition to his work on India, he has written on politics and human rights in Afghanistan and has worked with a number of human rights organizations.

JAMES D. SEYMOUR is Senior Research Scholar at Columbia University's East Asian Institute. He has also taught at New York University and the New School for Social Research. His most recent book is *China's Satellite Parties*, concerning the non-Communist political parties in the PRC. His other books include *China, the Politics of Revolutionary Reintegration*; *China Rights Annals*; *The Fifth Modernization: China's Human Rights Movement, 1978–1979*; and

Introduction to Comparative Government (co-author). He is a member of the National Advisory Committee of Amnesty International–USA.

EVELYNE HUBER STEPHENS is Associate Professor of political science at Nothwestern University. Her past work focused on workers' participation and self-management and on the politics of development in Latin America and the Caribbean. She has authored *The Politics of Workers' Participation: The Peruvian Approach in Comparative Perspective*, as well as articles on labor mobilization and workers' control in Europe and Latin America. She is the coauthor (with John D. Stephens) of *Democratic Socialism in Jamaica: The Political Movement and Social Transformation in Dependent Capitalism* and a number of related articles. Now she is working on a book (with Dietrich Rueschemeyer and John D. Stephens) on the relationship between socioeconomic development and political democracy, and on a comparative-historical analysis of government-sponsored capital/labor accommodations in Latin America.

JOHN D. STEPHENS is Associate Professor of political science and sociology at Northwestern University. His past research has focused on the welfare state and social democracy in Europe, which is the topic of his book *The Transition from Capitalism to Socialism* and of a number of articles on the Swedish case. He is the coauthor (with Evelyne Huber Stephens) of *Democratic Socialism in Jamaica: The Political Movement and Social Transformation in Dependent Capitalism* and a number of related articles. Currently he is working on a book (with Dietrich Rueschemeyer and Evelyne Huber Stephens) on the relationship between socioeconomic development and political democracy, and on a comparative-historical analysis of capital/labor compromises in Europe.